FV

 St. Louis Community College

Forest Park
Florissant Valley
Meramec

Instructional Resources
St. Louis, Missouri

FILMED BOOKS AND PLAYS

FILMED BOOKS AND PLAYS

A LIST OF BOOKS AND PLAYS FROM WHICH FILMS HAVE BEEN MADE, 1928–86

by
A. G. S. ENSER, FLA, FRSA

Gower

Published by
Gower Publishing Company Limited, Gower House, Croft Road, Aldershot, Hampshire GU11 3HR, England

Gower Publishing Company, Old Post Road, Brookfield, Vermont 05036, USA

First published November 1968 by
Andre Deutsch Limited, 105 Great Russell Street, London W.C.1.
Revised edition published March 1971
Second impression of revised edition May 1972
Revised cumulated edition published 1975
Supplementary edition 1975–1981 published 1982
Revised edition 1985, 1987
Reprinted 1989

British Library Cataloguing in Publication Data

Enser, A.G.S.
    Filmed books and plays: a list of books
    and plays from which films have been made,
    1928–86.—Rev. ed.
    I. Film adaptations—Bibliography
    I. Title
    011'.37   Z5784.M9

Library of Congress Cataloging-in-Publication Data

Enser, A.G.S.
    Filmed books and plays.
    1. Film adaptations—Bibliography.   I. Title.
    Z5784.M9E563   1987   (PN1997.85   016.8088   87–157)

ISBN 0 566 03564 2

CONTENTS

PREFACE

Scope

This list of films made from books or plays covers films produced between 1928 and 1986. It is a cumulated list comprising *Filmed Books and Plays, 1928–1974*, *Filmed Books and Plays, 1975–1981*, and *Filmed Books and Plays, 1928–1983*.

The commencing date 1928 was chosen because from that year onwards most films produced for public viewing were talking pictures. Nearly all the films listed are either British or American in origin.

For any compiler of such a book as this, there are many pitfalls, and what was correct at one period of time can be incorrect later. Both film companies and publishers create difficulties for the bibliographer. The former may announce a film using the published title of the book or play from which the film is taken, then present the film under an entirely different title. Or, they announce a film using a different title to that of the published book, but on presentation may revert to the published title or even use another title altogether. Then, the film title as well as the book title may vary in different countries. Publishers too, as a film tie-in, may republish the book using a title chosen by the film company. Occasionally, it is stated that the film is based on the novel by . . . only for the compiler of this bibliography to find the novel is unpublished.

A new development is the making of films from books and plays for television showing only, as opposed to cinema theatre screening. Advantage has been taken, therefore, to include such films, thereby increasing the coverage of this bibliography, by the inclusion of (TV) by the side of the relevant entry. Also the symbol (V) is inserted after the title of the film to indicate it is available on video tape.

Once again, it is not claimed that the list is completely exhaustive, and I shall be pleased to be informed of omissions and errors.

Arrangement

There are three indexes, namely:

(a) Film Title Index
(b) Author Index
(c) Change of Original Title Index

The articles 'The', 'A', or 'An' are placed at the end of the title instead of at the beginning, and are ignored in alphabetical arrangement.

The Film Title Index is arranged alphabetically under the title of the film. Underneath is shown the name of the maker or distributing company (usually in abbreviation) and the year the film was registered.

Opposite is shown the name of the author of the book from which the film was made, and underneath, the name of the publisher. Where another title, in italics, follows the name of the author, this signifies that the film company changed the title of the book from the original shown in italics to that printed opposite. Where (P) is found, this signifies that the book is in play form.

The Author Index is arranged alphabetically under the names of authors with further alphabetical arrangement under each author of his works which have been filmed. Underneath the title of the work filmed is shown the name of the publisher. Opposite is shown the name of the maker of the film or distributing company. Should a title in italics follow, this signifies the title under which the film was presented. It will be noted that in this author index liberty has been taken to use an author's pseudonym, where employed, in preference to his real name. Reference in such cases is made from the real name to the pseudonym used, e.g.,

STURE-VASA, Mary *see* **O'HARA, Mary**, *pseud*

In the case of dual authors, the author entry is made under the name of the first mentioned on the title page. The second author's name is also listed but reference given to the name of the first author, under which the entry will be found, e.g.,

SIMONS, S.J. *jt. author see* **BRAHMS, C.**

The Change of Original Title Index is an alphabetical arrangement of the original book titles differing from their film titles. Underneath the original book title is found the name of the author. Opposite is found the title of the film, with underneath the name of the maker or distributing company and the year the film was registered.

How to use the Indexes

If the name of the film is known but not the name of the author of the book, refer to the Film Title Index. Ignore any article 'The', 'A' or 'An'.

If the name of the author is known but not that of the book nor film, refer to the Author Index where, under the author's name, will be found in alphabetical arrangement the titles of his works which have been filmed.

If it is desired to know what works of a particular author have been filmed, refer to the Author Index.

If the original title of the book is known but not that given to the film, nor the author's name refer to the Change of Original Title Index.

The Indexes are intended for the use of information services in public and special libraries, as well as film societies and all concerned with the film industry.

Acknowledgements

I am grateful both to reviewers and personal correspondents who have pointed out errors and omissions. In particular, I wish to thank Mr. H. A. Thevent of Buenos Aires, Mr. David F. Cheshire, and Mr. Robin Wade.

For this latest cumulated edition I wish to acknowledge the facilities placed at my disposal by Mr. Eric Rhodes, and the staff of the East Sussex County Libraries, especially to the County Library Local Government Unit.

A.G.S. ENSER
Eastbourne

August 1986

LIST OF ABBREVIATIONS

AA	Anglo-Amalgamated Film Company
AB	Associated British Film Distributors
ABC	American Broadcasting Corporation
ABP	Associated British and Pathé Film Distributors
ALL	Alliance Productions Limited
ANGLIA	Anglia Television
ARC	The Archers Film Productions Ltd
AUT	Auten Films
BBC	British Broadcasting Corporation
BD	British and Dominion Films Ltd
BI	British International Films
BL	British Lion Films Ltd
BN	British National Films Ltd
CFF	Children's Film Foundation
CHANNEL 4	Channel 4 Television
CIC	Cinema International Corporation
CIN	Cineguild Incorporated
COL	Columbia Productions Ltd
CONT	Continental Films Ltd
EAL	Ealing Studios Ltd
EL	Eagle Lion Distributors Ltd
EMI	Thorn EMI Films
FOX	Fox and Twentieth Century Fox Ltd

GB	Gaumont British Ltd
GFD	General Film Distributors Ltd
GTO	GTO Films
GUO	GUO Film Distributors
HTV	Harlech Television (Wales)
ID	First Division Films
IN	International Motion Pictures
ITC	ITC Film Distribution
ITV	Independent Television Corporation
jt. author	*joint author*
LF	London Films
LWT	London Weekend Television
MGM	Metro-Goldwyn-Mayer Ltd
MON	Monogram Films
NBC	National Broadcasting Corporation
NY	New York
OLY	Olympic Films
PAR	Paramount Productions Ltd
PRC	Producers' Releasing Corporation
pseud	*pseudonym*
PSO	Producers' Sales Organisation
RANK	J. Arthur Rank Film Distribution
REN	Renown Pictures Corporation Ltd
REP	Republic Pictures
RKO	R.K.O. Radio Pictures Ltd
SF	SAFIR Films
STV	Southern Television
TC	Two Cities Films Ltd
TV	Television Film
UA	United Artists' Corporation
UI	Universal International Motion Pictures
UIP	United International Pictures
UN	Universal Motion Pictures Ltd
(V)	*video tape*
WAR	Warner Brothers Pictures Ltd
WW	World Wide Films Ltd

FILM TITLE INDEX

A

ABBESS, THE
SCOTIA-BARBER 1976

Spark, M. (*Abbess of Crewe, The*)
Viking, N.Y.

ABDICATION, THE
COL—WAR 1974

Wolff, R. (P)
Paperback Library

ABDUCTION
HEMDALE 1977

James, H.
Whirlwind, N.Y.

ABE LINCOLN IN ILLINOIS
RKO 1940

Sherwood, R.E. (*Abe Lincoln of . . .*)
(P)
Scribner, N.Y.

ABOUT FACE
WAR 1952

Monks, J. *and* Finklehoffe, F.F.
(*Brother rat*) (P)
Random House, N.Y.

ABOUT LAST NIGHT
TRI-STAR 1986

Mamet, D. (*Sexual Perversity in Chicago*)
Grove, N.Y.

ABOUT MRS LESLIE
PAR 1954

Delmar, V.
Hale

ABOVE SUSPICION
MGM 1943

McInnes, H.
Harrap

ABOVE US THE WAVES (V)
GFD 1954

Warren, C.E.T. *and* Benson, J.
Harrap

ABSOLUTE BEGINNERS (V)
VIRGIN 1985

MacInnes, C.
Allison & Busby

ACCENT ON YOUTH
PAR 1935

Raphaelson, S. (P)
French

ACCIDENT
MON 1967

Mosley, N.
Hodder & Stoughton

ACCOUNT RENDERED
RANK 1957

Barrington, P.
Barker

1

TITLE OF FILM	AUTHOR AND PUBLISHER
ACCUSED, THE PAR 1949	Truesdell J. (*Be still my love*) Boardman
ACCUSED OF MURDER REP 1956	Burnett, W.R. (*Vanity Row*) Corgi
ACES HIGH (V) EMI 1976	Sherriff, R.C. (*Journey's End*) Gollancz
ACROSS 110th STREET (V) UA 1972	Ferris, W. Harper, N.Y.
ACROSS THE BRIDGE RANK 1957	Greene, G. Heinemann
ACROSS THE WIDE MISSOURI MGM 1951	De Voto, B. Eyre & Spottiswoode
ACTION FOR SLANDER UA 1938	Borden, M. Heinemann
ACTION IN THE NORTH ATLANTIC WAR 1943	Gilpatric, G. Dutton, N.Y.
ACT OF LOVE UA 1954	Hayes, A. (*Girl on the Via Flaminia, The*) Gollancz
ACT OF MURDER, AN UN 1948	Lothar, E. (*Mills of God, The*) Secker
ACT ONE WAR 1963	Moss, H. Secker & Warburg
ACTRESS, THE MGM 1953	Gordon, R. (*Leading lady*) (P) Dramatists, N.Y.
ADA DALLAS MGM 1960	Williams, W. Muller
ADAM HAD FOUR SONS COL 1941	Bonner, C. (*Nor perfume nor wine*) Cassell
ADDING MACHINE, THE RANK 1970	Rice, E. (P) Viking, N.Y.

TITLE OF FILM	AUTHOR AND PUBLISHER
ADDRESS UNKNOWN COL 1944	Taylor, K. Hamilton
ADMIRABLE CRICHTON, THE COL 1957	Barrie, *Sir* J.M. (P) Hodder & Stoughton
ADOLF HITLER—MY PART IN HIS **DOWNFALL** UA 1972	Milligan, S. Joseph
ADVENTURE MGM 1945	Davis, C.B. (*Anointed, The*) Barker
ADVENTURE IN IRAQ WAR 1943	Archer, W. (*Green goddess, The*) (P) Heinemann
ADVENTURE IN THE HOPFIELDS ABP 1954	Lavin, N. *and* Thorp, M. (*Hop dog, The*) Oxford U.P.
ADVENTURE ISLAND PAR 1947	Stevenson, R.L. (*Ebb tide*) Various
ADVENTURERS, THE PAR 1968	Robbins, H. Blond
ADVENTURES OF BULLWHIP GRIFFIN, **THE** DISNEY 1967	Fleischman, S. (*Bullwhip Griffin*) Penguin
ADVENTURES OF GERARD, THE UA 1970	Doyle, *Sir* A.C. (*Exploits of Brigadier Gerard, The*) Murray
ADVENTURES OF HAJJI BABA, THE FOX 1954	Morier, J.J. (*Adventures of Hajji Baba Ispahan*) Modern Library, N.Y.
ADVENTURES OF HUCKLEBERRY **FINN, THE** (V) MGM 1939 MGM 1960	Twain, M. (*Huckleberry Finn*) Various
ADVENTURES OF MARTIN EDEN, THE COL 1942	London, J. (*Martin Eden*) Heinemann

3

TITLE OF FILM	AUTHOR AND PUBLISHER
ADVENTURES OF QUENTIN DURWARD MGM 1955	Scott, *Sir* W. (*Quentin Durward*) Various
ADVENTURES OF ROBINSON CRUSOE, THE UA 1954	Defoe, D. Various
ADVENTURES OF SHERLOCK HOLMES, THE GRANADA 1983 (TV)	Doyle, *Sir* A.C. Murray
ADVENTURES OF TOM SAWYER, THE (V) UA 1938	Twain, M. (*Tom Sawyer*) Various
ADVISE AND CONSENT BL 1962	Drury, A. Collins
AERODROME, THE (V) BBC 1983 (TV)	Warner, R. Oxford U.P.
AFFAIR AT THE VILLA FIORITA, THE WAR 1964	Godden, R. (*Battle of the Villa Fiorita*) Macmillan
AFFAIRS OF CAPPY RICKS, THE REP 1937	Kyne, P.B. (*Cappy Ricks*) Hodder & Stoughton
AFFAIRS OF CELLINI UA 1934	Mayer, E.J. (*Firebrand, The*) (P) French
AFRICAN FURY ABP 1955	Michael, G. Joseph
AFRICAN QUEEN, THE ROMULUS 1951	Forester, C.S. Joseph
AFTER OFFICE HOURS BI 1932	Druten, J. van (*London Wall*) (P) Gollancz
AFTER THE BALL BL 1957	De Frece, *Lady* (*Recollections of Vesta Tilly*) Hutchinson

TITLE OF FILM	AUTHOR AND PUBLISHER
AGENCY CAROLCO 1980	Gottlieb, P. Sphere
AGE OF CONSENT COL 1968	Lindsay, N. Laurie
AGE OF INNOCENCE RKO 1934	Wharton, *Mrs* E. Appleton-Century, N.Y.
AGONY AND THE ECSTACY, THE FOX 1964	Stone, I. Collins
AH WILDERNESS MGM 1935	O'Neill, E.G. (P) Cape
AIN'T LIFE WONDERFUL ABP 1953	Williams, B. (*Uncle Willie and the bicycle shop*) Harrap
AIRPORT RANK 1969	Hailey, A. Joseph *and* Souvenir
AKENFIELD ANGLE FILMS 1975	Blythe, R. Penguin
ALFIE (V) PAR 1965	Naughton, B. (P) French
ALFIE (V) PAR 1965	Naughton, B. MacGibbon & Kee
ALIBI, THE WAR 1935	Lardner, R. Garden City, N.Y.
ALICE HEMDALE 1980	Carroll, L. (*Alice in Wonderland*) Various
ALICE ADAMS RKO 1935	Tarkington, B. Odyssey Press, N.Y.
ALICE IN WONDERLAND PAR 1933 RKO 1951	Carroll, L. Various

TITLE OF FILM	AUTHOR AND PUBLISHER
ALICE'S ADVENTURES IN WONDERLAND (V) FOX 1972	Carroll, L. Various
ALL CREATURES GREAT AND SMALL (V) EMI 1974 BBC 1985 (TV)	Herriot, J. (*If Only They Could Talk; It Shouldn't Happen to a Vet*) Joseph (*Lord God made them all, The*) Pan
ALLEGHENY UPRISING (V) RKO 1939	Swanson, N.H. (*First Rebel, The*) Grosset, N.Y.
ALL FALL DOWN MGM 1961	Herlihy, J.L. Dutton, N.Y.
ALLIGATOR NAMED DAISY, AN RANK, 1955	Terrot, C. Collins
ALL MEN ARE ENEMIES FOX 1934	Aldington, R. Heinemann
ALL NEAT IN BLACK STOCKINGS WAR 1968	Gaskell, J. Hodder & Stoughton
ALL OVER THE TOWN WESSEX 1948	Delderfield, R.F. (P) French
ALL PASSION SPENT BBC 1986 (TV)	Sackville-West, V.
ALL QUIET ON THE WESTERN FRONT (V) UN 1930 ITC 1980	Remarque, E.M. Putnam
ALL THAT MONEY CAN BUY RKO 1941	Benet, S.V. (*Devil and Daniel Webster, The*) Oxford U.P.
ALL THE FINE YOUNG CANNIBALS MGM 1960	Marshall, R. (*Brixby girls, The*) Heinemann
ALL THE KING'S MEN COL 1949	Warren, R.P. Eyre & Spottiswoode

TITLE OF FILM	AUTHOR AND PUBLISHER
ALL THE PRESIDENT'S MEN (V) COL—WAR 1976	Bernstein, C. & Woodward, R. Secker & Warburg
ALL THE RIVERS RUN CHANNEL 4 1984 (TV)	Cato, N. New English Library
ALL THE WAY HOME PAR 1963	Agee, J. (*Death in the family, A*) Gollancz
ALL THIS AND HEAVEN TOO WAR 1940	Field, R. Collins
ALL THIS AND MONEY TOO UA 1963	Hardy, L. (*Grand Duke and Mr Pimm, The*) Cape
ALMOST MARRIED FOX 1932	Soutar, A. (*Devil's triangle*) Hutchinson
ALONG CAME JONES RKO 1945	LeMay, A. (*Useless cowboy, The*) Collins
ALPHABET MURDERS, THE MGM 1966	Christie, A. (*ABC murders, The*) Collins
ALTERED STATES (V) COL 1981	Chayefsky, P. Harper, N.Y.
ALWAYS CANNON 1984	Meldal-Johnsen, T. Avon, N.Y.
AMADEUS (V) ORION 1983	Shaffer, P. (P) Penguin
AMATEUR, THE (V) FOX 1981	Littell, R. Simon & Schuster, N.Y.
AMATEUR GENTLEMAN, THE UA 1936	Farnol, J. Sampson Low
AMAZING DR CLITTERHOUSE, THE WAR 1938	Lyndon, B. (P) Hamilton
AMAZING MR BLUNDEN, THE HEMDALE 1972	Barber, A. (*Ghosts*) Cape

TITLE OF FILM	AUTHOR AND PUBLISHER
AMAZING QUEST, THE KLEMENT, 1936	Oppenheim, E.P. (*Amazing quest of Mr Ernest Bliss, The*) Hodder & Stoughton
AMBASSADOR, THE CANNON 1984	Leonard, E. (*52 Pick-up*) Avon, N.Y.
AMBUSH MGM 1950	Short, L. Collins
AMBUSHES, THE COL 1968	Hamilton, D. Coronet
AMERICAN FRIEND, THE (V) CINEGATE 1978	Highsmith, P. Hodder & Stoughton
AMERICANIZATION OF EMILY, THE MGM 1963	Huie, W.B. W.H. Allen
AMITYVILLE HORROR, THE (V) AMERICAN INTERNATIONAL 1979	Anson, J. Bantam, N.Y.
AMITYVILLE II: THE POSSESSION COL—EMI—WAR 1982	Holzer, H. (*Murder in Amityville*) Futura
AMOROUS ADVENTURES OF MOLL FLANDERS, THE PAR 1964	Defoe, D. (*Moll Flanders*) Various
AMOROUS PRAWN, THE BL 1962	Kimmins, A. (P) French
AMOS (V) PRECISION 1985 (TV)	West, S. Rawson, N.Y.
ANASTASIA FOX 1956	Bolton, G. (P) French
ANATOLIAN SMILE, THE WAR 1964	Kazan, E. (*America, America*) Collins
ANATOMY OF A MURDER COL 1959	Traver, R. Faber

8

TITLE OF FILM	AUTHOR AND PUBLISHER
ANDERSON TAPES, THE (V) COL 1971	Sanders, L. Coronet
ANDERSONVILLE COL 1959	Kantor, M. W.H. Allen
AND NOW MIGUEL UI 1965	Krumgold, J. Cowell-Collier, N.Y.
AND NOW TOMORROW PAR 1944	Field, R. Collins
AND ONE WAS WONDERFUL MGM 1940	Miller, A.D. Methuen
ANDROCLES AND THE LION RKO 1952	Shaw, G.B. (P) Constable
ANDROMEDA STRAIN, THE (V) RANK 1971	Crichton, M. Cape
AND THEN THERE WERE NONE (V) ABP 1965	Christie, A. (*Ten little niggers*) Collins
ANGEL BABY CONT DIS 1961	Barber, E.O. (*Jenny Angel*) Putnam
ANGEL LEVINE UA 1970	Malamud, B. Eyre & Spottiswoode
ANGEL WHO PAWNED HER HARP, THE BL 1954	Terrot, C. Collins
ANGEL WITH THE TRUMPET BL 1950	Lothar, E. Harrap
ANGRY HILLS, THE MGM 1959	Uris, L. Wingate
ANIMAL FARM ABP 1954	Orwell, G. Secker & Warburg
ANIMAL KINGDOM, THE RKO 1932	Barry, L. (P) French, N.Y.

9

TITLE OF FILM	AUTHOR AND PUBLISHER
ANNA AND THE KING OF SIAM FOX 1946	Landon, M. Harrap
ANNA CHRISTIE MGM 1930	O'Neill, E.G. (P) Random House, N.Y.
ANNA KARENINA (V) MGM 1935 BL 1948	Tolstoy, L.N. Various
ANNA LUCASTA COL 1948	Yordon, P. Random House, N.Y.
ANNA OF THE FIVE TOWNS BBC 2 1985 (TV)	Bennett, A. Methuen
ANNE OF GREEN GABLES RKO 1934 SULLIVAN FILMS 1985 (TV)	Montgomery, L.M. Harrap
ANNE OF THE THOUSAND DAYS (V) RANK 1969	Anderson, M. (P) Crown, N.Y.
ANNE OF WINDY POPLARS RKO 1940	Montgomery, L.M. (*Anne of Windy Willows*) Harrap
ANNIE'S COMING OUT (V) ENTERPRISE 1984	Crossley, R. *and* McDonald A. Penguin
ANNIVERSARY, THE WAR 1968	MacIlwraith, W. (P) Evans
ANN VICKERS RKO 1933	Lewis, S. Cape
ANOTHER COUNTRY (V) GOLDCREST 1983	Mitchell, J. (P) French
ANOTHER LANGUAGE MGM 1933	Franken, R. (P) Rich & Cowan
ANOTHER MAN'S POISON EROS 1952	Sands, L. (*Intent to murder*) (P) English Theatre

TITLE OF FILM	AUTHOR AND PUBLISHER
ANOTHER PART OF THE FOREST UN 1948	Hellman, L.F. (P) Viking, N.Y.
ANOTHER TIME, ANOTHER PLACE PAR 1958	Coffee, L. (*Weep no more*) Cassell
ANOTHER TIME, ANOTHER PLACE (V) CINEGATE 1983	Kesson, J. Chatto & Windus
ANTAGONISTS, THE (V) UA 1980	Gann, E.K. (U.S. Title: *Masada*) New American Library, N.Y.
ANTHONY ADVERSE WAR 1936	Allen, H. Gollancz
ANTONY AND CLEOPATRA (V) RANK 1972	Shakespeare, W. (P) Various
ANYTHING CAN HAPPEN PAR 1952	Papashvily, G. *and* Papashvily, H. Heinemann
ANY WEDNESDAY WAR 1966	Resnik, M. (*Son of any Wednesday*) (P) Stein & Day, N.Y.
APACHE UA 1954	Wellman, P.I. (*Bronco Apache*) News of the World
APACHE TERRITORY COL 1958	L'Amour, L. (*Burning Hills*) Jason Press, N.Y.
APPLE DUMPLING GANG, THE (V) DISNEY 1974	Bickham, J.M. Hale
APPOINTMENT WITH VENUS GFD 1951	Tickell, J. Hodder & Stoughton
APPENTICESHIP OF DUDDY KRAVITZ, THE (V) RANK 1975	Richler, M. Deutsch
ARCH OF TRIUMPH (V) UA 1948 HTV 1984 (TV)	Remarque, E.M. Hutchinson

TITLE OF FILM	AUTHOR AND PUBLISHER
ARE HUSBANDS NECESSARY PAR 1942	Rorick, I.S. (*Mr and Mrs Cugat*) Jarrolds
AREN'T MEN BEASTS AB 1937	Sylvaine, V. (P) French
AREN'T MEN BEASTS AB 1937	Sylvaine, V. Jenkins
AREN'T WE ALL PAR 1932	Lonsdale, F. (P) Heinemann
ARE YOU IN THE HOUSE ALONE ITV 1984 (TV)	Peck, R.H. Dell, N.Y.
ARIZONA COL 1940	Kelland, C.B. Harper, N.Y.
ARKANSAS JUDGE REP 1941	Stone, I. (*False witness*) Doubleday, N.Y.
ARMS AND THE MAN GB 1940 ARGENT 1982 (TV)	Shaw, G.B. (P) Various
ARMY BRAT MGM 1946	Waddleton, T.D. (*Little Mr Jim*) Coward-McCann, N.Y.
AROUND THE WORLD IN EIGHTY DAYS (V) UA 1957	Verne, J. Various
ARRANGEMENT, THE WAR 1969	Kazan, E. Collins
ARRIVEDERCI, BABY! PAR 1967	Deming, R. (*Careful Man, The*) W.H. Allen
ARROWHEAD PAR 1953	Burnett, W.R. (*Adobe Walls*) Knopf, N.Y.
ARROW IN THE DUST ABP 1954	Foreman, L.L. (*Road to San Jacinto*) Dutton, N.Y.

TITLE OF FILM	AUTHOR AND PUBLISHER
ARROWSMITH UA 1931	Lewis, S. (*Martin Arrowsmith*) Cape
ARSENE LUPIN MGM 1932	LeBlanc, M. Newnes
ARSENIC AND OLD LACE WAR 1944	Kesselring, J.O. (P) Random House, N.Y.
ARTURO'S ISLAND GALA 1963	Morante, E. Collins
ASHANTI (V) COL—EMI 1979	Vasquez-Figuero, A. (*Ebano*) Hale
AS HUSBANDS GO FOX 1934	Crothers, R. (P) French
ASK ANY GIRL MGM 1959	Wolfe, W. Hammond
AS LONG AS THEY'RE HAPPY GFD 1954	Sylvaine, V. (P) French
ASPERN CONNOISSEUR 1981	James, H. (*Aspern Papers, The*) Macmillan
ASPHALT JUNGLE, THE MGM 1950	Burnett, W.R. Heinemann
ASSASSINATION BUREAU, THE PAR 1969	London, J. *and* Fish, R. Deutsch
ASSAULT (V) RANK 1971	Young, K. (*Ravine, The*) Pan
ASSAULT ON A QUEEN PAR 1966	Finney, J. Eyre & Spottiswoode
ASSIGNMENT IN BRITTANY MGM 1943	MacInnes, H. Harrap
ASSIGNMENT 'K' COL 1968	Howard, H. Collins

TITLE OF FILM	AUTHOR AND PUBLISHER
ASSIGNMENT—PARIS COL 1952	Gallico, P. (*Trial by Terror*) Joseph
ASSISI UNDERGROUND, THE CANNON 1985	Ramati, A. (*While the Pope kept silent*) Allen & Unwin
AS THE EARTH TURNS WAR 1934	Carroll, G. Macmillan
ASTONISHED HEART, THE GFD 1949	Coward, N. (P) Heinemann
AS YOU DESIRE ME MGM 1932	Frank, L. (*Carl and Anna*) Davis
AS YOU LIKE IT FOX 1933	Shakespeare, W. (P) Various
ATLANTIC BI 1930	Raymond, E. (*Berg, The*) (P) Benn
ATTEMPTS TO KILL AA 1961	Wallace, E. (*Lone House Mystery, The*) Collins
AT THE EARTH'S CORE (V) BL 1976	Burroughs, E.R. Ace, N.Y.
AT THE VILLA ROSE AB 1940	Mason, A.E.W. Hodder & Stoughton
ATTICA (V) ITV 1985 (TV)	Wicker, T. (*Time to die*) Bodley Head
AT WAR WITH THE ARMY (V) PAR 1951	Allardice, J. (P) French, N.Y.
AUDREY ROSE (V) UA 1977	De Felitta, F. Collins
AUNT CLARA BL 1954	Streatfeild, N. Collins

14

TITLE OF FILM	AUTHOR AND PUBLISHER

AUNTIE MAME
WAR 1958

Dennis, P.
Vanguard, N.Y.

AUNTIE MAME
WAR 1958

Lawrence, J. *and* Lee, R.E. (P)
Vanguard, N.Y.

AUTOBIOGRAPHY OF MISS JANE PITTMAN, THE
SAGA 1975

Gaines, E.J.
Bantam

AUTUMN CROCUS
BI 1930

Anthony, C.L. (P)
Gollancz

AVALANCHE
PRC 1946

Boyle K.
Faber

AVALANCHE EXPRESS (V)
FOX 1979

Forbes, C.
Dutton, N.Y.

AVENGERS, THE
REP 1950

Beach, R.E. (*Don Careless*)
Hutchinson

AWAKENING, THE (V)
COL—EMI—WAR 1980

Stoker, B. (*Jewel of the Seven Stars*)
Jarrolds

AWAY ALL BOATS
UI 1955

Dodson, K.
Angus and Robertson

B

BABBIT
IN 1934

Lewis, S.
Cape

BABY AND THE BATTLESHIP, THE
BL 1956

Thorne, A.
Heinemann

BABY DOLL
WAR 1956

Williams, T. (P)
Secker & Warburg

BABY LOVE
AVCO EMBASSY 1969

Christian, T.C.
Cape

BABY, THE RAIN MUST FALL
COL 1965

Foote, H. (*Travelling Lady, The*) (P)
Dramatists, N.Y.

TITLE OF FILM	AUTHOR AND PUBLISHER
BACHELOR GIRL APARTMENT WAR 1966	Resnik, M. (*Any Wednesday*) (P) English Theatre
BACHELOR IN PARADISE MGM 1961	Caspary, V. Pan
BACHELOR PARTY, THE COL 1957	Chayefsky, P. (P) Simon & Schuster, N.Y.
BACHELOR'S FOLLY WW 1932	Wallace, E. (*Calendar, The*) (P) Collins
BACK FROM THE DEAD FOX 1957	Turney, C. (*Other One, The*) Holt, N.Y.
BACKGROUND ABP 1953	Chetham-Strode, W. (P) French
BACKGROUND TO DANGER WAR 1943	Ambler, E. (*Uncommon Danger*) Hodder & Stoughton
BACKSTAIRS AT THE WHITE HOUSE BBC 2 1984 (TV)	Parks, L.A. (*It was fun working at the White House*) Fleet, N.Y.
BACK STREET UN 1931 UN 1941 UN 1961	Hurst, F. Cape
BACK TO GOD'S COUNTRY GFD 1953	Curwood, J.O. Triangle Bks, N.Y.
BAD DAY AT BLACK ROCK MGM 1955	Niall, M. Muller
BADGER'S GREEN HIGHBURY 1949	Sherriff, R.C. (P) Gollancz
BAD MEN OF TOMBSTONE ABP 1949	Monoghan, J. (*Last of the Badmen*) Bobbs-Merrill, Indianapolis
BAD SEED WAR 1956	March, W. Hamilton

16

TITLE OF FILM	AUTHOR AND PUBLISHER
BAHAMA PASSAGE PAR 1941	Hayes, N. (*Dido Cay*) Davies
BALCONY, THE BL 1963	Genet, J. (P) Faber
BAMBI RKO 1942	Salten, F. Cape
BANANA RIDE ABP 1941	Travers, B. (P) French
BAND OF ANGELS WAR 1956	Warren, R.P. Eyre & Spottiswoode
BANG THE DRUM SLOWLY GUILD HOME VIDEO (TV) 1982	Harris, M. Buccaneer, Cutchogue, N.Y.
BANK SHOT, THE UA 1974	Westlake, D.E. Simon & Schuster, N.Y.
BARABBAS (V) COL 1962	Lagerkvist, P. Four Square Bks
BARCHESTER CHRONICLES, THE BBC 1982 (TV)	Trollope, A. (*Barchester Towers:* *Warden, The*) Various
BAREFOOT IN THE PARK (V) PAR 1967	Simon, N. (P) French, N.Y.
BAREFOOT MAILMAN, THE COL 1951	Pratt, T. Cassell
BARRETTS OF WIMPOLE STREET, THE MGM 1934 MGM 1956	Besier, R. (P) Gollancz
BARRETTS OF WIMPOLE STREET, THE MGM 1934 MGM 1956	Besier, R. Gollancz
BAR 20 UA 1943	Mulford, C.E. Hodder & Stoughton

TITLE OF FILM	AUTHOR AND PUBLISHER
BAR 20 RIDES AGAIN PAR 1935	Mulford, C.E. Hodder & Stoughton
BAT, THE WAR 1959	Rinehart, M.R. (P) French
BATTLE CRY WAR 1954	Uris, L. Wingate
BATTLE FOR ANZIO, THE (V) COL 1968	Vaughan Thomas, W. (*Anzio*) Longmans
BATTLE HYMN UI 1956	Hess, D.E. Davies
BATTLE OF BRITAIN, THE UA 1969	Wood, D. *and* Dempster, D. (*Narrow Margin, The*) Arrow
BATTLE OF THE BULGE (V) CINERAMA 1965	Merriam, R.E. Panther
BATTLE OF THE RIVER PLATE, THE (V) RANK 1956	Powell, M. (*Graf Spee*) Hodder & Stoughton
BAT WHISPERS, THE UA 1931	Rinehart, M.R. (*Bat, The*) Cassell
BAWDY ADVENTURES OF TOM JONES, THE CIC 1976	Fielding, H. (*Tom Jones*) Various
BAXTER! MGM—EMI 1972	Platt, K. (*Boy Who Could Make Himself Disappear, The*) Chilton, Philadelphia
BEACHCOMBER GFD 1954	Maugham, W.S. (*Vessel of Wrath*) Heinemann
BEACHHEAD UA 1953	Hubler, R.G. (*I've Got Mine*) Putnam, N.Y.
BEAR ISLAND (V) COL—EMI—WAR 1979	MacLean, A. Collins

18

TITLE OF FILM	AUTHOR AND PUBLISHER
BEARS AND I, THE (V) DISNEY 1974	Leslie, R.F. Ballantine, N.Y.
BEAST FROM 20,000 FATHOMS, THE WAR 1953	Bradbury, R. (*Foghorn, The*) Doubleday, N.Y.
BEAST WITH FIVE FINGERS (V) WAR 1946	Harvey, W.F. Dent
BEAT THE DEVIL ROMULUS 1953	Helvick, J. Boardman
BEAU BRUMMELL MGM 1954	Fitch, C. (P) Lane, N.Y.
BEAU GESTE PAR 1939 UI 1966 BBC 1984 (TV)	Wren, P.C. Murray
BEAU IDEAL RKO 1931	Wren, P.C. Murray
BEAU JAMES PAR 1957	Fowler, G. Viking, N.Y.
BEAU SABREUR PAR 1928	Wren, P.C. Murray
BEAUTY FOR SALE MGM 1933	Baldwin, F. (*Beauty*) Sampson Low
BEAUTY'S DAUGHTER FOX 1935	Norris, K. Murray
BECAUSE THEY'RE YOUNG COL 1960	Farris, J. (*Harrison High*) Gollancz
BECKET (V) PAR 1963	Anouilh, J. (P) Methuen
BECKY SHARP RKO 1935	Thackerary, W.M. (*Vanity Fair*) Various

TITLE OF FILM	AUTHOR AND PUBLISHER
BEDELIA GFD 1946	Caspary, V. Eyre & Spottiswoode
BEDFORD INCIDENT, THE BL 1964	Rascovich, M. Secker & Warburg
BEDKNOB AND BROOMSTICK DISNEY 1971	Norton, M. Dent
BED SITTING ROOM, THE UA 1969	Milligan, S. *and* Antrobus, J. M. & J. Hobbs
BEFORE I WAKE GN 1955	Debrett, H. Dodd, N.Y.
BEGGARS OF LIFE PAR 1928	Tully, J. Chatto & Windus
BEGGAR'S OPERA, THE (V) BL 1953	Gay, J. (P) French
BEGUILED, THE UN 1971	Cullinan, T. Sphere
BEHIND THAT CURTAIN FOX 1930	Biggers, E.D. Harrap
BEHIND THE HEADLINES RANK 1956	Chapman, R. Laurie
BEHIND THE MASK BL 1958	Wilson, J.R. (*Mask, The*) Heinemann
BEHOLD A PALE HORSE COL 1964	Pressburger, E. (*Killing a Mouse on Sunday*) Harcourt, N.Y.
BEHOLD MY WIFE PAR 1935	Parker, G. (*Translations of a Savage*) Methuen
BEING THERE (V) ITC 1980	Kosinski, J. Bantam, N.Y.
BELL, THE BBC 1982 (TV)	Murdock, I. Chatto & Windus

TITLE OF FILM	AUTHOR AND PUBLISHER
BELLA DONNA OLY 1935 UN 1945	Hichens, R. Heinemann
BELL, BOOK AND CANDLE COL 1958	Druten, J. van (P) French
BELL JAR, THE AVCO EMBASSY 1978	Plath, S. Harper, N.Y.
BELLE DE JOUR CURZON 1967	Kessel, J. Barker
BELLE OF NEW YORK, THE MGM 1952	McLellan, C.M.S. (P) French
BELL FOR ADANO, A FOX 1945	Hersey, J.R. Gollancz
BELLS ARE RINGING MGM 1960	Comden, B. *and* Green, A. (P) Random House, N.Y.
BELLS GO DOWN, THE EAL 1943	Methuen
BELLS ON THEIR TOES FOX 1952	Gilbreth, F.B. *and* Carey, E.` Heinemann
BELOVED INFIDEL FOX 1959	Graham, S. *and* Frank, G. Cassell
BELOVED VAGABOND, THE COL 1937	Locke, W.J. Lane
BELOW THE BELT (V) PRODUCTIONS ASSOCIATED 1982	Drexler, R. (*Submission of a Lady Wrestler*) Mayflower
BELSTONE FOX, THE (V) FOX—RANK 1973	Rook, D. (*Ballad of . . .*) Hodder & Stoughton
BEN HUR (V) MGM 1931 MGM 1959	Wallace, L. Various

TITLE OF FILM	AUTHOR AND PUBLISHER
BENSON MURDER CASE, THE PAR 1930	Dine, S.S. van Benn
BEQUEST TO THE NATION UN 1972	Rattigan, T. (P) Hamilton
BERKELEY SQUARE FOX 1933	Balderston, J.L. (P) French
BERLIN AFFAIR, THE CANNON 1986	Tanizaki, J. (*Buddhist cross, The*) Putnam, N.Y.
BERLIN ALEXANDERPLATZ CHANNEL 4 1985 (TV)	Doblin, A. Penguin
BERLIN TUNNEL BBC 1984 (TV)	Lindquist, D. Methuen
BERNARDINE FOX 1957	Chase, M. (P) Oxford U.P.
BEST DEFENCE UIP 1984	Grossbach, R. (*Easy and hard ways out*) Carroll & Graf, N.Y.
BEST MAN, THE UA 1968	Vidal, G. (P) Little, Brown, Boston
BEST MAN WINS, THE COL 1948	Twain, M. (*Celebrated Jumping Frog of Calaveras, The*) Various
BEST OF EVERYTHING, THE FOX 1959	Jaffé, R. Cape
BEST YEARS OF OUR LIVES, THE RKO 1946	Kantor, M. (*Glory for me*) Coward-McCann, N.Y.
BETRAYAL VIRGIN 1983	Pinter, H. (P) Eyre-Methuen
BETRAYAL FROM THE EAST RKO 1945	Hynd, A. McBride, N.Y.

TITLE OF FILM	AUTHOR AND PUBLISHER
BETSY, THE (V) UA 1978	Robbins, H. New English Library
BETWEEN HEAVEN AND HELL FOX 1956	Gwaltney, F.I. (*Day the Century Ended, The*) Secker & Warburg
BETWEEN TWO WORLDS WAR 1944	Vane, S. (*Outward Bound*) (P) Chatto & Windus
BEWARE MY LOVELY RKO 1952	Dineli, M. (*Man, The*) (P) Dramatists, N.Y.
BEWARE OF PITY TC 1946	Zweig, S. Cassell
BEYOND REASONABLE DOUBT (V) J & M FILMS 1980	Yallop, D. Hodder & Stoughton
BEYOND THE CURTAIN RANK 1960	Wallis, A.J. *and* Blair, C.E. (*Thunder Above*) Jarrolds
BEYOND THE FOREST WAR 1951	Engstrand, S.D. Cape
BEYOND THE POSEIDON ADVENTURE (V) COL—EMI—WAR 1979	Gallico, P. Joseph
BEYOND THE RIVER FOX 1955	Simenon, G. (*Bottom of the Bottle*) Doubleday, N.Y.
BEYOND THIS PLACE REN 1959	Cronin, A.J. Gollancz
BHOWANI JUNCTION MGM 1955	Masters, J. Joseph
BICYCLE THIEVES (V) MGM 1949	Bartolini, L. Joseph
BIG BANKROLL WAR 1961	Katcher, L. Gollancz

TITLE OF FILM	AUTHOR AND PUBLISHER
BIG BOUNCE, THE WAR 1968	Leonard, E. Hale
BIG CLOCK, THE PAR 1948	Fearing, K. Lane
BIG COUNTRY, THE UA 1958	Hamilton, D. Wingate
BIG FISHERMAN, THE DISNEY 1959	Douglas, L.C. Davies
BIG FIX, THE CIC 1979	Simon, R.L. Pocket Books, N.Y.
BIG HEAT, THE COL 1953	McGivern, W.P. Hamilton
BIG HOUSE, THE MGM 1930	Robinson, L. Macmillan
BIG JACK MGM 1949	Flexner, J.T. (*Doctors on Horseback*) Heinemann
BIG KNIFE, THE UA 1955	Odets, C. (P) Random House, N.Y.
BIG NIGHT, THE UA 1951	Ellin, S. (*Dreadful Summit*) Simon & Schuster, N.Y.
BIG RED (V) DISNEY 1962	Kjelgaard, J.A. Grosset, N.Y.
BIG SKY, THE (V) RKO 1952	Guthrie, A.B. Boardman
BIG SLEEP, THE (V) WAR 1946 ITC 1978	Chandler, R. Hamilton
BIG SNATCH, THE GALA 1963	Trinian, J. (*Big Grab, The*) Pyramid Bks
BIG STICK UP AT BRINKS UN 1979	Behn, N. (*Brink's Job, The*) Putnam, N.Y.

BILLIE
UA 1965

Alexander, R. (*Time Out For Ginger*) (P)
Dramatists, N.Y.

BILLION DOLLAR BRAIN (V)
UA 1967

Deighton, L.
Cape

BILL OF DIVORCEMENT, A (V)
RKO 1932
RKO 1940

Dane, C. (P)
Heinemann

BILLY BUDD
ANGLO-ALLIED 1962

Melville, H.
Various

BILLY BUDD
ANGLO-ALLIED 1962

Coxe, L.O. *and* Chapman, R.H. (P)
Hill and Wang, N.Y.

BILLY LIAR (V)
WAR 1962

Waterhouse, K.
Joseph

BILLY LIAR (V)
WAR 1962

Waterhouse, K. *and* Hall, W. (P)
Joseph

BILLY THE KID
MGM 1941

Burns, W.N. (*Saga of Billy the Kid*)
Grosset, N.Y.

**BINGO LONG TRAVELLING ALL STARS
AND MOTOR KINGS, THE**
CIC 1976

Brashler, W.
Harper, N.Y.

BIOGRAPHY OF A BACHELOR GIRL
MGM 1935

Behrman, S.N. (*Biography*) (P)
French

BIRD MAN OF ALCATRAZ
UA 1962

Gaddis, T.E.
Four Square Books

BIRDS, THE (V)
RANK 1963

Du Maurier, D.
Gollancz

BIRDY
TRI-STAR 1984 (TV)

Wharton, W.
Knopf, N.Y.

BIRTHDAY PARTY, THE (V)
CINERAMA 1968

Pinter, H. (P)
Methuen

TITLE OF FILM	AUTHOR AND PUBLISHER
BISHOP MURDER CASE, THE MGM 1930	Dine, S.S. van Cassell
BISHOP'S WIFE, THE RKO 1947	Nathan, R. (*In Barley Fields*) Constable
BITCH, THE (V) BRENT—WALKER 1979	Collins, J. Pan
BITTER HARVEST (V) RANK 1962	Hamilton, P. (*Twenty Thousand Streets Under the Sky*) Constable
BITTER SWEET MGM 1940	Coward, N. (P) Heinemann
BITTER TEA OF GENERAL YEN, THE COL 1933	Stone, *Mrs* G. Bobbs-Merrill, Indianapolis
BLACK ACES UN 1937	Payne, S. Wright & Brown
BLACK ANGEL UN 1946	Woolrich, C. Doubleday, N.Y.
BLACK ARROW (V) COL 1948 DISNEY 1985 (TV)	Stevenson, R.L. Various
BLACKBEARD'S GHOST DISNEY 1968	Stahl, B. Houghton, Mifflin, Boston
BLACK BEAUTY (V) FOX 1946 TIGON 1971	Sewell, A. Various
BLACK BIRD, THE COL—WAR 1975	Hammett, D. (*Maltese Falcon, The*) Cassell
BLACKBOARD JUNGLE MGM 1954	Hunter, E. Constable
BLACK CAMEL FOX 1931	Biggers, E.D. Cassell

TITLE OF FILM	AUTHOR AND PUBLISHER
BLACK CAT, THE UN 1934	Poe, E.A. Various
BLACK CAULDRON, THE DISNEY 1985	Alexander, L. Collins
BLACK EAGLE COL 1948	Henry, O. (*Passing of Black Eagle*) Various
BLACK EYE COL—WAR 1973	Jacks, J. (*Murder on the Wild Side*) Fawcett, N.Y.
BLACK FLOWERS FOR THE BRIDE FOX 1970	Kressing, H. (*Cook, The*) Panther
BLACK JACK (V) ENTERPRISE 1980	Garfield, L. Longmans
BLACK LIMELIGHT ALL 1939	Sherry, G. (P) French
BLACK MAGIC UA 1949	Dumas, A. (*Memoirs of a Physician*) Routledge
BLACKMAIL BI 1929	Bennett, C. (P) Rich & Cowan
BLACKMAILER GFD 1951	Myers, E. (*Mrs Christopher*) Chapman & Hall
BLACK MARBLE, THE (V) AVCO EMBASSY 1980	Wambaugh, J. Dell, N.Y.
BLACK NARCISSUS (V) ARC 1947	Godden, R. Davies
BLACK ROSE, THE FOX 1949	Costain, T.B. Staples
BLACK SHIELD OF FALWORTH, THE UI 1954	Pyle, H. (*Men of Iron*) Various
BLACK STALLION (V) UA 1979	Farley, W. Random House, N.Y.

TITLE OF FILM	AUTHOR AND PUBLISHER

BLACK STALLION RETURNS (V)
MGM 1984

Farley, W.
Hodder & Stoughton

BLACK SUNDAY (V)
PAR 1977

Harris, T.
Hodder & Stoughton

BLACK SWAN, THE
FOX 1942

Sabatini, R.
Hutchinson

BLACK TOWER, THE
ANGLIA 1985 (TV)

James, P.D.
Sphere

BLACK TULIP, THE
CINERAMA 1965

Dumas, A.
Various

BLACK WIDOW
FOX 1954

Quentin, P.
Simon & Schuster, N.Y.

BLACK WINDMILL, THE
PAR 1974

Egleton, C. (*Seven Days to a Killing*)
Hodder & Stoughton

BLADE RUNNER (V)
COL—EMI—WAR 1982

Dick, P.K. (*Do Androids Dream of Electric Sheep?*)
Ballantine, N.Y.

BLANCHE FURY
CIN 1948

Shearing, J.
Heinemann

BLAZE AT NOON
PAR 1947

Gann, E.K.
Aldor

BLAZE OF THE SUN
PAR 1959

Hougron, J.
Hurst & Blackett

BLEAK HOUSE
BBC 2 1985 (TV)

Dickens, C.
Various

BLESS THE BEASTS AND CHILDREN
COL 1971

Swarthout, G.
Secker & Warburg

BLIND DATE (V)
RANK 1959

Howard, L.
Longmans

BLINDFOLD
UI 1965

Fletcher, L.
Eyre & Spottiswoode

BLIND GODDESS, THE
FOX 1948

Hastings, *Sir* P. (P)
French

BLISS
NEW SOUTH WALES 1984

Carey, P.
Faber

BLITHE SPIRIT
CIN 1945

Coward, N. (P)
Heinemann

BLOCKADE
RKO 1928

Chatterton, E.K. (*'Q' Ships and their Story*)
Sidgwick & Jackson

BLOOD ALLEY
WAR 1955

Fleischman, A.S.
Corgi

BLOOD AND SAND
FOX 1941

Ibanez, V.B.
Grosset, N.Y.

BLOODBROTHERS (V)
COL—WAR 1978

Price, R.
Bantam, N.Y.

BLOOD FROM THE MUMMY'S TOMB (V)
MGM—EMI 1971

Stoker, B. (*Jewel of the Seven Stars*)
Jarrolds

BLOODHOUNDS OF BROADWAY
FOX 1952

Runyon, D.
Various

BLOOD HUNT
BBC 2 1986 (TV)

Gunn, N.
Souvenir

BLOODLINE (V)
CIC 1979

Sheldon, S.
Morrow, N.Y.

BLOOD OF OTHERS, THE
ORION 1985 (TV)

De Beauvoir, S.
Penguin

BLOOD ON MY HANDS
UI 1949

Butler, G. (*Kiss the Blood off my Hands*)
Jarrolds

BLOOD RELATIVES
RANK 1978

McBain, E.
Hamilton

TITLE OF FILM	AUTHOR AND PUBLISHER
BLOTT ON THE LANDSCAPE BBC 1985 (TV)	Sharpe, T. Secker & Warburg
BLUE ANGEL, THE PAR 1930 FOX 1959	Mann, H. Jarrolds
BLUEBELL BBC 1986 (TV)	Perry, G. Pavilion
BLUE BIRD, THE FOX 1940 FOX 1976	Maeterlinck, M. (P) Various
BLUE FIN SOUTH AUSTRALIA FILM 1978	Thiele, C. Collins
BLUE JEANS FOX 1959	Herlihy, J.L. *and* Noble, W. (*Blue Denim*) (P) Random House, N.Y.
BLUE LAGOON (V) INDIVIDUAL 1949 COL 1980	Stacpoole, H. de V. Various
BLUE MAX, THE (V) FOX 1965	Hunter, J.D. Muller
BLUE NIGHT, THE BUTCHER 1973	Wambaugh, J. Joseph
BOAT, THE (V) COL—EMI—WAR 1982	Buchheim, L-G. Knopf, N.Y.
BOB AND CAROL AND TED AND ALICE (V) COL 1970	Welles, P. Corgi
BOBBY DEERFIELD (V) COL—WAR 1977	Remarque, E.M. (*Heaven has no Favourites*) Harcourt, N.Y.
BOBO, THE WAR 1967	Cole, B. (*Olimpia*) W.H. Allen

TITLE OF FILM	AUTHOR AND PUBLISHER
BODY, THE KESTREL ANGLO-EMI 1971	Smith, A. Allen & Unwin
BODY IN THE LIBRARY, THE BBC 1984 (TV)	Christie, A. Collins
BODY SNATCHER, THE RKO 1945	Stevenson, R.L. Various
BOFORS GUN, THE UI 1968	McGrath, J. (*Events whilst Guarding the Bofors Gun*) (P) Methuen
BOMBAY MAIL UN 1934	Blochman, L.G. Collins
BONAVENTURE GFD 1951	Hastings, C. (P) French
BONJOUR TRISTESSE COL 1957	Sagan, F. Murray
BON VOYAGE DISNEY 1962	Hayes, M. *and* Hayes, J.A. Deutsch
BON VOYAGE BBC 1985 (TV)	Coward, N. Methuen
BOOM UI 1968	Williams, T. (*Milk Train doesn't stop here anymore*) (P) Secker & Warburg
BORDER LEGION PAR 1930	Grey, Z. Hodder & Stoughton
BORDERLINES UA 1965	Telfer, D. (*Caretakers, The*) Macdonald
BORN AGAIN (V) AVCO EMBASSY 1979	Colson, C. Bantam, N.Y.
BORN FREE (V) BL 1965	Adamson, J. Collins

TITLE OF FILM	AUTHOR AND PUBLISHER
BORN RECKLESS FOX 1930	Clarke, D.H. (*Louis Beretti*) Long
BORN TO BE BAD RKO 1950	Parrish, A. (*All Kneeling*) Benn
BORN TO KILL RKO 1947	Gunn, J.E. (*Deadlier than the Male*) World, N.Y.
BORN YESTERDAY COL 1951 CANNON 1986	Kanin, G. (P) Viking, N.Y.
BOSTONIANS, THE (V) RANK 1984	James, H. Various
BOSTON STRANGLER, THE (V) FOX 1968	Frank, G. Cape
BOTANY BAY PAR 1952	Nordhoff, C. *and* Hall, J.N. Chapman & Hall
BOUGHT WAR 1931	Henry, H. (*Jackdaws Strut*) Paul
BOUND FOR GLORY UA 1977	Guthrie, W. Dutton, N.Y.
BOUNTY, THE (V) COL—EMI—WAR 1984	Hough, R. (*Captain Bligh and Mr. Christian*) Hutchinson
BOX OF DELIGHT, THE BBC 1984 (TV)	Masefield, J. Heinemann
BOYD'S SHOP RANK 1960	Ervine, St. J.G. (P) Allen & Unwin
BOY FRIEND, THE MGM—EMI 1971	Wilson, S. (P) Penguin
BOY IN THE BUSH, THE CHANNEL 4 1984 (TV)	Lawrence, D.H. *and* Skinner, M.L. Heinemann

BOY ON A DOLPHIN, THE
FOX 1957

Divine, D.
Murray

BOY WHO DRANK TOO MUCH, THE
MTM 1980 (TV)

Greene, S.
Viking, N.Y.

BOYS FROM BRAZIL, THE (V)
ITC 1978

Levin, I.
Joseph

BOYS IN BROWN
GFD 1949

Beckwith, R. (P)
Marshall

BOYS IN THE BAND, THE
WAR 1969

Crowley, M. (P)
Secker & Warburg

BRAMBLE BUSH
WAR 1959

Mergendahl, C.
Muller

BRANDED
PAR 1950

Evans, E.
Various

BRANDY FOR THE PARSON
MGM 1952

Household, G.
Joseph

BRASHER DOUBLOON, THE
MGM 1947

Chandler, R. (*High Window, The*)
Hamilton

BRASS BOTTLE, THE
RANK 1964

Anstey, F.
Murray

BRASS TARGET
MGM 1978

Nolan, F. (*Algonquin Project, The*)
Morrow, N.Y.

BRAT
FOX 1931

Fulton, M. (P)
Longmans, N.Y.

BRAT FARRAR
HAMMER 1950
BBC 1986 (TV)

Tey, J.
Davies

BRAVADOS, THE
FOX 1958

O'Rourke, F.
Heinemann

BRAVE BULLS, THE
COL 1950

Lea, T.
Heinemann

TITLE OF FILM	AUTHOR AND PUBLISHER
BREAKFAST AT TIFFANYS (V) PAR 1961	Capote, T. Hamilton
BREAKHEART PASS (V) UA 1975	MacLean, A. Collins
BREAKING POINT WAR 1950	Hemingway, E. (*To Have and Have not*) Cape
BREAKING POINT, THE BUTCHER 1960	Meynell, L. Collins
BREAK IN THE CIRCLE EXCLUSIVE 1954	Loraine, P. Hodder & Stoughton
BREAKOUT (V) COL—WAR 1975	Asinof, C. (*Ten Second Jailbreak*) Joseph
BREAKOUT CFTF 1984	Gillham, B. (*Place to hide, A*) Deutsch
BREATH OF SCANDAL, A PAR 1960	Molnar, F. (*Olympia*) (P) Brentano, N.Y.
BREWSTER'S MILLIONS (V) UA 1945 CUIP 1985 (TV)	McCutcheon, G.B. Various
BRIDAL PATH, THE BL 1959	Tranter, N. Hodder & Stoughton
BRIDES ARE LIKE THAT IN 1936	Conners, B. (*Applesauce*) (P) French, N.Y.
BRIDE WORD BLACK, THE UA 1968	Irish, W. Sphere
BRIDESHEAD REVISITED ITV 1982 (TV)	Waugh, E. Penguin
BRIDGE AT REMAGEN, THE UA 1968	Hechler, K. Pan

TITLE OF FILM	AUTHOR AND PUBLISHER
BRIDGE IN THE JUNGLE, THE UA 1971	Traven, B. Cape
BRIDGE OF SAN LUIS RAY, THE MGM 1929 UA 1944	Wilder, T. Longmans
BRIDGE ON THE RIVER KWAI, THE COL 1957	Boulle, P. Fontana
BRIDGES AT TOKO-RI, THE (V) PAR 1954	Michener, J.A. Secker & Warburg
BRIDGE TOO FAR, A (V) UA 1977	Ryan, C. Hamilton
BRIDGE TO THE SUN MGM 1961	Terasaki, G. Joseph
BRIEF ENCOUNTER (V) CIN 1946	Coward, N. (*Still Life*) (P) French
BRIGADOON (V) MGM 1954	Lerner, A.J. (P) Theatre Arts
BRIGHT LEAF WAR 1950	Fitz-Simons, F. Rinehart, N.Y.
BRIGHTON ROCK (V) AB 1948	Greene, G. Heinemann
BRIGHT VICTORY UI 1951	Kendrick, B.H. (*Lights Out*) W.H. Allen
BRITANNIA OF BILLINGSGATE GB 1933	Jope-Slade, C. *and* Stokes, S. (P) French
BRITISH AGENT IN 1934	Lockhart, *Sir* R.H.B. (*Memoirs of a* . . .) Putnam
BROKEN ARROW FOX 1950	Arnold, E. (*Blood Brother*) Collins

TITLE OF FILM	AUTHOR AND PUBLISHER
BROTHER ORCHID WAR 1940	Connell, R.E. (P) French, N.Y.
BROTHER RAT FOX 1938	Monks, J. *and* Finklehoffe, F.R. (P) Random House, N.Y.
BROTHERS, THE FOX 1947	Strong, L.A.G. Gollancz
BROTHERS IN LAW BL 1956	Cecil, H. Joseph
BROTHERS KARAMAZOV, THE MGM 1957 COL—WAR 1972	Dostoevski, F. Various
BROTHERS RICO COL 1957	Simenon, G. Doubleday, N.Y.
BROTHER'S TALE, A GRANADA 1983 (TV)	Barstow, S. Corgi
BROWNING VERSION, THE GFD 1951	Rattigan, T. (P) French
BROWN ON 'RESOLUTION' GB 1933	Forester, C.S. Lane
BUCCANEER, THE PAR 1938	Saxon, L. (*LaFitte the Pirate*) Appleton-Century, N.Y.
BUG (V) PAR 1975	Page, T. (*Hephaestus Plague, The*) Putnam
BUGLES IN THE AFTERNOON WAR 1952	Haycox, E. Hodder & Stoughton
BUILD MY GALLOWS HIGH RKO 1947	Homes, G. Grosset, N.Y.
BULLDOG DRUMMOND AT BAY REP 1937	'Sapper' Hodder & Stoughton
BULLDOG DRUMMOND COMES BACK PAR 1937	'Sapper' (*Female of the Species, The*) Hodder & Stoughton

BULLDOG DRUMMOND IN AFRICA
PAR 1938

'Sapper' (*Challenge, The*)
Hodder & Stoughton

BULLDOG DRUMMOND'S PERIL
PAR 1938

'Sapper' (*Third Round, The*)
Hodder & Stoughton

BULLDOG DRUMMOND'S SECRET POLICE
PAR 1939

'Sapper' (*Temple Tower*)
Hodder & Stoughton

BULLITT (V)
WAR 1968

Pike, R.L. (*Mute Witness*) (P)
Deutsch

BUNKER BEAN
RKO 1936

Wilson, H.L.
Lane

BUNNY LAKE IS MISSING
COL 1965

Piper, E.
Secker & Warburg

BURIED ALIVE
AIRTIME 1983

Bennett, A.
Penguin

BURN 'EM UP O'CONNOR
MGM 1939

Campbell, *Sir* M. (*Salute to the Gods*)
Cassell

BURNT OFFERINGS
UA 1976

Marasco, R.
Coronet

BUSMAN'S HOLIDAY
MGM 1940

Sayers, D.L. (*Busman's Honeymoon*)
Gollancz

BUSMAN'S HOLIDAY
MGM 1940

Sayers, D.L. *and* Byrne, M. St. C.
(*Busman's Honeymoon*) (P)
Harcourt, N.Y.

BUS STOP
FOX 1956

Inge, W. (P)
Random House, N.Y.

BUSY BODY, THE
PAR 1968

Westlake, D.E.
Boardman

BUTLEY
SEVEN KINGS 1973

Gray, S. (P)
Viking, N.Y.

TITLE OF FILM	AUTHOR AND PUBLISHER
BUT NOT FOR ME PAR 1959	Raphaelson, S. (*Accent on Youth*) (P) Gollancz
BUTTERCUP CHAIN, THE COL 1969	Elliot, J. Panther
BUTTERFIELD 8 MGM 1960	O'Hara, J. Cresset Press
BUTTERFLIES ARE FREE COL 1972	Gershe, L. Random House, N.Y.
BUTTERFLY (V) J & M FILMS 1981	Cain, J.M. Random House, N.Y.
BUT THE FLESH IS WEAK MGM 1932	Novello, I. (*Truth Game, The*) (P) French, N.Y.
BY LOVE POSSESSED UA 1961	Cozzens, J.G. Longmans
BY THE LIGHT OF THE SILVERY MOON WAR 1953	Tarkington, B. (*Penrod*) Hodder & Stoughton
BY THE SWORD DIVIDED BBC 1983 (TV)	Adair, J. Century

C

CABARET (V) CINERAMA 1972	Druten, J. van (*I am a Camera*) (P) Evans
CACTUS FLOWER (V) COL 1969	Burrows, A. (P) French, N.Y.
CADDIE (V) HEMDALE 1976	Brink, C.R. (*Caddie Woodlawn*) Collier-Macmillan
CAESAR AND CLEOPATRA (V) PASCAL 1945	Shaw, G.B. (P) Various
CAINE MUTINY, THE COL 1954	Wouk, H. Cape

TITLE OF FILM	AUTHOR AND PUBLISHER
CAIRO MGM 1963	Burnett, W.R. (*Asphalt Jungle, The*) Corgi
CAL (V) WAR 1984	MacLaverty, B. Cape
CALENDAR, THE GFD 1932 GFD 1948	Wallace, E. (P) French, N.Y.
CALIFORNIA SUITE (V) COL 1979	Simon, N. (P) Random House, N.Y.
CALLAN EMI 1974	Mitchell, J. (*Red File for Callan, A*) Simon & Schuster, N.Y.
CALL HER SAVAGE FOX 1932	Thayer, T. Long
CALLING BULLDOG DRUMMOND MGM 1951	Fairlie, G. Hodder & Stoughton
CALLING PHILO VANCE WAR 1940	Dine, S.S. van (*Kennel Murder Case, The*) Cassell
CALL IT A DAY WAR 1937	Smith, D. (P) Gollancz
CALL OF THE WILD, THE (V) UA 1935 MGM—EMI 1972	London, J. Heinemann
CALLING DR KILDARE MGM 1935	Brand, M. Hodder & Stoughton
CALLING OF DAN MATTHEWS, THE COL 1946	Wright, H.B. Hodder & Stoughton
CALYPSO BL 1956	Poe, E.A. (*Gold Bug, The and Telltale Heart, The*) Various
CAMELOT (V) WAR 1967	White, T.H. (*Once and Future King, The*) Collins

TITLE OF FILM	AUTHOR AND PUBLISHER
CAMILLE MGM 1936 ROSEMOUNT 1984 (TV)	Dumas, A. *fils* (*La Dame aux Camélias*) Various
CAMPBELL'S KINGDOM (V) RANK 1957	Innes, H. Collins
CANARY MURDER CASE, THE PAR 1929	Dine, S.S. van Benn
CANCEL MY RESERVATION MGM—EMI 1972	L'Amour, L. (*Broken Gun, The*) Corgi
CANDLESHOE (V) DISNEY 1977	Innes, M. (*Christmas at Candleshoe*) Gollancz
CANDY CINERAMA 1968	Southern, T. *and* Hoffenberg, M. Geis
CANNERY ROW (V) MGM 1981	Steinbeck, J. Heinemann
CANTERBURY TALES, THE UA 1972	Chaucer, G. Various
CANTERVILLE GHOST, THE MGM 1944	Wilde, O. Collins
CANYON PASSAGE UN 1946	Haycox, E. Hodder & Stoughton
CAPE FEAR UI 1962	Macdonald, J.D. (*Executioners, The*) Hale
CAPPY RICKS RETURNS REP 1935	Kyne, P.B. (*Cappy Ricks Comes Back*) Hodder & Stoughton
CAPTAIN BLOOD (V) WAR 1936	Sabatini, R. Hutchinson
CAPTAIN BLOOD, FUGITIVE COL 1952	Sabatini, R. (*Captain Blood Returns*) Hutchinson

CAPTAIN BOYCOTT INDIVIDUAL 1947	Rooney, P. Talbot Press
CAPTAIN CAUTION UA 1940	Roberts, K. Collins
CAPTAIN FROM CASTILLE FOX 1948	Shellabarger, S. Macmillan
CAPTAIN HORATIO HORNBLOWER, R.N. WAR 1951	Forester, C.S. (*Captain Hornblower, R.N.*) Joseph
CAPTAIN IS A LADY, THE MGM 1940	Crothers, R. (*Old Lady 31*) (P) Various
CAPTAIN LIGHTFOOT UI 1954	Burnett, W.R. Macdonald
CAPTAIN NEWMAN, M.D. UI 1963	Rosten, L. Gollancz
CAPTAINS COURAGEOUS MGM 1937	Kipling, R. Macmillan
CAPTAIN'S DOLL, THE BBC 1982 (TV)	Lawrence, D.H. Secker
CAPTAIN'S TABLE, THE RANK 1958	Gordon, R. Joseph
CAPTIVE CITY, THE WAR 1965	Appleby, J. Hodder & Stoughton
CARAVAN FOX 1934 BL 1947	Smith, *Lady* E. Hutchinson
CARAVANS BORDEAUX FILMS 1979	Michener, J.A. Random House, N.Y.
CARAVAN TO VACCARES (V) RANK 1974	MacLean, A. Collins

CARD, THE (V)
GFD 1951

Bennett, A.
Methuen

CARDINAL, THE
COL 1963

Robinson, H.M.
Macdonald

CAREER
PAR 1959

Lee, J. (P)
Random House, N.Y.

CAREER
RKO 1939

Stong, P.D.
Grosset, N.Y.

'CAREFUL HE MIGHT HEAR YOU' (V)
SYME 1983

Elliott, S. (*Signs of life*)
Penguin

CARETAKER, THE
BL 1963

Pinter, H. (P)
Methuen

CAREY TREATMENT, THE (V)
MGM—EMI 1972

Hudson, J. (*Case of Need, The*)
Heinemann

CARNIVAL
COL 1935
TC 1946

Mackenzie, *Sir* C.
Various

CAROLINE CHERIE
WAR 1968

St. Laurent, C.
Pan

CARPETBAGGERS, THE
PAR 1963

Robbins, H.
Blond

CARRIE (V)
PAR 1950
UA 1976

Dreiser, T. (*Sister Carrie*)
Constable

CARRINGTON, V.C. (V)
INDEPENDENT 1954

Christie, D. *and* Christie, C. (P)
Heinemann

CARRY ON, ADMIRAL
REN 1957

Hay, I. *and* King-Hall, S. (*Off the Record*) (P)
French

CARVE HER NAME WITH PRIDE
RANK 1957

Minney, R.J.
Newnes

TITLE OF FILM	AUTHOR AND PUBLISHER
CASE AGAINST MRS AMES, THE PAR 1936	Roche, A.S. Melrose
CASE OF ELINOR NORTON, THE FOX 1935	Rinehart, M.R. Cassell
CASE OF SERGEANT GRISCHA, THE RKO 1930	Zweig, A. Secker
CASE OF THE BLACK CAT, THE IN 1936	Gardner, E.S. (*Case of the Caretaker's Cat, The*) Cassell
CASE OF THE CURIOUS BRIDE, THE IN 1935	Gardner, E. S. Cassell
CASE OF THE HOWLING DOG, THE WAR 1934	Gardner, E.S. Grosset, N.Y.
CASE OF THE LUCKY LEGS, THE WAR 1935	Gardner, E.S. Cassell
CASE OF THE STUTTERING BISHOP, THE WAR 1937	Gardner, E.S. Cassell
CASE OF THE VELVET CLAWS, THE IN 1936	Gardner, E.S. Cassell
CASH McCALL WAR 1959	Hawley, C. Hammond
CASINO MURDER CASE, THE MGM 1935	Dine, S.S. van Cassell
CASINO ROYALE COL 1966	Fleming, I. Cape
CASS TIMBERLANE MGM 1947	Lewis, S. Cape
CAST A DARK SHADOW EROS 1955	Green, J. (*Murder Mistaken*) (P) Evans

CAST A GIANT SHADOW
UA 1965

Berkman, T.
Doubleday, N.Y.

CAST A LONG SHADOW
UA 1959

Overholster, W.D.
Ward Lock

CASTAWAY
VIRGIN 1985

Irvine, L.
Gollancz

CASTAWAYS, THE
DISNEY 1961

Verne, J.
Various

CASTLE IN THE AIR
ABP 1952

Melville, A. (P)
French

CASTLE KEEP
COL 1969

Eastlake, W.
Joseph

CATACOMBS
BL 1964

Bennett, J.
Abelard-Schuman

CAT AND MOUSE (V)
EROS 1958

Halliday, M.
Hodder & Stoughton

CAT AND THE CANARY, THE (V)
PAR 1939
GALA 1981

Willard, J. (P)
Hudson

CAT BALLOU (V)
COL 1965

Chansler, R. (*Ballad of Cat Ballou, The*)
Little, Brown, Boston

CAT CHASER
EMI 1984

Leonard, E.
Arbor, N.Y.

CATCH ME A SPY
RANK 1971

Marton, G. *and* Meray, T.
W.H. Allen

CATCH 22 (V)
PAR 1969

Heller, J.
Cape

CAT CREEPS, THE
UN 1930

Willard, J. (*Cat and the Canary, The*)
Hudson

TITLE OF FILM	AUTHOR AND PUBLISHER

CATHEDRAL
UNICORN 1984 (TV)

Macaulay, D.
Collins

CATLOW
MGM—EMI 1972

L'Amour, L.
Corgi

CAT ON A HOT TIN ROOF (V)
MGM 1958

Williams, T. (P)
Secker & Warburg

CATTLE ANNIE AND LITTLE BRITCHES
HEMDALE 1980

Ward, R.
Ace, N.Y.

CAUGHT (V)
MGM 1948

Block, L. (*Wild Calendar*)
World, N.Y.

CAVALCADE
FOX 1933
FOX 1955

Coward, N. (P)
Heinemann

CELEBRITY (V)
NBC 1984 (TV)

Thompson, T.
Doubleday, N.Y.

CELL 2455, DEATH ROW
COL 1955

Chessman, C.
Longmans

CENTENNIAL SUMMER
FOX 1946

Idell, A.E.
Sampson, Low

CERTAIN SMILE, A.
FOX 1958

Sagan, F.
Murray

CHAD HANNA
FOX 1940

Edmonds, W.D.
Collins

CHAIN, THE
COL 1952

Wellman, P.I.
Laurie

CHALK GARDEN, THE
RANK 1963

Bagnold, E. (P)
French

CHALLENGE TO LASSIE
MGM 1949

Atkinson, E. (*Greyfriar's Bobby*)
Hamilton

CHAMPIONS (V)
EMBASSY 1983

Champion, B. *and* Powell, J.
(*Champion's Story*)
Gollancz

CHANT OF JIMMIE BLACKSMITH, THE
FOX 1979

Keneally, T.
Angus & Robertson

CHAPMAN REPORT, THE
WAR 1962

Wallace, I.
Cassell

CHAPTER TWO (V)
COL—EMI—WAR 1980

Simon, N. (P)
Random House, N.Y.

CHARGE IS MURDER, THE
MGM 1963

Dewlen, A.
Longmans

CHARIOTS OF FIRE (V)
ALLIED STARS 1981

Kennaway, J. (*Dollar bottom and Taylor's finest hour*)
Mainstream

CHARLEY AND THE ANGEL
DISNEY 1974

Stanton, W. (*Golden Evenings of Summer, The*)
Lancer, N.Y.

CHARLEY MOON
BL 1956

Arkell, R.
Joseph

CHARLEY'S AUNT
COL 1930
FOX 1941

Thomas, B. (P)
French, N.Y.

CHARLEY VARRICK
UN 1973

Reese, J. (*Looters, The*)
Hale

CHARLIE CHAN CARRIES ON
FOX 1931

Biggers, E.D.
Cassell

CHARLIE MUGGIN
EUSTON FILMS 1979

Freemantle, B. (*Charlie M*)
Doubleday, N.Y.

CHARLOTTE'S WEB
SCOTIA-BARBER 1972

White, R.B.
Penguin

CHARLY
CINERAMA 1968

Keyes, D. (*Flowers for Algernon*)
Cassell

CHARTERS AND CALDICOTT
BBC 1985 (TV)

Bingham, S.
BBC

TITLE OF FILM	AUTHOR AND PUBLISHER
CHASE, THE COL 1965	Foote, H. (P) Dramatists, N.Y.
CHASING YESTERDAY RKO 1935	France, A. (*Crime of Silvester Bonnard, The*) Collins
CHEAPER BY THE DOZEN FOX 1950	Gilbreth, F.B. *and* Carey, E.G. Heinemann
CHEERS FOR MISS BISHOP UA 1941	Aldrich, *Mrs* B. (*Miss Bishop*) Hodder & Stoughton
CHERRY PICKER, THE (V) FOX—RANK 1972	Phillips, M. (*Pick up Sticks*) Joseph
CHEYENNE AUTUMN WAR 1964	Sandoz, M. McGraw-Hill, N.Y.
CHICKEN CHRONICLES, THE (V) ALPHA 1980	Diamond, P. Dell, N.Y.
CHICKEN EVERY SUNDAY FOX 1948	Taylor, R. Methuen
CHICKEN-WAGON FAMILY FOX 1935	Benefield, B. Triangle Bks, N.Y.
CHILD IN THE HOUSE EROS 1956	McNeill, J. Hodder & Stoughton
CHILD IS BORN, A WAR 1940	Axelson, *Mrs* M.M. Cladwell, Idaho
CHILD OF DIVORCE RKO 1946	Atlas, L. (*Wednesday's Child*) (P) French, N.Y.
CHILDREN OF SANCHEZ, THE HALL BARTLETT 1978	Lewis, O. Random House, N.Y.
CHILDREN'S HOUR UA 1962	Hellman, L. (P) Dramatists, N.Y.
CHILDREN'S WAR, THE STAFFORD 1984	Eisner, J. (*Survivor, The*) Bantam, N.Y.

TITLE OF FILM	AUTHOR AND PUBLISHER
CHILD'S PLAY (V) PAR 1972	Marasco, R. (P) Random House, N.Y.
CHILTERN HUNDREDS, THE TC 1949	Home, W.D. (P) French
CHINA SEAS MGM 1935	Garstin, C. Chatto & Windus
CHINA SKY RKO 1945	Buck, P. Blue Ribbon Bks, N.Y.
CHIP OF THE FLYING U UN 1940	Bower, B.M. Grosset, N.Y.
CHIPS ARE DOWN, THE LOPERT 1949	Sartre, J-P. Rider
CHITTY, CHITTY BANG BANG (V) UA 1968	Fleming, I. Cape
CHOCOLATE SOLDIER, THE MGM 1941	Molnar, F. (*Guardsman, The*) (P) Macey-Masius, N.Y.
CHOIRBOYS, THE (V) GTO 1977	Wambaugh, J. Weidenfeld & Nicolson
CHOSEN, THE (V) CONTEMPORARY 1982	Polok, C. Fawcett, N.Y.
CHRISTIANE F (V) FOX 1982	F., C. Arlington
CHRISTINE (V) COL—EMI—WAR 1984	King, S. New English Library
CHRISTINE JORGENSEN STORY, THE UA 1970	Jorgensen, C. Eriksson, N.Y.
CHRISTMAS CAROL MGM 1938 ENTERPRISE 1984	Dickens, C. Various
CHRISTMAS HOLIDAY UN 1944	Maugham, W.S. Heinemann

Title	Author and Publisher
CHRISTMAS PRESENT, A CHANNEL 4 1985 (TV)	Dickens, C. (*Christmas carol, A*) Various
CHRISTMAS TREE, THE FOX 1969	Bataille, M. Murray
CHRISTOPHER BEAN MGM 1933 FOX 1956	Fauchois, R. (*Late Christopher Bean, The*) (P) Gollancz
CHRISTOPHER COLUMBUS GFD 1949	Sabatini, R. (*Columbus*) Hutchinson
CHRISTOPHER STRONG RKO 1933	Frankau, G. Hutchinson
CHRIST STOPPED AT EBOLI ARTIFICIAL EYE 1982	Levi, C. Gollancz
CHUKA PAR 1967	Jessup, R. Jenkins
CIMARRON RKO 1931 MGM 1960	Ferber, E. Heinemann
CINCINNATI KID, THE (V) MGM 1965	Jessup, R. Gollancz
CINDERELLA LIBERTY FOX 1974	Ponicsan, D. Harper, N.Y.
CIRCLE OF CHILDREN, A FOX 1977 (TV)	MacCracken, M. Sphere
CIRCLE OF DECEPTION FOX 1960	Waugh, A. (*Guy Renton*) Consul Bks
CIRCLE OF TWO (V) BORDEAUX FILMS 1982	Baird, M.T. (*Lesson in Love, A*) Various
CIRCUS QUEEN MURDER COL 1933	Abbot, A. (*Murder of the Circus Queen, The*) Collins

CITADEL, THE
MGM 1938
BBC 1983 (TV)

Cronin, A.J.
Gollancz

CITY ACROSS THE RIVER
UI 1949

Shulman, I. (*Amboy Dukes, The*)
Doubleday, N.Y.

CITY FOR CONQUEST
WAR 1940

Kandel, A.
Joseph

CITY JUNGLE, THE
WAR 1959

Powell, R. (*Philadelphian, The*)
Hodder & Stoughton

CLAIRVOYANT, THE (V)
GB 1935

Lothar, E.
Secker

CLAN OF THE CAVE BEAR
RANK 1985

Auel, J.M.
Crown, N.Y.

CLARENCE
PAR 1937

Tarkington, B. (P)
French, N.Y.

CLASH BY NIGHT
RKO 1952

Odets, C. (P)
Random House, N.Y.

CLASS OF MISS MacMICHAEL, THE
GALA 1980

Hutson, S. (*Eff Off*)
Corgi

CLASS RELATIONS
ARTIFICIAL EYE 1985

Kafka, F. (*Amerika*)
Secker & Warburg

CLAUDIA
FOX 1943

Franken, R.
W.H. Allen

CLAUDIA
FOX 1943

Franken, R. (P)
French, N.Y.

CLAUDIA AND DAVID
FOX 1946

Franken, R.
W.H. Allen

CLEOPATRA
FOX 1963

Franzero, C.M. (*Life and Times of
. . .*)
Redman

TITLE OF FILM	AUTHOR AND PUBLISHER
CLIVE OF INDIA UA 1935	Lipscombe, W.P. *and* Minney, R.J. (P) Gollancz
CLOCHEMERLE BLUE RIBBON 1951	Chevalier, G. Secker & Warburg
CLOCKWORK ORANGE, THE WAR 1971	Burgess, A. Heinemann
CLUE OF THE TWISTED CANDLE, THE AA 1960	Wallace, E. Newnes
CLUNY BROWN FOX 1946	Sharpe, M. Collins
COAL MINER'S DAUGHTER UN 1980	Lynn, L. *and* Vecsey, G. Warner
COAST OF SKELETONS BL 1964	Wallace, E. (*Sanders of the River*) Ward Lock
COCKFIGHTER EMI 1974	Willeford, C. Crown, N.Y.
COCOON FOX 1984	Saperstein, D. Granada
CODE OF THE WEST (V) RKO 1947	Grey, Z. Hodder & Stoughton
COLDITZ STORY, THE (V) BL 1954	Reid, R.P. Hodder & Stoughton
COLD WAR SWAP, THE UA 1969	Thomas, R. (*Spy in the Vodka*) Hodder & Stoughton
COLD WIND IN AUGUST UA 1961	Wohl, B. Mayflower
COLLECTOR, THE (V) BL 1964	Fowles, J. Cape
COLONEL EFFINGHAM'S RAID FOX 1945	Fleming, B. Various

TITLE OF FILM	AUTHOR AND PUBLISHER
COLOR PURPLE, THE WAR 1986	Walker, A. Harbrace, N.Y.
COMA (V) CIC 1978	Cook, R. Little, Brown, Boston
COMANCHEROS, THE FOX 1961	Wellman, P.I. Doubleday, N.Y.
COME AND GET IT UA 1936	Ferber, E. Heinemann
COME BACK CHARLESTON BLUE COL—WAR 1972	Hime, C. (*Heat's On, The*) Berkeley, N.Y.
COME BACK, LITTLE SHEBA PAR 1952	Inge, W.M. (P) Random House, N.Y.
COME BLOW YOUR HORN PAR 1963	Simon, N. (P) Doubleday, N.Y.
COMEDIANS, THE MGM 1967	Greene, G. Bodley Head
COMEDY MAN, THE BL 1964	Hayes, D. Abelard-Schuman
COME FLY WITH ME MGM 1963	Glemser, B. (*Girl on a Wing*) Macdonald
COMMAND DECISION MGM 1948	Haines, W.W. Cassell
COMMAND DECISION MGM 1948	Haines, W.W. (P) Random House, N.Y.
COMPANY OF COWARDS MGM 1965	Schaefer, J. Mayflower
COMPANY OF WOLVES PALACE 1984	Carter, A. *and* Wolf, A. Harper, N.Y.
COMPROMISING POSITIONS UIP 1986	Isaacs, S. Penguin

COMPULSION
FOX 1959

Levin, M.
Muller

CONDEMNED
UA 1939

Niles, B. (*Condemned to Devil's Island*)
Cape

CONDEMNED OF ALTONA, THE
FOX 1964

Satre, J-P. (*Loser Wins*) (P)
Hamilton

CONDORMAN
DISNEY 1981

Sheckley, R. (*Game of X, The*)
Sphere

CONDUCT UNBECOMING (V)
BL 1975

England, B. (P)
French

CONE OF SILENCE
BL 1959

Beatty, D.
Secker & Warburg

CONFESSIONS FROM A HOLIDAY CAMP (V)
COL—WAR 1977

Lea, T.
Sphere

CONFESSIONS OF A COUNTER-SPY
RANK 1960

Morros, B. (*My Ten Years as a Counter-Spy*)
Laurie

CONFESSIONS OF A DRIVING INSTRUCTOR (V)
COL—WAR 1976

Lea, T.
Sphere

CONFESSIONS OF A POP PERFORMER (V)
COL—WAR 1975

Lea, T. (*Confessions from the Pop Scene*)
Futura

CONFESSIONS OF A WINDOW CLEANER (V)
COL—WAR 1974

Lea, T.
Sphere

CONFESSIONS OF FELIX KRULL (V)
SAFIR 1983

Mann, T. (. . . *Confidence Man*)
Secker & Warburg

CONFESSIONS OF NAT TURNER, THE
FOX 1969

Styron, W.
Cape

TITLE OF FILM	AUTHOR AND PUBLISHER
CONFIDENTIAL AGENT WAR 1945	Greene, G. Heinemann
CONFIDENTIAL REPORT WAR 1955	Welles, O. (*Mr Arkadin*) W.H. Allen
CONFLICT OF WINGS BL 1954	Sharp, D. Putnam, N.Y.
CONFORMIST, THE CURZON 1971	Moravia, A. Penguin
CONGO MAISIE MGM 1940	Collinson, W. (*Congo Landing*) McBride, N.Y.
CONNECTICUT YANKEE FOX 1931	Twain, M. (*Yankee at the Court of King Arthur, A*) Chatto & Windus
CONNECTION, THE CONT 1962	Gelber, J. Faber
CONQUERING HORDE PAR 1931	Hough, E. (*North of 36*) Appleton-Century, N.Y.
CONQUEROR, THE RKO 1955	Clou, J. (*Caravan to Carnal, A*) Redman
CONQUEST OF SPACE PAR 1955	Bonestell, C. *and* Ley, W. Sidgwick
CONRACK FOX 1974	Conroy, P. (*Water is Wide, The*) Houghton, Mifflin, Boston
CONSENTING ADULT CHANNEL 4 1986 (TV)	Hobson, L. Warner, N.Y.
CONSPIRATOR MGM 1949	Slater, H. Lehmann
CONSPIRATORS, THE WAR 1944	Prokosch, F. Chatto & Windus

CONSTANT NYMPH, THE
FOX 1934
WAR 1943

Kennedy, M.
Heinemann

CONSTANT NYMPH, THE
FOX 1934
WAR 1943

Kennedy, M. (P)
Doubleday, N.Y.

CONTACT
POLYGRAM 1982

Sagan, C. (*Cosmic Connection*)
Macmillan

CONVICTED
COL 1950

Flavin, M. (*One Way Out*) (P)
French, N.Y.

COOL BREEZE
MGM—EMI 1972

Burnett, W.R. (*Asphalt Jungle, The*)
Kaye & Ward

COOL HAND LUKE (V)
WAR 1968

Pearce, D.
Penguin

COOL WORLD, THE
WISEMAN 1963

Miller, W.
Secker & Warburg

COPS AND ROBBERS
UA 1974

Westlake, D.E.
Hodder & Stoughton

CORN IS GREEN, THE
WAR 1945

Williams, E. (P)
Heinemann

CORONER CREEK
COL 1948

Short, L.
Collins

CORRIDOR OF MIRRORS
GFD 1948

Massie, C.
Faber

CORSICAN BROTHERS, THE (V)
WAR 1968
CBS 1985 (TV)

Dumas, A. (*Deux Frères*)
Macmillan

COTTAGE TO LET
GFD 1941

Kerr, G. (P)
French

COTTON COMES TO HARLEM
UA 1969

Himes, C.
Muller

TITLE OF FILM	AUTHOR AND PUBLISHER
COUNSELLOR AT LAW UN 1933	Rice, E. (P) Gollancz
COUNTERFEIT TRAITOR, THE PAR 1962	Klein, A. (*Double Dealers*) Faber
COUNTERPOINT UI 1968	Sillitoe, A. (*General, The*) W.H. Allen
COUNTESS DRACULA (V) RANK 1970	Penrose, V. (*Bloody Countess, The*) Caldar & Boyars
COUNT 5 AND DIE FOX 1957	Wynne, B. Souvenir Press
COUNT OF MONTE CRISTO, THE (V) UA 1934 SCOTIA BARBER 1976	Dumas, A. Various
COUNTRY GIRL, THE PAR 1954	Odets, C. (*Winter Journey*) (P) Viking Press, N.Y.
COUNTRY GIRLS, THE (V) CHANNEL 4 1983 (TV)	O'Brien, E. Penguin
COUNT YOUR BLESSINGS MGM 1959	Mitford, N. (*Blessing, The*) Hamilton
COURT MARTIAL OF GEORGE AMSTRONG CUSTER, THE BBC 2 1984 (TV)	Jones, D.C. Scribner, N.Y.
COURTSHIP OF EDDIE'S FATHER, THE MGM 1963	Toby, M. Gibbs & Phillips
COVENANT WITH DEATH, A WAR 1966	Becker, S. Hamilton
COVER HER FACE ANGLIA 1985 (TV)	James, P.D. Hamilton
COWBOY COL 1957	Harris, F. (*On the Trail*) Lane

COWBOYS, THE
COL—WAR 1972

Jennings, W.D.
Bruce & Watson

COW COUNTRY
ABP 1953

Bishop, C. (*Shadow Range*)
Macmillan, N.Y.

CRACKER FACTORY, THE
BBC 1984 (TV)

Rebeta, J.
Bantam, N.Y.

CRACK IN THE MIRROR
FOX 1960

Haedrich, M.
W.H. Allen

CRADLE WILL FALL, THE
BBC 1983 (TV)

Clark, M.H.
Dell, N.Y.

CRAIG'S WIFE
COL 1936

Kelly, G. (P)
French

CRASHING THRU'
MON 1939

Erskine, L.Y. (*Renfrew Rides the Range*)
Appleton-Century, N.Y.

CRAZE (V)
EMI 1974

Seymour, H. (*Infernal Idol*)
Avon, N.Y.

CRAZY FOR YOU
GUBER PETERS 1985

Davis, T. (*Vision quest*)
Viking, N.Y.

CREATOR
PSO 1985

Leven, J.
Penguin

CRIME AND PUNISHMENT
COL 1935
WAR 1958

Dostoevski, F.M.
Various

CRIME BY NIGHT
WAR 1946

Homes, G. (*Forty Whacks*)
Grosset, N.Y.

CRIMSON CIRCLE, THE
NEW ERA 1930

Wallace, E.
Hodder & Stoughton

CRISS CROSS
UI 1949

Tracy, D.
Constable

TITLE OF FILM	AUTHOR AND PUBLISHER

CRITIC'S CHOICE
WAR 1962

Levin, I. (P)
Random House, N.Y.

CROOKED ROAD, THE
GALA 1964

West, M.L. (*Big Story, The*)
Heinemann

CROSS AND THE SWITCHBLADE, THE
FOX 1970

Wilkerson, D.
Oliphants

CROSS COUNTRY
COL—EMI—WAR 1983

Kastle, H.
Mayflower

CROSS CREEK (V)
EMI 1984

Rawlings, M.K. (*Mocking bird*)
Ga:St. Simon's Island

CROSSED SWORDS
FOX 1977

Twain, M. (*Prince and the Pauper, The*)
Various

CROSSFIRE
RKO 1947

Brooks, R. (*Brick Foxhole, The*)
Harper, N.Y.

CROSS OF IRON
EMI 1976

Heinrich, W. (*Willing Flesh*)
Corgi

CROSSWINDS
PAR 1951

Burtis, T. (*New Guinea Gold*)
Doubleday, N.Y.

CROUCHING BEAST, THE
OLY 1936

Williams, V. (*Clubfoot*)
Hodder & Stoughton

CROWDED SKY, THE
WAR 1960

Searls, H.
Harper, N.Y.

CRUEL PASSION
TARGET 1978

De Sade, *Marquis* (*Justine*)
Various

CRUEL SEA, THE (V)
GFD 1952

Monsarrat, N.
Cassell

CRUISING (V)
LORIMAR 1980

Walker, G.
W.H. Allen

CRY FOR HAPPY
COL 1960

Campbell, G.
Harcourt, N.Y.

58

TITLE OF FILM	AUTHOR AND PUBLISHER
CRY FROM THE STREETS, A EROS 1958	Coxhead, E. (*Friend in Need, A*) Collins
CRY HAVOC MGM 1943	Kenward, A.R. (P) French
CRY IN THE NIGHT, A (V) WAR 1956	Masterson, W. (*All Through the Night*) W.H. Allen
CRY OF BATTLE WAR 1964	Appel, B. (*Fortress in the Rice*) Bobbs-Merrill, Indianapolis
CRY OF THE CITY FOX 1948	Helseth, H.E. (*Chair for Martin Rome, The*) Dodd, N.Y.
CRY, THE BELOVED COUNTRY BL 1951	Paton, A. Cape
CRY, THE BELOVED COUNTRY BL 1951	Anderson, M. (*Lost in the Stars*) (P) Sloane, N.Y.
CRY TOUGH UA 1959	Shulman, I. (*Children of the Dark*) Holt, N.Y.
CRY WOLF WAR 1947	Carleton, *Mrs* M.C. Sun Dial, N.Y.
CUCKOO IN THE NEST GB 1938	Travers, B. (P) Bickers
CUCKOO IN THE NEST GB 1938	Travers, B. Lane
CUJO (V) PSO 1982	King, S. Macdonald
CURE FOR LOVE, THE BL 1949	Greenwood, W. (P) French
CURSE OF FRANKENSTEIN, THE WAR 1957	Shelley, *Mrs* M.W. (*Frankenstein*) Various

TITLE OF FILM	AUTHOR AND PUBLISHER

CURSE OF THE WEREWOLF, THE
RANK 1960

Endore, G. (*Werewolf of Paris, The*)
Long

CURTAIN FALLS, THE
BL 1964

Druon, M.
Hart-Davies

CURTAIN UP
GFD 1952

King, P. (*On Monday Next*) (P)
French

CUSTARD BOYS, THE
FOREST HALL 1980

Rae, J.
Hart-Davis

CUTTER'S WAY (V)
UA 1981

Thornburg, N. (*Cutter and Bone*)
Heinemann

CYNARA
UA 1932

Harwood, H.M. *and* Brown, R.G.
Benn

CYRANO DE BERGERAC
UA 1950
RKO 1985 (TV)

Rostand, E. (P)
Simon & Schuster, N.Y.

D

DADDY LONG LEGS
FOX 1931
FOX 1955

Webster, J.
Hodder & Stoughton

DAISY KENYON
FOX 1947

Janeway, *Mrs* E.
Doubleday, N.Y.

DAISY MILLER
CIC 1974

Jones, H.
Hart-Davis

DAMAGED LIVES
PAR 1935

Eustace, C.J.
Putnam, N.Y.

DAM BUSTERS, THE (V)
ABP 1954

Brickhill, P.
Evans

DAMES DON'T CARE
FANCEY 1954

Cheyney, P.
Collins

TITLE OF FILM	AUTHOR AND PUBLISHER
DAMNATION ALLEY FOX 1978	Zelazny, R. Putnam, N.Y.
DAMNED, THE BL 1963	Lawrence, H.L. (*Children of the Light*) Macdonald
DAMSEL IN DISTRESS, A (V) RKO 1937	Wodehouse, P.G. Jenkins
DANCE OF DEATH, THE PAR 1969	Strindberg, A. (P) Duckworth
DANCE OF THE DWARFS (V) DOVE 1982	Household, G. Henry
DANCE PRETTY LADY BI 1931	Mackenzie, *Sir* C. (*Carnival*) Various
DANDY IN ASPIC, A COL 1968	Marlowe, D. Gollancz
DANGER AHEAD MON 1940	Erskine, L.Y. (*Renfrew's Long Trail*) Grosset, N.Y.
DANGEROUS CORNER RKO 1934	Priestley, J.B. (P) Heinemann
DANGEROUS DAVIES—THE LAST DETECTIVE (V) INNER CIRCLE FILMS 1980	Thomas, L. Eyre & Methuen
DANGEROUS DAYS OF KIOWA JONES, THE MGM 1966	Adams, C. Collins
DANGEROUS EXILE RANK 1957	Wilkins, V. (*King Reluctant, A*) Cape
DANGEROUS JOURNEY CHANNEL 4 1985 (TV)	Bunyan, J. (*Pilgrim's progress*) Various
DANGEROUS LOVE BRUT 1978	Christman, E. (*Nice Italian Girl, A*) Dodd, N.Y.

DANGEROUS PARADISE PAR 1930	Conrad, J. (*Victory*) Various
DANGER ROUTE UA 1968	York, A. (*Eliminator, The*) Hutchinson
DANGER SIGNAL WAR 1945	Bottome, P. (*Murder in the Bud*) Faber
DANGER WITHIN BL 1958	Gilbert, M. (*Death in Captivity*) Pan
DANIEL (V) PAR 1983	Doctorow, E.L. (*Book of Daniel, The*) Random House, N.Y.
DANNY JONES (V) CINERAMA 1972	Collier, J.L. (*Fires of Youth*) Penguin
DARK AT THE TOP OF THE STAIRS, THE WAR 1960	Inge, W.M. (P) Random House, N.Y.
DARK COMMAND REP 1940	Burnett, W.R. Heinemann
DARKER THAN AMBER FOX 1970	Macdonald, J.D. Hale
DARK MAN, THE GFD 1951	Dell, J. (*Nobody Ordered Wolves*) Heinemann
DARK PAGE, THE COL 1952	Fuller, S. Duell, N.Y.
DARK PASSAGE WAR 1947	Goodis, D. World, N.Y.
DARK VICTORY (V) WAR 1939	Brewer, G.E. *and* Bloch, B. (P) Dramatists, N.Y.
DARK WATERS UA 1944	Cockrell, F.M. *and* Cockrell, M. World, N.Y.

TITLE OF FILM	AUTHOR AND PUBLISHER
DAUGHTER OF DARKNESS PAR 1948	Catto, M. (*They Walk Alone*) (P) Secker & Warburg
DAUGHTER OF THE DRAGON PAR 1931	Rohmer, S. (*Daughter of Fu Manchu*) Cassell
DAVID AND LISA BL 1963	Rubin, T.I. (*Lisa and David*) Macmillan
DAVID COPPERFIELD MGM 1935 FOX 1969 BBC 1986 (TV)	Dickens, C. Various
DAWN PATROL, THE IN 1930 WAR 1938	Saunders, J.M. Queensway Press
DAY OF THE DOLPHIN, THE (V) UA 1973	Merle, R. Weidenfeld & Nicolson
DAY OF THE JACKAL, THE (V) UA 1973	Forsyth, F. Hutchinson
DAY OF THE LOCUST PAR 1974	West, N. Penguin
DAY OF THE OUTLAW UA 1959	Wells, L.E. Hale
DAY OF THE TRIFFIDS, THE (V) RANK 1962 BBC 1982 (TV)	Wyndham, J. Joseph
DAY THE UNIVERSE CHANGED, THE BBC 1985 (TV)	Burke, J. BBC
DAY THEY ROBBED THE BANK OF ENGLAND, THE MGM 1959	Brophy, J. Fontana
DAY TO REMEMBER, A GFD 1953	Tickell, J. (*Hand and the Flower, The*) Hodder & Stoughton

TITLE OF FILM	AUTHOR AND PUBLISHER

D DAY SIXTH OF JUNE
FOX 1956

Shapiro, L. (*Sixth of June, The*)
Collins

DEAD CERT
UA 1974

Francis, D.
Joseph

DEAD END
UA 1937

Kingsley, S. (P)
Dramatists, N.Y.

DEADFALL
FOX 1968

Cory, D.
Muller

DEADLINE AT DAWN (V)
RKO 1946

Irish, W.
Lippincott, Philadelphia

DEADLY AFFAIR
BL 1966

Le Carré, J. (*Call for the Dead*)
Gollancz

DEADLY COMPANIONS, THE
WAR 1961

Fleischman, A.S. (*Yellowleg*)
Muller

DEADLY DUO, THE
UA 1962

Jessup, R.
Boardman

DEADLY HARVEST (V)
BBC 1984 (TV)

Household, G. (*Watcher in the shadows*)
Penguin

DEADLY IS THE FEMALE
UA 1949

Kantor, M.
Coward-McCann, NY.

DEADLY RECORD
AA 1959

Hooke, N.W.
Hale

DEADLY TRAP (V)
NATIONAL GENERAL 1972

Cavanaugh, A. (*Children are gone, The*)
Simon & Schuster, N.Y.

DEAD MEN TELL NO TALES
ALL 1939

Beeding, F. (*Norwich Victims, The*)
Hodder & Stoughton

DEAD ZONE, THE (V)
COL—EMI—WAR 1984

King, S.
Fontana

TITLE OF FILM	AUTHOR AND PUBLISHER
DEALING WAR 1972	Douglas, M. Talmy-Franklin
DEAR AND GLORIOUS PHYSICIAN PAR 1963	Caldwell, T. Collins
DEAR BRIGITTE FOX 1965	Haase, J. (*Erasmus with Freckles*) Simon & Schuster, N.Y.
DEAR HEART WAR 1964	Mosel, T. (P) Obolensky, N.Y.
DEAR MR PROHACK GFD 1949	Bennett, A. (*Mr Prohack*) Various
DEAR OCTOPUS GFD 1943	Smith, D. (P) Heinemann
DEAR RUTH PAR 1947	Krasna, N. (P) Gollancz
DEATH AT BROADCASTING HOUSE PHOENIX 1935	Gielgud, V.H. Rich & Cowan
DEATH DRUMS ALONG THE RIVER PLANET 1963	Wallace, E. (*Sanders of the River*) Ward Lock
DEATH IN CANAAN, A BBC 1985 (TV)	Barthel, J. (*Death in California*) Penguin
DEATH IN VENICE (V) WAR 1971	Mann, T. Penguin
DEATH IS PART OF THE PROCESS BBC 1986 (TV)	Bernstein, H. Sinclair Browne
DEATH OF A GUNFIGHTER UI 1969	Patten, L.B. (*Law of the Gun*) Four Square Books
DEATH OF AN EXPERT WITNESS ANGLIA 1982 (TV)	James, P.D. Faber
DEATH OF A SALESMAN COL 1951	Miller, A. (P) Cresset Press

TITLE OF FILM	AUTHOR AND PUBLISHER
DEATH OF THE HEART, THE GRANADA 1985 (TV)	Bowen, E. Cape
DEATH ON THE DIAMOND MGM 1934	Fitzsimmons, C. Grosset, N.Y.
DEATH ON THE NILE (V) EMI 1978	Christie, A. Collins
DEATH SENTENCE CANNON 1981	Garfield, B. Evans
DEATH TRAP COL—EMI—WAR 1982	Levin, I. (P) French
DEATH WATCH (V) CONTEMPORARY 1979	Compton, D. (*Continuous Katherine Mortenhoe, The*) Arrow, N.Y.
DEATH WISH (V) CANNON 1981	Garfield, B. Hodder & Stoughton
DEATH WISH II (V) CANNON 1981	Garfield, B. Hodder & Stoughton
DECAMERON (V) UI 1971	Boccaccio, G. Various
DECAMERON NIGHTS EROS 1953	Boccaccio, G. (*Decameron, The*) Various
DECEPTION WAR 1946	Verneuil, L. (*Jealousy*) (P) French, N.Y.
DECEPTIONS BBC 1986 (TV)	Michael, J. Sphere
DECISION BEFORE DAWN FOX 1951	Howe, G.L. (*Call it Treason*) Hart-Davis
DECISION OF CHRISTOPHER BLAKE, THE WAR 1948	Hart, M. (*Christopher Blake*) (P) Random House, N.Y.

TITLE OF FILM	AUTHOR AND PUBLISHER
DECLINE AND FALL . . . OF A BIRDWATCHER FOX 1968	Waugh, E. (*Decline and Fall*) Chapman & Hall
DEEP, THE (V) COL—WAR 1977	Benchley, P. Deutsch
DEEP BLUE SEA, THE FOX 1955	Rattigan, T. (P) Hamilton
DEEP IN MY HEART MGM 1954	Arnold, E. Duell, N.Y.
DEEP SIX, THE (V) WAR 1957	Dibner, M. Cassell
DEEP VALLEY WAR 1947	Totheroh, D. Hutchinson
DEEP WATERS FOX 1948	Moore, R. (*Spoonhandle*) Grosset, N.Y.
DEER HUNTER, THE (V) COL—EMI 1979	Corder, E.M. Hodder & Stoughton
DEERSLAYER (V) REP 1943 FOX 1957	Cooper, F.J. Various
DELAVINE AFFAIR, THE MON 1954	Chapman, R. (*Winter Wears a Shroud*) Laurie
DELICATE BALANCE, A SEVEN KEYS 1974	Albee, E. Cape
DELIVERANCE (V) WAR 1973	Dickey, J. Hamilton
DELUGE, THE RKO 1933	Wright, S.F. Allied Press
DEMON SEED (V) MGM 1977	Koonntz, D. Bantam, Toronto

TITLE OF FILM	AUTHOR AND PUBLISHER
DENTIST IN THE CHAIR REN 1960	Finch, M. Ace
DE SADE MGM—EMI 1969	Lely, G. Elek
DESERT FURY PAR 1947	Stewart, R. World, N.Y.
DESERT GOLD PAR 1936	Grey, Z. Nelson
DESERT HEARTS MGM 1985	Rule, J. (*Desert of the heart*) Fl:Tallhassee
DESERT PURSUIT ABP 1952	Perkins, K. (*Desert Voices*) Wright & Brown
DESERT SAND UA 1955	Robb, J. (*Punitive Action*) Hamilton
DESIGN FOR LIVING PAR 1933	Coward, N. (P) Heinemann
DESIRÉE FOX 1954	Selinko, A. Heinemann
DESIRE ME MGM 1947	Frank, L. (*Carl and Anna*) Davies
DESIRE UNDER THE ELMS PAR 1958	O'Neill, E.G. (P) Cape
DESPAIR GALA 1978	Nabokov, V. Putnam, N.Y.
DESPERATE CHARACTERS (V) ITC 1971	Fox, P. Macmillan
DESPERATE HOURS, THE PAR 1954	Hayes, J. Deutsch
DESPERATE HOURS, THE PAR 1954	Hayes, J. (P) Random House, N.Y.

TITLE OF FILM	AUTHOR AND PUBLISHER
DESPERATE MAN, THE AA 1959	Somers, P. (*Beginners Luck*) Collins
DESPERATE MOMENT GFD 1953	Albrand, M. Chatto & Windus
DESPERATE ONES, THE (V) AMERICAN INT 1968	Ramati, A. (*Beyond the Mountains*) Penguin
DESPERATE SEARCH MGM 1952	Mayse, A. Harrap
DESTINATION TOKYO WAR 1943	Fisher, S.G. Appleton-Century, N.Y.
DESTRY UI 1954	Brand, M. (*Destry Rides Again*) Hodder & Stoughton
DESTRY RIDES AGAIN UN 1932 UN 1939	Brand, M. Hodder & Stoughton
DETECTIVE, THE FOX 1968	Thorp, R. Corgi
DETECTIVE, THE BBC 1985 (TV)	Ferris, P. Weidenfeld & Nicolson
DETECTIVE STORY PAR 1951	Kingsley, P. (P) Random House, N.Y.
DETOUR PRC 1946	Goldsmith, M.M. Hurst & Blackett
DEVIL AT 4 O'CLOCK, THE COL 1961	Catto, M. Pan
DEVIL COMMANDS, THE COL 1941	Sloane, W. (*Edge of Running Water, The*) Methuen
DEVIL-DOLL, THE MGM 1936	Merritt, A. (*Burn, Witch, Burn*) Methuen

TITLE OF FILM	AUTHOR AND PUBLISHER
DEVIL MAKES THREE, THE MGM 1952	Bachmann, L. (*Kiss of Death*) Knopf, N.Y.
DEVIL NEVER SLEEPS, THE FOX 1962	Buck, P. Pan
DEVIL RIDES OUT, THE ABP 1971	Wheatley, D. Hutchinson
DEVILS, THE (V) WAR 1971	Huxley, A. (*Devils of Loudon, The*) Chatto & Windus
DEVILS, THE (V) WAR 1971	Whiting, J. (P) French
DEVIL'S ADVOCATE, THE (V) RANK 1977	West, M. Heinemann
DEVIL'S BRIGADE, THE UA 1968	Adleman, R.H. *and* Walton, G. Transworld
DEVIL'S DAFFODIL, THE BL 1961	Wallace, E. (*Daffodil Mystery*) Ward Lock
DEVIL'S DISCIPLE, THE UA 1959	Shaw, G.B. (P) Constable
DEVIL'S OWN, THE FOX 1968	Curtis, P. Macdonald
DIAL 'M' FOR MURDER WAR 1954	Knott, F. (P) Random House, N.Y.
DIAL 999 AA 1955	Graeme, B. (*Way Out, The*) Hutchinson
DIAMOND HEAD COL 1962	Gilman, P. Joseph
DIAMOND JIM UN 1935	Morell, P. Hurst & Blackett
DIAMONDS ARE FOREVER (V) UA 1971	Fleming, I. Cape

TITLE OF FILM	AUTHOR AND PUBLISHER
DIANA BBC 1984 (TV)	Delderfield, R.F. (*There was a fair maid dwelling: The unjust skies*) Coronet
DIARY OF A COUNTRY PRIEST, THE GGT 1950	Bernanos, G. Lane
DIARY OF A MAD HOUSEWIFE UI 1971	Kaufman, S. Penguin
DIARY OF ANNE FRANK, THE FOX 1959	Frank, A. Gollancz
DIARY OF ANNE FRANK, THE FOX 1959	Goodrich, F. *and* Hackett, A. (P) French
DIARY OF MAJOR THOMPSON GALA 1957	Daninos, P. Cape
DIGBY—THE BIGGEST DOG IN THE WORLD RANK 1973	Key, T. Piccolo
DINNER AT EIGHT MGM 1933	Kaufman, G.S. *and* Ferber, E. (P) Heinemann
DIPLOMATIC COURIER FOX 1952	Cheyney, P. (*Sinister Errand*) Collins
DIRTY DINGUS MAGEE (V) MGM 1970	Markson, D. (*Ballad of Dingus Magee, The*) Blond
DIRTY DOZEN, THE (V) MGM 1966	Nathanson, E.M. Barker
DIRTY MARY, CRAZY LARRY FOX 1974	Unekis, R. (*Chase, The*) Walker, N.Y.
DIRTY TRICKS (V) FILMPLAN 1980	Clifford, T. (*Glendower Legacy, The*) Putnam
DISAPPEARANCE, THE CINEGATE 1977	Marlowe, D. (*Echos of Celandine*) Penguin

DISPUTED PASSAGE
PAR 1939

Douglas, L.C.
Davies

DISTANT TRUMPET, A
WAR 1964

Horgan, P.
Macmillan

DOC SAVAGE—MAN OF BRONZE
COL—WAR 1975

Robeson, K.
Corgi

DOCK BRIEF, THE
MGM 1962

Mortimer, J. (P)
Elek

DOCTOR AND THE GIRL, THE
MGM 1949

Meersch, M. van der. (*Bodies and Souls*)
Pilot Press

DOCTOR AT LARGE (V)
RANK 1957

Gordon, R.
Joseph

DOCTOR AT SEA (V)
BFD 1955

Gordon, R.
Joseph

DOCTOR BULL
FOX 1933

Cozzens, J.G. (*Cure of the Flesh*)
Longmans

DOCTOR DOLITTLE
FOX 1966

Lofting, H.
Cape

DOCTOR FAUSTUS (V)
COL 1968

Marlowe, C. (*Tragical History of . . .*)
(P)
Various

DOCTOR FISHER OF GENEVA
BBC 2 1984 (TV)

Greene, G.
Bodley Head

DOCTOR IN CLOVER (V)
RANK 1965

Gordon, R.
Joseph

DOCTOR IN LOVE (V)
RANK 1959

Gordon, R.
Joseph

DOCTOR IN THE HOUSE (V)
GFD 1954

Gordon, R.
Joseph

TITLE OF FILM	AUTHOR AND PUBLISHER
DOCTOR IN TROUBLE (V) RANK 1970	Gordon, R. (*Doctor on Toast*) Joseph
DOCTOR'S DILEMMA, THE MGM 1958	Shaw, G.B. (P) Constable
DOCTOR'S WIVES (V) COL 1971	Slaughter, F.G. Arrow
DOCTOR ZHIVAGO MGM 1965	Pasternak, B. Collins
DODSWORTH UA 1936	Lewis, S. Cape
DODSWORTH UA 1936	Howard, S.C. (P) Harcourt, N.Y.
DOG OF FLANDERS, A RKO 1935 FOX 1959	Ouida Chatto & Windus
DOGS OF WAR, THE (V) UA 1980	Forsyth, F. Hutchinson
DOG SOLDIERS UA 1978	Stone, R. Secker & Warburg
DOKTOR FAUSTUS SAFIR 1983	Mann, T. Secker & Warburg
DOLL'S HOUSE, A (V) BL 1973	Ibsen, H. (P) Various
DOMBEY BBC 1984 (TV)	Dickens, C. Various
DOMINANT SEX, THE AB 1937	Egan, M. (P) Gollancz
DOMINO KILLINGS, THE ITC 1978	Kennedy, A. (*Domino Principle, The*) Viking, N.Y.

DONA FLOR AND HER TWO HUSBANDS
FD 1978

Amado, J.
Avon, N.Y.

DON CAMILLO
CANNON 1982

Guareschi, G.
Murray

DON CHICAGO
BN 1945

Roberts, C.E.B.
Jarrolds

DON IS DEAD, THE
UN 1973

Albert, M.H.
Coronet

DON QUIXOTE
EUSTON 1985 (TV)

Greene, G.
Heinemann

DON'T BOTHER TO KNOCK
FOX 1952

Armstrong, C. (*Mischief*)
Davies

DON'T BOTHER TO KNOCK
WAR 1961

Hanley, C. (*Love from Everybody*)
Hutchinson

DON'T DRINK THE WATER
AVCO EMBASSY 1969

Allen, W. (P)
Random House, N.Y.

DON'T GO NEAR THE WATER
MGM 1957

Brinkley, W.
Cape

**DON'T JUST LIE THERE, SAY
SOMETHING**
RANK 1975

Pertwee, M. (P)
French

DON'T JUST STAND THERE
RANK 1969

Williams, C.
Cassell

DON'T LOOK NOW (V)
BL 1973

Du Maurier, D.
Doubleday, N.Y.

DON'T MAKE WAVES
MGM 1966

Wallach, I. (*Muscle Beach*)
Gollancz

**DON'T RAISE THE BRIDGE, LOWER
THE RIVER**
BL 1967

Wilk, M.
Heinemann

TITLE OF FILM	AUTHOR AND PUBLISHER
DON'T STEAL MY BABY BBC 1985 (TV)	Christman, E. (*Nice Italian girl, A*) Dodd, N.Y. U.S. title *Black Market baby*
DOOR IN THE WALL ABP 1956	Wells, H.G. Benn
DORIAN GRAY (V) HEMDALE 1973	Wilde, O. (*Picture of . . .*) Unicorn Press
DOUBLE CONFESSION ABP 1950	Garden, J. (*All on a Summer's Day*) Joseph
DOUBLE IMAGE FOX 1959	MacDougall, R. *and* Allan, E. (P) French
DOUBLE INDEMNITY PAR 1944	Cain, J.M. Hale
DOUBLE MAN, THE (V) WAR 1966	Maxfield, H.S. (*Legacy of a Spy*) Heinemann
DOUBTING THOMAS FOX 1935	Kelly, G. (*Torch-bearers*) (P) French, N.Y.
DOUGHGIRLS, THE WAR 1944	Fields, J. (P) Random House, N.Y.
DOVE, THE (V) EMI 1974	Graham, R.L. *and* Gill, D. Angus & Robertson
DOWNHILL RACERS, THE (V) PAR 1969	Hall, O. Bodley Head
DOWN 3 DARK STREETS UA 1954	Gordon, *Mrs* M. *and* Gordon, G. (*Case File F.B.I.*) Doubleday, N.Y.
DRACULA (V) UN 1931 UI 1957 EMI 1973 CIC 1979	Stoker, B. (P) Rider

TITLE OF FILM	AUTHOR AND PUBLISHER
DRACULA'S DAUGHTER UN 1936	Stoker, B. (*Dracula's Guest*) Jarrolds
DRACULA SUCKS KODIAK 1979	Stoker, B. (*Dracula*) Various
DRAGON SEED MGM 1944	Buck, P. Methuen
DRAGONWYCK FOX 1946	Seton, A. Hodder & Stoughton
DR. BULL FOX 1933	Cozzens, J.G. (*Last Adam*) Harcourt, Brace, N.Y.
DREAM GIRL PAR 1947	Rice, E. (P) Coward-McCann, N.Y.
DREAM OF KINGS, A WAR 1969	Petraskis, H.M. Barker
DRESSER, THE (V) COL 1983	Harwood, R. (P) Amber Lane
DR FAUSTUS (V) BL 1966	Marlowe, C. (P) Various
DRIFT FENCE PAR 1935	Grey, Z. Hodder & Stoughton
DRIVE, HE SAID COL 1971	Larner, J. Mayflower
DR JEKYLL AND MR HYDE PAR 1932 MGM 1941	Stevenson, R.L. Various
DR KILDARE'S CRISIS MGM 1940	Brand, M. Hodder & Stoughton
DR NO (V) UA 1962	Fleming, I. Cape
DROWNING POOL, THE COL—WAR 1975	Macdonald, R. Fontana

TITLE OF FILM	AUTHOR AND PUBLISHER
DR STRANGELOVE; OR HOW I LEARNED TO STOP WORRYING AND LOVE THE BOMB COL 1963	George, P. (*Two Hours to Doom*) Corgi
DR SYN GB 1937 DISNEY 1963	Thorndike, R. Various
DRUM (V) PAR 1976	Onstott, K. Pan
DRUMS UA 1938	Mason, A.E.W. (*Drum, The*) Hodder & Stoughton
DRUMS ALONG THE MOHAWK FOX 1939	Edmonds, W.D. Jarrolds
DRUMS IN THE DEEP SOUTH RKO 1952	Noble, H. (*Woman with a Sword*) Doubleday, N.Y.
DRUMS OF DESTINY NEW REALM 1962	Michael, G. (*Michaels in Africa, The*) Muller
DRUMS OF FU MANCHU REP 1943	Rohmer, S. Cassell
DRY ROT BL 1956	Chapman, J. (P) English Theatre Guild
DUBAI AMERICAN COMMUNICATIONS INDUSTRIES 1980	Moore, R. Doubleday, N.Y.
DUEL AT DIABLO UA 1966	Albert, M. (*Apache Rising*) Muller
DUEL IN THE SUN (V) MGM 1946	Busch, N. W.H. Allen
DUELLISTS, THE (V) CIC 1977	Conrad, J. Fontana
DUET FOR ONE CANNON 1983	Kempinski, T. (P) French

TITLE OF FILM	AUTHOR AND PUBLISHER
DULCIMA MGM—EMI 1972	Bates, H.E. Penguin
DULCY MGM 1940	Kaufman, G.S. *and* Connelly, M. (P) Various
DUMBO (V) DISNEY 1972	Aberson, H. *and* Pearl, H. Disney Classic, Purnell
DUNE (V) UN 1983	Herbert, F. Gollancz
DUNKIRK MGM 1958	Trevor, E. (*Big Pick-Up*) Heinemann
DUNWICH HORROR (V) AMERICAN INT 1969	Lovecraft, H.P. (*Shuttered Room, The*) Gollancz
DURRELL IN RUSSIA CHANNEL 4 1986 (TV)	Durrell, G. *and* Durrell, L. Macdonald
DUST DASKA FILMS 1985	Coetzee, J.M. (*In the heart of the country*) Penguin
DUST IN THE SUN WAR 1958	Cleary, J. (*Justin Bayard*) Collins
DUSTY ERMINE TWICKENHAM 1936	Grant, N. (P) French

E

EACH DAWN I DIE WAR 1939	Odlum, J. Various
EAGLE HAS LANDED, THE (V) ITC 1976	Higgins, J. Collins
EARL OF CHICAGO MGM 1940	Williams, B. Harrap

TITLE OF FILM	AUTHOR AND PUBLISHER
EARTH V. THE FLYING SAUCERS COL 1956	Keyhoe, D.E. (*Flying Saucers from Outer Space*) Hutchinson
EASIEST WAY, THE MGM 1931	Walter, E. (P) Dodd, N.Y.
EAST LYNNE FOX 1931	Wood, *Mrs* H. Various
EAST OF EDEN (V) WAR 1954	Steinbeck, J. Heinemann
EAST RIVER MGM 1949	Asch, S. Macdonald
EAST SIDE, WEST SIDE MGM 1950	Davenport, M. Collins
EASY COME, EASY GO PAR 1947	McNulty, J.L. (*Third Avenue, New York*) Little, Brown, Boston
EASY LIVING PAR 1937	Caspary, V. Longmans
EASY STREET POLYGRAM 1982	Berman, S. Dial, N.Y.
EBB TIDE PAR 1937	Stevenson, R.L. Various
EBONY TOWER ITV 1984 (TV)	Fowles, J. Cape
ECHO OF BARBARA RANK 1960	Burke, J. Long
ECLIPSE GALA 1976	Woolaston, N. Macmillan
EDGE OF DARKNESS WAR 1943	Woods, W.H. Grosset, N.Y.

TITLE OF FILM	AUTHOR AND PUBLISHER
EDGE OF DOOM RKO 1950	Brady, L. Cresset Press
EDGE OF FURY UA 1958	Coates, R.M. (*Wisteria Cottage*) Gollancz
EDUCATING RITA (V) RANK 1983	Russell, W. (P) French
EDWARD, MY SON MGM 1949	Morley, R. *and* Langley, N. (P) French
EFFECT OF GAMMA RAYS ON MAN-IN-THE-MOON MARIGOLDS, THE FOX-RANK 1972	Zindel, P. (P) French
EGG AND I, THE UN 1947	Macdonald, B. Hammond
EGYPTIAN, THE FOX 1954	Waltari, M. (*Sinuhe the Egyptian*) Putnam
EIGER SANCTION, THE (V) CIC 1975	Trevanion, Heinemann
EIGHT IRON MEN COL 1952	Brown, H. (*Sound of Hunting, A*) Knopf, NY.
8 MILLION WAYS TO DIE PSO 1985	Block, L. (*Stab in the dark*) Arbor, N.Y.
80,000 SUSPECTS RANK 1963	Trevor, E. (*Pillars of Midnight, The*) Heinemann
EL DORADO PAR 1967	Brown, H. (*Stars in their Courses, The*) Cape
ELECTRA UA 1963	Euripedes (P) Various
ELENI CBS 1985 (TV)	Gage, N. Random, N.Y.

TITLE OF FILM	AUTHOR AND PUBLISHER
ELEPHANT BOY (V) UA 1937	Kipling, R. (*Toomai of the Elephants*) Macmillan
ELEPHANT WALK PAR 1954	Standish, R. Davies
11 HARROWHOUSE FOX 1974	Browne, G.A. Arbor House, N.Y.
ELLERY QUEEN AND THE PENTHOUSE MYSTERY COL 1941	Queen, E. (*Penthouse Mystery*) Grosset, N.Y.
ELLERY QUEEN AND THE PERFECT CRIME COL 1941	Queen, E. (*Perfect Crime, The*) Grosset, N.Y.
ELLERY QUEEN, MASTER DETECTIVE COL 1940	Queen, E. Grosset, N.Y.
ELMER GANTRY (V) UA 1959	Lewis, S. Cape
ELUSIVE PIMPERNEL, THE BL 1950	Orczy, *Baroness* E. Hutchinson
EMBASSY HEMDALE 1972	Coulter, S. Heinemann
EMIL AND THE DETECTIVES UFA 1931 DISNEY 1964	Kastner, E. Cape
EMMANUELLE (V) SF 1975	Arsan, E. Mayflower
EMPEROR JONES UA 1933	O'Neill, E.G. (P) Cape
EMPEROR'S CANDLESTICKS, THE MGM 1937	Orczy, *Baroness* E. Hodder & Stoughton
EMPIRE OF THE ANTS (V) BRENT WALKER 1978	Wells, H.G. (*Valley of the Ants, The*) Fontana

TITLE OF FILM	AUTHOR AND PUBLISHER
EMPTY SADDLES UN 1936	Wilson, C. Ward Lock
ENCHANTED APRIL RKO 1935	'Elizabeth' Macmillan
ENCHANTED COTTAGE, THE RKO 1945	Pinero, *Sir* A.W. (P) Heinemann
ENCHANTED ISLAND (V) WAR 1958	Melville, H. (*Typee*) Dent
ENCHANTMENT RKO 1949	Godden, R. (*Fugue in Time*) Joseph
ENCORE GFD 1951	Maugham, W.S. Heinemann
END AS A MAN COL 1957	Willingham, C. Barker
END AS A MAN COL 1957	Willingham, C. (*Strange One, The*) (P) Grosset, N.Y.
ENDLESS LOVE (V) BARBER 1981	Spencer, S. Knopf, N.Y.
ENDLESS NIGHT BL 1971	Christie, A. Collins
END OF AUGUST, THE ENTERPRISE 1981	Chopin, K. (*Awakening, The*) Avon, N.Y.
END OF THE AFFAIR, THE COL 1954	Greene, G. Heinemann
END OF THE RIVER, THE ARCHERS 1947	Holdridge, D. (*Death of a Common Man*) Hale
END OF THE ROAD CONT 1969	Barth, J. Penguin

TITLE OF FILM	AUTHOR AND PUBLISHER

ENEMY BELOW, THE
FOX 1957

Rayner, D.A. (*Escort*)
Kimber

ENEMY OF THE PEOPLE (V)
ENTERPRISE 1978

Ibsen, H. (P)
Various

ENGLAND MADE ME
HEMDALE 1972

Greene, G.
Heinemann

ENIGMA (V)
COL—EMI—WAR 1983

Barak, M. (*Enigma Sacrifice*)
Futura

ENTERTAINER, THE
BL 1960
SEVEN KEYS 1975

Osborne, J. (P)
Evans

ENTERTAINING MR. SLOANE
WAR 1969

Orton, J. (P)
Hamilton

ENTITY, THE (V)
FOX 1982

De Felitta, F.
Warner, N.Y.

EQUUS (V)
UA 1977

Shaffer, P.
Deutsch

**ERROL FLYNN: MY WICKED WICKED
WAYS**
ITV 1985 (TV)

Flynn, E.
Berkeley, N.Y.

ESCAPADE
EROS 1955

McDougall, R. (P)
Heinemann

ESCAPADE IN FLORENCE
DISNEY 1963

Fenton, E. (*Mystery in Florence*)
Constable

ESCAPE
RKO 1930
FOX 1948

Galsworthy, J. (P)
Duckworth

ESCAPE
MGM 1940

Vance, E.
Collins

ESCAPE ARTIST, THE (V)
POLYGRAM 1982 (TV)

Wagoner, D.
Ballantine, N.Y.

TITLE OF FILM	AUTHOR AND PUBLISHER
ESCAPE FROM ALCATRAZ (V) CIC 1979	Bruce, J.C. McGraw, N.Y.
ESCAPE FROM ZAHREIN PAR 1962	Barrett, M. (*Appointment in Zahrein*) Pan
ESCAPE IN THE DESERT WAR 1945	Sherwood, R.E. (*Petrified Forest, The*) (P) Scribner, N.Y.
ESCAPE ME NEVER UA 1935	Kennedy, M. (P) Heinemann
ESCAPE ME NEVER UA 1935	Kennedy, M. Heinemann
ESCAPE TO WITCH MOUNTAIN (V) DISNEY 1974	Key, A. Various
ESTHER WATERS WESSEX 1948	Moore, G. (P) Heinemann
ESTHER WATERS WESSEX 1948	Moore, G. Various
EUROPEANS, THE GB 1979	James, H. Penguin
EVE GALA 1963	Chase, J.H. Panther
EVE OF ST. MARK, THE FOX 1944	Anderson, M. (P) Lane
EVERY LITTLE CROOK AND NANNY MGM 1972	Hunter, E. Constable
EVERYTHING IS THUNDER GB 1936	Hardy, J.L. Lane
EVERYTHING YOU EVER WANTED TO KNOW ABOUT SEX BUT WERE AFRAID TO ASK (V) UA 1972	Reuben, D. W.H. Allen

84

TITLE OF FILM	AUTHOR AND PUBLISHER
EVERY WHICH WAY BUT LOOSE (V) COL—EMI—WAR 1980	Kronberg, J.J. Hale
EVIL THAT MEN DO (V) ITC 1983	Hill, R.L. Hodder & Stoughton
EVIL UNDER THE SUN COL 1981	Christie, A. Collins
EXCALIBUR (V) COL—EMI—WAR 1981	Malory, *Sir* T. (*Morte d'Arthur, Le*) Various
EXECUTIONER'S SONG, THE (V) GOLDFARB 1982	Mailer, N. Arrow
EXECUTIVE SUITE MGM 1954	Hawley, C. Hammond
EX-FLAME TIFFANY 1931	Wood, *Mrs* H. (*East Lynne*) Various
EXODUS (V) UA 1960	Uris, L. Wingate
EXORCIST, THE (V) WAR 1973	Blatty, W.P. Bond & Briggs
EXPERIENCES OF AN IRISH RM CHANNEL 4 1982 (TV)	Somerville, E. *and* Ross, M. Dent
EXPERIMENT PERILOUS RKO 1944	Carpenter, M. Harrap
EXPERT, THE WAR 1932	Ferber, E. (*Old Man Minick*) Doubleday, N.Y.
EXTRAORDINARY ADVENTURES OF **THE MOUSE AND THE CHILD, THE** AMBASSADOR 1977 (*U.S. title:* Mouse and the Child)	Hoban, R. Faber
EXTRAORDINARY SEAMAN MGM 1967	Rock, P. Souvenir Press

TITLE OF FILM	AUTHOR AND PUBLISHER

EYE OF THE DEVIL
MGM 1968

Loraine, P. (*Day of the Arrow*)
Collins

EYE OF THE NEEDLE (V)
UA 1981

Follett, K.
New American Library, N.Y.

EYES IN THE NIGHT
MGM 1942

Kendrick, B.H. (*Odour of Violets*)
Methuen

EYEWITNESS (V)
MGM 1970

Hebden, M. (*Eye-witness*)
Harrap

F

FABIAN OF THE YARD
EROS 1954

Fabian, R.
Naldrett Press

FABIOLA
BL 1951

Wiseman, N.P.S. (*Cardinal*)
Various

FACE IN THE CROWD, A
WAR 1957

Schulberg, B.W. (*Some Faces in the crowd*)
Lane

FACE IN THE NIGHT
GN 1956

Graeme, B. (*Suspense*)
Hutchinson

FACE TO FACE
RKO 1952

Crane, S. (*Bride Comes to Yellow Sky, The*)
Knopf, N.Y.

FAHRENHEIT 451
UI 1966

Bradbury, R.
Hart-Davis

FAIL SAFE
BL 1963

Burdick, E. *and* Wheeler, H.
Hutchinson

FAIR WARNING
FOX 1931

Brand, M. (*Untamed, The*)
Hodder & Stoughton

FAIR WIND TO JAVA (V)
REP 1953

Roark, G.
Falcon Press

TITLE OF FILM	AUTHOR AND PUBLISHER
FAITHFUL HEART, THE GFD 1932	Hoffe, M. (P) Heinemann
FALCON AND THE SNOWMAN RANK 1984	Lindsey, R. Penguin
FALCON TAKES OVER, THE RKO 1942	Chandler, R. (*Farewell, My Lovely*) Hamilton
FALLEN ANGEL FOX 1945	Holland, M. Dutton, N.Y.
FALLEN IDOL, THE (V) FOX 1948	Greene, G. (*Basement Room, The*) Cresset Press
FALLEN SPARROW, THE RKO 1943	Hughes, D.B. Nicholson & Watson
FALL OF THE HOUSE OF USHER, THE AA 1960	Poe, E.A. Various
FAME IS THE SPUR TC 1947 BBC 1982 (TV)	Spring, H. Collins
FAMILY DOCTOR FOX 1957	Fleming, J. (*Deeds of Mr Deadcert, The*) Hutchinson
FAMILY HONEYMOON UN 1949	Croy, H. Hurst & Blackett
FAMILY PLOT UN 1976	Canning, V. (*Rainbird Pattern, The*) Heinemann
FAMILY WAR, THE BL 1966	Naughton, B. (*All in Good Time*) (P) French
FANATIC COL 1965	Blaisdell, A. (*Nightmare*) Gollancz
FAN, THE CIC 1981	Randall, B. Random House, N.Y.

TITLE OF FILM	AUTHOR AND PUBLISHER
FANNY WAR 1960	Behrman, S.N. *and* Logan, J. (P) Random House, N.Y.
FANNY BY GAS LIGHT GFD 1944 BBC 1982 (TV)	Sadleir, M. Constable
FANNY HILL (V) GALA 1965 BRENT WALKER 1983	Cleland, J. Luxor Press
FAREWELL, MY LOVELY (V) RKO 1944 FOX—RANK 1975	Chandler, R. Hamilton
FAREWELL TO ARMS, A (V) PAR 1932 FOX 1957	Hemingway, E. Cape
FAR FROM THE MADDING CROWD (V) WAR 1966	Hardy, T. Macmillan
FAR HORIZONS, THE PAR 1955	Emmons, D.G. (*Sacajawea of the Shoshones*) Binfords, Portland, Oregon
FARMER TAKES A WIFE, THE FOX 1953	Edmonds, W.D. (*Rome Haul*) Triangle Bks, N.Y.
FARMER'S WIFE, THE AB 1940	Phillpotts, E. (P) French
FAR PAVILIONS, THE (V) GOLDCREST 1983	Kaye, M.M. Lane
FAST AND LOOSE MGM 1939	Page, M. (*Fast Company*) Heinemann
FAST TIMES (V) UIP 1982	Crowe, C. (*Fast Times at Ridgemont High*) Simon & Schuster, N.Y.
FAT CITY COL—WAR 1972	Gardner, L. Hart-Davis

TITLE OF FILM	AUTHOR AND PUBLISHER
FATE IS THE HUNTER FOX 1964	Gann, E.K. Hodder & Stoughton
FATHER, THE BBC 2 1985 (TV)	Strindberg, A. (P) Duckworth
FATHER BROWN COL 1954	Chesterton, G.K. (*Father Brown Stories*) Cassell
FATHER BROWN, DETECTIVE (V) PAR 1935	Chesterton, G.K. (*Wisdom of Father Brown, The*) Cassell
FATHER OF THE BRIDE MGM 1950	Streeter, E. Hamilton
FATHER'S DOING FINE ABP 1952	Langley, N. (*Little Lambs eat Ivy*) (P) French
FATHOM FOX 1968	Forrester, L. (*Girl Called Fathom, A*) Heinemann
FBI STORY, THE (V) WAR 1958	Whitehead, D. Panther
FDR'S LAST YEAR CHANNEL 4 1984 (TV)	Bishop, J. Hart-Davis
FEAR IS THE KEY (V) MGM—EMI 1972	MacLean, A. Collins
FEAR ON TRIAL CHANNEL 4 1985 (TV)	Faulk, J.H. University of Texas
FEDORA (V) MAINLINE 1979	Tryon, T. (*Crowned Heads*) Fawcett, N.Y.
FEET OF THE SNAKE, THE WELLER/MYERS 1985	Chubin, B. Arbor, N.Y.
FELLINI SATYRICON (V) UA 1970	Petronius (*Satyricon*) Various

TITLE OF FILM	AUTHOR AND PUBLISHER
FEMININE TOUCH, THE RANK 1956	Russell, S.M. (*Lamp is Heavy, A*) Angus & Robertson
FERRY TO HONG KONG (V) RANK 1959	Kent, S. Hutchinson
FEVER IN THE BLOOD WAR 1960	Pearson, W. Macmillan
FIERCEST HEART, THE FOX 1960	Cloete, S. Collins
FIFTH MUSKETEER, THE (V) SASCH WIEN FILMS 1978	Dumas, A. (*Man in the Iron Mask, The*) Various
55 DAYS AT PEKING (V) RANK 1962	Edwards, S. Bantam, N.Y.
FIGHTER, THE (V) UA 1952	London, J. (*Mexican, The*) Appleton-Century, N.Y.
FIGHTING CARAVANS PAR 1931	Grey, Z. Hodder & Stoughton
FIGHTING GUARDSMAN, THE COL 1945	Dumas, A. (*Companions of Jehu, The*) Dent
FIGHTING MAD MON 1939	Erskine, L.Y. (*Renfrew Rides Again*) Appleton-Century, N.Y.
FIGURES IN A LANDSCAPE FOX 1970	England, B. Cape
FINAL ACT, THE SAWBUCK 1980	Hudson, C. Joseph
FINAL PROGRAMME, THE MGM—EMI 1973	Moorcock, M. Alison & Busby
FINDERS KEEPERS (V) RANK 1984	Dennis, C. (*Next-to-last train ride, The*) Macmillan

TITLE OF FILM	AUTHOR AND PUBLISHER
FINE MADNESS, A WAR 1965	Baker, E. Joseph
FINN AND HATTIE PAR 1931	Stewart, D.O. (*Mr and Mrs Haddock* *abroad*) Doran, N.Y.
FIRE DOWN BELOW COL 1957	Kent, S. Hutchinson
FIREFOX (V) COL—EMI—WAR 1982	Thomas, C. Joseph
FIRE OVER ENGLAND (V) UA 1937	Mason, A.E.W. Hodder & Stoughton
FIRE SALE FOX 1978	Klane, R. Fawcett, N.Y.
FIRESTARTER (V) UIP 1984	King, S. Macdonald
FIRST AMONG EQUALS ITV 1986 (TV)	Archer, J. Hodder & Stoughton
FIRST BLOOD (V) ORION 1982	Morrell, D. Pan
FIRST COMES COURAGE COL 1943	Arnold, E. (*Commandos, The*) Rich & Cowan
FIRST DEADLY SIN, THE (V) CIC 1981	Sanders, L. Macmillan, N.Y.
FIRST GENTLEMAN, THE COL 1948	Ginsbury, N. (P) Hammond
FIRST GREAT TRAIN ROBBERY, THE (V) UA 1979	Crichton, M. (*Great Train Robbery*) Cape
FIRST LEGION, THE UA 1951	Lavery, E.G. (P) French, N.Y.

TITLE OF FILM	AUTHOR AND PUBLISHER

FIRST MEN IN THE MOON, THE
COL 1963

Wells, H.G.
Various

FIRST MRS FRASER, THE
STERLING 1932

Ervine, St. J. (P)
Chatto & Windus

F.I.S.T. (V)
UA 1978

Eszterhas, J.
Dell, N.Y.

FITZWOLLY STRIKES BACK
UA 1968

Tyler, P. (*Garden of Cucumbers, A*)
Gollancz

FIVE AND TEN
MGM 1931

Hurst, F.
Cape

FIVE FINGER EXERCISE
COL 1962

Shaffer, P. (P)
French

FIVE FINGERS
FOX 1952

Moyzisch, L.C. (*Operation Cicero*)
Wingate

FIVE HAVE A MYSTERY TO SOLVE
CFF 1964

Blyton, E.
Hodder & Stoughton

FIVE LITTLE PEPPERS AND HOW THEY GREW
COL 1939

Sidley, M.
Various

FIVE ON A TREASURE ISLAND
BL 1957

Blyton, E.
Hodder & Stoughton

FIVE WEEKS IN A BALLOON
FOX 1962

Verne, J.
Various

FIXER, THE
MGM 1969

Malamud, B.
Eyre & Spottiswoode

FLAME IN THE STREETS
RANK 1961

Willis, T. (*Hot Summer Night*) (P)
French

FLAMINGO ROAD
WAR 1949

Wilder, R.
Grosset, N.Y.

FLAMING STAR
FOX 1960

Huffaker, C. (*Flaming Lance*)
Simon & Schuster, N.Y.

TITLE OF FILM	AUTHOR AND PUBLISHER
FLASHPOINT (V) EMI 1984	La Fontaine, G. Mayflower
FLASH THE OTTER DISNEY 1969	Liers, E. (*Otter's Story*) Hodder & Stoughton
FLASH THE SHEEPDOG CFF 1966	Fidler, K. Lutterworth
FLAT TWO AA 1962	Wallace, E. Long
FLEA IN HER EAR, A FOX 1968	Feydeau, G. (P) Methuen
FLESH AND BLOOD BL 1951	Bridie, J. (*Sleeping Clergyman, A*) (P) French
FLESH AND FANTASY UN 1943	Wilde, O. (*Lord Arthur Savile's Crime*) Various
FLESH IS WEAK, THE EROS 1957	Miller, G. Corgi
FLETCH UIP 1985	McDonald G. Gollancz
FLIGHT FROM ASHIYA UA 1963	Arnold, E. Muller
FLIGHT OF THE DOVES COL 1971	Macken, W. Macmillan
FLIGHT OF THE PHOENIX, THE FOX 1965	Trevor, E. Heinemann
FLIGHT OF THE WHITE STALLION, THE DISNEY 1963	Podhajsky, A. (*White Stallions of Vienna, The*) Harrap
FLIM-FLAM MAN, THE FOX 1966	Owen, G. (*Ballad of the Flim-Flam Man*) Macmillan, N.Y.

TITLE OF FILM	AUTHOR AND PUBLISHER
FLOATING DUTCHMAN, THE AA 1953	Bentley, N. Joseph
FLOODS OF FEAR RANK 1958	Hawkins, J. *and* Hawkins, W. Eyre & Spottiswoode
FLORENTINE DAGGER, THE WAR 1935	Hecht, B. Harrap
FLORIAN MGM 1940	Salten, F. Cape
FLOWER DRUM SONG UI 1961	Lee, C.Y. Gollancz
FLOWERS IN THE ATTIC NEW WORLD 1985	Andrews, V.C. Hall, Boston: Mass
FLY AWAY PETER GFD 1948	Dearsley, A.P. (P) French
FOLLOW ME UN 1972	Shaffer, P. (*Public Eye, The*) (P) French
FOLLOW ME BOYS! DISNEY 1967	Kantor, M. (*God and my Country*) World, N.Y.
FOLLOW THAT DREAM UA 1962	Powell, R. (*Pioneer Go Home*) Hodder & Stoughton
FOLLOW THAT HORSE WAR 1959	Mason, H. (*Photo Finish*) Joseph
FOLLY TO BE WISE BL 1952	Bridie, J. (*It Depends what you mean*) (P) Constable
FOOL FOR LOVE CANNON 1986	Shepard, S. (P) San Francisco
FOOLS PARADE COL 1971	Grubb, D. (*Fools Paradise*) Hodder & Stoughton
FOOLS RUSH IN PINEWOOD 1949	Horn, K. (P) French

94

TITLE OF FILM	AUTHOR AND PUBLISHER
FOOTSTEPS IN THE FOG COL 1955	Jacobs, W.W. (*Interruption, The*) Methuen
FOOTSTEPS IN THE NIGHT AUTEN 1932	Simpson, *Mrs* C.F. Methuen
FOR BEAUTY'S SAKE FOX 1941	Kelland, C.B. (*Skin Deep*) Various
FOR BETTER, FOR WORSE (V) ABP 1954	Watkyn, A. (P) Elek
FORBIDDEN ENTERPRISE 1984 (TV)	Gross, L. (*Last Jews in Berlin, The*) Simon & Schuster, N.Y.
FORBIDDEN FRUIT CAMEO-POLY 1952	Simenon, G. (*Act of Passion*) Routledge
FORBIDDEN TERRITORY HOFFBERG 1938	Wheatley, D. Hutchinson
FORBIDDEN VALLEY UN 1938	Hardy, S. Macaulay, N.Y.
FORBIN PROJECT, THE UN 1972	Jones, D.F. (*Colossus*) Hart-Davis
FORCE OF EVIL MGM 1949	Wolfert, I (*Tucker's People*) Gollancz
FORCE 10 FROM NAVARONE (V) COL—WAR 1978	MacLean, A. Collins
FOREIGN CORRESPONDENT UA 1940	Sheean, V. Hamilton
FOREVER AMBER FOX 1947	Winsor, K. Macdonald
FOREVER FEMALE PAR 1953	Barrie, *Sir* J.M. (*Rosalind*) (P) Hodder & Stoughton
FORGOTTEN STORY, THE HTV 1982 (TV)	Graham, W. Bodley Head

FORGOTTEN VILLAGE, THE
MGM 1941

Steinbeck, J.
Viking Press, N.Y.

FORLORN RIVER
PAR 1937

Grey, Z.
Hodder & Stoughton

FOR LOVE ALONE
WARRANTY, AUSTRALIA 1985

Stead, C.
Angus & Robertson

FORMULA, THE
MGM 1980

Shagan, S.
Bantam, N.Y.

FORSYTE SAGA, THE
MGM 1950

Galsworthy, J. (*Man of Property, The*)
Heinemann

FOR THEM THAT TRESPASS
ABP 1949

Raymond, E.
Cassell

FOR THE TERM OF HIS NATURAL LIFE
FILMO 1985 (TV)

Clarke, M.
Angus & Robertson

FOR THOSE I LOVED (V)
GALA 1984

Gray, M. *and* Gallo, M.
New American Library, N.Y.

FORTUNE IS A WOMAN
COL 1957

Graham, W.
Hodder & Stoughton

FORTUNES OF CAPTAIN BLOOD, THE
COL 1950

Sabatini, R.
Hutchinson

FOR WHOM THE BELL TOLLS (V)
PAR 1943
MANLEY 1984

Hemingway, E.
Cape

FOR YOUR EYES ONLY (V)
UA 1981

Fleming, I.
Cape

FOUNTAIN, THE
RKO 1934

Morgan, C.
Macmillan

FOUNTAINHEAD
WAR 1949

Rand, A.
Cassell

TITLE OF FILM	AUTHOR AND PUBLISHER

FOUR DAYS WONDER
UN 1937

Milne, A.A.
Methuen

FOUR FACES WEST
UA 1948

Rhodes, E.M. (*Paso Por Acqui*)
Houghton Mifflin, Boston

FOUR FEATHERS, THE (V)
PAR 1930
UA 1939
TRIDENT BARBER 1978

Mason, A.E.W.
Murray

**FOUR HORSEMEN OF THE
APOCALYPSE, THE**
MGM 1961

Blasco-Ibanez, C.
Various

FOUR HOURS TO KILL
PAR 1935

Krasna, N. (*Small Miracle*) (P)
French, N.Y.

FOUR JUST MEN, THE
EARLING 1939

Wallace, E.
Various

FOUR POSTER, THE
COL 1952

Hartog, J. de (P)
Sampson Low

FOUR MUSKETEERS, THE
FOX—RANK 1974

Dumas, A. (*Three Musketeers, The*)
Various

FOUR-SIDED TRIANGLE
EXCLUSIVE 1952

Temple, W.F.
Long

FOURTH PROTOCOL
FOURTH PROTOCOL 1986

Forsyth, F.
Hutchinson

FOX, THE
WAR 1968

Lawrence, D.H.
Heinemann

FOX AND THE HOUND
DISNEY 1981

Mannix, D.
Various

FOXES OF HARROW, THE
FOX 1947

Yerby, F.
Heinemann

FOXFIRE
UI 1954

Seton, A.
Hodder & Stoughton

FOXHOLE IN CAIRO (V)
BL 1960

Mosley, L. (*Cat and the Mice, The*)
Barker

FRAGMENT OF FEAR
COL 1969

Bingham, J.
Panther

FRAMED (V)
CIC 1974

Powers, A. *and* Misenheimer, M.
Pinnacle

FRANCHISE AFFAIR, THE
ABP 1951

Tey, J.
Davies

FRANCIS
UI 1949

Stern, D.
Farrar, N.Y.

FRANKENSTEIN (V)
UN 1931
YORKSHIRE 1984 (TV)

Shelley, *Mrs* M.W.
Dent

FRAULEIN
FOX 1957

McGovern, J.
Calder

FREAKY FRIDAY
DISNEY 1976

Rodgers, M.
Hamilton

FRECKLES
FOX 1960

Porter, G.S.
Hodder & Stoughton

FREEDOM ROAD (V)
ENTERPRISE 1980

Fast, H.
Various

FRENCH ARE A FUNNY RACE, THE
CONTINENTAL 1957

Daninos, P. (*Major Thompson Lives in France*)
Cape

FRENCH CONNECTION, THE (V)
FOX 1971

Moore, R.
Hodder & Stoughton

FRENCH LEAVE
AB 1937

Berkeley, R. (P)
French

FRENCH LIEUTENANT'S WOMAN, THE
(V)
UA 1981

Fowles, J.
Cape

TITLE OF FILM	AUTHOR AND PUBLISHER
FRENCHMAN'S CREEK PAR 1944	Du Maurier, D. Gollancz
FRENCH MISTRESS, A BL 1960	Monro, R. (P) French
FRENCH WITHOUT TEARS PAR 1940	Rattigan, T. (P) French
FRENZY (V) RANK 1971	La Bern, A. (*Goodbye Piccadilly,* *Farewell Leicester Square*) Pan
FREUD BBC 1984 (TV)	Harrison, C. Weidenfeld & Nicolson
FRIEDA EALING 1947	Millar, R. (P) English Theatre Guild
FRIENDLY FIRE (V) BBC 1984 (TV)	Bryan, C.D.B. Bantam, N.Y.
FRIENDLY PERSUASION MGM 1956	West, J. Hodder & Stoughton
FRIEND OR FOE (V) CFF 1982	Morpurgo, M. Macmillan
FRIENDS AND LOVERS RKO 1931	Dekobra, M. (*Sphinx has Spoken,* *The*) Laurie
FRIENDS OF EDDIE COYLE, THE PAR 1973	Higgins, G.V. Secker & Warburg
FRIGHTENED LADY, THE BL 1941	Wallace, E. (P) French, N.Y.
FRIGHTENED LADY, THE BL 1932 BL 1941	Wallace, E. (*Case of the Frightened* *Lady, The*) Hodder & Stoughton
FROG PRINCE, THE (V) WAR 1985	Rootes, N. Arrow

FROM BEYOND
EMPIRE 1986

Lovecraft, H.P.
Various

FROM BEYOND THE GRAVE
EMI 1974

Chetwynd-Hayes, R. (*Elemental, The*)
Fontana

FROM HERE TO ETERNITY
COL 1953

Jones, J.
Collins

FROM NOON TILL THREE
UA 1975

Gilroy, F.D.
Doubleday, N.Y.

FROM RUSSIA WITH LOVE (V)
UA 1963

Fleming, I.
Cape

FROM THE EARTH TO THE MOON
WAR 1958

Verne, J.
Various

FROM THE TERRACE
FOX 1960

O'Hara, J.
Cresset Press

FROM THIS DAY FORWARD
RKO 1946

Bell, T. (*All Brides are Beautiful*)
Grosset, N.Y.

FRONTIER MARSHAL
FOX 1939

Lake, S. (*Wyatt Earp*)
Various

FRONTIER RANGERS
MGM 1959

Roberts, K. (*North-West Passage*)
Collins

FRONT PAGE, THE
UA 1931
CIC 1974

Hecht, B. *and* MacArthur, C.C. (P)
Covici, N.Y.

FRONT PAGE STORY
BL 1953

Gaines, R. (*Final Night*)
Heinemann

FUGITIVE, THE (V)
RKO 1947

Greene, G. (*Power and the Glory, The*)
Heinemann

FUGITIVE KIND, THE
UA 1960

Williams, T. (*Orpheus Descending*)
Secker & Warburg

FULL CIRCLE
CIC 1978

Straub, P. (*Julia*)
  Cape

FULL HOUSE
FOX 1952

Henry, O.
  Hodder & Stoughton

FULL OF LIFE
COL 1957

Fante, J.
  Little, Brown, Boston

FULL TREATMENT, THE
COL 1960

Thorn, R.S.
  Heinemann

FUMED OAK
GFD 1952

Coward, N. (P)
  Heinemann

FUNERAL IN BERLIN
PAR 1966

Deighton, L.
  Cape

FURIES, THE
PAR 1950

Busch, N.
  W.H. Allen

FUTZ
COMMONWEALTH 1969

Owens, R. (*Futz and What Came After*) (P)
  Random House, N.Y.

FUZZ (V)
UA 1972

McBain, E.
  Hamilton

FUZZY PINK NIGHTGOWN, THE
UA 1957

Tate, S.
  Harper, N.Y.

G

GABY
MGM 1955

Sherwood, R.E. (*Waterloo Bridge*) (P)
  Scribner, N.Y.

GAILY, GAILY
UA 1969

Hecht, B.
  Elek

GAMBIT
UI 1966

Lane, K.
  Hodder & Stoughton

TITLE OF FILM	AUTHOR AND PUBLISHER
GAMBLERS, THE FOX—RANK 1974	Gogol, N. (P) Dent
GAME FOR THREE LOSERS WAR 1965	Lustgarten, E. Museum Press
GAME FOR VULTURES (V) COL—EMI—WAR 1979	Hartman, M. Pan
GAME IS OVER, THE COL 1967	Zola, E. (*Kill, The*) Arrow
GAMES, THE (V) FOX 1969	Atkinson, H. Cassell
GANG THAT COULDN'T SHOOT STRAIGHT, THE MGM—EMI 1972	Breslin, J. Hutchinson
GARDEN MURDER CASE, THE MGM 1936	Dine, S.S. van Cassell
GARDEN OF ALLAH, THE (V) UA 1936	Hichens, R. Methuen
GASLIGHT BN 1940 MGM 1944	Hamilton, P. (P) French
GAUNT WOMAN, THE RKO 1950	Gilligan, E. Scribner, N.Y.
GAY CABALLERO FOX 1932	Gill, T. (*Gay Bandit of the Border*) Collins
GEMINI CONTENDERS, THE ITC 1978	Ludlum, R. Dell, N.Y.
GENERAL CRACK WAR 1930	Preedy, G. Lane
GENERAL DIED AT DAWN, THE PAR 1936	Booth, C.G. Bell

GENERATION
AVCO EMBASSY 1969

Goodhart, W. (P)
Doubleday, N.Y.

GENTLE ANNIE
MGM 1944

Kantor, M.
Various

GENTLE GIANT
PAR 1968

Morley, W. (*Gentle Ben*)
Dutton, N.Y.

GENTLE GUNMAN, THE
GFD 1952

Macdougall, R. (P)
Elek

GENTLE JULIA
FOX 1936

Tarkington, B.
Grosset, N.Y.

GENTLEMEN MARRY BRUNETTES
UA 1955

Loos, A. (*But . . .*)
Brentano, N.Y.

GENTLEMEN PREFER BLONDES (V)
FOX 1953

Loos, A.
Cape

GENTLEMEN'S AGREEMENT
FOX 1947

Hobson, *Mrs* L.
Cassell

GEORDIE
BL 1955

Walker, D.
Collins

GEORGE AND MARGARET
WAR 1940

Savory, G. (P)
French, N.Y.

GEORGE WASHINGTON SLEPT HERE
WAR 1942

Kaufman, G.S. *and* Hart, M. (P)
Random House, N.Y.

GEORGY GIRL
COL 1966

Forster, M.
Secker & Warburg

GETAWAY, THE (V)
CINERAMA 1972

Thompson, J.
W. H. Allen

GET CARTER
MGM 1971

Lewis, T. (*Jack's Return Home*)
Joseph

GETTING OF WISDOM, THE (V)
TEDDERWICK 1979

Richardson, H.H.
Heinemann

GETTING STRAIGHT
COL 1969

Kolb, K.
Barrie & Rockliff

GHOST AND MRS MUIR, THE
FOX 1947

Dick, R.A.
Harrap

GHOSTS OF BERKELEY SQUARE, THE
BN 1947

Brahms, C. *and* Simon, S.J. (*No Nightingales*)
Joseph

GHOST STORY (V)
UN 1981

Straub, P.
Coward-McCann, N.Y.

GHOST TRAIN, THE (V)
GFD 1931
GFD 1941

Ridley, A. (P)
French, N.Y.

GIANT
WAR 1956

Ferber, E.
Gollancz

GIDEON'S DAY
COL 1958

Marric, J.J.
Hodder & Stoughton

GIDGET
COL 1959

Kohner, F.
Joseph

GIFT FROM THE BOYS, A
COL 1959

Buchwald, A.
Harper, N.Y.

GIGI (V)
MGM 1958

Colette
Secker & Warburg

GIRL FROM ALASKA, THE
REP 1942

Case, R.O. (*Golden Portage, The*)
Jarrolds

GIRL FROM MANDALAY
REP 1936

Campbell, R. (*Death in Tiger Valley*)
Hodder & Stoughton

GIRL FROM PETROVKA
UN 1975

Feifer, G.
Macmillan

GIRL HE LEFT BEHIND, THE
WAR 1957

Hargrove, M.
Viking Press, N.Y.

GIRL HUNTERS, THE
FOX 1964

Spillane, M.
Barker

GIRL IN THE HEADLINES, THE
BL 1963

Payne, L. (*Nose on my Face, The*)
Hodder & Stoughton

GIRL IN THE NEWS
FOX 1941

Vickers, R.
Jenkins

GIRL IN WHITE, THE
MGM 1952

Barringer, E.D. (*Bowery to Bellevue*)
Norton, N.Y.

GIRL MUST LIVE, A
UN 1941

Bonett, E.
Miles

GIRL NAMED TAMIKO, A
PAR 1963

Kirkbride, R.
Pan

GIRL OF THE LIMBERLOST, A
MON 1934

Porter, G.S.
Hodder & Stoughton

GIRL OF THE NIGHT
WAR 1960

Greenwald, H. (*Call Girl, The*)
Elek

GIRL ON THE BOAT, THE
UA 1962

Wodehouse, P.G.
Jenkins

GIRL ON THE MOTORCYCLE, THE
BL 1965

Mandiargues, A.P. de
Calder

GIRLS OF PLEASURE ISLAND, THE
PAR 1953

Maier, W. (*Pleasure Island*)
Wingate

GIRLS OF SUMMER
PAR 1959

Nash, N.R. (P)
French, N.Y.

GIRL WHO COULDN'T QUIT, THE
MON 1949

Marks, L. (P)
French

GIRL WHO DARED, THE
REP 1944

Field, M. (*Blood on her Shoe*)
Jarrolds

GIRL WITH GREEN EYES (V)
UA 1964

O'Brien, E. (*Lonely Girl, The*)
Cape

TITLE OF FILM	AUTHOR AND PUBLISHER
GIVE ME YOUR HEART WAR 1936	Mallory, J. (*Sweet Aloes*) Cassell
GIVE US THE MOON GFD 1944	Brahms, C. *and* Simon, S.J. (*Elephant in White, The*) Joseph
GIVE US THIS DAY GFD 1949	Di Donato, P. (*Christ in Concrete*) World, N.Y.
GLAD TIDINGS EROS 1953	Delderfield, R.F. (P) Rylee
GLASS CAGE, THE EXCLUSIVE 1955	Martin, A.E. (*Curious Crime*) Muller
GLASS KEY, THE PAR 1935 PAR 1942	Hammett, D. Cassell
GLASS MENAGERIE WAR 1950	Williams, T. (P) Lehmann
GLITTER DOME, THE (V) EMI 1984	Wambaugh, J. Morrow, N.Y.
GLORY BOYS, THE YORKSHIRE 1984 (TV)	Seymour, G. Random, N.Y.
GLORY GUYS UA 1965	Birney, H. (*Dice of God, The*) Holt, N.Y.
GNOMOBILE (V) DISNEY 1966	Stern, G.B. Laurie
GO-BETWEEN, THE (V) MGM—EMI 1971	Hartley, L.P. Penguin
GODFATHER, THE (V) PAR 1971	Puzo, M. Heinemann
GODFATHER PART II, THE (V) CIC 1974	Puzo, M. Heinemann

TITLE OF FILM	AUTHOR AND PUBLISHER
GOD IS MY CO-PILOT WAR 1945	Scott, R.L. Hodder & Stoughton
GODSEND, THE (V) CANNON 1980	Taylor, B. Avon, N.Y.
GOD'S LITTLE ACRE (V) UA 1958	Caldwell, E. Heinemann
GOLD HEMDALE 1974	Smith, W. (*Gold Mine*) Heinemann
GOLD BUG, THE BL 1956	Poe, E.A. Various
GOLDEN BOY COL 1938	Odets, C. (P) Gollancz
GOLDEN EAR-RINGS PAR 1947	Foldes, Y. Hale
GOLDEN GATE, THE ITC 1978	MacLean, A. Collins
GOLDEN GIRL (V) AVCO EMBASSY 1980	Lear, P. Cassell
GOLDEN HAWK, THE COL 1952	Yerby, F. Heinemann
GOLDEN HEAD, THE CINERAMA 1965	Pilkington, R. (*Nepomuk of the River*) Macmillan
GOLDEN RENDEZVOUS (V) RANK 1977	MacLean, A. Collins
GOLDEN SALAMANDER GFD 1949	Canning, V. Hodder & Stoughton
GOLDEN SEAL, THE NEW REALM 1984	Marshall, J.V. (*River ran out of Eden, A*) Heinemann

TITLE OF FILM	AUTHOR AND PUBLISHER
GOLDFINGER (V) UA 1963	Fleming, I. Cape
GOLD FOR THE CAESARS MGM 1963	Seward, F.A. Redman
GOLD OF THE SEVEN SAINTS WAR 1961	Frazee, S. (*Desert Guns*) World, N.Y.
GO NAKED IN THE WORLD MGM 1960	Chamales, T. Deutsch
GONE TO EARTH BL 1950	Webb, M. Cape
GONE WITH THE WIND (V) MGM 1939	Mitchell, M. Macmillan
GOODBYE AGAIN UA 1961	Sagan, F. (*Aimez-vous Brahms?*) Murray
GOODBYE CHARLIE FOX 1965	Axelrod, G. (P) French, N.Y.
GOODBYE COLUMBUS PAR 1969	Roth, P. Deutsch
GOODBYE GEMINI CINERAMA 1970	Hall, J. (*Ask Agememnon*) Sphere
GOODBYE MR CHIPS MGM 1939	Hilton, J. Hodder & Stoughton
GOODBYE MR CHIPS MGM 1969	Hilton, J. *and* Burnham, B. (P) French, N.Y.
GOODBYE, MY FANCY WAR 1951	Kanin, F. (P) French, N.Y.
GOODBYE, MY LADY WAR 1956	Street, J.H. Invincible Press
GOOD COMPANIONS, THE FOX 1933 ABP 1957	Priestley, J.B. Heinemann

TITLE OF FILM	AUTHOR AND PUBLISHER
GOOD COMPANIONS, THE FOX 1933 ABP 1957	Priestley, J.B. *and* Knoblock, E. (P) French, N.Y.
GOOD EARTH, THE MGM 1937	Buck, P. Methuen
GOOD FAIRY, THE UN 1934	Molnar, F. (P) Crown, N.Y.
GOOD FATHER, THE FILM FOUR 1986	Prince, P. Carroll & Graf, N.Y.
GOOD MORNING, MISS DOVE FOX 1955	Patton, F.G. Gollancz
GOOD NEIGHBOUR SAM COL 1965	Finney, J. Eyre & Spottiswoode
GOOD-TIME GIRL GFD 1948	La Bern, A.J. (*Night darkens the Streets*) Nicholson & Watson
GORILLA WAR 1931 FOX 1939	Spence, R. (P) French
GORKY PARK (V) ORION 1983	Smith, M.C. Collins
GO TELL IT ON THE MOUNTAIN PRICE 1985 (TV)	Baldwin, J. Corgi
GRACIE ALLEN MURDER CASE, THE PAR 1939	Dine, S.S. van Cassell
GRADUATE, THE (V) UA 1968	Webb, C. Penguin
GRAND CANARY FOX 1934	Cronin, A.J. Gollancz
GRAND CENTRAL MURDER MGM 1942	McVeigh, S. Houghton, Mifflin, Boston

TITLE OF FILM	AUTHOR AND PUBLISHER
GRAND HOTEL MGM 1932	Baum, V. Bles
GRAND NATIONAL NIGHT REN 1953	Christie, D. *and* Christie, C. (P) French
GRAND TOUR, THE TRI-STAR 1984	Prochau, W. (*Trinity's child*) Putnam, N.Y.
GRAPES OF WRATH, THE FOX 1940	Steinbeck, J. Heinemann
GRASSHOPPER, THE NATIONAL GENERAL LECTURES 1969	McShane, M. (*Passing of Evil, The*) Cassell
GRASS IS GREENER, THE UI 1960	Williams, H. *and* Williams, M. (P) Gollancz
GRASS IS SINGING, THE MAINLINE 1981	Lessing, D. Heinemann
GRAY LADY DOWN CIC 1977	Lavallee, D. (*Event One Thousand*) Coronet
GREAT BANK ROBBERY, THE WAR 1969	O'Rourke, F. Sphere
GREAT CATHERINE WAR 1968 PAR 1973	Shaw, G.B. (P) Constable
GREAT DAY IN THE MORNING (V) RKO 1955	Andrew, R.H. Lane
GREAT DIVIDE, THE IN 1930	Moody, W.V. (P) Macmillan
GREAT ESCAPE, THE (V) UA 1963	Brickhill, P. Faber
GREATEST, THE COL—WAR 1977	Muhammad, Ali Hart-Davis

GREATEST STORY EVER TOLD, THE
UA 1965

Oursler, F.
Worlds Work

GREAT EXPECTATIONS (V)
UN 1934
CINEGUILD 1946
SCOTIA BARBER 1975

Dickens, C.
Various

GREAT GAME, THE
ADELPHI 1953

Thomas, B. (*Shooting Star*) (P)
Deane

GREAT GATSBY, THE (V)
PAR 1949
PAR 1973

Fitzgerald, F.S.K.
Grey Walls Press

GREAT IMPERSONATION, THE
UN 1936
UN 1942

Oppenheim, E.P.
Hodder & Stoughton

GREAT IMPOSTER, THE
UI 1960

Crichton, R.
Gollancz

GREAT MAN, THE
UI 1956

Morgan, A.
Dutton, N.Y.

GREAT MEADOW, THE
MGM 1931

Roberts, E.M.
Cape

GREAT MOUSE DETECTIVE, THE
DISNEY 1986

Titus, E. (*Basil of Baker Street*)
Archway, N.Y.

GREAT SANTINI, THE (V)
COL—EMI—WAR 1981

Conroy, P.
Avon, N.Y.

GREAT SINNER, THE
MGM 1949

Dostoevski, F.M. (*Great Gambler*)
Macmillan

GREAT WHITE HOPE, THE (V)
FOX 1971

Sackler, H. (P)
Faber

GREEN BERETS, THE (V)
WAR 1968

Moore, R.
Crown, N.Y.

GREEN DOLPHIN STREET
MGM 1947

Goudge, E.
Hodder & Stoughton

GREEN EYES CHESTERFIELD 1934	Ashbrook, H. (*Murder of Stephen Kester*) Eyre & Spottiswoode
GREEN FINGERS BN 1947	Arundel, E. (*Persistent Warrior, The*) Jenkins
GREEN FOR DANGER INDIVIDUAL 1947	Brand, C. Lane
GREENGAGE SUMMER, THE RANK 1960	Godden, R. Macmillan
GREEN GODDESS, THE WAR 1930	Archer, W. (P) Heinemann
GREEN GRASS OF WYOMING FOX 1949	O'Hara, M. Eyre & Spottiswoode
GREEN GROW THE RUSHES BL 1951	Clewes, H. Lane
GREEN HELL UN 1940	Duguid, J. Various
GREEN HELMET, THE MGM 1960	Cleary, J. Collins
GREEN ICE (V) ITC 1981	Browne, G.A. Delacorte, N.Y.
GREEN LIGHT, THE WAR 1937	Douglas, L.C. Davies
GREEN MAN, THE BL 1956	Maunder, F. *and* Gilliat, S. (*Meet a Body*) (P) French
GREEN MANSIONS MGM 1958	Hudson, W.H. Various
GREEN PACK, THE BL 1936	Wallace, E. (P) French

TITLE OF FILM	AUTHOR AND PUBLISHER
GREEN PACK, THE BL 1936	Wallace, E. *and* Curtis, R.G. Hutchinson
GREEN PASTURES WAR 1936	Connelly, M. (P) Gollancz
GREEN SCARF, THE BL 1954	Cars, G. des (*Brute, The*) Wingate
GREEN YEARS, THE MGM 1946	Cronin, A.J. Gollancz
GREYSTOKE (V) WAR 1984	Burroughs, E.R. (*Tarzan of the apes*) Various
GRIP OF FEAR, THE COL 1962	Gordons, The (*Operation Terror*) Macdonald
GRISSOM GANG, THE (V) CINERAMA 1971	Chase, J.H. (*No Orchids for Miss Blandish*) Panther
GROUNDSTAR CONSPIRACY RANK 1972	Davies, L.P. (*Alien, The*) Barrie & Jenkins
GROUP, THE UA 1965	McCarthy, M. Weidenfeld & Nicolson
GUADACANAL DIARY FOX 1943	Tregaskis, R.W. Wells & Gardner
GUARDSMAN, THE MGM 1931	Molnar, F. (P) Macy-Masius, N.Y.
GUEST IN THE HOUSE UA 1944	Wilde, H. *and* Eunson, D. (*Dear Evelyn*) (P) French
GUIDE FOR THE MARRIED MAN, THE FOX 1968	Tarloff, F. Price, Sterm, Sloan, Los Angeles
GUILT IS MY SHADOW ABP 1950	Curtis, P. (*You're Best Alone*) Macdonald

TITLE OF FILM	AUTHOR AND PUBLISHER
GUILTY? GN 1956	Gilbert, M. (*Death has Deep Roots*) Pan
GUINEA PIG, THE PILGRIM-PATHE 1949	Strode, W.S. (P) Sampson Low
GULLIVER'S TRAVELS PAR 1939 EMI 1976	Swift, J. Various
GUNFIGHTERS COL 1947	Grey, Z. (*Twin Sombreros*) Hodder & Stoughton
GUN FURY COL 1954	Granger, K.R.G. (*Ten Against Caesar*) Houghton, Mifflin, Boston
GUN GLORY MGM 1957	Yordan, P. (*Man of the West*) Deutsch
GUN RUNNERS, THE SEVEN ARTS 1958	Hemingway, E. (*To Have and Have Not*) Cape
GUNS AT BATASI FOX 1964	Holles, R. (*Siege of Battersea, The*) Joseph
GUNS IN THE HEATHER DISNEY 1969	Amerman, L. Harcourt, Brace, N.Y.
GUNSMOKE GFD 1952	Fox, N.A. (*Roughshod*) Dodd, N.Y.
GUNS OF AUGUST, THE RANK 1964	Tuchman, R. (*August, 1914*) Constable
GUNS OF DARKNESS WAR 1964	Clifford, F. (*Act of Mercy*) Hamilton
GUNS OF DIABLO MGM 1964	Taylor, R.L. (*Travels of Jaimie McPheeters, The*) Macdonald
GUNS OF NAVARONE, THE (V) COL 1959	MacLean, A. Collins

GUNS OF THE TIMBERLANDS (V)
WAR 1959

L'Amour, L.
Jason Press, N.Y.

GUY NAMED JOE, A
MGM 1943

Cairn, J.
Hollywood Pubns

GYPSY
WAR 1962

Lee, G.R.
Pan

GYPSY AND THE GENTLEMAN, THE
RANK 1957

Hooke, N.W. (*Darkness I Leave You*)
Hale

H

HAIL, HERO
CINEMA CENTER 1969

Weston, J.
Mackay, N.Y.

HAIRY APE, THE
UA 1944

O'Neill, E.G. (P)
Cape

HALLELUJAH TRAIL, THE
UA 1965

Gullick, B.
Doubleday, N.Y.

HAMLET (V)
TC 1948
CLASSIC CINEMAS 1964
COL 1969

Shakespeare, W. (P)
Various

HAMMERHEAD
COL 1968

Mayo, J.
Heinemann

HAMMER THE TOFF
BUTCHER 1952

Creasey, J.
Long

HAND, THE (V)
SERENDIPITY 1981

Brandel, M. (*Lizard's Tail, The*)
Simon & Schuster, N.Y.

HANGED MAN, THE
RANK 1964

Hughes, D.B. (*Expendable Man, The*)
Deutsch

HANGING TREE, THE
WAR 1958

Johnson, D.M.
Deutsch

TITLE OF FILM	AUTHOR AND PUBLISHER
HANGMEN ALSO DIE UA 1943	Habe, H. (*Thousand Shall Fall, A*) Harrap
HANGOVER SQUARE FOX 1945	Hamilton, P. Constable
HANSEL AND GRETEL RKO 1954	Grimm, J.K. *and* Grimm, W.K. Various
HAPPENING, THE PAR 1967	Curry, E. Corgi
HAPPIEST DAYS OF YOUR LIFE, THE BL 1949	Dighton, J. (P) Elek
HAPPIEST MILLIONAIRE, THE (V) DISNEY 1968	Biddle, C.D. *and* Crichton, K. Sphere
HAPPINESS OF THREE WOMEN, THE ADELPHI 1954	Evans, E. (*Wishing Well*) (P) French
HAPPY ANNIVERSARY UA 1959	Fields, J. *and* Chodorov, J. (*Anniversary Waltz*) (P) Random House, N.Y.
HAPPY FAMILY, THE APEX 1952	Hutton, M.G. (P) Deane
HAPPY HOOKER, THE SCOTIA BARBER 1975	Hollander, X. Talmy-Franklin
HAPPY LAND FOX 1943	Kantor, M. Longmans
HAPPY THIEVES, THE UA 1961	Condon, R. (*Oldest Confession, The*) Longmans
HAPPY TIME, THE COL 1952	Fontaine, R.L. Hamilton
HAPPY TIME, THE COL 1952	Taylor, S.A. (P) Dramatists, N.Y.
HARDER THEY FALL COL 1956	Schulberg, B.W. Lane

HARD MAN, THE
COL 1957

Katcher, L.
Macmillan, N.Y.

HARLOW
PAR 1964

Shulman, I.
Mayflower

HARPER
WAR 1967

Macdonald, R. (*Moving Target, The*)
Pan

HARRAD EXPERIMENT, THE
FOX 1974

Rimmer, R.H.
New English Library

HARRIET CRAIG
COL 1950

Kelly, G. (*Craig's Wife*) (P)
French

HARRY BLACK
FOX 1958

Walker, D.
Collins

HARRY'S GAME (V)
YORKSHIRE 1982 (TV)

Seymour, G.
Collins

HARVESTER, THE
REP 1936

Porter, G.S.
Hodder & Stoughton

HARVEY
GFD 1950

Chase, M. (P)
Dramatists, N.Y.

HATE SHIP
BI 1930

Graeme, B.
Hutchinson

HATFUL OF RAIN, A.
FOX 1957

Gazzo, M.V. (P)
Random House, N.Y.

HATTER'S CASTLE
PAR 1942

Cronin, A.J.
Gollancz

HAUNTED PALACE, THE
AMERICAN INT 1963

Lovecraft, H.P. (*Case of Charles
Dexter, The*)
Panther

HAUNTING, THE
MGM 1963

Jackson, S. (*Haunting of Hill House,
The*)
Joseph

HAVING WONDERFUL CRIME
RKO 1945

Rice, E.
Nicholson & Watson

HAVING WONDERFUL TIME
RKO 1938

Kober, A. (P)
Dramatists, N.Y.

HAWAII
UA 1965

Michener, J.A.
Secker & Warburg

HAYWIRE
BBC 2 1984 (TV)

Hayward, B.
Bantam, N.Y.

HAZARD
PAR 1948

Chanslor, R.
Various

HEAD OVER HEELS
UA 1979

Beattie, A. (*Chilly Scenes of Winter*)
Popular Library, N.Y.

HEART BEAT
COL—EMI—WAR 1980

Cassady, C.
Creative Arts, Berkeley: Cal.

HEARTBREAK PASS
UA 1975

MacLean, A.
Collins

HEART IS A LONELY HUNTER, THE (V)
WAR 1968

McCullers, C.
Penguin

HEART KEEPER, THE
FOX 1969

Sagan, F.
Murray

HEART OF A CHILD
RANK 1958

Bottome, P.
Faber

HEART OF THE DRAGON, THE
CHANNEL 4 1984 (TV)

Clayre, A.
Harvill

HEART OF THE MATTER
BL 1953

Greene, G.
Heinemann

HEAT AND DUST (V)
ENTERPRISE 1983

Jhabvala, R.P.
Murray

HEAT LIGHTING
WAR 1934

Hull, H.R.
Cobden Sanderson

HEAVEN CAN WAIT FOX 1943	Ackland, R. (*Birthday*) (P) French, N.Y.
HEAVEN KNOWS MR. ALLISON FOX 1957	Shaw, C. Muller
HEDDA SCOTIA BARBER 1977	Ibsen, H. (*Hedda Gabler*) (P) Various
HEFFERAN FAMILY, THE FOX 1956	Taylor, R. (*Chicken Every Sunday*) Methuen
HEIDI FOX 1937 UA 1954	Spyri, J. Various
HEIDI'S SONG HANNA-BARBERA 1982	Spyri, J. (*Heidi*) Various
HEIRESS, THE PAR 1949	Goetz, R. *and* Goetz, A. (P) Reinhardt & Evans
HEIRESS, THE PAR 1949	James, H. (*Washington Square*) Macmillan
HE KNEW WOMEN RKO 1930	Behrman, S.N. (*Second Man*) (P) Various
HELL BELOW ZERO COL 1953	Innes, H. (*White South, The*) Collins
HELLCATS OF THE NAVY COL 1957	Lockwood, C.A. *and* Adamson, H.C. (*Hellcats of the Sea*) Greenberg, N.Y.
HELLER IN PINK TIGHTS PAR 1960	L'Amour, L. (*Heller With A Gun*) Muller
HELL IS A CITY WAR 1959	Procter, M. Hutchinson
HELL IS EMPTY RANK 1967	Straker, J.F. Harrap

HELL IS FOR HEROES
PAR 1962

Anders, C.
Corgi

HELL IS SOLD OUT
EROS 1951

Dekobra, M.
Laurie

HELLO DOLLY! (V)
FOX 1968

Stewart, M. (P)
D.B.S. Pubs., N.Y.

HELL ON FRISCO BAY (V)
WAR 1955

McGivern, W.P. (*Darkest Hour*)
Collins

HELL'S HEROES
UN 1930

Kyne, P.B. (*Three Godfathers, The*)
Various

HELL'S OUTPOST
REP 1954

Short, L. (*Silver Rock*)
Collins

HELTER SKELTER (V)
HEMDALE 1976

Bugliosi, V. *and* Gentry, C. (*Manson Murders, The*)
Bodley Head

HENRY V
TC 1945

Shakespeare, W. (P)
Various

HE RAN ALL THE WAY
UA 1951

Ross, S.
Farrar, N.Y.

HERE COMES MR. JORDAN
COL 1941

Segall, H. (*Halfway to Heaven*) (P)
French

HERE COME THE HUGGETTS
GFD 1948

Constanduros, M. *and* Constanduros, D.
Sampson Low

HERE WE GO ROUND THE MULBERRY BUSH
UA 1967

Davies, H.
Pan

HER FIRST ROMANCE
MON 1940

Porter, G.S. (*Her Father's Daughter*)
Murray

HERITAGE OF THE DESERT
PAR 1933
PAR 1939

Grey, Z.
Nelson

HEROES OF THE TELEMARK (V)
RANK 1965

Drummond, J.D. (*But for These Men*)
W.H. Allen

HEROIN GANG, THE
MGM 1968

Wilder, R. (*Fruit of the Poppy*)
W.H. Allen

HER SISTER'S SECRET
PRC 1946

Kaus, G. (*Dark Angel*)
Cassell

HER STRANGE DESIRE
POWERS 1932

Middleton, E. (*Potiphar's Wife*)
Laurie

HER TWELVE MEN
MGM 1954

Baker, L.
McGraw-Hill, N.Y.

HER WONDERFUL LIFE
COL 1950

Moss, A. *and* Marvel, E. (*Legend of the Latin Quarter*)
W.H. Allen

HESTER STREET
CONNOISSEUR 1975

Cahen, A. (*Yekl*)
Peter Smith

HIAWATHA
ABP 1952
CHANNEL 4 1984 (TV)

Longfellow, H.W. (Poem)
Various

HIDDEN HOMICIDE
RANK 1958

Capon, P. (*Death at Shinglestrand*)
Ward Lock

HIDEAWAYS, THE (V)
UA 1973

Konigsburg, E.L. (*From the Mixed-up Files of Mr. Basil E. Frankwester*)
Macmillan

HIDE IN PLAIN SIGHT (V)
CIC 1980

Waller, L.
Dell, N.Y.

HIDING PLACE, THE (V)
WORLD WIDE FILMS 1974

Boom, Corie Ten
Hodder & Stoughton

HIGH AND THE MIGHTY, THE
WAR 1954

Gann, E.K.
Hodder & Stoughton

HIGH BARBAREE, THE
MGM 1947

Nordhoff, C.B. *and* Hall, J.N.
Faber

TITLE OF FILM	AUTHOR AND PUBLISHER
HIGH BRIGHT SUN, THE RANK 1964	Black, I.S. Hutchinson
HIGH HELL PAR 1958	Frazee, S. (*High Cage*) Macmillan, N.Y.
HIGH ROAD TO CHINA (V) MIRACLE 1984	Cleary, J. Warner, N.Y.
HIGH SIERRA WAR 1941	Burnett, W.R. Heinemann
HIGH SOCIETY MGM 1956	Barry, P. (*Philadelphia Story, The*) (P) French
HIGH VERMILION PAR 1951	Short, L. Collins
HIGH WIND IN JAMAICA, A FOX 1964	Hughes, R. Chatto & Windus
HIGH WINDOW, THE FOX 1947	Chandler, R. Hamilton
HILDA CRANE FOX 1956	Raphaelson, S. (P) Random House, N.Y.
HILL, THE MGM 1965	Rigby, K. *and* Allen, R.S. Mayflower
HILL IN KOREA, A BL 1956	Catto, M. Hutchinson
HILL'S ANGELS (V) DISNEY 1980	Hill, A.F. (*North Avenue Irregulars*) Berkeley, N.Y.
HILLS OF OLD WYOMING PAR 1937	Mulford, C.E. (*Round-up, The*) Hodder & Stoughton
HINDENBURG, THE (V) CIC 1975	Mooney, M.M. Hart-Davis

TITLE OF FILM	AUTHOR AND PUBLISHER
HINDLE WAKES GB 1932 MON 1952	Houghton, S. (P) Various
HIRELING, THE COL—WAR 1973	Hartley, L.P. Penguin
HIS DOUBLE LIFE PAR 1933	Bennett, A. (*Great Adventure*) Methuen
HIS EXCELLENCY GFD 1951	Arlington, A. Chatto & Windus
HIS EXCELLENCY GFD 1951	Christie, D. *and* Christie, P. (P) Elek
HIS GIRL FRIDAY COL 1940	Hecht, B. *and* MacArthur, C.C. (*Front Page, The*) (P) Covici, N.Y.
HIS MAJESTY O'KEEFE WAR 1954	Klingman, L. *and* Green, G. Hale
HIS WOMAN PAR 1931	Collins, D. (*Sentimentalists*) Little, Brown, Boston
HISTORY OF MR. POLLY TC 1949	Wells, H.G. Various
HITLER: A CAREER GTO 1978	Fest, J. Harcourt, N.Y.
HITLER'S CHILDREN RKO 1943	Ziemer, G. (*Education for Death*) Constable
HIT THE DECK MGM 1954	Osborne, H. (*Shore Leave*) (P) French, N.Y.
H.M. PULHAM, Esq MGM 1941	Marquand, J.P. Hale
H.M.S. DEFIANT COL 1962	Tilsley, F. (*Mutiny*) Eyre & Spottiswoode

TITLE OF FILM	AUTHOR AND PUBLISHER

HOBSON'S CHOICE (V)
BL 1931
BL 1953

Brighouse, H. (P)
French

HOFFMAN
WAR 1969

Gebler, E. (*Shall I Eat You Now?*)
(P)
Pan

HOLCROFT CONVENTION, THE (V)
COL—EMI—WAR 1985

Ludlum, R. (*Holcroft Covenant, The*)
Hart-Davis

HOLD BACK THE DAWN
PAR 1941

Frings, *Mrs*. K.
Duell, N.Y.

HOLD BACK THE NIGHT
ABP 1956

Frank, P.
Hamilton

HOLE IN THE HEAD, A
UA 1959

Schulman, A. (P)
Random House, N.Y.

HOLLOW TRIUMPH
EL 1948

Forbes, M.
Martin

HOLLY AND THE IVY, THE
BL 1952

Browne, W. (P)
Elek

HOLLYWOOD WIVES (V)
WAR 1985 (TV)

Collins, J.
Collins

HOLY MATRIMONY
PAR 1943

Bennett, A. (*Great Adventure*)
Methuen

HOMBRE
FOX 1966

Leonard, E.
Hale

HOME AT SEVEN
BL 1951

Sherriff, R.C. (P)
Gollancz

HOME BEFORE DARK
WAR 1958

Bassing, E.
Longmans

HOMECOMING, THE
SEVEN KEYS 1973

Pinter, H. (P)
Grove, N.Y.

HOME FROM THE HILL MGM 1959	Humphrey, W. Pan
HOME IS THE HERO BL 1959	Macken, W. (P) Macmillan
HOME OF THE BRAVE UA 1949	Laurents, A. (P) Dramatists, N.Y.
HOME ON THE RANGE PAR 1935	Grey, Z. (*Code of the West*) Hodder & Stoughton
HOME SWEET HOMICIDE FOX 1946	Rice, C. World, N.Y.
HONDO WAR 1953	L'Amour, L. Muller
HONDO AND THE APACHES MGM 1966	L'Amour, L. Muller
HONEY PAR 1930	Miller, A.D. *and* Thomas, A.E. (*Come out of the Kitchen*) (P) French
HONEYMOON FOR THREE WAR 1941	Scott, A. *and* Haight, G. (*Goodbye Again*) (P) French, N.Y.
HONEYMOON MACHINE MGM 1961	Semple, L. (*Golden Fleecing, The*) (P) French, N.Y.
HONEY POT, THE UA 1966	Sterling, T. (*Evil of the Day, The*) Penguin
HONEY POT, THE UA 1966	Jonson, B. (*Volpone*) (P) Various
HONKEYTONK MAN (V) COL—EMI—WAR 1983	Carlile, C. Simon & Schuster, N.Y.
HONOR THY FATHER FOX 1973	Talese, G. Souvenir Press

TITLE OF FILM	AUTHOR AND PUBLISHER
HONORARY CONSUL (V) PAR 1983	Greene, G. Heinemann
HOP-ALONG-CASSIDY PAR 1935	Mulford, C.E. Hodder & Stoughton
HOP-ALONG-CASSIDY RETURNS PAR 1936	Mulford, C.E. Hodder & Stoughton
HOPSCOTCH (V) RANK 1980	Garfield, B. Evans
HORIZONTAL LIEUTENANT, THE MGM 1962	Cotler, G. (*Bottletop Affair, The*) Panther
HORSE IN THE GREY FLANNEL SUIT, **THE** (V) DISNEY 1968	Hatch, E. (*Year of the Horse, The*) Crown, N.Y.
HORSEMEN, THE COL 1971	Kessel, J. Barker
HORSE'S MOUTH, THE UA 1958	Cary, J. Joseph
HORSE SOLDIERS, THE UA 1959	Sinclair, H. Muller
HORSE WITHOUT A HEAD, THE DISNEY 1963	Berna, P. (*Hundred Million Frames,* *A*) Penguin
HOSTAGES PAR 1943	Heym, S. Putnam
HOSTILE WITNESS UA 1968	Roffey, J. (P) Evans
HOTEL WAR 1966	Haley, A. Pan
HOTEL BERLIN WAR 1945	Baum, V. (*Berlin Hotel*) Joseph

HOTEL DU LAC
BBC 2 1986 (TV)

Brookner, A.
Cape

HOTEL NEW HAMPSHIRE
EMI 1984

Irving, J.
Cape

HOTEL PARADISO
MGM 1971

Feydeau, G. *and* Desvallieres, M. (P)
Heinemann

HOTEL RESERVE
RKO 1944

Ambler, E. (*Epitaph for a Spy*)
Hodder & Stoughton

HOT ENOUGH FOR JUNE
RANK 1963

Davidson, L. (*Night of Wenceslas*)
Gollancz

HOUDINI
PAR 1953

Kellock, H.
Heinemann

HOUND DOG MAN
FOX 1959

Gipson, F.B. (*Circles Round the Wagon*)
Joseph

HOUND OF THE BASKERVILLES, THE
(V)
ID 1932
FOX 1939
UA 1959
HEMDALE 1978
EMBASSY 1983

Doyle, *Sir* A.C.
Murray

HOUR BEFORE DAWN
PAR 1944

Maugham, W.S.
Doubleday, N.Y.

HOUSE ACROSS THE LAKE, THE
ABP 1954

Hughes, K. (*High Wray*)
Gifford

HOUSE BY THE RIVER, THE
REP 1950

Herbert, *Sir* A.P.
Methuen

HOUSE DIVIDED, A
UN 1932

Buck, P.
Methuen

HOUSE IN MARSH ROAD, THE
GN 1960

Meynell, L.
Collins

TITLE OF FILM	AUTHOR AND PUBLISHER

HOUSE IN THE SQUARE, THE
FOX 1951

Balderston, J.L. (*Berkeley Square*)
(P)
French

HOUSE IS NOT A HOME, A
PAR 1964

Adler, P.
Heinemann

HOUSEKEEPER'S DAUGHTER, THE
UA 1939

Clarke, D.H.
Laurie

HOUSEKEEPING
CANNON 1986

Robinson, M.
Farrar, N.Y.

HOUSEMAN'S TALE, A
BBC 1985 (TV)

Douglas, C.
Fontana

HOUSE OF A THOUSAND CANDLES,
THE
REP 1936

Nicolson, M.
Hale

HOUSE OF CARDS
RANK 1968

Ellin, S.
Macdonald

HOUSE OF FEAR
UN 1945

Doyle, *Sir* A.C. (*Adventure of the*
Five Orange Pips)
Murray

HOUSE OF NUMBERS
MGM 1957

Finney, J.
Eyre & Spottiswoode

HOUSE OF SECRETS, THE
RANK 1956

Noel, S.
Deutsch

HOUSE OF THE ARROW
AB 1940
ABP 1953

Mason, A.E.W.
Hodder & Stoughton

HOUSE OF THE LONG SHADOWS, THE
CANNON 1982

Biggers, E.D. (*Seven Keys to*
Baldpate)
Grosset, N.Y.

HOUSE OF THE SEVEN GABLES, THE
UN 1940

Hawthorne, N.
Various

TITLE OF FILM	AUTHOR AND PUBLISHER
HOUSE OF THE SEVEN HAWKS, THE MGM 1959	Canning, V. (*House of the Seven Flies, The*) Hodder & Stoughton
HOUSE OF THE SPANIARD, THE GB 1936	Behrend, A. Heinemann
HOUSE ON GARIBALDI STREET, THE (V) ITC 1979	Harel, I. Deutsch
HOUSE ON GREENAPPLE STREET, THE MGM 1970	Daniels, H.R. Deutsch
HOUSE ON TELEGRAPH HILL, THE FOX 1951	Lyon, D. (*Tentacles*) Harper, N.Y.
HOUSEMASTER ALL 1939	Hay, I. Hodder & Stoughton
HOUSEMASTER ALL 1939	Hay, I. (P) French
HOWARDS OF VIRGINIA, THE COL 1940	Page, E. (*Tree of Liberty*) Collins
HOW DO I LOVE THEE? (V) CIRO 1970	De Vries, P. (*Let Me Count the Ways*) Gollancz
HOW GREEN WAS MY VALLEY FOX 1941	Llewellyn, R. Joseph
HOW HE LIED TO HER HUSBAND BI 1931	Shaw, G.B. (P) Constable
HOW I WON THE WAR UA 1967	Ryan, P. Muller
HOWLING, THE (V) AVCO EMBASSY 1981	Brandner, G. Fawcett, N.Y.
HOWLING IN THE WOODS, A UN 1971 (TV)	Johnston, V. Dodd, N.Y.

TITLE OF FILM	AUTHOR AND PUBLISHER
HOW SWEET IT IS WAR 1968	Resnik, M. (*Turquoise Bikini, The*) Transworld
HOW TO STEAL A DIAMOND IN FOUR **UNEASY LESSONS** UA 1972	Westlake, D.E. (*Hot Rock*) Hodder & Stoughton
HOW TO SUCCEED IN BUSINESS **WITHOUT REALLY TRYING** UA 1966	Mead, J. Macdonald
HOW WARS END CHANNEL 4 1985 (TV)	Taylor, A.J.P. Hamilton
HUCKLEBERRY FINN (V) UA 1974	Twain, M. Various
HUCKSTERS, THE MGM 1947	Wakeman, F. Falcon Press
HUD PAR 1963	McMurtry, L. (*Horseman, Pass By*) Hamilton
HUGGETTS ABROAD, THE HGF 1949	Constanduros, M. *and* Constanduros, D. Sampson Low
HUMAN COMEDY, THE MGM 1943	Saroyan, W. Faber
HUMAN DESIRE COL 1954	Zola, E. (*La Bête Humaine*) Various
HUMAN FACTOR, THE (V) RANK 1980	Greene, G. Heinemann
HUMORESQUE WAR 1946	Hurst, F. Smith, N.Y.
HUNCHBACK OF NOTRE DAME, THE (V) RKO 1939 RANK 1957	Hugo, V. Various

HUNGER, THE
UIP 1983

Strieber, W.
  Morrow, N.Y.

HUNGRY HILL
TC 1947

Du Maurier, D.
  Gollancz

HUNTER, THE (V)
PAR 1980

Keane, C.
  Arbor House, N.Y.

HUNTERS, THE
FOX 1958

Salter, J.
  Heinemann

HUNTINGTOWER
PAR 1928

Buchan, J.
  Hodder & Stoughton

HURRICANE (V)
UA 1937
ITC 1980

Nordhoff, C.B. *and* Hall, J.N.
  Chapman & Hall

HURRY SUNDOWN
PAR 1966

Gilden, K.B.
  Heinemann

HUSBAND'S HOLIDAY
PAR 1931

Pascal, E. (*Marriage Bed, The*)
  Allen & Unwin

HUSTLER, THE
FOX 1961

Tevis, W.
  Joseph

I

I AM A CAMERA (V)
BL 1955

Druten, J. van (P)
  Random House, N.Y.

I AM A FUGITIVE
WAR 1932

Burns, R.E. (*I am a Fugitive from the Chain Gang*)
  Paul

I AM THE CHEESE
ALMI 1984

Cormier, R.
  Panther, N.Y.

I BELIEVE IN YOU
EALING 1953

Stokes, S. (*Court Circular*)
  Joseph

TITLE OF FILM	AUTHOR AND PUBLISHER
ICE COLD IN ALEX (V) ABP 1957	Landon, C. Heinemann
ICEMAN COMETH, THE AMERICAN FILM THEATRE 1975	O'Neill, E. (P) Cape
ICE PALACE WAR 1960	Ferber, E. Gollancz
ICE STATION ZEBRA (V) MGM 1968	MacLean, A. Collins
I CLAUDIUS BBC 1976 (TV)	Graves, R. Methuen
IDEAL HUSBAND, AN (V) BL 1948	Wilde, O. (P) Methuen
I DIED A THOUSAND TIMES WAR 1955	Burnett, W.R. (*High Sierra*) Various
IDIOT'S DELIGHT MGM 1939	Sherwood, R.E. (P) Heinemann
IDLE ON PARADE COL 1959	Camp, W. MacGibbon
IDLE RICH MGM 1929	Ellis, E. (*White Collars*) (P) French, N.Y.
IF GB 1967	Sherwin, D. Sphere
IF A MAN ANSWERS RANK 1962	Wolfe, W. Hammond
IF I HAD A MILLION PAR 1932	Andrews, R.H. Hurst & Blackett
IF I WERE FREE RKO 1933	Druten, J. van (*Behold We Live*) (P) Gollancz
IF I WERE KING PAR 1938	McCarthy, J.H. Heinemann

132

TITLE OF FILM	AUTHOR AND PUBLISHER
IF WINTER COMES MGM 1947	Hutchinson, A.S.M. Hodder & Stoughton
IF YOU COULD SEE WHAT I CAN HEAR SUNN-CLASSIC 1982	Sullivan, T. *and* Gill, D. New American Library, N.Y.
I KILLED THE COUNT GN 1939	Coppel, A. (P) Heinemann
I LIVED WITH YOU GB 1935	Novello, I. (P) Methuen
I'LL CRY TOMORROW MGM 1955	Roth, L. Gollancz
I'LL GET YOU FOR THIS (V) BL 1951	Chase, J.H. Jarrolds
ILL MET BY MOONLIGHT RANK 1956	Moss, W.S. Corgi
ILLUSTRATED MAN, THE WAR 1968	Bradbury, R. Hart-Davis
I LOVE TROUBLE COL 1948	Huggins, R. (*Double Take*) Grosset, N.Y.
I'M ALRIGHT JACK (V) BL 1959	Hackney, A. (*Private Life*) Gollancz
I MARRIED A DOCTOR IN 1936	Lewis, S. (*Main Street*) Cape
I MARRIED ADVENTURE COL 1940	Johnson, O.H. Hutchinson
I'M FROM MISSOURI PAR 1939	Croy, H. (*Sixteen Hands*) Hamilton
IMITATION GENERAL MGM 1958	Chamberlain, W. (*Trumpets of Company K*) Ballantine, N.Y.

TITLE OF FILM	AUTHOR AND PUBLISHER
IMITATION OF LIFE UN 1934 RANK 1959	Hurst, F. (*Anatomy of Me*) Cape
IMMORTAL SERGEANT, THE FOX 1943	Brophy, J. Collins
IMPATIENT MAIDEN UN 1932	Clarke, D.H. (*Impatient Virgin*) Long
IMPORTANCE OF BEING EARNEST, **THE** (V) GFD 1952	Wilde, O. (P) Heinemann
INADMISSIBLE EVIDENCE PAR 1968	Osborne, J. (P) Faber
IN A LONELY PLACE COL 1950	Hughes, D.B. Duell, N.Y.
IN CELEBRATION SEVEN KEYS 1976	Storey, D. (P) Cape
INCENSE FOR THE DAMNED GN 1970	Raven, S. (*Doctors Wear Scarlet*) Panther
IN COLD BLOOD COL 1968	Capote, T. Hamilton
INCREDIBLE JOURNEY, THE (V) DISNEY 1962	Burnford, S. Hodder & Stoughton
INCREDIBLE SHRINKING MAN, THE RANK 1957	Matherson, R. Chamberlain Press, Philadelphia
INCUBUS (V) NEW REALM 1982	Russell, R. Sphere
INDECENT OBSESSION, AN PBL AUSTRALIA 1985	McCullough, C. Macdonald
INDISCREET WAR 1958	Krasna, N. (*Kind Sir*) (P) Dramatists, N.Y.

TITLE OF FILM	AUTHOR AND PUBLISHER
I NEVER PROMISED YOU A ROSE GARDEN (V) NEW WORLD 1979	Greenberg, J. New American Library, N.Y.
I NEVER SANG FOR MY FATHER COL 1971	Anderson, R.W. (P) Random House, N.Y.
INFORMER, THE RKO 1935	O'Flaherty, L. Cape
INFORMERS, THE RANK 1963	Warner, D. (*Death of a Snout*) Cassell
IN HARM'S WAY COL 1965	Bassett, J. (*Harm's Way*) Heinemann
INHERIT THE WIND UA 1960	Lawrence, J. *and* Lee, R.E. (P) Random House, N.Y.
IN HIS STEPS GN 1936	Sheldon, C.M. Warne
IN LOVE AND WAR FOX 1958	Myrer, A. (*Big War, The*) Hamilton
IN NAME ONLY RKO 1939	Breuer, B. (*Memory of Love*) Rich & Cowan
INNOCENT BYSTANDERS SCOTIA-BARBER 1972	Munro, J. Barrie & Jenkins
INNOCENT SINNERS RANK 1957	Godden, R. (*Episode of Sparrows, An*) Macmillan
INNOCENTS, THE FOX 1961	James, H. (*Turn of the Screw, The*) Dent
INNOCENTS OF CHICAGO BI 1934	Drawbell, J.W. Collins
INNOCENTS WITH DIRTY HANDS FOX—RANK 1975	Neely, R. Star

INN OF THE SIXTH HAPPINESS, THE
FOX 1958

Burgess, A. (*Small Woman, The*)
Evans

IN PRAISE OF OLDER WOMEN (V)
COL—EMI—WAR 1978

Vizinczey, S.
Macmillan

INQUISITOR, THE
GALA 1982

Wainwright, J. (*Brainwash*)
Macmillan

IN SEARCH OF THE CASTAWAYS
DISNEY 1962

Verne, J. (*Captain Grant's Children*)
Various

IN SEARCH OF THE TROJAN WAR
BBC 2 1985 (TV)

Wood, M.
BBC

INSIDE DAISY CLOVER
WAR 1965

Lambert, G.
Hamilton

INSIDE MOVES (V)
BARBER 1981

Walton, T.
New American Library, N.Y.

INSIDE THE LINES
RKO 1930

Biggers, E.D. (P)
French, N.Y.

INSPECTOR, THE
FOX 1962

Hartog, J. de
Hamilton

INSPECTOR CALLS, AN
BL 1954

Priestley, J.B. (P)
French

INSPECTOR GENERAL, THE (V)
WAR 1949

Gogol, N.V. (P)
French, N.Y.

INSURANCE MAN, THE
BBC 2 1986 (TV)

Kafka, F. (*Trial, The*)
Secker & Warburg

INTENT TO KILL
FOX 1958

Bryan, M.
Eyre & Spottiswoode

INTERPOL
COL 1957

Forrest, A.J.
Wingate

IN THE CHINESE ROOM
FOX 1959

Connell, V. (*Chinese Room, The*)
Secker & Warburg

TITLE OF FILM	AUTHOR AND PUBLISHER
IN THE COOL OF THE DAY MGM 1963	Ertz, S. Collins
IN THE DOGHOUSE RANK 1961	Duncan, A. (*It's a Vet's Life*) Joseph
IN THE FRENCH STYLE COL 1963	Shaw, I. Cape
IN THE HEAT OF THE NIGHT (V) UA 1967	Ball, J. Joseph
IN THE SECRET STATE BBC 2 1985 (TV)	McCrum, R. Hamilton
IN THE WAKE OF A STRANGER BUTCHER 1959	Black, I.S. Dakers
IN THIS HOUSE OF BREDE CHANNEL 4 1984 (TV)	Godden, R. Futura
IN THIS OUR LIFE WAR 1942	Glasgow, E. Cape
INTRUDER, THE (V) BL 1953	Maugham, R. (*Line on Ginger*) Chapman & Hall
INTRUDER IN THE DUST MGM 1949	Faulkner, W. Random House, N.Y.
INVASION OF THE BODY SNATCHERS, THE (V) COL 1956 UA 1979	Finney, J. (*Body Snatchers, The*) Eyre & Spottiswoode
INVESTIGATION OF MURDER, AN FOX 1974	Sjowall, M. *and* Wahloo, P. (*Laughing Policeman, The*) Gollancz
INVINCIBLE SIX, THE PAR 1968	Barrett, M. (*Heroes of Yucca, The*) Hale
INVISIBLE MAN, THE UN 1933 BBC 1984 (TV)	Wells, H.G. Various

TITLE OF FILM	AUTHOR AND PUBLISHER
I OUGHT TO BE IN PICTURES TCF 1982	Simon, N. (P) Random, N.Y.
I PASSED FOR WHITE WAR 1960	Bradley, M.H. Davies
IPCRESS FILE, THE (V) RANK 1964	Deighton, L. Hodder & Stoughton
IPHIGENIA UA 1978	Euripides (P) Various
I REMEMBER MAMMA RKO 1948	Druten, J. van (P) Dramatists, N.Y.
IRENE ARGYLE 1950	Marsh, R.J. Chatto & Windus
I RING DOORBELLS PRC 1946	Birdwells, R. Messner, N.Y.
IRISHMAN, THE SOUTH AUSTRALIA FILMS 1978	O'Connor, E. Angus & Robertson
IRON CURTAIN FOX 1948	Gouzenko, I. (*This was my Choice*) Dent
IRON DUKE, THE GB 1935	Lindsay, P. Queensway Press
IRON MAN (V) UI 1951	Burnett, W.R. Heinemann
IRON MISTRESS, THE WAR 1952	Wellman, P.I. Laurie
ISADORA UI 1969	Duncan, I. (*My Life*) Gollancz
ISADORA UI 1969	Stokes, S. (*Isadora Duncan*) Pan
I SHALL RETURN FOX 1950	Wolfert, I. (*American Guerilla in the Philippines*) Gollancz

ISLAND, THE (V)
CIC 1980

Benchley, P.
Doubleday, N.Y.

ISLAND AT THE TOP OF THE WORLD, THE (V)
DISNEY 1974

Cameron, I.
Hutchinson

ISLAND IN THE SKY
WAR 1953

Gann, E.K.
Joseph

ISLAND IN THE SUN
FOX 1957

Waugh, A.
Cassell

ISLAND OF DR. MOREAU, THE
AMERICAN INTERNATIONAL 1977

Wells, H.G.
Heinemann

ISLAND OF LOST SOULS
EROS 1959

Wells, H.G. (*Island of Dr. Moreau, The*)
Heinemann

ISLAND OF THE BLUE DOLPHINS
RANK 1964

O'Dell, S.
Constable

ISLANDS IN THE STREAM
PAR 1977

Hemingway, E.
Collins

ISLE OF SINNERS
REGENT 1952

Quefflec, H.
Verschoyle

ISN'T IT ROMANTIC?
PAR 1948

Nolan, J. (*Gather ye Rosebuds*)
Appleton-Century, N.Y.

IS PARIS BURNING?
PAR 1965

Collins, L. *and* Lapierre, D.
Gollancz

I START COUNTING
UA 1970

Lindop, A.E.
Collins

IS YOUR HONEYMOON REALLY NECESSARY?
ADELPHI 1953

Tidmarsh, E.V. (P)
Deane

I TAKE THIS WOMAN
PAR 1931

Rinehart, M.R. (*Lost Ecstasy*)
Doran, N.Y.

TITLE OF FILM	AUTHOR AND PUBLISHER
IT ALL CAME TRUE WAR 1940	Bromfield, L. (*Better Than Life*) Cassell
IT ALWAYS RAINS ON SUNDAYS EALING 1948	La Bern, A.J. Nicholson & Watson
I THANK A FOOL MGM 1962	Lindop, A.E. Collins
IT HAPPENED ONE NIGHT COL 1934	Adams, S.H. (*Night Bus*) Longmans
IT HAPPENS EVERY SPRING FOX 1950	Davies, V. Farrar, N.Y.
IT HAPPENS EVERY THURSDAY GFD 1953	McIlvaine, J. McRae-Smith
I, THE JURY (V) UA 1953 COL—EMI—WAR 1982	Spillane, M. Barker
IT PAYS TO ADVERTISE PAR 1931	Hackett, W. *and* Megrue, R.C. (P) French
IT'S A DOG'S LIFE MGM 1955	Davis, R.H. (*Bar Sinister, The*) Scribner, N.Y.
IT SHOULDN'T HAPPEN TO A VET (V) EMI 1976	Herriot, J. (*All Things Bright and Beautiful*) Joseph
IT'S NEVER TOO LATE ABP 1956	Douglas, F. (P) Evans
IT STARTED IN TOKYO WAR 1961	Gruber, F. (*Twenty Plus Two*) Boardman
IT'S TOUGH TO BE FAMOUS IN 1932	McCall, M. (*Gold Fish Bowl, The*) Paul
IVANHOE (V) MGM 1951	Scott, *Sir* W. Various

IVY
UI 1947

Lowndes, *Mrs.* M.B. (*Story of Ivy*)
Eyre & Spottiswoode

I WAKE UP SCREAMING
FOX 1941

Fisher, S.
Hale

I WALK THE LINE (V)
COL 1971

Jones, M. (*Exile, An*)
Deutsch

I WANT TO LIVE
UA 1958

Rawson, T.
Muller

I WANT WHAT I WANT
CINERAMA 1972

Brown, G.
Panther

I WAS A SPY
FOX 1934

McKenna, M.
Jarrolds

I WAS MONTY'S DOUBLE
ABP 1958

James, M.E.C.
Rider

I WOULDN'T BE IN YOUR SHOES
MON 1948

Irish, W.
Lippincott, Philadelphia

J

JALNA
RKO 1935

Roche, M. de la
Macmillan

JAMAICA INN
PAR 1939
HTV 1983 (TV)

Du Maurier, D.
Gollancz

JANE EYRE (V)
MON 1934
FOX 1944
BL 1970
BBC 1984 (TV)

Bronte, C.
Various

JANE'S HOUSE
COL 1983

Smith, R.K.
Pan

JANIE
WAR 1944

Bentham, J. *and* Williams, H.V. (P)
French, N.Y.

TITLE OF FILM	AUTHOR AND PUBLISHER
JASSY GFD 1947	Lofts, N. Joseph
JAVA HEAD ID 1935	Hergesheimer, J. Heinemann
JAZZ SINGER (V) EMI 1980 (TV)	Raphaelson, S. University of Wisconsin
JEALOUSY PAR 1929	Verneuil, L. (P) French
JEANNIE TANSA 1942	Stuart, A. (P) Hamilton
JENNIE GERHARDT PAR 1933	Dreiser, T. Constable
JENNIFER ON MY MIND UA 1971	Simon, R.L. (*Heir*) Macdonald
JENNY'S WAR HTV 1985 (TV)	Stoneley, J. Hamlyn
JEREMIAH JOHNSON COL—WAR 1972	Fisher, V. Four Square Books
JESSICA UA 1961	Sandstrom, F. (*Midwife of Pont Clery, The*) Ace
JEWEL IN THE CROWN, THE GRANADA 1983 (TV)	Scott, P. (*Raj Quartet, The*) Heinemann
JEW SÜSS GB 1935	Feutchwanger, L. (P) Hutchinson
JEW SÜSS GB 1935	Feutchwanger, L. Hutchinson
JEZEBEL WAR 1938	Frankau, P. Rich & Cowan
JIGSAW BL 1962	Waugh, H. (*Sleep Long My Love*) Gollancz

JIGSAW MAN, THE
J & M FILMS 1984

Bennett, D.
Corgi

JOAN OF ARC (V)
RKO 1948

Anderson, M. (*Joan of Lorraine*) (P)
Anderson House, N.Y.

JOE EGG
COL 1971

Nichols, P. (*Day in the Death of . . .*)
(P)
Faber

JOEY BOY
BL 1965

Chapman, E.
Cassell

JOHN AND MARY
FOX 1969

Jones, M.
Cape

JOHN BROWN'S BODY
FOX 1968

Benet, S.V.
Holt, Rinehart & Winston, N.Y.

JOHN LOVES MARY
WAR 1949

Krasna, N. (P)
Dramatists, N.Y.

JOHNNY ANGEL
RKO 1945

Booth, C.G. (*Mr. Angel Comes Aboard*)
Doubleday, N.Y.

JOHNNY BELINDA
WAR 1948

Harris, E. (P)
French

JOHNNY COOL
UA 1964

McPartland, J. (*Kingdom of Johnny Cool, The*)
Muller

JOHNNY GOT HIS GUN
RANK 1971

Trumbo, D.
Corgi

JOHNNY GUITAR
REP 1954

Chanslor, R.
Hale

JOHNNY ONE-EYE
UA 1950

Runyon, D.
Constable

JOHNNY ON THE SPOT
FANCY 1954

Cronin, M. (*Paid in Full*)
Museum Press

TITLE OF FILM	AUTHOR AND PUBLISHER
JOHNNY TREMAIN DISNEY 1957	Forbes, E. Constable
JOHNNY VAGABOND UA 1943	Bromfield, L. (*McLeod's Folly*) Cassell
JOKER IS WILD PAR 1957	Cohn, A. Random House, N.Y.
JOLLY BAD FELLOW, A BL 1964	Vulliamy, C.E. (*Don Among the Dead Men*) Joseph
JONATHAN LIVINGSTONE SEAGULL PAR 1974	Bach, R. Turnstone Press
JORY FOX—RANK 1974	Bass, M.R. Putnam
JOSEPH AND HIS BRETHREN COL 1954	Parker, L.N. (P) Bodley Head
JOSEPH ANDREWS UA 1976	Fielding, H. Various
JOURNEY FOR MARGARET MGM 1942	White, W.L. Hurst & Blackett
JOURNEY INTO FEAR (V) RKO 1942	Ambler, E. Hodder & Stoughton
JOURNEY'S END TIFFANY 1930	Sherriff, R.C. (P) Gollancz
JOURNEY'S END TIFFANY 1930	Sherriff, R.C. *and* Bartlett, V. Gollancz
JOURNEY TO SHILOH UI 1968	Henry, W. Gollancz
JOURNEY TO THE CENTRE OF THE EARTH FOX 1959 CANNON 1986	Verne, J. Various

TITLE OF FILM	AUTHOR AND PUBLISHER
JOY UGC 1984	Laurey, J. W.H. Allen
JOY IN THE MORNING MGM 1965	Smith, B. Heinemann
JUAREZ WAR 1939	Harding, B. (*Phantom Crown*) Harrap
JUBAL COL 1956	Wellman, P.I. (*Jubal Troop*) Grosset, N.Y.
JUBILEE TRAIL REP 1954	Bristow, G. Eyre & Spottiswoode
JUGGLER, THE COL 1953	Blankfort, M. Dobson
JULIA (V) FOX 1977	Hellman, L. (*Pentimento*) Macmillan
JULIA MISBEHAVES MGM 1948	Sharp, M. (*Nutmeg Tree*) Various
JULIUS CAESAR (V) MGM 1953 MGM 1969	Shakespeare, W. (P) Various
JUNGLE BOOK, THE (V) DISNEY 1966	Kipling, R. Macmillan
JUNIOR MISS FOX 1945	Benson, *Mrs.* S. Sun Dial, N.Y.
JUNIOR MISS FOX 1945	Chodorov, J. *and* Fields, J. (P) Dramatists, N.Y.
JUNO AND THE PAYCOCK BI 1930	O'Casey, S. (P) Macmillan
JUPITER'S DARLING MGM 1954	Sherwood, R.E. (*Road to Rome, The*) (P) French, N.Y.

TITLE OF FILM	AUTHOR AND PUBLISHER

JUST FOR YOU
PAR 1952

Benet, S.V. (*Famous*)
Farrar, N.Y.

JUSTINE (V)
FOX 1969
THE OTHER CINEMA 1976

Durrell, L. (*Alexandria Quartet*)
Faber

JUST WILLIAM
AB 1940

Crompton, R.
Newnes

K

KANE AND ABEL
BBC 1986 (TV)

Archer, J.
Hodder & Stoughton

KANGAROO
WORLD FILM 1985

Lawrence, D.H.
Heinemann

KATE PLUS TEN
WAINWRIGHT 1938

Wallace, E.
Ward Lock

KAZAN, THE WOLF DOG
COL 1949

Curwood, J.O.
Grosset, N.Y.

KEEPER OF THE BEES
MON 1935

Porter, G.S.
Hutchinson

KEEPER OF THE FLAME
MGM 1942

Wylie, I.A.R.
Cassell

KEEPERS OF YOUTH
POWERS 1932

Ridley, A.
Benn

KENNEL MURDER CASE, THE
WAR 1933

Dine, S.S. van
Cassell

KENTUCKIAN, THE
UA 1955

Holt, F. (*Gabriel Horn*)
Various

KENTUCKY
FOX 1938

Foote, J.T. (*Look of Eagles*)
Appleton-Century, N.Y.

KES (V)
UA 1969

Hines, B. (*Kestrel for a Knave, A*)
Joseph

146

KEY, THE
COL 1958

Hartog, J. de (*Stella*)
Hamilton

KEY, THE
ENTERPRISE 1985

Tanizaki, J.
Putnam, N.Y.

KEY EXCHANGE
FOX 1985

Wade, K. (P)
Avon, N.Y.

KEY LARGO (V)
WAR 1948

Anderson, M. (P)
Random House, N.Y.

KEYS OF THE KINGDOM
FOX 1944

Cronin, A.J.
Gollancz

KEY TO REBECCA, THE
WORLD VISION 1985 (TV)

Follett, K.
Hamilton

KHARTOUM
CINERAMA 1966

Caillou, A.
W.H. Allen

KID FOR TWO FARTHINGS, A
INDEPENDENT 1954

Mankowitz, W.
Deutsch

KID GALAHAD
WAR 1937
UA 1962

Wallace, F.
Hale

KIDNAPPED (V)
FOX 1938
MON 1949
DISNEY 1959
RANK 1972

Stevenson, R.L. (*Catriona*)
Various

KIDNAPPING OF THE PRESIDENT, THE
(V)
BORDEAUX FILMS 1981

Templeton, C.
Avon, N.Y.

KILLER
CINECENTA 1969

Blake, N. (*Beast Must Die, The*)
Collins

KILLER ELITE, THE (V)
UA 1976

Rostand, Robert
Dell, N.Y.

TITLE OF FILM	AUTHOR AND PUBLISHER
KILLER ON A HORSE MGM 1966	Doctorow, E.L. (*Welcome to Hard Times*) Simon & Schuster, N.Y.
KILLERS, THE (V) UN 1946 RANK 1964	Hemingway, E. Cape
KILLERS OF KILIMANJARO COL 1959	Hunter, J.A. (*African Bush Adventures*) Various
KILLER WALKS, A GN 1952	Barton, R. (*Envy my Simplicity*) Chapman & Hall
KILLING, THE UA 1956	White, L. (*Clean Break*) Boardman
KILLING FIELDS, THE WAR 1984	Schanberg, S. (*Death and Life of Dith Pran, The*) Pan
KILLING OF SISTER GEORGE, THE (V) CINERAMA 1968	Marcus, F. (P) French
KIM MGM 1949 LF 1984 (TV)	Kipling, R. Macmillan
KIND LADY MGM 1935 MGM 1951	Chodorov, E. (P) French
KIND OF ALASKA, A CENTRAL 1985 (TV)	Pinter, H. (P) Grove, N.Y.
KIND OF LOVING, A (V) AA 1962	Barstow, S. Joseph
KING AND COUNTRY WAR 1965	Hodson, J.L. (*Return to Woods*) Gollancz
KING AND COUNTRY WAR 1965	Wilson, J. (*Hamp*) (P) Evans

TITLE OF FILM	AUTHOR AND PUBLISHER
KING AND I, THE (V) FOX 1956	Landon, M. (*Anna and the King of Siam*) Harrap
KING CREOLE (V) PAR 1958	Robbins, H. (*Stone for Danny Fisher, A*) Hale
KING DAVID UIP 1985	The Bible (*Samuel I & II: Chronicles I*)
KING IN SHADOW BL 1959	Neumann, R. (*Queen's Doctor, The*) Gollancz
KING LEAR COL 1970 GRANADA 1982 (TV) CANNON 1986	Shakespeare, W. (P) Various
KING OF THE GRIZZLIES (V) DISNEY 1969	Seton, E.T. (*Biography of a Grizzly, The*) Hodder & Stoughton
KING OF THE GYPSIES CIC 1980	Maas, P. Bantam, N.Y.
KING OF THE KHYBER RIFLES FOX 1954	Mundy, T. Hutchinson
KING RAT BL 1965	Clavell, J. Joseph
KING RICHARD AND THE CRUSADERS WAR 1954	Scott, *Sir* W. (*Talisman, The*) Various
KINGS GO FORTH UA 1958	Brown, J.D. Cassell
KING SOLOMON'S MINES GB 1937 MGM 1950 CANNON 1985	Haggard, *Sir* R.H. Cassell
KING SOLOMON'S TREASURE (V) BARBER ROSE 1979	Haggard, *Sir* R.H. (*Alan Quatermain*) Various

KING'S ROW
WAR 1941

Bellamann, H.
Cape

KIPPS
FOX 1941

Wells, H.G.
Various

KISMET
IN 1931
MGM 1955

Knoblock, E. (P)
Methuen

KISS AND TELL
COL 1945

Herbert, F.H. (P)
Longmans

KISS BEFORE DYING, A
UA 1956

Levin, I.
Joseph

KISS ME DEADLY
UA 1954

Spillane, M.
Barker

KISS ME KATE
MGM 1953

Shakespeare, W. (*Taming of the Shrew*) (P)
Various

KISS OF FIRE
GFD 1955

Lauritzen, J. (*Rose and the Flame, The*)
Hurst & Blackett

KISS OF THE SPIDER WOMAN
PALACE 1985

Puig, M.
Knopf, N.Y.

KISS THE BOYS GOODBYE
PAR 1941

Boothe, C. (P)
Various

KISS THEM FOR ME
FOX 1957

Wakeman, F. (*Shore Leave*)
Farrar, N.Y.

KISS TOMORROW GOODBYE
WAR 1950

McCoy, H.
Barker

KITCHEN, THE
BL 1961

Wesker, A. (P)
Faber

KITTY
PAR 1945

Marshall, *Mrs*. R.
Collins

TITLE OF FILM	AUTHOR AND PUBLISHER
KITTY FOYLE RKO 1940	Morley, C.D. Lippincott, Philadelphia
KLANSMAN, THE (V) PAR 1974	Huie, W.B. Sphere
KNACK, THE UA 1965	Jellicoe, A. (P) Dell, N.Y.
KNAVE OF HEARTS ABP 1954	Hemon, L. (*M. Ripois and his Nemesis*) Allen & Unwin
KNIGHTS OF THE RANGE PAR 1940	Grey, Z. Hodder & Stoughton
KNIGHTS OF THE ROUND TABLE MGM 1954	Malory, *Sir* T. (*Morte d'Arthur, Le*) Various
KNIGHT WITHOUT ARMOUR (V) UA 1937	Hilton, J. Macmillan
KNOCKBACK BBC 1985 (TV)	Adams, P. *and* Cooklin, S. Duckworth
KNOCK ON ANY DOOR COL 1949	Motley, W. Collins
KNOTS CINEGATE 1975	Laing, R.D. Random House, N.Y.
KON-TIKI RKO 1951	Heyerdahl, T. (*Kontiki expedition*) Allen & Unwin
KOTCH CINERAMA 1972	Topkins, K. Panther
KRAMER vs KRAMER (V) COL—EMI—WAR 1979	Corman, A. New American Library, N.Y.
KREMLIN LETTER, THE (V) FOX 1969	Behn, N. W.H. Allen

L

LA BRAVA
CANNON 1986

Leonard, E.
Avon, N.Y.

LABURNUM GROVE
APB 1935

Priestley, J.B. (P)
Heinemann

LACE
LORIMAR 1984 (TV)

Conran, S.
Penguin

LADDIE
RKO 1935

Porter, G.S.
Murray

LADIES IN RETIREMENT
COL 1941

Percy, E. *and* Denham, R. (P)
Random House, N.Y.

LADY AND THE TRAMP, THE
DISNEY 1955

Greene, W.
Simon & Schuster, N.Y.

LADY CHATTERLEY'S LOVER (V)
COL 1956
COL—EMI—WAR 1981

Lawrence, D.H.
Heinemann

LADY FROM SHANGHAI, THE
COL 1948

King, S.
Worlds Work

LADY IN CEMENT
FOX 1969

Albert, M.H.
Sphere

LADY IN THE CAR, THE
COL 1969

Japrisot, S. (. . . *with Glasses and a Gun*)
Souvenir Press

LADY IN THE DARK, THE
PAR 1944

Pryce, M.
Lane

LADY IN THE LAKE
MGM 1946

Chandler, R.
Hamilton

LADY IN THE MORGUE
UN 1938

Latimer, J.
Methuen

LADY L
MGM 1965

Gary, R.
Joseph

TITLE OF FILM	AUTHOR AND PUBLISHER
LADY MISLAID, A ABP 1958	Horne, K. (P) English Theatre Guild
LADY OF SCANDAL, THE MGM 1930	Lonsdale, F. (*High Road, The*) (P) Collins
LADY POSSESSED, A REP 1951	Kellino, P. (*Del Palma*) Hale
LADY SINGS THE BLUES CINEMA INT 1972	Holiday, B. Barrie & Jenkins
LADY SURRENDERS, A UN 1930	Erskine, J. (*Experiment in Sincerity*) Putnam
LADY TO LOVE, A MGM 1930	Howard, S. (*They Knew What They Wanted*) (P) Chatto & Windus
LADY VANISHES, THE (V) MGM 1938 RANK 1978	White, E.L. (*Wheel Spins, The*) Collins
LADY WINDERMERE'S FAN FOX 1949	Wilde, O. (P) Methuen
LADY WITH A LAMP, THE BL 1951	Berkeley, R. (P) Gollancz
LAMB CANNON 1986	MacLaverty, B. Cape
LAMP STILL BURNS, THE TC 1943	Dickens, M. (*One Pair of Feet*) Joseph
LANDFALL AB 1948	Shute, N. Heinemann
LANDLORD, THE UA 1970	Hunter, K. Pan
LAND THAT TIME FORGOT (V) BL 1974	Burroughs, E.R. Methuen

TITLE OF FILM	AUTHOR AND PUBLISHER
LANGUAGE OF LOVE GN 1971	Hegeler, I. *and* Hegeler, S. (*ABZ of Love, The*) Spearman
LA RONDE BL 1964	Schnitzler, A. Ace
LA RONDE (V) COMMERCIAL 1951	Schnitzler, A. (*Merry Go Round*) Weidenfield & Nicolson
LASH, THE IN 1931	Bartlett, L. *and* Bartlett, V.S. (*Adios*) Murray
LASSIE COME HOME MGM 1943	Knight, E.M. Cassell
LAST ANGRY MAN, THE COL 1959	Greene, G. Pan
LAST BATTLE, THE MGM 1968	Ryan, C. Collins
LAST CHANCE, THE MGM 1945	Schweizer, R. Drummond & Secker
LAST DAYS OF POMPEII, THE (V) COL 1983 (TV)	Lytton, *1st baron* Various
LAST DETAIL (V) COL 1973	Ponicsan, D. Dial Press, N.Y.
LAST EMBRACE, THE (V) UA 1984	Bloom, M.T. (*13th Man, The*) Star
LAST FRONTIER, THE COL 1955	Roberts, R.E. (*Gilded Rooster, The*) Laurie
LAST GRENADE, THE CINERAMA 1969	Sherlock, J. (*Ordeal of Major Grigsby, The*) Hutchinson
LAST HARD MAN, THE FOX—RANK 1976	Garfield, B. (*Gun Down*) Dell, N.Y.

TITLE OF FILM	AUTHOR AND PUBLISHER
LAST HUNT, THE MGM 1955	Lott, M. Houghton, Mifflin, Boston
LAST HURRAH, THE COL 1958	O'Connor, E. Pan
LAST MAN ON EARTH, THE GOLDEN ERA 1964	Matheson, R. (*I Am Legend*) Bantam, N.Y.
LAST MAN TO HANG COL 1956	Bullett, G. (*Jury, The*) Dent
LAST OF MRS CHEYNEY, THE MGM 1937	Lonsdale, F. (P) Collins
LAST OF THE MOHICANS, THE (V) UA 1936 RANK 1977	Cooper, J.F. Various
LAST OF THE REDSKINS COL 1949	Cooper, J.F. (*Last of the Mohicans, The*) Various
LAST OF THE RED HOT LOVERS PAR 1972	Simon, N. (P) Random House, N.Y.
LAST PAGE, THE EXCLUSIVE 1952	Chase, J.H. (P) French
LAST PICTURE SHOW, THE COL 1972	McMurtry, L. Sphere
LAST PLACE ON EARTH, THE RENEGADE FILMS 1984 (TV)	Huntford, R. (*Scott and Amundsen*) Pan
LAST ROUND UP, THE PAR 1934	Grey, Z. (*Border Legion, The*) Hodder & Stoughton
LAST SAFARI, THE PAR 1968	Hanley, G. (*Gilligan's Last Elephant*) Collins
LAST SHOT YOU HEAR, THE FOX 1969	Fairchild, W. (*Sound of Murder, The*) (P) French

TITLE OF FILM	AUTHOR AND PUBLISHER
LAST SUMMER FOX 1969	Hunter, E. Constable
LAST TIME I SAW PARIS, THE MGM 1954	Fitzgerald, F.S. (*Babylon Revisited*) Scribner, N.Y.
LAST TRAIL, THE FOX 1933	Grey, Z. Hodder & Stoughton
LAST TYCOON, THE (V) PAR 1977	Fitzgerald, F.S. Penguin
LAST UNICORN SUNN CLASSIC 1982	Beagle, P.S. Ballantine, N.Y.
LAST VALLEY, THE CINERAMA 1971	Pick, J.B. Sphere
LAST WARNING, THE UN 1939	Latimer, J. (*Dead Don't Care, The*) Methuen
LAST WARRIOR, THE WAR 1970	Huffaker, C. (*Nobody Loves a Drunken Indian*) Sphere
LATE EDWINA BLACK, THE GFD 1951	Dinner, W. *and* Morum, W. (P) French
LATE GEORGE APLEY, THE FOX 1947	Marquand, J.P. Hale
LATE GREAT PLANET EARTH, THE (V) ENTERPRISE 1979	Lindsay, H. *and* Carlson, C.C. Zonderman, Chicago
LAUGHING ANNE REP 1953	Conrad, J. (*Within the Tides*) Dent
LAUGHTER IN THE DARK UA 1969	Nabokov, V. Weidenfeld & Nicholson
LAURA (V) FOX 1944	Caspary, V. Eyre & Spottiswoode
LAURA (V) FOX 1944	Caspary, V. *and* Sklar, G. (P) Dramatists, N.Y.

TITLE OF FILM	AUTHOR AND PUBLISHER
L'AVEU WAR 1970	London, A. (*On Trial*) Macdonald
LAW AND DISORDER BL 1957	Roberts, D. (*Smugglers' Circuit*) Methuen
LAW AND ORDER UN 1932	Burnett, W.R. (*'Saint Johnson'*) Heinemann
LAW AND THE LADY, THE MGM 1951	Lonsdale, F. (*Last of Mrs. Cheyney, The*) (P) Collins
LAWLESS EIGHTIES, THE BL 1957	Smith, A.J. (*Brother Van*) Various
LAWLESS STREET, A COL 1955	Ward, B. (*Marshal of Medicine Bend, The*) Hodder & Stoughton
LAW OF THE TROPICS WAR 1941	Hobart, A.T. (*Oil for the Lamps of China*) Cassell
LAWRENCE OF ARABIA (V) BL 1962	Lawrence, T.E. (*Seven Pillars of Wisdom*) Cape
LAXDALE HALL ABP 1953	Linklater, E. Cape
LEAGUE OF FRIGHTENED MEN, THE COL 1937	Stout, R. Cassell
LEAGUE OF GENTLEMEN, THE (V) RANK 1960	Boland, J. Boardman
LEARNING TREE, THE WAR 1969	Parks, G. Hodder & Stoughton
LEASE OF LIFE EALING 1954	Baker, F. Angus & Robertson
LEATHER BOYS, THE BL 1962	George, E. Blond

TITLE OF FILM	AUTHOR AND PUBLISHER
LEATHER BURNERS, THE UA 1943	Lomax, B. Muller
LEAVE HER TO HEAVEN FOX 1945	Williams, B.A. Hale
LEFT HAND OF GOD, THE FOX 1955	Barrett, W.E. Corgi
LEGEND OF HELL HOUSE, THE FOX—RANK 1973	Matheson, R. (*Hell House*) Corgi
LEGEND OF LOBO, THE DISNEY 1962	Seton, E.T. (*Lobo and Other Stories*) Hodder & Stoughton
LEMON DROP KID, THE PAR 1951	Runyon, D. Lippincott, Philadelphia
LENNY (V) UA 1975	Barry, J. (P) Random House, N.Y.
LEOPARD, THE FOX 1962	Lampedusa, G. di Collins
LEOPARD IN THE SNOW (V) ANGLO—CANADIAN 1977	Mather, A. Mills & Boon
LEOPARD MAN, THE RKO 1943	Woolrich, C. (*Black Alibi*) Simon & Schuster, N.Y.
LES MISERABLES (V) UA 1935 FOX 1952	Hugo, V. Various
LET NO MAN WRITE MY EPITAPH COL 1960	Motley, W. Collins
LET'S BE HAPPY ABP 1957	Stuart, A. (*Jeannie*) (P) French, N.Y.
LET'S DO IT AGAIN COL 1953	Richman, A. (*Not so Long Ago*) (P) French, N.Y.
LET'S KILL UNCLE UI 1967	O'Grady, R. Longmans

TITLE OF FILM	AUTHOR AND PUBLISHER
LET THE PEOPLE SING BN 1942	Priestley, J.B. Heinemann
LETTER, THE PAR 1929 WAR 1940	Maugham, W.S. (P) Heinemann
LETTER FROM AN UNKNOWN **WOMAN, A** (V) UI 1948 UN 1979	Zweig, S. Cassell
LETTER TO THREE WIVES (V) FOX 1948	Klemper, J. (*Letter to Five Wives*) Scribner, N.Y.
LETTY LYNTON MGM 1932	Lowndes, *Mrs*. M.B. Benn
LIBEL MGM 1959	Wooll, E. (P) French
LIBERATION OF LORD BYRON JONES, **THE** COL 1969	Ford, J.H. Bodley Head
LIE, THE SELVAGGIA 1986	Moravia, A. Woodhill, N.Y.
LIFE AND ADVENTURES OF NICHOLAS **NICKLEBY, THE** PRIMETIME 1984 (TV)	Dickens, C. (*Nicholas Nickleby*) Various
LIFE AND LOVES OF A SHE-DEVIL BBC 1986 (TV)	Weldon, F. Hodder & Stoughton
LIFEFORCE CANNON 1985	Wilson, C. (*Space vampires*) Random, N.Y.
LIFE FOR RUTH RANK 1962	Drummond, W. Corgi
LIFE WITH FATHER WAR 1947	Day, C. Chatto & Windus

TITLE OF FILM	AUTHOR AND PUBLISHER
LIGHT AT THE EDGE OF THE WORLD, THE (V) MGM 1972	Verne, J. (*Lighthouse at the End of the World*) Sampson Low
LIGHT IN THE FOREST, THE DISNEY 1958	Richter, C. Gollancz
LIGHT IN THE PIAZZA MGM 1962	Spencer, E. Heinemann
LIGHTNING STRIKES TWICE WAR 1951	Echard, M. (*Dark Fantastic*) Invincible Press
LIGHT OF HEART, THE FOX 1942	Williams, E. (P) Heinemann
LIGHT OF WESTERN STARS, THE PAR 1930 PAR 1940	Grey, Z. Nelson
LIGHTSHIP, THE RANK 1985	Lenz, S. (*Das Feuerschiff*) Various
LIGHT THAT FAILED, THE PAR 1939	Kipling, R. Macmillan
LIGHT UP THE SKY BRYANSTON 1960	Storey, R. (*Touch it Light*) (P) French
LILIES OF THE FIELD, THE UA 1963	Barrett, W.E. Heinemann
LILIOM FOX 1930	Molnar, F. (P) Simon & Schuster, N.Y.
LILITH BL 1965	Salamanca, J.R. Heinemann
LILY CHRISTINE PAR 1932	Arlen, M. Collins
LIMBO UN 1972	Silver, J. *and* Gottlieb, L. Heinemann

TITLE OF FILM	AUTHOR AND PUBLISHER
LIMBO LINE, THE (V) MONARCH 1968	Canning, V. Heinemann
LION, THE FOX 1962	Kessell, J. Hart-Davis
LION AND THE LAMB COL 1931	Oppenheim, E.P. Hodder & Stoughton
LIONHEART CFF 1968	Fullerton, A. Hodder & Stoughton
LION IN THE STREETS, A WAR 1953	Langley, A.L. McGraw-Hill, N.Y.
LION IN WINTER, THE (V) AVCO EMBASSY 1969	Goldman, J. (P) French
LIQUIDATOR, THE MGM 1965	Gardner, J. Muller
LIST OF ADRIAN MESSENGER UI 1963	Macdonald, P. Penguin
LITTLE ARK, THE (V) FOX 1971	Hartog, J. de Four Square Books
LITTLE BIG MAN (V) CINEMA CENTER 1969	Bergner, T. Eyre & Spottiswoode
LITTLE BOY LOST PAR 1953	Laski, M. Cresset Press
LITTLE CAESAR IN 1930	Burnett, W.R. Cape
LITTLE COLONEL FOX 1935	Johnston, A.F. Various
LITTLE DRUMMER GIRL, THE (V) WAR 1984 (TV)	Le Carré, J. Hodder & Stoughton
LITTLE FOXES, THE RKO 1941	Hellman, L.F. (P) Hamilton

TITLE OF FILM	AUTHOR AND PUBLISHER
LITTLE GIRL WHO LIVES DOWN THE LANE RANK 1976	Koenig, L. Souvenir
LITTLE GLORIA—HAPPY AT LAST ITV 1983 (TV)	Goldsmith, B. Macmillan
LITTLE HUT, THE MGM 1957	Roussin, A. (P) Random House, N.Y.
LITTLE LORD FAUNTLEROY (V) UA 1936 POLYGRAM 1981	Burnett, F.H. Warne
LITTLE MAN, WHAT NOW? UN 1934	Fallada, H. Putnam
LITTLE MEN RKO 1940	Alcott, L.M. Various
LITTLE MINISTER, THE RKO 1934	Barrie, *Sir* J.M. Cassell
LITTLE MURDERS FOX 1971	Feiffer, J. (P) Cape
LITTLE ORVIE (V) RKO 1940	Tarkington, B. Heinemann
LITTLE PRINCE, THE CIC 1974	Saint-Expury, A. Various
LITTLE PRINCESS, THE FOX 1939	Burnett, F.H. Various
LITTLE ROMANCE, A COL—EMI—WAR 1979	Cauvin, P. (*Blind Love*) Fawcett, N.Y.
LITTLE SHEPHERD OF KINGDOM COME, THE FOX 1961	Fox, J. Scribner, N.Y.
LITTLE WOMEN RKO 1933 MGM 1948	Alcott, L.M. Various

LITTLE WORLD OF DON CAMILLO, THE
LF 1952

Guareschi, G.
Gollancz

LIVE AND LET DIE (V)
UA 1974

Fleming, I.
Cape

LIVE NOW, PAY LATER
REGAL 1962

Story, J.T.
Secker & Warburg

LIVES OF A BENGAL LANCER, THE
PAR 1935

Brown, F.Y. (*Bengal Lancer*)
Gollancz

LIVING FREE
COL 1971

Adamson, J.
Collins

LIZZIE
MGM 1957

Jackson, S. (*Bird's Nest, The*)
Farrar, N.Y.

LOCK UP YOUR DAUGHTERS
COL 1968

Miles, B. (P)
French

LOCK UP YOUR DAUGHTERS
COL 1968

Vanbrugh, *Sir* J. (*Relapse, The*) (P)
Various

LOCK UP YOUR DAUGHTERS
COL 1968

Fielding, H. (*Rape Upon Rape*) (P)
Various

LODGER, THE
FOX 1944

Lowndes, *Mrs.* M.B.
Benn

LOGAN'S RUN (V)
MGM 1976

Nolan, W. *and* Johnson, G.
Gollancz

LOLITA
MGM 1962

Nabokov, K.
Corgi

LOLLY-MADONNA WAR, THE
MGM—EMI 1973

Grafton, S.
Owen

LONDON BELONGS TO ME
UN 1948

Collins, N.
Collins

LONDON NOBODY KNOWS, THE
BL 1969

Fletcher, G.
Penguin

**LONELINESS OF THE LONG DISTANCE
RUNNER, THE**
BL 1962

Sillitoe, A.
W.H. Allen

LONELY ARE THE BRAVE
UI 1962

Abbey, E. (*Brave Cowboy, The*)
Eyre & Spottiswoode

LONELYHEARTS
UA 1959

West, N. (*Miss Lonelyhearts*)
Grey Walls Press

LONELY HEARTS (V)
GALA 1981

Strindberg, A. (*Father, The*) (P)
Various

LONELY LADY, THE (V)
COL—EMI—WAR 1983

Robbins, H.
PB., N.Y.

LONE STAR RANGER
FOX 1930
FOX 1942

Grey, Z.
Harper

LONG WOLF RETURNS
COL 1936

Vance, J.L.
Grosset, N.Y.

**LONG AND THE SHORT AND THE
TALL, THE**
WAR 1960

Hall, W. (P)
Heinemann

LONG DAY'S DYING, THE
PAR 1968

White, A.
Hodder & Stoughton

LONG DAY'S JOURNEY INTO NIGHT
(V)
FOX 1962

O'Neill, E.G. (P)
Cape

LONGEST DAY, THE (V)
FOX 1962

Ryan, C.
Gollancz

LONG GOODBYE, THE (V)
UA 1973

Chandler, R.
Hamilton

LONG GRAY LINE
COL 1954

Maher, M. *and* Campion, N.R.
(*Bringing up the Brass*)
McKay, N.Y.

TITLE OF FILM	AUTHOR AND PUBLISHER
LONG HAUL, THE COL 1957	Mills, M. Pan
LONG, HOT SUMMER, THE (V) FOX 1957	Faulkner, W. (*Hamlet, The*) Chatto & Windus
LONG KNIFE, THE AA 1958	Truss, S. (*Long Night, The*) Hodder & Stoughton
LONG, LONG TRAILER, THE MGM 1954	Twiss, C. Crowell, N.Y.
LONG MEMORY, THE GFD 1953	Clewes, H. Macmillan
LONG RIDE HOME, THE COL 1967	Wolford, N. *and* Wolford, S. (*Southern Blade, The*) Morrow, N.Y.
LONG SHIPS, THE BL 1963	Bengtsson, F. Collins
LONG VOYAGE HOME, THE UA 1940	O'Neill, E.G. (P) Cape
LONG WAIT, THE UA 1954	Spillane, M. Barker
LOOK BACK IN ANGER (V) ABP 1959	Osborne, J. (P) Faber
LOOKING FOR MR GOODBAR (V) CIC 1978	Rossner, J. Cape
LOOKING FORWARD MGM 1933	Anthony, C.L. (*Service*) (P) French
LOOKING GLASS WAR, THE (V) COL 1969	Le Carré, J. Gollancz
LOOT (V) BL 1971	Orton, J. (P) Methuen
LORD BABS GFD 1932	Howard, K. Benn

LORD CAMBER'S LADIES BI 1932	Vachell, H.A. (*Case of Lady Camber The*) (P) French
LORD JIM COL 1964	Conrad, J. Dent
LORD LOVE A DUCK UA 1965	Hine, A. Atheneum Press, N.Y.
LORD MOUNTBATTEN (V) WALKER 1986 (TV)	Butler, D. Methuen
LORD OF THE FLIES BL 1963	Golding, W. Faber
LORD OF THE RINGS (V) UA 1980	Tolkien, J.R.R. (*Fellowship of the Rings : Two Towers, The*) Allen & Unwin
LORDS OF DISCIPLINE, THE PAR 1982	Conroy, P. Secker & Warburg
LORNA DOONE ATP 1935 COL 1951	Blackmore, R.D. Various
LOSER TAKES ALL BL 1956	Greene, G. Heinemann
LOST COMMAND (V) COL 1966	Larteguy, J. (*Centurions, The*) Hutchinson
LOST CONTINENT, THE WAR 1968	Wheatley, D. (*Uncharted Seas*) Hutchinson
LOST EMPIRES GRANADA 1985 (TV)	Priestley, J.B. Heinemann
LOST HORIZON COL 1937 COL 1973	Hilton, J. Macmillan
LOST MAN, THE RANK 1969	Green, F.L. Joseph

TITLE OF FILM	AUTHOR AND PUBLISHER
LOST MOMENT, THE (V) UN 1947	James, H. (*Aspern Papers, The*) Macmillan
LOST PATROL RKO 1934	Macdonald, P. (*Patrol*) Collins
LOST PEOPLE, THE GFD 1949	Boland, B. (*Cockpit*) (P) Elek
LOST STAGE VALLEY COL 1951	Bonham, F. Simon & Schuster, N.Y.
LOST WEEK-END, THE PAR 1945	Jackson, C. Lane
LOST WORLD, THE FOX 1960	Doyle, *Sir* A.C. Murray
LOUDEST WHISPER, THE UA 1962	Hellman, L. (*Children's Hour, The*) (P) Dramatists, N.Y.
LOVE BAN, THE BL 1972	Laffan, K. (*It's a 2 ft 6 inch Above The Ground World*) (P) Faber
LOVE BEGINS AT TWENTY IN 1936	Flavin, M. (*Broken Dishes*) (P) French, N.Y.
LOVE BOCCACCIO STYLE PRODUCTION ASSOCIATES 1977	Boccaccio, G. (*Decameron, The*) Various
LOVE CAGE, THE MGM 1965	Keene, D. (*Joy House*) Consul Bks
LOVED ONE, THE MGM 1965	Waugh, E. Chapman & Hall
LOVE FROM A STRANGER UA 1937	Vosper, F. (P) French
LOVE IN AMSTERDAM MONARCH 1968	Freeling, N. Penguin

TITLE OF FILM	AUTHOR AND PUBLISHER
LOVE IS A MANY SPLENDOURED THING FOX 1955	Han Suyin (*Many Splendoured Thing, A*) Cape
LOVE LETTERS PAR 1945	Massie, C. (*Pity my Simplicity*) Faber
LOVE LETTERS OF A STAR UN 1936	King, R. (*Case of the Constant God*) Methuen
LOVELY TO LOOK AT MGM 1952	Miller, A.D. (*Gowns by Roberta*) Various
LOVE MACHINE, THE COL 1971	Susann, J. W.H. Allen
LOVE ON THE DOLE UA 1941	Greenwood, W. Cape
LOVE ON THE DOLE UA 1941	Gow, R. *and* Greenwood, W. (P) French
LOVERS MUST LEARN WAR 1962	Fineman, I. (*These Our Lovers*) Long
LOVES OF JOANNA GODDEN, THE GFD 1947	Smith, S.K. (*Joanna Godden*) Cassell
LOVE STORY BI 1941	Drawbell, J.W. (*Love and Forget*) Collins
LOVE STORY (V) PAR 1970	Segal, E.W. Hodder & Stoughton
LOVING COL 1969	Ryan, J.M. (*Brook Wilson Ltd*) Hodder Fawcett
LOVIN' MOLLY GALA 1975	McMurtry, L. (*Leaving Cheyenne*) Popular Library, N.Y.
LOYALTIES AUT 1934	Galsworthy, J. (P) Duckworth
L SHAPED ROOM, THE BL 1962	Banks, L.R. Chatto & Windus

168

TITLE OF FILM	AUTHOR AND PUBLISHER
LUCK OF BARRY LYNDON, THE (V) WAR 1974	Thackeray, W.M. (*Barry Lyndon*) Various
LUCK OF GINGER COFFEY, THE BL 1965	Moore, B. Deutsch
LUCK OF THE IRISH FOX 1948	Jones, G.P. *and* Jones, C.B. Random House, N.Y.
LUCKY JIM (V) BL 1957	Amis, K. Gollancz
LUCKY STIFF, THE UA 1948	Rice, C. World, N.Y.
LUCY MAME WAR 1974	Dennis, P. (*Auntie Mame*) Muller
LUMMOX UA 1930	Hurst, F. Cape
LUST FOR LIFE MGM 1956	Stone, I. Bodley Head
LUTHER SEVEN KEYS 1973	Osborne, J. (P) Faber
LUV BL 1966	Schisgal, M. (P) Coward-McCann, N.Y.
LUXURY LINER PAR 1933	Kaus, G. Cassell
LYDIA BAILEY FOX 1952	Roberts, K. Collins

M

McCABE AND MRS. MILLER WAR 1972	Naughton, E. (*McCabe*) Panther
MACABRE ABP 1957	Durrant, T. (*Marble Forest*) Wingate

MACBETH (V)
REP 1948
BL 1960
COL—WAR 1971

Shakespeare, W. (P)
Various

McGUFFIN, THE
BBC 2 1986 (TV)

Bowen, J.
Hamilton

MACKENNA'S GOLD
COL 1969

Henry, W.
Hammond

McKENZIE BREAK, THE
UA 1971

Shelley, S.
Sphere

MACKINTOSH MAN, THE (V)
COL—WAR 1973

Bagley, D. (*Freedom Trap, The*)
Collins

MACOMBER AFFAIR, THE
UA 1947

Hemingway, E.
Cape

McVICAR (V)
BRENT WALKER 1980

McVicar, J. (*McVicar Himself*)
Hutchinson

MADAME BOVARY
MGM 1949

Flaubert, G.
Cape

MADAME CURIE
MGM 1943

Curie, E.
Heinemann

MADAME CURIE
BBC 1984 (TV)

Reid, R.
Collins

MAD DEATH OF NIGEL
BBC (Scotland) 1985 (TV)

Slater, N.
Granada

MADHOUSE
EMI 1974

Hall, A. (*Devilday — Madhouse*)
Sphere

MADIGAN
UI 1968

Dougherty, R. (*Commissioner, The*)
Hart-Davis

MADISON AVENUE
FOX 1960

Kirk, J. (*Build-up Boys, The*)
Hart-Davis

TITLE OF FILM	AUTHOR AND PUBLISHER
MADNESS OF THE HEART TC 1949	Sandstrom, F. Cassell
MADONNA OF THE SEVEN MOONS GFD 1945	Lawrence, M. Hurst & Blackett
MADONNA OF THE STREETS COL 1930	Maxwell, W.B. (*Ragged Messenger,* *The*) Butterworth
MAD ROOM, THE COL 1968	Denham, R. *and* Percy, E. (*Ladies in* *Retirement*) (P) Random House, N.Y.
'MAGGIE, THE' (V) EALING 1954	White, J.D. Heinemann
MAGIC (V) FOX 1978	Goodman, W. Dial, N.Y.
MAGIC BOW GFD 1946	Komroff, M. Heinemann
MAGIC BOX, THE BL 1951	Allister, R. (*Friese-Greene*) Marsland
MAGIC CHRISTIAN, THE (V) COMMONWEALTH 1969	Southern, T. Deutsch
MAGIC FIRE REP 1956	Harding, B. Harrap
MAGIC GARDEN OF STANLEY **SWEETHEART, THE** MGM 1970	Westbrook, R. W.H. Allen
MAGICIAN, THE FOX 1972	Stein, S. New English Library
MAGICIAN OF LUBLIN, THE (V) CENTURY CINEMA 1979	Singer, I. Cape
MAGIC MOUNTAIN, THE SAFIR 1983	Mann, T. Secker & Warburg

TITLE OF FILM	AUTHOR AND PUBLISHER
MAGNIFICENT AMBERSONS, THE (V) RKO 1942	Tarkington, B. Grosset, N.Y.
MAGNIFICENT OBSESSION UN 1935 UI 1954	Douglas, L.C. Allen & Unwin
MAGNIFICENT YANKEE, THE MGM 1950	Biddle, F. (*Mr. Justice Holmes*) Scribner, N.Y.
MAGUS, THE FOX 1969	Fowles, J. Cape
MAIDS, THE ELY LANDAU 1974	Genet, J. (P) Faber
MAJOR BARBARA PASCAL 1941	Shaw, G.B. (P) Various
MAJORITY OF ONE, A WAR 1961	Spigelgass, L. (P) French, N.Y.
MAKE HASTE TO LIVE REP 1954	Gordon, M. *and* Gordon, G. Doubleday, N.Y.
MAKE ME AN OFFER BL 1954	Mankowitz, W. Deutsch
MAKE ME A STAR PAR 1932	Wilson, H.L. (*Merton of the Movies*) Cape
MAKE MINE MINK RANK 1960	Coke, P. (*Breath of Spring*) (P) French
MAKE WAY FOR A LADY RKO 1936	Jordan, E.G. (*Daddy and I*) Grosset, N.Y.
MAKE WAY FOR TOMORROW PAR 1937	Lawrence, J. (*Years Are So Long, The*) Harrap
MAKING IT FOX 1971	Leigh, J. (*What can you do?*) Panther

TITLE OF FILM	AUTHOR AND PUBLISHER
MALE ANIMAL WAR 1942	Thurber, J. *and* Nugent, E. (P) Random House, N.Y.
MALEVIL POLYGRAM 1981	Merle, R. Warner, N.Y.
MALPAS MYSTERY, THE AA 1960	Wallace, E. (*Face in the Night*) Long
MALTESE FALCON, THE (V) WAR 1941	Hammett, D. Cassell
MAN, THE PAR 1972	Wallace, I. New English Library
MAN ABOUT THE HOUSE, A LF 1947	Young, F.B. Heinemann
MAN ABOUT THE HOUSE, A LF 1947	Young, F.B. (P) Heinemann
MAN ABOUT TOWN FOX 1932	Clift, D. Long
MAN AT THE CARLTON TOWER AA 1961	Wallace, E. (*Man At the Carlton*) Hodder & Stoughton
MAN CALLED HORSE, A (V) CINEMA CENTER 1969	Johnson, D.M. Deutsch
MAN CALLED NOON, THE SCOTIA-BARBER 1973	L'Amour, L. Corgi
MAN CALLED PETER, A FOX 1954	Marshall, C. (*Story of Peter Marshall, The*) Davies
MANCHURIAN CANDIDATE UA 1962	Condon, R. Pan
MAN COULD GET KILLED, A RANK 1966	Walker, D.E. (*Adventure in Diamonds*) Evans

MANDARINS, THE FOX 1969	De Beauvoir, S. Fontana
MAN DETAINED AA 1961	Wallace, E. (*Debt Discharged, A*) Ward Lock
MANDINGO (V) PAR 1975	Onstott, K. Pan
MANDY GFD 1952	Lewis, H. (*Day is Ours, The*) Macdonald
MANEATERS ARE LOOSE! BBC 1984 (TV)	Willis, T. (*Man-eater*) Pan
MAN FOR ALL SEASONS, A (V) COL 1966	Bolt, R. (P) French
MAN FROM BITTER RIDGE, THE GFD 1955	Raine, W.M. (*Rawhide Justice*) Hodder & Stoughton
MAN FROM DAKOTA, THE MGM 1940	Kantor, M. (*Arouse and Beware*) Gollancz
MANHUNT FOX 1941	Household, G. (*Rogue Male*) Chatto & Windus
MANHUNT FOX 1958	Locke, C.O. (*Road to Socorro, The*) Hutchinson
MAN IN GREY, THE GFD 1943	Smith, *Lady* E. Hutchinson
MAN IN HALF-MOON STREET PAR 1944	Lyndon, B. (P) Hamilton
MAN INSIDE, THE COL 1958	Chaber, M.E. Eyre & Spottiswoode
MAN IN THE ATTIC, THE FOX 1953	Lowndes, *Mrs.* M.B. (*Lodger, The*) Benn
MAN IN THE GREY FLANNEL SUIT, THE FOX 1956	Wilson, S. Cassell

TITLE OF FILM	AUTHOR AND PUBLISHER
MAN IN THE IRON MASK, THE (V) UA 1939 ITC 1976	Dumas, A. Collins
MAN IN THE MIDDLE FOX 1963	Fast, H. (*Winston Affair, The*) Methuen
MAN IN THE NET, THE UA 1958	Quentin, P. Gollancz
MAN IN THE ROAD, THE GN 1956	Armstrong, A. (*He was Found in the Road*) Methuen
MAN IN THE SHADOW AA 1957	Davis, S. (*One Man's Secret*) Boardman
MAN IN THE VAULT RKO 1957	Gruber, F. (*Lock and the Key, The*) Worlds Work
MANITOU (V) ENTERPRISE 1978	Masterton, G. Pinnacle, N.Y.
MAN OF ARAN GB 1934	Mullen, P. Faber
MAN OF LA MANCHA UA 1972	Wasserman, D. (P) Random House, N.Y.
MAN OF THE FOREST PAR 1935	Grey, Z. Hodder & Stoughton
MAN OF THE WEST UA 1958	Brown, W.C. (*Border Jumpers, The*) Muller
MAN OF THE EIFFEL TOWER, THE BL 1950	Simenon, G. (*Battle of Nerves, A*) Routledge
MAN-PROOF MGM 1938	Lea, F.H. (*Four Marys*) Nicholson & Watson
MANSFIELD PARK BBC 1983 (TV)	Austen, J. Various

TITLE OF FILM	AUTHOR AND PUBLISHER

MANSLAUGHTER
PAR 1930

Miller, A.D.
Dodd, N.Y.

MAN THEY COULDN'T ARREST, THE
GB 1933

'Seamark'
Hodder & Stoughton

MAN TRAP
EXCLUSIVE 1953

Trevor, E. (*Queen in Danger*)
Boardman

MAN TRAP
PAR 1961

Macdonald, J.P. (*Restless*)
Pan Bks

MANUELA
BL 1957

Woods, W.
Hart-Davis

MAN WHO CAME TO DINNER, THE
WAR 1941

Kaufman, G.S. *and* Hart, M. (P)
Random House, N.Y.

MAN WHO COULD CHEAT DEATH, THE
PAR 1959

Lyndon, B. (*Man in Half-Moon Street, The*) (P)
Hamilton

MAN WHO COULD WORK MIRACLES, THE
UA 1937

Wells, H.G.
Cresset Press

MAN WHO FELL TO EARTH, THE (V)
BL 1976

Tevis, W.
Pan

MAN WHO HAD POWER OVER WOMEN, THE
AVCO EMBASSY 1970

Williams, G.
Secker & Warburg

MAN WHO LOVED CAT DANCING, THE (V)
MGM 1973

Durham, M.
Macmillan

MAN WHO LOVED REDHEADS, THE
BL 1954

Rattigan, T. (*Who is Sylvia?*) (P)
Hamilton

MAN WHO NEVER WAS, THE
FOX 1955

Montague, E.E.S.
Evans

MAN WHO UNDERSTOOD WOMEN
FOX 1959

Gary, R. (*Colours of the Day, The*)
Joseph

176

MAN WHO WAS NOBODY, THE
AA 1960

Wallace, E.
Ward Lock

MAN WHO WATCHED THE TRAINS GO BY, THE
EROS 1952

Simenon, G.
Routledge

MAN WHO WOULD BE KING, THE
COL 1976

Kipling, R.
Macmillan

MAN WHO WOULDN'T DIE, THE
FOX 1942

Rawson, C. (*No Coffin for the Corpse*)
Little, Brown, Boston

MAN WITHIN, THE
FOX 1947

Greene, G.
Heinemann

MAN WITH MY FACE, THE
UA 1951

Taylor, S.W.
Hodder & Stoughton

MAN WITHOUT A STAR
UI 1955

Linford, D.
Morrow, N.Y.

MAN WITH THE DEADLY LENS (V)
COL—EMI—WAR 1982
U.S. title: Wrong is Right

McCarry, C. (*Better Angels, The*)
Arrow

MAN WITH THE GOLDEN ARM, THE
UA 1955

Algren, N.
Doubleday, N.Y.

MAN WITH THE GOLDEN GUN (V)
UA 1974

Fleming, I.
Cape

MAN WITH THE TWISTED LIP, THE
GN 1951

Doyle, *Sir* A.C.
Murray

MAN WITH THIRTY SONS, THE
MGM 1952

Bowen, C.D. (*Yankee from Olympus*)
Benn

MAN, WOMAN AND CHILD (V)
COL—EMI—WAR 1983

Segal, E.
Gollancz

MAPP AND LUCIA
CHANNEL 4 1985 (TV)

Benson, E.F.
Heinemann

TITLE OF FILM	AUTHOR AND PUBLISHER
MARACAIBO PAR 1958	Silliphant, S. Farrar, N.Y.
MARATHON MAN PAR 1976	Goldman, W. Dial, N.Y.
MARAUDERS, THE WAR 1962	Ogburn, C. (*Merrill's Marauders*) Hodder & Stoughton
MARCHING ALONG FOX 1952	Sousa, J.P. Hale
MARGIN FOR ERROR FOX 1943	Boothe, C. (P) Hamilton
MARIA CHAPDELAINE ASTRAL FILMS 1983	Hemon, L. Macmillan
MARIE COL—EMI—WAR 1986	Maas, P. Random, N.Y.
MARIE ANTOINETTE MGM 1938	Zweig, S. Cassell
MARILYN: THE UNTOLD STORY RANK 1980	Mailer, N. Warner, N.Y.
MARJORIE MORNINGSTAR WAR 1957	Wouk, H. Cape
MARK, THE (V) FOX 1961	Israel, C.E. Macmillan
MARK OF CAIN, THE TC 1948	Shearing, J. (*Airing in a Closed Carriage*) Hutchinson
MARK OF THE RENEGADE UI 1951	McCulley, J. (*Mark of Zorro*) Grosset, N.Y.
MARK OF ZORRO, THE (V) FOX 1940	McCulley, J. Grosset, N.Y.
MARLOWE MGM 1969	Chandler, R. (*Little Sister, The*) Hamilton

178

TITLE OF FILM	AUTHOR AND PUBLISHER
MARNIE UI 1964	Graham, W. Hodder & Stoughton
MAROONED (V) COL 1969	Caidin, M. Hodder & Stoughton
MARRIAGE IS A PRIVATE AFFAIR MGM 1944	Kelly, J. Cassell
MARRIAGE OF A YOUNG STOCKBROKER, THE FOX 1971	Webb, C. Deutsch
MARRIAGE OF CONVENIENCE AA 1960	Wallace, E. (*Three Oak Mystery, The*) Ward Lock
MARRIAGE PLAYGROUND, THE PAR 1929	Wharton, E. (*Children, The*) Appleton Century, N.Y.
MARRIED MAN, A LWT 1985 (TV)	Read, P.P. Avon, N.Y.
MARTIAN CHRONICLES, THE BBC 2 1984 (TV)	Bradbury, R. Bantam, N.Y.
MARTIN (V) MIRACLE INTERNATIONAL 1979	Romero, G.A. Futura
MARTY COL 1956	Chayevsky, P. (P) Simon & Schuster, N.Y.
MARY, MARY WAR 1963	Kerr, J. (P) Doubleday, N.Y.
MARY OF SCOTLAND RKO 1936	Anderson, M. (P) Harcourt, Brace, N.Y.
MARY POPPINS (V) DISNEY 1964	Travers, P.L. Penguin
M.A.S.H. (V) FOX 1969	Hooker, R. (*Mash*) Morrow, N.Y.
MASK OF DIMITRIOS, THE WAR 1944	Ambler, E. Hodder & Stoughton

TITLE OF FILM	AUTHOR AND PUBLISHER
MASK OF DOUBT EXCLUSIVE 1954	White, J.E.M. (*Mask of Dust*) Hodder & Stoughton
MASK OF FU MANCHU MGM 1932	Rohmer, S. Cassell
MASQUE OF THE RED DEATH, THE AA 1964	Poe, E.A. Various
MASQUERADE UA 1965	Canning, V. (*Castle Minerva*) Hodder & Stoughton
MASSACRE IN ROME (V) GN 1975	Katz, R. (*Death in Rome*) Cape
MASS APPEAL UN 1985	Davis, B.C. (P) Avon, N.Y.
MASTER OF BALLANTRAE, THE WAR 1953 CBS 1983 (TV)	Stevenson, R.L. Various
MASTER OF BANKDAM, THE ALL 1947	Armstrong, T. (*Crowthers of Bankdam, The*) Collins
MASTER OF THE GAME (V) ROSEMOUNT 1984 (TV)	Sheldon, S. Collins
MASTER OF THE ISLANDS UA 1970	Michener, J.A. (*Hawaii*) Secker & Warburg
MASTER OF THE WORLD AA 1961	Verne, J. Sampson Low
MASTER SPY GN 1962	Jennings, D.K. (*They Also Serve*) Badger Bks
MATCHMAKER, THE PAR 1958	Wilder, T. (P) French
MATILDA (V) RANK 1979	Gallico, P. Berkeley, N.Y.

MATING GAME, THE
MGM 1959

Bates, H.E. (*Darling Buds of May, The*)
Joseph

MAVERICK QUEEN, THE
REP 1956

Grey, Z.
Hodder & Stoughton

MAXIE
RANK 1985

Finney, J. (*Marion's Wall*)
Eyre & Spottiswoode

MAYBE IT'S LOVE
WAR 1934

Anderson, M. (*Saturday's Children*)
(P)
Longmans, N.Y.

MAYDAY : 40,000 FT
COL—WAR 1976

Ferguson, A. (*Jet Stream*)
Arrow

MAYERLING (V)
WAR 1968

Anet, C.
Frewin

MAZES AND MONSTERS
PROCTOR & GAMBLE 1982 (TV)

Jaffe, R.
Dell, N.Y.

ME AND THE GIRLS
BBC 1985 (TV)

Coward, N.
Methuen

MEAN SEASON
ORION 1985

Katzenbach, J. (*In the Heat of the Summer*)
Joseph

MEDAL FOR THE GENERAL, A
BN 1944

Ronald, J.
Hodder & Stoughton

MEDUSA TOUCH, THE (V)
ITC 1978

Van Greenaway, P.
Stein & Day, N.Y.

MEETINGS WITH REMARKABLE MEN
ENTERPRISE 1979

Gurdjieff, G.I.
Dutton, N.Y.

MEET ME IN ST LOUIS (V)
MGM 1944

Benson, *Mrs*. S.
Random House, N.Y.

MEET ME TONIGHT
GFD 1952

Coward, N. (P)
Heinemann

MEET MR. CALLAGHAN
EROS 1954

Cheyney, P. (*Urgent Hangman, The*)
Collins

MEET MR. CALLAGHAN
EROS 1954

Verner, G. (P)
French

MEET MR. LUCIFER
GFD 1953

Ridley, A. (*Beggar My Neighbour*)
(P)
Evans

MEET NERO WOLFE
COL 1936

Stout, R. (*Fer de Lance*)
Cassell

MELVILLE GOODWIN, USA
WAR 1956

Marquand, J.P.
Hale

MEMBER OF THE WEDDING, THE
COL 1952

McCullers, C.
Cresset Press

MEMED MY HAWK (V)
EMI 1984

Kemal, Y.
Writers and Readers

MEMOIRS OF A SURVIVOR (V)
EMI 1981

Lessing, D.
Picador

MENACE, THE
COL 1932

Wallace, E. (*Feathered Serpent*)
Hodder & Stoughton

MENACE ON THE MOUNTAIN
DISNEY 1972

Hancock, M.A.
Macrae, Smith, N.Y.

MEN AGAINST SPEED
FOX 1958

Ruesch, H. (*Racer, The*)
Hurst & Blackett

MEN ARE LIKE THAT
PAR 1929

Kelly, G. (*Show-off, The*) (P)
French, N.Y.

MEN ARE SUCH FOOLS
WAR 1938

Baldwin, F.
Sampson Low

MEN BEHIND BARS
ABP 1954

Duffy, C. *and* Kenning, D. (*San Quentin*)
Davies

TITLE OF FILM	AUTHOR AND PUBLISHER
MEN IN HER LIFE COL 1941	Smith, *Lady* E. (*Ballerina*) Gollancz
MEN IN WAR UA 1957	Praag, V.V. (*Day Without End*) Sloane, N.Y.
MEN IN WHITE MGM 1934	Kingsley, S. Gollancz
MEN OF TOMORROW MUNDUS 1935	Gibbs, A.H. (*Young Apollo, The*) Hutchinson
MEPHISTO WALTZ (V) FOX 1971	Stewart, F. (*Mustard*) Joseph
MERCHANT OF VENICE, THE (V) PRECISION 1974	Shakespeare, W. (P) Various
MERRY CHRISTMAS, MR. LAWRENCE (V) CINEVENTURE 1983	Post, *Sir* L. van der (*Seed and the Sower, The*) Hogarth
MERTON OF THE MOVIES MGM 1947	Wilson, H.L. Cape
MESSAGE TO GARCIA FOX 1936	Hubbard, E. Lothian, N.Y.
MICHAEL AND MARY UN 1932	Milne, A.A. (P) Chatto & Windus
MICHAEL O'HALLORAN REP 1937 MON 1949	Porter, G.S. Murray
MICHAEL STROGOFF RKO 1937	Verne, J. Various
MICKY EL 1948	Goodin, P. (*Clementine*) Dutton, N.Y.
MIDDLE OF THE NIGHT COL 1959	Chayefsky, P. (P) Random House, N.Y.

TITLE OF FILM	AUTHOR AND PUBLISHER
MIDDLE WATCH BI 1930 AB 1940	Hay, I. *and* Hall, S.K. (P) French
MIDNIGHT COWBOY, THE (V) UA 1969	Herlihy, J.L. Cape
MIDNIGHT EPISODE COL 1951	Simenon, G. (*Monsieur La Souris*) Gallimard, Paris
MIDNIGHT EXPRESS (V) COL—WAR 1978	Hayes, B. *and* Hoffer, W. Dutton, N.Y.
MIDNIGHT MAN, THE UN 1974	Anthony, D. (*Midnight Lady and the Mourning Man*) Fontana
MIDSHIPMAID, THE GB 1932	Hay, I. *and* Hall, S.K. (P) French
MIDSHIPMAN EASY ATP 1935	Marryat, F. (*Mr. Midshipman Easy*) Various
MIDSUMMER NIGHT'S DREAM, A (V) WAR 1935 EAGLE 1969 MAINLINE 1985	Shakespeare, W. (P) Various
MIGHTY TREVE, THE UN 1937	Terhune, A.P. (*Treve*) Grosset, N.Y.
MIKADO, THE (V) UN 1939	Gilbert, *Sir* W.S. (P) Macmillan
MILDRED PIERCE WAR 1945	Cain, J.M. Hale
MILLIE RKO 1931	Clarke, D.H. Long
MILLIE'S DAUGHTER COL 1947	Clarke, D.H. Laurie
MILLIONAIRESS, THE FOX 1960	Shaw, G.B. (P) Constable

184

MILLION POUND NOTE, THE (V)
GFD 1953

Twain, M.
Harper, N.Y.

MILL ON THE FLOSS, THE
STANDARD 1939

Eliot, G.
Various

MILL ON THE PO
LUX 1950

Bacchelli, R.
Hutchinson

MIN AND BILL
MGM 1930

Moon, L. (*Dark Star*)
Gollancz

MIND BENDERS, THE
AA 1963

Kennaway, J.
Pan Bks

MIND OF MR. REEDER, THE
RAYMOND 1939

Wallace, E. (*Mind of Mr. J.G.
Reeder, The*)
Hodder & Stoughton

MIND OF MR. SOAMES, THE
COL 1969

Maine, C.E.
Panther

MINE OWN EXECUTIONER
BL 1948

Balchin, N.
Collins

MINE WITH THE IRON DOOR, THE
COL 1936

Wright, H.B.
Appleton-Century, N.Y.

MINISTRY OF FEAR
PAR 1944

Greene, G.
Heinemann

MIRACLE IN THE RAIN
WAR 1956

Hecht, B.
Knopf, N.Y.

MIRACLE OF THE BELLS
PAR 1944

Janney, R.
W.H. Allen

MIRACLE ON 34TH STREET
FOX 1948
FOX 1956

Davies, V.
Harcourt, N.Y.

MIRACLES FOR SALE
MGM 1939

Rawson, C. (*Death From a Top Hat*)
Collins

TITLE OF FILM	AUTHOR AND PUBLISHER
MIRACLE WORKER, THE UA 1962	Gibson, W. (P) Knopf, N.Y.
MIRAGE UI 1965	Fast, H. Mayflower
MIRROR CRACK'D, THE (V) EMI 1981	Christie, A. (*Mirror Crack'd from Side to Side, The*) Fontana
MISHIMA COL—EMI—WAR 1985	Mishima, Y. (*Runaway Horses*) Knopf, N.Y. (*Temple of the Golden Pavilion*) Putnam, N.Y.
MISSING (V) POLYGRAM 1982	Hauser, T. (*Execution of Charles Horman, The*) Harbrace, N.Y.
MISSION GOLDCREST 1986	Bolt, R. Penguin
MISSION OF DANGER MGM 1959	Roberts, K. (*North-west Passage*) Collins
MISSION TO MOSCOW WAR 1943	Davies, J.E. Gollancz
MISS JULIE (V) LF 1951 TIGON 1972	Strindberg, J.A. (P) Dent
MISS ROBIN CRUSOE FOX 1954	Defoe, D. (*Adventures of Robinson Crusoe, The*) Various
MISSOURI TRAVELLER, THE DISNEY 1958	Burress, J. Vanguard, N.Y.
MISS SADIE THOMPSON COL 1954	Maugham, W.S. (*Rain*) (P) French
MISS SUSIE SLAGLE'S PAR 1945	Tucker, A. Grosset, N.Y.

TITLE OF FILM	AUTHOR AND PUBLISHER
MISTER BUDDWING MGM 1967	Hunter, E. (*Buddwing*) Constable
MISTER MOSES UA 1965	Catto, M. Heinemann
MISTER QUILP EMI 1975	Dickens, C. (*Old Curiosity Shop,* *The*) Various
MISTER ROBERTS (V) WAR 1955	Heggen, T. Nicholson
MISTER ROBERTS (V) WAR 1955	Heggen, T. *and* Logan, J. (P) Random House, N.Y.
MISTER SCOUTMASTER FOX 1953	Cochran, R.E. (*Be Prepared*) Sloane, N.Y.
MISTRAL'S DAUGHTER (V) ITV 1986 (TV)	Krantz, J. Sidgwick & Jackson
MISTRESS PAMELA MGM—EMI 1973	Richardson, S. (*Pamela*) Various
MISTY FOX 1961	Henry, M. (*Misty of Chincoteague*) Collins
MIX ME A PERSON BL 1962	Story, J.T. Corgi
MOBY DICK (V) WAR 1930 WAR 1954	Melville, H. Various
MODERATO CANTABILE R.J. LEVY 1960	Duras, M. Calder
MODESTY BLAISE (V) FOX 1965	O'Donnell, P. Souvenir Press
MOG LWT 1985 (TV)	Tinniswood, P. Hodder & Stoughton

TITLE OF FILM	AUTHOR AND PUBLISHER
MOGAMBO MGM 1953	Collison, W. (*Farewell to Women*) (P) McBride, N.Y.
MOLL FLANDERS FOX 1954	Defoe, D. Various
MOLLY MAGUIRES, THE PAR 1969	Lewis, A.H. (*Lament for Molly Maguires*) Longmans
MOMENT OF DANGER ABP 1959	Mackenzie, D. Pan
MOMMIE DEAREST (V) PAR 1981	Crawford, C. Hart-Davis
MONEY FROM HOME PAR 1953	Runyon, D. Various
MONEY TRAP, THE MGM 1965	White, L. Boardman
MONKEY GRIP (V) PAVILION FILMS 1982	Garner, H. Penguin
MONKEY ON MY BACK UA 1957	Brown, W. Elek
MONKEYS, GO HOME! DISNEY 1967	Wilkinson, G.R. (*Monkeys, The*) Macdonald
MONKEY'S PAW, THE RKO 1932 BUTCHER 1948	Jacobs, W.W. *and* Parker, L.N. (P) Harrap
MONOCLED MUTINEER, THE BBC 1986 (TV)	Allison, W. *and* Fairley, J. Quartet
MONSIEUR BEAUCAIRE PAR 1946	Tarkington, B. Grosset, N.Y.
MONSIGNOR FOX 1983	Leger, J.A. (*Monsignore*) Dell, N.Y.

TITLE OF FILM	AUTHOR AND PUBLISHER
MONSTER CLUB, THE ITC 1981	Chetwynd-Hayes, R. Kimber
MONSTER OF TERROR AMERICAN INT 1965	Lovecraft, H.P. (*Color Out of Space, The*) World Pubs, N.Y.
MONTE WALSH CINEMA CENTER 1969	Schaefer, J. Deutsch
MOON AND SIXPENCE, THE UA 1942	Maugham, W.S. Heinemann
MOONCUSSERS, THE DISNEY 1971	Vinton, I. (*Flying Ebony*) Macdonald
MOONFLEET MGM 1955	Faulkner, J.M. Little, Brown, Boston
MOON IS BLUE, THE UA 1953	Herbert, F.H. (P) Random House, N.Y.
MOON IS DOWN, THE FOX 1943	Steinbeck, J. (P) Viking Press, N.Y.
MOON IS DOWN, THE FOX 1943	Steinbeck, J. Heinemann
MOONRAKER (V) UA 1979	Fleming, I. Cape
MOONSHINE WAR, THE MGM 1970	Leonard, E. Hale
MOON'S OUR HOME, THE PAR 1936	Baldwin, F. Sampson Low
MOONSPINNERS, THE DISNEY 1964	Stewart, M. Hodder & Stoughton
MOONSTONE, THE MON 1934	Collins, W. Various
MOONTIDE FOX 1942	Robertson, W. Hamilton

TITLE OF FILM	AUTHOR AND PUBLISHER
MORALS OF MARCUS, THE GB 1935	Locke, W.J. (*Morals of Marcus Ordeyne, The*) Lane
MORGAN—A SUITABLE CASE FOR TREATMENT (V) BL 1966	Mercer, D. (P) Calder
MORNING DEPARTURE GFD 1950	Woollard, K. (P) French
MORTAL STORM, THE MGM 1940	Bottome, P. Faber
MOSS ROSE FOX 1947	Shearing, J. Heinemann
MOST DANGEROUS MAN IN THE WORLD, THE RANK 1969	Kennedy, J.R. Joseph
MOTHER DIDN'T TELL ME FOX 1950	Bard, M. (*Doctor Wears Three Faces, The*) Hammond
MOULIN ROUGE (V) UA 1952	La Mure, P. Collins
MOUNTAIN, THE PAR 1956	Troyat, H. Allen & Unwin
MOUNTAIN IS YOUNG, THE PAR 1959	Han Suyin Cape
MOUNTAIN ROAD, THE COL 1959	White, T.H. Cassell
MOURNING BECOMES ELECTRA RKO 1948	O'Neill, E.G. (P) Cape
MOUSE AND THE WOMAN, THE (V) FACELIFT FILMS 1981	Thomas, D. Dent
MOUSE ON THE MOON UA 1962	Wibberly, L. (*Mouse that Roared, The*) Hale

TITLE OF FILM	AUTHOR AND PUBLISHER
MOUSE THAT ROARED, THE (V) COL 1959	Wibberly, L. (*Wrath of Grapes*) Hale
MOVING TARGET, THE WAR 1966	Macdonald, R. Fontana
MR. & MRS. EDGEHILL BBC 1985 (TV)	Coward, N. Methuen
MR. AND MRS. NORTH MGM 1941	Davis, O. (P) French, N.Y.
MR. BELVEDERE RINGS THE BELL FOX 1951	McEnroe, R.E. (*Silver Whistle, The*) (P) Theatre Arts
MR. BLANDINGS BUILDS HIS DREAM HOUSE (V) RKO 1948	Hodgins, E. Joseph
MR DEEDS GOES TO TOWN COL 1936	Kelland, C.B. Barker
MR. DENNING DRIVES NORTH BL 1951	Coppel, A. Harrap
MR. DODDS TAKES THE AIR WAR 1937	Kelland, C.B. (*Great Crooner, The*) Barker
MR. EMMANUEL TC 1944	Golding, L. Rich & Cowan
MR. FORBUSH AND THE PENGUINS BL 1971	Billing, G. Coronet
MR. HOBBS TAKES A VACATION FOX 1962	Streeter, E. (*Mr. Hobbs' Holiday*) Hamilton
MR. MOSES UA 1965	Catto, M. (*Mister Moses*) Heinemann
MR. PEABODY AND THE MERMAID UN 1948	Jones, G.P. *and* Jones, C.B. (*Peabody's Mermaid*) Joseph

TITLE OF FILM	AUTHOR AND PUBLISHER
MR. PERRIN AND MR. TRAILL TC 1948	Walpole, H. Various
MR. PYE CHANNEL 4 1986 (TV)	Peake, M. (*Mister Pye*) Penguin
MRS. CAPPER'S BIRTHDAY BBC 1985 (TV)	Coward, N. Methuen
MRS. GIBBONS' BOYS BL 1962	Clickman, W. *and* Stein, J. (P) French, N.Y.
MR. SKEFFINGTON WAR 1944	'Elizabeth' Heinemann
MRS. MIKE UA 1950	Freedman, B. *and* Freedman, N. Hamilton
MRS. MINIVER MGM 1942	Struther, J. Chatto & Windus
MR. SMITH GOES TO WASHINGTON COL 1939	Landery, C. Dent
MRS. PARKINGTON MGM 1944	Bromfield, L. Cassell
MRS. POLLIFAX—SPY UA 1971	Colman, D. (*Unexpected Mrs. Pollifax, The*) Hale
MRS. WIGGS OF THE CABBAGE PATCH PAR 1934	Rice, A.C. Grosset, N.Y.
MR. WINKLE GOES TO WAR COL 1944	Pratt, T. Duell, N.Y.
MUDLARK, THE FOX 1950	Bonnet, T. W.H. Allen
MURDER BI 1930	Dane, C. *and* Simpson, H. de G. Hodder & Stoughton
MURDER AHOY MGM 1964	Christie, A. (*Miss Marple*) Collins

TITLE OF FILM	AUTHOR AND PUBLISHER
MURDER AT THE GALLOP MGM 1963	Christie, A. (*After the Funeral*) Collins
MURDER BY PROXY EXCLUSIVE 1954	Nielson, H. Gollancz
MURDERER'S ROW (V) BL 1966	Hamilton, D. Muller
MURDER INC. WAR 1952	Eastwood, J. Dakers
MURDER, INCORPORATED FOX 1960	Turkus, B. *and* Feder, S. Gollancz
MURDER IN THE CATHEDRAL FILM TRADERS 1951	Eliot, T.S. (P) Faber
MURDER IN THE PRIVATE CAR MGM 1934	Rose, E.E. (*Rear Car*) (P) French, N.Y.
MURDER IN THE RUE MORGUE AMERICAN INT 1971	Poe, E.A. Various
MURDER IN THORNTON SQUARE MGM 1944	Hamilton, P. (*Gaslight*) (P) French
MURDER IS ANNOUNCED, A BBC 1985 (TV)	Christie, A. Collins
MURDER IS EASY BBC 2 1982 (TV)	Christie, A. Collins
MURDER IS MY BUSINESS PRC 1946	Halliday, B. Dodd, N.Y.
MURDER MOST FOUL MGM 1963	Christie, A. (*Mrs. McGinty's Dead*) Collins
MURDER, MY SWEET (V) RKO 1944	Chandler, R. (*Farewell, My Lovely*) Hamilton
MURDER OF A MODERATE MAN BBC 1985 (TV)	Howlett, J. Arrow

TITLE OF FILM	AUTHOR AND PUBLISHER
MURDER OF DR. HARRIGAN IN 1936	Eberhart, M.G. (*From This Dark Stairway*) Heinemann
MURDER ON A BRIDLE PATH RKO 1936	Palmer, S. (*Puzzle of the Briar Pipe*) Collins
MURDER ON A HONEYMOON RKO 1935	Palmer, S. (*Puzzle of the Pepper Tree*) Jarrolds
MURDER ON DIAMOND ROW UA 1937	Wallace, E. (*Squeaker, The*) Hodder & Stoughton
MURDER ON THE ORIENT EXPRESS (V) EMI 1974	Christie, A. Collins
MURDER ON THE SECOND FLOOR, THE WAR 1941	Vosper, F. (P) French
MURDER REPORTED COL 1957	Chapman, R. (*Murder for the Millions*) Laurie
MURDER SHE SAID MGM 1961	Christie, A. (*4.50 from Paddington*) Collins
MURDERS IN THE RUE MORGUE UN 1932	Poe, E.A. Various
MURDER WITHOUT CRIME ABP 1950	Thompson, J.L. (P) French
MURDER WITH PICTURES PAR 1936	Coxe, G.H. Heinemann
MURPHY'S ROMANCE COL—EMI—WAR 1985	Schott, M. Capra: Santa Barbara
MURPHY'S WAR (V) PAR 1971	Catto, M. Heinemann
MUSIC LOVERS, THE (V) UA 1971	Bowen, C.D. Hodder & Stoughton

TITLE OF FILM	AUTHOR AND PUBLISHER
MUTINY ON THE BOUNTY (V) MGM 1935 MGM 1962	Nordhoff, J.N. *and* Hall, C. Chapman & Hall
MY BRILLIANT CAREER (V) GUO 1979	Franklin, M. St. Martin's, N.Y.
MY BROTHER JONATHAN AB 1948 BBC 1985 (TV)	Young, F.B. Heinemann
MY COUSIN RACHEL FOX 1952 NBC 1984 (TV)	Du Maurier, D. Gollancz
MY DAUGHTER JOY BL 1950	Nemirowsky, I. (*David Golden*) Constable
MY DEATH IS A MOCKERY ADELPHI 1952	Baber, D. Heinemann
MY FAIR LADY (V) WAR 1964	Lerner, A.J. (P) Constable
MY FAIR LADY WAR 1964	Shaw, G.B. (*Pygmalion*) (P) Constable
MY FORBIDDEN PAST RKO 1951	Banks, P. (*Carriage Entrance*) Putnam, N.Y.
MY FRIEND FLICKA FOX 1943	O'Hara, M. Eyre & Spottiswoode
MY GLORIOUS BROTHERS UA 1959	Fast, H. Panther
MY GUN IS QUICK UA 1957	Spillane, M. Barker
MY LOVER, MY SON MGM 1969	Grierson, E. (*Reputation for a Song*) Chatto & Windus
MY MAN GODFREY UN 1936 UI 1957	Hatch, E. Barker

TITLE OF FILM	AUTHOR AND PUBLISHER
MY NAME IS JULIA ROSS COL 1945	Gilbert, A. (*Woman in Red, The*) Collins
MY OLD MAN (V) AMERICAN NAT.ENT. 1984	Hemingway, E. Cape
MY OWN TRUE LOVE PAR 1948	Foldes, Y. (*Make You a Fine Wife*) Hutchinson
MY PLEASURE IS MY BUSINESS (V) MIRACLE FILMS 1975	Hollander, X. (*Happy Hooker, The*) Talmy-Franklin
MYRA BRECKENRIDGE FOX 1969	Vidal, G. Blond
MY REPUTATION WAR 1946	Jaynes, C. World, N.Y.
MY SIDE OF THE MOUNTAIN PAR 1968	George, J. Bodley Head
MY SISTER AND I GFD 1948	Bonett, E. (*High Pavement*) Heinemann
MY SISTER EILEEN COL 1942 COL 1955	Fields, J. *and* Chodorov, J. (P) Macmillan
MY SISTER EILEEN COL 1942 COL 1955	McKenney, R. Chatto & Windus
MY SIX CONVICTS COL 1952	Wilson, D.P. Hamilton
MY SON, MY SON UA 1940	Spring, H. Collins
MYSTERIES OF THE GODS EMI 1976	Daniken, E. (*Chariots of the Gods*) Corgi
MYSTERIOUS DR. FU MANCHU PAR 1929	Rohmer, S. (*Mystery of Dr. Fu Manchu, The*) Methuen

TITLE OF FILM	AUTHOR AND PUBLISHER
MYSTERIOUS ISLAND COL 1962	Verne, J. Dent
MYSTERIOUS RIDER, THE PAR 1933 PAR 1938	Grey, Z. Hodder & Stoughton
MYSTERY HOUSE WAR 1938	Eberhart, M.G. (*Mystery of Hunting's End*) Lane
MYSTERY OF EDWIN DROOD UN 1935	Dickens, C. Various
MYSTERY OF MARIE ROGET UN 1942	Poe, E.A. Various
MYSTERY OF ROOM 13 ALL 1941	Wallace, E. (*Room 13*) Allied Press
MY WIFE'S FAMILY ABP 1956	Duprez, F. (P) French

N

NADIA CHANNEL 4 1986 (TV)	Comaneci, N. Duckworth
NAKED AND THE DEAD, THE (V) WAR 1958	Mailer, N. Wingate
NAKED COUNTRY NEW SOUTH WALES 1984	West, M. Coronet
NAKED EDGE, THE UA 1961	Ehrlich, M. (*First Train to Babylon*) Gollancz
NAKED FACE, THE (V) CANNON 1983	Sheldon, S. Morrow, N.Y.
NAKED HEART, THE BL 1950	Hemon, L. (*Maria Chapdelaine*) Macmillan

NAKED HOURS, THE
COMPTON 1965

Moravia, A. (*Appointment at the Beach*)
Secker & Warburg

NAKED IN THE SUN
RKO 1956

Slaughter, F.G. (*Warrior, The*)
Doubleday, N.Y.

NAKED JUNGLE, THE
PAR 1953

Stephenson, C. (*Leiningen Versus the Ants*)
Barker

NAKED RUNNER, THE
WAR 1966

Clifford, F.
Hodder & Stoughton

NANA (V)
MGM 1933
GALA 1955
CANNON 1983

Zola, E.
Various

NANNY, THE
WAR 1965

Piper, E.
Secker & Warburg

NARROW CORNER
WAR 1933

Maugham, W.S.
Heinemann

NARROWING CIRCLE, THE
EROS 1955

Symons, J.
Gollancz

NASTY HABITS (V)
SCOTIA BARBER 1976
U.S. title: The Abbess

Spark, M. (*Abbess of Crewe, The*)
Penguin

NATIONAL HEALTH
COL—WAR 1973

Nichols, P. (P)
Faber

NATIONAL VELVET
MGM 1944

Bagnold, E. (P)
Heinemann

NATIVE SON
CLASSIC 1951

Wright, R.
Gollancz

NATIVE SON
CLASSIC 1951

Green, P. *and* Wright, R. (P)
Harper, N.Y.

TITLE OF FILM	AUTHOR AND PUBLISHER
NATURAL, THE (V) COL—EMI—WAR 1984	Malamud, B. Chatto & Windus
NEGATIVES WALTER READE 1979	Everett, P. Cape
NEIGHBORS COL—EMI—WAR 1981	Berger, T. Dell, N.Y.
NEITHER THE SEA NOR THE SAND TIGON 1972	Honeycombe, G. Hutchinson
NELLY'S VERSION MITHRAS 1983	Figes, E. (*Waking, The*) Hamilton
NET, THE GFD 1952	Pudney, J. Joseph
NEVADA PAR 1935	Grey, Z. Hodder & Stoughton
NEVADA SMITH PAR 1963	Robbins, H. (*Carpetbaggers, The*) Blond
NEVER A DULL MOMENT RKO 1950	Swift, K. (*Who Could Ask For Anything More*) Simon & Schuster, N.Y.
NEVER BACK LOSERS AA 1962	Wallace, E. (*Green Ribbon, The*) Hutchinson
NEVER CRY WOLF DISNEY 1983	Mowat, F. Bantam, N.Y.
NEVER ENDING STORY, THE WAR 1985	Ende, M. Lane
NEVER GIVE AN INCH (V) RANK 1972	Kesey, K. (*Sometimes a Great Notion*) Methuen
NEVER LET ME GO MGM 1953	Bax, R. (*Come the Dawn*) Hutchinson
NEVER LOVE A STRANGER ABP 1957	Robbins, H. Corgi

TITLE OF FILM	AUTHOR AND PUBLISHER
NEVER SO FEW MGM 1959	Chamales, T. Pan
NEVER TAKE NO FOR AN ANSWER INDEPENDENT 1951	Gallico, P.W. (*Small Miracle, The*) Joseph
NEVER THE TWAIN SHALL MEET MGM 1931	Kyne, P.B. Various
NEVER TOO LATE WAR 1965	Long, S.A. (P) French, N.Y.
NEW INTERNS, THE COL 1964	Frede, R. (*Interns, The*) Corgi
NEW MORALS FOR OLD MGM 1932	Druten, J. van (*After All*) (P) Gollancz
NICE GIRL LIKE ME, A (V) AVCO EMBASSY 1969	Piper, A. (*Sweet and Plenty*) Heinemann
NICHOLAS AND ALEXANDRA (V) COL 1971	Massie, R.K. Gollancz
NICHOLAS NICKLEBY (V) EALING 1947 CHANNEL 4 1982 (TV)	Dickens, C. Various
NIGHT AND THE CITY FOX 1950	Kersh, G. Heinemann
NIGHTCOMERS RANK 1959	Ambler, E. Hodder & Stoughton
NIGHTCOMERS, THE AVCO EMBASSY 1972	Hastings, M. Pan
NIGHT COMES TOO SOON BUTCHER 1947	Lytton, B. (*Haunted and the Haunters, The*) (P) Various
NIGHT DIGGER, THE MGM 1971	Cowley, J. (*Nest in a Falling Tree*) Secker & Warburg

NIGHTFALL
HEMDALE 1982

Asimov, I.
Panther

NIGHT GAMES (V)
GALA 1966

Zetterling, M.
Constable

NIGHT HAS A THOUSAND EYES
PAR 1948

Hopley, G.
Oxford U.P.

NIGHT HAS EYES, THE
ANGLO-AMERICAN 1952

Kennington, A.
Jarrolds

NIGHT IN HAVANA
UA 1957

Sylvester, R. (*Big Boodle, The*)
Random House, N.Y.

NIGHT IN NEW ORLEANS, A
PAR 1942

Langham, J.R. (*Sing a Song of Murder*)
Hale

NIGHT LIFE OF THE GODS
UN 1935

Smith, T.
Methuen

NIGHTMARE ALLEY
FOX 1947

Gresham, W.
Heinemann

NIGHTMARE IN DUBLIN
RANK 1957

Loraine, P. (*Dublin Nightmare*)
Hodder & Stoughton

NIGHT MUST FALL
MGM 1937
MGM 1964

Williams, E. (P)
Gollancz

NIGHT OF JANUARY 16TH
PAR 1941

Rand, A. (P)
Longmans

NIGHT OF THE BIG HEAT
PLANET 1967

Lymington, J.
Hodder & Stoughton

NIGHT OF THE DEMON
COL 1957

James, M.R. (*Casting the Runes*)
Arnold

NIGHT OF THE GENERALS, THE (V)
BL 1966

Kirst, H.H.
Collins

TITLE OF FILM	AUTHOR AND PUBLISHER
NIGHT OF THE HUNTER, THE UA 1955	Grubb, D. Hamilton
NIGHT OF THE IGUANA, THE MGM 1963	Williams, T. (P) Secker & Warburg
NIGHT OF THE LEPUS MGM—EMI 1972	Braddon, R. (*Year of the Angry Rabbit, The*) Pan
NIGHT OF THE QUARTER MOON MGM 1959	Coen, F. Corgi
NIGHT TO REMEMBER, A (V) RANK 1957	Lord, W. Longmans
NIGHT UNTO NIGHT WAR 1949	Wylie, P. Farrar, N.Y.
NIGHT WAS OUR FRIEND MONARCH 1951	Pertwee, M. (P) English Theatre Guild
NIGHT WATCH AVCO EMBASSY 1973	Fletcher, L. (P) Random House, N.Y.
NIGHTWING (V) COL—EMI—WAR 1980	Smith, M.C. Norton, N.Y.
NIGHT WITHOUT STARS GFD 1951	Graham, W. Hodder & Stoughton
NIJINSKY PAR 1980	Nijinsky, R. AMS, N.Y.
NIJINSKY PAR 1980	Nijinsky, V. University of California
NIKKI, WILD DOG OF THE NORTH DISNEY 1961	Curwood, J.O. (*Nomads of the North*) Nelson
9½ WEEKS PALACE 1986	McNeill, E. Sphere
NINE HOURS TO RAMA FOX 1962	Wolpert, S. Hamilton

TITLE OF FILM	AUTHOR AND PUBLISHER
1915 BBC 2 1985 (TV)	Macdonald, R. Faber
1984 (V) ABP 1956	Orwell, G. Gollancz
NINE TILL SIX ATP 1932	Stuart, A. *and* Stuart, P. (P) French, N.Y.
NINTH CONFIGURATION, THE (V) ITC 1979	Blatty, W. Bantam, N.Y.
92 IN THE SHADE (V) ITC 1975	McGuane, T. Farrar, N.Y.
NO BLADE OF GRASS MGM—EMI 1972	Christopher, J. (*Death of Grass*) Penguin
NOBODY LIVES FOREVER (V) WAR 1946	Burnett, W.R. World, N.Y.
NOBODY RUNS FOREVER RANK 1968	Cleary, J. (*High Commissioner, The*) Collins
NO DOWN PAYMENT FOX 1957	McPartland, J. Macdonald
NO HANDS ON THE CLOCK PAR 1941	Homes, G. Various
NO HIGHWAY FOX 1951	Shute, N. Heinemann
NO KIDDING AA 1960	Anderson, V. (*Beware of Children*) Hart-Davis
NO LOVE FOR JOHNNIE RANK 1960	Fienburgh, W. Hutchinson
NO MAN OF HER OWN PAR 1950	Irish, W. (*I Married a Dead Man*) Lippincott, Philadelphia
NO MORE ORCHIDS COL 1932	Perkins, G. Wright & Brown

TITLE OF FILM	AUTHOR AND PUBLISHER
NONE BUT THE LONELY HEART RKO 1944	Llewellyn, R. Joseph
NO ONE MAN PAR 1932	Hughes, R. Jarrolds
NO ORCHIDS FOR MISS BLANDISH ALL 1948	Chase, J.H. Jarrolds
NOOSE FOR A LADY AA 1953	Verner, G. (*Whispering Woman*) Wright & Brown
NO PLACE FOR JENNIFER ABP 1949	Hambledon, P. (*No Difference to me*) Sampson Low
NO RESTING PLACE ABP 1951	Niall, I. Heinemann
NO ROAD BACK RKO 1956	Cary, F.L. *and* Weathers, P. (*Madam Tic-Tac*) (P) French
NO ROOM AT THE INN BN 1948	Temple, J. (P) Sampson Low
NO ROOM FOR THE GROOM UI 1952	Teilhet, D.L. (*My True Love*) Gollancz
NORTH AND SOUTH WAR 1985 (TV)	Jakes, J. Collins
NORTH DALLAS FORTY (V) PAR 1980	Gent, P. Morrow, N.Y.
NOR THE MOON BY NIGHT RANK 1958	Packer, J. Eyre & Spottiswoode
NORTHERN PATROL ABP 1954	Curwood, J.O. (*Nomads of the North*) Various
NORTH OF THE RIO GRANDE PAR 1937	Mulford, C.E. (*Cottonwood Gulch*) Hodder & Stoughton
NORTH SEA HIJACK CIC 1980	Davies, J. (*Esther, Ruth and Jennifer*) W.H. Allen

TITLE OF FILM	AUTHOR AND PUBLISHER
NORTH STAR RKO 1933	Hellman, L.F. Macmillan
NORTH STAR CRUSADE ITC 1978	Katz, W. Arrow
NORTH-WEST MOUNTED POLICE PAR 1940	Fetherstonhaugh, R.C. (*Royal Canadian Mounted Police*) Various
NORTH-WEST PASSAGE MGM 1940	Roberts, K. Collins
NORWOOD PAR 1971	Portis, C. Cape
NO SAD SONGS FOR ME COL 1950	Southard, R. Doubleday, N.Y.
NO SEX PLEASE—WE'RE BRITISH (V) COL—WAR 1974	Marriott, A. (P) French
NOT AS A STRANGER UA 1955	Thompson, M. Joseph
NOT FOR HONOUR AND GLORY COL 1965	Larteguy, J. (*Yellow Fever*) Hutchinson
NOTHING BUT THE NIGHT FOX—RANK 1972	Blackburn, J. Cape
NO TIME FOR COMEDY WAR 1940	Behrman, S.N. (P) Random House, N.Y.
NO TIME FOR SERGEANTS WAR 1958	Hyman, M. Dent
NO TIME FOR SERGEANTS WAR 1958	Levin, I. *and* Hyman, M. (P) Random House, N.Y.
NOT NOW DARLING (V) MGM 1972	Chapman, J. *and* Cooney, R. (P) English Theatre
NOTORIOUS LANDLADY, THE COL 1962	Shulman, I. Gold Medal Bks

NOT QUITE JERUSALEM
RANK 1985

Kember, P. (P)
Methuen

NOW AND FOREVER (V)
ABP 1955

Delderfield, R.F. (*Orchard Walls, The*) (P)
French

NO WAY TO TREAT A LADY
PAR 1968

Goldman, W.
Coronet

NOW BARRABAS WAS A ROBBER
WAR 1949

Home, W.D. (*Now Barrabas*)
Longmans

NOWHERE TO GO
MGM 1958

Mackenzie, D.
Elek

NOWHERE TO RUN
MGM 1978 (TV)

Einstein, J. (*Blackjack Hijack*)
Fawcett, N.Y.

NOW, VOYAGER (V)
WAR 1949

Prouty, O.
Hodder & Stoughton

NUN'S STORY, THE
WAR 1958

Hulme, K.
Muller

NURSE
CHANNEL 4 1984 (TV)

Anderson, P.
Star

NURSE ON WHEELS
WAR 1963

Jones, J. (*Nurse is a Neighbour*)
Joseph

NURSE'S SECRET, THE
WAR 1941

Rinehart, M.R. (*Miss Pinkerton*)
Various

O

OBLONG BOX, THE (V)
AA 1969

Poe, E.A.
Collins

OBSESSION (V)
GFD 1949

Coppel, A. (*Man About a Dog, A*)
Harrap

OCTOBER MAN, THE
GFD 1947

Ambler, E.
Hodder & Stoughton

TITLE OF FILM	AUTHOR AND PUBLISHER
OCTOPUSSY (V) UIP 1983	Fleming, I. Cape
ODD MAN OUT (V) TC 1947	Green, F.L. Joseph
ODDS AGAINST TOMORROW UA 1959	McGivern, W. Fontana
ODESSA FILE, THE COL 1974	Forsyth, F. Hutchinson
ODETTE, G.C. BL 1950	Tickell, J. Chapman & Hall
OEDIPUS THE KING UI 1968	Sophocles (P) Various
OEDIPUS REX OEDIPUS REX 1956	Sophocles (P) Various
OFFENCE, THE UA 1972	Hopkins, J. (*This Story of Yours*) (P) Penguin
OFFICER AND A GENTLEMAN, AN (V) COL 1984	Smith, S. Avon, N.Y.
OFFICE WIFE WAR 1930	Baldwin, F. Sampson Low
OF HUMAN BONDAGE RKO 1934 WAR 1946 MGM 1963	Maugham, W.S. Heinemann
OF MICE AND MEN UA 1939	Steinbeck, J. Heinemann
OF MICE AND MEN UA 1939	Steinbeck, J. (P) Covici, N.Y.
OH DAD, POOR DAD PAR 1966	Kopit, A. (. . . *Mama's Hung You In The Closet and I'm Feeling So Sad*) (P) Methuen

TITLE OF FILM	AUTHOR AND PUBLISHER
OH! FOR A MAN! FOX 1957	Axelrod, G. (*Will Success Spoil Rock Hunter?*) (P) Random House, N.Y.
OH! GOD! (V) COL—WAR 1977	Corman, A. Simon & Schuster, N.Y.
OH! MEN! OH! WOMEN! FOX 1957	Chodorov, E. (P) French
OH! SAILOR BEHAVE! WAR 1931	Rice, E. (*See Naples and Die*) (P) French, N.Y.
OIL FOR THE LAMPS OF CHINA WAR 1935	Hobart, *Mrs.* A.T. Cassell
OLD ACQUAINTANCE WAR 1943	Druten, J. van (P) Random House, N.Y.
OLD DARK HOUSE, THE UN 1932 BL 1963	Priestley, J.B. (*Benighted*) Heinemann
OLD ENGLISH WAR 1930	Galsworthy, J. (P) Duckworth
OLD FASHIONED GIRL, AN EL 1948	Alcott, L.M. Sampson Low
OLD MAID, THE WAR 1939	Wharton, *Mrs.* E.N. Grosset, N.Y.
OLD MAN AND THE SEA WAR 1957	Hemingway, E. Cape
OLD MAN AT THE ZOO, THE BBC 1983 (TV)	Wilson, A. Panther
OLD YELLER (V) DISNEY 1958	Gipson, F.B. Harper, N.Y.
OLIVER (V) COL 1968	Dickens, C. (*Oliver Twist*) Various

TITLE OF FILM	AUTHOR AND PUBLISHER
OLIVER'S STORY CIC 1979	Segal, E. Harper, N.Y.
OLIVER TWIST (V) MON 1933 CINEGUILD 1948 TRIDENT 1982 BBC 1985 (TV)	Dickens, C. Various
OLIVIA FDF 1950	'Olivia' Hogarth Press
OMEGA MAN, THE COL—WAR 1971	Matheson, R. (*I am Legend*) Bantam
OMEN, THE (V) FOX 1976	Seltzer, D. Futura
ON APPROVAL FOX 1944	Lonsdale, F. (P) Collins
ON BORROWED TIME MGM 1939	Watkins, L.E. Davies
ON BORROWED TIME MGM 1939	Osborne, P. (P) Dramatists, N.Y.
ONCE A JOLLY SWAGMAN WESSEX 1949	Slater, M. Lane
ONCE IS NOT ENOUGH PAR 1975	Susann, J. W.H. Allen
ONCE MORE MY DARLING UI 1949	Davis, *Mrs.* L. (*Come Be My Love*) Doubleday, N.Y.
ONCE MORE, WITH FEELING COL 1959	Kurnitz, H. (P) Random House, N.Y.
ONCE UPON A TIME IN AMERICA (V) COL—EMI—WAR 1983	Hays, L. New American Library, N.Y.
ONE DAY IN THE LIFE OF IVAN DENIZOVICH CINERAMA 1971	Solzhenitsyn, A. Bodley Head

TITLE OF FILM	AUTHOR AND PUBLISHER
ONE DESIRE UI 1955	Richter, C. (*Tracy Cromwell*) Knopf, N.Y.
ONE EYED JACKS PAR 1960	Neider, C. (*Authentic Death of Hendry Jones, The*) Harper, N.Y.
ONE FLEW OVER THE CUCKOO'S NEST (V) UA 1975	Kersey, K. Viking, N.Y.
ONE FOOT IN HEAVEN WAR 1941	Spence, H. Harrap
ONE HUNDRED AND ONE DALMATIANS DISNEY 1960	Smith, D. Heinemann
100 RIFLES FOX 1969	MacLeod, R. (*Californio, The*) Coronet
ONE JUMP AHEAD GFD 1955	Chapman, R. Laurie
ONE MORE RIVER UN 1934	Galsworthy, J. (*Over the River*) Heinemann
ONE MORE SPRING FOX 1950	Nathan, R. Cassell
ONE MORE TOMORROW WAR 1946	Barry, P. (*Animal Kingdom*) (P) French, N.Y.
ONE NIGHT IN LISBON PAR 1941	Druten, J. van (*There's Always Juliet*) (P) French, N.Y.
ONE OF OUR DINOSAURS IS MISSING (V) DISNEY 1975	Forrest, D. (*Great Dinosaur Robbery, The*) Hodder & Stoughton
ONE OF THOSE THINGS RANK 1971	Bodelsen, A. (*Hit, and Run, Run, Run*) Joseph

TITLE OF FILM	AUTHOR AND PUBLISHER
ONE ROMANTIC NIGHT UA 1930	Molnar, F. (*Swan, The*) (P) Longmans, N.Y.
ONE SHOE MAKES IT MURDER LORIMAR 1983 (TV)	Beresvici, E. Dell, N.Y.
ONE SUNDAY AFTERNOON PAR 1933 WAR 1948	Hagan, P. (P) French, N.Y.
ONE THAT GOT AWAY, THE (V) RANK 1957	Burt, K. *and* Leasor, J. Collins *and* Joseph
ONE THIRD OF A NATION PAR 1939	Arent, A. *ed*. Random House, N.Y.
ONE TOUCH OF VENUS UN 1948	Perelman, S.J. *and* Nash, O. (P) Little, Brown, Boston
ONE WAY PENDULUM UA 1964	Simpson, N.F. (P) Methuen
ONE WAY TICKET COL 1935	Turner, E. Constable
ONE WILD OAT EROS 1951	Sylvaine, V. (P) French
ON FRIDAY AT 11 BL 1961	Chase, J.H. (*World In My Pocket, The*) Pan
ON GOLDEN POND (V) CIC 1981	Thompson, E. (P) Dodd, N.Y.
ON HER MAJESTY'S SECRET SERVICE (V) UA 1969	Fleming, I. Cape
ONION FIELD, THE AVCO 1979	Wambaugh, J. Delacorte, N.Y.
ONIONHEAD WAR 1958	Hill, W. Deutsch

TITLE OF FILM	AUTHOR AND PUBLISHER
ONLY GAME IN TOWN, THE FOX 1969	Gilroy, F.D. (P) Random House, N.Y.
ONLY THE VALIANT WAR 1950	Warren, C.M. Macmillan, N.Y.
ONLY TWO CAN PLAY (V) BL 1961	Amis, K. (*That Uncertain Feeling*) Gollancz
ONLY WHEN I LARF (V) PAR 1969	Deighton, L. Sphere
ONLY WHEN I LAUGH (V) COL 1981	Simon, N. (*Gingerbread Lady*) (P) French
ON THE BEACH UA 1959	Shute, N. Heinemann
ON THE FIDDLE AA 1961	Delderfield, R.F. (*Stop at a Winner*) Hodder & Stoughton
ON THE NIGHT OF THE FIRE SOMLO 1939	Green, F.L. Joseph
ON THE RUN CFF 1969	Bawden, N. Gollancz
OPERATION AMSTERDAM (V) RANK 1958	Walker, D.E. (*Adventure in Diamonds*) Evans
OPERATION DAYBREAK (V) COL—WAR 1975	Burgess, A. (*Seven Men at Daybreak*) Mayflower
OPERATION MADBALL COL 1962	Carter, A. (P) French, N.Y.
OPERATION UNDERCOVER UA 1975	Mills, J. Farrar, N.Y.
OPPOSITE SEX, THE MGM 1956	Booth, C. (*Women, The*) (P) Dramatists Play Service
OPTIMISTS OF NINE ELMS, THE SCOTIA-BARBER 1973	Simmons, H. Methuen

TITLE OF FILM	AUTHOR AND PUBLISHER
ORDEAL BY INNOCENCE (V) CANNON 1985	Christie, A. Collins
ORDERS ARE ORDERS (V) BL 1954	Hay, I. *and* Armstrong, A. (P) French
ORDINARY PEOPLE PAR 1981	Guest, J. Viking, N.Y.
OREGON PASSAGE ABP 1957	Shirrefs, G.D. (*Trails End*) Avalon, N.Y.
ORIENT EXPRESS FOX 1934	Greene, G. (*Stamboul Train*) Heinemann
OSCAR, THE PAR 1965	Sale, R. Cassell
OSTERMAN WEEKEND, THE (V) J & M FILMS 1983	Ludlum, R. Hart-Davis
OTHELLO UA 1956 EAGLE FILMS 1966	Shakespeare, W. (P) Various
OTHELLO THE BLACK COMMANDO M B DIFFUSION 1982 (TV)	Shakespeare, W. (*Othello*) (P) Various
OTHER, THE FOX 1972	Tryon, T. Knopf, N.Y.
OTHER HALVES CONT 1986	McCauley, S. Hodder & Stoughton
OTHER SIDE OF MIDNIGHT, THE (V) FOX 1977	Sheldon, S. Hodder & Stoughton
OTLEY COL 1969	Waddell, M. Hodder & Stoughton
OUR BETTERS RKO 1933	Maugham, W.S. (P) Heinemann
OUR HEARTS WERE YOUNG AND GAY PAR 1944	Skinner, C.O. *and* Kimbrugh, E. Constable

OUR MAN IN HAVANA
COL 1959

Greene, G.
Heinemann

OUR MOTHER'S HOUSE
MGM 1967

Gloag, J.
Pan

OUR TOWN
UA 1940

Wilder, T.N. (P)
Coward-McCann, N.Y.

OUR VINES HAVE TENDER GRAPES
MGM 1945

Martin, G.V. (*For . . .*)
Joseph

OUT
CINEGATE 1982

Sukenick, R.
Swallow

OUTCAST LADY
MGM 1935

Arlen, M. (*Green Hat, The*)
Collins

OUTCAST OF THE ISLANDS, AN
LF 1951

Conrad, J.
Various

OUTCASTS OF POKER FLAT
RKO 1937
FOX 1952

Harte, B.
Various

OUTFIT, THE (V)
MGM 1973

Stark, R.
Coronet

OUTLAW JOSEY WALES, THE (V)
COL—WAR 1976

Carter, F. (*Gone to Texas*)
Delacorte, N.Y.

OUT OF AFRICA
UN 1985

Thurman, J. (*Isak Dinesen*)
Weidenfeld & Nicolson

OUT OF AFRICA
UN 1985

Trzebinski, E. (*Silence Will Speak*)
Heinemann

OUT OF THE DARKNESS
CFF 1984 (TV)

Hoyland, J. (*Ivy Garland, The*)
Allison & Busby

OUT OF THE FOG
GN 1962

Graeme, B. (*Fog for a Killer*)
Hutchinson

OUT OF THE FOG
WAR 1941

Shaw, I. (*Gentle People, The*) (P)
Dramatists, N.Y.

OUTRAGE MGM 1964	Kanin, F. *and* Kanin, M. (*Rashomon*) (P) Random House, N.Y.
OUTSIDER, THE (V) PAR 1968	Camus, A. Hamilton
OUTSIDERS, THE WAR 1982	Hinton, S.E. Gollancz
OUTWARD BOUND WAR 1930	Vane, S. (P) Boni, N.Y.
OVERLANDERS, THE EALING 1946	Butler, D. World Film Pubns
OVER 21 COL 1945	Gordon, R. (P) Dramatists, N.Y.
OWD BOB BG 1937	Olivant, A. Various
OWL AND THE PUSSYCAT, THE (V) COL 1970	Manhoff, B. (P) French
OX-BOW INCIDENT, THE FOX 1956	Clark, W. van T. Gollancz
OXBRIDGE BLUES BBC 1984 (TV)	Raphaelson, F. Penguin

P

PACIFIC DESTINY BL 1956	Grimble, *Sir* A. (*Pattern of Islands*) Murray
PACK, THE COL—WAR 1977	Fisher, D. W.H. Allen
PAD, THE (AND HOW TO USE IT) UI 1967	Shaffer, P. (*Private Ear, The*) (P) French
PADDY FOX 1969	Dunne, L. (*Goodbye to the Hill*) Hutchinson

TITLE OF FILM	AUTHOR AND PUBLISHER
PADDY THE NEXT BEST THING FOX 1933	Page, G. Hurst & Blackett
PAGANINI STRIKES AGAIN CFF 1973	Lee, B. Hutchinson
PAINTED HILLS MGM 1951	Hull, A. (*Shep of the Painted Hills*) Chapman & Hall
PAINTED VEIL, THE MGM 1934	Maugham, W.S. Heinemann
PAIR OF BRIEFS RANK 1961	Brooke, H. *and* Bannerman, K. (*How Say You?*) (P) Evans
PAJAMA GAME WAR 1957	Bissell, R.P. (*7½ cents*) Little, Brown, Boston
PAJAMA GAME WAR 1957	Abbott, G. *and* Bissell, R.P. (P) Random House, N.Y.
PALE RIDER COL—EMI—WAR 1985	Foster, A.D. Arrow
PAL JOEY COL 1957	O'Hara, J. Cresset Press
PANIC IN NEEDLE PARK, THE (V) FOX 1971	Mills, J. Sphere
PANTHER'S MOON GFD 1950	Canning, V. Hodder & Stoughton
PAPER CHASE FOX 1974	Osborn, J.J. Houghton, Mifflin, Boston
PAPER MOON PAR 1973	Brown, J.D. (*"Addie Pray"*) Hodder & Stoughton
PAPER ORCHID COL 1949	La Bern, A.J. Marlowe
PAPILLON (V) COL 1973	Charriere, H. Hart-Davis

216

PARADINE CASE, THE (V) BI 1949	Hichens, R. Convoy Bks
PARADISE FOR THREE MGM 1938	Kastner, E. (*Three Men in the Snow*) Cape
PARADISE POSTPONED EUSTON 1986 (TV)	Mortimer, J. Penguin
PARALLAX VIEW, THE (V) HEMDALE 1978	Singer, L. Doubleday, N.Y.
PARENT TRAP, THE DISNEY 1961	Kastner, E. (*Lottie and Lisa*) Cape
PARIS BLUES UA 1961	Flender, H. Panther
PARIS-UNDERGROUND UA 1945	Shiber, *Mrs.* E. Harrap
PARK IS MINE, THE RAMBLE 1985 (TV)	Peters, S. Blondi & Briggs
PARNELL MGM 1937	Schauffler, E. (P) Gollancz
PAROLE FIXER PAR 1940	Hoover, J.E. (*Persons in Hiding*) Dent
PARRISH WAR 1960	Savage, M. Longmans
PARSON OF PANAMINT, THE PAR 1941	Kyne, P.B. Grosset, N.Y.
PARTNERS IN CRIME AA 1960	Wallace, E. (*Man Who Knew, The*) Newnes
PASSAGE, THE (V) HEMDALE 1978	Nicolaysen, B. (*Perilous Passage, The*) Playboy, N.Y.
PASSAGE FROM HONG KONG WAR 1941	Biggers, E.D. (*Agony Column*) Bobbs-Merrill, Indianapolis

PASSAGE HOME
GFD 1955

Armstrong, R.
Dent

PASSAGES FROM JAMES JOYCE'S
FINNEGAN'S WAKE
CONT 1969

Joyce, J. (*Finnegan's Wake*)
Faber

PASSAGE TO INDIA, A. (V)
COL—EMI 1984

Forster, E.M.
Dent

PASSENGERS
COL—WAR 1976

Dwyer, K.R. (*Shattered*)
Barker

PASSING OF THE THIRD FLOOR BACK,
THE
GB 1936

Jerome, J.K.
Hurst & Blackett

PASSIONATE FRIENDS, THE
CINEGUILD 1949

Wells, H.G.
Benn

PASSIONATE SUMMER, THE
RANK 1958

Mason, R. (*Shadow and the Peak,*
The)
Collins

PASSION FLOWER
MGM 1930

Norris, K.
Murray

PASSPORT TO TREASON
EROS 1956

O'Brine, M.
Hammond

PASSWORD IS COURAGE, THE
MGM 1962

Castle, J.
Souvenir Press

PASTOR HALL
UA 1940

Toller, E. (P)
Lane

PATCH OF BLUE, A
MGM 1966

Kata, E. (*Be Ready With Bells and*
Drums)
Penguin

PATHFINDER, THE
COL 1953

Cooper, J.F.
Various

PATHS OF GLORY
UA 1957

Cobb, H.
Heinemann

TITLE OF FILM	AUTHOR AND PUBLISHER
PATIENT IN ROOM 18, THE WAR 1938	Eberhart, M.G. Heinemann
PATTON: LUST FOR GLORY (V) FOX 1970	Farago, L. (*Patton*) Mayflower
PAWNBROKER, THE (V) PAR 1964	Wallant, E.L. Gollancz
PAYMENT DEFERRED MGM 1932	Forester, C.S. Lane
PAYMENT DEFERRED MGM 1932	Forester, C.S. (P) Lane
PAYROLL AA 1960	Bickerton, D. Eyre & Spottiswoode
PEARL, THE RKO 1948	Steinbeck, J. Heinemann
PEARL OF DEATH UN 1944	Doyle, *Sir* A.C. (*Six Napoleons*) Murray
PEEPER (V) FOX—RANK 1975	Laumer, K. (*Deadfall*) Hale
PENELOPE MGM 1966	Cunningham, E.V. Deutsch
PENROD AND SAM IN 1931 WAR 1937	Tarkington, B. (*Penrod*) Hodder & Stoughton
PEOPLE AGAINST O'HARA, THE MGM 1951	Lipsky, E. Wingate
PEOPLE THAT TIME FORGOT, THE (V) BRENT WALKER 1977	Burroughs, E.R. Various
PEOPLE VERSUS DR. KILDARE, THE (V) MGM 1941	Brand, M. (*Dr. Kildare's Trial*) Dodd, N.Y.

TITLE OF FILM	AUTHOR AND PUBLISHER
PERCY (V) MGM—EMI 1971	Hitchcock, R. Sphere
PERFECT ALIBI, THE RKO 1931	Milne, A.A. (P) Putnam, N.Y.
PERFECT MARRIAGE, THE PAR 1946	Raphaelson, S. (P) Dramatists, N.Y.
PERIL FOR THE GUY PAR 1956	Kennett, J. Brockhampton
PERILOUS JOURNEY, A REP 1953	Roe, V. (*Golden Tide, The*) Cassell
PERIOD OF ADJUSTMENT MGM 1962	Williams, T. (P) Secker & Warburg
PERRI (V) DISNEY 1957	Salten, F. Cape
PERSONAL PROPERTY MGM 1937	Harwood, H.M. (*Man in Possession*) (P) Benn
PERSONS IN HIDING PAR 1939	Hoover, J.E. Dent
PETE 'N' TILLIE UN 1972	De Vries, P. (*Witch's Milk*) Gollancz
PETER IBBETSON PAR 1935	Du Maurier, G. Various
PETER PAN RKO 1953 DISNEY 1974	Barrie, *Sir* J.M. (P) Hodder & Stoughton
PETRIFIED FOREST, THE WAR 1936	Sherwood, R.E. (P) Scribner, N.Y.
PETULIA WAR 1968	Haase, J. (*Me and the Arch Kook Petulia*) Heinemann

TITLE OF FILM	AUTHOR AND PUBLISHER
PEYTON PLACE FOX 1957	Metalious, G. Muller
PHANTOM FRIEND, THE OLY 1935	Lowndes, *Mrs.* M.B. (*Lodger, The*) Methuen
PHANTOM LADY UN 1944	Irish, W. Lippincott, Philadelphia
PHANTOM OF THE OPERA, THE (V) UN 1943 UI 1962	Leroux, G. Various
PHANTOM OF THE RUE MORGUE WAR 1954	Poe, E.A. (*Murder in the Rue Morgue*) Various
PHANTOM STRIKES, THE MON 1939	Wallace, E. (*Ringer, The*) (P) Hodder & Stoughton
PHANTOM TOLLBOOTH, THE MGM 1969	Juster, N. Collins
PHILADELPHIA STORY MGM 1940	Barry, P. (P) French
PHYSICAL ASSAULT (V) TITAN 1973	Kolpacoff, V. (*Prisoners of Quai Dong, The*) Sphere
PICCADILLY JIM MGM 1936	Wodehouse, P.G. Jenkins
PICKWICK PAPERS, THE REN 1952 BBC 1985 (TV)	Dickens, C. Various
PICNIC COL 1955	Inge, W. (P) Random House, N.Y.
PICTURE OF DORIAN GRAY, THE MGM 1945	Wilde, O. Various
PIECES OF DREAMS UA 1975	Barrett, W.E. (*Wine and the Music, The*) Heinemann

PIED PIPER FOX 1942	Shute, N. Heinemann
PIGEON THAT TOOK ROME, THE PAR 1962	Downes, D. (*Easter Dinner, The*) Rinehart, N.Y.
PIGEON THAT WORKED A MIRACLE DISNEY 1958	Liggett, T. (*Pigeon Fly Home*) Holiday, N.Y.
PILGRIMAGE FOX 1933	Wylie, I.A.R. Cassell
PINK JUNGLE, THE UI 1968	Williams, A. (*Snake Water*) Panther
PINK STRING AND SEALING WAX EALING 1946	Pertwee, R. (P) English Theatre Guild
PINKY FOX 1949	Sumner, *Mrs.* C.R. (*Quality*) Dymock
PIRATE, THE MGM 1948	Behrman, S.N. (P) Random House, N.Y.
PIT AND THE PENDULUM, THE (V) AA 1961	Poe, E.A. Various
PITFALL UA 1948	Dratler, J. Oxford, U.P.
PIT OF DARKNESS BUTCHER 1961	McCutcheon, H. (*To Duty Death*) Long
PLACE IN THE SUN, A PAR 1951	Dreiser, T. (*American Tragedy, An*) Various
PLACE OF ONE'S OWN, A GFD 1945	Sitwell, *Sir* O. Macmillan
PLACE TO GO, A BL 1964	Fisher, M. (*Bethnal Green*) Cassell
PLAGUE DOGS, THE (V) DOLBY STEREO 1982	Adams, R.G. Lane

TITLE OF FILM	AUTHOR AND PUBLISHER
PLAINSMAN, THE PAR 1936	Wilstach, F. (*Wild Bill Hickok*) Sun Dial, N.Y.
PLANET OF THE APES FOX 1968	Boulle, P. (*Monkey Planet*) Penguin
PLAYBOY OF THE WESTERN WORLD, THE CHANNEL 4 1986 (TV)	Synge, J.M. (P) Methuen
PLAY IT AGAIN, SAM (V) PAR 1972	Allen, W. (P) Random House, N.Y.
PLAY IT AS IT LAYS UN 1972	Didion, J. Weidenfeld & Nicolson
PLAZA SUITE (V) PAR 1972	Simon, N. (P) French
PLEASE DON'T EAT THE DAISIES MGM 1960	Kerr, J. Heinemann
PLEASE TURN OVER AA 1959	Thomas, B. (*Book of the Month*) (P) French
PLEASURE OF HIS COMPANY, THE PAR 1959	Taylor, S.A. *and* Skinner, C.O. (P) Heinemann
PLEASURE SEEKERS, THE FOX 1965	Secondari, J.H. (*Coins in the Fountain*) Eyre & Spottiswoode
PLENTY (V) COL—EMI—WAR 1985	Hare, D. (P) New American Library, N.Y.
PLOUGH AND THE STARS, THE RKO 1936	O'Casey, S. (P) Macmillan
PLUNDER WILCOX 1937	Travers, B. (P) Bickers
PLUNDER OF THE SUN WAR 1953	Dodge, D. Random House, N.Y.

TITLE OF FILM	AUTHOR AND PUBLISHER
PLYMOUTH ADVENTURE, THE MGM 1952	Gebler, E. Cassell
POCKET FULL OF RYE, A BBC 1985 (TV)	Christie, A. Collins
POCKET MONEY (V) FIRST ARTISTS 1972	Brown, J.P.S. Sphere
POET'S PUB AQUILA 1949	Linklater, E. Cape
POINT BLANK (V) MGM 1967	Stark, R. Coronet
POISON PEN AB 1940	Llewellyn, R. (P) French
POLLYANNA DISNEY 1960	Porter, G.S. Harrap
POLLY FULTON MGM 1949	Marquand, J.P. Hale
POOKIE PAR 1969	Nichols, J. (*Sterile Cuckoo, The*) Pan
POOR COW WAR 1967	Dunn, N. McGibbon, & Kee
POPE OF GREENWICH VILLAGE, THE MGM/UA 1984	Patrick, V. Hodder & Stoughton
PORK CHOP HILL UA 1959	Marshall, S.L.A. Panther
PORT AFRIQUE COL 1956	Dryer, B.V. Cassell
PORTNOY'S COMPLAINT (V) COL—WAR 1972	Roth, P. Cape
PORTRAIT OF CLARE ABP 1949	Young, F.B. Heinemann

TITLE OF FILM	AUTHOR AND PUBLISHER
PORTRAIT OF THE ARTIST AS A YOUNG MAN ULYSSES FILM 1977	Joyce, J. Cape
POSEIDON ADVENTURE, THE (V) FOX 1972	Gallico, P. Pan
POSSESSION OF JOEL DELANEY, THE SCOTIA-BARBER 1971	Stewart, R. Deutsch
POSTMAN ALWAYS RINGS TWICE, THE (V) MGM 1946 ITC 1981	Cain, J.M. Cape
POWDERSMOKE RANGE RKO 1935	Macdonald, W.C. Collins
POWER, THE MGM 1968	Robinson, F. Sphere
POWER AND THE GLORY, THE PAR 1962	Greene, G. Heinemann
POWER AND THE PRIZE, THE MGM 1956	Swiggett, H. Hodder & Stoughton
PRECINCT 45—LOS ANGELES POLICE COL 1972	Wambaugh, J. (*New Centurians, The*) Little, Brown, Boston
PRELUDE TO FAME GFD 1950	Huxley, A.L. (*Young Archimedes*) Chatto & Windus
PREMATURE BURIAL, THE AA 1962	Poe, E.A. Various
PRESIDENT'S LADY, THE FOX 1953	Stone, I. (*Immortal Wife*) Invincible Press
PRESS FOR TIME (V) JARFID 1966	McGill, A. (*Yea, Yea, Yea*) Secker & Warburg
PRESSURE POINT UA 1963	Lindner, R. (*Fifty Minute Hour, The*) Corgi

TITLE OF FILM	AUTHOR AND PUBLISHER
PRETTY MAIDS ALL IN A ROW MGM—EMI 1971	Pollini, F. Spearman
PRETTY POISON (V) FOX 1968	Geller, S. (*She Let Him Continue*) Dutton, N.Y.
PRETTY POLLY RANK 1967	Coward, N. (*Pretty Polly Barlow*) Mayflower
PRICE, THE CHANNEL 4 1985 (TV)	Ransley, P. Corgi
PRICE OF SILENCE, THE GN 1959	Meynell, L. (*One Step From Murder*) Collins
PRICK UP YOUR EARS GAVIN 1986	Lahr, J. Avon, N.Y.
PRIDE AND PREJUDICE (V) MGM 1940	Austen, J. Various
PRIDE AND THE PASSION, THE UA 1957	Forester, C.S. (*Gun, The*) Joseph
PRIDE OF THE MARINES WAR 1945	Butterfield, R.P. (*Al Schmid, Marine*) Norton, N.Y.
PRIEST OF LOVE, THE (V) ENTERPRISE 1981	Moore, H.T. Heinemann
PRIME OF MISS JEAN BRODIE, THE FOX 1969	Spark, M. Macmillan
PRINCE AND THE PAUPER WAR 1937 DISNEY 1961 FOX 1977	Twain, M. Chatto & Windus
PRINCE OF FOXES FOX 1949	Shellabarger, S. Macmillan
PRINCE OF PLAYERS FOX 1954	Ruggles, E. Davies

TITLE OF FILM	AUTHOR AND PUBLISHER
PRINCE OF THE CITY (V) COL—EMI—WAR 1981	Daley, R. Hart-Davis
PRINCESS DAISY (V) ITV 1984 (TV)	Krantz, J. Sidgwick & Jackson
PRINCE WHO WAS A THIEF, THE GFD 1951	Dreiser, T. World, N.Y.
PRISONER, THE COL 1955	Boland, B. (P) Elek
PRISONER OF SECOND AVENUE, THE (V) COL—WAR 1975	Simon, N. (P) Random House, N.Y.
PRISONER OF ZENDA UA 1937 MGM 1952 CIC 1979 BBC 1984 (TV)	Hope, A. Harrap
PRIVATE AFFAIRS OF BEL AMI, THE UA 1947	De Maupassant, G. (*Bel Ami*) Various
PRIVATE ANGELO ABP 1949	Linklater, E. Cape
PRIVATE LIVES MGM 1931	Coward, N. (P) Heinemann
PRIVATE LIVES OF ELIZABETH AND ESSEX, THE WAR 1939	Anderson, M. (*Elizabeth the Queen*) (P) Longmans, N.Y.
PRIVATE'S PROGRESS, A BL 1956	Hackney, A. Gollancz
PRIVATE WORLDS PAR 1935	Bottome, P. Lane
PRIZE, THE MGM 1963	Wallace, I. Cassell

PRIZE OF GOLD, A
COL 1954

Catto, M.
Heinemann

PRIZE OF PERIL, THE
SAADA 1983

Sheckley, R.
Sphere

PRIZZI'S HONOUR
FOX 1985

Condon, R.
Joseph

PROFESSIONALS, THE (V)
COL 1966

O'Rourke, F. (*Mule for the Marquesa, A*)
Fontana

PROFESSOR TIM
RKO 1957

Sheils, G. (P)
Macmillan

PROMISE AT DAWN
AVCO EMBASSY 1971

Taylor, S. (*First Love*) (P)
Dramatists, N.Y.

PROMISE AT DAWN
AVCO EMBASSY 1971

Gary, R.
Joseph

PROUD AND PROFANE
PAR 1956

Crockett, L.H. (*Magnificent Devils*)
Dymock

PROUD ONES
FOX 1956

Athanas, V.
Rich & Cowan

PRUDENCE AND THE PILL
FOX 1968

Mills, H.
Triton

PSYCHE 59
BL 1964

Ligneris, F. (*Psyche 63*)
Spearman

PSYCHO (V)
PAR 1960

Block, R.
Hale

PT 109
WAR 1963

Donovan, R.J. (*Wartime Adventures of President John Kennedy, The*)
Panther

PUBLIC DEFENDER
RKO 1931

Goodchild, G. (*Splendid Crime, The*)
Hodder & Stoughton

TITLE OF FILM	AUTHOR AND PUBLISHER
PUMPKIN EATER, THE BL 1963	Mortimer, P. Penguin
PUMPING IRON CINEGATE 1976	Gaines, C. *and* Butler, G. Simon & Schuster, N.Y.
PUMPING IRON II BLUE DOLPHIN 1984	Gaines, C. *and* Butler, G. Simon & Schuster, N.Y.
PUPPET ON A CHAIN (V) SCOTIA-BARBER 1971	MacLean, A. Collins
PURPLE NOON HILLCREST 1961	Highsmith, P. (*Talented Mr. Ripley, The*) Pan
PURPLE PLAIN, THE (V) GFD 1954	Bates, H.E. Joseph
PURSUIT (V) BARBER 1981	Reed, J.D. (*Freefall*) Delacorte, N.Y.
PURSUIT OF HAPPINESS, THE COL 1971	Rogers, T. Bodley Head
PYGMALION MGM 1938	Shaw, G.B. (P) Constable

Q

QUALITY STREET RKO 1937	Barrie, *Sir* J.M. (P) Hodder & Stoughton
QUARE FELLOW, THE BL 1962	Behan, B. (P) Methuen
QUARTET FOX 1981	Rhys, J. Harper, N.Y.
QUARTETTE GFD 1949	Maugham, W.S. Heinemann
QUATERMAIN CANNON 1985	Haggard, *Sir* R. (*Allan Quatermain*) Various

TITLE OF FILM	AUTHOR AND PUBLISHER
QUEEN BEE COL 1955	Lee, E. Hurst & Blackett
QUEEN OF SPADES, THE AB 1949	Pushkin, A.S. Various
QUEEN OF THE MOB PAR 1940	Hoover, J.E. (*Persons in Hiding*) Dent
QUEST FOR FIRE (V) FOX 1982	Rosny, J.H. Ballantine, N.Y.
QUICK, BEFORE IT MEETS MGM 1964	Benjamin, P. Gollancz
QUIET DAYS IN CLICHY MIRACLE FILMS 1974	Miller, H. Calder
QUIET AMERICAN, THE UA 1957	Greene, G. Heinemann
QUIET FLOWS THE DON GALA 1958	Sholokhov, M. (*And Quiet Flows the Don*) Putnam
QUIET MAN, THE REP 1952	Walsh, M. Angus & Robertson
QUIET WEDDING PAR 1941	MacCracken, E. (P) French
QUIET WEEK END AB 1946	MacCracken, E. (P) French
QUILLER MEMORANDUM, THE (V) JARFID 1966	Hall, A. (*Berlin Memorandum, The*) Collins
QUO VADIS? (V) IN 1929 MGM 1949 CHANNEL 4 1986 (TV)	Sienkiewicz, H. Various

R

RABBIT, RUN
WAR 1969

Updike, J.
Deutsch

RACERS, THE
FOX 1954

Ruesch, H. (*Racer, The*)
Hurst & Blackett

RACHEL, RACHEL
WAR 1968

Laurence, M. (*Jest of God, A*)
Macmillan

RACKET, THE
RKO 1952

Cormack, B. (P)
French, N.Y.

RAFFLES
UA 1930
UA 1940

Hornung, E.W.
Grayson

RAGE IN HEAVEN
MGM 1941

Hilton, J. (*Dawn of Reckoning*)
Butterworth

RAGE OF ANGELS (V)
NBC 1983 (TV)

Sheldon, S.
Morrow, N.Y.

RAGE TO LIVE, A
UA 1964

O'Hara, J.
Cresset Press

RAGING BULL (V)
UA 1981

La Motta, J.
Bantam, N.Y.

RAGING MOON, THE (V)
MGM 1971

Marshall, P.
Tandem

RAGING TIDE, THE
UI 1951

Gann, E.K. (*Fiddler's Green*)
Sloane, N.Y.

RAGMAN'S DAUGHTER, THE (V)
FOX 1972

Sillitoe, A.
W.H. Allen

RAGTIME (V)
COL—EMI—WAR 1981

Doctorow, E.L.
Macmillan

RAILWAY CHILDREN, THE (V)
MGM 1970

Nesbit, E.
Various

RAIN
UA 1932

Maugham, W.S. (P)
Heinemann

RAINBOW TRAIL
FOX 1932

Grey, Z.
Harper

RAINMAKER, THE
PAR 1956

Nash, N.R. (P)
Random House, N.Y.

RAINS CAME, THE
FOX 1939

Bromfield, L.
Cassell

RAINS OF RANCHIPUR, THE
FOX 1955

Bromfield, L. (*Rains Came, The*)
Cassell

RAINTREE COUNTRY
MGM 1957

Lockridge, R.
Macdonald

RAISE THE TITANIC (V)
ITC 1980

Cussler, C.
Joseph

RAISING A RIOT
BL 1954

Toombs, A.
Hammond

RAISIN IN THE SUN, A
COL 1960

Hansberry, L. (P)
Methuen

"RALLY ROUND THE FLAG, BOYS"
FOX 1958

Shulman, M.
Heinemann

RAMONA
FOX 1936

Jackson, *Mrs*. H.M.
Sampson Low

RAMPAGE
WAR 1963

Caillou, A.
Davies

RAMROD
UA 1947

Short, L.
Collins

RANDOM HARVEST
MGM 1942

Hilton, J.
Macmillan

RAPE, THE
MIRACLE FILMS 1976

Freeling, N. (*Because of the Cats*)
Penguin

RAPTURE FOX 1964	Hastings, P. (*Rapture in my Rags*) Dent
RASCAL DISNEY 1969	North, S. (*Little Rascal*) Brockhampton
RAT, THE RKO 1938	Bottome, P. Allan
RAT RACE, THE PAR 1960	Kanin, G. (P) Dramatists, N.Y.
RATTLE OF A SIMPLE MAN (V) WAR 1964	Dyer, C. (P) French
RAVEN, THE UN 1935	Poe, E.A. Various
RAWHIDE YEARS, THE UI 1955	Fox, N.A. Collins
RAZORBACK (V) WAR 1983	Brennan, P. Jove, N.Y.
RAZOR'S EDGE, THE (V) FOX 1946 COLGEMS 1983	Maugham, W.S. Heinemann
REACH FOR GLORY GALA 1962	Rae, J. (*Custard Boys, The*) Hart-Davis
REACH FOR THE SKY (V) RANK 1956	Brickhill, P. Collins
REACH FOR TOMORROW COL 1959	Motley, W. (*Let No Man Write My Epitaph*) Longmans
REACHING FOR THE SUN PAR 1941	Smitter, W. (*F.O.B. Detroit*) Dent
REAL GLORY, THE UA 1939	Clifford, C.L. Heinemann

RE-ANIMATOR
EMPIRE 1985

Lovecraft, H.P. (*Herbert West—The Re-Animator*)
Various

REAP THE WILD WIND
PAR 1942

Strabel, T.
Collins

REBECCA (V)
UA 1940

Du Maurier, D.
Gollancz

REBECCA OF SUNNYBROOK FARM
FOX 1932
FOX 1938

Wiggins, *Mrs.* K.D.
Various

REBEL WITHOUT A CAUSE, A
WAR 1955

Schulman, I. (*Children of the Dark*)
World, N.Y.

RECKLESS MOMENT, THE
COL 1949

Holding, *Mrs.* E. (*Blank Wall*)
Simon & Schuster, N.Y.

RECKONING, THE
COL 1969

Hall, P. (*Harp That Once, The*)
Heinemann

RED BADGE OF COURAGE, THE
MGM 1951

Crane, S.
Various

RED BERET, THE
COL 1953

Saunders, H. St. G.
Joseph

RED CANYON
UN 1949

Grey, Z. (*Wildfire*)
Hodder & Stoughton

RED DANUBE
MGM 1949

Marshall, B.
Constable

RED DUST
MGM 1932

Collinson, W.
McBride, N.Y.

RED HOUSE, THE
UA 1947

Jerusalem, E.
Laurie

RED PEPPERS
GFD 1952

Coward, N. (P)
Heinemann

TITLE OF FILM	AUTHOR AND PUBLISHER
RED PONY, THE (V) BL 1949 BL 1976	Steinbeck, J. Viking Press, N.Y.
RED RIVER UA 1948	Chase, B. Sampson Low
RED SKY AT MORNING UN 1971	Bradford, R. Hodder & Stoughton
RED WAGON ALL 1935	Smith, *Lady* E. Gollancz
REFLECTION OF FEAR, A (V) COL—WAR 1972	Forbes, S. (*Go to thy Deathbed*) Hale
REFLECTIONS ARTIFICIAL EYE 1984	Banville, J. (*Newton Letter, The*) Secker & Warburg
REFLECTIONS IN A GOLDEN EYE WAR 1966	McCullers, C. Cresset Press
REILLY ACE OF SPIES EUSTON 1983 (TV)	Lockhart, R.B. Futura
REINCARNATION OF PETER PROUD, THE FOX RANK 1975	Ehrlich, M. W.H. Allen
REIVERS, THE WAR 1969	Faulkner, W. Chatto & Windus
RELUCTANT DEBUTANTE, THE MGM 1958	Home, W.D. (P) French
RELUCTANT HEROES (V) ABP 1951	Morris, C. (P) English Theatre Guild
RELUCTANT WIDOW, THE GFD 1950	Heyer, G. Heinemann
REMAINS TO BE SEEN MGM 1953	Lindsay, H. *and* Crouse, R. (P) Dramatists, N.Y.

REMEMBER THAT FACE
COL 1951

Findley, F.
Reinhardt & Evans

REMO
RANK 1985

Murphy, W. *and* Sapin, R.
Fiesta, N.Y.

RENEGADE CANYON
COL 1953

Dawson, P.
Collins

RENDEZVOUS
PAR 1950

Barrie, *Sir* J.M. (*Alice Sit By the Fire*)
(P)
Hodder & Stoughton

RENDEZVOUS
MGM 1935

Yardley, H.O. (*American Black Chamber, The*)
Faber

REPORT TO THE COMMISSIONER (V)
UA 1975

Mills, J. (*Operation Undercover*)
Farrow, N.Y.

REPRIEVE
WAR 1962

Resko, J.
MacGibbon

REPRISAL
COL 1956

Gordon, A.
Hamilton

RESCUERS
DISNEY 1977

Sharp, M. (*Rescuers and Miss Bianca, The*)
Dell, N.Y.

RESPECTABLE PROSTITUTE, THE
GALA 1955

Sartre, J-P. (P)
Penguin

RESURRECTION
UN 1931

Tolstoy, L.N.
Various

RETURN FROM THE ASHES
UA 1965

Monteilhet, H.
Panther

RETURN OF DON CAMILLO, THE
MIRACLE FILMS 1954

Guareschi, G. (*Don Camillo and the Prodigal Son*)
Gollancz

RETURN OF DR. FU MANCHU
PAR 1930

Rohmer, S.
Hurst & Blackett

TITLE OF FILM	AUTHOR AND PUBLISHER
RETURN OF SHERLOCK HOLMES PAR 1929	Doyle, *Sir* A.C. Murray
RETURN OF THE BIG CAT DISNEY 1974	Dietz, L. (*Year of the Big Cat*) Little, Brown, Boston
RETURN OF THE SOLDIER (V) BRENT WALKER 1981	West, R. Virago
RETURN TO PARADISE UA 1953	Michener, J.A. Random House, N.Y.
RETURN TO PEYTON PLACE FOX 1960	Metalious, G. Muller
REUBEN, REUBEN (V) FOX 1984	De Vries, P. Penguin
REUNION IN VIENNA MGM 1933	Sherwood, R.E. (P) Scribner, N.Y.
REVOLT OF MAMIE STOVER, THE FOX 1956	Huie, W.B. W.H. Allen
REVOLUTIONARY, THE UA 1971	Koningsberger, H. Deutsch
REWARD, THE FOX 1965	Barrett, M. Longmans
RHAPSODY MGM 1954	Richardson, H.H. (*Maurice Guest*) Heinemann
RHODES GB 1936	Millin, S.G. Chatto & Windus
RHUBARB PAR 1951	Smith, H.A. Barker
RICH AND FAMOUS MGM 1981	Druten, J. van (*Old Acquaintance*) (P) French
RICHARD'S THINGS SOUTHERN PICTURES 1980	Raphael, F. Cape

TITLE OF FILM	AUTHOR AND PUBLISHER
RICHARD III BL 1955	Shakespeare, W. (P) Various
RICH MAN, POOR GIRL MGM 1938	Ellis, E. (*White Collars*) (P) French, N.Y.
RICH MAN, POOR MAN ABC 1975 (TV)	Shaw, I. Cape
RICH MAN'S FOLLY PAR 1931	Dickens, C. (*Dombey and Son*) Various
RIDDLE OF THE SANDS, THE (V) RANK 1979	Childers, E. Various
RIDE A WILD PONY DISNEY 1975	Aldridge, J. (*Sporting Proposition, A*) Dell, N.Y.
RIDE BEYOND VENGEANCE COL 1966	Dewlen, A. (*Night of the Tiger, The*) Longmans
RIDERS OF THE PURPLE SAGE FOX 1931 FOX 1941	Grey, Z. Harper, N.Y.
RIDE THE HIGH WIND BUTCHER 1965	Harding, G. (*North of Bushman's Rock*) Hale
RIDE THE PINK HORSE UI 1947	Hughes, D.B. Duell, N.Y.
RIGHT STUFF, THE (V) COL—EMI—WAR 1982	Wolfe, T. Cape
RIGHT TO LIVE WAR 1935	Maugham, W.S. (*Sacred Flame, The*) (P) Heinemann
RING, THE UA 1953	Shulman, I. (*Cry Tough*) Dial Press, N.Y.
RINGER, THE ID 1932 REGENT 1952	Wallace, E. Hodder & Stoughton

238

TITLE OF FILM	AUTHOR AND PUBLISHER
RINGER, THE ID 1932 REGENT 1952	Wallace, E. (P) Hodder & Stoughton
RING OF BRIGHT WATER (V) RANK 1968	Maxwell, G. Longmans
RIO CONCHOS FOX 1964	Huffaker, C. (*Guns of the Rio Conchos*) Muller
RIOT, THE PAR 1969	Elli, F. Heinemann
RISE AND SHINE FOX 1941	Thurber, J. (*My Life and Hard Times*) Hamilton
RISING OF THE MOON WAR 1957	Gregory, *Lady* I.A. (P) Putnam
RITZ, THE (V) COL—WAR 1976	McNally, T. (P) Dodd, N.Y.
RIVER, THE UA 1951	Godden, R. Joseph
RIVER LADY UN 1948	Brach, H. *and* Water, F. Cassell
RIVER OF DEATH CANNON 1986	McLean, A. Doubleday, N.Y.
RIVER'S END WAR 1930 WAR 1940	Curwood, J.O. Grosset, N.Y.
ROAD BACK UN 1937	Remarque, E.M. Putnam
ROAD TO SINGAPORE WAR 1931	Pertwee, R. (*Heat Wave*) (P) French, N.Y.
ROARIN' LEAD REP 1937	Macdonald, W.C. Collins

ROBBER'S ROOST FOX 1933 UA 1955	Grey, Z. Hodder & Stoughton
ROBBERY UNDER ARMS RANK 1957	Boldrewood, R. Macmillan
ROBE, THE (V) FOX 1953	Douglas, L.C. Davies
ROBERTA RKO 1935	Miller, A.D. (*Gowns by Roberta*) Various
ROCKETS GALORE RANK 1958	Mackenzie, *Sir* C. Chatto & Windus
ROCKETS IN THE DUNES RANK 1960	Lamplugh, L. Cape
ROCKING HORSE WINNER, THE TC 1949	Lawrence, D.H. Heinemann
ROGUE COP MGM 1954	McGivern, W.P. Collins
ROMANCING THE STONE (V) FOX 1984	Wilder, J. Corgi
ROMANOFF AND JULIET RANK 1961	Ustinov, P. (P) Heinemann Educational
ROMAN SPRING OF MRS. STONE, THE WAR 1961	Williams, T. Ace
ROMANTIC CONGRESSWOMAN, THE FOX RANK 1975	Wiseman, T. Cape
ROMEO AND JULIET (V) MGM 1936 GFD 1954 GALA 1956 RANK 1966 PAR 1968	Shakespeare, W. (P) Various

ROMMEL—DESERT FOX (V) FOX 1951	Young, D. (*Rommel*) Collins
ROOKERY NOOK MGM 1930	Travers, B. Lane
ROOKERY NOOK MGM 1930	Travers, B. (P) Bickers
ROOM AT THE TOP (V) BL 1958	Braine, J. Eyre & Spottiswoode
ROOM FOR ONE MORE WAR 1952	Rose, A.P. Houghton, Mifflin, Boston
ROOM IN THE HOUSE MON 1955	Evans, E.E. (*Bless this House*) (P) French
ROOM WITH A VIEW, A GOLDCREST 1985	Forster, E.M. Arnold
ROONEY RANK 1958	Cookson, C. Macdonald
ROOSTER COGBURN UN 1975	Portis, C. (*True Grit*) Simon & Schuster, N.Y.
ROOTS ABC 1977 (TV)	Haley, A. Hall
ROOTS OF HEAVEN, THE FOX 1958	Gary, R. Joseph
ROPE (V) WAR 1948	Hamilton, P. (P) French
ROSEANNA McCOY RKO 1951	Bannum, A. Holt, N.Y.
ROSEBUD UA 1974	Hemingway, J. *and* Bonnecarrere, P. Morrow, N.Y.
ROSEMARY'S BABY (V) PAR 1968	Levin, I. Joseph

TITLE OF FILM	AUTHOR AND PUBLISHER
ROSES OF PICARDY, THE EXCELLENT 1930	Mottram, R.H. (*Spanish Farm, The*) Chatto & Windus
ROSE TATTOO PAR 1954	Williams, T. (P) Secker & Warburg
ROSIE FRIES 1982 (TV)	Clooney, R. *and* Strait, R. (*This For Remembrance*) Robson
ROSIE DIXON—NIGHT NURSE COL—WAR 1977	Dixon, R. (*Confessions of a Night Nurse*) Futura
ROUGH AND THE SMOOTH, THE MGM 1959	Maugham, R. Chapman & Hall
ROUGH COMPANY COL 1954	Hamilton, D. Wingate
ROUGH CUT PAR 1980	Lambert, D. (*Touch of the Lion's Paw, A*) Corgi
ROUGHLY SPEAKING WAR 1945	Pierson, *Mrs.* L. Simon & Schuster, N.Y.
ROUGH SHOOT UA 1953	Household, G. Joseph
ROUNDERS, THE MGM 1965	Evans, M. Macmillan, N.Y.
ROYAL BED RKO 1931	Sherwood, R.E. (*Queen's Husband, The*) (P) Scribner, N.Y.
ROYAL FAMILY OF BROADWAY PAR 1930	Kaufman, G.S. *and* Ferber, E. (*Royal Family, The*) (P) French, N.Y.
ROYAL FLASH FOX RANK 1976	Fraser, G.M. Barrie *and* Jenkins

TITLE OF FILM	AUTHOR AND PUBLISHER
ROYAL HUNT OF THE SUN, THE RANK 1968	Shaffer, P. (P) Pan
RUDDIGORE GALA 1967	Gilbert, *Sir* W.S. (P) Macmillan
RUGGLES OF RED GAP PAR 1935	Wilson, H.L. Various
RULING CLASS, THE UA 1971	Barnes, P. (P) Heinemann
RUMBLE FISH (V) PSO 1982	Hinton, S.E. Gollancz
RUMBLES ON THE DOCKS COL 1957	Paley, F. Crown, N.Y.
RUN, COUGAR, RUN DISNEY 1972	Murphy, R. (*Mountain Lion, The*) Dutton, N.Y.
RUNNING MAN, THE COL 1963	Smith, S. (*Ballad of the Running Man*) Hamilton
RUNNING OF THE TIDE MGM 1949	Forbes, E. Houghton, Mifflin, Boston
RUNNING SCARED (V) CINEMA INT 1973	McDonald, G. Astor-Honor, N.Y.
RUN SILENT, RUN DEEP UA 1958	Beach, E.L. Wingate
RUSSIAN ROULETTE (V) FOX RANK 1975	Ardies, T. (*Kosygin is Coming*) Doubleday, N.Y.
RUSSIANS ARE COMING—THE RUSSIANS ARE COMING UA 1966	Benchley, N. (*Off Islanders, The*) Penguin
RUTHLESS EL 1948	Stoddart, D. (*Prelude to Night*) Coward-McCann, N.Y.

S

ST. IVES (V)
COL—WAR 1976

Bleeck, O. (*Procane Chronicle, The*)
Morrow, N.Y.

SABOTAGE (V)
GB 1936

Conrad, J. (*Secret Agent, The*)
Various

SABRINA FAIR
PAR 1954

Taylor, S. (P)
Random House, N.Y.

SACRED FLAME, THE
WAR 1939

Maugham, W.S. (P)
Heinemann

SAIL A CROOKED SHIP
COL 1961

Benchley, N.
Hutchinson

SAILOR BEWARE!
BL 1956

King, P. *and* Cary, F.L. (P)
Elek

SAILOR FROM GIBRALTAR, THE
UA 1967

Duras, M.
Calder

SAILOR'S RETURN, THE
ARIEL 1978

Garnett, D.
Chatto & Windus

**SAILOR WHO FELL FROM GRACE
WITH THE SEA** (V)
FOX RANK 1976

Mishima, Y.
Putnam, N.Y.

SAINT IN NEW YORK, THE
RKO 1938

Charteris, L.
Hodder & Stoughton

SAINT JACK
NEW WORLD 1979

Theroux, P.
Ballantine, N.Y.

SAINT JOAN
UA 1957

Shaw, G.B. (P)
Constable

SAINT MEETS THE TIGER, THE
REP 1943

Charteris, L. (*Meet the Tiger*)
Ward Lock

SAINT'S VACATION, THE
RKO 1941

Charteris, L. (*Getaway*)
Hodder & Stoughton

TITLE OF FILM	AUTHOR AND PUBLISHER
SALAAMBO FOX 1959	Flaubert, G. Dent
SALAMANDER, THE (V) ITC 1981	West, M. Morrow, N.Y.
SALEM'S LOT (V) WAR 1981 (TV)	King, S. New English Library
SALLY IN OUR ALLEY ABP 1932	McEvoy, C. (*Likes of 'er, The*) Harrap
SAL OF SINGAPORE PATHE 1929	Collins, D. (*Sentimentalists*) Little, Brown, Boston
SALOME CANNON 1986	Wilde, O. (P) Various
SALON KITTY FOX 1977	Norden, P. (*Madame Kitty*) Abelard-Schuman
SALOON BAR EALING 1942	Harvey, J. *Jun.* (P) French
SALUTE JOHN CITIZEN BN 1942	Greenwood, R. (*Mr. Bunting at War*) Dent
SALUTE THE TOFF BUTCHER 1951	Creasey, J. Long
SALZBURG CONNECTION, THE FOX 1972	MacInnes, H. Collins
SAME TIME NEXT YEAR (V) CIC 1979	Slade, B. (P) Dell, N.Y.
SAMMY GOING SOUTH BL 1962	Canaway, W.H. Hutchinson
SAN ANTONE REP 1952	Carroll, C. (*Golden Herd*) Morrow, N.Y.
SANCTUARY FOX 1960	Faulkner, W. Chatto & Windus

TITLE OF FILM	AUTHOR AND PUBLISHER
SANCTUARY FOX 1960	Faulkner, W. (*Requiem for a Nun*) Chatto & Windus
SAND FOX 1949	James, W. Cassell
SANDERS OF THE RIVER UA 1935	Wallace, E. Ward Lock
SAND PEBBLES, THE FOX 1966	McKenna, R. Gollancz
SANDS OF THE KALAHARI PAR 1965	Mulvihill, W. Longmans
SAN FRANCISCO STORY, THE WAR 1952	Summers, R.A. (*Vigilante*) Duell, N.Y.
SANGAREE PAR 1933	Slaughter, F.G. Jarrolds
SANTE FE COL 1951	Marshall, J.L. Random House, N.Y.
SAPPHIRE (V) RANK 1959	Cousins, E.G. Panther
SARABAND FOR DEAD LOVERS EL 1949	Simpson, H. Heinemann
SARACEN BLADE, THE COL 1954	Yerby, F. Heinemann
SARATOGA TRUNK WAR 1945	Ferber, E. Heinemann
SATAN BUG, THE UA 1964	Stuart, I. Collins
SATAN MET A LADY FIRST NATIONAL 1937	Hammett, D. (*Maltese Falcon, The*) Cassell
SATURDAY ISLAND RKO 1951	Brooke, H. Heinemann

TITLE OF FILM	AUTHOR AND PUBLISHER

**SATURDAY NIGHT AND SUNDAY
MORNING**
BL 1960

Sillitoe, A.
W.H. Allen

SATURDAY'S CHILDREN
WAR 1940

Anderson, M. (P)
Longmans, N.Y.

SATURDAY'S HERO
COL 1950

Lampell, M. (*Hero, The*)
Messner, N.Y.

SAVAGE, THE
PAR 1952

Foreman, L.L. (*Don Desperado*)
Cassell

SAVAGE INNOCENTS, THE (V)
RANK 1960

Ruesch, H. (*Top of the World*)
Gollancz

SAVAGE MESSIAH
MGM—EMI 1972

Ede, H.S.
Fraser

SAVAGE SAM
DISNEY 1963

Gipson, F.
Hodder & Stoughton

SAVE THE TIGER
PAR 1973

Shagan, S.
Joseph

SAVING GRACE
RANK 1986

Gittelson, C.
Knopf, N.Y.

SAXON CHARM, THE
UI 1948

Wakeman, F.
Rinehart, N.Y.

SAYONARA (V)
WAR 1957

Michener, J.A.
Secker & Warburg

SCANDALOUS JOHN
DISNEY 1971

Gardner, R.M.
Constable

SCAPEGOAT, THE
MGM 1958

Du Maurier, D.
Gollancz

SCAR, THE
ABP 1949

Holding, C.H.
Eerdmans, Grand Rapids

SCARAMOUCHE
MGM 1952

Sabatini, R.
Hutchinson

TITLE OF FILM	AUTHOR AND PUBLISHER
SCARFACE UA 1932	Trail, A. Long
SCARFACE MOB, THE WAR 1959	Ness, E. *and* Fraley, O. (*Untouchables, The*) Messner, N.Y.
SCARLET AND THE BLACK (V) ITC 1983 (TV)	Gallagher, H.J. (*Scarlet Pimpernel of the Vatican*) Collins
SCARLET LETTER, THE MAJESTIC 1934 CHANNEL 4 1986 (TV)	Hawthorne, N. Various
SCARLET PIMPERNEL, THE UA 1935 LONDON F.P. 1982	Orczy, *Baroness* E. Hodder & Stoughton
SCATTERGOOD BAINES RKO 1941	Kelland, C.B. Hodder & Stoughton
SCHOOL FOR SCOUNDRELS WAR 1960	Potter, S. (*Gamesmanship, Oneupmanship, Lifemanship*) Hart-Davis
SCREAM AND SCREAM AGAIN AMERICAN INT 1969	Saxon, P. (*Disorientated Man, The*) Baker
SCREAMING MIMI COL 1957	Brown, F. Boardman
SCROOGE PAR 1935 REN 1951 FOX 1970	Dickens, C. (*Christmas Carol, A*) Various
SCRUPLES AMERICAN TV 1983 (TV)	Krantz, J. Futura
SCUDDA HOO! SCUDDA HAY! FOX 1948	Chamberlain, G.A. Grosset, N.Y.
SEA AROUND US, THE RKO 1953	Carson, R.L. Staples

SEA CHASE, THE
WAR 1954

Geer, A.
Collins

SEA GOD, THE
PAR 1930

Russell, J. (*Where the Pavement Ends*)
Butterworth

SEAGULL, THE
WAR 1969

Chekhov, A. (P)
Various

SEAGULLS OVER SORRENTO
MGM 1954

Hastings, H. (P)
Elek

SEA HAWK, THE
WAR 1940
CANNON 1985 (TV)

Sabatini, R.
Various

SEALED VERDICT
PAR 1948

Shapiro, L.
Doubleday, N.Y.

SEAL MORNING
ITV 1986 (TV)

Farre, R.
Hutchinson

SEANCE ON A WET AFTERNOON
RANK 1964

McShane, M.
Cassell

SEA OF GRASS
MGM 1947

Ritchter, C.M.
Constable

SEARCHERS, THE
WAR 1956

LeMay, A.
Collins

SEARCH FOR BRIDEY MURPHY, THE
PAR 1956

Bernstein, M.
Hutchinson

SEARCHING WIND, THE
PAR 1946

Hellman, L.F. (P)
Viking Press, N.Y.

SEA SHALL NOT HAVE THEM, THE
EROS 1954

Harris, J.
Hurst & Blackett

SEA WALL
RANK 1957

Duras, M. (*Sea of Troubles*)
Methuen

TITLE OF FILM	AUTHOR AND PUBLISHER
SEAWEED CHILDREN, THE PENRITH 1978	Trollope, A. (*Malachi's Cove*) Various
SEA-WIFE FOX 1957	Scott, J.D. (*Sea Wyf and Biscuit*) Heinemann
SEA WOLF, THE FOX 1930 WAR 1941	London, J. Heinemann
SEA WOLVES, THE (V) RANK 1980	Leasor, J. (*Boarding Party*) Bantam
SECOND HAND WIFE FOX 1933	Norris, K. Murray
SECOND HONEYMOON CONT 1931	Ayres, R.M. Hodder & Stoughton
SECOND MRS. TANQUERAY, THE VANDYKE 1952	Pinero, *Sir* A.W. (P) Heinemann
SECONDS PAR 1965	Ely, D. Deutsch
SECOND TIME ROUND FOX 1961	Roberts, R.E. (*Star in the West*) Pocket Bks
SECRET AGENT (V) GB 1936	Maugham, W.S. (*Ashenden*) Heinemann
SECRET ARMY, THE BBC 1977 (TV)	Brason, J. BBC
SECRET BEYOND THE DOOR, THE (V) UI 1948	King, R. Various
SECRET DIARY OF ADRIAN MOLE, AGED 13¾ THAMES 1985 (TV)	Townsend, S. Methuen
SECRET FOUR, THE MON 1940	Wallace, E. (*Four Just Men, The*) Various

SECRET GARDEN, THE
MGM 1949

Burnett, F.H.
Heinemann

SECRET INTERLUDE
FOX 1955

Basso, H. (*View from Pompey's
Head*)
Collins

SECRET LIFE OF WALTER MITTY
RKO 1949

Thurber, J.
World, N.Y.

SECRET OF DR. KILDARE, THE
MGM 1939

Brand, M.
Hodder & Stoughton

SECRET OF NIMH, THE
UIP 1982

O'Brien, R.C. (*Mrs. Brisby and the
Rats of Nimh*)
Gollancz

SECRET OF SANTA VITTORIA, THE
UA 1969

Crichton, R.
Hodder & Stoughton

SECRET OF STAMBOUL, THE
HOB 1939

Wheatley, D. (*Eunuch of Stamboul,
The*)
Hutchinson

SECRET OF ST. IVES, THE
COL 1949

Stevenson, R.L. (*St. Ives*)
Various

SECRET PLACES
RANK 1983

Elliott, J.
Hodder & Stoughton

SECRET SERVANT, THE
BBC 1985 (TV)

Lyall, G.
Viking, N.Y.

SECRET TENT
BL 1956

Addyman, E. (P)
English Theatre Guild

SECRETS OF THE PURPLE REEF, THE
FOX 1960

Cottrell, D. (*Silent Reef*)
Hodder & Stoughton

SECRET WAYS, THE
RANK 1960

McLean, A. (*Last Frontier*)
Collins

SEED
UN 1931

Norris, C.G.
Heinemann

TITLE OF FILM	AUTHOR AND PUBLISHER
SEE HERE, PRIVATE HARGROVE MGM 1944	Hargrove, M. Hodder & Stoughton
SEE HOW THEY RUN BL 1955 CHANNEL 4 1984 (TV)	King, P. (P) French
SEE YOU IN HELL, DARLING WAR 1966	Mailer, N. (*American Dream, An*) Deutsch
SEMINOLE UPRISING EROS 1955	Brandon, C. (*Bugle's Wake*) Dutton, N.Y.
SEMI-TOUGH UA 1978	Jenkins, D. New American Library, N.Y.
SENTINEL, THE UN 1977	Konvitz, J. Secker & Warburg
SEPARATE BEDS MGM 1964	Goodman, G.J.W. (*Wheeler-Dealers, The*) Doubleday, N.Y.
SEPARATE PEACE PAR 1972	Knowles, J. Heinemann
SEPARATE TABLES (V) UA 1958	Rattigan, T. (P) French
SEQUOIA MGM 1934	Hoyt, V.J. Grosset, N.Y.
SERENADE WAR 1956	Cain, J.M. Penguin
SERGEANT, THE WAR 1968	Murphy, D. Sphere
SERGEANT YORK WAR 1941	Cowan, S.K. (*Sergeant York and his People*) Various
SERIOUS CHARGE EROS 1959	King, P. (P) French

TITLE OF FILM	AUTHOR AND PUBLISHER
SERPICO (V) PAR 1974	Maas, P. Fontana
SERVANT, THE (V) WAR 1963	Maugham, R. Heinemann
SEVEN ALONE (V) HEMDALE 1974	Morrow, H. (*On to Oregon*) Morrow, N.Y.
SEVEN BRIDES FOR SEVEN BROTHERS (V) MGM 1954	Benet, S.V. (*Sobbin' Women, The*) Heinemann
SEVEN CITIES OF GOLD FOX 1955	Ziegler, I.G. (*Nine Days of Father Serra*) Longmans
SEVEN DAYS IN MAY PAR 1963	Knebel, F. *and* Bailey, C.W. Corgi
SEVEN DAYS' LEAVE PAR 1930	Barrie, *Sir* J.M. (*Old Lady Shows her Medals, The*) (P) Hodder & Stoughton
SEVEN KEYS TO BALDPATE RKO 1930 RKO 1935 RKO 1947	Biggers, E.D. Grosset, N.Y.
SEVEN MINUTES, THE FOX 1971	Wallace, I. New English Library
SEVEN-PER-CENT SOLUTION, THE (V) UN 1977	Meyer, N. Dutton, N.Y.
SEVENTEEN PAR 1940	Tarkington, B. (P) French, N.Y.
SEVENTH CROSS, THE MGM 1944	Seghers, A. Hamilton
7TH DAWN UA 1964	Keon, M. (*Durian Tree, The*) Hamilton

TITLE OF FILM	AUTHOR AND PUBLISHER
SEVENTH HEAVEN, THE FOX 1937	Strong, A. (P) French, N.Y.
SEVEN THIEVES FOX 1960	Catto, M. (*Lions at the Kill*) Hutchinson
SEVENTH SIN, THE MGM 1957	Maugham, W.S. (*Painted Veil, The*) Heinemann
SEVEN THUNDERS RANK 1957	Croft-Cooke, R. Macmillan
79 PARK AVENUE UN 1977 (TV)	Robbins, H. New English Library
SEVEN-UPS, THE (V) FOX—RANK 1974	Posner, R. Futura
SEVEN WAYS FROM SUNDOWN UI 1960	Huffaker, C. Muller
SEVEN YEAR ITCH, THE FOX 1954	Axelrod, G. (P) Random House, N.Y.
SEVEN YEARS IN TIBET CURZON 1956	Harrer, H. Hart-Davis
SEVERED HEAD, A COL 1969	Murdoch, I. Chatto & Windus
SEVERED HEAD, A COL 1969	Murdoch, I. *and* Priestley, J.B. (P) Chatto & Windus
SEX AND THE SINGLE GIRL WAR 1964	Brown, H.G. Muller
SEX SYMBOL, THE WAR 1974	Bessie, A. (*Symbol, The*) Sphere
SHADOW, THE GLOBE 1936	Stuart, D. Wright & Brown
SHADOWLANDS BBC 1985 (TV)	Straub, P. Collins

SHADOW OF A WOMAN
WAR 1946

Perdue, V. (*He Fell Down Dead*)
Doubleday, N.Y.

SHAFT
MGM 1971

Tidyman, E.
Joseph

SHAKE HANDS WITH THE DEVIL
UA 1959

Conner, R.
Dent

SHALAKO
WAR 1968

L'Amour, L.
Bantam

SHANE (V)
PAR 1953

Schaefer, J.W.
Deutsch

SHAPE OF THINGS TO COME, THE
BARBER DANN 1979

Wells, H.G.
Hutchinson

SHARE OUT, THE
AA 1962

Wallace, E. (*Jack O'Judgement*)
Ward Lock

SHARKEY'S MACHINE (V)
COL—EMI—WAR 1982

Diehl, W.
Sphere

SHE
RKO 1935
WAR 1964
CONTINENTAL 1984

Haggard, *Sir* H.R.
Macdonald

SHE DIDN'T SAY NO!
ABP 1958

Troy, U. (*We Are Seven*)
Heinemann

SHEPHERD OF THE HILLS, THE
PAR 1941

Wright, H.B.
Grosset, N.Y.

SHERLOCK HOLMES AND THE VOICE OF TERROR
UN 1942

Doyle, *Sir* A.C. (*His Last Bow*)
Various

SHE SHALL HAVE MURDER
BL 1950

Ames, D.
Hodder & Stoughton

SHE'S WORKING HER WAY THROUGH COLLEGE
WAR 1952

Thurber, J. *and* Nugent, E. (*Male Animal, The*) (P)
Random House, N.Y.

SHETLAND BUS, THE FORLONG 1954	Howarth, D. Nelson
SHIELD FOR MURDER UA 1954	McGivern, W.P. Dodd, N.Y.
SHINING, THE (V) COL—EMI—WAR 1980	King, S. New American Library, N.Y.
SHINING HOUR, THE MGM 1938	Winter, K. (P) Heinemann
SHINING VICTORY WAR 1941	Cronin, A.J. (*Jupiter Laughs*) (P) Gollancz
SHIPBUILDERS, THE BN 1944	Blake, G. Faber
SHIP FROM SHANGHAI MGM 1930	Collins, D. (*Ordeal, The*) Allan
SHIP OF FOOLS COL 1964	Porter, K.A. Secker & Warburg
SHIRALEE, THE MGM 1957	Niland, D'A. Angus & Robertson
SHOCK TREATMENT FOX 1964	Van Atta, W. Doubleday, N.Y.
SHOES OF THE FISHERMAN, THE MGM 1972	West, M.L. Heinemann
SHOGUN (V) PAR 1981	Clavell, J. Dell, N.Y.
SHOOTING PARTY, THE REEVE 1984 (TV)	Colegate, I. Avon, N.Y.
SHOOTIST, THE PAR 1976	Swarthout, G. Doubleday, N.Y.
SHOP AT SLY CORNER, THE BL 1946	Percy, E. (P) French

SHORT CUT TO HELL PAR 1957	Greene, G. (*Gun For Sale, A*) Heinemann
SHORT GRASS ABP 1951	Blackburn, T.W. Sampson Low
SHOUT AT THE DEVIL (V) HEMDALE 1976	Smith, W. Heinemann
SHOW BOAT UN 1929 UN 1936 MGM 1951	Ferber, E. Heinemann
SHOW-OFF, THE MGM 1934	Kelly, G. (P) French, N.Y.
SHRIKE, THE UI 1955	Kramm, J. (P) Random House, N.Y.
SHUTTERED ROOM, THE WAR 1966	Lovecraft, H.P. Gollancz
SICILIAN, THE EMI 1986	Puzo, M. Linden, N.Y.
SIDDHARTHA COL—WAR 1973	Hesse, H. Picador
SIDELONG GLANCES OF A PIGEON KICKER, THE BUTCHER 1970	Boyer, D. Macdonald
SIDE SHOW OF LIFE WAR 1931	Locke, W.J. (*Mounteback*) Lane
SIDNEY SHELDON'S BLOODLINE CIC 1979	Sheldon, S. (*Bloodline*) Morrow, N.Y.
SIERRA BARON FOX 1958	Blackburn, T.W. Random House, N.Y.
SIGN OF FOUR (V) WW 1932 EMBASSY 1984	Doyle, *Sir* A.C. Various

SIGN OF THE CROSS, THE
PAR 1932
PAR 1944

Barrett, W.
Various

SIGN OF THE RAM, THE
COL 1949

Ferguson, M.
Hale

SIGNPOST TO MURDER
MGM 1965

Doyle, M. (P)
French

SILAS MARNER
BBC 1985 (TV)

Eliot, G.
Various

SILENCERS, THE
COL 1965

Hamilton, D.
Hodder & Stoughton

SILENT DUST
ABP 1952

Pertwee, R. *and* Pertwee, M.
(*Paragon, The*) (P)
English Theatre Guild

SILENT ENEMY, THE
ROMULUS 1958

Pugh, M. (*Commander Crabb*)
Macmillan

SILENT PARTNER, THE (V)
ENTERPRISE 1978

Bodelsen, A.
Penguin

SILENT WORLD, THE
RANK 1955

Cousteau, J.
Hamilton

SILVER BEARS, THE (V)
EMI 1978

Erdman, P.
Hutchinson

SILVER CHALICE, THE
WAR 1954

Costain, T.B.
Hodder & Stoughton

SILVER DARLINGS, THE
ALL 1947

Gunn, N.M.
Faber

SILVER FOX AND SAM DAVENPORT
DISNEY 1962

Seton, E.T. (*Biography of a Silver Fox, The*)
Appleton

SILVER HORDE, THE
RKO 1930

Beach, R.
Hodder & Stoughton

TITLE OF FILM	AUTHOR AND PUBLISHER
SILVER WHIP, THE FOX 1953	Schaefer, J.W. (*Big Range*) Deutsch
SIMON AND LAURA RANK 1955	Melville, A. (P) French
SINFUL DAVEY UA 1969	Haggart, D. (*Life of David Haggart, The*) Sphere
SINGER NOT THE SONG, THE (V) RANK 1960	Lindop, A.E. Heinemann
SINGLE HANDED FOX 1952	Forester, C.S. (*Brown on 'Resolution'*) Lane
SINISTER MAN, THE AA 1961	Wallace, E. Hodder & Stoughton
SINK THE BISMARCK FOX 1960	Forester, C.S. (*Hunting the Bismarck*) Joseph
SINCE YOU WENT AWAY (V) UA 1944	Wilder, M.A. McGraw-Hill, N.Y.
SING SING NIGHTS MON 1934	Keeler, H.S. Ward Lock
SINNER TAKES ALL MGM 1936	Chambers, W. (*Murder for a Wanton*) Melrose
SIN OF MADELON CLAUDET MGM 1931	Knoblock, E. (*Lullaby, The*) (P) Putnam
SINS OF RACHEL CADE, THE WAR 1960	Mercer, C. (*Rachael Cade*) Collins
SIROCCO COL 1951	Kessel, J. Random House, N.Y.
SISTER KENNY RKO 1946	Kenny, E. *and* Ostenso, M. (*And They Shall Walk*) Dodd, N.Y.

TITLE OF FILM	AUTHOR AND PUBLISHER
SISTERS, THE WAR 1938	Brinig, M. Cobden-Sanderson
SITTING PRETTY FOX 1948	Davenport, *Mrs. G.* (*Belvedere*) Bobbs, Merrill, Indianapolis
SITTING TARGET (V) MGM—EMI 1972	Henderson, L. Harrap
SITUATION HOPELESS BUT NOT **SERIOUS** PAR 1964	Shaw, R. (*Hiding Place, The*) Chatto & Windus
SIX BRIDGES TO CROSS GFD 1954	Dinneen, J.F. (*Anatomy of a Crime*) Scribner, N.Y.
633 SQUADRON UA 1964	Smith, F.E. Hutchinson
SIX WEEKS POLYGRAM 1982	Stewart, F.M. Corgi
SKIN GAME BI 1931	Galsworthy, J. (P) Duckworth
SKINNER STEPS OUT UA 1929	Dodge, H.I. *and others* (*Skinner's Dress Suit*) (P) French, N.Y.
SKYJACKED (V) MGM 1972	Harper, D. (*Hijacked*) Corgi
SKYLARK PAR 1941	Raphaelson, S. (P) Various
SKYSCRAPER SOULS MGM 1932	Baldwin, F. (*Skyscraper*) Sampson Low
SLAPSTICK INTERNATIONAL 1981	Vonnegut, K. Delacorte, N.Y.
SLAPSTICK OF ANOTHER KIND LORIMAR 1984	Vonnegut, K. (*Slapstick*) Cape

TITLE OF FILM	AUTHOR AND PUBLISHER
SLAUGHTER-HOUSE-FIVE UN 1972	Vonnergut, K. Cape
SLAUGHTER ON 10TH AVENUE UI 1957	Keating, W.J. *and* Carter, H. (*Man Who Rocked the Boat, The*) Harper, N.Y.
SLAYGROUND (V) EMI 1983	Westlake, D. (*Butcher's Moon*) Coronet
SLEEPERS EAST FOX 1934	Nebel, F. Collins
SLEEPING TIGER, THE INSIGNIA 1954	Moiseiwitsch, M. Heinemann
SLEUTH (V) FOX 1972	Shaffer, A. (P) Calder
SLIGHT CASE OF MURDER, A WAR 1938	Runyan, D. *and* Lindsay, H. (P) Dramatists, N.Y.
SLIGHTLY HONOURABLE UA 1939	Presnell, F.G. (*Send Another Coffin*) Heinemann
SMALL BACK ROOM, THE LF 1949	Balchin, N. Collins
SMILEY FOX 1955	Raymond, M. Sylvan Press
SMILEY'S PEOPLE BBC 1982 (TV)	Le Carré, J. Hodder & Stoughton
SMOKE DISNEY 1970	Corbin, W. Harrap
SMOKY FOX 1933 FOX 1946	James, W. Various
SNAKE PIT, THE FOX 1948	Ward, M.J. Cassell

SNOWBOUND
RKO 1948

Innes, M.H. (*Lonely Skier, The*)
Collins

SNOW DOG
ABP 1951

Curwood, J.O. (*Tentacles of the North*)
Various

SNOW GOOSE, THE
BBC 1971

Gallico, P.
Joseph

SNOWS OF KILIMANJARO, THE
FOX 1952

Hemingway, E.
Cape

SNOW TREASURE
TIGON 1968

McSwigan, M. (*All Aboard for Freedom*)
Dent

SO BIG
WAR 1932
WAR 1953

Ferber, E.
Heinemann

SO BRIGHT THE FLAME
MGM 1952

Barringer, E.D. (*Bowery to Bellevue*)
Norton, N.Y.

SO DEAR TO MY HEART
RKO 1948

North, S.
Odhams

SO ENDS OUR NIGHT
UA 1941

Remarque, E.M. (*Flotsam*)
Hutchinson

SO EVIL MY LOVE
PAR 1948

Shearing, J. (*For Her to See*)
Hutchinson

SOFT BEDS, HARD BATTLES
FOX—RANK 1974

Evans, P.
New English Library

SO GOES MY LOVE
UN 1946

Maxim, H.P.
World, N.Y.

SOHO INCIDENT
COL 1956

Westerby, R. (*Wide Boys Never Work*)
Methuen

SOLDIER AND THE LADY, THE
RKO 1937

Verne, J. (*Michael Strogoff*)
Sampson Low

TITLE OF FILM	AUTHOR AND PUBLISHER
SOLDIER BLUE (V) AVCO EMBASSY 1971	Olsen, T.V. White Lion
SOLDIER IN THE RAIN WAR 1965	Goldman, W. Eyre & Spottiswoode
SOLDIER OF FORTUNE FOX 1955	Gann, E.K. Hodder & Stoughton
SOLDIER'S STORY, A COL—EMI—WAR 1985	Fuller, C. (*Soldier's Play, A*) (P) Hill & Wang, N.Y.
SOLDIERS THREE MGM 1951	Kipling, R. Macmillan
SOLID GOLD CADILLAC, THE COL 1956	Teichman, H. *and* Kaufman, G.S. (P) Random House, N.Y.
SOLITARY CHILD, THE BL 1957	Bawden, N. Collins
SOLO FOR SPARROW AA 1962	Wallace, E. (*Gunner, The*) Long
SOLOMON AND SHEBA UA 1959	Williams, J. Macdonald
SO LONG AT THE FAIR (V) GFD 1950	Thorne, A. Heinemann
SOMBRERO MGM 1953	Niggli, J. (*Mexican Village, A*) Sampson Low
SOMEONE IS KILLING THE GREAT CHEFS OF EUROPE LORIMAR 1978	Lyons, N. *and* Lyons, I. Cape
SOMEBODY UP THERE LIKES ME MGM 1956	Graziano, R. Hammond
SOME CAME RUNNING MGM 1958	Jones, J. Collins
SOME KIND OF HERO (V) UIP 1981	Kirkwood, J. New American Library, N.Y.

TITLE OF FILM	AUTHOR AND PUBLISHER
SOME LIKE IT HOT UA 1959	Wilder, W. *and* Diamond, I.A.L. Panther
SOMETHING OF VALUE MGM 1957	Ruark, R. Hamilton
SOMETHING TO HIDE AVCO EMBASSY 1973	Monsarrat, N. Pan
SOMETHING WICKED THIS WAY COMES DISNEY 1983	Bradbury, R. Hart-Davis
SOMETHING WILD UA 1962	Karmel, A. (*Mary Ann*) Secker & Warburg
SOMEWHERE IN TIME CIC 1980	Matheson, R. (*Bid Time Return*) Sphere
SONG OF BERNADETTE, THE FOX 1943	Werfel, F.V. Hamilton
SONG TO REMEMBER, A COL 1945	Leslie, D. (*Polonaise*) Hutchinson
SON OF INDIA MGM 1931	Crawford, F.M. (*Mr. Isaacs*) Macmillan
SONS AND LOVERS FOX 1960	Lawrence, D.H. Heinemann
SOPHIA LOREN—HER OWN STORY BBC 1985 (TV)	Hotchner, A.E. (*Sophia Living and Loving*) Morrow, N.Y.
SOPHIE'S CHOICE (V) ITC 1982	Styron, W. Bantam, N.Y.
SORCERER CIC 1978	Arnaud, G. (*Wages of Fear, The*) British Publishers Guild
SO RED THE ROSE PAR 1935	Young, S. Cassell

TITLE OF FILM	AUTHOR AND PUBLISHER
SORORITY HOUSE RKO 1939	Chase, M.C. (P) French, N.Y.
SORRELL AND SON UA 1934 YORKSHIRE 1984 (TV)	Deeping, W. Cassell
SO THIS IS LOVE WAR 1953	Moore, G. (*You're Only Human Once*) Invincible Press
SO THIS IS NEW YORK UA 1948	Lardner, R.W. (*Big Town, The*) Garden City, N.Y.
SOUND AND THE FURY, THE FOX 1959	Faulkner, W. Chatto & Windus
SOUNDER (V) FOX 1972	Armstrong, W.H. Gollancz
SOUND OF MUSIC, THE (V) FOX 1965	Trapp, M.A. (*Story of the Trapp Family Singers*) Bles
SOUND OF THE FURY, THE UA 1951	Pagano, J. (*Condemned, The*) Invincible Press
SOUTH BY JAVA HEAD RANK 1960	MacLean, A. Collins
SOUTHERN CROSS GEOFF REEVES 1983 (TV)	Coleman, T. Hutchinson
SOUTHERNER, THE UA 1945	Perry, G.S. (*Hold Autumn in your Hands*) Sun Dial, N.Y.
SOUTHERN STAR, THE COL 1969	Verne, J. (*Southern Star Mystery, The*) Arco
SOUTH PACIFIC (V) TODD AO 1958	Michener, J.A. (*Tales from the South Pacific*) Collins

SOUTH RIDING
UA 1938

Holtby, W.
Collins

SOUTHWEST TO SONORA
UI 1966

MacLeod, R. (*Appaloosa, The*)
Muller

SO WELL REMEMBERED
RKO 1947

Hilton, J.
Macmillan

SOYLENT GREEN (V)
MGM—EMI 1973

Harrison, H. (*Make Room, Make Room!*)
Sidgwick & Jackson

SPACE
PAR 1985 (TV)

Michener, J.A.
Secker & Warburg

SPACEMAN AND KING ARTHUR, THE
(V)
DISNEY 1980

Twain, M. (*Yankee at King Arthur's Court*)
Various

SPACE VAMPIRES
CANNON 1984

Wilson, C.
Random House, N.Y.

SPANIARD'S CURSE, THE
BL 1957

Pargeter, E. (*Assize of the Dying, The*)
Heinemann

SPANISH CAPE MYSTERY, THE
REP 1935

Queen, E.
Gollancz

SPANISH GARDENER, THE
RANK 1956

Cronin, A.J.
Gollancz

SPARE THE ROD
BL 1961

Croft, M.
Pan

SPARKLING CYANIDE
WAR 1984 (TV)

Christie, A.
Collins

SPARROWS CAN'T SING
WAR 1962

Lewis, S. (*Sparrers can't Sing*) (P)
Evans

SPARTACUS (V)
RANK 1959

Fast, H.
Panther

SPEAK EASILY
MGM 1932

Kelland, C.B.
Harper, N.Y.

SPELL BOUND (V)
UA 1945

Beeding, F.
World, N.Y.

SPENCER'S MOUNTAIN
WAR 1963

Hamner, E.
Dial Press, N.Y.

SPHINX (V)
COL—EMI—WAR 1980

Cook, R.
Putnam, N.Y.

SPIDER'S WEB, THE
UA 1960
BBC 2 1985 (TV)

Christie, A. (P)
French

SPIKES GANG, THE
UA 1974

Tippette, G. (*Harry Spikes*)
Futura

SPINSTER, THE
MGM 1962

Ashton-Warner, S.
Secker & Warburg

SPIRAL ROAD, THE
UI 1962

Hartog, J. de
Hamilton

SPIRAL STAIRCASE, THE (V)
RKO 1946
COL—WAR 1975

White, E.L. (*Some Must Watch*)
Ward Lock

SPIRIT IS WILLING, THE
PAR 1968

Benchley, N. (*Visitors, The*)
Hutchinson

SPIRIT OF ST. LOUIS, THE
WAR 1956

Lindbergh, C.A. (*We*)
Putnam, N.Y.

SPLIT, THE
MGM 1968

Stark, R.
Hodder Fawcett

SPOILERS, THE
UN 1942
UN 1955

Beach, R.
Cassell

SPORTING CLUB, THE
AVCO EMBASSY 1968

McGuane, T.
Deutsch

SPOT OF BOTHER, A
AB 1938

Sylvaine, V. (P)
French

SPRING AND PORT WINE
AA 1969

Naughton, B. (P)
French

SPY IN BLACK, THE
COL 1938

Clouston, J.S.
Blackwood

SPY OF NAPOLEON
TWICKENHAM 1931

Orczy, *Baroness* E.
Hodder & Stoughton

SPY STORY (V)
GALA 1976

Deighton, L.
Cape

**SPY WHO CAME IN FROM THE COLD,
THE**
PAR 1964

Le Carré, J.
Gollancz

SPY WHO LOVED ME, THE (V)
UA 1977

Wood, C.
Cape

SQUARE RING, THE
GFD 1953

Peterson, R.
Barker

SQUEAKER, THE
GB 1937

Wallace, E. (P)
Hodder & Stoughton

SQUEAKER, THE
GB 1937

Wallace, E.
Hodder & Stoughton

SQUEEZE, THE (V)
COL—WAR 1977

Craig, D.
Stein & Day, N.Y.

STAB IN THE DARK
PSO 1985

Block, L. (*8 Million Ways to Die*)
Arbor, N.Y.

STAGECOACH (V)
UA 1939
FOX 1965

Haycox, E. (*Stage to Lordsburgh*)
Hodder & Stoughton

STAGE DOOR
RKO 1937

Kaufman, G.S. *and* Ferber, E. (P)
Heinemann

STAGE FRIGHT WAR 1949	Jepson, S. (*Man Running*) Macdonald
STAIRCASE FOX 1969	Dyer, C. W.H. Allen
STAIRCASE FOX 1969	Dyer, C. (P) French
STALAG 17 (V) PAR 1953	Bevan, D. *and* Trzcinski, E. (P) Dramatists, N.Y.
STALKING MOON, THE WAR 1968	Olsen, T.V. Sphere
STALLION ROAD WAR 1947	Longstreet, S. Jarrolds
STAMPEDE ABP 1950	Mann, E.B. Triangle Bks, N.Y.
STAND BY YOUR MAN JNP 1981 (TV)	Wynette, T. PB, N.Y.
STAND UP VIRGIN SOLDIERS (V) COL—WAR 1977	Thomas, L. Eyre & Methuen
STAR IN THE DUST UN 1956	Leighton, L. (*Law Man*) Worlds Work
STAR QUALITY BBC 1985 (TV)	Coward, N. Methuen
STARS IN MY CROWN MGM 1950	Brown, J.D. Hodder & Stoughton
STARS LOOK DOWN, THE GN 1940	Cronin, A.J. Gollancz
STARTING OVER (V) PAR 1980	Wakefield, D. Dell, N.Y.
STATE FAIR FOX 1945 FOX 1962	Stong, P.D. Grosset, N.Y.

TITLE OF FILM	AUTHOR AND PUBLISHER
STATION WEST RKO 1948	Short, L. Collins
STAY AWAY, JOE (V) MGM 1969	Cushman, D. Bantam
STAY HUNGRY (V) UA 1976	Gaines, C. Chatto & Windus
STAYING ON GRANADA 1985 (TV)	Scott, P. Heinemann
STEAMBOAT ROUND THE BEND FOX 1935	Burman, B.L. Nelson
STEAMING (V) COL—EMI—WAR 1985	Dunn, N. (P) Amber Lane
STEEL CAGE, THE GN 1956	Duffy, C.T. (*San Quentin*) Davies
STELLA FOX 1950	Disney, D.M. (*Family Skeleton*) Doubleday, N.Y.
STELLA DALLAS UA 1937	Prouty, *Mrs.* O. Hodder & Stoughton
STEPFORD WIVES, THE (V) CONTEMPORARY 1978	Levin, I. Random House, N.Y.
STEP LIVELY (V) RKO 1944	Murray, J. *and* Boret, A. (*Room Service*) (P) Random House, N.Y.
STEPPENWOLF CONTEMPORARY 1978	Hesse, H. Various
STICK CIC 1985	Leonard, E. Lane
STILETTO (V) AVCO EMBASSY 1970	Robbins, H. Mayflower
STOLEN AIRLINER, THE BL 1955	Pudney, J. (*Thursday Adventure*) Evans

TITLE OF FILM	AUTHOR AND PUBLISHER
STONE KILLER, THE (V) COL 1973	Gardner, J. (*Complete State of Death, A*) Cape
STONE LEOPARD, THE ITC 1978	Forbes, C. Collins
STOPOVER TOKYO FOX 1957	Marquand, J.P. Collins
STOP, YOU'RE KILLING ME WAR 1952	Runyon, D. *and* Lindsay, H. (*Slight Case of Murder, A*) (P) Dramatists, N.Y.
STORM CENTRE COL 1956	Taradash, D. *and* Moll, E. Panther
STORM FEAR UA 1955	Seeley, C. Holt, N.Y.
STORM IN A TEACUP LF 1937	Bridie, J. (P) French
STORM OVER THE NILE GFD 1955	Mason, A.E.W. (*Four Feathers, The*) Hodder & Stoughton
STORY OF DR. WASSELL, THE PAR 1944	Hilton, J. Macmillan
STORY OF ESTHER COSTELLO, THE COL 1957	Monsarrat, N. Cassell
STORY OF G.I. JOE, THE UA 1945	Pyle, E.T. Various
STORY OF GILBERT AND SULLIVAN, THE BL 1953	Baily, L. (*Gilbert and Sullivan Book, The*) Cassell
STORY OF MANKIND, THE WAR 1957	Van Loon, H.W. Harrap
STORY OF O, THE (V) NEW REALM 1976	Reage, P. Olympia

TITLE OF FILM	AUTHOR AND PUBLISHER
STORY OF PRIVATE POOLEY, THE CONTEMPORARY 1962	Jolly, C. (*Vengeance of Private Pooley, The*) Heinemann
STORY OF TEMPLE DRAKE, THE PAR 1933	Faulkner, W. (*Sanctuary*) Chatto & Windus
STRAIGHT TIME COL—WAR 1978	Bunker, E. (*No Beast so Fierce*) Dell, N.Y.
STRANGE AFFAIR, THE PAR 1968	Toms, B. Constable
STRANGE AFFAIR OF UNCLE HARRY, THE UN 1945	Job, T. (*Uncle Harry*) (P) French
STRANGE AWAKENING, THE AA 1958	Quentin, P. (*Puzzle for Fiends*) Gollancz
STRANGE BOARDERS GB 1938	Oppenheim, E.P. (*Strange Boarders of Palace Crescent*) Hodder & Stoughton
STRANGE CARGO MGM 1940	Sale, R. (*Not Too Narrow, Not Too Deep*) Cassell
STRANGE DOOR, THE UI 1951	Stevenson, R.L. (*Sire of Maletroit's Door, The*) Various
STRANGE INCIDENT FOX 1943	Clark, W. van T. (*Ox-Bow Incident, The*) Gollancz
STRANGE INTERLUDE MGM 1932	O'Neill, E.G. (P) Cape
STRANGE INTRUDER ABP 1957	Fowler, H.M. (*Shades Will Not Vanish*) Angus & Robertson
STRANGER, THE GN 1963	Beaumont, C. (*Intruder, The*) Muller

272

TITLE OF FILM	AUTHOR AND PUBLISHER
STRANGER CAME HOME EXCLUSIVE 1954	Sanders, G. (*Stranger at Home*) Pilot Press
STRANGER IN MY ARMS, A UI 1958	Wilder, R. (*And Ride a Tiger*) W.H. Allen
STRANGER IN THE HOUSE (V) JARFID 1966	Simenon, G. (*Strangers in the House*) Routledge
STRANGER IN TOWN EROS 1957	Chitterden, F. (*Uninvited, The*) Boardman
STRANGERS IN LOVE PAR 1932	Locke, W.J. (*Shorn Lamb, The*) Lane
STRANGERS MAY KISS MGM 1931	Parrott, U. Cape
STRANGERS ON A TRAIN (V) WAR 1951	Highsmith, P. Cresset Press
STRANGERS ON HONEYMOON GB 1937	Wallace, E. (*Northing Tramp, The*) Hodder & Stoughton
STRANGER'S RETURN MGM 1933	Stong, P.D. Harcourt, N.Y.
STRANGERS WHEN WE MEET COL 1959	Hunter, E. Constable
STRANGER WALKED IN, THE REN 1949	Vosper, F. (*Love From a Stranger*) (P) Collins
STRANGE WOMAN, THE UA 1946	Williams, B.A. Houghton, Mifflin, Boston
STRANGE WORLD OF PLANET X, THE EROS 1958	Ray, R. Jenkins
STRAWBERRY BLONDE, THE WAR 1941	Hagan, J. (*One Sunday Afternoon*) (P) French, N.Y.

STRAWBERRY ROAN BN 1944	Street, A.G. Faber
STRAW DOGS (V) CINERAMA 1971	Williams, G.M. (*Siege at Trencher's Farm, The*) Mayflower
STRAW MAN, THE UA 1953	Disney, D.M. Doubleday, N.Y.
STREETCAR NAMED DESIRE, A (V) WAR 1951 PSO 1984	Williams, T. (P) Lehmann
STREET OF CHANCE PAR 1942	Woolrich, C. (*Black Curtain, The*) Grosset, N.Y.
STREET OF SHADOWS AA 1953	Meynell, L. (*Creaking Chair, The*) Collins
STREET SCENE UA 1931	Rice, E. (P) French, N.Y.
STRICTLY DISHONOURABLE UN 1931 MGM 1951	Sturges, P. (P) Liveright, N.Y.
STRIKE ME PINK UA 1936	Kelland, C.B. (*Dreamland*) Miles
STRIP-TEASE MURDERS UA 1943	Lee, G.R. Lane
STRONGER THAN FEAR RKO 1952	Brady, L. (*Edge of Doom*) Cresset Press
STRONG MEDICINE STV 1986 (TV)	Hailey, A. Joseph
STUD, THE (V) BRENT WALKER 1978	Collins, J. Mayflower
STUDS LONIGAN UA 1964	Farrell, J.T. W.H. Allen

TITLE OF FILM	AUTHOR AND PUBLISHER
STUDY IN SCARLET, THE WW 1933	Doyle, *Sir* A.C. Ward Lock
STUNTMAN, THE (V) FOX 1979	Canutt, Y. *and* Drake, G. Walker, N.Y.
SUBMARINE BBC 1985 (TV)	Crane, J. BBC
SUBTERRANEANS, THE MGM 1960	Kerouac, J. Deutsch
SUCH GOOD FRIENDS PAR 1972	Gould, L. Weidenfeld & Nicolson
SUDDEN FEAR RKO 1952	Sherry, E. Hodder & Stoughton
SUDDENLY, LAST SUMMER COL 1959	Williams, T. (P) Secker & Warburg
SUGARFOOT WAR 1951	Kelland, C.B. Grosset, N.Y.
SUICIDE MISSION EROS 1957	Howarth, D. (*Shetland Bus, The*) Nelson
SUMMER AND SMOKE PAR 1959	Williams, T. (P) Secker & Warburg
SUMMER HOLIDAY MGM 1948	O'Neill, E.G. (*Ah Wilderness*) (P) Cape
SUMMER LIGHTNING BD 1932	Wodehouse, P.G. Jenkins
SUMMER LIGHTNING CHANNEL 4 1986 (TV)	Turganev, I. (*First Love*) Hogarth
SUMMER MADNESS UA 1955	Laurents, A. (*Time of the Cuckoo, The*) (P) Random House, N.Y.

TITLE OF FILM	AUTHOR AND PUBLISHER
SUMMER MAGIC DISNEY 1963	Wiggins, K.D. (*Mother Carey's Chickens*) Hodder & Stoughton
SUMMER OF FEAR (V) BRENT WALKER 1978	Duncan, L. Dell, N.Y.
SUMMER OF '42 (V) WAR 1971	Raucher, H. W.H. Allen
SUMMER OF THE SEVENTEENTH DOLL, THE UA 1959	Lawler, R. (P) Fontana
SUMMER PLACE, A WAR 1959	Wilson, S. Cassell
SUN ALSO RISES, THE FOX 1957 NBC 1984 (TV)	Hemingway, E. (*Fiesta*) Cape
SUNDAY IN NEW YORK MGM 1964	Krasna, N. (P) Random House, N.Y.
SUNDOWN UA 1941	Lyndon, B. Lane
SUNDOWNERS, THE WAR 1960	Cleary, J. (*Back of Beyond*) Collins
SUNDOWN JIM FOX 1942	Haycox, E. Paul
SUNRISE AT CAMPOBELLO WAR 1960	Schary, D. (P) Random House, N.Y.
SUNSET PASS PAR 1933 RKO 1946	Grey, Z. Hodder & Stoughton
SUNSHINE BOYS, THE (V) CIC—MGM 1975	Simon, N. (P) Random House, N.Y.
SUN SHINES BRIGHT, THE REP 1953	Cobb, I.S. (*Old Judge Priest*) Grosset, N.Y.

TITLE OF FILM	AUTHOR AND PUBLISHER
SUPER COPS, THE MGM 1974	Whitemore, L.H. Futura
SUPERFLY PAR 1972	Penty, P. Sphere
SURPRISE PACKAGE COL 1960	Buckwald, A. Gollancz
SURRENDER—HELL ABP 1959	Harkins, P. (*Blackburn's Headhunters*) Cassell
SURVIVE (V) STIGWOOD 1976	Blair, C. *jun.* Mayflower
SURVIVOR, THE (V) HEMDALE 1980	Herbert, J. New American Library, N.Y.
SUSAN AND GOD MGM 1940	Crothers, R. (P) Random House, N.Y.
SUSAN SLADE WAR 1962	Hume, D. (*Sins of Susan Slade, The*) Dell, N.Y.
SUSPECT BL 1960	Balchin, N. (*Sort of Traitor, A*) Collins
SUSPECT, THE UN 1944	Ronald, J. (*This Way Out*) Rich & Cowan
SUSPICION RKO 1941	Iles, F. (*Before the Fact*) Gollancz
SUTTAR'S GOLD UN 1983	Cendrars, B. Various
SUZY MGM 1936	Gorman, H. Cassell
SVENGALI (V) WAR 1931 REN 1954	Du Maurier, G. (*Trilby*) Various

SWALLOWS AND AMAZONS (V)
EMI 1973

Ransome, A.
Cape

SWAMP WATER
FOX 1941

Bell, V.
Collins

SWAN, THE
MGM 1956

Molnar, F. (P)
Boni, N.Y.

SWARM, THE (V)
COL—WAR 1978

Herzog, A.
Heinemann

SWEET BIRD OF YOUTH
MGM 1962

Williams, T. (P)
Secker & Warburg

SWEET HOSTAGE
BBC 1984 (TV)

Benchley, N.
Chicago University Press

SWEETLOVE, BITTER
FILM 2 1969

Williams, J. (*Night Song*)
Collins

SWEET RIDE, THE
FOX 1968

Murray, W.
W.H. Allen

SWEET WILLIAM
ITC 1980

Bainbridge, B.
Duckworth

SWISS FAMILY ROBINSON (V)
RKO 1940
DISNEY 1960
DISNEY 1977

Wyss, J.D.
Various

SWORD AND THE ROSE, THE
RKO 1953

Kester, P. (*When Knighthood was in Flower*) (P)
French, N.Y.

SWORD AND THE ROSE, THE
RKO 1953

Major, C. (*When Knighthood was in Flower*)
Grayson

SWORD IN THE STONE
DISNEY 1963

White, T.H.
Collins

SYBIL
BARBER DANN 1979

Schreiber, F.R.
Warner, N.Y.

TITLE OF FILM	AUTHOR AND PUBLISHER

SYLVIA
PAR 1963

Cunningham, E.V.
Deutsch

SYLVIA
ENTERPRISE 1985

Ashton-Warner, S. (*Teacher I Passed This Way*)
Virago

SYLVIA SCARLETT
RKO 1935

Mackenzie, *Sir* C.
Various

SYMPHONY IN TWO FLATS
GFD 1931

Novello, I. (P)
Methuen

SYNDICATE, THE
WAR 1968

Rhodes, D.
Four Square Books

T

TAGGART
UI 1965

L'Amour, L.
Corgi

TAI PAN
MGM 1968
ORION 1986

Clavell, J.
Joseph

TAKE, THE
COL—WAR 1974

Newman, G.F. (*Sir, You Bastard*)
W.H. Allen

TAKE A GIANT STEP
UA 1959

Peterson, L.S. (P)
French, N.Y.

TAKE A GIRL LIKE YOU
COL 1971

Amis, K.
Gollancz

TAKE CARE OF MY LITTLE GIRL
FOX 1951

Goodin, P.
Dutton, N.Y.

TAKE HER, SHE'S MINE
MGM 1963

Ephron, P. *and* Ephron, H. (P)
Random House, N.Y.

TAKE ME WHILE I'M WARM
BORDER 1965

Sulzberger, C.L. (*My Brother Death*)
Hamilton

TAKE MY LIFE
EL 1948

Graham, W.
Ward Lock

TAKING OF PELHAM 123, THE (V)
UA 1974

Godey, J.
Hodder & Stoughton

TALE OF TWO CITIES, A (V)
MGM 1935
RANK 1957
BBC 1982 (TV)

Dickens, C.
Various

TALES OF TERROR
WAR 1963

Poe, E.A. (*Morella; Black Cat, The;
Case of Dr. Valdemar*)
Various

TALK OF A MILLION
ABP 1951

D'Alton, L.L. (*Money Doesn't
Matter*) (P)
Duffy, Dublin

TALL HEADLINES, THE
GN 1951

Lindop, A.E.
Heinemann

TALL MAN RIDING
WAR 1955

Fox, N.A.
Collins

TALL MEN, THE
FOX 1955

Fisher, C.
Houghton, Mifflin, Boston

TALL STORY
WAR 1960

Nemerov, H. (*Homecoming Game,
The*)
Gollancz

TALL STORY
WAR 1960

Lindsay, H. *and* Crouse, R. (P)
Random House, N.Y.

TAMAHINE
WAR 1963

Niklaus, T.
Lane

TAMANGO
COL 1959

Merimee, P.
Blackie

TAMARIND SEED, THE (V)
SCOTIA-BARBER 1974

Anthony, E.
Hutchinson

TITLE OF FILM	AUTHOR AND PUBLISHER
TAMING OF THE SHREW, THE (V) INDIVIDUAL 1933 COL 1968	Shakespeare, W. (P) Various
TAMMY TELL ME TRUE RANK 1961	Sumner, G. Bobbs, Merrill, Indianapolis
TAP ROOTS UI 1948	Street, J. Sun Dial, N.Y.
TAPS (V) FOX 1982	Freeman, D. (*Father Sky*) Secker & Warburg
TARAS BULBA UA 1962	Gogol, N. Dent
TARKA THE OTTER (V) RANK 1978	Williamson, H. Cape
TARNISHED ANGELS, THE UI 1957	Faulkner, W. (*Pylon*) Chatto & Windus
TARZAN, THE APE MAN (V) MGM 1982	Burroughs, E.R. Various
TASTE OF EXCITEMENT MONARCH 1969	Healey, B. (*Waiting for a Tiger*) Hale
TASTE OF HONEY, A BRYANSTON 1961	Delaney, S. (P) Methuen
TAXI TO TOBRUK MIRACLE FILMS 1961	Havard, R. Collins
TEA AND SYMPATHY MGM 1956	Anderson, R. (P) Random House, N.Y.
TEAHOUSE OF THE AUGUST MOON, THE MGM 1957	Patrick, J. (P) Heinemann
TEAHOUSE OF THE AUGUST MOON, THE MGM 1957	Sneider, V.J. Macmillan

TITLE OF FILM	AUTHOR AND PUBLISHER
TELEFON (V) CIC 1978	Wager, W. Barker
TELL ENGLAND CAPITOL 1931	Raymond, E. Cassell
TELL ME THAT YOU LOVE ME, JANIE MOON PAR 1971	Kellogg, M. Secker & Warburg
TELL TALE HEART, THE ABP 1960	Poe, E.A. Various
TELL THEM WILLIE BOY IS HERE (V) RANK 1969	Lawton, H. (*Willie Boy*) Paisano Press, California
TEMPEST (V) PAR 1959	Pushkin, A. (*Captain's Daughter, The*) Various
TEMPEST, THE (V) RAFTERS 1969 MAINLINE 1979	Shakespeare, W. (P) Various
TEMPTATION COL 1930	Hichens, R. (*Bella Donna*) Heinemann
TEMPTATION HARBOUR AB 1947	Simenon, G. (*Newhaven–Dieppe*) Routledge
TEN DAYS TO DIE INTERCONTINENTAL 1955	Musmanno, M.A. Davies
TEN DAYS WONDER HEMDALE 1971	Queen, E. Gollancz
TENDERFOOT DISNEY 1964	Tevis, J.H. (*Arizona in the 50's*) Univ. of New Mexico Pr. Albuquerque
TENDER IS THE NIGHT FOX 1959 BBC 2 1985 (TV)	Fitzgerald, F.S.K. Grey Walls Press

TENDER TRAP
MGM 1955

Shulman, M. *and* Smith, R.P. (P)
Random House, N.Y.

TEN LITTLE INDIANS (V)
ABP 1965

Christie, A. (*Ten Little Niggers*) (P)
French

TEN LITTLE INDIANS (V)
ABP 1965

Christie, A. (*Ten Little Niggers*)
Collins

TEN LITTLE NIGGERS (V)
FOX 1945

Christie, A. (P)
French

TEN LITTLE NIGGERS (V)
FOX 1945

Christie, A.
Collins

TEN MINUTE ALIBI
SOSKIN 1934

Armstrong, A. *and* Shaw, H.
Methuen

TEN MINUTE ALIBI
SOSKIN 1934

Armstrong, A. (P)
Gollancz

TENNESSEE'S PARTNER
RKO 1955

Harte, B.
Various

TEN NORTH FREDERICK
FOX 1958

O'Hara, J.
Cresset Press

10 RILLINGTON PLACE (V)
COL 1971

Kennedy, L.
Panther

TEN SECONDS TO HELL
UA 1958

Bachmann, L. (*Phoenix*)
Collins

TENSION AT TABLE ROCK (V)
RKO 1956

Gruber, G. (*Bitter Sage*)
Wright & Brown

10.30 p.m. SUMMER
UA 1965

Duras, M. (*10.30 p.m. on a Summer Night*)
Calder

TERM OF TRIAL
WAR 1962

Barlow, J.
Hamilton

TERRIBLE BEAUTY, A
UA 1960

Roth, A.
Hutchinson

TERRONAUTS, THE AVCO EMBASSY 1967	Leinster, M. (*Wailing Asteroid, The*) Sphere
TERROR, THE ALL 1941	Wallace, E. Collins
TERROR, THE ALL 1941	Wallace, E. (P) French
TESS (V) COL 1979	Hardy, T. (*Tess of the d'Urbervilles*) Macmillan
TESS OF THE STORM COUNTRY FOX 1960	White, G.M. Various
THANK YOU, JEEVES FOX 1936	Wodehouse, P.G. Jenkins
THANK YOU MR. MOTO FOX 1937	Marquand, J.P. Jenkins
THARK GB 1932	Travers, B. (P) Bickers
THAT CERTAIN FEELING PAR 1956	Kerr, J. *and* Brooke, E. (*King of Hearts*) (P) Doubleday, N.Y.
THAT COLD DAY IN THE PARK COMMONWEALTH 1969	Miles, R. Souvenir Press
THAT DANGEROUS AGE LF 1948	Kennedy, M. (*Autumn*) (P) French
THAT DARN CAT (V) DISNEY 1964	Gordons, The (*Undercover Cat*) Macdonald
THAT FORSYTE WOMAN MGM 1949	Galsworthy, J. (*Forsyte Saga*) Heinemann
THAT LADY FOX 1954	O'Brien, K. Heinemann
THAT WAS THEN . . . THIS IS NOW MIRACLE 1986	Hinton, S.E. Macmillan

THAT WOMAN OPPOSITE
MON 1957

Carr, J.D. (*Emperor's Snuffbox, The*)
Hamilton

THEIR SECRET AFFAIR
WAR 1956

Marquand, J.P. (*Melville Goodwin, USA*)
Hale

THERE GOES THE BRIDE
ENTERPRISE 1981

Cooney, R. *and* Chapman, J. (P)
English Theatre Guild

THERE'S A GIRL IN MY SOUP (V)
COL 1970

Frisby, T. (P)
French

THERE'S A GIRL IN MY SOUP (V)
COL 1970

Hitchcock, R.
W.H. Allen

THÉRESE
GALA 1965

Mauriac, F.
Eyre & Spottiswoode

THESE CHARMING PEOPLE
PAR 1931

Arlen, M.
Collins

THESE THOUSAND HILLS
FOX 1958

Guthrie, A.B.
Hutchinson

THESE THREE
UA 1936

Hellman, L.F. (*Children's Hour, The*)
(P)
Knopf, N.Y.

THEY CAME BY NIGHT
FOX 1940

Lyndon, B. (P)
Hamilton

THEY CAME TO A CITY
EALING 1945

Priestley, J.B. (P)
Heinemann

THEY CAME TO CORDURA
COL 1959

Swarthout, G.
Heinemann

THEY DRIVE BY NIGHT
WAR 1940

Bezzerides, A.I. (*Long Haul*)
Cape

THEY FOUND A CAVE
CFF 1962

Chauncy, N.
O.U.P.

TITLE OF FILM	AUTHOR AND PUBLISHER
THEY GAVE HIM A GUN MGM 1937	Cowen, W.J. Heinemann
THEY KNEW MR. KNIGHT GFD 1946	Whipple, D. Murray
THEY KNEW WHAT THEY WANTED RKO 1940	Howard, S.C. (P) Harcourt, N.Y.
THEY MADE ME A FUGITIVE WAR 1947	Budd, J. (*Convict has Escaped, A*) Joseph
THEY'RE A WEIRD MOB (V) RANK 1965	Culotta, N. Kaye
THEY SAVED LONDON EROS 1957	Newman, B. Hamilton
THEY SHOOT HORSES, DON'T THEY (V) CINERAMA 1969	McCoy, H. Methuen
THEY WERE EXPENDABLE MGM 1945	White, W.L. Hamilton
THEY WERE SISTERS GFD 1945	Whipple, D. Murray
THEY WON'T FORGET WAR 1937	Greene, W. (*Death in the Deep South*) Cassell
THIEF (V) UA 1981	Hohimer, F. (*Home Invader, The*) Chicago Review, Chicago
THIEF WHO CAME TO DINNER (V) COL—WAR 1973	Smith, J.L. Doubleday, N.Y.
THIEVES' HIGHWAY FOX 1949	Bezzarides, A.I. (*Thieves' Market*) Scribner, N.Y.
THIEVES LIKE US UA 1974	Anderson, E. Avon, N.Y.
THING FROM ANOTHER WORLD, THE RKO 1951	Campbell, J.W. (*Who Goes There?*) Shasta Pubns, Chicago

TITLE OF FILM	AUTHOR AND PUBLISHER
THINGS HAPPEN AT NIGHT REN 1947	Harvey, F. (*Poltergeist, The*) (P) Dent
THINGS TO COME (V) UA 1936	Wells, H.G. (*Shape of Things to Come, The*) Hutchinson
THINGS TO COME (V) UA 1936	Wells, H.G. (P) Cresset Press
THIN MAN, THE MGM 1934	Hammett, D. Barker
THIN RED LINE, THE PLANET 1964	Jones, J. Collins
THIRD DAY, THE WAR 1965	Hayes, J. W.H. Allen
THIRD MAN, THE (V) GFD 1950	Greene, G. Heinemann
THIRD MAN ON THE MOUNTAIN DISNEY 1959	Ullman, J.R. (*Banner in the Sky*) Collins
THIRD PARTY RISK EXCLUSIVE 1955	Bentley, N. Joseph
THIRD TIME LUCKY ANGOFILM 1948	Butler, G. (*They Cracked her Glass Slipper*) Jarrolds
THIRTEEN AT DINNER (V) WAR 1985	Christie, A. (*Lord Edgware Dies*) Collins
13 WEST STREET BL 1962	Brackett, L. (*Tiger amongst us, The*) Boardman
THIRTY-NINE STEPS, THE (V) GB 1935 RANK 1959 RANK 1978	Buchan, J. Various
THIRTY SECONDS OVER TOKYO MGM 1944	Lawson, T. Hammond

TITLE OF FILM	AUTHOR AND PUBLISHER
THIS ABOVE ALL FOX 1942	Knight, E.M. Cassell
THIS EARTH IS MINE UI 1959	Hobart, *Mrs*. A.T. (*Cup and the* *Sword, The*) Cassell
THIS GUN FOR HIRE PAR 1942	Greene, G. (*Gun for Sale, A*) Various
THIS HAPPY BREED (V) TC 1944	Coward, N. (P) Heinemann
THIS HAPPY FEELING RANK 1958	Herbert, F.H. (*For Love or Money*) (P) Dramatists, N.Y.
THIS ISLAND EARTH UI 1955	Jones, R.F. Shasta Pubns, Chicago
THIS IS MY AFFAIR FOX 1951	Weidman, J. (*I Can Get It For You* *Wholesale*) Heinemann
THIS IS MY STREET WAR 1963	Maynard, N. Corgi
THIS PROPERTY IS CONDEMNED PAR 1966	Williams, T. (P) New Directions, Norfolk, Conn.
THIS SPORTING LIFE (V) RANK 1962	Storey, D. Longmans
THIS SWEET SICKNESS ARTIFICIAL EYE 1979	Highsmith, P. Heinemann
THIS WAS A WOMAN FOX 1948	Morgan, J. (P) French
THIS WOMAN IS MINE UN 1941	Gabriel, G.W. (*I, James Lewis*) Doubleday, N.Y.
THORN BIRDS, THE PISCES 1979	McCullough, C. Harper, N.Y.

TITLE OF FILM	AUTHOR AND PUBLISHER
THOSE CALLOWAYS (V) DISNEY 1965	Annixter, P. (*Swift Water*) Houghton, Mifflin, Boston
THOSE WERE THE DAYS PAR 1940	Pinero, *Sir* A.W. (*Magistrate, The*) (P) Heinemann
THOUSAND CLOWNS, A UA 1964	Gardner, H. (P) Random House, N.Y.
1,000 PLANE RAID, THE UA 1968	Barker, R. (*Thousand Plan, The*) Chatto & Windus
THREE UA 1969	Shaw, I. (*Then There Were Three*) Cape
THREE CAME HOME FOX 1949	Keith, A. Joseph
THREE COINS IN THE FOUNTAIN FOX 1954	Secondari, J. (*Coins in the Fountain*) Eyre & Spottiswoode
THREE COMRADES MGM 1938	Remarque, E.M. Hutchinson
3 DAYS OF THE CONDOR PAR 1975	Grady, J. (*Six Days of the Condor*) Norton, N.Y.
THREE FACES OF EVE, THE FOX 1957	Thigpen, C.H. *and* Cleckley, H.M. Secker & Warburg
3 FOR BEDROOM C INT 1952	Lieberson, G. Doubleday, N.Y.
THREE FOR THE SHOW FOX 1948 COL 1954	Maugham, W.S. (*Home and Beauty*) (P) Heinemann
THREE GODFATHERS, THE MGM 1936	Kyne, P.B. Various
THREE IN A CELLAR NEW REALM 1970	Hall, A. (*Late Boy Wonder, The*) Barrie & Jenkins

TITLE OF FILM	AUTHOR AND PUBLISHER
THREE IN A FAMILY UA 1944	Ephron, P. *and* Ephron, H. (P) French, N.Y.
THREE IN THE ATTIC (V) WAR 1968	Yafa, S. Sphere
THREE INTO TWO WON'T GO UI 1968	Newman, A. Triton
THREE LIVES OF THOMASINA, THE DISNEY 1963	Gallico, P. (*Thomasina*) Joseph
THREE MEN IN A BOAT BL 1956	Jerome, J.K. Various
THREE MUSKETEERS, THE (V) RKO 1935 FOX 1939 MGM 1949 FOX—RANK 1974	Dumas, A. Various
THREE ON A SPREE UA 1961	McCutcheon, G.B. (*Brewster's Millions*) Various
THREE SISTERS (V) BL 1970	Chekhov, A. (P) Chatto & Windus
THREE WEIRD SISTERS, THE BN 1948	Armstrong, C. (*Case of the Weird Sisters, The*) Gifford
THREE WORLDS OF GULLIVER, THE COL 1959	Swift, J. (*Gulliver's Travels*) Various
THUMB TRIPPING (V) AVCO EMBASSY 1972	Mitchell, D. Cape
THUNDERBALL (V) UA 1964	Fleming, I. Cape
THUNDERHEAD, SON OF FLICKA FOX 1945	O'Hara, M. Eyre & Spottiswoode

TITLE OF FILM	AUTHOR AND PUBLISHER
THUNDER IN THE EAST PAR 1951	Moorehead, A. (*Rage of the Vulture, The*) Hamilton
THUNDER MOUNTAIN FOX 1935	Grey, Z. Hodder & Stoughton
THUNDERING HERD PAR 1933	Grey, Z. Hodder & Stoughton
THUNDER ROCK MGM 1943	Ardrey, R. (P) Hamilton
TIARA TAHITI (V) RANK 1962	Cotterell, G. Eyre & Spottiswoode
TIGER BY THE TAIL EROS 1955	Chase, J.H. Hale
TIGER IN THE SMOKE RANK 1956	Allingham, M. Chatto & Windus
TIGER MAKES OUT, THE COL 1968	Schisgal, M. (*Typists and the Tiger, The*) (P) Cape
TIGERS DON'T CRY (V) RANK 1978	Burmeister, J. (*Running Scared*) Sphere
TIGER WALKS, A DISNEY 1964	Niall, I. Heinemann
TILL THE END OF TIME RKO 1946	Busch, N. (*They Dream of Home*) Grosset, N.Y.
TIMBER FURY EL 1950	Curwood, J.O. (*Retribution*) Various
TIMBERJACK REP 1954	Cushman, D. (*Ripper from Rawhide*) Macmillan, N.Y.
TIME AFTER TIME COL—EMI—WAR 1979	Alexander, K. Delacorte, N.Y.
TIME GENTLEMEN, PLEASE! ABP 1952	Minney, R.J. (*Nothing to Lose*) Macdonald

TIME MACHINE, THE (V)
MGM 1960

Wells, H.G.
Heinemann

TIME OF INDIFFERENCE
CONT 1967

Moravia, A.
Secker & Warburg

TIME OF YOUR LIFE
UA 1948

Saroyan, W. (P)
Faber

TIME OUT OF MIND
UN 1947

Field, R.
Macmillan

TIME TO LOVE AND A TIME TO DIE
RANK 1957

Remarque, E.M.
Hutchinson

TIME TO REMEMBER
AA 1962

Wallace, E. (*Man who bought London*)
Ward Lock

TIME WITHOUT PITY
HARLEQUIN 1957

Williams, E. (*Somebody Waiting*) (P)
Dramatists, N.Y.

TIMOTHY'S QUEST
PAR 1936

Wiggin, K.D.
Partridge

TIN DRUM
UA 1979

Grass, G.
Cape

TISH
MGM 1942

Rinehart, M.R. (*Tish Marches On*)
Cassell

TOBACCO ROAD
FOX 1941

Caldwell, E.
Falcon Press

TOBACCO ROAD
FOX 1941

Caldwell, E. *and* Kirkland, J. (P)
Falcon Press

TOBY TYLER
DISNEY 1959

Kaler, J.O.
Various

TO CATCH A KING (V)
GAYLORD 1983

Patterson, H.
Hutchinson

TO CATCH A THIEF
PAR 1955

Dodge, D.
Penguin

TITLE OF FILM	AUTHOR AND PUBLISHER
TO DOROTHY, A SON BL 1954	Macdougall, R. (P) Evans
TO FIND A MAN COL—WAR 1971	Wilson, S.J. W.H. Allen
TO HAVE AND HAVE NOT WAR 1944	Hemingway, E. Cape
TO HAVE AND TO HOLD LWT 1986 (TV)	Moggach, D. Penguin
TO HELL AND BACK UI 1955	Murphy, A. Hammond
TO KILL A MOCKING BIRD UI 1962	Lee, H. Penguin
TO LIVE AND DIE IN LA MGM/UA 1985	Petievich, G. Arbor, N.Y.
TOMAHAWK TRAIL, THE UA 1950	Cooper, J.F. (*Leather Stocking Tales*) Various
TO MARY—WITH LOVE FOX 1936	Sherman, R. Faber
TOM BROWN'S SCHOOLDAYS RKO 1940 REN 1951	Hughes, T. Various
TOM HORN (V) COL—EMI—WAR 1980	Horn, T. University of Oklahoma
TOM JONES (V) UA 1962	Fielding, H. Various
TOMORROW IS FOREVER RKO 1946	Bristow, G. Heinemann
TOMORROW THE WORLD UA 1944	D'Usseau, A. *and* Gow, J. (*Deep are the Roots*) (P) Dramatists, N.Y.

TITLE OF FILM	AUTHOR AND PUBLISHER
TOM SAWYER UA 1973	Twain, M. (*Adventures of . . .*) Various
TOM THUMB MGM 1958	Grimm, J.L.K. *and* Grimm, W.K. Various
TONIGHT AT 8.30 GFD 1952	Coward, N. (P) Heinemann
TONIGHT IS OURS PAR 1933	Coward, N. (*Queen was in the* *Parlour, The*) (P) Heinemann
TONIGHT WE SING FOX 1953	Hurok, S. *and* Goode, R. (*Impressario*) Macdonald
TONKA (V) DISNEY 1958	Appel, D. (*Comanche*) Various
TOO LATE THE HERO (V) CIRO 1971	Hughes, W. Sphere
TOO MANY CHEFS LORIMAR 1979	Lyons, N. *and* Lyons, I. (*Someone is* *Killing the Great Chefs of Europe*) Cape
TOO MANY HUSBANDS COL 1948	Maugham, W.S. (*Home and Beauty*) (P) Heinemann
TOO MUCH, TOO SOON WAR 1958	Barrymore, D. *and* Frank, G. Muller
TOO YOUNG TO MARRY WAR 1931	Flavin, M. (*Broken Dishes*) (P) French, N.Y.
TOPAZ UI 1968	Uris, L. Kimber
TOPKAPI (V) UA 1964	Ambler, E. (*Light of Day, The*) Heinemann
TOPPER MGM 1937	Smith, T. Sun Dial, N.Y.

TITLE OF FILM	AUTHOR AND PUBLISHER
TOPPER TAKES A TRIP UA 1939	Smith, T. Methuen
TORCH BEARERS, THE FOX 1935	Kelly, G. (P) French, N.Y.
TORTILLA FLAT MGM 1942	Steinbeck, J. Penguin
TO SERVE THEM ALL MY DAYS BBC 1982 (TV)	Delderfield, R.F. Hodder & Stoughton
TO SIR, WITH LOVE COL 1966	Braithwaite, E.R. Bodley Head
TO THE DEVIL, A DAUGHTER (V) EMI 1976	Wheatley, D. Hutchinson
TO THE LAST MAN PAR 1933	Grey, Z. Hodder & Stoughton
TO THE LIGHTHOUSE (V) BBC 1983 (TV)	Woolf, V. Dent
TO THE PUBLIC DANGER GFD 1948	Hamilton, P. (P) Constable
TOUCHED BY LOVE (V) COL 1980	Canada, L. (*To Elvis with Love*) Everest House, N.Y.
TOUCH OF EVIL UN 1958	Masterson, W. (*Badge of Evil*) Corgi
TOUCH OF LARCENY, A PAR 1959	Garve, A. (*Megstone Plot, The*) Collins
TOUCH OF LOVE, A BL 1969	Drabble, M. (*Millstone, The*) Penguin
TOUGH GUYS DON'T DANCE CANNON 1986	Mailer, N. Random, N.Y.
TOWERING INFERNO (V) COL—WAR 1975	Stern, R.M. (*Tower, The*) Pan

TITLE OF FILM	AUTHOR AND PUBLISHER
TOWERING INFERNO (V) COL—WAR 1975	Scortia, T.M. *and* Robinson, F.M. (*Glass Inferno, The*) Hodder & Stoughton
TOWN LIKE ALICE, A (V) RANK 1956 BBC 1984 (TV)	Shute, N. Heinemann
TOWN TAMER PAR 1965	Gruber, F. Barker
TOWN WITHOUT PITY UA 1961	Gregor, M. Heinemann
TOYS IN THE ATTIC UA 1963	Hellman, L. (P) Random House, N.Y.
TRACK OF THE CAT WAR 1954	Clark, W. van T. Gollancz
TRADER HORN MGM 1931 MGM 1973	Horn, A. Cape
TRAIL DUST PAR 1936	Mulford, C.E. Hodder & Stoughton
TRAIL OF THE YUKON MONOGRAM 1949	Curwood, J.O. (*Gold Hunters, The*) Various
TRAITOR'S GATE COL 1965	Wallace, E. Hodder & Stoughton
TRANSCONTINENTAL EXPRESS REP 1950	Nevins, F.J. (*Yankee Dared, A*) By the Author, Chicago
TRANS-SIBERIAN EXPRESS ITC 1978	Adler, W. Macmillan
TRAPEZE UA 1956	Catto, M. (*Killing Frost, The*) Heinemann
TRAVELLERS BY NIGHT TVS 1985 (TV)	Alcock, V. Methuen

TRAVELLER'S JOY GFD 1951	Macrae, A. (P) French
TRAVELS WITH MY AUNT MGM 1972	Greene, G. Bodley Head
TREAD SOFTLY APEX 1952	Verner, G. (*Show Must Go On, The*) Wright & Brown
TREASURE HUNT BL 1952	Farrel, M.J. *and* Perry, J. (P) Collins
TREASURE ISLAND (V) MGM 1934 RKO 1949 MGM—EMI 1971 CANNON 1986	Stevenson, R.L. Various
TREASURE OF LOST CANYON, THE UI 1952	Stevenson, R.L. (*Treasure of Franchard*) Various
TREASURE OF MATECUMBRE DISNEY 1976	Taylor, R.L. (*Journey to Matecumbre*) New American Library, N.Y.
TREASURE OF SIERRA MADRE (V) WAR 1948	Traven, B. Cape
TREASURE OF THE GOLDEN CONDOR FOX 1953	Marshall, E. (*Jewel of Mahabar*) Hodder & Stoughton
TREE GROWS IN BROOKLYN, A FOX 1945	Smith, B. Heinemann
TRENT'S LAST CASE BL 1952	Bentley, E.C. Various
TRESPASSER, THE COLIN GREGG 1983	Lawrence, D.H. Heinemann
TRIAL MGM 1955	Mankiewicz, D.M. Deutsch

TRIAL, THE
BL 1963
BBC 2 1986 (TV)

Kafka, F.
Secker & Warburg

TRIAL OF MARY DUGAN, THE
MGM 1929

Veiller, B. (P)
French

TRIAL OF THE CATONVILLE MINE
CINERAMA 1972

Berrigan, D. (P)
Bantam, N.Y.

TRIALS OF OSCAR WILDE, THE
EROS 1960

Hyde, H.M.
Hodge

TRIO
GFD 1950

Maugham, W.S.
Heinemann

TRIPLE CROSS, THE (V)
AA 1967

Owen, F. (*Eddie Chapman Story, The*)
Hamilton

TRIPLE ECHO, THE
HEMDALE 1972

Bates, H.E.
Joseph

TROJAN BROTHERS, THE
BN 1946

Johnson, P.H.
Joseph

TROJAN WOMEN, THE
CINERAMA 1971

Euripides (P)
Various

TROPIC OF CANCER
PAR 1969

Miller, H.
Calder

TROPIC ZONE
PAR 1953

Gill, T. (*No Place for Women*)
Putnam, N.Y.

TROTTIE TRUE
TC 1949

Brahms, C. *and* Simon, S.J.
Joseph

TROUBLE FOR TWO
MGM 1936

Stevenson, R.L. (*Suicide Club, The*)
Various

TROUBLE IN THE GLEN
REP 1954

Walsh, M.
Chambers

TITLE OF FILM	AUTHOR AND PUBLISHER
TROUBLE WITH ANGELS, THE COL 1965	Trahey, J. (*Life with Mother Superior*) Joseph
TROUBLE WITH GIRLS, THE (V) MGM 1969	Keene, D. *and* Babcock, D. (*Chautuaqua*) Four Square Books
TROUBLE WITH HARRY, THE (V) PAR 1955	Story, J.T. Boardman
TRUE AS A TURTLE RANK 1957	Coates, J. Gollancz
TRUE CONFESSIONS UA 1981	Dunne, J.G. Weidenfeld & Nicolson
TRUE GRIT (V) PAR 1969	Portis, C. Cape
TRUSTED OUTLAW, THE REP 1937	McCulley, J. Hutchinson
TUMULT ATHENA 1969	Allen, J. Hogarth Press
TUNES OF GLORY UA 1960	Kennaway, J. Putnam
TUNNEL OF LOVE, THE MGM 1959	De Vries, P. Gollancz
TUNNEL OF LOVE, THE MGM 1959	Fields, J. *and* De Vries, P. (P) French
TURNABOUT UA 1940	Smith, T. Methuen
TURN THE KEY SOFTLY GFD 1953	Brophy, J. Collins
TURTLE DIARY RANK 1985	Hoban, R. Random, N.Y.

TITLE OF FILM	AUTHOR AND PUBLISHER
TUTTLES OF TAHITI, THE RKO 1942	Nordhoff, C.B. *and* Hall, J.N. (*No more Gas*) Chapman & Hall
TWELVE O'CLOCK HIGH FOX 1949	Lay, B. *and* Bartlett, S. Harper, N.Y.
27TH DAY COL 1957	Mantley, J. Joseph
21 HOURS AT MUNICH (V) ALPHA 1976	Groussard, S. (*Blood of Israel, The*) Morrow, N.Y.
20,000 LEAGUES UNDER THE SEA (V) DISNEY 1954 DISNEY 1979	Verne, J. Various
20,000 YEARS IN SING SING IN 1933	Lawes, L.E. Garden City, N.Y.
TWENTY-ONE DAYS LF 1940	Galsworthy, J. (*First and the Last, The*) Heinemann
29 ACACIA AVENUE COL 1945	Constanduros, M. *and* Constanduros, D. (*Acacia Avenue*) (P) French
TWICE ROUND THE DAFFODILS AA 1962	Cargill, P. *and* Beale, J. (*Ring for Catty*) (P) French
TWILIGHT FOR THE GODS RANK 1957	Gann, E.K. Hodder & Stoughton
TWILIGHTS LAST GLEAMING HEMDALE 1977	Wager, W. (*Viper Three*) Macmillan
TWIST OF SAND, A UA 1968	Jenkins, G. Collins
TWO FACES OF DR. JEKYLL, THE COL 1958	Stevenson, R.L. (*Dr. Jekyll and Mr. Hyde*) Various

TITLE OF FILM	AUTHOR AND PUBLISHER
TWO FOR THE ROAD FOX 1967	Raphael, F. Cape
TWO FOR THE SEESAW UA 1962	Gibson, W. (P) French
TWO GENTLEMEN SHARING PAR 1969	Leslie, D.S. Pan
TWO IN THE DARK RKO 1936	Burgess, G. (*Two O'Clock Courage*) Triangle Bks, N.Y.
TWO KINDS OF WOMAN PAR 1932	Sherwood, R.E. (*This is New York*) (P) Scribner, N.Y.
TWO LEFT FEET BL 1965	Leslie, D.S. (*In My Solitude*) Hutchinson
TWO-LETTER ALIBI BL 1962	Garve, A. (*Death and the Sky Above Us*) Pan
TWO LOVES MGM 1960	Ashton-Warner, S. Secker & Warburg
TWO MINUTE WARNING UN 1976	La Fontaine, G. Coward-McCann, N.Y.
TWO MRS CARROLLS, THE WAR 1947	Vale, M. (P) Allen & Unwin
TWO RODE TOGETHER COL 1961	Cooke, W.E. Mills & Boon
2001, A SPACE ODYSSEY (V) MGM 1968	Clarke, A.C. Hutchinson
2010 (V) MGM 1985	Clarke, A.C. Granada
TWO WEEKS IN ANOTHER TOWN MGM 1962	Shaw, I. Cape

TWO YEARS BEFORE THE MAST
PAR 1946

Dana, R.H.
Various

U

UGLY AMERICAN, THE
UI 1962

Lederer, W.J. *and* Burdick, E.L.
Gollancz

UGLY DACHSHUND, THE
DISNEY 1966

Stern, G.B.
Cassell

ULYSSES (V)
ARCHWAY 1954

Homer (*Iliad*)
Various

ULYSSES
BL 1966

Joyce, J.
Lane

UNCHAINED
WAR 1954

Scudder, K.J. (*Prisoners are People*)
Doubleday, N.Y.

UNCLE SILAS
TC 1947

Le Fanu, S.
Oxford U.P.

UNCONQUERED
PAR 1947

Swanson, N.H.
Doubleday, N.Y.

UNDER CAPRICORN (V)
WAR 1949
SOUTH AUSTRALIA FILM 1983

Simpson, H.
Heinemann

UNDER MILK WOOD (V)
RANK 1971

Thomas, D. (P)
Dent

UNDER MY SKIN
FOX 1950

Hemingway, E. (*My Old Man*)
Cape

UNDER NEW MANAGEMENT
BUTCHER 1946

Jacobs, N.
Hutchinson

UNDER THE CARIBBEAN
BL 1954

Hass, H. (*Diving for Adventure*)
Jarrolds

UNDER THE RED ROBE
FOX 1937

Weyman, S.
Various

UNDER THE TONTO RIM
PAR 1933

Grey, Z.
Hodder & Stoughton

UNDER THE VOLCANO (V)
FOX 1984

Lowry, M.
Harper, N.Y.

UNDER TWO FLAGS
FOX 1936

Ouida
Chatto & Windus

UNEASY TERMS
BN 1948

Cheyney, P.
Collins

UNEXPECTED UNCLE
RKO 1941

Hatch, E.
Farrar, N.Y.

UNFAITHFUL, THE
WAR 1947

Maugham, W.S. (*Letter, The*) (P)
French

UNFORGIVEN, THE
UA 1960

LeMay, A. (*Siege at Dancing Bird, The*)
Collins

UNGUARDED HOUR, THE
MGM 1936

Merivale, B. (P)
French

UNHOLY LOVE
HP 1932

Flaubert, G. (*Madame Bovary*)
Cape

UNINVITED, THE
PAR 1944

Macardle, D. (*Uneasy Freehold*)
Doubleday, N.Y.

UNION STATION
PAR 1950

Walsh, T. (*Nightmare in Manhattan*)
Little, Brown, Boston

UNSEEN, THE
PAR 1945

White, E.L. (*Her Heart in Her Throat*)
Grosset, N.Y.

UNSUITABLE JOB FOR A WOMAN, AN
(V)
BOYD 1981

James, P.D.
Sphere

UNSUSPECTED, THE
WAR 1947

Armstrong, C.
Harrap

TITLE OF FILM	AUTHOR AND PUBLISHER
UNTAMED PAR 1940	Lewis, S. (*Mantrap*) Cape
UNTAMED FOX 1955	Moray, H. Museum Press
UNTIL THEY SAIL MGM 1957	Michener, J.A. (*Return to Paradise*) Secker & Warburg
UP FROM THE BEACH FOX 1964	Barr, G. (*Epitaph for an Enemy*) Hutchinson
UP FRONT UI 1951	Maudlin, W.H. Various
UP PERISCOPE WAR 1959	White, R. Collins
UPSTAIRS AND DOWNSTAIRS RANK 1959	Thorn, R.S. Spearman
UP THE DOWN STAIRCASE WAR 1966	Kaufman, B. Barker
UP THE JUNCTION PAR 1968	Dunn, N. Macgibbon & Kee
UP THE SANDBOX (V) CINERAMA 1973	Roiphe, A.R. Secker & Warburg
URBAN COWBOY (V) CIC 1980	Latham, A. Bantam, N.Y.

V

V WAR 1984 (TV)	Crispin, A.C. New English Library
VAGABOND KING, THE PAR 1930 PAR 1956	McCarthy, J.H. (P) French
VALACHI PAPERS, THE (V) CINEMA INT 1972	Maas, P. Panther

304

TITLE OF FILM	AUTHOR AND PUBLISHER
VALDEZ IS COMING (V) UA 1971	Leonard, E. Hale
VALENTINO UA 1977	Steiger, B. *and* Mane, C. Corgi
VALIANT IS THE WORD FOR CARRIE PAR 1938	Benefield, B. Heinemann
VALLEY OF DECISION MGM 1945	Davenport, M. Collins
VALLEY OF THE DOLLS FOX 1968	Susann, J. Cassell
VALLEY OF THE GIANTS WAR 1938	Kyne, P.B. Hodder & Stoughton
VALLEY OF THE HORSES PSO 1984	Auel, J.M. Bantam, N.Y.
VALLEY OF THE SUN RKO 1942	Kelland, C.B. Various
VALUE FOR MONEY RANK 1955	Boothroyd, D. Laurie
VANESSA MGM 1935	Walpole, *Sir* H. Macmillan
VANISHING AMERICAN, THE REP 1955	Grey, Z. Hodder & Stoughton
VANISHING VIRGINIAN, THE MGM 1941	Williams, *Mrs.* R. (*Father was a Handful*) Joseph
VANITY FAIR HOL 1932	Thackeray, W.M. Various
VEILED WOMAN FOX 1929	Reed, M. (*Spinner in the Sun*) Putnam
VENDETTA RKO 1951	Merimee, P. (*Columbia*) Hamilton

VENETIAN AFFAIR, THE
MGM 1966

McInnes, H.
Collins

VENETIAN BIRD
GFD 1952

Canning, V.
Hodder & Stoughton

VENGEANCE
BL 1963

Siodmak, C. (*Donovan's Brain*)
Corgi

VENGEANCE VALLEY
MGM 1950

Short, L.
Collins

VENOM (V)
HANDMADE 1982

Scholefield, A.
Heinemann

VENUS IN FURS
COMMONWEALTH 1970

Sacher-Masoch, L.
Various

VERDICT, THE (V)
FOX 1983

Reed, B.
Bantam, N.Y.

VERTIGO (V)
PAR 1958

Boileau, P. *and* Narcejac, T. (*Living and the Dead, The*)
Arrow

VESSEL OF WRATH, THE
PAR 1938

Maugham, W.S. (*Beachcomber*)
Heinemann

VICE VERSA
TC 1948

Anstey, F.
Murray

VICKI
FOX 1953

Fisher, S. (*I Wake Up Screaming*)
Hale

VICTORIA REGINA
RKO 1937

Housman, L. (P)
Cape

VICTORS, THE
BL 1963

Barons, A. (*Human Kind, The*)
Cape

VICTORY
PAR 1940

Conrad, J.
Various

VIEW FROM THE BRIDGE, A
TRANSCONTINENTAL 1961

Miller, A.
Penguin

TITLE OF FILM	AUTHOR AND PUBLISHER
VIKINGS, THE UA 1958	Marshall, E. (*Viking, The*) Muller
VILLAGE OF THE DAMNED, THE MGM 1960	Wyndham, J. (*Midwich Cuckoos, The*) Penguin
VILLAIN EMI—MGM 1971	Barlow, J. (*Burden of Proof*) Pan
VINTAGE, THE MGM 1957	Keir, U. Collins
VIOLATERS, THE RKO 1957	Beckhardt, I. *and* Brown, W. Arco
VIOLENT ENEMY, THE MONARCH 1969	Marlowe, H. (*Candle for the Dead, A*) Abelard-Schuman
VIOLENT SATURDAY FOX 1955	Heath, W.L. Hamilton
VIOLENT STREET (V) UA 1981	Hohimer, F. (*Home Invader*) Chicago Review, Chicago
V.I.P.'s, THE MGM 1963	Albert, M. Mayflower
VIRGIN AND THE GYPSY, THE LONDON SCREENPLAYS 1971	Lawrence, D.H. Heinemann
VIRGINIAN, THE PAR 1929	Wister, O. Various
VIRGIN ISLAND BL 1958	White, R. (*Our Virgin Island*) Gollancz
VIRGIN SOLDIERS, THE (V) COL 1969	Thomas, L. Constable
VIRGIN WITCH (V) TIGON 1970	Vogel, K. Corgi

TITLE OF FILM	AUTHOR AND PUBLISHER
VIRTUOUS HUSBAND UN 1931	Davis, D. (*Apron Strings*) (P) French, N.Y.
VISIT, THE FOX 1964	Durrenmatt, F. (P) French, N.Y.
VISIT TO A SMALL PLANET PAR 1959	Vidal, G. (P) Little, Toronto
VIVA ZAPATA! FOX 1952	Pinchon, E. (*Zapata the* *Unconquerable*) Doubleday, N.Y.
VOICE OF BUGLE ANN MGM 1936	Kantor, M. Selwyn & Blount
VOICE OF THE TURTLE WAR 1947	Druten, J. van (P) Joseph
VOICES (V) HEMDALE 1973	Lortz, R. (*Children of the Night*) (P) Dell, N.Y.
VOLPONE SIRITZKY 1947	Jonson, B. (P) Allen & Unwin
VON RYAN'S EXPRESS FOX 1964	Westheimer, D. Joseph
VOYAGE OF THE DAMNED (V) ITC 1976	Thomas, G. *and* Witts, G.M. Hodder & Stoughton

W

WACO PAR 1967	Sanford, H. *and* Lamb, M. (*Emporia* Hale
WAGES OF FEAR FILMS DE FRANCE 1953 CIC 1978	Arnaud, G. British Publishers' Guild
WAGON WHEELS PAR 1934	Grey, Z. (*Fighting Caravans*) Hodder & Stoughton

TITLE OF FILM	AUTHOR AND PUBLISHER
WAHOO BOBCAT, THE DISNEY 1963	Lippincott, J.W. Lippincott, Philadelphia
WAIT UNTIL DARK WAR 1968	Knott, F. (P) French
WAKE ME WHEN IT'S OVER FOX 1960	Singer, H. Putnam, N.Y.
WAKE OF THE RED WITCH REP 1948	Roark, G. Aldor
WAKE UP AND LIVE FOX 1937	Brande, D. Barker
WALKABOUT FOX 1971	Marshall, J.V. Joseph
WALKING STICK, THE MGM 1969	Graham, W. Collins
WALK IN THE SPRING RAIN, A COL 1969	Maddux, R. Doubleday, N.Y.
WALK IN THE SUN, A FOX 1945	Brown, H.P.M. Secker & Warburg
WALK ON THE WILD SIDE, A COL 1962	Algren, N. Ace
WALK WITH LOVE AND DEATH, A FOX 1968	Koningberger, H. Pan
WALLENBERG: THE LOST HERO BERYL—STONEHENGE 1985 (TV)	Werbell, F. *and* Clarke, T. (*Lost Hero*) McGraw, N.Y.
WALLS OF GOLD FOX 1933	Norris, K. Murray
WALLS OF JERICHO, THE FOX 1949	Wellman, P.I. Laurie
WALTZ OF THE TOREADORS RANK 1962	Anouilh, J. (P) French

TITLE OF FILM	AUTHOR AND PUBLISHER
WANDERER OF THE WASTELAND PAR 1935 RKO 1945	Grey, Z. Hodder & Stoughton
WANDERERS, THE WAR 1980	Price, R. Avon, N.Y.
WANDERING JEW, THE OLY 1935	Thurston, E.T. (P) Putnam
WAR AND PEACE PAR 1956	Tolstoy, L. Macmillan
WAR CORRESPONDENT INT 1951	Pyle, E.T. (*Here's Your War*) Various
WARE CASE, THE FOX 1939	Bancroft, G.P. (P) Methuen
WARLOCK FOX 1959	Hall, O. Bodley Head
WAR LORD, THE RANK 1965	Stevens, L. (*Lovers, The*) (P) French
WAR LOVER, THE COL 1963	Hersey, J. Hamilton
WARN THAT MAN AB 1942	Sylvaine, V. (P) French
WARNING TO WANTONS, A AQUILA 1949	Mitchell, M. Heinemann
WAR OF THE WORLDS (V) PAR 1953	Wells, H.G. Heinemann
WAR WAGON UI 1966	Huffaker, C. (*Badman*) Muller
WATCHER IN THE WOODS (V) DISNEY 1982	Randall, F.E. Atheneum, N.Y.
WATCH IT SAILOR COL 1961	Cary, F.L. *and* King, P. (P) Elek

TITLE OF FILM	AUTHOR AND PUBLISHER
WATCH ON THE RHINE (V) WAR 1943	Hellman, L.F. (P) Random House, N.Y.
WATER BABIES, THE (V) PRODUCER ASSOCIATES 1979	Kingsley, C. Various
WATERFRONT GFD 1950	Brophy, J. Various
WATER GYPSIES, THE SDC 1932	Herbert, *Sir* A.P. Methuen
WATERLOO BRIDGE UN 1932 MGM 1940	Sherwood, R.E. (P) Scribner, N.Y.
WATERSHIP DOWN (V) CIC 1978	Adams, R. Penguin
WATUSI MGM 1958	Haggard, *Sir* H.R. (*King Solomon's Mines*) Various
WAY OF A GAUCHO FOX 1952	Childs, H. (*Gaucho*) Prentice-Hall, N.Y.
WAYS AND MEANS GFD 1952	Coward, N. (P) Heinemann
WAY TO THE GOLD, THE FOX 1957	Steele, W.D. Doubleday, N.Y.
WAYWARD BUS, THE FOX 1957	Steinbeck, J. Heinemann
WAY WEST, THE UA 1966	Guthrie, A.B. Corgi
WAY WE WERE, THE COL 1973	Laurents, A. W.H. Allen
W.C. FIELDS AND ME UN 1976	Monti, C. *and* Rice, C. Joseph

TITLE OF FILM	AUTHOR AND PUBLISHER
WEAK AND THE WICKED, THE APB 1953	Henry, J. (*Who Lie in Gaol*) Gollancz
WEAKER SEX, THE TC 1948	McCracken, E. (*No Medals*) (P) French
WE ARE NOT ALONE WAR 1939	Hilton, J. Macmillan
WEATHER IN THE STREETS, THE BBC 2 1984 (TV)	Lehmann, R. Doubleday, N.Y.
WEDDING, THE TYNE-TEES 1983 (TV)	Pritchett, V.S. Chatto & Windus
WE DIE ALONE REN 1959	Howarth, D. (*Escape Alone*) Collins
WEEKEND AT DUNKIRK FOX 1965	Merle, R. (*Weekend at Zuydcoote*) Lehmann
WEEK-END AT THE WALDORF MGM 1945	Bolton, G. Grosset, N.Y.
WEEK-END MARRIAGE IN 1932	Baldwin, F. (*Part-time Wives*) Sampson Low
WEEK-ENDS ONLY FOX 1932	Fabian, W. (*Week-end Girl*) Paul
WEE WILLIE WINKIE FOX 1937	Kipling, R. Macmillan
WE JOINED THE NAVY WAR 1962	Winton, J. Joseph
WELCOME TO THE CLUB COL 1970	Wood, C.B. Panther
WE LIVE AGAIN UA 1934	Tolstoy, L.N. (*Resurrection*) Various
WE OF THE NEVER NEVER (V) ADAMS PACKER 1982	Gunn, *Mrs*. A. Angus & Robertson

TITLE OF FILM	AUTHOR AND PUBLISHER
WE'RE IN THE MINK RANK 1959	Coke, P. (*Breath of Spring*) (P) French
WE'RE NO ANGELS PAR 1955	Husson, A. (*My Three Angels*) (P) Random House, N.Y.
WEST II WAR 1963	Del Rivo, L. (*Furnished Room, The*) Hutchinson
WEST LAND CASE, THE UN 1937	Latimer, J. (*Headed for a Hearse*) Methuen
WEST OF THE PECOS RKO 1934 RKO 1945	Grey, Z. Hodder & Stoughton
WET PARADE MGM 1932	Sinclair, U. Laurie
WE WERE DANCING MGM 1942	Coward, N. (P) French
WE WERE STRANGERS COL 1949	Sylvester, R. (*Rough Sketch*) Dial Press, N.Y.
WHAT BECAME OF JACK AND JILL? FOX 1971	Moody, L. (*Ruthless Ones, The*) Hale
WHATEVER HAPPENED TO AUNT ALICE? (V) PALOMAR 1969	Curtiss, U. (*Forbidden Garden, The*) Eyre & Spottiswoode
WHATEVER HAPPENED TO BABY JANE? (V) WAR 1962	Farrell, H. (*Baby Jane*) Eyre & Spottiswoode
WHAT EVERY WOMAN KNOWS MGM 1934	Barrie, *Sir* J.M. (P) Hodder & Stoughton
WHAT EVERY WOMAN WANTS ADELPHI 1954	Lewis, E. (*Relations are Best Apart*) (P) Playscripts
WHAT LOLA WANTS WAR 1958	Addler, R. *and* Ross, J. (*Damn Yankees*) (P) Random House, N.Y.

313

WHAT MAD PURSUIT
BBC 1985 (TV)

Coward, N.
Methuen

WHAT PRICE GLORY
FOX 1952

Anderson, M. *and* Stallings, L. (P)
Dodd, N.Y.

WHEN EIGHT BELLS TOLL
RANK 1971

MacLean, A.
Collins

WHEN LADIES MEET
MGM 1941

Crothers, R. (P)
French, N.Y.

WHEN THE BOYS MEET THE GIRLS
MGM 1965

Bolton, G. *and* McGowan, J. (*Girl
Crazy*) (P)
Dramatic, Chicago

WHEN THE LEGENDS DIE
FOX 1972

Borland, H.
Penguin

WHEN TIME RAN OUT (V)
COL—EMI—WAR 1980

Thomas, G. *and* Witt, M. (*Day the
World Ended, The*)
Stein & Day, N.Y.

WHEN WE ARE MARRIED
BN 1943

Priestley, J.B. (P)
Heinemann

WHEN WORLDS COLLIDE
PAR 1951

Balmer, E. *and* Wylie, P.
Paul

WHERE DOES IT HURT?
HEMDALE 1971

Amateau, R. *and* Robinson, B.
(*Operator, The*)
Sphere

WHERE EAGLES DARE (V)
MGM 1969

MacLean, A.
Collins

WHERE LOVE HAS GONE
PAR 1964

Robbins, H.
Blond

WHERE SINNERS MEET
RKO 1934

Milne, A.A. (*Dover Road*) (P)
Houghton, Mifflin, Boston

WHERE'S POPPA?
UA 1971

Klane, R.
Random House, N.Y.

TITLE OF FILM	AUTHOR AND PUBLISHER
WHERE THE BOYS ARE (V) MGM 1960	Swarthout, G. Heinemann
WHERE THE LILIES BLOOM UA 1974	Cleaver, V. *and* Cleaver, B. Penguin
WHERE THE RED FERN GROWS EMI 1974	Rawls, W. Doubleday, N.Y.
WHERE THERE'S A WILL EROS 1955	Delderfield, R.F. (P) French
WHERE THE RIVER BENDS UI 1952	Gullick, B. (*Bend of the Snake*) Museum Press
WHERE THE SIDEWALK ENDS FOX 1950	Stuart, W.L. (*Night Cry*) Dial Press, N.Y.
WHERE THE SPIES ARE MGM 1965	Leasor, J. (*Passport to Oblivion*) Heinemann
WHEREVER SHE GOES ABP 1950	Abrahall, C.H. (*Prelude*) Oxford U.P.
WHILE PARENTS SLEEP SOSKIN 1936	Kimmins, A. (P) French
WHILE THE PATIENT SLEPT IN 1935	Eberhart, M.G. Heinemann
WHILE THE SUN SHINES ABP 1947	Rattigan, T. (P) Hamilton
WHIRLPOOL FOX 1951	Endore, G. (*Methinks the Lady*) Cresset Press
WHISKY GALORE (V) EALING 1949	Mackenzie, *Sir* C. Chatto & Windus
WHISPERERS, THE UA 1966	Nicolson, R. (*Mrs. Ross*) Constable
WHISPERING SMITH PAR 1948	Spearman, F.H. Grosset, N.Y.

TITLE OF FILM	AUTHOR AND PUBLISHER
WHISPERING SMITH SPEAKS FOX 1935	Spearman, F.H. (*Whispering Smith*) Grosset, N.Y.
WHISTLE DOWN THE WIND (V) RANK 1961	Bell, M.H. Boardman
WHISTLE-STOP UA 1946	Wolff, M.M. Constable
WHITE BANNERS WAR 1938	Douglas, L.C. Davies
WHITE BUFFALO, THE EMI 1978	Sale, R. Simon & Schuster, N.Y.
WHITE CARGO BI 1930 MGM 1942	Gordon, L. (P) Various
WHITE COCKATOO WAR 1935	Eberhart, M.G. Lane
WHITE COLT, THE COL 1969	Rook, D. Hodder & Stoughton
WHITE CORRIDORS GFD 1951	Ashton, H. (*Yeoman's Hospital*) Collins
WHITE DAWN, THE CIC 1974	Houston, J. Heinemann
WHITE FANG FOX 1936 FOX 1974	London, J. Methuen
WHITE SISTER MGM 1933	Crawford, F.M. Bles
WHITE TOWER, THE (V) RKO 1950	Ullman, J.R. Collins
WHITE UNICORN, THE CORNFIELD 1947	Sandstrom, F. (*Milk White Unicorn, The*) Cassell

TITLE OF FILM	AUTHOR AND PUBLISHER
WHITE WITCH DOCTOR FOX 1953	Stinetorf, L.A. Westminster Press, Philadelphia
WHO GOES NEXT? FOX 1938	Simpson, R. *and* Drawbell, J.W. (P) French
WHO GOES THERE? BL 1952	Dighton, J. (P) Elek
WHO IS HOPE SCHUYLER? FOX 1942	Ransome, S. (*Hearses Don't Hurry*) Doubleday, N.Y.
WHO IS THE RUNNING MAN? PSO 1986	Bachmann, R. New English Library
WHO KILLED AUNT MAGGIE? REP 1940	Field, M. Jarrolds
WHO KILLED THE CAT? GN 1966	Ridley, A. *and* Borer, M. (*Tabitha*) (P) French
WHO'LL STOP THE RAIN? (V) UA 1978	Stone, R. (*Dog Soldiers*) Secker & Warburg
WHO'S AFRAID OF VIRGINIA WOOLF? (V) WAR 1965	Albee, E. (P) Cape
WHOSE LIFE IS IT ANYWAY? CIC 1981	Clark, B. (P) Avon, N.Y.
WHO'S GOT THE ACTION? PAR 1963	Rose, A. (*Four Punters are Missing*) Hamilton
WHO WAS THAT LADY? COL 1960	Krasna, N. (*Who Was That Lady I Saw You With?*) (P) Random House, N.Y.
WHY NOT STAY FOR BREAKFAST? ENTERPRISE 1979	Stone, G. *and* Cooney, R. (P) French
WHY SHOULD I LIE? (V) MGM 1980	Hodges, H. (*Fabricator, The*) Avon, N.Y.

TITLE OF FILM	AUTHOR AND PUBLISHER
WICKED LADY, THE (V) GFD 1946 CANNON 1982	King-Hall, M. (*Life and Death of the Wicked Lady Skelton, The*) Davies
WILBY CONSPIRACY, THE (V) UA 1974	Driscoll, P. Macdonald
WILD AFFAIR, THE BL 1965	Sansom, W. (*Last Hours of Sandra Lee, The*) Hogarth Press
WILD AND THE WILLING, THE RANK 1962	Dobie, L. *and* Sloman, R. (*Tinker, The*) (P) French
WILD COUNTRY, THE (V) DISNEY 1971	Moody, R. (*Little Britches*) Harcourt, Brace, N.Y.
WILD GEESE, THE (V) RANK 1978	Carney, D. Heinemann
WILD GEESE II (V) COL—EMI—WAR 1985	Carney, D. (*Square Circle, The*) Firecrest
WILD HARVEST GN 1961	Longstreet, S. Muller
WILD HORSE MESA PAR 1932	Grey, Z. Hodder & Stoughton
WILD IN THE COUNTRY FOX 1961	Salamanca, J.R. (*Lost Country, The*) Four Square Books
WILD RIVER FOX 1960	Deal, B. (*Dunbar's Cove*) Hutchinson
WILL ANY GENTLEMAN . . . ? ABP 1953	Sylvaine, V. (P) French
WILLARD CINERAMA 1971	Gilbert, S. (*Ratman's Notebook*) Joseph
WILLIE WONKA AND THE CHOCOLATE FACTORY PAR 1971	Dahl, R. (*Charlie and the Chocolate Factory*) Allen & Unwin

TITLE OF FILM	AUTHOR AND PUBLISHER
WIND CANNOT READ, THE RANK 1958	Mason, R. Hodder & Stoughton
WINDOM'S WAY RANK 1957	Ullman, J.R. Collins
WINDOW TO THE SKY, A UN 1975	Valens, E.G. (*Long Way Up, A*) Harper, N.Y.
WINDS OF WAR, THE PAR 1983 (TV)	Wouk, H. Collins
WINDWALKER PACIFIC 1981	Yorgason, B. Bookcraft, Salt Lake City
WINGED VICTORY FOX 1944	Hart, M. (P) Various
WINNIE THE POOH AND THE HONEY TREE DISNEY 1965	Milne, A.A. Methuen
WINSLOW BOY, THE (V) IS 1949	Rattigan, T. (P) Hamilton
WINSTANLEY THE OTHER CINEMA 1975	Caute, D. (*Comrade Jacob*) Quartet
WINTER KILLS (V) AVCO EMBASSY 1979	Condon, R. Dial, N.Y.
WINTER MEETING WAR 1948	Vance, G. Collins
WINTERSET RKO 1936	Anderson, M. (P) Lane
WINTER'S TALE, A WAR 1968	Shakespeare, W. (P) Various
WIRETAPPER, THE EXCLUSIVE 1955	Vaus, J. (*Why I Quit Syndicated Crime*) Van Kempen, Wheaton, Ill.

TITLE OF FILM	AUTHOR AND PUBLISHER
WISE BLOOD ARTIFICIAL EYE 1979	O'Connor, F. Farrar, N.Y.
WITCHES, THE HAMMER 1966	Curtis, P. (*Devil's Own, The*) Pan
WITCHES OF SALEM, THE FILMS DE FRANCE 1957	Miller, A. (*Crucible, The*) (P) Secker & Warburg
WITCHFINDER GENERAL (V) TIGON 1968	Bassett, R. Jenkins
WITHOUT APPARENT MOTIVE FOX 1972	McBain, E. (*Ten Plus One*) Simon & Schuster, N.Y.
WITHOUT A TRACE (V) FOX 1983	Gutcheon, B. (*Still Missing*) Joseph
WITHOUT LOVE MGM 1945	Barry, P. (P) Coward-McCann, N.Y.
WITHOUT RESERVATIONS (V) RKO 1946	Allen, J. *and* Livingston, M. (*Thanks God, I'll Take it From Here*) Faber
WITH REGRET PAR 1935	Pertwee, R. *and* Dearden, H. (*Interference*) (P) French, N.Y.
WITNESS FOR THE PROSECUTION UA 1957	Christie, A. (P) French
WITNESS VANISHES, THE UN 1939	Ronald, J. (*They Can't Hang Me*) Rich & Cowan
WIZ, THE (V) DISNEY 1979	Baum, F. (*Wonderful Wizard of Oz, The*) Various
WIZARD OF OZ, THE (V) MGM 1939	Baum, L.F. Hutchinson
WOLFEN, THE (V) WAR 1980	Strieben, W. Morrow, N.Y.

TITLE OF FILM	AUTHOR AND PUBLISHER
WOLF HUNTERS, THE MONOGRAM 1949	Curwood, J.O. Various
WOLF LARSEN ABP 1959	London, J. (*Sea Wolf, The*) Heinemann
WOMAN IN THE DARK REP 1952	Cosentino, N. (*Moon Over Mulberry Street*) (P) Dramatic Pubns, Chicago
WOMAN IN THE HALL, THE GFD 1947	Stern, G.B. Cassell
WOMAN IN THE NIGHT WW 1929	Barcynska, *Countess* (*Tesha*) Hurst & Blackett
WOMAN IN THE WINDOW, THE RKO 1944	Wallis, J.H. (*Once Off Guard*) Jarrolds
WOMAN IN WHITE, THE WAR 1948	Collins, W. Various
WOMAN I STOLE, THE COL 1933	Hergesheimer, J. (*Tampico*) Various
WOMAN OBSERVED, THE FOX 1959	Mantley, J. (*Snow Birch, The*) Joseph
WOMAN OF AFFAIRS, A MGM 1929	Arlen, M. (*Green Hat, The*) Collins
WOMAN OF ROME, A EXCLUSIVE 1956	Moravia, A. Secker & Warburg
WOMAN OF STRAW UA 1964	Arley, C. Collins
WOMAN OF SUBSTANCE, A CHANNEL 4 1985 (TV)	Bradford, B.T. Avon, N.Y.
WOMAN OF SUMMER FOX 1963	Inge, W. (*Loss of Roses, A*) (P) Random House, N.Y.
WOMAN OF THE DUNES, THE CONTEMPORARY 1965	Abe, K. Secker & Warburg

321

TITLE OF FILM	AUTHOR AND PUBLISHER
WOMAN OF THE WORLD MGM 1935	Arlen, M. (*Green Hat, The*) Collins
WOMAN REBELS, A RKO 1936	Syrett, N. (*Portrait of a Rebel*) Bles
WOMAN'S ANGLE, A ABP 1951	Feiner, R. (*Three Cups of Coffee*) Dakers
WOMAN'S ROOM, THE BBC 2 1984 (TV)	French, M. Deutsch
WOMAN'S SECRET, A RKO 1949	Baum, V. (*Mortgage on Life*) Doubleday, N.Y.
WOMAN'S VENGEANCE, A UN 1947	Huxley, A.L. (*Gioconda Smile, The*) Harper
WOMAN WITH NO NAME, THE ABP 1950	Charles, T. (*Happy Now I Go*) Longmans
WOMAN WITHOUT A FACE MGM 1968	Hunter, E. (*Buddwing*) Constable
WOMEN, THE MGM 1939	Boothe, C. (P) Gollancz
WOMEN AREN'T ANGELS AB 1943	Sylvaine, V. (P) French
WOMEN IN LOVE (V) UA 1969	Lawrence, D.H. Heinemann
WOMEN OF TWILIGHT ROMULUS 1952	Rayman, S. (P) Evans
WOMEN WHO PLAY GB 1932	Lonsdale, F. (*Spring Cleaning*) (P) Collins
WONDERFUL COUNTRY, THE UA 1959	Lea, T. Heinemann
WONDERFUL WORLD OF THE BROTHERS GRIMM, THE MGM 1962	Grimm, J.L.K. *and* Grimm, W.K. (*Grimms' Fairy Tales*) Dent

TITLE OF FILM	AUTHOR AND PUBLISHER
WOODEN HORSE, THE (V) BL 1950	Williams, E. Collins
WORK IS A FOUR LETTER WORD UI 1968	Livings, H. (P) Methuen
WORLD ACCORDING TO GARP, THE (V) COL—EMI—WAR 1982	Irving, J. Gollancz
WORLD AND HIS WIFE, THE MGM 1948	Lindsay, H. *and* Crouse, R. (*State of the Union*) (P) Dramatists, N.Y.
WORLD IN HIS ARMS, THE GFD 1952	Beach, R. Hutchinson
WORLD IS FULL OF MARRIED MEN, THE (V) NEW REALM 1978	Collins, J. W.H. Allen
WORLD OF HENRY ORIENT, THE UA 1964	Johnson, N. Gollancz
WORLD OF SUZIE WONG, THE PAR 1959	Mason, R. Collins
WORLD OF SUZIE WONG, THE PAR 1959	Osborn, P. (P) Random House, N.Y.
WORLD, THE FLESH AND THE DEVIL, THE MGM 1959	Shiel, M.P. (*Purple Cloud, The*) Gollancz
WORM'S EYE VIEW ABP 1951	Delderfield, R.F. (P) Sampson Low
W PLAN RKO 1931	Seton, G. Butterworth
WRATH OF GOD, THE MGM—EMI 1973	Graham, J. Macmillan
WRECKING CREW, THE COL 1969	Hamilton, D. Coronet

TITLE OF FILM	AUTHOR AND PUBLISHER
WRECK OF THE MARY DEARE, THE MGM 1959	Innes, H. (*Mary Deare, The*) Collins
WRITTEN ON THE WIND UN 1956	Wilder, R. Corgi
WRONG BOX, THE COL 1965	Stevenson, R.L. *and* Osbourne, L. Longmans
WUSA PAR 1972	Stone, R. (*Hall of Mirrors, A*) Bodley Head
WUTHERING HEIGHTS (V) UA 1939 MGM—EMI 1970	Bronte, E.J. Various
WYNNE AND PENKOVSKY BBC 1985 (TV)	Wynne, G. (*Man from Moscow, A*) Arrow

Y

YANGTSE INCIDENT BL 1957	Earl, L. (*Escape of the Amethyst, The*) Harrap
YANK AT OXFORD, A MGM 1938	Garland, A.P. Collins
YANKEE PASHA GFD 1954	Marshall, E. Redman
YANK IN ERMINE, A MON 1955	Carstairs, J.P. (*Solid! Said the Earl*) Hurst & Blackett
YEARLING, THE MGM 1946	Rawlings, *Mrs.* M. Heinemann
YEAR OF LIVING DANGEROUSLY, THE UIP 1983	Koch, C.J. Sphere
YEAR OF THE DRAGON COL—EMI—WAR 1985	Daley, R. Coronet
YEARS BETWEEN, THE FOX 1946	Du Maurier, D. (P) Gollancz

TITLE OF FILM	AUTHOR AND PUBLISHER
YELLOW CANARY, THE FOX 1963	Masterson, W. (*Evil Come, Evil Go*) W.H. Allen
YELLOW SANDS, THE AB 1938	Phillpotts, E. (P) Duckworth
YELLOWSTONE KELLY WAR 1959	Fisher, C. Houghton, Mifflin, Boston
YES, MY DARLING DAUGHTER WAR 1939	Reed, M.W. (P) French, N.Y.
YIELD TO THE NIGHT ABP 1956	Henry, J. Gollancz
YOU CAN'T ESCAPE ABP 1955	Kennington, A. (*She Died Young*) Jarrolds
YOU CAN'T SEE ROUND CORNERS UI 1969	Cleary, J. Collins
YOU CAN'T TAKE IT WITH YOU COL 1938	Kaufman, G.S. *and* Hart, M. (P) Barker
YOU KNOW WHAT SAILORS ARE GFD 1953	Hyams, E. (*Sylvester*) Longmans
YOU'LL LIKE MY MOTHER UN 1972	Hintze, N.A. Fawcett, N.Y.
YOUNG AND EAGER WAR 1961	Caldwell, E. (*Claudelle*) Pan
YOUNG AND WILLING UA 1943	Swan, F. (*Out of the Frying Pan*) (P) French, N.Y.
YOUNG BESS MGM 1953	Irwin, M. Chatto & Windus
YOUNG BILLY YOUNG UA 1969	Henry, W. (*Who Rides with Wyatt?*) Bantam, N.Y.
YOUNGBLOOD HAWKE WAR 1963	Wouk, H. Cape

TITLE OF FILM	AUTHOR AND PUBLISHER
YOUNG CASSIDY MGM 1962	O'Casey, S. (*Mirror in my House*) Macmillan
YOUNG DOCTORS, THE UA 1961	Hailey, A. (*Final Diagnosis, The*) Joseph
YOUNG DON'T CRY, THE COL 1957	Jessup, R. (*Man in Charge*) Secker & Warburg
YOUNG DR. KILDARE, THE MGM 1938	Brand, M. Hodder & Stoughton
YOUNG EMMANUELLE NEW REALM 1977	Arsan, E. Hart-Davis
YOUNGEST PROFESSION, THE MGM 1943	Day, L. Laurie
YOUNG HAVE NO TIME, THE CROSS CHANNEL 1959	Allen, J. (*Young Love*) Pan
YOUNG IN HEART, THE UA 1938	Wylie, I.A.R. Cassell
YOUNG LIONS, THE (V) FOX 1957	Shaw, I. Cape
YOUNG LOVERS, THE MGM 1964	Halevy, J. Mayflower
YOUNG MAN OF MANHATTAN PAR 1930	Brush, K. Cassell
YOUNG MAN OF MUSIC (V) WAR 1950	Baker, D. (*Young Man with a Horn*) Gollancz
YOUNG SAVAGES, THE UA 1960	Hunter, E. (*Matter of Conviction, A*) Constable
YOUNG VISITORS, THE CHANNEL 4 1984 (TV)	Ashford, D. Chatto & Windus
YOUNG WARRIORS (V) RANK 1966	Matheson, R. (*Beardless Warriors*) Corgi

TITLE OF FILM	AUTHOR AND PUBLISHER
YOUNG WIDOW UA 1946	Cushman, C. Triangle Bks, N.Y.
YOUNG WINSTON COL—WAR 1972	Churchill, *Sir* W.S. (*My Early Life*) Fontana
YOUNG WIVES' TALE ABP 1951	Jeans, R. (P) French
YOUNG WOODLEY BI 1930	Druten, J. van (P) Putnam
YOUNG WOODLEY BI 1930	Druten, J. van Gollancz
YOU ONLY LIVE TWICE (V) UA 1966	Fleming, I. Cape
YOU PAY YOUR MONEY BUTCHER 1956	Cronin, M. Museum Press
YOU'RE A BIG BOY NOW WAR 1966	Benedictus, D. Blond
YOU'RE ONLY YOUNG TWICE ABP 1952	Bridie, J. (*What Say They*) (P) Constable
YOUR TICKET IS NO LONGER VALID (V) CAROLCO 1983	Gary, R. Braziller, N.Y.
YUKON FLIGHT MON 1940	Erskine, L.Y. (*Renfrew Rides North*) Grosset, N.Y.

Z

Z WAR 1969	Vassilikos, V. Macdonald
ZARAK COL 1956	Bevan, A.J. (*Story of Zarak Khan, The*) Jarrolds

TITLE OF FILM	AUTHOR AND PUBLISHER
ZASTROZZI CHANNEL 4 1986 (TV)	Shelley, P.B. Various
ZAZIE CONNOISSEUR 1962	Queneau, R. Lane
ZOO 2000 BBC 1984 (TV)	Cherfas, J. BBC
ZORBA THE GREEK FOX 1964 CANNON 1986	Kazantzakis, N. Faber

AUTHOR INDEX

Author's works which have been filmed are listed under the original title. Film titles which differ from the original are shown in italics.

A

ABBEY, Edward
BRAVE COWBOY, THE
(Hodder & Stoughton)

UI 1962
(*Lonely are the Brave*)

ABBOTT, Anthony
MURDER OF THE CIRCUS QUEEN,
THE
(Collins)

COL 1933
(*Circus Queen Murder*)

ABBOTT, George *and* **BISSELL, Richard Pike**
PAJAMA GAME (P)
(Random House, N.Y.)

WAR 1957

ABE, Kobo
WOMAN OF THE DUNES, THE
(Secker & Warburg)

CONTEMPORARY 1965

ABERSON, Helen *and* **PEARL, Harold**
DUMBO
(Disney Classic, Purnell)

DISNEY 1972

ABRAHALL, Clare Hoskyns
PRELUDE
(Oxford U.P.)

ABP 1950
(*Wherever She Goes*)

ABRAHAMS, Doris Caroline *see* **BRAHMS, C.** *pseud.*

ACKLAND, Rodney
BIRTHDAY (P)
(French, N.Y.)

FOX 1943
(*Heaven Can Wait*)

ADAMS, Clifton
DANGEROUS DAYS OF KIOWA
JONES, THE
(Collins)

MGM 1966

ADAMS, R.G.
PLAGUE DOGS, THE
(Lane)

DOLBY STEREO 1982

ADAMS, Peter *and* **COOKLIN, S.**
KNOCKBACK
(Duckworth)

BBC 1985 (TV)

ADAMS, Richard
WATERSHIP DOWN   CIC 1978
(Penguin)

ADAMS, Samuel Hopkins
NIGHT BUS   COL 1934
(Longmans)   (*It Happened One Night*)

ADAMSON, Hans Christian *see* **LOCKWOOD, C.A.** *jt. author*

ADAMSON, Joy
BORN FREE   BL 1964
(Collins)
LIVING FREE   COL 1971
(Collins)

ADDYMAN, Elizabeth
SECRET TENT (P)   BL 1956
(English Theatre Guild)

ADLEMAN, Robert H. *and* **WALTON, George**
DEVIL'S BRIGADE, THE   UA 1968
(Transworld)

ADLER, Polly
HOUSE IS NOT A HOME, A   PAR 1964
(Heinemann)

ADLER, Richard *and* **ROSS, Jerry**
WHAT LOLA WANTS (P)   WAR 1958
(Random House, N.Y.)

ADLER, Warren
TRANS-SIBERIAN EXPRESS   ITC 1978
(Macmillan)

AGEE, James
DEATH IN THE FAMILY, A   PAR 1963
(Gollancz)   (*All The Way Home*)

ALBEE, Edward
DELICATE BALANCE, A   SEVEN KEYS 1974
(Cape)

WHO'S AFRAID OF VIRGINIA   WAR 1965
WOOLF? (P)
(Cape)

ALBERT, Marvin H.
APACHE RISING   UA 1966
(Muller)   (*Duel at Diablo*)
DON IS DEAD, THE   UN 1973
(Coronet)
LADY IN CEMENT   FOX 1969
(Sphere)
V.I.P.'s, THE   MGM 1963
(Mayflower)

ALBRAND, Martha
DESPERATE MOMENT   GFD 1953
(Chatto & Windus)

ALCOCK, Vivien
TRAVELLERS BY NIGHT   TVS 1985 (TV)
(Methuen)

ALCOTT, Louise May
LITTLE MEN   RKO 1940
(Various)
LITTLE WOMEN   RKO 1933
(Various)   MGM 1948
OLD FASHIONED GIRL, AN   EL 1948
(Sampson Low)

ALDINGTON, Richard
ALL MEN ARE ENEMIES   FOX 1934
(Heinemann)

ALDRICH, *Mrs.* Bess
MISS BISHOP   UA 1941
(Hodder & Stoughton)   (*Cheers for Miss Bishop*)

ALDRIDGE, James
SPORTING PROPOSITION, A DISNEY 1975
(Dell, N.Y.)   (*Ride a Wild Pony*)

ALEXANDER, Karl
TIME AFTER TIME   COL—EMI—WAR 1979
(Delacorte, N.Y.)

ALEXANDER, Lloyd
BLACK CAULDRON, THE   DISNEY 1985
(Collins)

ALEXANDER, Ronald
TIME OUT FOR GINGER (P)   UA 1965
(Dramatists, N.Y.)   (*Billie*)

ALGREN, Nelson
MAN WITH THE GOLDEN ARM,   UA 1955
THE
(Doubleday, N.Y.)
WALK ON THE WILD SIDE, A   COL 1962
(Ace)

ALLAN, Edward *see* **MACDOUGALL, R.** *jt. author*

ALLARDICE, James
AT WAR WITH THE ARMY (P)   PAR 1951
(French, N.Y.)

ALLEN, Henry *see* **FISHER, Clay** *pseud.*

ALLEN, Hervey
ANTHONY ADVERSE   WAR 1936
(Gollancz)

ALLEN, Jane *pseud. and* **LIVINGSTONE, May**
THANKS GOD, I'LL TAKE IT FROM   RKO 1946
HERE   (*Without Reservation*)
(Faber)

ALLEN, Johannes
TUMULT   ATHENA 1969
(Hogarth Press)
YOUNG LOVE   CC 1959
(Pan)   (*Young Have No Time, The*)

ALLEN, R.S. *see* **RIGBY, Kay** *jt. author*

ALLEN, Woody
DON'T DRINK THE WATER (P)   AVCO EMBASSY 1969
(Random House, N.Y.)
PLAY IT AGAIN, SAM (P)   PAR 1972
(Random House, N.Y.)

AUTHOR AND ORIGINAL TITLE	FILM TITLE

ALLINGHAM, Margery
TIGER IN THE SMOKE   RANK 1956
(Chatto & Windus)

ALLISON, W. and FAIRLEY, J.
MONOCLED MUTINEER, THE   BBC 1986 (TV)
(Quartet)

ALLISTER, Ray
FRIESE-GREENE   BL 1951
(Marsland)   (*Magic Box, The*)

AMADO, Jorge
DONA FLOR AND HER TWO   FD 1978
HUSBANDS
(Avon, N.Y.)

AMATEAU, Rodney and ROBINSON, Budd
OPERATOR, THE   HEMDALE 1971
(Sphere)   (*Where Does it Hurt?*)

AMBLER, Eric
EPITAPH FOR A SPY   RKO 1944
(Hodder & Stoughton)   (*Hotel Reserve*)
JOURNEY INTO FEAR   RKO 1942
(Hodder & Stoughton)
LIGHT OF DAY, THE   UA 1964
(Heinemann)   (*Topkapi*)
MASK OF DIMITRIOS, THE   WAR 1944
(Hodder & Stoughton)
NIGHTCOMERS   RANK 1959
(Hodder & Stoughton)
OCTOBER MAN, THE   GFD 1947
(Hodder & Stoughton)
UNCOMMON DANGER   WAR 1943
(Hodder & Stoughton)   (*Background in Danger*)

AMERMAN, Lockhart
GUNS IN THE HEATHER   DISNEY 1969
(Harcourt, Brace, N.Y.)

AMES, Delano L.
SHE SHALL HAVE MURDER   BL 1950
(Hodder & Stoughton)

AMIS, Kingsley
LUCKY JIM   BL 1957
(Gollancz)
TAKE A GIRL LIKE YOU   COL 1971
(Gollancz)
THAT UNCERTAIN FEELING BL 1961
(Gollancz)   HTV 1986 (TV)
           (*Only Two Can Play*)

ANDERS, Curt
HELL IS FOR HEROES   PAR 1962
(Corgi)

ANDERSON, Edward
THIEVES LIKE US   UA 1974
(Avon, N.Y.)

ANDERSON, Maxwell
ANNE OF THE THOUSAND DAYS COL 1969
(P)
(*In* Best American plays: Crown, N.Y.)
BAD SEED (P)   WAR 1956
(Dodd, N.Y.)
ELIZABETH THE QUEEN (P) WAR 1939
(Longmans, N.Y.)   (*Private Lives of Elizabeth and Essex,*
           The)
EVE OF ST. MARK, THE (P) FOX 1944
(Lane)
JOAN OF LORRAINE (P)   RKO 1948
(Anderson House, N.Y.)   (*Joan of Arc*)
KEY LARGO (P)   WAR 1948
(Anderson House, N.Y.)
LOST IN THE STARS (P)   BL 1951
(Sloane, N.Y.)   (*Cry, The Beloved Country*)
MARY OF SCOTLAND (P)   RANK 1969
(Harcourt, Brace, N.Y.)
SATURDAY'S CHILDREN (P) WAR 1934
(Longmans, N.Y.)   (*Maybe It's Love*)
           WAR 1940
WINTERSET (P)   RKO 1936
(Lane)

ANDERSON, Maxwell *and* **STALLINGS, Laurence**
WHAT PRICE GLORY (P)   FOX 1952
(*In* Best Plays of 1924–25: Dodd, N.Y.)

ANDERSON, Peggy
NURSE
(Star)   CHANNEL 4 1984 (TV)

ANDERSON, Robert
I NEVER SANG FOR MY FATHER (P)   COL 1971
(Random House, N.Y.)
TEA AND SYMPATHY (P)   MGM 1956
(Random House, N.Y.)

ANDERSON, Verily
BEWARE OF CHILDREN   AA 1960
(Hart-Davis)   (*No Kidding*)

ANDREWS, Robert Hardy
GREAT DAY IN THE MORNING   RKO 1955
(Lane)
IF I HAD A MILLION   PAR 1932
(Hurst & Blackett)

ANDREWS, V.C.
FLOWERS IN THE ATTIC   NEW WORLD 1985
(Hall, Boston, Mass.)

ANET, Claude
MAYERLING   WAR 1968
(Frewin)

ANNIXTER, Paul
SWIFT WATER   DISNEY 1965
(Houghton, Mifflin, Boston)   (*Those Calloways*)

ANOUILH, Jean
BECKET (P)   PAR 1963
(Methuen)
WALTZ OF THE TOREADORS (P)   RANK 1962
(French)

ANSON, Jay
AMITYVILLE HORROR, THE   AMERICAN INTERNATIONAL
(Bantam, N.Y.)   1979

ANSTEY, F. *pseud.*
BRASS BOTTLE, THE   RANK 1964
(Murray)

ANSTEY, F. *pseud.* (*Continued*)
VICE VERSA   TC 1948
(Murray)

ANTHONY, C.L. *pseud.*
AUTUMN CROCUS (P)   AUT 1934
(Gollancz)
SERVICE (P)   MGM 1933
(French)   (*Looking Forward*)

ANTHONY, David
MIDNIGHT LADY AND THE   UN 1974
MOURNING MAN   (*Midnight Man, The*)
(Fontana)

ANTHONY, Evelyn
TAMARIND SEED, THE   SCOTIA-BARBER 1974
(Hutchinson)

ANTROBUS, John *see* **MILLIGAN, Spike** *jt. author*

APPEL, Benjamin
FORTRESS IN THE RICE   WAR 1964
(Bobbs-Merrill, Indianapolis)   (*Cry of Battle*)

APPEL, David
COMANCHE   DISNEY 1958
(Various)   (*Tonka*)

APPLEBY, John
CAPTIVE CITY, THE   WAR 1965
(Hodder & Stoughton)

ARCHER, Jeffrey
FIRST AMONG EQUALS   ITV 1986 (TV)
(Hodder & Stoughton)
KANE AND ABEL   BBC 1986 (TV)
(Hodder & Stoughton)

ARCHER, William
GREEN GODDESS, THE (P)   WAR 1930
(Heinemann)

ARDIES, Tom
KOSYGIN IS COMING   FOX—RANK 1975
(Doubleday, N.Y.)   (*Russian Roulette*)

ARDREY, Robert
THUNDER ROCK (P)   MGM 1943
(Hamilton)

ARENT, Arthur *ed.*
ONE THIRD OF A NATION (P)   PAR 1939
(*In* Federal Theatre Plays: Random
House, N.Y.)

ARKELL, Reginald
CHARLEY MOON   BL 1956
(Joseph)

ARLEN, Michael
GREEN HAT, THE   MGM 1929
(Collins)   (*Woman of Affairs, A*)
                         MGM 1935
                 (*Outcast Lady*)
                         MGM 1935
                 (*Woman of the World*)
LILY CHRISTINE   PAR 1932
(Collins)
THESE CHARMING PEOPLE   PAR 1931
(Collins)

ARLEY, Catherine
WOMAN OF STRAW   UA 1964
(Collins)

ARMSTRONG, Anthony
HE WAS FOUND IN THE ROAD   GN 1956
(Methuen)   (*Man in the Road, The*)
TEN MINUTE ALIBI (P)   SOSKIN 1934
(Gollancz)

ARMSTRONG, Anthony *see also* **HAY, Ian** *jt. author*

ARMSTRONG, Anthony *and* **SHAW, Herbert**
TEN MINUTE ALIBI   SOSKIN 1934
(Methuen)

ARMSTRONG, Charlotte
MISCHIEF   FOX 1952
(Davies)   (*Don't Bother to Knock*)

ARMSTRONG, Charlotte (*Continued*)
THREE WEIRD SISTERS
(Gifford)
UNSUSPECTED, THE
(Harrap)

BN 1948
(*Case of the Weird Sisters, The*)
WAR 1947

ARMSTRONG, Richard
PASSAGE HOME
(Dent)

GFD 1955

ARMSTRONG, Thomas
CROWTHERS OF BANKDAM, THE
(Collins)

ALL 1947
(*Master of Bankdam, The*)

ARMSTRONG, William H.
SOUNDER
(Gollancz)

FOX 1972

ARNAUD, Georges
WAGES OF FEAR
(British Publishers' Guild)

FILMS DE FRANCE 1953
CIC 1978
(U.S. title: *Sorcerer*)

ARNOLD, Elliott
BLOOD BROTHER
(Collins)
COMMANDOS, THE
(Rich & Cowan)
DEEP IN MY HEART
(Duell, N.Y.)
FLIGHT FROM ASHIYA
(Muller)

FOX 1950
(*Broken Arrow*)
COL 1943
(*First Comes Courage*)
MGM 1954

UA 1963

ARSAN, Emmanuelle
EMMANUELLE
(Mayflower)
YOUNG EMMANUELLE
(Hart Davis)

SF 1975

NEW REALM 1977

ARUNDEL, Edith
PERSISTENT WARRIORS, THE
(Jenkins)

BN 1947
(*Green Fingers*)

ASCH, Scholem
EAST RIVER
(Macdonald)

MGM 1949

ASHBROOK, Harriet
  MURDER OF STEPHEN KESTER   CHESTERFIELD 1934
  (Eyre & Spottiswoode)   (*Green-eyes*)

ASHFORD, Daisy
  YOUNG VISITORS, THE   CHANNEL 4 1984 (TV)
  (Chatto & Windus)

ASHTON, Helen
  YEOMAN'S HOSPITAL   GFD 1951
  (Collins)   (*White Corridors*)

ASHTON, Winifred *see* **DANE, Clemence** *pseud.*

ASHTON-WARNER, Sylvia
  SPINSTER, THE   MGM 1960
  (Secker & Warburg)   (*Two Loves*)
  TEACHER, I PASSED THIS WAY   ENTERPRISE 1985
  (Virago)   (*Sylvia*)

ASIMOV, Isaac
  NIGHT FALL   HEMDALE 1982
  (Panther)

ASINOE, E.
  TEN SECOND JAILBREAK   COL—WAR 1975
  (Joseph)   (*Breakout*)

ATHANAS, Verne
  PROUD ONES   FOX 1956
  (Rich & Cowan)

ATKINSON, Eleanor
  GREYFRIAR'S BOBBY   MGM 1949
  (Hamilton)   (*Challenge to Lassie*)

ATKINSON, Hugh
  GAMES, THE   FOX 1969
  (Cassell)

ATLAS, Leopold
  WEDNESDAY'S CHILD (P)   RKO 1946
  (French, N.Y.)   (*Child of Divorce*)

AUEL, Jean M.
CLAN OF THE CAVE BEAR   RANK 1985
(Crown, N.Y.)
VALLEY OF THE HORSES   PSO 1984
(Bantam, N.Y.)

AUSTEN, Jane
MANSFIELD PARK   BBC 1983 (TV)
(Various)
PRIDE AND PREJUDICE   MGM 1940
(Various)

AXELROD, George
GOODBYE CHARLIE (P)   FOX 1965
(French, N.Y.)
SEVEN YEAR ITCH, THE (P)   FOX 1955
(Heinemann)
WILL SUCCESS SPOIL ROCK   FOX 1957
HUNTER? (P)   (*Oh! For a Man!*)
(Random House, N.Y.)

AXELSON, *Mrs.* Mary Dougal
CHILD IS BORN, A   WAR 1940
(Caldwell, Idaho)

AYRES, Ruby Mildred
SECOND HONEYMOON   CONTINENTAL 1931
(Hodder & Stoughton)

B

BABCOCK, Dwight *see* **KEENE, D.** *jt. author*

BABER, Douglas
MY DEATH IS A MOCKERY   ADELPHI 1952
(Heinemann)

BACCHELLI, Riccardo
MILL ON THE PO   LUX FILMS 1950
(Hutchinson)

BACH, Richard
JONATHAN LIVINGSTONE   PAR 1974
SEAGULL
(Turnstone Press)

BACHMANN, Lawrence
KISS OF DEATH
(Knopf, N.Y.)
PHOENIX
(Collins)

MGM 1952
(*Devil Makes Three, The*)
UA 1958
(*Ten Seconds to Hell*)

BACHMANN, Richard
WHO IS THE RUNNING MAN?
(New English Library)

PSO 1986

BAGLEY, Desmond
FREEDOM TRAP, THE
(Collins)

COL—WAR 1973
(*Mackintosh Man, The*)

BAGNOLD, Enid
CHALK GARDEN, THE (P)
(French)
NATIONAL VELVET (P)
(Heinemann)

RANK 1963

MGM 1944

BAILEY, C.W. *see* **KNEBEL, F.** *jt. author*

BAILY, Leslie
GILBERT AND SULLIVAN BOOK,
THE
(Cassell)

BL 1953
(*Story of Gilbert and Sullivan, The*)

BAINBRIDGE, Beryl
SWEET WILLIAM
(Deutsch)

ITC 1980

BAIRD, Marie Thérèse
LESSON IN LOVE, A
(Various)

BORDEAUX FILMS 1981
(*Circle of Two*)

BAKER, Dorothy
YOUNG MAN WITH A HORN
(Gollancz)

WAR 1950
(*Young Man of Music*)

BAKER, Elliott
FINE MADNESS, A
(Joseph)

WAR 1965

BAKER, Frank
LEASE OF LIFE
(Angus & Robertson)

EALING 1954

BAKER, Louise
  HER TWELVE MEN   MGM 1954
  (McGraw-Hill, N.Y.)

BALCHIN, Nigel
  MINE OWN EXECUTIONER   BL 1948
  (Collins)
  SMALL BACK ROOM, THE   LF 1949
  (Collins)
  SORT OF TRAITOR, A   BL 1960
  (Collins)   (*Suspect*)

BALDERSTON, John Lloyd
  BERKELEY SQUARE (P)   FOX 1933
  (French)   FOX 1951
                  (*House in the Square, The*)

BALDWIN, Faith
  BEAUTY   MGM 1933
  (Sampson Low)   (*Beauty For Sale*)
  MEN ARE SUCH FOOLS   WAR 1938
  (Sampson Low)
  MOON'S OUR HOME, THE   PAR 1936
  (Sampson Low)
  OFFICE WIFE   WAR 1930
  (Sampson Low)
  PART-TIME WIVES   IN 1932
  (Sampson Low)   (*Week-end Marriage*)
  SKYSCRAPER   MGM 1932
  (Sampson Low)   (*Skyscraper Souls*)

BALDWIN, James
  GO TELL IT ON THE MOUNTAIN PRICE 1985
  (Corgi)

BALL, John
  IN THE HEAT OF THE NIGHT   UA 1967
  (Joseph)

BALMER, Edwin *and* **WYLIE, Philip**
  WHEN WORLDS COLLIDE   PAR 1951
  (Paul)

BANCROFT, George Pleydell
  WARE CASE, THE (P)   FOX 1939
  (Methuen)

BANKS, Lynne Reid
L-SHAPED ROOM, THE   BL 1962
(Chatto & Windus)

BANNERMAN, K. *see* **BROOKE, H.** *jt. author*

BANVILLE, John
NEWTON LETTER, THE   ARTIFICIAL EYE 1984
(Secker & Warburg)   (*Reflections*)

BARAK, Michael
ENIGMA SACRIFICE   COL—EMI—WAR 1982
(Futura)   (*Enigma*)

BARBER, Antonia
GHOSTS   HEMDALE 1972
(Cape)   (*Amazing Mr. Blunden, The*)

BARBER, Elsie Oaks
JENNY ANGEL   CONT 1961
(Putnam)   (*Angel Baby*)

BARCYNSKA, *Countess*
TESHA   WW 1929
(Hurst & Blackett)   (*Woman in the Night, The*)

BARD, Mary
DOCTOR WEARS THREE FACES,   FOX 1950
THE   (*Mother didn't Tell Me*)
(Hammond)

BARKER, Ralph
THOUSAND PLAN, THE   UA 1968
(Chatto & Windus)   (*1,000 Plane Raid, The*)

BARLING, Maurice *see* **BARRINGTON, Pamela** *pseud.*

BARLOW, James
BURDEN OF PROOF   *EMI—MGM 1971*
(Pan) *also published under film title*   (*Villain*)
TERM OF TRIAL   WAR 1962
(Hamilton)

BARNES, Peter
RULING CLASS, THE (P)   UA 1971
(Heinemann)

BARON, Alexander
HUMAN KIND, THE   BL 1963
(Cape)   (*Victors, The*)

BARR, George
EPITAPH FOR AN ENEMY   FOX 1964
(Hutchinson)   (*Up From the Beach*)

BARRETT, Michael
APPOINTMENT IN ZAHREIN   PAR 1962
(Pan)   (*Escape from Zahrein*)
HEROES OF YUCCA, THE   PAR 1968
(Hale)   (*Invincible Six, The*)
REWARD, THE   FOX 1965
(Longmans)

BARRETT, William Edward
LEFT HAND OF GOD, THE   FOX 1955
(Corgi)
LILIES OF THE FIELD, THE   UA 1963
(Heinemann)
WINE AND THE MUSIC, THE   UA 1975
(Heinemann)   (*Pieces of Dreams*)

BARRETT, Wilson
SIGN OF THE CROSS, THE   PAR 1932
(Various)   PAR 1944

BARRIE, *Sir* **James Matthew**
ADMIRABLE CRICHTON, THE (P)   COL 1957
(Hodder & Stoughton)
ALICE SIT BY THE FIRE   PAR 1950
(Hodder & Stoughton)   (*Rendezvous*) (U.S. title: *Darling
                                      How Could You?*)
LITTLE MINISTER, THE   RKO 1934
(Cassell)
OLD LADY SHOWS HER MEDALS,   PAR 1930
THE (P)   (*Seven Days' Leave*)
(Hodder & Stoughton)
PETER PAN (P)   RKO 1953
(Hodder & Stoughton)   DISNEY 1974

QUALITY STREET (P)   RKO 1937
(Hodder & Stoughton)
ROSALIND (P)   PAR 1953
(Hodder & Stoughton)   (*Forever Female*)
WHAT EVERY WOMAN KNOWS (P)   MGM 1934
(Hodder & Stoughton)

BARRINGER, Emily Dunning
BOWERY TO BELLEVUE   MGM 1952
(Norton, N.Y.)   (*Girl in White, The*)
                                    MGM 1952
                                    (*So Bright the Flame*)

BARRINGTON, Pamela *pseud.*
ACCOUNT RENDERED   RANK 1957
(Barker)

BARRY, Julian
LENNY (P)   UA 1975
(Random House, N.Y.)

BARRY, Philip
ANIMAL KINGDOM, THE (P)   RKO 1932
(French, N.Y.)   WAR 1946
                                    (*One More Tomorrow*)
PHILADELPHIA STORY (P)   MGM 1940
(French, N.Y.)   MGM 1956
                                    (*High Society*)
WITHOUT LOVE (P)   MGM 1945
(Coward-McCann, N.Y.)

BARRYMORE, Diana *and* **FRANK, Gerold**
TOO MUCH, TOO SOON   WAR 1958
(Muller)

BARSTOW, Stanley
BROTHER'S TALE, A   GRANADA 1983 (TV)
(Corgi)
KIND OF LOVING, A   AA 1962
(Joseph)

BARTH, John
END OF THE ROAD   CONTEMPORARY 1969
(Penguin)

BARTHEL, Joan
  DEATH IN CALIFORNIA   BBC 1985 (TV)
  (Penguin)   (*Death in Canaan, A*)

BARTLETT, Lanier *and* **BARTLETT, Virginia Stievers**
  ADIOS   IN 1931
  (Murray)   (*Lash, The*)

BARTLETT, Sy *see* **LAY, B.** *jt. author*

BARTLETT, V. *see* **SHERRIFF, R.C.** *jt. author*

BARTLETT, V.S. *see* **BARTLETT, L.** *jt. author*

BARTOLINI, Luigi
  BICYCLE THIEVES   MGM 1949
  (Joseph)

BARTON, Reyner
  ENVY MY SIMPLICITY   GN 1932
  (Chapman & Hall)   (*Killer Walks, A*)

BASS, Milton, R.
  JORY   FOX—RANK 1972
  (Putnam)

BASSETT, James
  HARM'S WAY   COL 1965
  (Heinemann)   (*In Harm's Way*)

BASSETT, Ronald
  WITCHFINDER GENERAL   TIGON 1968
  (Jenkins)

BASSING, Eileen
  HOME BEFORE DARK   WAR 1958
  (Longmans)

BASSO, Hamilton
  VIEW FROM POMPEY'S HEAD FOX 1955
  (Collins)   (*Secret Interlude*)

BATAILLE, Michel
  CHRISTMAS TREE, THE   FOX 1969
  (Murray)

BATES, Herbert Ernest
DARLING BUDS OF MAY, THE   MGM 1959
(Joseph)   (*Mating Game, The*)
DULCIMA   MGM—EMI 1972
(Penguin)
PURPLE PLAIN, THE   GFD 1954
(Joseph)
TRIPLE ECHO, THE   HEMDALE 1972
(Joseph)

BAUM, Lyman Frank
WIZARD OF OZ, THE   MGM 1939
(Hutchinson)   DISNEY 1979
       (*Wiz, The*)

BAUM, Vicki
BERLIN HOTEL   WAR 1945
(Joseph)   (*Hotel Berlin*)
GRAND HOTEL   MGM 1932
(Bles)
MORTGAGE ON LIFE   RKO 1949
(Doubleday, N.Y.)   (*Woman's Secret, A*)

BAWDEN, Nina
ON THE RUN   CFF 1969
(Gollancz)
SOLITARY CHILD, THE   BL 1957
(Collins)

BAX, Roger *pseud.*
CAME THE DAWN   MGM 1953
(Hutchinson)   (*Never Let Me Go*)

BEACH, Rex Ellingwood
ALASKA   UN 1942
(Harper, N.Y.)   (*Spoilers, The*)
DON CARELESS   REP 1950
(Hutchinson)   (*Avengers, The*)
SILVER HORDE, THE   RKO 1930
(Hodder & Stoughton)
SON OF THE GODS   IN 1930
(Hutchinson)   PAR 1930
       UN 1942
SPOILERS, THE   UI 1955
(Harper, N.Y.)

BEACH, Rex Ellingwood (*Continued*)
WORLD IN HIS ARMS, THE   GFD 1952
(Hutchinson)

BEAGLE, Peter S.
LAST UNICORN   SUNN CLASSIC 1982
(Ballantine, N.Y.)

BEALE, J. *see* **CARGILL, P.** *jt. author*

BEATTIE, Ann
CHILLY SCENES OF WINTER   UA 1979
(Popular Library, N.Y.)   (*Head Over Heels*)

BEATTY, David
CONE OF SILENCE   BL 1959
(Secker & Warburg)

BEAUMONT, Charles
INTRUDER, THE   GN 1963
(Muller)   (*Stranger, The*)

BECKER, Stephen
COVENANT WITH DEATH, A   WAR 1966
(Hamilton)

BECKHARDT, Israel *and* **BROWN, Wezel**
VIOLATORS, THE   RKO 1957
(Arco)

BECKWITH, Reginald
BOYS IN BROWN (P)   GFD 1949
(Marshall)

BEEDING, Francis *pseud.*
NORWICH VICTIMS, THE   ALL 1939
(Hodder & Stoughton)   (*Dead Men Tell No Tales*)
SPELL BOUND   UA 1945
(World, N.Y.)
Formerly published as
The House of Dr. Edwardes

BEHAN, Brendan
QUARE FELLOW, THE (P)   BL 1962
(Methuen)

BEHN, Noel
BIG STICK UP AT BRINK'S   COL—EMI—WAR 1979
(Putnam, N.Y.)   (*Brink's Job, The*)
KREMLIN LETTER, THE   FOX 1969
(W.H. Allen)

BEHREND, Arthur
HOUSE OF THE SPANIARD, THE   GB 1936
(Heinemann)

BEHRMAN, Samuel Nathaniel
BIOGRAPHY (P)   MGM 1934
(French)   (*Biography of a Bachelor Girl*)
NO TIME FOR COMEDY (P)   WAR 1940
(Hamilton)
PIRATE, THE (P)   MGM 1948
(Random House, N.Y.)
SECOND MAN (P)   RKO 1930
(Various)   (*He Knew Women*)

BEHRMAN, Samuel Nathaniel *and* **LOGAN, Joshua**
FANNY (P)   WAR 1960
(Random House, N.Y.)

BEITH, *Sir* **John Hay** *see* **HAY, Ian** *pseud.*

BELL, John Keble *see* **HOWARD, Keble** *pseud.*

BELL, Mary Hayley
WHISTLE DOWN THE WIND   RANK 1961
(Boardman)

BELL, Thomas
ALL BRIDES ARE BEAUTIFUL   RKO 1946
(Grosset, N.Y.)   (*From This Day Forward*)

BELL, Vereen
SWAMP WATER   FOX 1941
(Collins)   FOX 1952
                                       (*Lure of the Wilderness*)

BELLAMANN, Henry
KING'S ROW   WAR 1941
(Cape)

AUTHOR AND ORIGINAL TITLE	FILM TITLE

BENCHLEY, Nathaniel
OFF-ISLANDERS, THE
(Penguin)

UA 1966
(*Russians Are Coming—The Russians Are Coming, The*)

SAIL A CROOKED SHIP
(Hutchinson)

COL 1961

SWEET HOSTAGE
(*In* Benchley roundup: Chicago U.P.)

BBC 1984 (TV)

VISITORS, THE
(Hutchinson)

PAR 1968
(*Spirit is Willing, The*)

BENCHLEY, Peter
DEEP, THE
(Deutsch)

COL—WAR 1977

ISLAND, THE
(Doubleday, N.Y.)

CIC 1980

BENEDICTUS, David
YOU'RE A BIG BOY NOW
(Blond)

WAR 1966

BENEFIELD, Barry
CHICKEN-WAGON FAMILY
(Triangle Bks, N.Y.)

FOX 1939

VALIANT IS THE WORD FOR
CARRIE
(Heinemann)

PAR 1936

BENET, Stephen Vincent
DEVIL AND DANIEL WEBSTER,
THE
(Oxford U.P.)

RKO 1941
(*All That Money Can Buy*)

FAMOUS
(*In* Last Circle: Farrar, N.Y.)

PAR 1952
(*Just For You*)

JOHN BROWN'S BODY
(Holt, Rinehart & Winston, N.Y.)

FOX 1968

SOBBIN' WOMEN, THE
(*In* Thirteen o'clock: Heinemann)

MGM 1954
(*Seven Brides for Seven Brothers*)

BENGTSSON, Franz
LONG SHIPS, THE
(Collins)

BL 1963

BENJAMIN, Philip
QUICK BEFORE IT MEETS   MGM 1964
(Gollancz)

BENNETT, Arnold
ANNA OF THE FIVE TOWNS   BBC 2 1985 (TV)
(Methuen)
BURIED ALIVE   AIRTIME 1983
(Penguin)
CARD, THE   GFD 1951
(Methuen)
GREAT ADVENTURE   PAR 1933
(Methuen)   (*His Double Life*)
     PAR 1943
     (*Holy Matrimony*)
MR. PROHACK   GFD 1949
(Various)   (*Dear Mr. Prohack*)

BENNETT, Charles
BLACKMAIL (P)   BI 1929
(Rich & Cowan)

BENNETT, Dorothea
JIGSAW MAN, THE   J. & M. FILMS 1984
(Corgi)

BENNETT, Jay
CATACOMBS   BL 1964
(Abelard-Schuman)

BENSON, E.F.
MAPP AND LUCIA   CHANNEL 4 1985 (TV)
(Heinemann)

BENSON, *Mrs.* Sally
JUNIOR MISS   FOX 1945
(Sun Dial, N.Y.)
MEET ME IN ST. LOUIS   MGM 1944
(Random House, N.Y.)

BENTHAM, Josephine *and* WILLIAMS, Herschel V.
JANIE (P)   WAR 1944
(French, N.Y.)

BENTLEY, Edmund Clerihew
TRENT'S LAST CASE   BL 1952
(Various)

BENTLEY, Nicolas
FLOATING DUTCHMAN, THE   AA 1953
(Joseph)
THIRD PARTY RISK   EXCLUSIVE 1955
(Joseph)

BERESVICI, Eric
ONE SHOE MAKES IT MURDER   LORIMAR 1983
(Dell, N.Y.)

BERGER, Thomas
NEIGHBORS   COL—EMI—WAR 1981
(Dell, N.Y.)

BERGNER, Thomas
LITTLE BIG MAN   CINEMA CENTER 1969
(Eyre & Spottiswoode)

BERKELEY, Reginald
FRENCH LEAVE (P)   AB 1937
(French)
LADY WITH A LAMP, THE (P)   BL 1951
(Gollancz)

BERKMAN, Ted
CAST A GIANT SHADOW   UA 1965
(Doubleday, N.Y.)

BERMAN, Susan
EASY STREET   POLYGRAM 1982
(Dial, N.Y.)

BERNA, Paul
HUNDRED MILLION FRAMES, A   DISNEY 1963
(Penguin)   (*Horse Without a Head*)

BERNANOS, Georges
DIARY OF A COUNTRY PRIEST   GCT 1950
(Lane)

AUTHOR AND ORIGINAL TITLE	FILM TITLE

BERNSTEIN, Carl *and* **WOODWARD, R.**
ALL THE PRESIDENT'S MEN   COL—WAR 1978
(Secker & Warburg)

BERNSTEIN, Hilda
DEATH IS PART OF THE PROCESS   BBC 1986
(Sinclair Browne)

BERNSTEIN, Morey
SEARCH FOR BRIDEY MURPHY,   PAR 1956
THE
(Hutchinson)

BERRIGAN, Daniel
TRIAL OF THE CATONSVILLE MINE   CINERAMA 1972
(P)
(Bantam, N.Y.)

BESIER, Rudolf
BARRETTS OF WIMPOLE STREET,   MGM 1934
THE   MGM 1956
(Gollancz)
BARRETTS OF WIMPOLE STREET,   MGM 1934
THE (P)   MGM 1956
(Gollancz)

BESSIE, Alvah
SYMBOL, THE   WAR 1974
(Sphere)   (*Sex Symbol, The*)

BEVAN, Anthony J.
STORY OF ZARAK KHAN, THE   COL 1956
(Jarrolds)   (*Zarak*)

BEVAN, Donald *and* **TRZCINSKI, Edmund**
STALAG 17 (P)   PAR 1953
(Dramatists, N.Y.)

BEZZERIDES, Albert Isaac
LONG HAUL   WAR 1940
(Cape)   (*They Drive by Night*)
THIEVES' MARKET   FOX 1949
(Scribner, N.Y.)   (*Thieves' Highway*)

THE BIBLE
   (SAMUEL I & II: CHRONICLES I)   UIP 1985
                                       (*King David*)

BICKERTON, Derek
   PAYROLL   AA 1961
   (Eyre & Spottiswoode)

BICKHAM, Jack M.
   APPLE DUMPLING GANG, THE   DISNEY 1974
   (Hale)

BIDDLE, Cordelia Drexel *and* CRICHTON, Kyle
   HAPPIEST MILLIONAIRE, THE   DISNEY 1968
   (Sphere)

BIDDLE, Francis
   MR. JUSTICE HOLMES   MGM 1950
   (Scribner, N.Y.)   (*Magnificent Yankee, The*)

BIGGERS, Earl Derr
   AGONY COLUMN   WAR 1941
   (Bobbs-Merrill, Indianapolis)   (*Passage from Hong Kong*)
   BEHIND THAT CURTAIN   FOX 1930
   (Harrap)
   BLACK CAMEL   FOX 1931
   (Cassell)
   CHARLIE CHAN CARRIES ON   FOX 1931
   (Cassell)
   INSIDE THE LINES (P)   RKO 1930
   (French, N.Y.)
   SEVEN KEYS TO BALDPATE   RKO 1930
   (Grosset, N.Y.)   RKO 1935
                              RKO 1947
                              CANNON 1982
                              (*House of the Long Shadows*)

BILLING, Graham
   FORBUSH AND THE PENGUINS   BL 1971
   (Coronet)

BINGHAM, John
   FRAGMENT OF FEAR   COL 1969
   (Panther)

BINGHAM, Stella
CHARTERS AND CALDICOTT   BBC 1985 (TV)
(BBC)

BIRDWELL, Russell
I RING DOORBELLS   PRC 1946
(Messner, N.Y.)

BIRNEY, Hoffman
DICE OF GOD, THE   UA 1965
(Holt, N.Y.)   (*Glory Guys*)

BIRTLES, D.
OVERLANDERS, THE   EALING 1946
(World Film Pubns.)

BISHOP, Curtis
SHADOW RANGE   ABP 1953
(Macmillan, N.Y.)   (*Cow Country*)

BISHOP, Curtis *see also* **BRANDON, Curt** *pseud.*

BISHOP, Jim
FDR'S LAST YEAR   CHANNEL 4 1984 (TV)
(Hart-Davis)

BISSELL, Richard Pike
7½ CENTS   WAR 1957
(Little, Brown, Boston)   (*Pajama Game*)

BLACK, Ian Stewart
HIGH BRIGHT SUN, THE   RANK 1964
(Hutchinson)
IN THE WAKE OF A STRANGER   BUTCHER 1959
(Dakers)

BLACKBURN, John
NOTHING BUT THE NIGHT   FOX—RANK 1972
(Cape)

BLACKBURN, Thomas Wakefield
SHORT GRASS   ABP 1951
(Sampson Low)
SIERRA BARON   FOX 1958
(Random House, N.Y.)

BLACKMORE, Richard Doddridge
LORNA DOONE   ATP 1935
(Various)   COL 1951

BLAIR, C.F. *jt. author see* **WALLIS, A.J.**

BLAIR, Clay *jun.*
SURVIVE   STIGWOOD 1976
(Macmillan, N.Y.)

BLAIR, Eric *see* **ORWELL, George** *pseud.*

BLAISDELL, Anne *pseud.*
NIGHTMARE   COL 1965
(Gollancz)   (*Fanatic*)

BLAKE, George
SHIPBUILDERS, THE   BN 1944
(Faber)

BLAKE, Nicholas
BEAST MUST DIE, THE   CINECENTA 1969
(Collins)   (*Killer*)

BLANKFORT, Michael
JUGGLER, THE   COL 1953
(Dobson)

BLASCO IBANEZ, Vicente
BLOOD AND SAND   FOX 1941
(Benn)
FOUR HORSEMEN OF THE MGM 1961
APOCALYPSE, THE
(Various)

BLATTY, William Peter
EXORCIST, THE   WAR 1973
(Blond & Briggs)
NINTH CONFIGURATION, THE ITC 1979
(Bantam, N.Y.)

BLEECK, Oliver
PROCANE CHRONICLE, THE COL—WAR 1976
(Morrow, N.Y.)   (*St. Ives*)

BLOCH, B. *see* **BREWER, G.E.** *jt. author*

BLOCH, Robert
PSYCHO
(Hale)

PAR 1960

BLOCHMAN, Lawrence Goldtree
BOMBAY MAIL
(Collins)

UN 1934

BLOCK, Lawrence
STAB IN THE DARK
(Arbor, N.Y.)

PSO 1985
(*8 Million Ways to Die*)

BLOCK, Libbie
WILD CALENDAR
(World, N.Y.)

MGM 1948
(*Caught*)

BLOOM, Murray, T.
13th Man, The (Star)

UA 1984
(*Last Embrace, The*)

BLYTHE, Ronald
AKENFIELD
(Penguin)

ANGLE FILMS 1975

BLYTON, Enid
FIVE HAVE A MYSTERY TO SOLVE
(Hodder & Stoughton)
FIVE ON TREASURE ISLAND
(Hodder & Stoughton)

CFF 1964

BL 1957

BOCCACCIO, Giovanni
DECAMERON, THE
(Various)

EROS 1953
(*Decameron Nights*)
UA 1971
PRODUCTION
ASSOCIATES 1977
(*Love Boccaccio Style*)

BODELSEN, Anders
HIT, AND RUN RUN RUN
(Joseph)
SILENT PARTNER, THE
(Penguin)

RANK 1971
(*One of Those Things*)
ENTERPRISE 1978

BOILEAU, Pierre *and* **NARCEJAC, Thomas**
LIVING AND THE DEAD, THE   PAR 1958
(Arrow)   *(Vertigo)*

BOLAND, Bridget
COCKPIT (P)   GFD 1949
(*In* Plays of the year, 1948–49: Elek)   *(Lost People, The)*
PRISONER, THE (P)   COL 1955
(Elek)

BOLAND, John
LEAGUE OF GENTLEMEN, THE   RANK 1960
(Boardman)

BOLDREWOOD, Rolf
ROBBERY UNDER ARMS   RANK 1957
(Macmillan)

BOLT, Robert
MAN FOR ALL SEASONS, A (P)   COL 1966
(French)
MISSION   GOLDCREST 1986
(Penguin)

BOLTON, Guy
WEEK-END AT THE WALDORF   MGM 1945
(Grosset, N.Y.)

BOLTON, Guy *adaptor*
ANASTASIA (P)   FOX 1956
(French)

BOLTON, Guy *and* **McGOWAN, John**
GIRL CRAZY (P)   MGM 1965
(Dramatic, Chicago)   *(When the Boys Meet the Girls)*

BONESTELL, Chesley *and* **LEY, Willy**
CONQUEST OF SPACE   PAR 1954
(Sidgwick)

BONETT, Emery *pseud.*
GIRL MUST LIVE, A   UA 1941
(Miles)
HIGH PAVEMENT   GFD 1948
(Heinemann)   *(My Sister and I)*

BONHAM, Frank
  LOST STAGE VALLEY   COL 1951
  (Simon & Schuster, N.Y.)

BONNECARRE, P. *see* **HEMINGWAY, Joan** *jt. author*

BONNER, Charles
  NOR PERFUME NOR WINE   COL 1941
  (Cassell)   (*Adam Had Four Sons*)
  Formerly published as Legacy

BONNET, Theodore
  MUDLARK, THE   FOX 1950
  (W.H. Allen)

BOOM, Carrie Ten
  HIDING PLACE, THE   WORLD WIDE FILMS 1974
  (Hodder & Stoughton)

BOOTH, Charles Gordon
  GENERAL DIED AT DAWN, THE   PAR 1936
  (Bell)
  MR. ANGEL COMES ABOARD   RKO 1945
  (Doubleday, N.Y.)   (*Johnny Angel*)

BOOTHE, Clare
  KISS THE BOYS GOODBYE (P)   PAR 1941
  (Various)
  MARGIN FOR ERROR (P)   FOX 1943
  (*In* Five plays of 1940: Hamilton)
  WOMEN, THE (P)   MGM 1939
  (*In* Famous plays of 1937: Gollancz) MGM 1956
                      (*Opposite Sex, The*)

BOOTHROYD, Derrick
  VALUE FOR MONEY   RANK 1955
  (Laurie)

BORDEN, Mary
  ACTION FOR SLANDER   UA 1938
  (Heinemann)

BORER, Mary *see* **RIDLEY, Arnold** *jt. author*

BORLAND, Hal
WHEN THE LEGENDS DIE   FOX 1972
(Penguin)

BOTTOME, Phyllis
HEART OF A CHILD   RANK 1958
(Faber)
MORTAL STORM, THE   MGM 1940
(Faber)
MURDER IN THE BUD   WAR 1945
(Faber)   (*Danger Signal*)
PRIVATE WORLDS   PAR 1935
(Lane)
RAT, THE   RKO 1938
(Allan)

BOULLE, Pierre
BRIDGE ON THE RIVER KWAI, THE   COL 1957
(Collins)
MONKEY PLANET   FOX 1968
(Penguin)   (*Planet of the Apes*)

BOWEN, Catherine Drinker
MUSIC LOVERS, THE   UA 1971
(Hodder & Stoughton)
YANKEE FROM OLYMPUS   MGM 1952
(Benn)   (*Man With Thirty Sons, The*)

BOWEN, Elizabeth
DEATH OF THE HEART, THE   GRANADA 1985 (TV)
(Cape)

BOWEN, John
McGUFFIN, THE   BBC 2 1986 (TV)
(Hamilton)

BOWER, B.M.
CHIP OF THE FLYING U   UN 1940
(Grosset, N.Y.)

BOYER, David
SIDELONG GLANCES OF A PIGEON   BUTCHER 1970
KICKER, THE
(Macdonald)

BOYLE, Kay
AVALANCHE   PRC 1946
(Faber)

BRACKETT, Leigh
TIGER AMONGST US, THE   BL 1962
(Boardman)   (*13 West Street*)

BRADBURY, Ray
FAHRENHEIT 451   UI 1966
(Hart-Davis)
FOGHORN, THE   WAR 1953
(*In* Twice twenty-two: Doubleday, N.Y.) (*Beast from 20,000 Fathoms, The*)
ILLUSTRATED MAN, THE   WAR 1968
(Hart-Davis)
MARTIAN CHRONICLES, THE   BBC 2 1984 (TV)
(Bantam, N.Y.)
SOMETHING WICKED THIS WAY   DISNEY 1983
COMES
(Hart-Davis)

BRADDON, Russell
YEAR OF THE ANGRY RABBIT,   MGM—EMI 1972
THE   (*Night of the Lepus*)
(Pan)

BRADFORD, Barbara T.
WOMAN OF SUBSTANCE, A   CHANNEL 4 1985 (TV)
(Avon, N.Y.)

BRADFORD, Richard
RED SKY AT MORNING   UN 1971
(Hodder & Stoughton)

BRADLEY, Mary Hastings
I PASSED FOR WHITE   WAR 1960
(Davies)

BRADY, Leo
EDGE OF DOOM   RKO 1950
(Cresset Press)   RKO 1952
          (*Stronger Than Fear*)

BRAHMS, Caryl *and* **SIMON, S.J.** *pseud.*
ELEPHANT IN WHITE, THE   GFD 1944
(Joseph)   (*Give Us The Moon*)

BRAHMS, Caryl *and* **SIMON, S.J.** *pseud.* (*Continued*)
NO NIGHTINGALES   BN 1947
(Joseph)   (*Ghosts of Berkeley Square, The*)
TROTTIE TRUE   TC 1949
(Joseph)

BRAINE, John
LIFE AT THE TOP   BL 1965
(Eyre & Spottiswoode)
ROOM AT THE TOP   BL 1958
(Eyre & Spottiswoode)

BRAITHWAITE, E.R.
TO SIR, WITH LOVE   COL 1966
(Bodley Head)

BRANCH, Houston *and* **WATERS, Frank**
RIVER LAY   UN 1948
(Cassell)

BRAND, Christanna
GREEN FOR DANGER   INDIVIDUAL 1947
(Lane)

BRAND, Max *pseud.*
CALLING DR. KILDARE   MGM 1939
(Hodder & Stoughton)
DESTRY RIDES AGAIN   UN 1932
(Hodder & Stoughton)   UN 1939
                                   UI 1954
                                   (*Destry*)
DR. KILDARE'S CRISIS   MGM 1940
(Hodder & Stoughton)
DR. KILDARE'S TRIAL   MGM 1941
(Dodd, N.Y.)   (*People Versus Dr. Kildare, The*)
SECRET OF DR. KILDARE, THE   MGM 1939
(Hodder & Stoughton)
UNTAMED, THE   FOX 1931
(Wright & Brown)   (*Fair Warning*)
YOUNG DR. KILDARE, THE   MGM 1938
(Hodder & Stoughton)

BRANDE, Dorothea
WAKE UP AND LIVE   FOX 1937
(Barker)

BRANDNER, Gary
HOWLING, THE   AVCO EMBASSY 1981
(Fawcett, N.Y.)

BRANDON, Curt *pseud.*
BUGLE'S WAKE   EROS 1955
(Dutton, N.Y.)   (*Seminole Uprising*)

BRASHLER, William
BINGO LONG TRAVELLING ALL   CIC 1976
STARS AND MOTOR KINGS, THE
(Harper, N.Y.)

BRASON, John
SECRET ARMY, THE   BBC 1977 (TV)
(BBC)

BRENNAN, Peter
RAZORBACK   WAR 1983
(Jove, N.Y.)

BRESLIN, Jimmy
GANG THAT COULDN'T SHOOT   MGM—EMI 1972
STRAIGHT, THE
(Hutchinson)

BREUER, Bessie
MEMORY OF LOVE   RKO 1939
(Rich & Cowan)   (*In Name Only*)

BREWER, George Emerson *and* **BLOCH, Bertram**
DARK VICTORY (P)   WAR 1939
(Dramatists, N.Y.)

BRICKHILL, Paul
DAM BUSTERS, THE   ABP 1954
(Evans)
GREAT ESCAPE, THE   UA 1963
(Faber)
REACH FOR THE SKY   RANK 1956
(Collins)

BRIDIE, James *pseud.*
IT DEPENDS WHAT YOU MEAN (P)   BL 1952
(Constable)   (*Folly To Be Wise*)

BRIDIE, James *pseud.* (*Continued*)
SLEEPING CLERGYMAN, A (P)   BL 1951
(French)   (*Flesh and Blood*)
WHAT SAY THEY? (P)   ABP 1952
(Constable)   (*You're Only Young Twice*)

BRIGHOUSE, Harold
HOBSON'S CHOICE (P)   BI 1931
(French)   BL 1953

BRINIG, Myron
SISTERS, THE   WAR 1938
(Cobden Sanderson)

BRINK, Carol R.
CADDIE WOODLAWN   HEMDALE 1976
(Collier-Macmillan)   (*Caddie*)

BRINKLEY, William
DON'T GO NEAR THE WATER   MGM 1957
(Cape)

BRISTOW, Gwen
JUBILEE TRIAL   REP 1954
(Eyre & Spottiswoode)
TOMORROW IS FOREVER   RKO 1946
(Heinemann)

BROMFIELD, Louis
BETTER THAN LIFE   WAR 1940
(*In* A Collection of Nine Novels: Cassell)   (*It All Came True*)
McLEOD'S FOLLY   UA 1943
(*In* It takes all kinds: Cassell)   (*Johnny Vagabond*)
MRS. PARKINGTON   MGM 1944
(Cassell)
RAINS CAME, THE   FOX 1939
(Cassell)   FOX 1955
    (*Rains of Ranchipur, The*)

BRONTE, Charlotte
JANE EYRE   MON 1934
(Various)   FOX 1944
    BL 1970
    BBC 1981 (TV)

BRONTE, Emily Jane
  WUTHERING HEIGHTS   UA 1939
  (Various)   MGM—EMI 1970

BROOKE, E. *see* **KERR, J.** *jt. author*

BROOKE, Harold *and* **BANNERMAN, Kay**
  HOW SAY YOU? (P)   RANK 1961
  (Evans)   (*Pair of Briefs*)

BROOKE, Hugh
  SATURDAY ISLAND   RKO 1951
  (Heinemann)

BROOKNER, Anita
  HOTEL DU LAC   BBC 2 1986 (TV)
  (Cape)

BROOKS, Richard
  BRICK FOXHOLE, THE   RKO 1947
  (Harper, N.Y.)   (*Crossfire*)

BROPHY, John
  DAY THEY ROBBED THE BANK OF MGM 1959
  ENGLAND, THE
  (Collins)
  IMMORTAL SERGEANT, THE   FOX 1943
  (Collins)
  TURN THE KEY SOFTLY   GFD 1953
  (Collins)
  WATERFRONT   GFD 1950
  (Various)

BROWN, Francis Yeats *see* **YEATS-BROWN, F.**

BROWN, Frederic
  SCREAMING MIMI   COL 1957
  (Boardman)

BROWN, Geoffrey
  I WANT WHAT I WANT   CINERAMA 1972
  (Panther)

BROWN, Harry
SOUND OF HUNTING, A (P)   COL 1952
(Knopf, N.Y.)   (*Eight Iron Men*)

BROWN, Harry Peter McNab
STARS IN THEIR COURSES, THE   PAR 1967
(Cape)   (*El Dorado*)
WALK IN THE SUN, A   FOX 1945
(Secker & Warburg)

BROWN, Helen Gurney
SEX AND THE SINGLE GIRL   WAR 1964
(Muller)

BROWN, Joe David
"ADDIE PRAY"   PAR 1973
(Hodder & Stoughton)   (*Paper Moon*)
KINGS GO FORTH   UA 1958
(Cassell)
STARS IN MY CROWN   MGM 1950
(Hodder & Stoughton)

BROWN, J.P.S.
POCKET MONEY   FIRST ARTISTS 1972
(Sphere)

BROWN, R.G. *see* **HARWOOD, H.M.** *jt. author*

BROWN, Wenzell
MONKEY ON MY BACK   UA 1957
(Elek)

BROWN, Will C.
BORDER JUMPERS, THE   UA 1958
(Muller)   (*Man of the West*)

BROWNE, Gerald A.
11 HARROWHOUSE   FOX 1974
(Arbor House, N.Y.)
GREEN ICE   ITC 1981
(Delacorte, N.Y.)

BROWNE, Wynyard
HOLLY AND THE IVY, THE (P)   BL 1952
(French)

BRUCE, J.C.
ESCAPE FROM ALCATRAZ   CIC 1979
(McGraw, N.Y.)

BRUSH, Katherine
YOUNG MAN OF MANHATTAN   PAR 1930
(Cassell)

BRYAN, C.D.B.
FRIENDLY FIRE   BBC 1984 (TV)
(Bantam, N.Y.)

BRYAN, Michael
INTENT TO KILL   FOX 1958
(Eyre & Spottiswoode)

BUCHAN, John *1st Baron Tweedsmuir*
HUNTINGTOWER   PAR 1928
(Hodder & Stoughton)
THIRTY-NINE STEPS, THE   GB 1935
(Hodder & Stoughton)   RANK 1959
     RANK 1978

BUCHHEIM, Lothar-Guther
BOAT, THE   COL—EMI—WAR 1982
(Knopf, N.Y.)

BUCHWALD, Art
GIFT FROM THE BOYS, A   COL 1959
(Harper, N.Y.)
SURPRISE PACKAGE   COL 1960
(Gollancz)

BUCK, Pearl
CHINA SKY   RKO 1945
(Blue Ribbon Bks., N.Y.)
DEVIL NEVER SLEEPS, THE   FOX 1962
(Pan)
DRAGON SEED   MGM 1944
(Methuen)
GOOD EARTH, THE   MGM 1937
(Methuen)
HOUSE DIVIDED, A   UN 1932
(Methuen)

BUDD, Jackson
CONVICT HAS ESCAPED, A   WAR 1947
(Joseph)   (*They Made Me a Fugitive*)

BUGLIOSI, Vincent *and* **GENTRY, C.**
MANSON MURDERS, THE   HEMDALE 1976
(Bodley Head)   (*Helter Skelter*)

BULLETT, Gerald
JURY, THE   COL 1956
(Dent)   (*Last Man to Hang*)

BUNKER, Edward
NO BEAST SO FIERCE   COL—WAR 1978
(Dell, N.Y.)   (*Straight Time*)

BUNYAN, John
PILGRIM'S PROGRESS   CHANNEL 4 1985 (TV)
(Various)   (*Dangerous Journey*)

BURDICK, Eugene *and* **WHEELER, Harvey**
FAIL SAFE   BL 1963
(Hutchinson)

BURDICK, E. *see also* **LEDERER, W.J.** *jt. author*

BURGESS, Alan
SEVEN MEN AT DAYBREAK   COL—WAR 1975
(Mayflower)   (*Operation Daybreak*)
SMALL WOMAN, THE   FOX 1958
(Evans)   (*Inn of the Sixth Happiness, The*)

BURGESS, Anthony
CLOCKWORK ORANGE, A   WAR 1971
(Heinemann)

BURGESS, Gelett
TWO O'CLOCK COURAGE   RKO 1936
(Triangle Bks., N.Y.)   (*Two In the Dark*)

BURKE, James
DAY THE UNIVERSE CHANGED,   BBC 1985 (TV)
THE
(BBC)

AUTHOR AND ORIGINAL TITLE	FILM TITLE
BURKE, Jonathan ECHO OF BARBARA (Long)	RANK 1960
BURMAN, B.L. STEAMBOAT ROUND THE BEND (Nelson)	FOX 1935
BURMEISTER, J. RUNNING SCARED (Sphere)	RANK 1978 (*Tigers Don't Cry*)
BURNETT, Frances H. LITTLE LORD FAUNTLEROY (Various)	POLYGRAM 1981
BURNETT, William Riley ADOBE WALLS (Knopf, N.Y.) ASPHALT JUNGLE, THE (Corgi)	PAR 1953 (*Arrowhead*) MGM 1950 MGM 1963 (*Cairo*) MGM 1972 (*Cool Breeze*)
CAPTAIN LIGHTFOOT (Macdonald) DARK COMMAND (Heinemann) HIGH SIERRA (Heinemann)	UI 1954 REP 1940 WAR 1941 WAR 1955 (*I Died a Thousand Times*)
IRON MAN (Heinemann) LITTLE CAESAR (Cape) NOBODY LIVES FOREVER (World, N.Y.) SAINT JOHNSON (Heinemann) VANITY ROW (Corgi)	UI 1951 IN 1930 WAR 1946 UN 1932 (*Law and Order*) REP 1956 (*Accused of Murder*)

371

BURNFORD, Sheila
  INCREDIBLE JOURNEY, THE   DISNEY 1962
  (Hodder & Stoughton)

BURNHAM, B. *see* **HILTON, J.** *jt. author*

BURNS, Robert Elliott
  I AM A FUGITIVE FROM THE   WAR 1932
  CHAIN GANG   (*I Am a Fugitive*)
  (Paul)

BURNS, Walter Noble
  SAGA OF BILLY THE KID   MGM 1941
  (Grosset, N.Y.)   (*Billy The Kid*)

BURRESS, John
  MISSOURI TRAVELLER, THE   DISNEY 1958
  (Vanguard, N.Y.)

BURROUGHS, Edgar Rice
  AT THE EARTH'S CORE   BL 1976
  (Ace, N.Y.)
  LAND THAT TIME FORGOT   BL 1974
  (Methuen)
  PEOPLE THAT TIME FORGOT, THE   BRENT WALKER 1977
  (Various)
  TARZAN OF THE APES   WAR 1984
  (Various)   (*Greystoke*)
  TARZAN THE APE MAN   MGM 1982
  (Various)

BURROWS, Abe
  CACTUS FLOWER (P)   COL 1969
  (French, N.Y.)

BURT, Kendal *and* **LEASOR, James**
  ONE THAT GOT AWAY, THE   RANK 1957
  (Collins & Joseph)

BURTIS, Thomson
  NEW GUINEA GOLD   PAR 1951
  (Doubleday, N.Y.)   (*Crosswinds*)

BUSCH, Niven
  DUEL IN THE SUN   MGM 1946
  (W.H. Allen)

FURIES, THE   PAR 1950
(W.H. Allen)
THEY DREAM OF HOME   RKO 1946
(Grosset, N.Y.)   (*Till the End of Time*)

BUTLER, David
  LORD MOUNTBATTEN   WALKER 1986 (TV)
  (Methuen)

BUTLER, Gerald
  KISS THE BLOOD OFF MY HANDS   UI 1949
  (Jarrolds)   (*Blood On My Hands*)
  THEY CRACKED HER GLASS   ANGOFILM 1948
  SLIPPER   (*Third Time Lucky*)
  (Jarrolds)

BUTLER, Gerald *see* **GAINES, Charles** *jt. author*

BUTTERFIELD, Roger Place
  AL SCHMID, MARINE   WAR 1945
  (Norton, N.Y.)   (*Pride of the Marines*)

BYRNE, M. St. C. *see* **SAYERS, D.L.** *jt. author*

C

CAHAN, Abraham
  YEKL   CONNOISSEUR 1975
  (Peter Smith)   (*Hester Street*)

CAIDIN, Martin
  MAROONED   COL 1969
  (Hodder & Stoughton)

CAILLOU, Allan
  KHARTOUM   CINERAMA 1966
  (W.H. Allen)
  RAMPAGE   WAR 1963
  (Davies)

CAIN, James Mallahan
  BUTTERFLY   J & M FILMS 1981
  (Random House, N.Y.)

CAIN, James Mallahan (*Continued*)
DOUBLE INDEMNITY   PAR 1944
(Hale)   (*In* Three of a Kind)
MILDRED PIERCE   WAR 1945
(Hale)
POSTMAN ALWAYS RINGS TWICE,   MGM 1946
THE   ITC 1981
(Cape)
SERENADE   WAR 1956
(Penguin)

CAIRN, James
GUY NAMED JOE, A   MGM 1943
(Hollywood Pubns.)

CALDWELL, Erskine
CLAUDELLE   WAR 1961
(Pan)   (*Young and Eager*)
GOD'S LITTLE ACRE   UA 1958
(Heinemann)
TOBACCO ROAD   FOX 1941
(Falcon Press)

CALDWELL, Erskine *and* **KIRKLAND, Jack**
TOBACCO ROAD (P)   FOX 1941
(Falcon Press)

CALDWELL, Taylor
DEAR AND GLORIOUS PHYSICIAN   PAR 1963
(Collins)

CAMERON, Ian
ISLAND AT THE TOP OF THE   DISNEY 1974
WORLD, THE
(Hutchinson)

CAMP, William
IDLE ON PARADE   COL 1959
(MacGibbon)

CAMPBELL, George
CRY FOR HAPPY   COL 1960
(Harcourt, N.Y.)

CAMPBELL, John W.
WHO GOES THERE?   RKO 1951
(Shasta Pubns., Chicago)   (*Thing From Another World, The*)

CAMPBELL, *Sir* **Malcolm**
SALUTE TO THE GODS   MGM 1939
(Cassell)   (*Burn 'em Up O'Connor*)

CAMPBELL, Reginald
DEATH IN TIGER VALLEY   REP 1936
(Hodder & Stoughton)   (*Girl From Mandalay*)

CAMPION, N.R. *see* **MAHER, M.** *jt. author*

CAMUS, Albert
OUTSIDER, THE   PAR 1968
(Hamilton)

CANADA, Lena
TO ELLIS WITH LOVE   COL 1980
(Everest House, N.Y.)   (*Touched by Love*)

CANAWAY, W.H.
SAMMY GOING SOUTH   BL 1962
(Hutchinson)

CANNING, Victor
CASTLE MINERVA   UA 1965
(Hodder & Stoughton)   (*Masquerade*)
GOLDEN SALAMANDER   GFD 1949
(Hodder & Stoughton)
HOUSE OF THE SEVEN FLIES, THE   MGM 1959
(Hodder & Stoughton)   (*House of the Seven Hawks, The*)
LIMBO LINE, THE   MONARCH 1968
(Heinemann)
PANTHER'S MOON   GFD 1950
(Hodder & Stoughton)
RAINBIRD PATTERN, THE   UN 1976
(Heinemann)   (*Family Plot*)
VENETIAN BIRD   GFD 1952
(Hodder & Stoughton)

CANUTT, Yakina *and* **DRAKE, O.**
STUNTMAN, THE   FOX 1979
(Walker, N.Y.)

CAPON, Paul
DEATH AT SHINGLE STRAND   RANK 1958
(Ward Lock)   (*Hidden Homicide*)

CAPOTE, Truman
BREAKFAST AT TIFFANYS   PAR 1961
(Hamilton)
IN COLD BLOOD   COL 1968
(Hamilton)

CAREY, Peter
BLISS   NEW SOUTH WALES 1984
(Faber)

CARGILL, Patrick *and* BEALE, Jack
RING FOR CATTY (P)   AA 1962
(French)   (*Twice Round the Daffodils*)

CARLETON, *Mrs.* Marjorie Chalmers
CRY WOLF   WAR 1947
(Sun Dial, N.Y.)

CARLILE, Clancy
HONKEYTONK MAN   COL—EMI—WAR 1983
(Simon & Schuster, N.Y.)

CARLSON, C. *see* LINDSAY, Hal *jt. author*

CARNEY, Daniel
SQUARE CIRCLE, THE   COL—EMI—WAR 1985
(Firecrest)   (*Wild Geese II*)
WILD GEESE, THE   RANK 1978
(Heinemann)

CARPENTER, Margaret
EXPERIMENT PERILOUS   RKO 1944
(Harrap)

CARR, James Dickson
EMPEROR'S SNUFFBOX, THE   MON 1957
(Hamilton)   (*That Woman Opposite*)

CARROLL, Curt
GOLDEN HERD   REP 1952
(Morrow, N.Y.)   (*San Antone*)

CARROLL, Gladys
AS THE EARTH TURNS   WAR 1934
(Macmillan)

CARROLL, Lewis *pseud.*
ALICE IN WONDERLAND   PAR 1933
(Various)   RKO 1951
                              FOX 1972
                              (*Alice's Adventures in Wonderland*)
                              HEMDALE 1980
                              (*Alice*)

CARS, Guy des
BRUTE, THE   BL 1954
(Wingate)   (*Green Scarf, The*)

CARSON, Rachel L.
SEA AROUND US, THE   RKO 1953
(Staples)

CARSTAIRS, John Paddy
SOLID! SAID THE EARL   MON 1955
(Hurst & Blackett)   (*Yank in Ermine, A*)

CARTER, Angela *and* **WOLF, A.**
COMPANY OF WOLVES   PALACE 1984
(Harper, N.Y.)

CARTER, Arthur
OPERATION MADBALL (P)   COL 1962
(French, N.Y.)

CARTER, Felicity Winifred *see* **BONETT, Emery** *pseud.*

CARTER, Forrest
GONE TO TEXAS   COL—WAR 1976
(Delacorte, N.Y.)   (*Outlaw Josey Wales, The*)

CARTER, R. *see* **KEATING, W.J.** *jt. author*

CASE, Robert Ormond
GOLDEN PORTAGE, THE   REP 1942
(Jarrolds)   (*Girl From Alaska, The*)

CARY, E. *see* **GILBRETH, F.B.** *jt. author*

CARY, F.L. *see also* **KING, P.** *jt. author*

CARY, Falkland L. *and* **KING, Philip**
WATCH IT SAILOR (P)   COL 1961
(*In* Plays of the year 1961: Elek)

CARY, Falkland L. *and* **WEATHERS, Philip**
MADAM TIC-TAC (P)   RKO 1956
(French)   (*No Road Back*)

CARY, Joyce
HORSE'S MOUTH, THE   UA 1958
(Joseph)

CASPARY, Vera
BACHELOR IN PARADISE   MGM 1961
(Pan)
BEDELIA   GFD 1946
(Eyre & Spottiswoode)
EASY LIVING   PAR 1937
(Longmans)
LAURA   FOX 1944
(Eyre & Spottiswoode)

CASPARY, Vera *and* **SKLAR, George**
LAURA (P)   FOX 1944
(Dramatists, N.Y.)

CASSADY, Carolyn
HEART BEAT   COL—EMI—WAR 1980
(Creative Arts: Berkeley, Cal.)

CASTLE, John
PASSWORD IS COURAGE, THE   MGM 1962
(Souvenir Press)

CATO, Nancy
ALL THE RIVERS RUN   CHANNEL 4 1984 (TV)
(New English Library)

CATTO, Max
   DEVIL AT 4 O'CLOCK, THE   COL 1961
   (Pan)
   HILL IN KOREA, A   BL 1956
   (Hutchinson)
   KILLING FROST, A   UA 1956
   (Heinemann)   (*Trapeze*)
   LIONS AT THE KILL   FOX 1960
   (Hutchinson)   (*Seven Thieves*)
   MISTER MOSES   UA 1965
   (Heinemann)   (*Mr. Moses*)
   MURPHY'S WAR   PAR 1971
   (Heinemann)
   PRIZE OF GOLD, A   COL 1954
   (Heinemann)
   THEY WALK ALONE (P)   PAR 1948
   (Secker & Warburg)   (*Daughter of Darkness*)

CATTO, Max *see also* **KENT, Simon** *pseud.*

CAUTE, David
   COMRADE JACOB   THE OTHER CINEMA 1975
   (Quartet)   (*Winstanley*)

CAUVIN, Patrick
   BLIND LOVE   COL—EMI—WAR 1979
   (Fawcett, N.Y.)   (*Little Romance, A*)

CAVANAUGH, Arthur
   CHILDREN ARE GONE, THE   NATIONAL GENERAL 1972
   (Simon & Schuster, N.Y.)   (*Deadly Trap*)

CECIL, Henry
   BROTHERS IN LAW   BL 1956
   (Joseph)

CENDRARS, Blaise
   SUTTAR'S GOLD   UN 1983
   (Various)

CHABER, M.E. *pseud.*
   MAN INSIDE, THE   COL 1958
   (Eyre & Spottiswoode)

CHAMALES, Thomas T.
GO NAKED IN THE WORLD   MGM 1960
(Deutsch)
NEVER SO FEW   MGM 1959
(Pan)

CHAMBERLAIN, George Agnew
SCUDDA HOO! SCUDDA HAY!   FOX 1948
(Grosset, N.Y.)

CHAMBERLAIN, William
TRUMPETS OF COMPANY K   MGM 1958
(Ballantine, N.Y.)   (*Imitation General*)

CHAMBERS, Whitman
MURDER FOR A WANTON   MGM 1936
(Melrose)   (*Sinner Take All*)

CHAMPION, Bob *and* **POWELL, Jonathan**
CHAMPION'S STORY   EMBASSY 1983
(Gollancz)   (*Champions*)

CHANDLER, Raymond
BIG SLEEP, THE   WAR 1946
(Hamilton)   ITC 1978
FAREWELL, MY LOVELY   RKO 1942
(Hamilton)   (*Falcon Takes Over, The*)
            RKO 1944
            (*Murder My Sweet*)
            FOX—RANK 1975
HIGH WINDOW, THE   FOX 1947
(Hamilton)   (*Brasher Doubloon*)
LADY IN THE LAKE   MGM 1946
(Hamilton)
LITTLE SISTER, THE   MGM 1969
(Hamilton)   (*Marlowe*)
LONG GOODBYE, THE   UA 1973
(Hamilton)

CHANSLOR, Roy
BALLAD OF CAT BALLOU   COL 1965
(Little, Brown, Boston)   (*Cat Ballou*)
HAZARD   PAR 1948
(Various)

JOHNNY GUITAR   REP 1954
(Hale)

CHAPMAN, Edward
JOEY BOY   BL 1965
(Cassell)

CHAPMAN, John
DRY ROT (P)   BL 1956
(English Theatre Guild)

CHAPMAN, John *and* **COONEY, Ray**
NOT NOW DARLING (P)   MGM 1972
(English Theatre)

CHAPMAN, John *see* **COONEY, Ray** *jt. author*

CHAPMAN, Robert
BEHIND THE HEADLINES   RANK 1956
(Laurie)
MURDER FOR THE MILLIONS   COL 1957
(Laurie)   (*Murder Reported*)
ONE JUMP AHEAD   GFD 1955
(Laurie)
WINTER WEARS A SHROUD   MON 1954
(Laurie)   (*Delavine Affair, The*)

CHAPMAN, R.H. *see* **COXE, L.O.** *jt. author*

CHARRIERE, Henri
PAPILLON   COL—WAR 1973
(Hart-Davis)

CHARTERIS, Leslie
GETAWAY   RKO 1941
(Hodder & Stoughton)   (*Saint's Vacation, The*)
MEET THE TIGER   REP 1943
(Ward Lock)   (*Saint Meets the Tiger, The*)
SAINT IN NEW YORK, THE   RKO 1938
(Hodder & Stoughton)

CHASE, Borden
RED RIVER   UA 1948
(Sampson Low)

CHASE, James Hadley *pseud.*
  EVE   GALA 1963
  (Panther)
  I'LL GET YOU FOR THIS   BL 1951
  (Jarrolds)
  LAST PAGE, THE (P)   EXCLUSIVE 1952
  (French)
  NO ORCHIDS FOR MISS BLANDISH CINERAMA 1971
  (Jarrolds)   (*Grissom Gang, The*)
  TIGER BY THE TAIL   EROS 1955
  (Hale)
  WORLD IN MY POCKET, THE   BL 1961
  (Pan)   (*On Friday at 11*)

CHASE, Mary Coyle
  BERNARDINE (P)   FOX 1957
  (Oxford U.P.)
  HARVEY (P)   GFD 1950
  (Dramatists, N.Y.)
  SORORITY HOUSE (P)   RKO 1939
  (French, N.Y.)

CHATTERTON, Edward Keble
  'Q' SHIPS AND THEIR STORY   RKO 1928
  (Sidgwick & Jackson)   (*Blockade*)

CHAUCER, Geoffrey
  CANTERBURY TALES, THE   UA 1972
  (Various)

CHAUNCY, Nan
  THEY FOUND A CAVE   CFF 1962
  (Oxford U.P.)

CHAYEFSKY, Paddy
  ALTERED STATES   COL 1981
  (Harper, N.Y.)
  BACHELOR PARTY, THE (P)   COL 1957
  (*In* Television Plays: Simon & Schuster,
  N.Y.)
  MARTY (P)   COL 1956
  (Simon & Schuster, N.Y.)
  MIDDLE OF THE NIGHT (P)   COL 1959
  (Random House, N.Y.)

CHEKHOV, Anton
  SEAGULL, THE (P)   WAR 1969
  (Various)
  THREE SISTERS (P)   BL 1970
  (Chatto & Windus)

CHERFAS, Jeremy
  ZOO 2000   BBC 1984 (TV)
  (BBC)

CHESSMAN, Caryl
  CELL 2455, DEATH ROW   COL 1955
  (Longmans)

CHESTERTON, Gilbert Keith
  FATHER BROWN STORIES   COL 1954
  (Cassell)   (*Father Brown*)
  WISDOM OF FATHER BROWN, THE PAR 1935
  (Cassell)   (*Father Brown, Detective*)

CHETHAM-STRODE, Warren
  BACKGROUND (P)   ABP 1953
  (French)
  GUINEA PIG, THE (P)   PILGRIM-PATHE 1949
  (Sampson Low)

CHETWYND-HAYES, R.
  ELEMENTAL, THE   EMI 1974
  (Fontana)   (*From Beyond the Grave*)
  MONSTER CLUB, THE   ITC 1981
  (Kimber)

CHEVALIER, Gabriel
  CLOCHEMERLE   BLUE RIBBON 1951
  (Secker & Warburg)

CHEYNEY, Peter
  DAMES DON'T CARE   FANCEY 1954
  (Collins)
  SINISTER ERRAND   FOX 1952
  (Collins)   (*Diplomatic Courier*)
  UNEASY TERMS   BN 1948
  (Collins)
  URGENT HANGMAN, THE   EROS 1954
  (Collins)   (*Meet Mr. Callaghan*)

CHILDERS, Erskine
RIDDLE OF THE SANDS, THE   RANK 1979
(Various)

CHILDS, Herbert
GAUCHO   FOX 1952
(Prentice-Hall, N.Y.)   (*Way of a Gaucho*)

CHITTERDEN, Frank
UNINVITED, THE   EROS 1957
(Boardman)   (*Stranger in Town*)

CHODOROV, Edward
KIND LADY (P)   MGM 1935
(French)   MGM 1951
OH MEN! OH, WOMEN! (P)   FOX 1957
(French)

CHODOROV, Jerome *see also* **FIELDS, J.** *jt. author*

CHODOROV, Jerome *and* **FIELDS, Joseph**
JUNIOR MISS (P)   FOX 1945
(Dramatists, N.Y.)

CHOPIN, Kate
AWAKENING, THE   ENTERPRISE 1981
(Avon, N.Y.)   (*End of August, The*)

CHRISTIAN, Tina Chad
BABY LOVE   AVCO EMBASSY 1969
(Cape)

CHRISTIE, Agatha
ABC MURDERS, THE   MGM 1966
(Collins)   (*Alphabet Murders, The*)
AFTER THE FUNERAL   MGM 1963
(Collins)   (*Murder at the Gallop*)
BODY IN THE LIBRARY, THE   BBC 1984 (TV)
(Collins)
DEATH ON THE NILE   EMI 1978
(Collins)
ENDLESS NIGHT   BL 1971
(Collins)
EVIL UNDER THE SUN   COL 1981
(Collins)

4.50 FROM PADDINGTON	MGM 1961
(Collins)	(*Murder She Said*)
LORD EDGWARE DIES	WAR 1985 (TV)
(Collins)	(*Thirteen at Dinner*)
MIRROR CRACK'D FROM SIDE TO SIDE	EMI 1981
	(*Mirror Crack'd, The*)
(Collins)	
MISS MARPLE	MGM 1964
(Collins)	(*Murder Ahoy*)
MRS. McGINTY'S DEAD	MGM 1963
(Collins)	(*Murder Most Foul*)
MURDER IS ANNOUNCED, A	BBC 1985 (TV)
(Collins)	
MURDER IS EASY	BBC 2 1982 (TV)
(Collins)	
MURDER ON THE ORIENT EXPRESS	EMI 1974
(Collins)	
ORDEAL BY INNOCENCE	CANNON 1985
(Collins)	
POCKET FULL OF RYE, A	BBC 1985 (TV)
(Collins)	
SPARKLING CYANIDE	WAR 1984 (TV)
(Collins)	
SPIDER'S WEB, THE (P)	UA 1960
(French)	BBC 2 1985 (TV)
TEN LITTLE NIGGERS	FOX 1945
(Collins)	ABP 1965
	(*And Then There Was None*)
TEN LITTLE NIGGERS (P)	FOX 1945
(French)	ABP 1965
	(*Ten Little Indians*)
WITNESS FOR THE PROSECUTION (P)	UA 1957
(French)	

CHRISTIE, Dorothy *and* **CHRISTIE, Campbell**

CARRINGTON, V.C. (P)	INDEPENDENT 1954
(Heinemann)	
GRAND NATIONAL NIGHT (P)	REN 1953
(French)	
HIS EXCELLENCY (P)	GFD 1951
(*In* Plays of the year, 1950: Elek)	

CHRISTMAN, Elizabeth
NICE ITALIAN GIRL, A
(Dodd, N.Y.)

BRUT 1978
(*Dangerous Love*)
BBC 1985 (TV)
(*Don't Steal my Baby*: U.S. title *Black Market Baby*)

CHRISTOPHER, John
DEATH OF GRASS
(Penguin)

MGM—EMI 1972
(*No Blade of Grass*)

CHUBIN, Barry
FEET OF THE SNAKE, THE
(Arbor, N.Y.)

WELLER/MYERS 1985

CHURCHILL, *Sir* **Winston Spencer**
MY EARLY LIFE
(Fontana)

COL—WAR 1972
(*Young Winston*)

CLARK, Brian
WHOSE LIFE IS IT ANYWAY? (P)
(Avon, N.Y.)

CIC 1981

CLARK, Mary H.
CRADLE WILL FALL, THE
(Dell, N.Y.)

BBC 1983 (TV)

CLARK, Walter Van Tilburg
OX-BOW INCIDENT, THE
(Gollancz)

FOX 1943
(*Strange Incident*)
FOX 1956

TRACK OF THE CAT
(Gollancz)

WAR 1954

CLARKE, Arthur C.
2001, A SPACE ODYSSEY
(Hutchinson)
2010
(Granada)

MGM 1968

MGM 1985

CLARKE, Donald Henderson
HOUSEKEEPER'S DAUGHTER, THE
(Laurie)
IMPATIENT VIRGIN
(Long)

UA 1939

UN 1932
(*Impatient Maiden*)

LOUIS BERETTI	FOX 1930
(Long)	(*Born Reckless*)
MILLIE	RKO 1931
(Long)	
MILLIE'S DAUGHTER	COL 1947
(Laurie)	

CLARKE, Marcus
FOR THE TERM OF HIS NATURAL   FILMO 1985
LIFE
(Angus & Robertson)

CLARKE, Thurston *see* **WERBELL, F.** *jt. author*

CLAVELL, J.

KING RAT	BL 1964
(Joseph)	
SHOGUN	PAR 1981
(Dell, N.Y.)	
TAI PAN	MGM 1968
(Joseph	ORION 1986 (TV)

CLAYRE, Alistair
HEART OF THE DRAGON, THE   CHANNEL 4 1984 (TV)
(Harvill)

CLEARY, Jon

BACK OF SUNSET	WAR 1960
(Collins)	(*Sundowners, The*)
GREEN HELMET, THE	MGM 1960
(Collins)	
HIGH COMMISSIONER, THE	RANK 1968
(Collins)	
HIGH ROAD TO CHINA	MIRACLE 1984
(Warner, N.Y.)	
JUSTIN BAYARD	WAR 1958
(Collins)	(*Dust in the Sun*)
YOU CAN'T SEE ROUND CORNERS	UI 1969
(Collins)	

CLEAVER, Vera *and* **CLEAVER, Bill**
WHERE THE LILIES BLOOM   UA 1974
(Penguin)

CLECKLEY, H.M. *see* **THIGPEN, C.H.** *jt. author*

CLELAND, John
  FANNY HILL   GALA 1965
  (Luxor Press)   BRENT WALKER 1983

CLEMENS, Samuel Langhorne *see* **TWAIN, Mark** *pseud.*

CLEWES, Howard
  GREEN GROW THE RUSHES   BL 1951
  (Lane)
  LONG MEMORY, THE   GFD 1953
  (Macmillan)

CLIFFORD, Charles L.
  REAL GLORY, THE   UA 1939
  (Heinemann)

CLIFFORD, Francis
  ACT OF MERCY   WAR 1964
  (Hamilton)   (*Guns of Darkness*)
  NAKED RUNNER, THE   WAR 1966
  (Hodder & Stoughton)

CLIFT, Denison
  MAN ABOUT TOWN   FOX 1932
  (Long)

CLOETE, Stuart
  FIERCEST HEART, THE   FOX 1960
  (Collins)

CLOONEY, R. *and* **STRAIT, R.**
  THIS FOR REMEMBRANCE   FRIES 1982
  (Robson)   (*Rosie*)

CLOU, John
  CARAVAN TO CARNAL, A   RKO 1955
  (Redman)   (*Conqueror, The*)

CLOUSTON, J. Storer
  SPY IN BLACK, THE   COL 1938
  (Blackwood)

COATES, John
  TRUE AS A TURTLE   RANK 1957
  (Gollancz)

COATES, Robert M.
WISTERIA COTTAGE   UA 1958
(Gollancz)   (*Edge of Fury*)

COBB, Humphrey
PATHS OF GLORY   UA 1957
(Heinemann)

COBB, Irving Shrewsbury
OLD JUDGE PRIEST   REP 1953
(Grosset, N.Y.)   (*Sun Shines Bright, The*)

COCHRAN, Rice E.
BE PREPARED   FOX 1953
(Sloane, N.Y.)   (*Mister Scoutmaster*)

COCKRELL, Francis Marion *and* **COCKRELL, Marion**
DARK WATERS   UA 1944
(World, N.Y.)

COEN, Franklin
NIGHT OF THE QUARTER MOON   MGM 1959
(Corgi)

COETZEE, J.M.
IN THE HEART OF THE COUNTRY   DASKA FILMS 1985
(Penguin)   (*Dust*)

COFFEE, Lenore
WEEP NO MORE   PAR 1958
(Cassell)   (*Another Time, Another Place*)

COHN, Arthur
JOKER IS WILD   PAR 1957
(Random House, N.Y.)

COKE, Peter
BREATH OF SPRING (P)   RANK 1960
(French)   (*Make Mine Mink*)

COLE, Burt
OLIMPIA   WAR 1967
(W.H. Allen)   (*Bobo, The*)

COLEGATE, Isabel
SHOOTING PARTY, THE   REEVE 1984
(Avon, N.Y.)

COLEMAN, Terry
SOUTHERN CROSS   GEOFF REEVES 1983
(Hutchinson)

COLETTE
GIGI   MGM 1958
(Penguin)

COLLIER, James Lincoln
FIRES OF YOUTH   CINERAMA 1972
(Penguin)   (*Danny Jones*)

COLLINS, Dale
ORDEAL, THE   MGM 1930
(Allan)   (*Ship from Shanghai*)
SENTIMENTALISTS   PATHE 1929
(Little, Brown, Boston)   (*Sal of Singapore*)
      PAR 1931
      (*His Woman*)

COLLINS, Jackie
BITCH, THE   BRENT WALKER 1979
(Pan)
HOLLYWOOD WIVES   WAR 1985
(Collins)
STUD, THE   BRENT WALKER 1978
(Mayflower)
WORLD IS FULL OF MARRIED   NEW REALM 1978
MEN, THE
(W.H. Allen)

COLLINS, L. *and* **LAPIERRE, D.**
IS PARIS BURNING?   PAR 1965
(Gollancz)

COLLINS, Norman
LONDON BELONGS TO ME   UN 1948
(Collins)
American title is Dulcimer Street

COLLINS, Wilkie
MOONSTONE, THE   MON 1934
(Various)
WOMAN IN WHITE, THE   WAR 1948
(Various)

COLLINSON, W.
RED DUST   MGM 1932
(McBride, N.Y.)

COLLISON, Wilson *pseud.*
CONGO LANDING   MGM 1940
(McBride, N.Y.)   (*Congo Maisie*)
FAREWELL TO WOMEN (P)   MGM 1953
(McBride, N.Y.)   (*Mogambo*)

COLMAN, Dorothy
UNEXPECTED MRS. POLLIFAX,   UA 1971
THE   (*Mrs. Pollifax—Spy*)
(Hale)

COLSON, Charles
BORN AGAIN   AVCO EMBASSY 1979
(Bantam, N.Y.)

COMANECI, N.
NADIA   CHANNEL 4 1986 (TV)
(Duckworth)

COMBER, *Mrs.* **Elizabeth** *see* **HAN SUYIN** *pseud.*

COMDEN, Betty *and* **GREEN, Adolph**
BELLS ARE RINGING (P)   MGM 1960
(Random House, N.Y.)

COMPTON, David
CONTINUOUS KATHERINE   CONTEMPORARY 1979
MORTENHOE, THE   (*Death Watch*)
(Arrow, N.Y.)

CONDON, Richard
MANCHURIAN CANDIDATE   UA 1962
(Pan)
OLDEST CONFESSION, THE   UA 1961
(Longmans)   (*Happy Thieves, The*)

CONDON, Richard (*Continued*)
PRIZZI'S HONOUR   FOX 1985
(Joseph)
WINTER KILLS   AVCO EMBASSY 1979
(Dial, N.Y.)

CONNELL, Richard Edward
BROTHER ORCHID (P)   WAR 1940
(French, N.Y.)

CONNELL, Vivian
CHINESE ROOM, THE   FOX 1959
(Secker & Warburg)   (*In the Chinese Room*)

CONNELLY, Marc
GREEN PASTURES (P)   WAR 1936
(Gollancz)

CONNELLY, M. *see also* **KAUFMAN, G.S.** *jt. author*

CONNER, Rearden
SHAKE HANDS WITH THE DEVIL   UA 1959
(Dent)

CONNERS, Harry
APPLESAUCE (P)   IN 1936
(French, N.Y.)   (*Brides are like that*)

CONRAD, Joseph *pseud.*
DUELLISTS, THE   CIC 1977
(Fontana)
LORD JIM   COL 1964
(Dent)
OUTCAST OF THE ISLANDS, AN   LF 1951
(Various)
SECRET AGENT, THE   GB 1936
(Various)   (*Sabotage*)
VICTORY   PAR 1930
(Various)   (*Dangerous Paradise*)
      PAR 1940
WITHIN THE TIDES   REP 1953
(Dent)   (*Laughing Anne*)

CONRAN, Shirley
LACE   LORIMAR 1984
(Penguin)

CONROY, Pat
    GREAT SANTINI, THE   COL—-EMI—WAR 1981
    (Avon, N.Y.)
    LORDS OF DISCIPLINE, THE   PAR 1982
    (Secker & Warburg)
    WATER IS WIDE, THE   FOX 1974
    (Houghton, Mifflin, Boston)   (*Conrack*)

CONSTANDUROS, Mabel *and* **CONSTANDUROS, Denis**
    ACACIA AVENUE (P)   COL 1945
    (French)   (*29 Acacia Avenue*)
    HERE COME THE HUGGETTS   GFD 1948
    (Sampson Low)
    HUGGETTS ABROAD, THE   GFD 1949
    (Sampson Low)

COOK, Robin
    COMA   CIC 1978
    (Little, Brown, Boston)
    SPHINX   COL—EMI—WAR 1980
    (Putnam, N.Y.)

COOK, William Everett
    TWO RODE TOGETHER   COL 1961
    (Mills & Boon)

COOKLIN, Shirley *see* **ADAMS, Peter** *jt. author*

COOKSON, Catherine
    ROONEY   RANK 1958
    (Macdonald)

COONEY, Ray *see* **CHAPMAN, John** *jt. author*

COONEY, Ray *see* **STONE, Gene** *jt. author*

COOPER, James Fenimore
    DEERSLAYER, THE   REP 1943
    (Various)   FOX 1957
    LAST OF THE MOHICANS, THE UA 1936
    (Various)   COL 1949
                      (*Last of the Redskins*)
                     RANK 1977
    LEATHER STOCKING TALES   UA 1950
    (Various)   (*Tomahawk Trail, The*)

COOPER, James Fenimore (*Continued*)
   PATHFINDER, THE   COL 1953
   (Various)

COPPEL, Alec
   I KILLED THE COUNT (P)   GN 1939
   (Heinemann)
   I KILLED THE COUNT   GN 1939
   (Blackie)
   MAN ABOUT A DOG, A   GFD 1949
   (Harrap)   (*Obsession*)
   MR. DENNING DRIVES NORTH BL 1951
   (Harrap)

CORBIN, William
   SMOKE   DISNEY 1970
   (Harrap)

CORDER, E.M.
   DEER HUNTER, THE   COL—EMI—WAR 1979
   (Hodder & Stoughton)

CORMACK, Bartlett
   RACKET, THE (P)   RKO 1952
   (French, N.Y.)

CORMAN, Avery
   KRAMER vs KRAMER   COL—EMI—WAR 1979
   (New American Library, N.Y.)
   OH! GOD!   COL—WAR 1977
   (Simon & Schuster, N.Y.)

CORMIER, Robert
   I AM THE CHEESE   ALMI 1984
   (Panther, N.Y.)

CORY, Desmond
   DEADFALL   FOX 1968
   (Muller)

COSENTINO, Nicholas
   MOON OVER MULBERRY STREET REP 1952
   (P)   (*Woman in the Dark*)
   (Dramatic Pubns., Chicago)

AUTHOR AND ORIGINAL TITLE	FILM TITLE

COSTAIN, Thomas Bertram
BLACK ROSE, THE   FOX 1949
(Staples)
SILVER CHALICE, THE   WAR 1954
(Hodder & Stoughton)

COTLER, Gordon
BOTTLETOP AFFAIR, THE   MGM 1962
(Panther)   (*Horizontal Lieutenant, The*)

COTTERELL, Geoffrey
TIARA TAHITI   RANK 1962
(Eyre & Spottiswoode)

COTTRELL, Dorothy
SILENT REEFS   FOX 1960
(Hodder & Stoughton)   (*Secret of the Purple Reef, The*)

COULTER, Stephen
EMBASSY   HEMDALE 1972
(Heinemann)

COUSINS, E.G.
SAPPHIRE   RANK 1959
(Panther)

COUSTEAU, Jacques
SILENT WORLD, THE   RANK 1955
(Hamilton)

COWAN, Samuel Kinkade
SERGEANT YORK AND HIS PEOPLE   WAR 1941
(Various)   (*Sergeant York*)

COWARD, Noel
ASTONISHED HEART, THE (P)   GFD 1949
(*In* Tonight at 8.30: Heinemann)
BITTER SWEET (P)   MGM 1940
(Heinemann)
BLITHE SPIRIT (P)   CIN 1945
(Heinemann)
BON VOYAGE   BBC 1985 (TV)
(*In* Complete stories: Methuen)
CAVALCADE (P)   FOX 1933
(Heinemann)   FOX 1955

Coward, Noel (*Continued*)
DESIGN FOR LIVING (P)   PAR 1933
(Heinemann)
FUMED OAK (P)   GFD 1952
(French)
ME AND THE GIRLS   BBC 1985 (TV)
(*In* Complete stories: Methuen)
MEET ME TONIGHT (P)   GFD 1952
(Heinemann)
MR. & MRS. EDGEHILL   BBC 1985 (TV)
(*In* Complete stories: Methuen)
MRS. CAPPER'S BIRTHDAY   BBC 1985 (TV)
(*In* Complete stories: Methuen)
PRETTY POLLY BARLOW   RANK 1967
(Mayflower)   (*Pretty Polly*)
PRIVATE LIVES (P)   MGM 1931
(Heinemann)
QUEEN WAS IN THE PARLOUR,   PAR 1933
THE (P)   (*Tonight is Ours*)
(Heinemann)
RED PEPPERS (P)   GFD 1952
(Heinemann)
STAR QUALITY   BBC 1985 (TV)
(*In* Complete stories: Methuen)
STILL LIFE (P)   CIN 1946
(French)   (*Brief Encounter*)
THIS HAPPY BREED (P)   CIN 1944
(Heinemann)
TONIGHT AT 8.30 (P)   GFD 1952
(Heinemann)
WAYS AND MEANS (P)   GFD 1952
(Heinemann)
WE WERE DANCING (P)   MGM 1942
(French)
WHAT MAD PURSUIT   BBC 1985 (TV)
(*In* Complete stories: Methuen)

COWEN, William Joyce
THEY GAVE HIM A GUN   MGM 1937
(Heinemann)

COWLEY, Joy
NEST IN A FALLING TREE   MGM 1971
(Secker & Warburg)   (*Night Digger, The*)

COX, A.B. *see* **ILES, Francis** *pseud.*

COXE, George Harmon
  MURDER WITH PICTURES   PAR 1936
  (Heinemann)

COXE, Louis Osborne *and* **CHAPMAN, Robert H.**
  BILLY BUDD (P)   AA 1962
  (Hill & Wang, N.Y.)

COXHEAD, Elizabeth
  FRIEND IN NEED, A   EROS 1958
  (Collins)   (*Cry From The Streets, A*)

COZZENS, James Gould
  BY LOVE POSSESSED   UA 1961
  (Longmans)
  CURE OF THE FLESH   FOX 1933
  (Longmans)   (*Doctor Bull*)
  LAST ADAM   FOX 1933
  (Harcourt, Brace, N.Y.)   (*Dr. Bull*)

CRAIG, David
  SQUEEZE, THE   COL—WAR 1977
  (Stein & Day, N.Y.)

CRANE, Jonathan
  SUBMARINE   BBC 1985 (TV)
  (BBC)

CRANE, Stephen
  BRIDE COMES TO YELLOW SKY,   RKO 1952
  THE   (*Face to Face*)
  (*In* 20 stories: Knopf, N.Y.)
  RED BADGE OF COURAGE, THE   MGM 1951
  (Heritage, N.Y.)

CRAWFORD, Christina
  MOMMIE DEAREST   PAR 1981
  (Hart-Davis)

CRAWFORD, Francis Marion
  MR. ISAACS   MGM 1931
  (Macmillan)   (*Son of India*)
  WHITE SISTER   MGM 1933
  (Bles)

CREASEY, John
HAMMER THE TOFF   BUTCHER 1952
(Long)
SALUTE THE TOFF   BUTCHER 1951
(Long)

CREASEY, John *see also* **HALLIDAY, Michael** *pseud.* **MARRIC, J.J.** *pseud.*

CRICHTON, Kyle *see* **BIDDLE, C.D.** *jt. author*

CRICHTON, Michael
ANDROMEDA STRAIN, THE   RANK 1971
(Cape)
GREAT TRAIN ROBBERY, THE   UA 1979
(Cape)   (*First . . .*)

CRICHTON, Robert
GREAT IMPOSTER, THE   UI 1960
(Gollancz)
SECRET OF SANTA VITTORIA, THE   UA 1969
(Hodder & Stoughton)

CRISPIN, A.C.
V   WAR 1984
(New English Library)

CROCKETT, Lucy Heron
MAGNIFICENT DEVILS   PAR 1956
(Dymock)   (*Proud and Profane*)

CROFT, Michael
SPARE THE ROD   BL 1960
(Pan)

CROFT-COOKE, Rupert
SEVEN THUNDERS   RANK 1957
(Macmillan)

CROMPTON, Richmal
JUST WILLIAM   AB 1940
(Newnes)

CRONIN, Archibald Joseph
BEYOND THIS PLACE   REN 1959
(Gollancz)

CITADEL, THE	MGM 1938
(Gollancz)	BBC 1983 (TV)
GREEN YEARS, THE	MGM 1946
(Gollancz)	
HATTER'S CASTLE	PAR 1941
(Gollancz)	
JUPITER LAUGHS (P)	WAR 1941
(Gollancz)	(*Shining Victory*)
KEYS OF THE KINGDOM, THE	FOX 1944
(Gollancz)	
SPANISH GARDENER, THE	RANK 1956
(Gollancz)	
STARS LOOK DOWN, THE	GN 1940
(Gollancz)	

CRONIN, Michael

PAID IN FULL	FANCEY 1954
(Museum Press)	(*Johnny on the Spot*)
YOU PAY YOUR MONEY	BUTCHER 1956
(Museum Press)	

CROSS, *Mrs.* **Mary Ann** *see* **ELIOT, George** *pseud.*

CROSSLEY, Rosemary *and* **McDONALD Anne**

ANNIE'S COMING OUT	ENTERPRISE 1984
(Penguin)	

CROTHERS, Rachel

AS HUSBANDS GO (P)	FOX 1934
(French)	
'OLD LADY 31' (P)	MGM 1940
(Various)	(*Captain is a Lady, The*)
SUSAN AND GOD (P)	MGM 1940
(Random House, N.Y.)	
WHEN LADIES MEET (P)	MGM 1941
(French, N.Y.)	

CROUSE, R. *see* **LINDSAY, H.** *jt. author*

CROWE, Cameron

FAST TIMES AT RIDGEMONT HIGH	UIP 1982
(Simon & Schuster, N.Y.)	(*Fast Times*)

CROWLEY, Mart

BOYS IN THE BAND (P)	WAR 1969
(Secker & Warburg)	

AUTHOR AND ORIGINAL TITLE	FILM TITLE

CROY, Homer
   FAMILY HONEYMOON   UN 1949
   (Hurst & Blackett)
   SIXTEEN HANDS   PAR 1939
   (Hamilton)   (*I'm from Missouri*)

CULLINAN, Thomas
   BEGUILED, THE   UN 1971
   (Sphere)

CULOTTA, Nina
   THEY'RE A WEIRD MOB   RANK 1965
   (Kaye)

CUNNINGHAM, E.V. *pseud.*
   PENELOPE   MGM 1966
   (Deutsch)
   SYLVIA   PAR 1963
   (Deutsch)

CURIE, Eve
   MADAME CURIE   MGM 1943
   (Heinemann)

CURRY, Ellsworth
   HAPPENING, THE   PAR 1967
   (Corgi)

CURTIS, Peter
   DEVIL'S OWN, THE   HAMMER 1966
   (Pan)   (*Witches, The*)
   YOU'RE BEST ALONE   ABP 1950
   (Macdonald)   (*Guilt is my Shadow*)

CURTISS, Ursula
   FORBIDDEN GARDEN, THE   PALOMAR 1969
   (Eyre & Spottiswoode)   (*Whatever Happened to Aunt Alice?*)

CURWOOD, James Oliver
   BACK TO GOD'S COUNTRY   GFD 1953
   (Triangle Bks., N.Y.)
   GOLD HUNTERS, THE   MON 1949
   (Various)   (*Trail of the Yukon*)
   KAZAN THE WOLF DOG   COL 1949
   (Grosset, N.Y.)

AUTHOR AND ORIGINAL TITLE	FILM TITLE
NOMADS OF THE NORTH (Nelson)	ABP 1954 (*Northern Patrol*) DISNEY 1961 (*Nikki, Wild Dog of the North*)
RETRIBUTION (Various)	EL 1950 (*Timber Fury*)
RIVER'S END (Grosset, N.Y.)	WAR 1940
TENTACLES OF THE NORTH (Various)	ABP 1951 (*Snow Dog*)
WOLF HUNTERS, THE (Various)	MON 1949

CUSHMAN, Clarissa
YOUNG WIDOW   UA 1946
(Triangle Bks., N.Y.)

CUSHMAN, Dan
RIPPER FROM RAWHIDE   REP 1954
(Macmillan, N.Y.)   (*Timberjack*)
STAY AWAY, JOE   MGM 1969
(Bantam)

CUSSLER, Clive
RAISE THE TITANIC   ITC 1980
(Joseph)

D

DAHL, Roald
CHARLIE AND THE CHOCOLATE PAR 1971
FACTORY   (*Willie Wonka and the Chocolate*
(Allen & Unwin)   *Factory*)

DALEY, Robert
PRINCE OF THE CITY   COL—EMI—WAR 1981
(Hart-Davis)
YEAR OF THE DRAGON   COL—EMI—WAR 1985
(Coronet)

D'ALTON, Louis Lynch
MONEY DOESN'T MATTER (P) ABP 1951
(Duffy, Dublin)   (*Talk of a Million*)

DANA, Richard Henry
TWO YEARS BEFORE THE MAST   PAR 1946
(Various)

DANE, Clemence *pseud.*
BILL OF DIVORCEMENT, A (P)   RKO 1932
(Heinemann)   RKO 1940

DANE, Clemence *and* **SIMPSON, H. de G.**
ENTER SIR JOHN   BI 1930
(Hodder & Stoughton)   (*Murder*)

DANIELS, H.R.
HOUSE ON GREENAPPLE STREET,   MGM 1970
THE
(Deutsch)

DANIKEN, Erich von
CHARIOTS OF THE GODS   EMI 1976
(Corgi)   (*Mysteries of the Gods*)

DANINOS, Pierre
MAJOR THOMPSON LIVES IN   GALA 1957
FRANCE   (*Diary of Major Thompson, The*)
(Cape)   (U.S. title *French are a Funny Race,*
          The)

DANNAY, Frederic *see* **QUEEN, Ellery** *pseud.*

DAVENPORT, *Mrs.* **Gwen**
BELVEDERE   FOX 1948
(Bobbs-Merrill, Indianapolis)   (*Sitting Pretty*)

DAVENPORT, Marcia
EAST SIDE, WEST SIDE   MGM 1949
(Collins)
VALLEY OF DECISION, THE   MGM 1945
(Collins)

DAVIDSON, Lionel
NIGHT OF WENCELAS   RANK 1963
(Gollancz)   (*Hot Enough for June*)

DAVIES, Hunter
HERE WE GO ROUND THE   UA 1967
MULBERRY BUSH
(Panther)

DAVIES, Jack
ESTHER, RUTH AND JENNIFER   CIC 1980
(W.H. Allen)   (*North Sea Hijack*)

DAVIES, Joseph Edward
MISSION TO MOSCOW   WAR 1943
(Gollancz)

DAVIES, L.P.
ALIEN, THE   RANK 1972
(Barrie & Jenkins)   (*Groundstar Conspiracy, The*)

DAVIES, Valentine
IT HAPPENS EVERY SPRING   FOX 1950
(Farrar, N.Y.)
MIRACLE ON 34th STREET   FOX 1947
(Harcourt, N.Y.)   FOX 1956

DAVIS, B.C.
MASS APPEAL   UN 1985
(Avon, N.Y.)

DAVIS, Clyde Brion
ANOINTED, THE   MGM 1945
(Barker)   (*Adventure*)

DAVIS, Dorrence
APRON STRINGS (P)   UN 1931
(French, N.Y.)   (*Virtuous Husband*)

DAVIS, Frederick Clyde *see* **RANSOME, Stephen** *pseud.*

DAVIS, *Mrs.* Lavinia
COME BE MY LOVE   UN 1949
(Doubleday, N.Y.)   (*Once More My Darling*)

DAVIS, Owen
MR. AND MRS. NORTH (P)   MGM 1941
(French, N.Y.)

DAVIS, Richard Harding
BAR SINISTER, THE   MGM 1955
(Scribner, N.Y.)   (*It's a Dog's Life*)

DAVIS, Stratford
ONE MAN'S SECRET   AA 1957
(Boardman)   (*Man in the Shadow*)

DAVIS, Terry
VISION QUEST   GUBER PETERS 1985
(Viking, N.Y.)   (*Crazy for You*)

DAWSON, Peter
RENEGADE CANYON   COL 1953
(Collins)

DAY, Clarence
LIFE WITH FATHER (P)   WAR 1947
(Chatto & Windus)

DAY, Lillian
YOUNGEST PROFESSION, THE   MGM 1943
(Laurie)

DEAL, Borden
DUNBAR'S COVE   FOX 1960
(Hutchinson)   (*Wild River*)

DEARDON, H. *see* **PERTWEE, R.** *jt. author*

DEARSLEY, A.P.
FLY AWAY PETER (P)   GFD 1948
(French)

DE BEAUVOIR, Simone
BLOOD OF OTHERS, THE   ORION 1985 (TV)
(Penguin)
MANDARINS, THE   FOX 1969
(Fontana)

DEBRETT, Hal
BEFORE I WAKE   GN 1955
(Dodd, N.Y.)

DEEPING, Warwick
SORRELL AND SON   UA 1934
(Cassell)   YORKSHIRE TV 1984

DE FELITTA, Frank
AUDREY ROSE   UA 1977
(Collins)
ENTITY, THE   FOX 1982
(Warner, N.Y.)

DEFOE, Daniel
ADVENTURES OF ROBINSON   UA 1954
CRUSOE, THE   FOX 1954
(Various)   (*Miss Robin Crusoe*)
MOLL FLANDERS   FOX 1954
(Various)   PAR 1964
        (*Amorous Adventures of Moll
            Flanders, The*)

DE FRECE, *Lady*
RECOLLECTIONS OF VESTA   BL 1957
TILLEY   (*After the Ball*)
(Hutchinson)

DEIGHTON, Leonard
BILLION DOLLAR BRAIN   UA 1967
(Cape)
FUNERAL IN BERLIN   PAR 1966
(Cape)
IPCRESS FILE, THE   RANK 1964
(Hodder & Stoughton)
ONLY WHEN I LARF   PAR 1969
(Sphere)
SPY STORY   GALA 1976
(Cape)

DEKOBRA, Maurice
HELL IS SOLD OUT   EROS 1951
(Laurie)
SPHINX HAS SPOKEN, THE   RKO 1931
(Laurie)   (*Friends and Lovers*)

DELANEY, Shelagh
TASTE OF HONEY, A (P)   BL 1961
(Methuen)

DELDERFIELD, R.F.
ALL OVER THE TOWN (P)   WESSEX 1948
(French)
GLAD TIDINGS (P)   EROS 1953
(Rylee)
ORCHARD WALLS, THE (P)   ABP 1955
(French)   (*Now and Forever*)
STOP AT A WINNER   AA 1961
(Hodder & Stoughton)   (*On the Fiddle*)
THERE WAS A FAIR MAID   BBC 1984 (TV)
DWELLING: UNJUST SKIES, THE (*Diana*)
(Coronet)
TO SERVE THEM ALL MY DAYS BBC 1982 (TV)
(Hodder & Stoughton)
WHERE THERE'S A WILL (P)   EROS 1955
(French)
WORM'S EYE VIEW (P)   ABP 1951
(*In* Embassy Successes, Vol. I: Sampson
Low)

DELL, Jeffery
NOBODY ORDERED WOLVES   GFD 1951
(Heinemann)   (*Dark Man, The*)

DELMAR, Vina
ABOUT MRS. LESLIE   PAR 1954
(Hale)

DE RIVO, Laura
FURNISHED ROOM, THE   WAR 1963
(Hutchinson)   (*West II*)

DEMING, Richard
CAREFUL MAN, THE   PAR 1967
(W.H. Allen)   (*Arrivederci, Baby!*)

DEMPSTER, Derek *see* **WOOD, Derek** *jt. author*

DENHAM, Reginald *and* **PERCY, Edward**
LADIES IN RETIREMENT (P)   COL 1968
(Random House, N.Y.)   (*Mad Room, The*)

DENHAM, R. *see* **PERCY, E.** *jt. author*

AUTHOR AND ORIGINAL TITLE	FILM TITLE

DENNIS, Charles
NEXT-TO-LAST TRAIN RIDE, THE   RANK 1984
(Macmillan)   (*Finders Keepers*)

DENNIS, Patrick
AUNTIE MAME   WAR 1956
(Vanguard, N.Y.)   WAR 1974
    (*Lucy Mame*)

DE SADE, *Marquis*
JUSTINE   THE OTHER CINEMA 1976
(Various)   TARGET 1978
    (*Cruel Passion*)

DESVALLIERES, M. *see* **FEYDEAU, G.** *jt. author*

DE VOTO, Bernard
ACROSS THE WIDE MISSOURI   MGM 1951
(Eyre & Spottiswoode)

DE VRIES, Peter
LET ME COUNT THE WAYS   CIRO 1970
(Gollancz)   (*How Do I Love Thee?*)
REUBEN, REUBEN   FOX 1984
(Penguin)
TUNNEL OF LOVE, THE   MGM 1959
(Gollancz)
WITCH'S MILK   UN 1972
(*In* Cat's Pajamas and . . .: Gollancz)   (*Pete 'n' Tillie*)

DE VRIES, P. *see also* **FIELDS, J.** *jt. author*

DEWLEN, Al
NIGHT OF THE TIGER, THE   COL 1966
(Longmans)   (*Ride Beyond Vengeance*)
TWILIGHT OF HONOUR   MGM 1963
(Longmans)   (*Charge is Murder, The*)

DIAMOND, I.A.L. *see* **WILDER, W.** *jt. author*

DIAMOND, Paul
CHICKEN CHRONICLES, THE   ALPHA 1980
(Dell, N.Y.)

DIBNER, Martin
  DEEP SIX, THE   WAR 1957
  (Cassell)

DICK, Phillip, K.
  DO ANDROIDS DREAM OF   COL—EMI—WAR 1982
  ELECTRIC SHEEP?   (*Blade Runner*)
  (Ballantine, N.Y.)

DICK, R.A. *pseud.*
  GHOST AND MRS. MUIR, THE   FOX 1947
  (Harrap)

DICKENS, Charles
  BLEAK HOUSE   BBC 2 1985 (TV)
  (Various)
  CHRISTMAS CAROL, A   PAR 1935
  (Various)   MGM 1938
                  REN 1951
                  (*Scrooge*)
                  FOX 1970
                  (*Scrooge*)
                  ENTERPRISE 1984
                  CHANNEL 4 1985 (TV)
                  (*Christmas Present, A*)
  DAVID COPPERFIELD   MGM 1935
  (Various)   FOX 1969
  DOMBEY AND SON   BBC 1986 (TV)
  (Various   PAR 1931
                  BBC 1984 (TV)
  GREAT EXPECTATIONS   UN 1934
  (Various)   CINE 1946
                  SCOTIA BARBER 1978
  MYSTERY OF EDWIN DROOD, THE UN 1935
  (Various)
  NICHOLAS NICKLEBY   EALING 1948
  (Various)   CHANNEL 4 1982 (TV)
                  PRIMETIME 1984 (TV)
                  (*Life and Adventures of Nicholas
                     Nickleby*)
  OLD CURIOSITY SHOP   EMI 1975
  (Various)   (*Mister Quilp*)

AUTHOR AND ORIGINAL TITLE	FILM TITLE
OLIVER TWIST (Various)	MONOGRAM 1933 CINE 1948 COL 1968 (*Oliver*) TRIDENT 1982 BBC 1985 (TV)
PICKWICK PAPERS (Various)	REN 1952 BBC 1985 (TV)
TALE OF TWO CITIES, A (Various)	MGM 1935 RANK 1957 BBC 1982 (TV)

DICKENS, Monica
ONE PAIR OF FEET   TC 1943
(Joseph)   (*Lamp Still Burns, The*)

DICKEY, James
DELIVERANCE   WAR 1972
(Hamilton)

DIDION, Joan
PLAY IT AS IT LAYS   UN 1972
(Weidenfeld & Nicolson)

DI DONATO, Pietro
CHRIST IN CONCRETE   GFD 1949
(World, N.Y.)   (*Give Us This Day*)

DIEHL, William
SHARKEY'S MACHINE   COL—EMI—WAR 1982
(Sphere)

DIETZ, Lew
YEAR OF THE BIG CAT, THE DISNEY 1974
(Little, Brown, Boston)   (*Return of the Big Cat*)

DIGHTON, John
HAPPIEST DAYS OF YOUR LIFE,   BL 1949
THE (P)
(*In* Plays of the Year, 1948–49: Elek)
WHO GOES THERE? (P)   BL 1952
(*In* Plays of the Year, 1951: Elek)

DINE, S.S. van
BENSON MURDER CASE, THE   PAR 1930
(Benn)

DINE, S.S. van (*Continued*)
 BISHOP MURDER CASE, THE MGM 1930
 (Cassell)
 CANARY MURDER CASE, THE PAR 1929
 (Benn)
 CASINO MURDER CASE, THE MGM 1935
 (Cassell)
 GARDEN MURDER CASE, THE MGM 1936
 (Cassell)
 GRACIE ALLEN MURDER CASE, PAR 1939
 THE
 (Cassell)
 KENNEL MURDER CASE, THE WAR 1933
 (Cassell)   WAR 1940
             (*Calling Philo Vance*)

DINELLI, Mel
 MAN, THE (P)   RKO 1952
 (Dramatists, N.Y.)   (*Beware My Lovely*)

DINNEEN, Joseph F.
 ANATOMY OF A CRIME   GFD 1954
 (Scribner, N.Y.)   (*Six Bridges to Cross*)

DINNER, William *and* **MORUM, William**
 LATE EDWINA BLACK, THE (P) GFD 1951
 (French)

DISNEY, Doris Miles
 FAMILY SKELETON   FOX 1950
 (Doubleday, N.Y.)   (*Stella*)
 STRAW MAN, THE   UA 1953
 (Doubleday, N.Y.)

DIVINE, David *pseud.*
 BOY ON A DOLPHIN, THE FOX 1957
 (Murray)

DIXON, Rosie
 CONFESSIONS OF A NIGHT NURSE COL—WAR 1977
 (Futura)   (*Rosie Dixon—Night Nurse*)

DOBIE, Laurence *and* **SLOMAN, Robert**
 TINKER, THE (P)   RANK 1962
 (French)   (*Wild and Willing, The*)

DOBLIN, Alfred
BERLIN ALEXANDERPLATZ   CHANNEL 4 1985 (TV)
(Penguin)

DOCTOROW, E.L.
BOOK OF DANIEL, THE   PAR 1983
(Random House, N.Y.)   (*Daniel*)
RAGTIME   COL—EMI—WAR 1981
(Macmillan)
WELCOME TO HARD TIMES   MGM 1966
(Simon & Schuster, N.Y.)   (*Killer on a Horse*)

DODGE, David
PLUNDER OF THE SUN   WAR 1953
(Random House, N.Y.)
TO CATCH A THIEF   PAR 1955
(Penguin)

DODGE, Henry Irving *and others*
SKINNER'S DRESS SUIT (P)   UN 1929
(French, N.Y.)   (*Skinner Steps Out*)

DODGSON, Charles Lutwidge *see* **CARROLL, Lewis** *pseud.*

DODSON, Kenneth
AWAY ALL BOATS   UI 1955
(Angus & Robertson)

DONOVAN, Robert J.
WARTIME ADVENTURES OF   WAR 1963
PRESIDENT JOHN F. KENNEDY,   (*PT. 109*)
THE
(Panther)

DOSTOEVSKI, Fedor Mikhailovich
BROTHERS KARAMAZOV, THE   MGM 1957
(Various)   COL—WAR 1972
CRIME AND PUNISHMENT   COL 1935
(Various)   WAR 1958
                                     (*Crime and Punishment U.S.A.*)
GAMBLER AND OTHER STORIES,   MGM 1949
THE   (*Great Sinner, The*)
(Various)

DOUGHERTY, Richard
COMMISSIONER, THE   UI 1968
(Hart-Davis)   (*Madigan*)

DOUGLAS, Colin
HOUSEMAN'S TALE, A   BBC 1985 (TV)
(Fontana)

DOUGLAS, Felicity
IT'S NEVER TOO LATE (P)   ABP 1956
(Evans)

DOUGLAS, Lloyd Cassel
DISPUTED PASSAGE   PAR 1939
(Davies)
GREEN LIGHT, THE   WAR 1937
(Davies)
MAGNIFICENT OBSESSION   UN 1935
(Allen & Unwin)   UI 1954
ROBE, THE   FOX 1953
(Davies)
WHITE BANNERS   WAR 1938
(Davies)

DOUGLAS, Michael
DEALING   WAR 1972
(Talmy-Franklin)

DOWNES, Donald
EASTER DINNER, THE   PAR 1962
(Rinehart, N.Y.)   (*Pigeon that took Rome, The*)

DOYLE, *Sir* **Arthur Conan**
ADVENTURE OF THE FIVE PIPS   UN 1945
(Murray)
ADVENTURES OF SHERLOCK   GRANADA 1983 (TV)
HOLMES, THE
(Murray)
EXPLOITS OF BRIGADIER   UA 1970
GERARD, THE   (*Adventures of Gerard, The*)
(Murray)
HIS LAST BOW   UN 1942
(Murray)   (*Sherlock Holmes and the Voice of Terror*)

HOUND OF THE BASKERVILLES, THE (Murray)	ID 1932 FOX 1939 UA 1959 HEMDALE 1978 EMBASSY 1983
LOST WORLD, THE (Murray)	FOX 1960
MAN WITH THE TWISTED LIP, THE (*In* Adventures of Sherlock Holmes: Murray)	GN 1951
RETURN OF SHERLOCK HOLMES (Murray)	PAR 1929
SIGN OF FOUR (Murray)	WW 1932 EMBASSY 1984
SIX NAPOLEONS (Murray)	UN 1944 (*Pearl of Death*)
STUDY IN SCARLET, A (Murray)	WW 1933

DOYLE, Monte
SIGNPOST TO MURDER (P)   MGM 1965
(French)

DRABBLE, Margaret
MILLSTONE, THE   BL 1969
(Penguin)   (*Touch of Love, A*)

DRAKE, O. *see* **CANUTT, Y.** *jt. author*

DRATLER, Jay
PITFALL   UA 1948
(Oxford U.P.)

DRAWBELL, James Wedgwood
INNOCENTS OF CHICAGO   BI 1934
(Collins)
LOVE AND FORGET   BI 1940
(Collins)   (*Love Story*)

DRAWBELL, James Wedgwood *see also* **SIMPSON, Reginald** *jt. author*

DREISER, Theodore
AMERICAN TRAGEDY, AN   PAR 1931
(Constable)   PAR 1951
        (*Place in the Sun, A*)

DREISER, Theodore (*Continued*)
JENNIE GERHARDT   PAR 1933
(Constable)
SISTER CARRIE   PAR 1952
(Constable)   (*Carrie*)

DRESSER, Davis *see* **HALLIDAY, Brett** *pseud.*

DREXLER, Rosalyn
SUBMISSION OF A LAZY   PRODUCTION ASSOCIATES 1982
WRESTLER   (*Below the Belt*)
(Mayflower)

DRISCOL, Peter
WILBY CONSPIRACY, THE   UA 1974
(Macdonald)

DRUMMOND, John D.
BUT FOR THESE MEN   RANK 1965
(W.H. Allen)   (*Heroes of the Telemark*)

DRUMMOND, William
LIFE FOR RUTH   RANK 1962
(Corgi)

DRUON, Maurice
CURTAIN FALLS, THE   BL 1964
(Hart-Davis)

DRURY, Allen
ADVISE AND CONSENT   BL 1962
(Collins)

DRUTEN, John van
AFTER ALL (P)   MGM 1932
(*In* Famous Plays of 1931: Gollancz)   (*New Morals for Old*)
BEHOLD WE LIVE (P)   RKO 1933
(Gollancz)   (*If I Were Free*)
BELL, BOOK AND CANDLE (P)   COL 1958
(French)
I AM A CAMERA (P)   BL 1955
(Random House, N.Y.)   CINERAMA 1972
      (*Cabaret*)
I REMEMBER MAMA (P)   RKO 1948
(Dramatists, N.Y.)

AUTHOR AND ORIGINAL TITLE	FILM TITLE
LONDON WALL (P) (Gollancz)	BI 1931 (*After Office Hours*)
OLD ACQUAINTANCE (P) (French)	WAR 1943 MGM 1981 (*Rich and Famous*)
THERE'S ALWAYS JULIET (P) (French, N.Y.)	PAR 1941 (*One Night in Lisbon*)
VOICE OF THE TURTLE (P) (Joseph)	WAR 1947
YOUNG WOODLEY (P) (Putnam)	BI 1930
YOUNG WOODLEY (Gollancz)	BI 1930

DRYER, Bernard Victor

PORT AFRIQUE (Cassell)	COL 1956

DUFFY, Clinton *and* JENNINGS, Dean

SAN QUENTIN (Davies)	ABP 1954 (*Men Behind Bars*) GN 1956 (*Steel Cage, The*)

DUGUID, Julian

GREEN HELL (Various)	UN 1940

DUMAS, Alexandre (*père*)

BLACK TULIP (Various)	CINERAMA 1965
COMPANIONS OF JEHU, THE (Dent)	COL 1945 (*Fighting Guardsmen*)
COUNT OF MONTE CRISTO, THE (Various)	UA 1934 SCOTIA BARBER 1976
DEUX FRÈRES (Macmillan)	WAR 1968 CBS 1986 (TV) (*Corsican Brothers, The*)
MAN IN THE IRON MASK, THE (Collins)	UA 1939 ITC 1976 SASCHA WIEN FILMS 1978 (*Fifth Musketeer, The*)
MEMOIRS OF A PHYSICIAN (Routledge)	UA 1949 (*Black Magic*)

DUMAS, Alexandre (*père*) (*Continued*)
THREE MUSKETEERS, THE   RKO 1935
(Various)   FOX 1939
        MGM 1949
        FOX—RANK 1972
        FOX—RANK 1974
        (*Four Musketeers, The*)

DUMAS, Alexandre (*fils*)
LADY OF THE CAMELIAS, THE   MGM 1936
(Various)   (*Camille*)
        ROSEMOUNT 1984
        (*Camille*)

DU MAURIER, Daphne
BIRDS, THE   RANK 1963
(*In* Short Stories: Gollancz)
DON'T LOOK NOW   BL 1973
(Doubleday, N.Y.)
FRENCHMAN'S CREEK   PAR 1944
(Gollancz)
HUNGRY HILL   TC 1947
(Gollancz)
JAMAICA INN   PAR 1939
(Gollancz)   HTV 1983 (TV)
MY COUSIN RACHEL   FOX 1952
(Gollancz)   NBC 1984 (TV)
REBECCA   UA 1940
(Gollancz)
REBECCA (P)   UA 1940
(Gollancz)
SCAPEGOAT, THE   MGM 1958
(Gollancz)
YEARS BETWEEN, THE (P)   BOX 1946
(Gollancz)

DU MAURIER, George
PETER IBBOTSON   PAR 1935
(Various)
TRILBY   WAR 1931
(Various)   REN 1954
        (*Svengali*)

DUNCAN, Alex
IT'S A VET'S LIFE   RANK 1961
(Joseph)   (*In The Doghouse*)

DUNCAN, Isadora
MY LIFE   UI 1969
(Gollancz)   (*Isadora*)

DUNCAN, Lois
SUMMER OF FEAR   BRENT WALKER 1978
(Dell, N.Y.)

DUNN, Nell
POOR COW   WAR 1967
(McGibbon & Kee)
STEAMING (P)   COL—EMI—WAR 1985
(Amber Lane)
UP THE JUNCTION   PAR 1968
(McGibbon & Kee)

DUNNE, John G.
TRUE CONFESSIONS   UA 1981
(Weidenfeld & Nicolson)

DUNNE, Lee
GOODBYE TO THE HILL   FOX 1969
(Hutchinson)   (*Paddy*)

DUPREZ, Fred
MY WIFE'S FAMILY (P)   ABP 1956
(French)

DURAS, Marguerite
MODERATO CANTABILE   N.J. LEVY 1960
(Calder)
SAILOR FROM GIBRALTAR, THE   UA 1967
(Calder)
SEA OF TROUBLES, A   RANK 1958
(Methuen)   (*Sea Wall*)
10.30 p.m. ON A SUMMER NIGHT   UA 1965
(Calder)   (*10.30 p.m. Summer*)

DURHAM, Marilyn
MAN WHO LOVED CAT DANCING,   MGM 1973
THE
(Macmillan)

DURRANT, Theo
MARBLE FOREST   ABP 1957
(Wingate)   (*Macabre*)

DURRELL, Gerald *and* **DURRELL, Lee**
DURRELL IN RUSSIA   CHANNEL 4 1986 (TV)
(Macdonald)

DURRELL, Lawrence
JUSTINE   FOX 1969
(Faber)   (*Alexandria Quartet*)

DURRENMATT, Friedrich
VISIT, THE (P)   FOX 1964
(French, N.Y.)

D'USSEAU, Arnaud *and* **GOW, James**
DEEP ARE THE ROOTS (P)   UA 1944
(Dramatists, N.Y.)

DWYER, K.R.
SHATTERED   COL—WAR 1976
(Barker)   (*Passengers*)

DYER, Charles
RATTLE OF A SIMPLE MAN (P)   WAR 1964
(French)
STAIRCASE   FOX 1969
(W.H. Allen)
STAIRCASE (P)   FOX 1969
(French)

E

EARL, Lawrence
ESCAPE OF 'THE AMETHYST', THE   BL 1957
(Harrap)   (*Yangtse Incident*)

EASTLAKE, William
CASTLE KEEP   COL 1969
(Joseph)

EASTWOOD, James
MURDER INC.
(Dakers)

WAR 1952

EBERHART, Mignon G.
FROM THIS DARK STAIRWAY
(Heinemann)

IN 1936
(*Murder of Dr. Harrigan*)

ECHARD, Margaret
DARK FANTASTIC
(Invincible Press)

WAR 1951
(*Lightning Strikes Twice*)

EDE, H.S.
SAVAGE MESSIAH
(Fraser)

MGM—EMI 1972

EDMONDS, Walter Dumaux
ROME HAUL
(Triangle Bks., N.Y.)

FOX 1953
(*Farmer Takes a Wife, The*)

EDWARDS, Samuel
55 DAYS AT PEKING
(Bantam, N.Y.)

RANK 1962

EGLETON, Clive
SEVEN DAYS TO A KILLING
(Hodder & Stoughton)

PAR 1974
(*Black Windmill, The*)

EHRLICH, Max
FIRST TRAIN TO BABYLON
(Gollancz)
REINCARNATION OF PETER
PROUD, THE
(W.H. Allen)

UA 1961
(*Naked Edge, The*)
FOX—RANK 1975

EINSTEIN, James
BLACKJACK HIJACK
(Fawcett, N.Y.)

MGM 1978
(*Nowhere to Run*)

EISNER, Jack
SURVIVOR, THE
(Bantam, N.Y.)

STAFFORD 1984
(*Children's War, The*)

ELIOT, George
  SILAS MARNER   BBC 1985 (TV)
  (Various)

ELIOT, Thomas Stearns
  MURDER IN THE CATHEDRAL (P)   FILM TRADERS 1951
  (Faber)

ELLI, Frank
  RIOT, THE   PAR 1969
  (Heinemann)

ELLIN, Stanley
  DREADFUL SUMMIT   UA 1954
  (Simon & Schuster, N.Y.)   (*Big Night, The*)
  HOUSE OF CARDS   RANK 1968
  (Macdonald)

ELLIOTT, Janice
  BUTTERCUP CHAIN, THE   COL 1969
  (Panther)
  SECRET PLACES   RANK 1983
  (Hodder & Stoughton)

ELLIOTT, Sumner
  SIGNS OF LIFE   SYME 1983
  (Penguin)   (*"Careful He Might Hear You"*)

ELLIS, Ruth
  WHITE COLLARS (P)   MGM 1929
  (French, N.Y.)   (*Idle Rich*)

ELY, David
  SECONDS   PAR 1965
  (Deutsch)

EMMONS, Della Gould
  SACAJAWEA OF THE SHOSHONES PAR 1955
  (Binfords, Portland, Ore)   (*Far Horizons, The*)

ENDE, Michael
  NEVER ENDING STORY, THE   WAR 1985
  (Lane)

ENDORE, Guy
  METHINKS THE LADY   FOX 1951
  (Cresset Press)   (*Whirlpool*)
  WEREWOLF OF PARIS, THE   RANK 1960
  (Long)   (*Curse of the Werewolf, The*)

ENGLAND, Barry
  CONDUCT UNBECOMING (P)   BL 1975
  (French)
  FIGURES IN A LANDSCAPE   FOX 1970
  (Cape)

ENGSTRAND, Stuart David
  BEYOND THE FOREST   WAR 1951
  (Cape)

EPHRON, Phoebe *and* **EPHRON, Henry**
  TAKE HER, SHE'S MINE (P)   FOX 1963
  (Random House, N.Y.)
  THREE IS A FAMILY (P)   UA 1944
  (French, N.Y.)

ERDMAN, Paul
  SILVER BEARS, THE   EMI 1978
  (Hutchinson)

ERSKINE, John
  EXPERIMENT IN SINCERITY   UN 1930
  (Putnam)   (*Lady Surrenders, A*)

ERSKINE, Laurie York
  RENFREW'S LONG TRAIL   MON 1940
  (Grosset, N.Y.)   (*Danger Ahead*)
  RENFREW RIDES AGAIN   MON 1939
  (Appleton, N.Y.)   (*Fighting Mad*)
  RENFREW RIDES NORTH   MON 1940
  (Grosset, N.Y.)   (*Yukon Flight*)
  RENFREW RIDES THE RANGE   MON 1939
  (Appleton, N.Y.)   (*Crashing Thru'*)

ERTZ, Susan
  IN THE COOL OF THE DAY   MGM 1963
  (Collins)

ERVINE, St. John Green
BOYD'S SHOP (P)   RANK 1960
(Allen & Unwin)
FIRST MRS. FRASER, THE (P)   STERLING 1932
(Chatto & Windus)

ESZTERHAS, Joe
F.I.S.T.   UA 1978
(Dell, N.Y.)

EUNSON, D. *see* **WILDE, H.** *jt. author*

EURIPIDES
ELECTRA (P)   UA 1963
(Various)
IPHIGENIA (P)   UA 1978
(Various)
TROJAN WOMEN, THE   CINERAMA 1971
(Various)

EUSTACE, C.J.
DAMAGED LIVES   PAR 1935
(Putnam, N.Y.)

EVANS, E. Eynon
BLESS THIS HOUSE (P)   MON 1955
(French)   (*Room in the House*)
WISHING WELL (P)   ADELPHI 1954
(French)   (*Happiness of Three Women, The*)

EVANS, Evan
BRANDED   PAR 1950
(Various)

EVANS, Max
ROUNDERS, THE   MGM 1965
(Macmillan, N.Y.)

EVANS, Peter
SOFT BEDS, HARD BATTLES   FOX—RANK 1974
(New English Library)

EVERETT, Peter
NEGATIVES   WALTER READE 1970
(Cape)

F

F., Christiane
CHRISTIANE F   FOX 1982
(Arlington)

FABIAN, Robert
FABIAN OF THE YARD   EROS 1954
(Naldrett Press)

FABIAN, Warner
WEEK-END GIRL   FOX 1932
(Paul)   (*Week-ends Only*)

FAIRCHILD, William
SOUND OF MURDER, THE (P)   FOX 1969
(French)   (*Last Shot You Hear, The*)

FAIRLEY, J. *see* **ALLISON, W.** *jt. author*

FAIRLIE, Gerard
CALLING BULLDOG DRUMMOND   MGM 1951
(Hodder & Stoughton)

FALLADA, Hans
LITTLE MAN, WHAT NOW?   UN 1934
(Putnam)

FANTE, John
FULL OF LIFE   COL 1957
(Little, Brown, Boston)

FARAGO, Ladislas
PATTON: ORDEAL AND TRIUMPH   FOX 1970
(Mayflower)   (*Patton: Lust for Glory*)

FARLEY, Walter
BLACK STALLION   UA 1979
(Random House, N.Y.)
BLACK STALLION RETURNS   MGM 1984
(Hodder & Stoughton)

FARNOL, Jeffrey
AMATEUR GENTLEMAN, THE   UA 1936
(Sampson Low)

FARRE, Rowena
SEAL MORNING   ITV 1986 (TV)
(Hutchinson)

FARRELL, Henry
BABY JANE   WAR 1962
(Eyre & Spottiswoode)   (*Whatever Happened to Baby Jane?*)

FARRELL, James Thomas
STUDS LONIGAN   UA 1959
(W.H. Allen)   UA 1964

FARRELL, M.J. *and* **PERRY, John**
TREASURE HUNT (P)   BL 1952
(Collins)

FAST, Howard
FREEDOM ROAD   ENTERPRISE 1980
(Various)
MIRAGE   UI 1965
(Mayflower)
MY GLORIOUS BROTHERS UA 1959
(Panther)
SPARTACUS   RANK 1959
(Panther)
WINSTON AFFAIR, THE   FOX 1963
(Methuen)   (*Man in the Middle*)

FAST, Howard *see also* **CUNNINGHAM, E.V.** *pseud.*

FAUCHIOS, Rene
LATE CHRISTOPHER BEAN, THE MGM 1933
(P)   (*Christopher Bean*)
(Gollancz)

FAULK, John H.
FEAR ON TRIAL   CHANNEL 4 1985 (TV)
(U.P. of Texas)

FAULKNER, John Meade
MOONFLEET   MGM 1955
(Little, Brown, Boston)

FAULKNER, William
  HAMLET, THE   FOX 1957
  (Chatto & Windus)   (*Long Hot Summer, The*)
  INTRUDER IN THE DUST   MGM 1949
  (Random House, N.Y.)
  PYLON   UA 1957
  (Chatto & Windus)   (*Tarnished Angels, The*)
  REIVERS, THE   WAR 1969
  (Chatto & Windus)
  REQUIEM FOR A NUN   FOX 1960
  (Chatto & Windus)   (*Sanctuary*)
       PAR 1933
       (*Story of Temple Drake, The*)
  SANCTUARY   FOX 1960
  (Chatto & Windus)
  SOUND AND THE FURY, THE   FOX 1959
  (Chatto & Windus)

FAUST, Frederick *see* **BRAND, Max** *pseud.*

FEARING, Kenneth
  BIG CLOCK, THE   PAR 1948
  (Lane)

FEDER, S. *see* **TURKUS, B.** *jt. author*

FEIFER, George
  GIRL FROM PETROVA   UN 1975
  (Macmillan)

FEIFFER, Jules
  LITTLE MURDERS (P)   FOX 1971
  (Cape)

FEINER, Ruth
  THREE CUPS OF COFFEE   ABP 1951
  (Dakers)   (*Woman's Angle, A*)

FENTON, Edward
  MYSTERY IN FLORENCE   DISNEY 1963
  (Constable)   (*Escapade in Florence*)

FENTY, Philip
  SUPERFLY   PAR 1972
  (Sphere)

FERBER, Edna
CIMARRON   RKO 1931
(Gollancz)   MGM 1960
COME AND GET IT   UA 1936
(Heinemann)
GIANT   WAR 1956
(Gollancz)
ICE PALACE   WAR 1960
(Gollancz)
OLD MAN MINICK   WAR 1932
(Doubleday, N.Y.)   (*Expert, The*)
SARATOGA TRUNK   WAR 1945
(Heinemann)
SHOW BOAT   UN 1929
(Heinemann)   UN 1936
                             MGM 1951
SO BIG   WAR 1932
(Heinemann)   WAR 1953

FERBER, Edna *see also* **KAUFMAN, G.S.** *jt. author*

FERGUSON, Austin
JET STREAM   COL—WAR 1976
(Arrow, N.Y.)   (*Mayday: 40,000 ft.*)

FERGUSON, Margaret
SIGN OF THE RAM, THE   COL 1948
(Hale)

FERRIS, Paul
DETECTIVE, THE   BBC 1985 (TV)
(Weidenfeld & Nicolson)

FERRIS, Wally
ACROSS 110th STREET   UA 1972
(Harper, N.Y.)

FEST, Joachim
HITLER: A CAREER   GTO 1978
(Harcourt, N.Y.)

FETHERSTONHAUGH, Robert Collier
ROYAL CANADIAN MOUNTED   PAR 1940
POLICE   (*North West Mounted Police*)
(Various)

FEUCHTWANGER, Leon
JEW SÜSS (P)   GB 1935
(Hutchinson)
JEW SÜSS   GB 1935
(Hutchinson)

FEYDEAU, Georges
FLEA IN HER EAR, A (P)   FOX 1968
(Methuen)

FEYDEAU, Georges *and* **DESVALLIERES, M.**
HOTEL PARADISO (P)   MGM 1971
(Heinemann)

FIDLER, Kathleen
FLASH THE SHEEPDOG   CFF 1966
(Lutterworth)

FIELD, Medora
BLOOD ON HER SHOE   REP 1944
(Jarrolds)   (*Girl who Dared, The*)
WHO KILLED AUNT MAGGIE REP 1940
(Jarrolds)

FIELD, Rachel
ALL THIS AND HEAVEN TOO WAR 1940
(Collins)
AND NOW TOMORROW   PAR 1944
(Collins)
TIME OUT OF MIND   UA 1947
(Macmillan)

FIELDING, Henry
JOSEPH ANDREWS   UA 1976
(Various)
RAPE UPON RAPE (P)   COL 1968
(Various)   (*Lock Up Your Daughters*)
TOM JONES   UA 1962
(Dent)   CIC 1976
                 (*Bawdy Adventures of . . .*)

FIELDS, Joseph
DOUGHGIRLS, THE (P)   WAR 1944
(Random House, N.Y.)

FIELDS, Joseph *see also* **CHODOROV, J.** *jt. author*

FIELDS, Joseph *and* **CHODOROV, Jerome**
ANNIVERSARY WALTZ (P)   UA 1959
(Random House, N.Y.)   (*Happy Anniversary*)
MY SISTER EILEEN (P)   COL 1942
(Macmillan)   COL 1955

FIELDS, Joseph *and* **DE VRIES, Peter**
TUNNEL OF LOVE, THE (P)   MGM 1959
(French)

FIENBURGH, Wilfred
NO LOVE FOR JOHNNIE   RANK 1960
(Hutchinson)

FIGES, Eva
WAKING, THE   MITHRAS 1983
(Hamilton)   (*Nelly's Version*)

FINCH, M.
DENTIST IN THE CHAIR   REN 1960
(Ace)

FINDLEY, Ferguson *pseud.*
REMEMBER THAT FACE!   COL 1951
(Reinhardt & Evans)

FINEMAN, Irving
THESE OUR LOVERS   WAR 1962
(Long)   (*Lovers Must Learn*)

FINKLEHOFFE, F.R. *see* **MONKS, J.** *jt. author*

FINNEY, Jack
ASSAULT ON A QUEEN   PAR 1966
(Eyre & Spottiswoode)
BODY SNATCHERS, THE   COL 1956
(Eyre & Spottiswoode)   (*Invasion of the Body Snatchers, The*)
GOOD NEIGHBOUR SAM   COL 1965
(Eyre & Spottiswoode)
HOUSE OF NUMBERS   MGM 1957
(Eyre & Spottiswoode)
INVASION OF THE BODY   UA 1974
SNATCHERS
(Dell, N.Y.)

MARION'S WALL   RANK 1985
(Eyre & Spottiswoode)   (*Maxie*)

FISH, Robert *see* **LONDON, Jack** *jt. author*

FISHER, Clay
TALL MEN, THE   FOX 1955
(Houghton, Mifflin, Boston)
YELLOWSTONE KELLY   WAR 1959
(Houghton, Mifflin, Boston)

FISHER, Dave
PACK, THE   COL—WAR 1977
(W.H. Allen)

FISHER, Michael
BETHNAL GREEN   BL 1964
(Cassell)   (*Place To Go, A*)

FISHER, Stephen Gould
DESTINATION TOKYO   WAR 1943
(Appleton, N.Y.)

FISHER, Steve
I WAKE UP SCREAMING   FOX 1941
(Hale)   FOX 1953
     (*Vicki*)

FISHER, Vardis
JEREMIAH JOHNSON   COL—WAR 1972
(Four Square Books)

FITCH, Clyde
BEAU BRUMMELL (P)   MGM 1954
(Lane, N.Y.)

FITZGERALD, Francis Scott Key
BABYLON REVISITED   MGM 1954
(Scribner, N.Y.)   (*Last Time I Saw Paris, The*)
GREAT GATSBY, THE   PAR 1949
(Grey Walls Press)   PAR 1974
LAST TYCOON, THE   PAR 1977
(Penguin)
TENDER IS THE NIGHT   FOX 1962
(Grey Walls Press)   BBC 2 1985 (TV)

FITZ-SIMONS, Foster
  BRIGHT LEAF   WAR 1950
  (Rinehart, N.Y.)

FLAUBERT, Gustave
  MADAME BOVARY   HOLLYWOOD 1932
  (Cape)   *(Unholy Love)*
                          MGM 1949
  SALAAMBO   FOX 1959
  (Dent)

FLAVIN, Martin
  BROKEN DISHES (P)   IN 1936
  (French, N.Y.)   *(Love Begins at Twenty)*
                          WAR 1961
                          (Too Young to Marry)
  ONE WAY OUT (P)   COL 1950
  (French, N.Y.)   *(Convicted)*

FLEISCHMAN, Albert Sidney
  BLOOD ALLEY   WAR 1955
  (Corgi)
  BULLWHIP GRIFFIN   DISNEY 1968
  (Penguin)   *(Adventures of . . .)*
  YELLOWLEG   WAR 1961
  (Muller)   *(Deadly Companions, The)*

FLEMING, Berry
  COLONEL EFFINGHAM'S RAID   FOX 1945
  (Various)

FLEMING, Ian
  CASINO ROYALE   COL 1966
  (Cape)
  CHITTY, CHITTY BANG BANG   UA 1968
  (Cape)
  DIAMONDS ARE FOREVER   UA 1971
  (Cape)
  DR. NO   UA 1962
  (Cape)
  FOR YOUR EYES ONLY   UA 1981
  (Cape)
  FROM RUSSIA WITH LOVE   UA 1963
  (Cape)

GOLDFINGER   UA 1963
(Cape)
LIVE AND LET DIE   UA 1974
(Cape)
MAN WITH THE GOLDEN GUN,   UA 1974
THE
(Cape)
MOONRAKER   UA 1979
(Cape)
OCTOPUSSY   UNITED INTERNATIONAL 1983
(Cape)
ON HER MAJESTY'S SECRET   UA 1969
SERVICE
(Cape)
THUNDERBALL   UA 1964
(Cape)
YOU ONLY LIVE TWICE   UA 1966
(Cape)

FLEMING, Joan
DEEDS OF DR. DEADCERT, THE   FOX 1957
(Hutchinson)   (*Family Doctor*)

FLENDER, Harold
PARIS BLUES   UA 1961
(Panther)

FLETCHER, Geoffrey
LONDON NOBODY KNOWS, THE   BL 1969
(Penguin)

FLETCHER, Lucille
BLINDFOLD   UI 1965
(Eyre & Spottiswoode)
NIGHT WATCH (P)   AVCO EMBASSY 1973
(Random House, N.Y.)

FLEXNER, James Thomas
DOCTORS ON HORSEBACK   MGM 1949
(Heinemann)   (*Big Jack*)

FLYNN, Errol
ERROL FLYNN: MY WICKED   ITV 1985 (TV)
WICKED WAYS
(Berkeley, N.Y.)

FOLDES, Yolande
GOLDEN EARRINGS   PAR 1947
(Hale)
MAKE YOU A GOOD WIFE   PAR 1948
(Hutchinson)   (*My Own True Love*)

FOLLETT, Kenneth
EYE OF THE NEEDLE, THE   UA 1981
(New American Library, N.Y.)
KEY TO REBECCA, THE   WORLD VISION 1985
(Hamilton)

FONTAINE, Robert L.
HAPPY TIME, THE   COL 1952
(Hamilton)

FOOTE, Horton
CHASE, THE (P)   COL 1965
(Dramatists, N.Y.)
TRAVELLING LADY, THE (P) COL 1965
(Dramatists, N.Y.)   (*Baby, The Rain Must Fall*)

FOOTE, John Taintor
LOOK OF EAGLES   FOX 1938
(Appleton, N.Y.)   (*Kentucky*)

FORBES, Colin
AVALANCHE EXPRESS   FOX 1979
(Dutton, N.Y.)
STONE LEOPARD, THE   ITC 1978
(Collins)

FORBES, Esther
JOHNNY TREMAIN   DISNEY 1957
(Constable)
RUNNING OF THE TIDE, THE MGM 1949
(Houghton, Mifflin, Boston)

FORBES, Murray
HOLLOW TRIUMPH   EL 1948
(Martin)

FORBES, Stanton
GO TO THY DEATHBED   COL—WAR 1972
(Hale)   (*Reflection of Fear, A*)

AUTHOR AND ORIGINAL TITLE	FILM TITLE

FORD, Jesse Hill
LIBERATION OF LORD BYRON
JONES, THE
(Bodley Head)
COL 1969

FOREMAN, Leonard London
DON DESPERADO
(Cassell)
PAR 1952
(*Savage, The*)
ROAD TO SAN JACINTO
(Dutton, N.Y.)
ABP 1954
(*Arrow in the Dust*)

FORESTER, Cecil Scott
AFRICAN QUEEN, THE
(Joseph)
ROMULUS 1951
BROWN ON 'RESOLUTION'
(Lane)
GB 1933
FOX 1952
(*Single Handed*)

CAPTAIN HORNBLOWER, R.N.
(Joseph)
WAR 1951
(*Captain Horatio Hornblower, R.N.*)
GUN, THE
(Joseph)
UA 1957
(*Pride and the Passion, The*)
HUNT THE BISMARCK
(Joseph)
FOX 1960
(*Sink the Bismarck*)
PAYMENT DEFERRED
(Lane)
MGM 1932
PAYMENT DEFERRED (P)
(Lane)
MGM 1932

FORREST, A.J.
INTERPOL
(Wingate)
COL 1957

FORREST, David
GREAT DINOSAUR ROBBERY
(Hodder & Stoughton)
DISNEY 1975
(*One of our Dinosaurs is Missing*)

FORRESTER, Larry
GIRL NAMED FATHOM, A
(Heinemann)
FOX 1968
(*Fathom*)

FORSTER, E.M.
PASSAGE TO INDIA, A
(Dent)
COL—EMI—WAR 1984
ROOM WITH A VIEW, A
(Arnold)
GOLDCREST 1985

FORSTER, Margaret
GEORGY GIRL   COL 1966
(Secker & Warburg)

FORSYTH, Frederick
DAY OF THE JACKAL, THE   UN 1972
(Hutchinson)
DOGS OF WAR, THE   UA 1980
(Hutchinson)
FOURTH PROTOCOL   FOURTH PROTOCOL 1986
(Hutchinson)
ODESSA FILE, THE   COL 1974
(Hutchinson)

FOSTER, Alan D.
PALE RIDER   COL—EMI—WAR 1985
(Arrow)

FOWLER, Gene
BEAU JAMES   PAR 1957
(Viking, N.Y.)

FOWLER, Helen Marjorie
SHADES WILL NOT VANISH   ABP 1957
(Angus & Robertson)   (*Strange Intruder*)

FOWLES, John
COLLECTOR, THE   BL 1964
(Cape)
EBONY TOWER   ITV 1984 (TV)
(Cape)
FRENCH LIEUTENANT'S WOMAN,   UA 1981
THE
(Cape)
MAGUS, THE   FOX 1969
(Cape)

FOX, John
LITTLE SHEPHERD OF KINGDOM   FOX 1961
COME, THE
(Scribner, N.Y.)

FOX, Norman A.
RAWHIDE YEARS, THE   UI 1955
(Collins)

ROUGHSHOD   GFD 1952
(Dodd, N.Y.)   (*Gunsmoke*)
TALL MAN RIDING   WAR 1955
(Collins)

FOX, Paula
DESPERATE CHARACTERS   ITC 1971
(Macmillan)

FRAILEY, O. see **NESS, E.** *jt. author*

FRANCE, Anatole
CRIME OF SYLVESTRE BONNARD,   RKO 1935
THE   (*Chasing Yesterday*)
(Collins)

FRANCIS, Dick
DEAD CERT   UA 1974
(Joseph)

FRANK, Anne
DIARY OF ANNE FRANK, THE   FOX 1959
(Gollancz)

FRANK, Gerold
BOSTON STRANGLER, THE   FOX 1968
(Cape)

FRANK, Gerold see **BARRYMORE, D.** *jt. author*

FRANK, Leonhard
CARL AND ANNA   MGM 1932
(Various)   (*As You Desire Me*)

FRANK, Patrick
HOLD BACK THE NIGHT   ABP 1956
(Hamilton)

FRANKAU, Gilbert
CHRISTOPHER STRONG   RKO 1933
(Hutchinson)

FRANKAU, Pamela
JEZEBEL   WAR 1938
(Rich & Cowan)

FRANKEN, Rose
ANOTHER LANGUAGE (P)   MGM 1933
(Rich & Cowan)
CLAUDIA   FOX 1943
(W.H. Allen)
CLAUDIA (P)   FOX 1943
(French, N.Y.)
CLAUDIA AND DAVID   FOX 1946
(W.H. Allen)

FRANKLON, Miles
MY BRILLIANT CAREER   GUO 1979
(St. Martin's, N.Y.)

FRANZERO, Charles Marie
LIFE AND TIMES OF CLEOPATRA,   FOX 1963
THE   (*Cleopatra*)
(Redman)

FRASER, George M.
ROYAL FLASH   FOX—RANK 1976
(Barrie & Jenkins)

FRAZEE, Steve
DESERT GUNS   WAR 1961
(World, N.Y.)   (*Gold of the Seven Saints*)
HIGH CAGE   PAR 1958
(Macmillan, N.Y.)   (*High Hell*)

FREDE, Richard
INTERNS, THE   COL 1964
(Corgi)   (*New Interns, The*)

FREEDMAN, Benedict *and* **FREEDMAN, Nancy Mars**
MRS. MIKE   UA 1950
(Hamilton)

FREELING, Nicolas
BECAUSE OF THE CATS   MIRACLE FILMS 1976
(Penguin)   (*Rape, The*)
LOVE IN AMSTERDAM   MONARCH 1968
(Penguin)

FREEMAN, Devery
   FATHER SKY   FOX 1982
   (Secker & Warburg)   (*Taps*)

FREEMAN, Gillian *see* **GEORGE, Eliot** *pseud.*

FREEMANTLE, Brian
   CHARLIE M   EUSTON 1979
   (Doubleday, N.Y.)   (*Charlie Muggin*)

FRENCH, Marilyn
   WOMAN'S ROOM, THE   BBC 2 1984 (TV)
   (Deutsch)

FREY, Charles F. *see* **FINDLEY, Ferguson** *pseud.*

FRINGS, *Mrs.* Ketti
   HOLD BACK THE DAWN   PAR 1941
   (Duell, N.Y.)

FRISBY, Terence
   THERE'S A GIRL IN MY SOUP (P)   COL 1970
   (French)

FULLER, C.
   SOLDIER'S PLAY, A (P)   COL—EMI—WAR 1985
   (Hill & Wang, N.Y.)   (*Soldier's Story, A*)

FULLER, Samuel
   DARK PAGE, THE   COL 1952
   (Duell, N.Y.)

FULLERTON, Alexander
   LIONHEART   CFF 1968
   (Hodder & Stoughton)

FULTON, Maude
   BRAT (P)   FOX 1931
   (Longmans, N.Y.)

G

GABRIEL, Gilbert Wolf
   I, JAMES LEWIS   UN 1941
   (Doubleday, N.Y.)   (*This Woman is Mine*)

GADDIS, Thomas E.
  BIRD MAN OF ALCATRAZ   UA 1962
  (Four Square Books.)

GAGE, Nick
  ELENI   CBS 1985 (TV)
  (Random, N.Y.)

GAINES, Charles
  STAY HUNGRY   UA 1976
  (Chatto & Windus)

GAINES, Charles *and* **BUTLER, G.**
  PUMPING IRON   CINEGATE 1976
  (Simon & Schuster, N.Y.)
  PUMPING IRON II: THE   BLUE DOLPHIN 1984
  UNPRECEDENTED WOMAN
  (Simon & Schuster, N.Y.)

GAINES, E.J.
  AUTOBIOGRAPHY OF MISS JANE   SAGA 1975
  PITTMAN, THE
  (Bantam)

GAINES, Robert
  FINAL NIGHT   BL 1953
  (Heinemann)   (*Front Page Story*)

GALLAGHER, Hugh J.
  SCARLET PIMPERNEL OF THE   ITC 1983 (TV)
  VATICAN   (*Scarlet and the Black*)
  (Collins)

GALLICO, Paul
  BEYOND THE POSEIDON   COL—EMI—WAR 1979
  ADVENTURE
  (Joseph)
  MATILDA   RANK 1979
  (Berkeley, N.Y.)
  POSEIDON ADVENTURE, THE   FOX 1972
  (Pan)
  SMALL MIRACLE, THE   IND 1951
  (Joseph)   (*Never Take No For An Answer*)
  SNOW GOOSE, THE   BBC 1971
  (Joseph)

AUTHOR AND ORIGINAL TITLE	FILM TITLE
THOMASINA (Joseph)	DISNEY 1963 (*Three Lives of Thomasina, The*)
TRIAL BY TERROR (Joseph)	COL 1952 (*Assignment-Paris*)

GALLO, May *see* **GRAY, Martin** *jt. author*

GALSWORTHY, John

ESCAPE (P) (Duckworth)	RKO 1930 FOX 1948
FIRST AND THE LAST, THE (Heinemann)	LF 1940 (*Twenty-one Days*)
FORSYTE SAGA (Heinemann)	MGM 1949 (*That Forsyte Woman*)
LOYALTIES (P) (Duckworth)	AUTEN 1934
MAN OF PROPERTY, THE (Heinemann)	MGM 1949 (*Forsyte Saga, The*)
OLD ENGLISH (P) (Duckworth)	WAR 1930
OVER THE RIVER (Heinemann)	UN 1934 (*One More River*)
SKIN GAME (P) (Duckworth)	BI 1931

GANN, Ernest Kellogg

ANTAGONISTS, THE (New American Library, N.Y.)	UA 1980 (U.S. title: *Masada*)
BLAZE AT NOON (Aldor)	PAR 1937
FATE IS THE HUNTER (Hodder & Stoughton)	FOX 1964
FIDDLER'S GREEN (Sloane, N.Y.)	UI 1951 (*Raging Tide, The*)
HIGH AND THE MIGHTY, THE (Hodder & Stoughton)	WAR 1954
ISLAND IN THE SKY (Joseph)	WAR 1953
SOLDIER OF FORTUNE (Hodder & Stoughton)	FOX 1955
TWILIGHT FOR THE GODS (Hodder & Stoughton)	RANK 1957

GARDEN, John
   ALL ON A SUMMER'S DAY   ABP 1950
   (Joseph)   (*Double Confession*)

GARDNER, Erle Stanley
   CASE OF THE CARETAKER'S CAT,   IN 1936
   THE   (*Case of the Black Cat, The*)
   (Cassell)
   CASE OF THE CURIOUS BRIDE,   IN 1935
   THE
   (Cassell)
   CASE OF THE HOWLING DOG, THE   WAR 1934
   (Grosset, N.Y.)
   CASE OF THE LUCKY LEGS, THE   WAR 1935
   (Harrap)
   CASE OF THE STUTTERING   WAR 1937
   BISHOP, THE
   (Cassell)
   CASE OF THE VELVET CLAWS, THE   IN 1936
   (Harrap)

GARDNER, Herbert
   THOUSAND CLOWNS, A (P)   UA 1964
   (Random House, N.Y.)

GARDNER, John
   COMPLETE STATE OF DEATH, A   COL 1973
   (Cape)   (*Stone Killer, The*)
   LIQUIDATOR, THE   MGM 1965
   (Muller)

GARDNER, Leonard
   FAT CITY   COL—WAR 1972
   (Hart-Davis)

GARDNER, Richard M.
   SCANDALOUS JOHN   DISNEY 1971
   (Constable)

GARFIELD, Brian
   DEATH SENTENCE   CANNON 1981
   (Evans)
   DEATH WISH   CIC 1974
   (Hodder & Stoughton)

DEATH WISH II   CANNON 1981
(Hodder & Stoughton)
GUN DOWN   FOX—RANK 1976
(Dell, N.Y.)   (*Last Hard Man, The*)
HOPSCOTCH   RANK 1980
(Evans)

GARFIELD, Leon
   BLACK JACK   ENTERPRISE 1980
   (Longmans)

GARLAND, A.P.
   YANK AT OXFORD, A   MGM 1938
   (Collins)

GARNER, Helen
   MONKEY GRIP   PAVILION FILMS 1982
   (Penguin)

GARNETT, David
   SAILOR'S RETURN, THE   ARIEL 1978
   (Chatto & Windus)

GARSTIN, Crosbie
   CHINA SEAS   MGM 1935
   (Chatto & Windus)

GARVE, Andrew
   DEATH AND THE SKY ABOVE US   BL 1962
   (Pan)   (*Two-letter Alibi*)
   MEGSTONE PLOT, THE   PAR 1959
   (Collins)   (*Touch of Larceny, A*)

GARY, Romain
   COLOURS OF THE DAY, THE   FOX 1959
   (Joseph)   (*Man Who Understood Women*)
   LADY L   MGM 1965
   (Joseph)
   PROMISE AT DAWN   AVCO EMBASSY 1971
   (Joseph)
   ROOTS OF HEAVEN, THE   FOX 1958
   (Joseph)
   YOUR TICKET IS NO LONGER   CAROLOCO 1980
   VALID
   (Braziller, N.Y.)

GASKELL, Jane
   ALL NEAT IN BLACK STOCKINGS   WAR 1968
   (Hodder & Stoughton)

GAY, John
   BEGGAR'S OPERA, THE (P)   BL 1953
   (French)

GAZZO, Michael Vincente
   HATFUL OF RAIN, A (P)   FOX 1957
   (Random House, N.Y.)

GEBLER, Ernest
   PLYMOUTH ADVENTURE, THE   MGM 1952
   (Cassell)
   SHALL I EAT YOU NOW? (P)   WAR 1969
   (Pan)   (*Hoffman*)

GEER, Andrew Clare
   SEA CHASE, THE   WAR 1954
   (Collins)

GELBER, Jack
   CONNECTION, THE   CONT 1962
   (Faber)

GELLER, Stephen
   SHE LET HIM CONTINUE   FOX 1968
   (Bodley Head)   (*Pretty Poison*)

GENET, Jean
   BALCONY, THE (P)   BL 1963
   (Faber)
   MAIDS, THE (P)   ELY LANDAU 1974
   (Faber)

GENT, Peter
   NORTH DALLAS FORTY   PAR 1980
   (Morrow, N.Y.)

GENTRY, C. *see* **BULIOSI, V.** *jt. author*

GEORGE, Eliot *pseud.*
   LEATHER BOYS, THE   BL 1962
   (Blond)

GEORGE, J.
MY SIDE OF THE MOUNTAIN   PAR 1968
(Bodley Head)

GEORGE, Peter
TWO HOURS TO DOOM   COL 1963
(Corgi)   (*Dr. Strangelove: or How I Learned
                 to Stop Worrying and Love the
                 Bomb*)

GERSHE, Leonard
BUTTERFLIES ARE FREE   COL 1972
(Random House, N.Y.)

GIBBS, Anthony Hamilton
YOUNG APOLLO, THE   MUNDUS 1935
(Hutchinson)   (*Men of Tomorrow*)

GIBSON, William
MIRACLE WORKER, THE (P)   UA 1962
(Knopf, N.Y.)
TWO FOR THE SEESAW (P)   UA 1962
(French)

GIELGUD, Val Henry
DEATH AT BROADCASTING   PHOENIX 1935
HOUSE
(Rich & Cowan)

GIFFORD, Thomas
GLENDOWER LEGACY, THE   FILM PLAN 1980
(Putnam)   (*Dirty Tricks*)

GILBERT, Anthony *pseud.*
WOMAN IN RED, THE   COL 1945
(Collins)   (*My Name is Julia Ross*)

GILBERT, Michael
DEATH HAS DEEP ROOTS   GN 1956
(Pan)   (*Guilty?*)
DEATH IN CAPTIVITY   BL 1958
(Pan)   (*Danger Within*)

GILBERT, Stephen
RATMAN'S NOTEBOOK   CINERAMA 1971
(Joseph)   (*Willard*)

GILBERT, *Sir* **William Schwenck**
  MIKADO, THE (P)   UN 1939
  (Macmillan)
  PIRATES OF PENZANCE, THE (P)   UIP 1983
  (Macmillan)
  RUDDIGORE (P)   GALA 1967
  (Macmillan)

GILBRETH, Frank Bunker *and* **CAREY, Ernestine**
  BELLS ON THEIR TOES   FOX 1952
  (Heinemann)
  CHEAPER BY THE DOZEN   FOX 1950
  (Heinemann)

GILDEN, K.B.
  HURRY SUNDOWN   PAR 1966
  (Heinemann)

GILL, Derek *see* **SULLIVAN, Tom** *jt. author*

GILL, Tom
  GAY BANDIT OF THE BORDER   FOX 1932
  (Collins)   (*Gay Caballero*)
  NO PLACE FOR WOMEN   PAR 1953
  (Putnam, N.Y.)   (*Tropic Zone*)

GILLHAM, Bill
  PLACE TO HIDE, A   CFTF 1984
  (Deutsch)   (*Breakout*)

GILLIAT, S. *see* **LAUNDER, F.** *jt. author*

GILLIGAN, Edmund
  GAUNT WOMAN, THE   RKO 1950
  (Scribner, N.Y.)

GILMAN, Peter
  DIAMOND HEAD   COL 1962
  (Joseph)

GILPATRIC, Guy
  ACTION IN THE NORTH ATLANTIC   WAR 1943
  (Dutton, N.Y.)

GILROY, Frank D.
FROM NOON TILL THREE   UA 1975
(Doubleday, N.Y.)
ONLY GAME IN TOWN, THE (P)   FOX 1969
(Random House, N.Y.)

GINSBURY, Norman
FIRST GENTLEMAN, THE (P)   COL 1948
(Hammond)

GIPSON, Frederick Benjamin
CIRCLES ROUND THE WAGON   FOX 1959
(Joseph)   (*Hound Dog Man*)
OLD YELLER   DISNEY 1958
(Harper, N.Y.)
SAVAGE SAM   DISNEY 1963
(Hodder & Stoughton)

GLASGOW, Ellen
IN THIS OUR LIFE   WAR 1942
(Cape)

GLEMSER, Bernard
GIRL ON A WING   MGM 1963
(Macdonald)   (*Come Fly With Me*)

GLICKMAN, William *and* **STEIN, Joseph**
MRS. GIBBONS' BOYS (P)   BL 1962
(French, N.Y.)

GLOAG, Julian
OUR MOTHER'S HOUSE   MGM 1967
(Pan)

GODDEN, Rumer
BATTLE OF THE VILLA FIORITA,   WAR 1964
THE   (*Affair at the Villa Fiorita, The*)
(Macmillan)
BLACK NARCISSUS   ARCHERS 1947
(Davies)
EPISODE OF SPARROWS, AN   RANK 1957
(Macmillan)   (*Innocent Sinners*)
FUGUE IN TIME   RKO 1949
(Joseph)   (*Enchantment*)

GODDEN, Rumer (*Continued*)
GREENGAGE SUMMER, THE   RANK 1960
(Macmillan)
IN THIS HOUSE OF BREDE   CHANNEL 4 1984 (TV)
(Futura)
RIVER, THE   UA 1951
(Joseph)

GODEY, John
TAKING OF PELHAM 123, THE   UA 1974
(Hodder & Stoughton)

GOETZ, Ruth *and* **GOETZ, Augustus**
HEIRESS, THE (P)   PAR 1949
(Reinhardt & Evans)

GOGOL, Nikolai Vasilevich
GAMBLERS, THE (P)   FOX—RANK 1974
(*In* The Government Inspector and other
plays: Dent)
INSPECTOR GENERAL, THE (P)   WAR 1949
(French, N.Y.)
TARAS BULBA   UA 1962
(Dent)

GOLDING, Louis
MR. EMMANUEL   TC 1944
(Rich & Cowan)

GOLDING, William
LORD OF THE FLIES   BL 1963
(Faber)

GOLDMAN, James
LION IN WINTER, THE (P)   AVCO EMBASSY 1969
(French)

GOLDMAN, William
MAGIC   FOX 1978
(Dial, N.Y.)
MARATHON MAN   PAR 1976
(Dial, N.Y.)
NO WAY TO TREAT A LADY   PAR 1968
(Coronet)
SOLDIER IN THE RAIN   WAR 1965
(Eyre & Spottiswoode)

GOLDSMITH, Barbara
LITTLE GLORIA—HAPPY AT LAST   ITV 1983 (TV)
(Macmillan)

GOLDSMITH, Martin M.
DETOUR   PRC 1946
(Hurst & Blackett)

GOODCHILD, George
SPLENDID CRIME, THE   RKO 1931
(Hodder & Stoughton)   (*Public Defender*)

GOODE, R. *see* **HUROK, S.** *jt. author*

GOODHEART, William
GENERATION (P)   AVCO EMBASSY 1969
(Doubleday, N.Y.)

GOODIN, Peggy
CLEMENTINE   EL 1948
(Dutton, N.Y.)   (*Mickey*)
TAKE CARE OF MY LITTLE GIRL   FOX 1951
(Dutton, N.Y.)

GOODIS, David
DARK PASSAGE   WAR 1947
(World, N.Y.)

GOODMAN, George, J.W.
WHEELER-DEALERS, THE   MGM 1964
(Doubleday, N.Y.)   (*Separate Beds*)

GOODRICH, Frances *and* **HACKETT, Albert**
DIARY OF ANNE FRANK, THE (P)   FOX 1959
(French)

GORDON, Arthur
REPRISAL   COL 1956
(Hamilton)

GORDON, Leon
WHITE CARGO (P)   BI 1930
(Various)   MGM 1942

GORDON, *Mrs.* **Mildred** *and* **GORDON, G.**
  CASE FILE: F.B.I.   UA 1954
  (Doubleday, N.Y.)   (*Down 3 Dark Streets*)
  MAKE HASTE TO LIVE   REP 1954
  (Doubleday, N.Y.)
  OPERATION TERROR   COL 1962
  (Macdonald)   (*Grip of Fear*)
  UNDERCOVER CAT   DISNEY 1964
  (Macdonald)   (*That Darn Cat*)

GORDON, Richard
  CAPTAIN'S TABLE, THE   RANK 1958
  (Joseph)
  DOCTOR AT LARGE   RANK 1957
  (Joseph)
  DOCTOR AT SEA   BFD 1955
  (Joseph)
  DOCTOR IN CLOVER   RANK 1965
  (Joseph)
  DOCTOR IN LOVE   RANK 1959
  (Joseph)
  DOCTOR IN THE HOUSE   GFD 1954
  (Joseph)
  DOCTOR ON TOAST   RANK 1970
  (Joseph)   (*Doctor in Trouble*)

GORDON, Ruth
  LEADING LADY (P)   MGM 1953
  (Dramatists, N.Y.)   (*Actress, The*)
  OVER 21 (P)   COL 1945
  (Dramatists, N.Y.)

GORMAN, Herbert
  SUZY   MGM 1936
  (Cassell)

GOTTLIEB, Linda *see* **SILVER, Joan** *jt. author*

GOTTLIEB, Paul
  AGENCY   CAROLOCO 1980
  (Sphere)

GOUDGE, Elizabeth
  GREEN DOLPHIN STREET   MGM 1947
  (Hodder & Stoughton)

GOULD, Lois
SUCH GOOD FRIENDS   PAR 1972
(Weidenfeld & Nicolson)

GOUZENKO, Igor
THIS WAS MY CHOICE   FOX 1948
(Dent)   (*Iron Curtain*)

GOW, J. *see* **D'USSEAU, A.** *jt. author*

GRADY, James
SIX DAYS OF THE CONDOR   PAR 1975
(Norton, N.Y.)   (*3 Days of the Condor*)

GRAEME, Bruce *pseud.*
FOG FOR A KILLER   GN 1962
(Hutchinson)   (*Out of the Fog*)
HATE SHIP   BI 1930
(Hutchinson)
SUSPENSE   GN 1956
(Hutchinson)   (*Face in the Night*)
WAY OUT, THE   AA 1955
(Hutchinson)   (*Dial 999*)

GRAFTON, Sue
LOLLY-MADONNA WAR, THE   MGM—EMI 1973
(Owen)

GRAHAM, James
WRATH OF GOD, THE   MGM—EMI 1973
(Macmillan)

GRAHAM, Robin Lee *and* **GILL, Derek**
DOVE, THE   EMI 1974
(Angus & Robertson)

GRAHAM, Sheilah *and* **FRANK, Gerold**
BELOVED INFIDEL   FOX 1959
(Cassell)

GRAHAM, Winston
FORGOTTEN STORY, THE   HTV 1982 (TV)
(Bodley Head)
FORTUNE IS A WOMAN   COL 1957
(Hodder & Stoughton)

GRAHAM, Winston (*Continued*)
MARNIE   UI 1964
(Hodder & Stoughton)
NIGHT WITHOUT STARS   GFD 1951
(Hodder & Stoughton)
TAKE MY LIFE   EL 1948
(Ward Lock)
WALKING STICK, THE   MGM 1969
(Collins)

GRANGER, Kathleen R.G.
TEN AGAINST CAESAR   COL 1954
(Houghton, Mifflin, Boston) (*Gun Fury*)

GRANT, Neil
DUSTY ERMINE (P)   TWICKENHAM 1936
(French)

GRASS, Gunter
TIN DRUM   UA 1979
(Cape)

GRAVES, Robert
I, CLAUDIUS   BBC 1976 (TV)
(Methuen)

GRAY, Martin *and* **GALLO, May**
FOR THOSE I LOVED   GALA 1984
(New American Library, N.Y.)

GRAY, Simon
BUTLEY (P)   SEVEN KEYS 1973
(Viking, N.Y.)

GRAZIANO, Rocky
SOMEBODY UP THERE LIKES ME MGM 1956
(Hammond)

GREEN, A. *see* **COMDEN, B.** *jt. author*

GREEN, Frederick Lawrence
LOST MAN, THE   RANK 1969
(Joseph)
ODD MAN OUT   TC 1947
(Joseph)

ON THE NIGHT OF THE FIRE   SOMLO 1939
(Joseph)

GREEN, Gerald
LAST ANGRY MAN, THE   COL 1959
(Pan)

GREEN, G. *see* **KLINGMAN, L.** *jt. author*

GREEN, Janet
MURDER MISTAKEN (P)   EROS 1955
(Evans)   (*Cast a Dark Shadow*)

GREEN, Paul Eliot *and* **WRIGHT, Richard**
NATIVE SON (P)   CLASSIC 1951
(Harper, N.Y.)

GREENBERG, Joanne
I NEVER PROMISED YOU A ROSE   NEW WORLD 1979
GARDEN
(New American Library, N.Y.)

GREENE, Graham
ACROSS THE BRIDGE   RANK 1957
(*In* 21 Short Stories: Heinemann)
BASEMENT ROOM, THE   FOX 1948
(Cresset Press)   (*Fallen Idol, The*)
BRIGHTON ROCK   ABP 1948
(Heinemann)
COMEDIANS, THE   MGM 1967
(Heinemann)
CONFIDENTIAL AGENT   WAR 1945
(Heinemann)
DOCTOR FISHER OF GENEVA   BBC 2 1984 (TV)
(Bodley Head)
DON QUIXOTE   EUSTON 1985 (TV)
(Heinemann)
END OF THE AFFAIR, THE   COL 1954
(Heinemann)
ENGLAND MADE ME   HEMDALE 1972
(Heinemann)
GUN FOR SALE   PAR 1942
(Various)   (*This Gun For Sale*)
          PAR 1957
          (*Short Cut to Hell*)

GREENE, Graham (*Continued*)
  HEART OF THE MATTER, THE   BL 1953
  (Heinemann)
  HONORARY CONSUL   PAR 1983
  (Heinemann)
  HUMAN FACTOR, THE   RANK 1980
  (Heinemann)
  LOSER TAKES ALL   BL 1956
  (Heinemann)
  MAN WITHIN, THE   FOX 1947
  (Heinemann)
  MINISTRY OF FEAR   PAR 1944
  (Heinemann)
  OUR MAN IN HAVANA   COL 1959
  (Heinemann)
  POWER AND THE GLORY, THE   RKO 1947
  (Heinemann)   (*Fugitive, The*)
                            PAR 1962
  QUIET AMERICAN, THE   UA 1957
  (Heinemann)
  STAMBOUL TRAIN   FOX 1934
  (Heinemann)   (*Orient Express*)
  THIRD MAN, THE   GFD 1950
  (Heinemann)
  TRAVELS WITH MY AUNT   MGM 1972
  (Bodley Head)

GREENE, Shep
  BOY WHO DRANK TOO MUCH, THE   MTM 1980 (TV)
  (Viking, N.Y.)

GREENE, Ward
  DEATH IN THE DEEP SOUTH   WAR 1937
  (Cassell)   (*They won't Forget*)
  LADY AND THE TRAMP   DISNEY 1955
  (Simon & Schuster, N.Y.)

GREENWALD, Harold
  CALL GIRL, THE   WAR 1960
  (Elek)   (*Girl of the Night*)

GREENWOOD, Robert
  MR. BUNTING AT WAR   BN 1942
  (Dent)   (*Salute John Citizen*)

GREENWOOD, Walter
    CURE FOR LOVE, THE (P)   BL 1949
    (French)
    LOVE ON THE DOLE   UA 1941
    (Cape)

GREENWOOD, W. *see also* **GOW, R.** *jt. author*

GREGOR, Manfred
    TOWN WITHOUT PITY   UA 1961
    (Heinemann)

GREGORY, *Lady* **Isabella Augusta**
    RISING OF THE MOON (P)   WAR 1957
    (Putnam)

GRESHAM, W.
    NIGHTMARE ALLEY   FOX 1947
    (Heinemann)

GREY, Zane
    BORDER LEGION   PAR 1930
    (Hodder & Stoughton)   PAR 1934
                          (*Last Round Up, The*)
    CODE OF THE WEST   PAR 1935
    (Hodder & Stoughton)   (*Home on the Range*)
                          RKO 1947
    DESERT GOLD   PAR 1936
    (Nelson)
    DRIFT FENCE   PAR 1935
    (Hodder & Stoughton)
    FIGHTING CARAVANS   PAR 1931
    (Hodder & Stoughton)   PAR 1934
                          (*Wagon Wheels*)
    FORLORN RIVER   PAR 1937
    (Hodder & Stoughton)
    HERITAGE OF THE DESERT   PAR 1933
    (Nelson)   PAR 1939
    KNIGHTS OF THE RANGE   PAR 1940
    (Hodder & Stoughton)
    LAST TRAIL, THE   FOX 1933
    (Hodder & Stoughton)
    LIGHT OF WESTERN STARS, THE PAR 1930
    (Nelson)   PAR 1940

GREY, Zane (*Continued*)

LONE STAR RANGER	FOX 1930
(Harper)	FOX 1942
MAN OF THE FOREST	PAR 1933
(Hodder & Stoughton)	
MAVERICK QUEEN, THE	REP 1956
(Hodder & Stoughton)	
MYSTERIOUS RIDER, THE	PAR 1933
(Hodder & Stoughton)	PAR 1938
NEVADA	PAR 1935
(Hodder & Stoughton)	
RAINBOW TRAIL	FOX 1932
(Harper)	
RIDERS OF THE PURPLE SAGE	FOX 1931
(Harper)	FOX 1941
ROBBERS' ROOST	FOX 1933
(Hodder & Stoughton)	UA 1955
SUNSET PASS	PAR 1933
(Hodder & Stoughton)	
THUNDERING HERD	PAR 1933
(Hodder & Stoughton)	
THUNDER MOUNTAIN	FOX 1935
(Hodder & Stoughton)	
TO THE LAST MAN	PAR 1933
(Hodder & Stoughton)	
TWIN SOMBREROS	COL 1947
(Hodder & Stoughton)	(*Gunfighters*)
UNDER THE TONTO RIM	PAR 1933
(Hodder & Stoughton)	
VANISHING AMERICAN, THE	REP 1955
(Hodder & Stoughton)	
WANDERER OF THE WASTELAND	PAR 1935
(Hodder & Stoughton)	RKO 1945
WEST OF THE PECOS	RKO 1934
(Hodder & Stoughton)	RKO 1945
WILD FIRE	UN 1949
(Harper)	(*Red Canyon*)
WILD HORSE MESA	PAR 1932
(Hodder & Stoughton)	

GRIERSON, Edward

REPUTATION FOR A SONG	MGM 1969
(Chatto & Windus)	(*My Lover, My Son*)

GRIMBLE, *Sir* **Arthur**
PATTERN OF ISLANDS   BL 1956
(Murray)   (*South Pacific*)

GRIMM, Jakob Ludwig Karl *and* **GRIMM, Wilhelm Karl**
GRIMMS' FAIRY TALES   MGM 1962
(Dent)   (*Wonderful World of the Brothers*
          Grimm, The)
HANSEL AND GRETEL   RKO 1954
(Various)
TOM THUMB   MGM 1958
(Various)

GROSS, Leonard
LAST JEWS IN BERLIN, THE   ENTERPRISE 1984
(Simon & Schuster, N.Y.)   (*Forbidden*)

GROSSBACH, R.
EASY AND HARD WAYS OUT   UIP 1984
(Carroll & Graf, N.Y.)   (*Best Defence*)

GROUSSARD, Serge
BLOOD OF ISRAEL, THE   ALPHA 1976
(Morrow, N.Y.)   (*21 Hours at Munich*)

GROVER, C. *see* **GULLICK, Bill** *pseud.*

GRUBB, Davis
FOOLS PARADISE   COL 1971
(Hodder & Stoughton)   (*Fools Parade*)
NIGHT OF THE HUNTER, THE   UA 1955
(Hamilton)

GRUBER, Frank
BITTER SAGE   RKO 1956
(Wright & Brown)   (*Tension at Table Rock*)
LOCK AND THE KEY, THE   RKO 1957
(World Work)   (*Man in the Vault*)
TOWN TAMER   PAR 1965
(Barker)
TWENTY PLUS TWO   WAR 1961
(Boardman)   (*It started in Tokyo*)

GUARESCHI, Giovanni
DON CAMILLO   CANNON 1982
(Murray)

GUARESCHI, Giovanni (*Continued*)
DON CAMILLO AND THE   MIRACLE FILMS 1954
PRODIGAL SON   (*Return of Don Camillo, The*)
(Gollancz)
LITTLE WORLD OF DON CAMILLO,   LF 1952
THE
(Gollancz)

GUEST, Judith
ORDINARY PEOPLE   PAR 1981
(Viking, N.Y.)

GULLICK, Bill *pseud.*
BEND OF THE SNAKE   UI 1952
(Museum Press)   (*Where the River Bends*)
HALLELUJAH TRAIL, THE   UA 1965
(Doubleday, N.Y.)
Originally called Hallelujah Train, The

GUNN, Mrs. Aeneas
WE OF THE NEVER NEVER   ADAMS PACKER 1982
(Angus & Robertson)

GUNN, James Edward
DEADLIER THAN THE MALE   RKO 1947
(World, N.Y.)   (*Born to Kill*)

GUNN, Neil Miller
BLOOD HUNT   BBC 2 1986 (TV)
(Souvenir)
SILVER DARLINGS, THE   AA 1947
(Faber)

GURDJOEFF, G.I.
MEETINGS WITH REMARKABLE   ENTERPRISE 1979
MEN
(Dutton, N.Y.)

GUTCHEON, Beth
STILL MISSING   FOX 1983
(Joseph)   (*Without a Trace*)

GUTHRIE, Alfred B.
BIG SKY, THE   RKO 1952
(Boardman)

THESE THOUSAND HILLS   FOX 1958
(Hutchinson)
WAY WEST, THE   UA 1966
(Corgi)

GUTHRIE, Thomas Anstey *see* **ANSTEY, F.** *pseud.*

GUTHRIE, Woody
BOUND FOR GLORY   UA 1977
(Dutton, N.Y.)

GWALTNEY, Francis Irby
DAY THE CENTURY ENDED, THE   FOX 1956
(Secker & Warburg)   (*Between Heaven and Hell*)

H

HAASE, John
ERASMUS WITH FRECKLES   FOX 1965
(Simon & Schuster, N.Y.)   (*Dear Brigitte*)
ME AND THE ARCH KOOK   WAR 1968
PETULIA   (*Petulia*)
(Heinemann)

HABE, Hans
THOUSAND SHALL FALL, A   UA 1943
(Harrap)   (*Hangmen Also Die*)

HACKETT, A. *see* **GOODRICH, F.** *jt. author*

HACKETT, Walter *and* **MERGRUE, Roi Cooper**
IT PAYS TO ADVERTISE (P)   PAR 1931
(French)

HACKNEY, Alan
PRIVATE LIFE   BL 1959
(Gollancz)   (*I'm Alright Jack*)
PRIVATE'S PROGRESS, A   BL 1956
(Gollancz)

HAEDRICH, Marcel
CRACK IN THE MIRROR   FOX 1960
(W.H. Allen)

HAGAN, James
 ONE SUNDAY AFTERNOON (P) PAR 1933
 (French, N.Y.) WAR 1941
   (*Strawberry Blonde, The*)
   WAR 1948

HAGGARD, *Sir* **Henry Rider**
 ALLAN QUATERMAINE BARBER ROSE 1979
 (Various) (*King Solomon's Treasure*)
   CANNON 1985
   (*Quatermain*)
 KING SOLOMON'S MINES GB 1937
 (Cassell) MGM 1950
   MGM 1958
   (*Watusi*)
   CANNON 1985
 SHE RKO 1935
 (Macdonald) WAR 1964
   CONTINENTAL 1984

HAGGART, David
 LIFE OF DAVID HAGGART, THE UA 1969
 (Sphere) (*Sinful Davey*)

HAIGHT, G. *see* **SCOTT, A.** *jt. author*

HAILEY, Arthur
 AIRPORT RANK 1969
 (Joseph & Souvenir Press)
 FINAL DIAGNOSIS, THE UA 1961
 (Joseph) (*Young Doctors, The*)
 HOTEL WAR 1966
 (Pan)
 STRONG MEDICINE STV 1986 (TV)
 (Joseph)

HAINES, William Wister
 COMMAND DECISION MGM 1948
 (Cassell)
 COMMAND DECISION (P) MGM 1948
 (Random House, N.Y.)

HALEVY, Julian
 YOUNG LOVERS, THE MGM 1964
 (Mayflower)

AUTHOR AND ORIGINAL TITLE	FILM TITLE

HALEY, Alex
ROOTS — ABC 1977 (TV)
(Hall)

HALL, Adam
BERLIN MEMORANDUM, THE — RANK 1965
(Collins) — (*Quiller Memorandum, The*)

HALL, Angus
DEVIL DAY-MADHOUSE — EMI 1974
(Sphere) — (*Madhouse*)
LATE BOY WONDER, THE — NEW REALM 1970
(Barrie & Jenkins) — (*Three in a Cellar*)

HALL, Jenni
ASK AGEMEMNON — CINERAMA 1970
(Sphere) — (*Goodbye Gemini*)

HALL, J.N. *see* **NORDHOFF, C.** *jt. author*

HALL, Magdalen King *see* **KING-HALL, M.**

HALL, Oakley
DOWNHILL RACERS, THE — PAR 1969
(Bodley Head)
WARLOCK — FOX 1959
(Bodley Head)

HALL, Patrick
HARP THAT ONCE, THE — COL 1969
(Heinemann) — (*Reckoning, The*)

HALL, Willis
LONG AND THE SHORT AND THE — WAR 1960
TALL (P)
(Heinemann)

HALL, Willis *see also* **WATERHOUSE, K.** *jt. author*

HALLIDAY, Brett *pseud.*
MURDER IS MY BUSINESS — PRC 1946
(Dodd, N.Y.)

HALLIDAY, Michael *pseud.*
  CAT AND MOUSE   EROS 1958
  (Hodder & Stoughton)

HAMBLEDON, Phyllis
  NO DIFFERENCE TO ME   ABP 1950
  (Sampson Low)   (*No Place For Jennifer*)

HAMILTON, Donald
  AMBUSHES, THE   COL 1968
  (Coronet)
  BIG COUNTRY, THE   UA 1958
  (Wingate)
  MURDERER'S ROW   BL 1966
  (Muller)
  ROUGH COMPANY   COL 1954
  (Wingate)
  SILENCERS, THE   COL 1965
  (Hodder & Stoughton)
  WRECKING CREW, THE   COL 1969
  (Coronet)

HAMILTON, Patrick
  GASLIGHT (P)   BN 1940
  (French)   MGM 1944
                   (*Murder in Thornton Square*)
  HANGOVER SQUARE   FOX 1945
  (Constable)
  ROPE (P)   WAR 1948
  (French)
  TO THE PUBLIC DANGER (P)   GFD 1948
  (*In* Two Radio Plays: Constable)
  TWENTY THOUSAND STREETS RANK 1962
  UNDER THE SKY   (*Bitter Harvest*)
  (Constable)

HAMMETT, Dashiell
  GLASS KEY, THE   PAR 1935
  (Cassell)   PAR 1942
  MALTESE FALCON, THE   WAR 1931
  (Cassell)   FIRST NATIONAL 1937
                   (*Satan Met a Lady*)
                   WAR 1941
                   COL—WAR 1975
                   (*Black Bird, The*)

THIN MAN, THE   MGM 1934
(Barker)

HAMNER, Earl *jun.*
SPENCER'S MOUNTAIN   WAR 1963
(Dial Press, N.Y.)

HANCOCK, Mary A.
MENACE OF THE MOUNTAIN   DISNEY 1972
(Macrae, Smith, Philadelphia)

HANLEY, Clifford
LOVE FROM EVERYBODY   WAR 1961
(Hutchinson)   (*Don't Bother to Knock*)

HANLEY, Gerald
GILLIGAN'S LAST ELEPHANT   PAR 1968
(Collins)   (*Last Safari, The*)

HANNUM, *Mrs.* **Alberta**
ROSEANNA McCOY   RKO 1951
(Holt, N.Y.)

HANSBERRY, Loraine
RAISIN IN THE SUN, A (P)   COL 1960
(Methuen)

HAN SUYIN *pseud.*
MANY SPLENDOURED THING, A   FOX 1955
(Cape)   (*Love is a Many Splendoured Thing*)
MOUNTAIN IS YOUNG, THE   PAR 1959
(Cape)

HARDING, Bertita
MAGIC FIRE   REP 1956
(Harrap)
PHANTOM CROWN   WAR 1939
(Harrap)   (*Juarez*)

HARDING, George
NORTH OF BUSHMAN'S ROCK   BUTCHER 1965
(Hale)   (*Ride the High Wind*)

HARDY, Jocelyn Lee
EVERYTHING IS THUNDER   GB 1936
(Lane)

HARDY, Lindsay
GRAND DUKE AND MR. PIMM, THE   UA 1963
(Cape)   (*All This and Money Too*)

HARDY, Stuart *pseud.*
MOUNTAINS ARE MY KINGDOM   UN 1938
(Macaulay, N.Y.)   (*Forbidden Valley*)

HARDY, Thomas
FAR FROM THE MADDING CROWD WAR 1966
(Macmillan)
TESS OF THE D'URBERVILLES   COL 1979
(Macmillan)   (*Tess*)

HARE, David
PLENTY (P)   COL—EMI—WAR 1985
(New American Library, N.Y.)

HAREL, Isser
HOUSE ON GARIBALDI STREET,   ITC 1979
THE
(Deutsch)

HARGROVE, Marion
GIRL HE LEFT BEHIND, THE   WAR 1957
(Viking, N.Y.)
SEE HERE, PRIVATE HARGROVE MGM 1944
(Hodder & Stoughton)

HARKINS, Philip
BLACKBURN'S HEADHUNTERS   ABP 1959
(Cassell)   (*Surrender—Hell*)

HARPER, David
HIJACKED   MGM 1972
(Corgi)   (*Skyjacked*)

HARRER, Heinrich
SEVEN YEARS IN TIBET   CURZON 1956
(Hart-Davis)

HARRIS, Elmer
  JOHNNY BELINDA (P)   WAR 1948
  (French)

HARRIS, Frank
  ON THE TRAIL   COL 1957
  (Lane)   (*Cowboy*)

HARRIS, John
  SEA SHALL NOT HAVE THEM, THE   EROS 1954
  (Hurst & Blackett)

HARRIS, Mark
  BANG THE DRUM SLOWLY   GUILD HOME VIDEO 1982
  (Buccaneer, Cutchogue, N.Y.)

HARRIS, Thomas
  BLACK SUNDAY   PAR 1977
  (Hodder & Stoughton)

HARRISON, Carey
  FREUD   BBC 1984 (TV)
  (Weidenfeld & Nicolson)

HARRISON, Harry
  MAKE ROOM, MAKE ROOM!   MGM—EMI 1973
  (Sidgwick & Jackson)   (*Soylent Green*)

HART, Moss
  ACT ONE   WAR 1963
  (Secker & Warburg)
  CHRISTOPHER BLAKE (P)   WAR 1948
  (Random House, N.Y.)   (*Decision of Christopher Blake*)
  WINGED VICTORY (P)   FOX 1944
  (Various)

HART, Moss *see also* **KAUFMAN, G.S.** *jt. author*

HARTE, Bret
  OUTCASTS OF POKER FLAT   RKO 1937
  (Various)   FOX 1952
  TENNESSEE'S PARTNER   RKO 1955
  (Various)

HARTLEY, L.P.
GO-BETWEEN, THE   MGM—EMI 1971
(Penguin)
HIRELING, THE   COL—WAR 1973
(Penguin)

HARTMAN, Michael
GAME FOR VULTURES   COL—EMI—WAR 1979
(Pan)

HARTOG, Jan de
FOUR POSTER, THE (P)   COL 1952
(Sampson Low)
INSPECTOR, THE   FOX 1962
(Hamilton)
LITTLE ARK, THE   FOX 1971
(Four Square Books)
SPIRAL ROAD, THE   UI 1962
(Hamilton)
STELLA   COL 1958
(Hamilton)   *(Key, The)*

HARVEY, Frank
POLTERGEIST, THE (P)   REN 1947
(Deane)   *(Things Happen at Night)*

HARVEY, Frank *jun.*
SALOON BAR (P)   EALING 1942
(French)

HARVEY, William Fryer
BEAST WITH FIVE FINGERS   WAR 1946
(Dent)

HARWOOD, Harold Marsh
MAN IN POSSESSION (P)   MGM 1931
(Benn)   MGM 1937
                    (Personal Property)

HARWOOD, Harold Marsh *and* **BROWN, Robert Gore**
CYNARA   UA 1932
(Benn)

HARWOOD, Ronald
DRESSER, THE (P)   COL 1983
(Amber Lane)

AUTHOR AND ORIGINAL TITLE	FILM TITLE

HASS, Hans
DIVING TO ADVENTURE
(Jarrolds)

BL 1954
(*Under the Caribbean*)

HASTINGS, Charlotte
BONADVENTURE (P)
(French)

GFD 1951

HASTINGS, Hugh
SEAGULLS OVER SORRENTO (P)
(*In* Plays of the Year 1950: Elek)

MGM 1954

HASTINGS, Michael
NIGHTCOMERS, THE
(Pan)

AVCO EMBASSY 1972

HASTINGS, *Sir* Patrick
BLIND GODDESS, THE (P)
(French)

FOX 1948

HASTINGS, Phyllis
RAPTURE IN MY RAGS
(Dent)

FOX 1964
(*Rapture*)

HATCH, Eric
MY MAN GODFREY
(Barker)
UNEXPECTED UNCLE
(Farrar, N.Y.)
YEAR OF THE HORSE, THE
(Crown, N.Y.)

UN 1936
UI 1957
RKO 1941

DISNEY 1968
(*Horse in the Grey Flannel Suit, The*)

HAUSER, Thomas
EXECUTION OF CHARLES
HORMAN, THE
(Harbrace, N.Y.)

POLYGRAM 1982
(*Missing*)

HAVARD, René
TAXI TO TOBRUK
(Collins)

MIRACLE FILMS 1961

HAWKINS, John *and* **HAWKINS, Ward**
FLOODS OF FEAR
(Eyre & Spottiswoode)

RANK 1958

HAWLEY, Cameron
  CASH McCALL   WAR 1959
  (Hammond)
  EXECUTIVE SUITE   MGM 1954
  (Hammond)

HAWTHORNE, Nathaniel
  HOUSE OF THE SEVEN GABLES,   UN 1940
  THE
  (Various)
  SCARLET LETTER, THE   MAJESTIC 1934
  (Various)   CHANNEL 4 1986 (TV)

HAY, Ian *pseud.*
  HOUSEMASTER (P)   ALL 1939
  (French)
  HOUSEMASTER   ALL 1939
  (Hodder & Stoughton)

HAY, Ian *and* **ARMSTRONG, Anthony**
  ORDERS ARE ORDERS (P)   BL 1954
  (French)

HAY, Ian *and* **KING-HALL, Stephen**
  MIDDLE WATCH (P)   BI 1930
  (French)   AB 1940
  MIDSHIPMAID, THE (P)   GB 1932
  (French)
  OFF THE RECORD (P)   REN 1957
  (French)   (*Carry On Admiral*)

HAYCOX, Ernest
  BUGLES IN THE AFTERNOON   WAR 1952
  (Hodder & Stoughton)
  CANYON PASSAGE   UN 1946
  (Hodder & Stoughton)
  STAGE TO LORDSBURGH   UA 1939
  (*In* By Rope and Lead: (*Stagecoach*)
  Hodder & Stoughton)   FOX 1965
                                     (*Stagecoach*)
  SUNDOWN JIM   FOX 1942
  (Paul)

HAYES, Alfred
GIRL ON THE VIA FLAMINIA, THE   UA 1954
(Gollancz)   *(Act of Love)*

HAYES, Billy *and* **HOFFER, W.**
MIDNIGHT EXPRESS   COL—WAR 1978
(Dutton, N.Y.)

HAYES, Douglas
COMEDY MAN, THE   BL 1964
(Abelard-Schuman)

HAYES, Joseph
DESPERATE HOURS, THE   PAR 1955
(Deutsch)
DESPERATE HOURS, THE (P)   PAR 1955
(Random House, N.Y.)
THIRD DAY, THE   WAR 1965
(W.H. Allen)

HAYES, Marrijane *and* **HAYES, Joseph Arnold**
BONVOYAGE   DISNEY 1962
(Deutsch)

HAYES, Nelson
DILDO CAY   PAR 1941
(Davies)   *(Bahamas Passage)*

HAYES, R. Chetwynd *see* **CHETWYND-HAYES, R.**

HAYS, Lee
ONCE UPON A TIME IN AMERICA   COL—EMI—WAR 1983
(New American Library, N.Y.)

HAYWARD, Brooke
HAYWIRE   BBC 2 1984 (TV)
(Bantam, N.Y.)

HEALEY, Ben
WAITING FOR A TIGER   MONARCH 1969
(Hale)   *(Taste of Excitement)*

HEATH, W.L.
VIOLENT SATURDAY   FOX 1955
(Hamilton)

HEBDEN, Mark
 EYE-WITNESS   MGM 1970
 (Harrap)

HECHLER, Ken
 BRIDGE AT REMAGEN, THE   UA 1968
 (Panther)

HECHT, Ben
 FLORENTINE DAGGER, THE   WAR 1935
 (Harrap)
 GAILY, GAILY   UA 1969
 (Elek)
 MIRACLE IN THE RAIN   WAR 1956
 (Knopf, N.Y.)

HECHT, Ben *and* **MacARTHUR, Charles**
 FRONT PAGE, THE (P)   UA 1931
 (Covici, N.Y.)   COL 1940
    (*His Girl Friday*)
    CIC 1974

HEGELER, Inge *and* **HEGELER, Sten**
 ABZ OF LOVE, THE   GN 1971
 (Spearman)   (*Language of Love*)

HEGGEN, Thomas
 MISTER ROBERTS   WAR 1955
 (Nicholson)

HEGGEN, Thomas *and* **LOGAN, Joshua**
 MISTER ROBERTS (P)   WAR 1955
 (Random House, N.Y.)

HEINRICH, Willi
 WILLING FLESH   EMI 1976
 (Corgi)   (*Cross of Iron*)

HELLER, Joseph
 CATCH 22   PAR 1969
 (Cape)

HELLMAN, Lillian Florence
 ANOTHER PART OF THE FOREST   UN 1948
 (P)
 (Viking, N.Y.)

AUTHOR AND ORIGINAL TITLE	FILM TITLE
CHILDREN'S HOUR, THE (P) (Knopf, N.Y.)	UA 1936 (*These Three*) UA 1962 (*Loudest Whisper, The*)
LITTLE FOXES, THE (P) (Hamilton)	RKO 1941
NORTH STAR (Macmillan)	RKO 1943
PENTIMENTO (Macmillan)	FOX 1977 (*Julia*)
SEARCHING WIND, THE (P) (Viking, N.Y.)	PAR 1946
TOYS IN THE ATTIC (P) (Random House, N.Y.)	UA 1963
WATCH ON THE RHINE (P) (French, N.Y.)	WAR 1943

HELSETH, Henry Edward

CHAIR FOR MARTIN ROME, THE (Dodd, N.Y.)	FOX 1948 (*Cry of the City*)

HEMINGWAY, Ernest

FAREWELL TO ARMS, A (Cape)	PAR 1932 FOX 1957
FIESTA (Cape)	FOX 1957 (*Sun Also Rises, The*) NBC 1984 (TV)
FOR WHOM THE BELL TOLLS (Cape)	PAR 1943 MANLEY 1984
ISLANDS IN THE STREAM (Collins)	PAR 1977
KILLERS, THE (*In* First 49 Stories: Cape)	UN 1946 RANK 1964
MACOMBER AFFAIR, THE (*In* First 49 Stories: Cape)	UN 1947
MY OLD MAN (*In* First 49 Stories: Cape)	FOX 1950 (*Under My Skin*) AMERICAN NATIONAL 1984
OLD MAN AND THE SEA, THE (Cape)	WAR 1957
SNOWS OF KILIMANJARO, THE (Cape)	FOX 1952

HEMINGWAY, Ernest (*Continued*)
TO HAVE AND HAVE NOT
(Cape)

WAR 1944
WAR 1950
(*Breaking Point, The*)
SEVEN ARTS 1958
(*Gun Runners, The*)

HERMON, Louis
MARIA CHAPDELAINE
(Macmillan)

BL 1950
(*Naked Heart, The*)
ASTRAL FILMS 1983

M. RIPOIS AND HIS NEMESIS
(Allen & Unwin)

ABP 1954
(*Knave of Hearts*)

HENDERSON, Laurence
SITTING TARGET
(Harrap)

MGM—EMI 1972

HENRY, Harriet
JACKDAWS STRUT
(Paul)

WAR 1931
(*Bought*)

HENRY, Joan *pseud.*
WHO LIE IN GAOL
(Gollancz)
YIELD TO THE NIGHT
(Gollancz)

ABP 1953
(*Weak and the Wicked, The*)
ABP 1953

HENRY, Marguerite
MISTY OF CHINCOTEAGUE
(Collins)

FOX 1961
(*Misty*)

HENRY, O.
CLARION CALL, THE COP AND THE
ANTHEM, THE GIFT OF MAGI, THE
LAST LEAF, THE RANSOM OF RED
CHIEF, THE
(*In* Best of O. Henry: Hodder &
Stoughton)
PASSING OF THE BLACK EAGLE
(Various)

FOX 1952
(*Full House*)

COL 1948
(*Black Eagle*)

HENRY, Will
JOURNEY TO SHILOH
(Gollancz)

UI 1968

MACKENNA'S GOLD   COL 1969
(Hammond)
WHO RIDES WITH WYATT?   UA 1969
(Bantam)   (*Young Billy Young*)

HERBERT, *Sir* **Alan Patrick**
HOUSE BY THE RIVER, THE   REP 1950
(Methuen)
WATER GIPSIES, THE   SDC 1932
(Methuen)

HERBERT, Frank
DUNE   UN 1983
(Gollancz)

HERBERT, Frederick Hugh
FOR LOVE OR MONEY (P)   RANK 1958
(Dramatists, N.Y.)   (*This Happy Feeling*)
KISS AND TELL (P)   COL 1945
(Longmans)
MOON IS BLUE, THE (P)   UA 1953
(Random House, N.Y.)

HERBERT, James
SURVIVOR   HEMDALE 1980
(New American Library, N.Y.)

HERGESHEIMER, Joseph
JAVA HEAD   ID 1935
(Heinemann)
TAMPICO   COL 1933
(Various)   (*Woman I Stole, The*)

HERLIHY, James Leo
ALL FALL DOWN   MGM 1961
(Dutton, N.Y.)
MIDNIGHT COWBOY   UA 1969
(Cape)

HERLIHY, James Leo *and* **NOBLE, William**
BLUE DENIM (P)   FOX 1959
(Random House, N.Y.)   (*Blue Jeans*)

HERRIOT, James
   ALL THINGS BRIGHT AND   EMI 1976
   BEAUTIFUL   (*It Shouldn't Happen to a Vet*)
   (Joseph)
   IF ONLY THEY COULD TALK   EMI 1974
   (Joseph)   (*All Creatures Great and Small*)
   IT SHOULDN'T HAPPEN TO A VET   EMI 1974
   (Joseph)   (*All Creatures Great and Small*)
   LORD GOD MADE THEM ALL, THE   BBC 1985 (TV)
   (Pan)   (*All Creatures Great and Small*)

HERSEY, John Richard
   BELL FOR ADANO, A   FOX 1945
   (Gollancz)
   WAR LOVER, THE   COL 1963
   (Hamilton)

HERZOG, Arthur
   SWARM, THE   COL—WAR 1978
   (Heinemann)

HESSE, Dean E.
   BATTLE HYMN   UI 1956
   (Davies)

HESSE, Hermann
   SIDDHARTHA   COL—WAR 1973
   (Picador)
   STEPPENWOLF   CONTEMPORARY 1976
   (Various)

HEYER, Georgette *pseud.*
   RELUCTANT WIDOW, THE   GFD 1950
   (Heinemann)

HEYERDAHL, Thor
   KON-TIKI EXPEDITION   RKO 1951
   (Allen & Unwin)   (*Kon-Tiki*)

HEYM, Stefan
   HOSTAGES   PAR 1943
   (Putnam)

HICHENS, Robert
  BELLA DONNA   COL 1930
  (Heinemann)   OLY 1935
                     (*Temptation*)
                     UN 1945
  GARDEN OF ALLAH, THE   UA 1936
  (Methuen)
  PARADINE CASE, THE   BL 1949
  (Convoy)

HIGGINS, George V.
  FRIENDS OF EDDIE COYLE, THE   PAR 1973
  (Secker & Warburg)

HIGGINS, Jack
  EAGLE HAS LANDED, THE   ITC 1976
  (Collins)

HIGHSMITH, Patricia
  RIPLEY'S GAME   CINEGATE 1978
  (Hodder & Stoughton)   (*American Friend, The*)
  STRANGERS ON A TRAIN   WAR 1951
  (Cresset Press)
  TALENTED MR. RIPLEY, THE   HILLCREST 1961
  (Pan)   (*Purple Noon*)
  THIS SWEET SICKNESS   ARTIFICIAL EYE 1979
  (Heinemann)

HILL, Albert
  NORTH AVENUE IRREGULARS   DISNEY 1980
  (Berkeley, N.Y.)   (*Hill's Angels*)

HILL, R.L.
  EVIL THAT MEN DO, THE   ITC 1983
  (Hodder & Stoughton)

HILL, Weldon
  ONIONHEAD   WAR 1958
  (Deutsch)

HILTON, James
  DAWN OF RECKONING   MGM 1941
  (Butterworth)   (*Rage in Heaven*)
  GOODBYE MR. CHIPS   MGM 1939
  (Hodder & Stoughton)   MGM 1969

HILTON, James (*Continued*)
  KNIGHT WITHOUT ARMOUR   UA 1937
  (Macmillan)
  Originally called Without Armour
  LOST HORIZON   COL 1937
  (Macmillan)   COL 1973
  RANDOM HARVEST   MGM 1942
  (Macmillan)
  SO WELL REMEMBERED   RKO 1947
  (Macmillan)
  STORY OF DR. WASSELL, THE   PAR 1944
  (Macmillan)
  WE ARE NOT ALONE   WAR 1939
  (Macmillan)

HILTON, James *and* **BURNHAM, Barbara**
  GOODBYE MR. CHIPS (P)   MGM 1939
  (French, N.Y.)   MGM 1969

HIMES, C.
  COTTON COMES TO HARLEM   UA 1969
  (Muller)
  HEAT'S ON, THE   COL—WAR 1972
  (Berkeley, N.Y.)   (*Come Back Charleston Blue*)

HINE, Al
  LORD LOVE A DUCK   UA 1965
  (Atheneum Press, N.Y.)

HINES, Barry
  KESTREL FOR A KNAVE, A   UA 1969
  (Joseph)   (*Kes*)

HINTON, S.E.
  OUTSIDERS, THE   WAR 1982
  (Gollancz)
  RUMBLE FISH   PSO 1982
  (Gollancz)
  THAT WAS THEN . . . THIS IS NOW   MIRACLE 1986
  (Macmillan)

HINTZE, Naomi, A.
  YOU'LL LIKE MY MOTHER   UA 1972
  (Fawcett, N.Y.)

AUTHOR AND ORIGINAL TITLE	FILM TITLE

HITCHCOCK, Raymond
PERCY   MGM—EMI 1971
(Sphere)
THERE'S A GIRL IN MY SOUP   COL 1970
(W.H. Allen)

HOBAN, Russell
EXTRAORDINARY ADVENTURES   AMBASSADOR 1977
OF THE MOUSE AND THE CHILD,   (U.S. Title: *Mouse and the Child,*
THE   *The*)
(Faber)
TURTLE DIARY   RANK 1985
(Random, N.Y.)

HOBART, *Mrs.* **Alice Tisdale**
CUP AND THE SWORD, THE   UI 1959
(Cassell)   (*This Earth is Mine*)
OIL FOR THE LAMPS OF CHINA   WAR 1935
(Cassell)   WAR 1941
                                         (*Law of the Tropics*)

HOBSON, *Mrs.* **Laura**
CONSENTING ADULT   CHANNEL 4 1986
(Warner, N.Y.)
GENTLEMEN'S AGREEMENT   FOX 1947
(Cassell)

HODGES, Hollis
FABRICATOR, THE   MGM 1980
(Avon, N.Y.)   (*"Why Should I Lie?"*)

HODGINS, Eric
MR. BLANDINGS BUILDS HIS   RKO 1948
DREAM HOUSE
(Joseph)

HODSON, James Lansdale
RETURN TO WOODS   WAR 1965
(Gollancz)   (*King and Country*)

HOFFENBERG, M. *see* **SOUTHERN, Terry** *jt. author*

HOFFER, W. *see* **HAYES, Billy** *jt. author*

HOHIMER, Frank
HOME INVADER, THE
(Chicago Review, Chicago)

UA 1981
(*Violent Street*
U.S. Title: *Thief*)

HOLDING, Charles H.
SCAR, THE
(Eerdmans, Grand Rapids)

ABP 1949

HOLDING, *Mrs.* Elizabeth
BLANK WALL
(Simon & Schuster, N.Y.)

COL 1949
(*Reckless Moment, The*)

HOLDRIDGE, Desmond
DEATH OF A COMMON MAN
(Hale)

ARCHERS 1947
(*End of the River, The*)

HOLIDAY, Billie
LADY SINGS THE BLUES
(Barrie & Jenkins)

CINEMA INT 1972

HOLLAND, Marty
FALLEN ANGEL
(Dutton, N.Y.)

FOX 1945

HOLLANDER, Xaviera
HAPPY HOOKER, THE
(Talmy-Franklin)

SCOTIA BARBER 1975
MIRACLE FILMS 1975
(*My Pleasure is my Business*)

HOLLES, Robert
SIEGE OF BATTERSEA, THE
(Joseph)

FOX 1964
(*Guns at Batasi*)

HOLT, Felix
GABRIEL HORN
(Various)

UA 1955
(*Kentuckian, The*)

HOLTBY, Winifred
SOUTH RIDING
(Collins)

UA 1938

HOLZER, Hans
MURDER IN AMITYVILLE
(Futura)

COL—EMI—WAR 1982
(*Amityville II: The Possession*)

HOME, William Douglas
CHILTERN HUNDREDS, THE (P)   TC 1949
(French)
NOW BARABBAS (P)   WAR 1949
(Longmans)   (*Now Barabbas Was a Robber*)
RELUCTANT DEBUTANTE, THE (P)   MGM 1958
(French)

HOMER
ILIAD   ARCHWAY 1954
(Various)   (*Ulysses*)

HOMES, Geoffrey *pseud.*
BUILD MY GALLOWS HIGH   RKO 1947
(Grosset, N.Y.)
FORTY WHACKS   WAR 1946
(Grosset, N.Y.)   (*Crime by Night*)
NO HANDS ON THE CLOCK   PAR 1941
(Various)

HONEYCOMBE, Gordon
NEITHER THE SEA NOR THE SAND   TIGON 1972
(Hutchinson)

HOOKE, Nona Warner
DARKNESS I LEAVE YOU   RANK 1957
(Hale)   (*Gypsy and the Gentleman, The*)
DEADLY RECORD   AA 1959
(Hale)

HOOKER, Richard
MASH   FOX 1969
(Morrow, N.Y.)   (*M.A.S.H.*)

HOOVER, John Edgar
PERSONS IN HIDING   PAR 1939
(Dent)   PAR 1940
                                    (*Queen of the Mob*)
                                    PAR 1940
                                    (*Parole Fixer*)

HOPE, Anthony
PRISONER OF ZENDA   UA 1937
(Dent)   MGM 1952
                                    CIC 1979
                                    BBC 1984 (TV)

HOPKINS, John
THIS STORY OF YOURS (P)   UA 1972
(Penguin)   (*Offence, The*)

HOPLEY, George *pseud.*
NIGHT HAS A THOUSAND EYES   PAR 1948
(Oxford U.P.)

HORGAN, Paul
DISTANT TRUMPET, A   WAR 1964
(Macmillan)

HORN, Aloysius
TRADER HORN   MGM 1931
(Cape)   MGM 1973

HORN, Tom
TOM HORN   COL—EMI—WAR 1980
(University of Oklahoma)

HORNE, Kenneth
FOOLS RUSH IN (P)   PINEWOOD 1949
(French)
LADY MISLAID, A (P)   ABP 1958
(English Theatre Guild)

HORNUNG, Ernest William
RAFFLES   UA 1930
(Grayson)   UA 1940

HOTCHNER, A.E.
SOPHIA LIVING AND LOVING   BBC 1985 (TV)
(Morrow, N.Y.)   (*Sophia Loren—Her Own Story*)

HOUGH, Emerson
NORTH OF 36   PAR 1931
(Appleton, N.Y.)   (*Conquering Horde*)

HOUGH, Richard
CAPTAIN BLIGH AND MR.   COL—EMI—WAR 1984
CHRISTIAN   (*Bounty, The*)
(Hutchinson)

HOUGHTON, Stanley
HINDLE WAKES (P)   GB 1932
(Sidgwick)   MON 1952

HOUGRON, Jean
BLAZE OF THE SUN   PAR 1959
(Hurst & Blackett)

HOUSEHOLD, Geoffrey
BRANDY FOR THE PARSON   MGM 1952
(*In* Tales of Adventure: Joseph)
DANCE OF THE DWARFS   DOVE 1982
(Henry)
ROGUE MALE   FOX 1941
(Chatto & Windus)   (*Manhunt*)
ROUGH SHOOT   UA 1953
(Joseph)
WATCHER IN THE SHADOWS   BBC 1984 (TV)
(Penguin)   (*Deadly Harvest*)

HOUSMAN, Laurence
VICTORIA REGINA (P)   RKO 1937
(Cape)

HOUSTON, James
WHITE DAWN, THE   CIC 1974
(Heinemann)

HOWARD, Hartley
ASSIGNMENT 'K'   COL 1968
(Collins)

HOWARD, Keble *pseud.*
LORD BABS   GFD 1932
(Benn)

HOWARD, Leigh
BLIND DATE   RANK 1959
(Longmans)

HOWARD, Sidney Coe
DODSWORTH (P)   UA 1936
(Harcourt, N.Y.)

HOWARD, Sidney Coe (*Continued*)
THEY KNEW WHAT THEY WANTED
(P)
(*In* Modern Plays, edited by J.F.
MacDermott, Harcourt, N.Y.)

MGM 1930
(*Lady to Love, A*)
RKO 1940

HOWARTH, David
ESCAPE ALONE
(Collins)
SHETLAND BUS, THE
(Nelson)

REN 1959
(*We Die Alone*)
FORLONG 1954
EROS 1957
(*Suicide Mission*)

HOWE, George Locke
CALL IT TREASON
(Hart-Davis)

FOX 1951
(*Decision Before Dawn*)

HOWLETT, John
MURDER OF A MODERATE MAN
(Arrow)

BBC 1985 (TV)

HOYLAND, John
IVY GARLAND, THE
(Allison & Busby)

CFF 1985
(*Out of the Darkness*)

HOYT, Vance Joseph
SEQUOIA
(Grosset, N.Y.)

MGM 1934

HUBBARD, Elbert
MESSAGE TO GARCIA, A (Poem)
(Lothian, N.Y.)

FOX 1936

HUBLER, Richard Gibson
I'VE GOT MINE
(Putnam, N.Y.)

UA 1955
(*Beachhead*)

HUDSON, Christopher
FINAL ACT, THE
(Joseph)

SAWBUCK 1980

HUDSON, Jeffrey
CASE OF NEED, THE
(Heinemann)

MGM—EMI 1972
(*Carey Treatment, The*)

480

HUDSON, William Henry
GREEN MANSIONS   MGM 1959
(Various)

HUFFAKER, Clair
BADMAN   UI 1966
(Muller)   (*War Wagon*)
FLAMING LANCE   FOX 1960
(Simon & Schuster, N.Y.)   (*Flaming Star*)
GUNS OF THE RIO CONCHOS   FOX 1964
(Muller)   (*Rio Conchos*)
NOBODY LOVES A DRUNKEN
INDIAN   WAR 1970
(Sphere)   (*Last Warrior, The*)
SEVEN WAYS FROM SUNDOWN   UI 1960
(Muller)

HUGGINS, Roy
DOUBLE TAKE   COL 1948
(Grosset, N.Y.)   (*I Love Trouble*)

HUGHES, Dorothy Belle
EXPENDABLE MAN, THE   RANK 1964
(Deutsch)   (*Hanged Man, The*)
FALLEN SPARROW, THE   RKO 1943
(Nicholson & Watson)
IN A LONELY PLACE   COL 1950
(Duell, N.Y.)
RIDE THE PINK HORSE   UI 1947
(Duell, N.Y.)

HUGHES, Ken
HIGH WRAY   ABP 1954
(Gifford)   (*House Across the Lake, The*)

HUGHES, Richard
HIGH WIND IN JAMAICA, A   FOX 1964
(Chatto & Windus)

HUGHES, Rupert
NO ONE MAN   PAR 1932
(Jarrolds)

HUGHES, Thomas
TOM BROWN'S SCHOOLDAYS   RKO 1940
(Various)   REN 1951

HUGHES, William
TOO LATE THE HERO   CIRO 1971
(Sphere)

HUGO, Victor
HUNCHBACK OF NOTRE DAME,
THE   RKO 1939
(Various)   RANK 1957
LES MISERABLES   UA 1935
(Various)   FOX 1952

HUIE, William Bradford
AMERICANIZATION OF EMILY,
THE   MGM 1963
(W.H. Allen)
KLANSMAN, THE   PAR 1974
(W.H. Allen)
REVOLT OF MAMIE STOVER, THE
(W.H. Allen)   FOX 1956

HULL, Alexander
SHEP OF THE PAINTED HILLS   MGM 1951
(Chapman & Hall)   (*Painted Hills*)

HULL, Helen Rose
HEAT LIGHTNING   WAR 1934
(Cobden Sanderson)

HULME, Kathryn
NUN'S STORY, THE   WAR 1958
(Muller)

HUME, Doris
SIN OF SUSAN SLADE, THE   WAR 1962
(Duell, N.Y.)   (*Susan Slade*)

HUMPHREY, William
HOME FROM THE HILL   MGM 1959
(Pan)

HUNTER, Evan
BLACKBOARD JUNGLE   MGM 1954
(Constable)
BUDDWING   MGM 1967
(Constable)   (*Woman Without a Face*)

482

EVERY LITTLE CROOK AND
NANNY   MGM 1972
(Constable)
LAST SUMMER   FOX 1969
(Constable)
MATTER OF CONVICTION, A   UA 1960
(Constable)   (*Young Savages, The*)
STRANGERS WHEN WE MEET   COL 1959
(Constable)

HUNTER, Jack D.
BLUE MAX, THE   FOX 1965
(Muller)

HUNTER, John Alexander
AFRICAN BUSH ADVENTURES   COL 1959
(Various)   (*Killers of Kilimanjaro*)

HUNTER, Kristin
LANDLORD, THE   UA 1970
(Pan)

HUNTFORD, Roland
SCOTT AND AMUNDSEN   RENEGADE FILMS 1984
(Pan)   (*Last Place on Earth, The*)

HUROK, Sol *and* **GOODE, Ruth**
IMPRESSARIO   FOX 1953
(Macdonald)   (*Tonight We Sing*)

HURST, Fannie
ANATOMY OF ME   UN 1934
(Cape)   (*Imitation of Life*)
                     RANK 1959
                     (*Imitation of Life*)
BACK STREET   UN 1931
(Cape)   UN 1941
                     UI 1961
FIVE AND TEN   MGM 1931
(Cape)
HUMORESQUE   WAR 1946
(Smith, N.Y.)
LUMMOX   UA 1930
(Cape)

HUSSON, Albert
MY THREE ANGELS (P)   PAR 1955
(Random House, N.Y.)   (*We're No Angels*)

HUTCHINSON, Arthur Stuart-Menteth
IF WINTER COMES   MGM 1947
(Hodder & Stoughton)

HUTCHISON, Graham Seton *see* **SETON, G.** *pseud.*

HUTSON, Sandy
EFF OFF   GALA 1980
(Corgi)   (*Class of Miss MacMichael, The*)

HUTTON, Michael Clayton
HAPPY FAMILY, THE (P)   APEX 1952
(Deane)

HUXLEY, Aldous Leonard
DEVILS OF LOUDUN, THE   WAR 1971
(Chatto & Windus)   (*Devils, The*)
GIOCONDA SMILE, THE   UN 1947
(Harper, N.Y.)   (*Woman's Vengeance, A*)
YOUNG ARCHIMEDES   GFD 1950
(Chatto & Windus)   (*Prelude to Fame*)

HYAMS, Edward
SYLVESTER   GFD 1953
(Longmans)   (*You Know What Sailors Are*)

HYDE, Harford Montgomery
TRIALS OF OSCAR WILDE, THE   EROS 1960
(Hodge)

HYMAN, Max
NO TIME FOR SERGEANTS   WAR 1958
(Dent)

HYMAN, Max *see also* **LEVIN, I.** *jt. author*

HYND, Alan
BETRAYAL FROM THE EAST   RKO 1945
(MacBride, N.Y.)

I

IBANEZ, Vicente Blasco *see* **BLASCO, I.V.**

IBSEN, Henrik
DOLL'S HOUSE, A (P)   BL 1973
(Various)
ENEMY OF THE PEOPLE, AN (P)   ENTERPRISE 1978
(Various)
HEDDA GABLER (P)   SCOTIA BARBER 1977
(Various)   (*Hedda*)

IDELL, Albert Edward
CENTENNIAL SUMMER   FOX 1946
(Sampson Low)

ILES, Francis *pseud.*
BEFORE THE FACT   RKO 1941
(Gollancz)   (*Suspicion*)

INGE, William
BUS STOP (P)   FOX 1956
(Random House, N.Y.)
DARK AT THE TOP OF THE STAIRS,
THE (P)   WAR 1960
(Random House, N.Y.)
COME BACK LITTLE SHEBA (P) PAR 1952
(Random House, N.Y.)
LOSS OF ROSES, A (P)   FOX 1963
(Random House, N.Y.)   (*Stripper, The*)
                    FOX 1963
                    (*Woman of Summer*)
PICNIC (P)   COL 1955
(Random House, N.Y.)

INNES, Hammond
CAMPBELL'S KINGDOM   RANK 1957
(Collins)
LONELY SKIER, THE   RKO 1948
(Collins)   (*Snowbound*)
MARY DEARE, THE   MGM 1959
(Collins)   (*Wreck of the Mary Deare*)
WHITE SOUTH, THE   COL 1953
(Collins)

INNES, Michael
CHRISTMAS AT CANDLESHOE   DISNEY 1977
(Gollancz)   (*Candleshoe*)

IRISH, William *pseud.*
BRIDE WORE BLACK, THE   UA 1968
(Sphere)
DEADLINE AT DAWN   RKO 1946
(Lippincott, Philadelphia)
I MARRIED A DEAD MAN   PAR 1950
(Lippincott, Philadelphia)   (*No Man of Her Own*)
I WOULDN'T BE IN YOUR SHOES   MON 1948
(Lippincott, Philadelphia)
PHANTOM LADY   UN 1944
(Lippincott, Philadelphia)

IRVINE, Lucy
CASTAWAY   VIRGIN 1985
(Gollancz)

IRVING, John
HOTEL NEW HAMPSHIRE   EMI 1984
(Cape)
WORLD ACCORDING TO GARP,   COL—EMI—WAR 1982
THE
(Gollancz)

IRWIN, Margaret
YOUNG BESS   MGM 1953
(Chatto & Windus)

ISAACS, Susan
COMPROMISING POSITIONS   UIP 1986
(Penguin)

ISRAEL, Charles Edward
MARK, THE   FOX 1961
(Macmillan)

J

JACKS, Jeff
MURDER ON THE WILD SIDE   COL—WAR 1973
(Fawcett, N.Y.)   (*Black Eye*)

JACKSON, Charles Reginald
LOST WEEK-END, THE   PAR 1945
(Lane)

JACKSON, *Mrs.* **Helen Maria**
RAMONA   FOX 1936
(Sampson Low)

JACKSON, Shirley
BIRD'S NEST, THE   MGM 1957
(Farrar, N.Y.)   (*Lizzie*)
HAUNTING OF HILL HOUSE, THE   MGM 1963
(Joseph)   (*Haunting, The*)

JACOBS, Naomi
UNDER NEW MANAGEMENT   BUTCHER 1946
(Hutchinson)

JACOBS, William Wymark
INTERRUPTION, THE   COL 1955
(*In* Sea Whispers: Methuen)   (*Footsteps in the Fog*)

JACOBS, William Wymark *and* **PARKER, Louis Napoleon**
MONKEY'S PAW, THE (P)   RKO 1932
(*In* One-act Plays of Today, Series 2:   BUTCHER 1948
Harrap)

JAFFÉ, Rona
BEST OF EVERYTHING, THE   FOX 1959
(Cape)
MAZES AND MONSTERS   PROCTOR & GAMBLE 1982
(Dell, N.Y.)

JAKES, John
NORTH AND SOUTH   WAR 1985 (TV)
(Collins)

JAMES, Harrison
ABDUCTION   HEMDALE 1977
(Whirlwind, N.Y.)

JAMES, Henry
ASPERN PAPERS, THE   UN 1947
(Macmillan)   (*Last Moment, The*)
         CONNOISSEUR 1981
         (*Aspern*)

JAMES, Henry (*Continued*)
BOSTONIANS, THE   RANK 1984
(Various)
DAISY MILLER   CIC 1974
(*In* The Complete Tales, Vol. iv: Hart-Davis)
EUROPEAN, THE   GB 1979
(Penguin)
TURN OF THE SCREW, THE   FOX 1961
(Dent)   (*Innocents, The*)
WASHINGTON SQUARE   PAR 1949
(Macmillan)   (*Heiress, The*)

JAMES, Meyrich Edward Clifton
I WAS MONTY'S DOUBLE   ABP 1958
(Rider)

JAMES, Montague Rhodes
CASTING THE RUNES   COL 1957
(Arnold)   (*Night of the Demon*)

JAMES, P.D.
BLACK TOWER, THE   ANGLIA TV 1985
(Sphere)
COVER HER FACE   ANGLIA TV 1985 (TV)
(Hamilton)
DEATH OF AN EXPERT WITNESS   ANGLIA 1982 (TV)
(Faber)
UNSUITABLE JOB FOR A WOMAN,
AN   BOYD 1981
(Sphere)

JAMES, Will
SAND   FOX 1949
(Cassell)
SMOKY   FOX 1933
(Various)   FOX 1946

JANEWAY, *Mrs.* Elizabeth
DAISY KENYON   FOX 1947
(Doubleday, N.Y.)

JANNEY, Russell
MIRACLE OF THE BELLS, THE   RKO 1948
(W.H. Allen)

JAPRISOT, Sebastien
LADY IN THE CAR WITH GLASSES
AND A GUN, THE   COL 1969
(Souvenir Press)   (*Lady in the Car, The*)

JAYNES, Clare
MY REPUTATION   WAR 1946
(World, N.Y.)
(*Originally called* Instruct My Sorrows)

JEANS, Ronald
YOUNG WIVES' TALE (P)   ABP 1951
(*In* Plays of the Year, 1949–50: Elek)

JEFFRIES, Graham Montague *see* **GRAEME, Bruce** *pseud.*

JELLICOE, Ann
KNACK, THE (P)   UA 1965
(Dell, N.Y.)

JENKINS, Dan
SEMI-TOUGH   UA 1978
(New American Library, N.Y.)

JENKINS, Geoffrey
TWIST OF SAND, A   UA 1968
(Collins)

JENNINGS, D. *see* **DUFFY, C.** *jt. author*

JENNINGS, William Dale
COWBOYS, THE   COL—WAR 1972
(Bruce & Watson)

JEPSON, Selwyn
MAN RUNNING   WAR 1949
(Macdonald)   (*Stage Fright*)

JEROME, Jerome Klapka
PASSING OF THE THIRD FLOOR
BACK, THE   GB 1936
(Hurst & Blackett)
THREE MEN IN A BOAT   BL 1956
(Various)

JERUSALEM, Else
  RED HOUSE, THE   UN 1947
  (Laurie)

JESSUP, Richard
  CHUKA   PAR 1966
  (Jenkins)
  CINCINNATI KID, THE   MGM 1965
  (Gollancz)
  DEADLY DUO, THE   UA 1962
  (Boardman)
  MAN IN CHARGE   COL 1957
  (Secker & Warburg)   (*Young Don't Cry, The*)

JHABVALA, Ruth P.
  HEAT AND DUST   ENTERPRISE 1983
  (Murray)

JOB, Thomas
  UNCLE HARRY (P)   UN 1945
  (French)   (*Strange Affair of Uncle Harry, The*)

JOHNSON, Dorothy M.
  HANGING TREE, THE   WAR 1958
  (Deutsch)
  MAN CALLED HORSE, A   CINEMA CENTER 1969
  (Deutsch)

JOHNSON, G. *see* **NOLAN, W.F.** *jt. author*

JOHNSON, Nora
  WORLD OF HENRY ORIENT, THE   UA 1964
  (Gollancz)

JOHNSON, Osa Helen
  I MARRIED ADVENTURE   COL 1940
  (Hutchinson)

JOHNSON, Owen
  LAWRENCEVILLE SCHOOL TALES   MGM 1950
  (Grosset, N.Y.)   (*Happy Years, The*)

JOHNSON, Pamela Hansford
  TROJAN BROTHERS, THE   BN 1946
  (Joseph)

JOHNSTON, Annie Fellows
LITTLE COLONEL   FOX 1935
(Various)

JOHNSON, Velda
HOWLING IN THE WOODS, A   UN 1971
(Dodd, N.Y.)

JOLLY, Cyril
VENGEANCE OF PRIVATE
POOLEY, THE   CONT 1962
(Heinemann)   (*Story of Private Pooley, The*)

JONES, D.C.
COURT MARTIAL OF GEORGE
ARMSTRONG CUSTER, THE   BBC 2 1984 (TV)
(Scribner, N.Y.)

JONES, D.F.
COLOSSUS   UN 1972
(Hart-Davis)   (*Forbin Project, The*)

JONES, Guy Pearce *and* **JONES, Constance Bridges**
PEABODY'S MERMAID   UN 1948
(Joseph)   (*Mr. Peabody and the Mermaid*)
THERE WAS A LITTLE MAN   FOX 1948
(Random House, N.Y.)   (*Luck of the Irish*)

JONES, James
FROM HERE TO ETERNITY   COL 1953
(Collins)
SOME CAME RUNNING   MGM 1958
(Collins)
THIN RED LINE, THE   PLANET 1964
(Collins)

JONES, Joanna
NURSE IS A NEIGHBOUR   WAR 1963
(Joseph)   (*Nurse on Wheels*)

JONES, Madison
EXILE, AN   COL 1971
(Deutsch)   (*I Walk the Line*)

JONES, Mervyn
JOHN AND MARY   FOX 1969
(Cape)

JONES, Raymond F.
THIS ISLAND EARTH   UI 1955
(Sharta Pubns., Chicago)

JONSON, Ben
VOLPONE (P)   SIRITZKY 1947
(Allen & Unwin)   UA 1966
                   (Honey Pot, The)

JOPE-SLADE, Christine *and* **STOKES, Sewell**
BRITANNIA OF BILLINGSGATE (P)   GB 1933
(French)

JORDAN, Elizabeth Garver
DADDY AND I   RKO 1936
(Grosset, N.Y.)   *(Make Way for a Lady)*

JORGENSEN, Christine
CHRISTINE JORGENSEN STORY,   UA 1970
THE
(Eriksson, N.Y.)

JOYCE, James
FINNEGAN'S WAKE   CONT 1969
(Faber)   *(Passages from James Joyce's . . .)*
PORTRAIT OF THE ARTIST AS A
YOUNG MAN   ULYSSES 1977
(Cape)
ULYSSES   BL 1966
(Lane)

JUSTER, Norton
PHANTOM TOLLBOOTH, THE   MGM 1969
(Collins)

K

KAFKA, Franz
AMERIKA   ARTIFICIAL EYE 1985
(Secker & Warburg)   *(Class Relations)*

TRIAL, THE	BL 1963
(Secker & Warburg)	BBC 2 1986
	(*Insurance Man, The*)
KALER, James Otis	
TOBY TYLER	DISNEY 1959
(Various)	
KANDEL, Aben	
CITY FOR CONQUEST	WAR 1940
(Joseph)	
KANIN, Fay	
GOODBYE, MY FANCY (P)	WAR 1951
(French, N.Y.)	
KANIN, Fay *and* **KANIN, Michael**	
RASHOMON (P)	MGM 1964
(Random House, N.Y.)	(*Outrage*)
KANIN, Garson	
BORN YESTERDAY (P)	COL 1951
(Viking, N.Y.)	CANNON 1986
RAT RACE, THE (P)	PAR 1960
(Dramatists, N.Y.)	
KANTOR, Mackinlay	
ANDERSONVILLE	COL 1959
(W.H. Allen)	
AROUSE AND BEWARE	MGM 1940
(Gollancz)	(*Man from Dakota, The*)
GENTLE ANNIE	MGM 1944
(Various)	
GLORY FOR ME	RKO 1946
(Coward-McCann, N.Y.)	(*Best Years of our Lives, The*)
GOD AND MY COUNTRY	DISNEY 1967
(World, N.Y.)	(*Follow Me, Boys!*)
GUN CRAZY	UA 1949
(*In* Author's Choice: Coward-McCann,	(*Deadly is the Female*)
N.Y.)	
HAPPY LAND	FOX 1943
(Longmans)	
VOICE OF BUGLE ANN	MGM 1936
(Selwyn & Blount)	

KARMEL, Alex
MARY ANN
(Secker & Warburg)

UA 1962
(*Something Wild*)

KASTLE, Herbert
CROSS COUNTRY
(Mayflower)

COL—EMI—WAR 1983

KASTNER, Erich
EMIL AND THE DETECTIVES
(Cape)
LOTTIE AND LISA
(Cape)
THREE MEN IN THE SNOW
(Cape)

UFA 1931
DISNEY 1964
DISNEY 1961

MGM 1938
(*Paradise for Three*)

KATA, Elizabeth
BE READY WITH BELLS AND
DRUMS
(Penguin)

MGM 1966
(*Patch of Blue, A*)

KATCHER, Leon
BIG BANKROLL
(Gollancz)
HARD MAN, THE
(Macmillan, N.Y.)

WAR 1961

COL 1957

KATZ, Robert
DEATH IN ROME
(Cape)

GN 1975
(*Massacre in Rome*)

KATZ, William
NORTH STAR CRUSADE
(Arrow, N.Y.)

ITC 1978

KATZENBACH, John
IN THE HEAT OF THE SUMMER
(Joseph)

ORION 1985 (TV)
(*Mean Season*)

KAUFMAN, Bel
UP THE DOWN STAIRCASE
(Barker)

WAR 1966

KAUFMAN, George Simon *and* **CONNELLY, Marc**
DULCY (P)
(Various)

MGM 1940

494

KAUFMAN, George Simon *and* **FERBER, Edna**
DINNER AT EIGHT (P)   MGM 1933
(Heinemann)
ROYAL FAMILY, THE (P)   PAR 1930
(French, N.Y.)   (*Royal Family of Broadway*)
STAGE DOOR (P)   RKO 1937
(Heinemann)

KAUFMAN, George Simon *and* **HART, Moss**
GEORGE WASHINGTON SLEPT
HERE (P)   WAR 1942
(*In* Six Plays: Random House, N.Y.)
MAN WHO CAME TO DINNER, THE
(P)   WAR 1941
(Random House, N.Y.)
YOU CAN'T TAKE IT WITH YOU (P)
(Barker)   COL 1938

KAUFMAN, G.S. *see also* **TEICHMAN, H.** *jt. author*

KAUFMAN, Sue
DIARY OF A MAD HOUSEWIFE   UI 1971
(Penguin)

KAUS, Gina
DARK ANGEL   PRC 1946
(Cassell)   (*Her Sister's Secret*)
LUXURY LINER   PAR 1933
(Cassell)

KAYE, M.M.
FAR PAVILLIONS, THE   GOLDCREST 1983
(Lane)

KAYE-SMITH, Sheila
JOANNA GODDEN   GFD 1947
(Cassell)   (*Loves of Joanna Godden, The*)

KAZAN, Elia
AMERICA, AMERICA   WAR 1964
(Collins)   (*Anatolian Smile, The*)
ARRANGEMENT, THE   WAR 1969
(Collins)

KAZANTZAKIS, Nikes
ZORBA THE GREEK   FOX 1964
(Faber)   CANNON 1986

KEANE, Christopher
HUNTER, THE   PAR 1980
(Avon, N.Y.)

KEATING, William J. *and* **CARTER, Richard**
MAN WHO ROCKED THE BOAT,
THE   UI 1957
(Harper, N.Y.)   (*Slaughter on 10th Avenue*)

KEELER, Harry Stephen
SING SING NIGHTS   MON 1934
(Ward Lock)

KEENE, Day
JOY HOUSE   MGM 1965
(Consul Bks.)   (*Love Cage, The*)

KEENE, Day *and* **BABCOCK, Dwight**
CHAUTUAQUA   MGM 1969
(Four Square Books)   (*Trouble with Girls, The*)

KEIR, Ursula
VINTAGE, THE   MGM 1937
(Collins)

KEITH, Agnes
THREE CAME HOME   FOX 1949
(Joseph)

KELLAND, Clarence Buddington
ARIZONA   COL 1940
(Harper)
DREAMLAND   UA 1936
(Miles)   (*Strike me Pink*)
GREAT CROONER, THE   WAR 1937
(Barker)   (*Mr. Dodd Takes the Air*)
MR. DEEDS GOES TO TOWN   COL 1936
(Barker)
SCATTERGOOD BAINES   RKO 1941
(Hodder & Stoughton)

SKIN DEEP   FOX 1941
(Various)   (*For Beauty's Sake*)
SPEAK EASILY   MGM 1932
(Harper)
SUGARFOOT   WAR 1951
(Grosset, N.Y.)
VALLEY OF THE SUN   RKO 1942
(Various)

KELLINO, Pamela
DEL PALMA   REP 1951
(Hale)   (*Lady Possessed, A*)

KELLOCK, Harold
HOUDINI   PAR 1953
(Heinemann)

KELLOGG, Marjorie
TELL ME THAT YOU LOVE ME,
JANIE MOON   PAR 1971
(Secker & Warburg)

KELLY, George
CRAIG'S WIFE (P)   COL 1936
(French)   COL 1950
    (*Harriet Craig*)
SHOW-OFF, THE (P)   PAR 1929
(French, N.Y.)   (*Men Are Like That*)
    MGM 1934
TORCH BEARERS (P)   FOX 1935
(French, N.Y.)

KELLY, Judith
MARRIAGE IS A PRIVATE AFFAIR   MGM 1944
(Cassell)

KEMAL, Yashar
MEMED MY HAWK   EMI 1984
(Writers and Readers)

KEMBER, Paul
NOT QUITE JERUSALEM (P)   RANK 1985
(Methuen)

KEMPINSKI, Tom
DUET FOR ONE (P)   CANNON 1983
(French)

KENEALLY, Thomas
CHANT OF JIMMY BLACKSMITH,   FOX 1979
THE
(Angus & Robertson)

KENDRICK, Baynard Hardwick
LIGHTS OUT   UI 1951
(W.H. Allen)   (*Bright Victory*)
ODOUR OF VIOLETS   MGM 1942
(Methuen)   (*Eyes in the Night*)

KENNAWAY, James
DOLLAR BOTTOM AND TAYLOR'S
FINEST HOUR   ALLIED STARS 1981
(Mainstream)   (*Chariots of Fire*)
MIND BENDERS, THE   AA 1963
(Pan)
TUNES OF GLORY   UA 1960
(Putnam)

KENNEDY, Adam
DOMINO PRINCIPLE, THE   ITC 1978
(Viking, N.Y.)   (*Domino Killings, The*)

KENNEDY, Jay Richard
MOST DANGEROUS MAN IN THE
WORLD, THE   RANK 1969
(Joseph)

KENNEDY, Ludovic
10 RILLINGTON PLACE   COL 1971
(Panther)

KENNEDY, Margaret
AUTUMN (P)   LF 1949
(French)   (*That Dangerous Age*)
CONSTANT NYMPH, THE (P)   FOX 1934
(Heinemann)   WAR 1943
CONSTANT NYMPH, THE   FOX 1934
(Heinemann)   WAR 1943

ESCAPE ME NEVER   UA 1935
(Heinemann)

KENNETT, John
PERIL FOR THE GUY   BL 1953
(Brockhampton)

KENNINGTON, Alan
NIGHT HAS EYES, THE   ANGLO—AMERICAN 1952
(Jarrolds)
SHE DIED YOUNG   ABP 1955
(Jarrolds)   (*You Can't Escape*)

KENNY, Elizabeth *and* **OSTENSO, Martha**
AND THEY SHALL WALK   RKO 1946
(Dodd, N.Y.)   (*Sister Kenny*)

KENT, Simon *pseud.*
FERRY TO HONG KONG   RANK 1959
(Hutchinson)
FIRE DOWN BELOW   COL 1957
(Hutchinson)

KENT, Willis *see* **COLLISON, Wilson** *pseud.*

KENWARD, Alan Richard
CRY HAVOC (P)   MGM 1943
(French, N.Y.)

KEON, Michael
DURIAN TREE, THE   UA 1964
(Hamilton)   (*7th Dawn*)

KERR, Geoffrey
COTTAGE TO LET (P)   GFD 1941
(French)

KERR, Jean
MARY, MARY (P)   WAR 1963
(Doubleday, N.Y.)
PLEASE DON'T EAT THE DAISIES   MGM 1960
(Heinemann)

KERR, Jean *and* **BROOKE, Eleanor**
KING OF HEARTS (P)   PAR 1956
(Doubleday, N.Y.)   (*That Certain Feeling*)

KERSH, Gerald
NIGHT AND THE CITY   FOX 1950
(Heinemann)

KESEY, Ken
ONE FLEW OVER THE CUCKOO'S
NEST   UA 1975
(Viking, N.Y.)
SOMETIMES A GREAT NOTION   RANK 1972
(Methuen)   (*Never Give An Inch*)

KESSEL, Joseph
BELLE DE JOUR   CURZON 1967
(Barker)
HORSEMEN, THE   COL 1971
(Barker)
LION, THE   FOX 1962
(Hart-Davis)
SIROCCO   COL 1951
(Random House, N.Y.)

KESSELRING, Joseph Otto
ARSENIC AND OLD LACE (P)   WAR 1944
(French)

KESSON, Jessie
"ANOTHER TIME, ANOTHER   CINEGATE 1983
PLACE"
(Chatto & Windus)

KESTER, Paul
WHEN KNIGHTHOOD WAS IN   RKO 1953
FLOWER (P)   (*Sword and the Rose, The*)
(French, N.Y.)

KEY, Alexander
ESCAPE TO WITCH MOUNTAIN DISNEY 1974
(Various)

KEY, Ted
DIGBY—THE BIGGEST DOG IN THE
WORLD   RANK 1973
(Piccolo)

KEYES, Daniel
FLOWERS FOR ALGERNON   CINERAMA 1968
(Cassell)   (*Charly*)

KEYHOE, Donald E.
FLYING SAUCERS FROM OUTER   COL 1956
SPACE   (*Earth Versus the Flying Saucers*)
(Hutchinson)

KIMBROUGH, E. *see* **SKINNER, C.O.** *jt. author*

KIMMINS, Anthony
AMOROUS PRAWN, THE (P)   BL 1962
(French)
WHILE PARENTS SLEEP (P)   SOSKIN 1936
(French)

KING, Philip
ON MONDAY NEXT (P)   GFD 1952
(French)   (*Curtain Up*)
SEE HOW THEY RUN (P)   BL 1955
(French)   CHANNEL 4 1984
SERIOUS CHARGE (P)   EROS 1959
(French)

KING, Philip *see also* **CARY, F.L.** *jt. author*

KING, Philip *and* **CARY, Falkland L.**
SAILOR BEWARE (P)   BL 1956
(*In* Plays of the Year, Vol. 12: Elek)

KING, Rufus
CASE OF THE CONSTANT GOD   UN 1936
(Methuen)   (*Love Letters of a Star*)
SECRET BEYOND THE DOOR, THE
(Various)   UI 1948

KING, Sherwood
LADY FROM SHANGHAI, THE *or* I   COL 1948
DIE BEFORE I WAKE
(Worlds Work)

KING, Stephen
  CARRIE   UA 1976
  (New English Library)
  CHRISTINE   COL—EMI—WAR 1984
  (New English Library)
  CUJO   PSO 1982
  (Macdonald)
  DEAD ZONE   COL—EMI—WAR 1984
  (Futura)
  FIRESTARTER   UIP 1984
  (Macdonald)
  SALEM'S LOT   WAR 1981
  (New English Library)
  SHINING, THE   COL—EMI—WAR 1982
  (New American Library, N.Y.)

KING-HALL, Magdalen
  LIFE AND DEATH OF THE WICKED
  LADY SKELTON, THE   GFD 1946
  (Davies)   (*Wicked Lady, The*)
                                     CANNON 1982

KING-HALL, S. *see* **HAY, I.** *jt. author*

KINGSLEY, Charles
  WATER BABIES, THE   PRODUCER ASSOCIATES 1979
  (Various)

KINGSLEY, Sidney
  DEAD END (P)   UA 1937
  (Dramatists, N.Y.)
  DETECTIVE STORY (P)   PAR 1951
  (Random House, N.Y.)
  MEN IN WHITE   MGM 1934
  (Gollancz)

KIPLING, Rudyard
  CAPTAINS COURAGEOUS   MGM 1937
  (Macmillan)
  JUNGLE BOOK, THE   DISNEY 1966
  (Macmillan)
  KIM   MGM 1949
  (Macmillan)   LF 1984 (TV)
  LIGHT THAT FAILED, THE   PAR 1939
  (Macmillan)

MAN WHO WOULD BE KING, THE   COL 1976
(*In* Wee Willie Winkie and Other Stories:
Macmillan)
SOLDIERS THREE   MGM 1951
(Macmillan)
TOOMAI OF THE ELEPHANTS   UA 1937
(Macmillan)   (*Elephant Boy*)
WEE WILLIE WINKIE   FOX 1937
(Macmillan)

KIRK, Jeremy
  BUILD-UP BOYS, THE   FOX 1960
  (Hart-Davis)   (*Madison Avenue*)

KIRKBRIDE, Ronald
  GIRL NAMED TAMIKO, A   PAR 1963
  (Pan)

KIRKLAND, J. *see* **CALDWELL, E.** *jt. author*

KIRKWOOD, James
  SOME KIND OF HERO   UIP 1981
  (New American Library, N.Y.)

KIRST, Hans Helmuth
  NIGHT OF THE GENERALS, THE   BL 1966
  (Collins)

KJELGAARD, James Arthur
  BIG RED   DISNEY 1962
  (Grosset, N.Y.)

KLANE, Robert
  FIRE SALE   FOX 1978
  (Fawcett, N.Y.)
  WHERE'S POPPA   GEM TOBY 1975
  (Tandem)

KLEIN, Alexander
  DOUBLE DEALERS   PAR 1962
  (Faber)   (*Counterfeit Traitor, The*)

KLEMPNER, John
  LETTER TO FIVE WIVES, A   FOX 1948
  (Scribner, N.Y.)   (*Letter to Three Wives, A*)

KLINGMAN, Lawrence *and* **GREEN, Gerald**
    HIS MAJESTY O'KEEFE   WAR 1954
    (Hale)

KNEBEL, Fletcher *and* **BAILEY, Charles W.**
    SEVEN DAYS IN MAY   PAR 1963
    (Corgi)

KNIGHT, Eric Mowbray
    LASSIE COME HOME   MGM 1943
    (Cassell)
    THIS ABOVE ALL   FOX 1942
    (Cassell)

KNOBLOCK, Edward
    KISMET (P)   IN 1931
    (Methuen)   MGM 1955
    LULLABY, THE (P)   MGM 1931
    (Putnam)   (*Sin of Madelon Claudet, The*)

KNOTT, Frederick
    DIAL 'M' FOR MURDER (P)   WAR 1954
    (Random House, N.Y.)
    WAIT UNTIL DARK (P)   WAR 1968
    (French)

KNOWLES, John
    SEPARATE PEACE   PAR 1972
    (Heinemann)

KOBER, Arthur
    HAVING WONDERFUL TIME (P)   RKO 1938
    (Dramatist, N.Y.)

KOCH, C.J.
    YEAR OF LIVING DANGEROUSLY,
    THE   UIP 1983
    (Sphere)

KOENIG, Laird
    LITTLE GIRL WHO LIVES DOWN
    THE LANE   RANK 1976
    (Souvenir)

AUTHOR AND ORIGINAL TITLE	FILM TITLE

KOHNER, Frederick
GIDGET — COL 1959
(Joseph)

KOLB, Ken
GETTING STRAIGHT — COL 1969
(Barrie & Rockcliffe)

KOLPACOFF, Victor
PRISONERS OF QUAI DONG, THE — TITAN 1973
(Sphere) — (*Physical Assault*)

KOMROFF, Manuel
MAGIC BOW — GFD 1946
(Heinemann)

KONIGSBURG, E.L.
FORM THE MIXED-UP FILES OF MR.
BASIL E. FRANKWESTER — UA 1973
(Macdonald) — (*Hideaways, The*)

KONINGSBERGER, Hans
REVOLUTIONARY, THE — UA 1971
(Deutsch)
WALK WITH LOVE AND DEATH, A
(Pan) — FOX 1968

KONVITZ, Jeffrey
SENTINEL, THE — UN 1979
(Secker & Warburg)

KOONTZ, Dean
DEMON SEED — MGM 1977
(Bantam, Toronto)

KOPIT, Arthur
OH DAD, POOR DAD (P) — PAR 1966
(Methuen)

KOSINSKI, Jerzy
BEING THERE — ITC 1980
(Bantam, N.Y.)

KRAMM, Joseph
SHRIKE, THE (P)   UI 1955
(Random House, N.Y.)

KRANTZ, Judith
MISTRAL'S DAUGHTER   ITV 1986 (TV)
(Sidgwick & Jackson)
PRINCESS DAISY   ITV 1984 (TV)
(Sidgwick & Jackson)
SCRUPLES   AMERICAN TV 1983 (TV)
(Futura)

KRASNA, Norman
DEAR RUTH (P)   PAR 1947
(*In* Best Plays of 1944–45: Gollancz)
JOHN LOVES MARY (P)   WAR 1949
(Dramatists, N.Y.)
'KIND SIR' (P)   WAR 1958
(Dramatists, N.Y.)   (*Indiscreet*)
SMALL MIRACLE (P)   PAR 1935
(French, N.Y.)   (*Four Hours to Kill*)
SUNDAY IN NEW YORK (P)   MGM 1964
(Random House, N.Y.)
WHO WAS THAT LADY I SAW YOU
WITH? (P)   COL 1960
(Random House, N.Y.)   (*Who Was That Lady?*)

KRESSING, Harry
COOK, THE   FOX 1970
(Panther)   (*Black Flowers for the Bride*)

KRONBERG, Jeremy
EVERY WHICH WAY BUT LOOSE   COL—EMI—WAR 1980
(Hale)

KRUMGOLD, Joseph
AND NOW MIGUEL   UI 1965
(Cowell-Collier, N.Y.)

KURNITZ, Harry
ONCE MORE WITH FEELING (P)   COL 1959
(Random House, N.Y.)

KURNITZ, Harry *see also* **PAGE, M.** *pseud.*

AUTHOR AND ORIGINAL TITLE	FILM TITLE

KYNE, Peter Bernard
 CAPPY RICKS
 (Hodder & Stoughton)
 NEVER THE TWAIN SHALL MEET
 (Various)
 PARSON OF PANAMINT, THE
 (Grosset, N.Y.)
 THREE GODFATHERS
 (Various)

 VALLEY OF THE GIANTS
 (Hodder & Stoughton)

REP 1937
(*Affairs of Cappy Ricks, The*)
MGM 1931

PAR 1941

UN 1930
(*Hell's Heroes*)
MGM 1936
FOX 1948
WAR 1938

L

LA BERN, Arthur Jack
 GOODBYE PICCADILLY,
 FAREWELL LEICESTER SQUARE
 (Pan)
 IT ALWAYS RAINS ON SUNDAYS
 (Nicholson & Watson)
 NIGHT DARKENS THE STREETS
 (Nicholson & Watson)
 PAPER ORCHID
 (Marlowe)

RANK 1971
(*Frenzy*)
EALING 1948

GFD 1948
(*Good-timer Girl*)
COL 1949

LAFFAN, Kevin
 IT'S A 2ft 6in ABOVE THE GROUND
 WORLD (P)
 (Faber)

BL 1972
(*Love Ban, The*)

LA FONTAINE, George
 FLASHPOINT
 (Mayflower)
 TWO MINUTES WARNING
 (Coward-McCann, N.Y.)

EMI 1984

UN 1976

LAGERKVIST, Par
 BARABBAS
 (Four Square Books)

COL 1962

LAHR, John
 PRICK UP YOUR EARS
 (Avon, N.Y.)

GAVIN 1986

LAING, R.D.
  KNOTS (P)   CINEGATE 1975
  (Random House, N.Y.)

LAKE, Stuart N.
  WYATT EARP: FRONTIER
  MARSHAL   FOX 1939
  (Various)   (*Frontier Marshal*)

LAMBERT, Derek
  TOUCH OF THE LION'S PAW, A   PAR 1980
  (Corgi)   (*Rough Cut*)

LAMBERT, Gavin
  INSIDE DAISY CLOVER   WAR 1965
  (Hamilton)

LA MOTTA, J.
  RAGING BULL   UA 1981
  (Bantam, N.Y.)

L'AMOUR, Louis
  BROKEN GUN, THE   MGM—EMI 1972
  (Corgi)   (*Cancel my Reservation*)
  BURNING HILLS   COL 1958
  (Jason Press, N.Y.)   (*Apache Territory*)
  CATLOW   MGM—EMI 1972
  (Corgi)
  GUNS OF THE TIMBERLANDS WAR 1959
  (Jason Press, N.Y.)
  HELLER WITH A GUN   PAR 1960
  (Muller)   (*Heller in Pink Tights*)
  HONDO   WAR 1953
  (Muller)
  HONDO AND THE APACHES   MGM 1966
  (Muller)
  MAN CALLED NOON, THE   SCOTIA BARBER 1973
  (Corgi)
  SHALAKO   WAR 1968
  (Bantam)
  TAGGART   UI 1965
  (Corgi)

LAMPEDUSA, Guiseppe di
LEOPARD, THE   FOX 1962
(Collins)

LAMPELL, Millard
HERO, THE   COL 1951
(Messner, N.Y.)   (*Saturday's Hero*)

LAMPLUGH, Lois
ROCKETS IN THE DUNES RANK 1960
(Cape)

LA MURE, Pierre
MOULIN ROUGE   UA 1952
(Collins)

LANDERY, Charles
MR. SMITH GOES TO WASHINGTON
(Dent)   COL 1939

LANDON, Christopher
ICE COLD IN ALEX   ABP 1957
(Heinemann)

LANDON, Margaret
ANNA AND THE KING OF SIAM FOX 1946
(Harrap)   FOX 1956
        (*King and I, The*)

LANE, Kendall
GAMBIT   UI 1966
(Hodder & Stoughton)

LANGHAM, James R.
SING A SONG OF MURDER PAR 1942
(Hale)   (*Night in New Orleans, A*)

LANGLEY, Adria Locke
LION IN THE STREETS, A WAR 1953
(McGraw-Hill, N.Y.)

LANGLEY, Noel
LITTLE LAMBS EAT IVY (P) ABP 1952
(French)   (*Father's Doing Fine*)

LANGLEY, Noel *see also* **MORLEY, E.** *jt. author*

LAPIERRE, D. *see* **COLLINS, L.** *jt. author*

LARDNER, Ring Wilmer
  ALIBI IKE   WAR 1935
  (*In* Best Stories: Garden City Press, N.Y.)
  BIG TOWN, THE   UA 1948
  (*In* Best Stories: Garden City Press, N.Y.) (*So this is New York*)

LARNER, Jeremy
  DRIVE, HE SAID   COL 1971
  (Mayflower)

LARTEGUY, Jean
  CENTURIONS, THE   COL 1966
  (Hutchinson)   (*Lost Command*)
  YELLOW FEVER   COL 1965
  (Hutchinson)   (*Not For Honour and Glory*)

LASKI, Marghanita
  LITTLE BOY LOST   PAR 1953
  (Cresset Press)

LATHAM, Aaron
  URBAN COWBOY   CIC 1980
  (Bantam, N.Y.)

LATIMER, Jonathan
  DEAD DON'T CARE, THE   UN 1939
  (Methuen)   (*Last Warning, The*)
  HEADED FOR A HEARSE   UN 1937
  (Methuen)   (*Westland Case, The*)
  LADY IN THE MORGUE   UN 1938
  (Methuen)

LAUMER, Keith
  DEADFALL   FOX—RANK 1975
  (Hale)   (*Peeper*)

LAUNDER, Frank *and* **GILLIAT, Sidney**
  MEET A BODY (P)   BL 1956
  (French)   (*Green Man, The*)

LAURENCE, Margaret
  JEST OF GOD, A   WAR 1968
  (Macmillan)   (*Rachel, Rachel*)

LAURENTS, Arthur
  HOME OF THE BRAVE (P)   UA 1949
  (Dramatists, N.Y.)
  TIME OF THE CUCKOO, THE (P)   UA 1955
  (Random House, N.Y.)   (*Summer Madness*)
  WAY WE WERE, THE   COL 1972
  (W.H. Allen)

LAUREY, Joy
  JOY   UGC 1984
  (W.H. Allen)

LAURITZEN, Jonreed
  ROSE AND THE FLAME, THE   GFD 1955
  (Hurst & Blackett)   (*Kiss of Fire*)

LAVALLEE, David
  EVENT 1000   CIC 1977
  (Coronet)

LAVERY, Emmet Godfrey
  FIRST LEGION, THE (P)   UA 1951
  (French, N.Y.)

LAVIN, Nora *and* **THORP, Molly**
  HOP DOG, THE   ABP 1954
  (Oxford U.P.)   (*Adventure in the Hopfields*)

LAWES, Lewis Edward
  20,000 YEARS IN SING SING   IN 1933
  (Garden City Press, N.Y.)

LAWLER, Ray
  SUMMER OF THE SEVENTEENTH
  DOLL, THE (P)   UA 1959
  (Collins)

LAWRENCE, David Herbert
  CAPTAIN'S DOLL, THE   BBC 1982 (TV)
  (*In* The Tales of D.H. Lawrence: Secker)
  FOX, THE   WAR 1968
  (*In* Tales of D.H. Lawrence, The:
  Heinemann)
  KANGAROO   WORLD FILM ALLIANCE 1985
  (Heinemann)

LAWRENCE, David Herbert (*Continued*)
  LADY CHATTERLEY'S LOVER   COL 1956
  (Heinemann)   FOX 1981
  ROCKING HORSE WINNER, THE   TC 1949
  (*In* Complete Tales: Heinemann)
  SONS AND LOVERS   FOX 1960
  (Heinemann)
  TRESPASSER, THE   COLIN GREGG 1981
  (Heinemann)
  VIRGIN AND THE GYPSY, THE   LONDON SCREENPLAYS 1971
  (Heinemann)
  WOMEN IN LOVE   UA 1969
  (Heinemann)

LAWRENCE, David Herbert *and* **SKINNER, M.L.**
  BOY IN THE BUSH, THE   CHANNEL 4 1984 (TV)
  (Heinemann)

LAWRENCE, H.L.
  CHILDREN OF LIGHT   BL 1963
  (Macdonald)   (*The Damned, The*)

LAWRENCE, Jerome *and* **LEE, Robert, E.**
  AUNTIE MAME (P)   WAR 1958
  (Vanguard, N.Y.)
  INHERIT THE WIND (P)   UA 1960
  (Random House, N.Y.)

LAWRENCE, Josephine
  YEARS ARE SO LONG, THE   PAR 1937
  (Harrap)   (*Make Way For Tomorrow*)

LAWRENCE, Margery
  MADONNA OF THE SEVEN MOONS   GFD 1945
  (Hurst & Blackett)

LAWRENCE, Thomas Edward
  SEVEN PILLARS OF WISDOM   BL 1962
  (Cape)   (*Lawrence of Arabia*)

LAWSON, Ted
  THIRTY SECONDS OVER TOKIO   MGM 1944
  (Hammond)

LAWTON, Harry
  WILLIE BOY   RANK 1969
  (Paisano Press, Calif.)   (*Tell Them Willie Boy is Here*)

LAY, Beirne *and* **BARTLETT, Sy**
  TWELVE O'CLOCK HIGH   FOX 1949
  (Harper, N.Y.)

LEA, Fanny Heaslip
  FOUR MARYS   MGM 1938
  (Nicholson & Watson)   (*Man-proof*)

LEA, Thomas
  BRAVE BULLS, THE   COL 1950
  (Heinemann)
  WONDERFUL COUNTRY, THE   UA 1959
  (Heinemann)

LEA, Timothy
  CONFESSIONS FROM A HOLIDAY
  CAMP   COL—WAR 1977
  (Sphere)
  CONFESSIONS FROM THE POP
  SCENE   COL—WAR 1975
  (Futura)   (*Confessions of a Pop Performer*)
  CONFESSIONS OF A DRIVING
  INSTRUCTOR   COL—WAR 1976
  (Sphere)
  CONFESSIONS OF A WINDOW
  CLEANER   COL—WAR 1974
  (Futura)

LEAR, Robert
  GOLDEN GIRL   AVCO EMBASSY 1980
  (Cassell)

LEASOR, James
  BOARDING PARTY   RANK 1980
  (Bantam)   (*Sea Wolves, The*)
  PASSPORT TO OBLIVION   MGM 1965
  (Heinemann)   (*Where the Spies Are*)

LEBLANC, Maurice
  ARSENE LUPIN   MGM 1932
  (Newnes)

LE CARRÉ, John
    CALL FOR THE DEAD   BL 1966
    (Gollancz)   (*Deadly Affair, The*)
    LITTLE DRUMMER GIRL, THE   WAR 1984
    (Hodder & Stoughton)
    LOOKING GLASS WAR, THE   COL 1969
    (Gollancz)
    SMILEY'S PEOPLE   BBC 1982 (TV)
    (Hodder & Stoughton)
    SPY WHO CAME IN FROM THE
    COLD, THE   PAR 1963
    (Gollancz)

LEDERER, William Julius *and* **BURDICK, Eugene L.**
    UGLY AMERICAN, THE   UI 1962
    (Gollancz)

LEE, Benjamin
    PAGANINI STRIKES AGAIN   CFF 1973
    (Hutchinson)

LEE, Chin Yang
    FLOWER DRUM SONG   UI 1961
    (Gollancz)

LEE, Edna
    QUEEN BEE   COL 1955
    (Hurst & Blackett)

LEE, Gypsy Rose
    GYPSY   WAR 1962
    (Pan)
    STRIP-TEASE MURDERS   UA 1943
    (Lane)

LEE, Harper
    TO KILL A MOCKING BIRD   UI 1962
    (Penguin)

LEE, James
    CAREER (P)   PAR 1959
    (Random House, N.Y.)

LEE, Manfred *see* **QUEEN, Ellery,** *pseud.*

LEE, R.E. *see* **LAWRENCE, J.** *jt. author*

LE FANU, Sheridan
UNCLE SILAS   TC 1947
(Oxford U.P.)

LEGER, Jack A.
MONSIGNOR   FOX 1983
(Dell, N.Y.)   (*Monsignore*)

LEHMANN, Rosamund
WEATHER IN THE STREETS, THE   BBC 2 1984 (TV)
(Doubleday, N.Y.)

LEIGH, James
WHAT CAN YOU DO?   FOX 1971
(Panther)   (*Making It*)

LEIGHTON, Lee
LAW MAN   UN 1956
(Worlds Work)   (*Star in the Dust*)

LEINSTER, Murray
WAILING ASTEROID, THE   AVCO EMBASSY 1967
(Sphere)   (*Terronauts, The*)

LELY, Gilbert
DE SADE   MGM—EMI 1969
(Elek)

LeMAY, Alan
SEARCHERS, THE   WAR 1956
(Collins)
SIEGE AT DANCING BIRD, THE   UA 1960
(Collins)   (*Unforgiven, The*)
USELESS COWBOY, THE   RKO 1945
(Collins)   (*Along Came Jones*)

LENZ, S.
DAS FELUERSCHIFF   RANK 1985
(Various)   (*Lightship, The*)

LEONARD, Elmore
BIG BOUNCE   WAR 1968
(Hale)

LEONARD, Elmore (*Continued*)
CAT CHASER   EMI 1984
(Arbor, N.Y.)
52 PICK UP   CANNON 1986
(Avon, N.Y.)   (*Ambassador, The*)
HOMBRE   FOX 1966
(Hale)
LA BRAVA   CANNON 1986
(Avon, N.Y.)
MOONSHINE WAR, THE   MGM 1970
(Hale)
STICK   CIC 1985
(Lane)
VALDEZ IS COMING   UA 1971
(Hale)

LERNER, Alan Jay
BRIGADOON (P)   MGM 1954
(Theatre Arts)
MY FAIR LADY (P)   WAR 1964
(Constable)

LEROUX, Gaston
PHANTOM OF THE OPERA, THE   UN 1943
(Various)   UI 1962

LESLIE, David Stuart
IN MY SOLITUDE   BL 1965
(Hutchinson)   (*Two Left Feet*)
TWO GENTLEMEN SHARING   PAR 1969
(Pan)

LESLIE, Doris
POLONAISE   COL 1945
(Hutchinson)   (*Song to Remember, A*)

LESLIE, Robert F.
BEARS AND I, THE   DISNEY 1974
(Ballantine, N.Y.)

LESSING, Doris
GRASS IS SINGING, THE   MAINLINE 1981
(Heinemann)
MEMOIRS OF A SURVIVOR   EMI 1981
(Picador)

LEVEN, Jeremy
  CREATOR   PSO 1985
  (Penguin)

LEVI, Carlo
  CHRIST STOPPED AT EBOLI   ARTIFICIAL EYE 1982
  (Gollancz)

LEVIN, Ira
  BOYS FROM BRAZIL, THE   ITC 1978
  (Joseph)
  CRITIC'S CHOICE (P)   WAR 1962
  (Random House, N.Y.)
  DEATH TRAP (P)   COL—EMI—WAR 1982
  (French)
  KISS BEFORE DYING, A   UA 1956
  (Joseph)
  ROSEMARY'S BABY   PAR 1968
  (Joseph)
  STEPFORD WIVES, THE   CONTEMPORARY 1978
  (Random House, N.Y.)

LEVIN, Ira *and* **HYMAN, Mac**
  NO TIME FOR SERGEANTS (P)   FOX 1959
  (Random House, N.Y.)

LEVIN, Meyer
  COMPULSION   WAR 1958
  (Muller)

LEWIS, Arthur H.
  LAMENT FOR MOLLY MAGUIRES   PAR 1969
  (Longmans)   (*Molly Maguires, The*)

LEWIS, Edin
  RELATIVES ARE BEST APART (P)   ADELPHI 1954
  (Playscripts)   (*What Every Woman Wants*)

LEWIS, Hilda
  DAY IS OURS, THE   GFD 1952
  (Macdonald)   (*Mandy*)

LEWIS, Oscar
  CHILDREN OF SANCHEZ, THE   HALL BARRETT 1978
  (Random House, N.Y.)

LEWIS, Sinclair
ANN VICKERS   RKO 1933
(Cape)
BABBITT   IN 1934
(Cape)
CASS TIMBERLANE   MGM 1947
(Cape)
DODSWORTH   UA 1936
(Cape)
ELMER GANTRY   UA 1959
(Cape)
MAIN STREET   IN 1936
(Cape)   (*I Married a Doctor*)
MANTRAP   PAR 1940
(Cape)   (*Untamed*)
MARTIN ARROWSMITH   UA 1931
(Cape)   (*Arrowsmith*)

LEWIS, Stephen
SPARRERS CAN'T SING (P)   MGM 1962
(Evans)   (*Sparrows Can't Sing*)

LEWIS, Ted
JACK'S RETURN HOME   MGM 1972
(Joseph)   (*Get Carter*)

LEY, Willy *see* **BONESTELL, C.** *jt. author*

LIEBERSON, Goddard
3 FOR BEDROOM C   UI 1952
(Doubleday, N.Y.)

LIERS, Ernst
OTTER'S STORY   DISNEY 1969
(Hodder & Stoughton)   (*Flash the Otter*)

LIGGETT, Thomas
PIGEON FLY HOME   DISNEY 1958
(Holiday, N.Y.)   (*Pigeon that Worked a Miracle*)

LIGNERIS, Françoise de
PSYCHE 63   BL 1964
(Spearman)   (*Psyche 59*)

LINDBERGH, Charles Augustus
WE   WAR 1956
(Putnam, N.Y.)   (*Spirit of St. Louis, The*)

LINDFORD, Dee
MAN WITHOUT A STAR   UI 1955
(Morrow, N.Y.)

LINDNER, Robert
FIFTYMINUTE HOUR, THE   UA 1963
(Corgi)   (*Pressure Point*)

LINDOP, Audrey Erskine
I START COUNTING   UA 1970
(Collins)
I THANK A FOOL   MGM 1962
(Collins)
SINGER NOT THE SONG, THE   RANK 1960
(Heinemann)
TALL HEADLINES, THE   GN 1951
(Heinemann)

LINDSAY, Hal *and* **CARLSON, C.**
LATE GREAT PLANET EARTH, THE
(Zonderman, Chicago)   ENTERPRISE 1978

LINDSAY, Howard *and* **CROUSE, Russell**
LIFE WITH FATHER (P)   PAR 1946
(French)
REMAINS TO BE SEEN (P)   MGM 1953
(Dramatists, N.Y.)
STATE OF THE UNION (P)   MGM 1948
(Dramatists, N.Y.)   (*World and his Wife, The*)
TALL STORY (P)   WAR 1960
(Random House, N.Y.)

LINDSAY, Howard *see also* **RUNYON, D.** *jt. author*

LINDSAY, Norman
AGE OF CONSENT   COL 1968
(Laurie)

LINDSAY, Philip
IRON DUKE, THE   GB 1935
(Queensway Press)

519

LINDSEY, Robert
  FALCON AND THE SNOWMAN   RANK 1984
  (Penguin)

LINDQUIST, Donald
  BERLIN TUNNEL   BBC 1984 (TV)
  (Methuen)

LININGTON, Elizabeth *see* **BLAISDELL, Anne** *pseud.*

LINKLATER, Eric
  POET'S PUB   AQUILA 1949
  (Cape)
  LAXDALE HALL   ABP 1953
  (Cape)
  PRIVATE ANGELO   ABP 1949
  (Cape)

LIPPINCOTT, Joseph Wharton
  WAHOO BOBCAT, THE   DISNEY 1963
  (Lippincott, Philadelphia)

LIPSCOMB, William Percy *and* **MINNEY, R.J.**
  CLIVE OF INDIA (P)   UA 1935
  (Gollancz)

LIPSKY, Eleazar
  PEOPLE AGAINST O'HARA, THE   MGM 1951
  (Wingate)

LITTELL, Robert
  AMATEUR, THE   FOX 1981
  (Simon & Schuster, N.Y.)

LIVINGS, Henry
  WORK IS A FOUR LETTER WORD   UI 1968
  (P)
  (Methuen)

LLEWELLYN, Richard
  HOW GREEN WAS MY VALLEY   FOX 1941
  (Joseph)
  NONE BUT THE LONELY HEART   RKO 1944
  (Joseph)
  POISON PEN (P)   AB 1940
  (French)

LOCKE, C.O.
ROAD TO SOCORRO, THE   FOX 1958
(Hutchinson)   (*Manhunt*)

LOCKE, William John
BELOVED VAGABOND, THE   COL 1937
(Lane)
MORALS OF MARCUS ORDEYNE   GB 1935
(Lane)   (*Morals of Marcus, The*)
MOUNTEBANK   WAR 1931
(Lane)   (*Sideshow of Life*)
SHORN LAMB, THE   PAR 1932
(Lane)   (*Strangers in Love*)

LOCKHART, *Sir* Robert Hamilton Bruce
MEMOIRS OF A BRITISH AGENT   IN 1934
(Putnam)   (*British Agent*)

LOCKHART, Robin B.
REILLY—ACE OF SPIES   EUSTON 1983 (TV)
(Futura)

LOCKRIDGE, Ross
RAINTREE COUNTY   MGM 1957
(Macdonald)

LOCKWOOD, Charles Andrew *and* ADAMSON, Hans Christian
HELLCATS OF THE SEA   COL 1957
(Greenberg, N.Y.)   (*Hellcats of the Navy*)

LOFTING, Hugh
DR. DOLITTLE   FOX 1966
(Cape)

LOFTS, Norah
JASSY   GFD 1947
(Joseph)

LOGAN, J. *see* **BEHRMAN, S.N.** *jt. author and* **HEGGEN, T.** *jt. author*

LOMAX, Bliss
LEATHER BURNERS, THE   UA 1943
(Muller)

LONDON, Artur
  ON TRIAL   WAR 1970
  (Macdonald)   (*L'Aveu*)

LONDON, Jack
  CALL OF THE WILD   UA 1935
  (Heinemann)   MGM—EMI 1972
  MARTIN EDEN   COL 1942
  (Heinemann)   (*Adventures of Martin Eden*)
  MEXICAN, THE   UA 1952
  (*In* Nightborn and Other Stories: (*Fighter, The*)
  Appleton, N.Y.)
  SEA WOLF, THE   FOX 1930
  (Heinemann)   WAR 1941
             ABP 1959
             (*Wolf Larsen*)
  WHITE FANG   FOX 1936
  (Methuen)   FOX 1974

LONDON, Jack *and* **FISH, Robert**
  ASSASSINATION BUREAU, THE   PAR 1969
  (Deutsch)

LONG, Gabrielle Margaret Vere *see* **PREEDY, George** *pseud.* **SHEARING, Joseph** *pseud.*

LONG, Sumner Arthur
  NEVER TOO LATE (P)   WAR 1965
  (French, N.Y.)

LONGFELLOW, Henry Wadsworth
  HIAWATHA (Poem)   ABP 1952
  (Various)   CHANNEL 4 1984 (TV)

LONGSTREET, Stephen
  STALLION ROAD   WAR 1947
  (Jarrolds)
  WILD HARVEST   GN 1961
  (Muller)

LONSDALE, Frederick
  AREN'T WE ALL (P)   PAR 1932
  (Heinemann)
  HIGH ROAD, THE (P)   MGM 1930
  (Collins)   (*Lady of Scandal, The*)

LAST OF MRS. CHEYNEY, THE (P)   MGM 1937
(Collins)   MGM 1951
    (*Law and the Lady, The*)
ON APPROVAL (P)   FOX 1944
(Collins)
SPRING CLEANING (P)   GB 1932
(Collins)   (*Women who Play*)

LOOS, Anita
BUT GENTLEMEN MARRY
BRUNETTES   UA 1955
(Brentano, N.Y.)   (*Gentlemen marry Brunettes*)
GENTLEMEN PREFER BLONDES   FOX 1953
(Cape)

LORAINE, Philip
BREAK IN THE CIRCLE   EXCLUSIVE 1954
(Hodder & Stoughton)
DAY OF THE ARROW   MGM 1968
(Collins)   (*Eye of the Devil*)
DUBLIN NIGHTMARE   RANK 1957
(Hodder & Stoughton)   (*Nightmare in Dublin*)

LORD, Walter
NIGHT TO REMEMBER, A   RANK 1957
(Longmans)

LORTZ, Richard
CHILDREN OF THE NIGHT (P)   HEMDALE 1973
(Dell, N.Y.)   (*Voices*)

LOTHAR, Ernst
ANGEL WITH THE TRUMPET   BL 1950
(Harrap)
CLAIRVOYANT, THE   GB 1935
(Secker)
MILLS OF GOD, THE   UN 1948
(Secker)   (*Act of Murder, An*)

LOTT, Milton
LAST HUNT, THE   MGM 1955
(Houghton, Mifflin, Boston)

LOVECRAFT, H.P.
CASE OF CHARLES DEXTER, THE   AMERICAN INT 1963
(Panther)   (*Haunted Palace, The*)

LOVECRAFT, H.P. (*Continued*)
  COLOR OUT OF SPACE   AMERICAN INT 1965
  (*In* Best Supernatural Stories: World   (*Monster of Terror*)
  Pubs., N.Y.)
  FROM BEYOND   EMPIRE 1986
  (Various)
  RE-ANIMATOR   EMPIRE 1985
  (Various)   (*Herbert West—The Re-animator*)
  SHUTTERED ROOM, THE   AMERICAN INT 1969
  (Gollancz)   (*Dunwich Horror*)

LOWNDES, *Mrs.* **Marie Belloe**
  LETTY LYNTON   MGM 1932
  (Benn)
  LODGER, THE   FOX 1944
  (Benn)   FOX 1953
       (*Man in the Attic, The*)
  STORY OF IVY, THE   UI 1947
  (Eyre & Spottiswoode)   (*Ivy*)

LOWRY, Malcolm
  UNDER THE VOLCANO   FOX 1984
  (Harper, N.Y.)

LUDLUM, Robert
  GEMINI CONTENDERS, THE   ICT 1978
  (Dell, N.Y.)
  HOLCROFT COVENANT, THE   COL—EMI—WAR 1985
  (Hart-Davis)   (*Holcroft Convention, The*)
  OSTERMAN WEEKEND, THE   UN 1980
  (Dell, N.Y.)

LUSTGARTEN, Edgar
  GAME FOR THREE LOSERS   WAR 1965
  (Museum Press)

LYALL, Gavin
  SECRET SERVANT, THE   BBC 1985 (TV)
  (Viking, N.Y.)

LYMINGTON, John
  NIGHT OF THE BIG HEAT   PLANET 1967
  (Hodder & Stoughton)

MacARTHUR, C. *see* **HECHT, B.** *jt. author*

McBAIN, Ed.
  BLOOD RELATIVES   RANK 1978
  (Hamilton)
  FUZZ   UA 1972
  (Hamilton)
  TEN PLUS ONE   FOX 1972
  (Simon & Schuster, N.Y.)   (*Without Apparent Motive*)

McCALL, Mary
  GOLD FISH BOWL, THE   IN 1932
  (Paul)   (*It's Tough to be Famous*)

MACARDLE, Donald
  UNEASY FREEHOLD   PAR 1944
  (Doubleday, N.Y.)   (*Uninvited, The*)

McCARRY, Charles
  BETTER ANGELS, THE   COL—EMI—WAR 1982
  (Arrow, N.Y.)   (*Man with the Deadly Lens*)

McCARTHY, Justin Huntly
  IF I WERE KING   PAR 1938
  (Heinemann)
  VAGABOND KING, THE (P) PAR 1930
  (French)   PAR 1956

McCARTHY, Mary
  GROUP, THE   UA 1965
  (Weidenfeld & Nicolson)

McCAULEY, Sue
  OTHER HALVES   CONT 1986
  (Hodder & Stoughton)

McCOY, Horace
  KISS TOMORROW GOODBYE WAR 1950
  (Barker)
  THEY SHOOT HORSES DON'T CINERAMA 1969
  THEY?
  (Methuen)

McCRACKEN, Esther
  NO MEDALS (P)   TC 1948
  (French)   (*Weaker Sex, The*)

QUIET WEDDING (P)   PAR 1941
(French)
QUIET WEEK-END (P)   AB 1946
(French)

MacCRACKEN, Mary
CIRCLE OF CHILDREN, A   FOX 1977
(Sphere)

McCULLERS, *Mrs.* **Carson**
HEART IS A LONELY HUNTER, THE   WAR 1968
(Penguin)
MEMBER OF THE WEDDING, THE   COL 1952
(Cresset Press)
REFLECTIONS IN A GOLDEN EYE   WAR 1966
(Cresset Press)

McCULLEY, Johnston
MARK OF ZORRO, THE   FOX 1940
(Grosset, N.Y.)   UI 1951
      (Mark of the Renegade)
TRUSTED OUTLAW, THE   REP 1937
(Hutchinson)

McCULLOUGH, Colleen
INDECENT OBSESSION, AN   PBL (Australia) 1985
(Macdonald)
THORN BIRDS, THE   PISCES 1979
(Harper, N.Y.)   BBC 1983 (TV)

McCUTCHEON, George Barr
BREWSTER'S MILLIONS   UA 1945
(Various)   UA 1961
      (Three on a Spree)
      CUIP 1985

McCUTCHEON, Hugh
TO DUSTY DEATH   BUTCHER 1961
(Long)   *(Pit of Darkness)*

McDONALD, Anne *see* **CROSSLEY, Rosemary** *jt. author*

MACDONALD, Betty
EGG AND I, THE   UN 1947
(Hammond)

MACDONALD, Gregory
  FLETCH   UIP 1985
  (Gollancz)
  RUNNING SCARED   CINEMA INT 1973
  (Astor-Honor, N.Y.)

MACDONALD, John D.
  DARKER THAN AMBER   FOX 1970
  (Hale)
  EXECUTIONERS, THE   UI 1962
  (Hale)   (*Cape Fear*)
  RESTLESS   PAR 1961
  (Pan)   (*Man Trap*)

MACDONALD, Philip
  LIST OF ADRIAN MESSENGER UI 1963
  (Penguin)
  PATROL   RKO 1934
  (Collins)   (*Lost Patrol*)

MACDONALD, Roger
  1915   BBC 2 1985 (TV)
  (Faber)

MACDONALD, Ross
  DROWNING POOL, THE   COL—WAR 1975
  (Fontana)
  MOVING TARGET, THE   WAR 1967
  (Pan)   (*Harper*)

MACDONALD, William Colt
  POWDERSMOKE RANGE   RKO 1935
  (Collins)
  ROARIN' LEAD   REP 1937
  (Collins)

MACDOUGALL, Roger
  ESCAPADE (P)   EROS 1955
  (Heinemann)
  GENTLE GUNMAN, THE (P)   GFD 1952
  (*In* Plays of the Year 1950–51: Elek)
  TO DOROTHY, A SON (P)   BL 1954
  (Evans)

MACDOUGALL, Roger *and* **ALLAN, Edward**
  DOUBLE IMAGE (P)   FOX 1959
  (French)

McENROE, Robert G.
  SILVER WHISTLE, THE (P)   FOX 1951
  (Theatre Arts)   (*Mr. Belvedere Rings the Bell*)

McEVOY, Charles
  LIKES OF 'ER, THE (P)   ABP 1932
  (*In* Great Modern British Plays: Harrap)   (*Sally in our Alley*)

McGILL, Angus
  YEA, YEA, YEA   RANK 1966
  (Secker & Warburg)   (*Press for Time*)

McGIVERN, William P.
  BIG HEAT, THE   COL 1953
  (Hamilton)
  DARKEST HOUR   WAR 1955
  (Collins)   (*Hell on Frisco Bay*)
  ODDS AGAINST TOMORROW   UA 1959
  (Collins)
  ROGUE COP   MGM 1954
  (Collins)
  SHIELD FOR MURDER   UA 1954
  (Dodd, N.Y.)

McGOVERN, James
  FRAULEIN   FOX 1957
  (Calder)

McGOWAN, John *see* **BOLTON, G.** *jt. author*

McGRATH, John
  EVENTS WHILST GUARDING THE
  BOFORS GUN (P)   UI 1968
  (Methuen)   (*Bofors Gun, The*)

McGUANE, Thomas
  92 IN THE SHADE   ITC 1975
  (Farrar, N.Y.)
  SPORTING CLUB, THE   AVCO EMBASSY 1968
  (Deutsch)

McILVAINE, Jane
  IT HAPPENS EVERY THURSDAY   GFD 1953
  (McRae-Smith)

MacILWRAITH, William
  ANNIVERSARY, THE (P)   WAR 1968
  (Evans)

MACINNES, Colin
  ABSOLUTE BEGINNERS   VIRGIN 1985
  (Allison & Busby)

MacINNES, Helen
  ABOVE SUSPICION   MGM 1943
  (Harrap)
  ASSIGNMENT IN BRITTANY   MGM 1943
  (Harrap)
  SALZBURG CONNECTION, THE   FOX 1972
  (Collins)
  VENETIAN AFFAIR, THE   MGM 1966
  (Collins)

MACKEN, Walter
  FLIGHT OF THE DOVES   COL 1971
  (Macmillan)
  HOME IS THE HERO (P)   BL 1959
  (Macmillan)

McKENNA, Marthe
  I WAS A SPY   FOX 1934
  (Jarrolds)

McKENNA, Richard
  SAND PEBBLES, THE   FOX 1966
  (Gollancz)

McKENNEY, Ruth
  MY SISTER EILEEN   COL 1942
  (Chatto & Windus)   COL 1955

MACKENZIE, *Sir* **Compton**
  CARNIVAL   BI 1931
  (Various)   (*Dance Pretty Lady*)
              COL 1935
              TC 1946

ROCKETS GALORE   RANK 1958
(Chatto & Windus)
SYLVIA SCARLETT   RKO 1935
(Various)
WHISKY GALORE   EALING 1949
(Chatto & Windus)

MACKENZIE, Donald
MOMENT OF DANGER   ABP 1959
(Pan)
NOWHERE TO GO   MGM 1958
(Elek)

MACKINTOSH, Elizabeth *see* **TEY, Josephine** *pseud.*

MACLAVERTY, Bernard
CAL   WAR 1984
(Cape)
LAMB   CANNON 1986
(Cape)

MACLEAN, Alistair
BEAR ISLAND   COL—EMI—WAR 1979
(Collins)
BREAKHEART PASS   UA 1975
(Collins)   (*Heartbreak Pass*)
CARAVAN TO VACCARES   RANK 1974
(Collins)
FEAR IS THE KEY   MGM—EMI 1972
(Collins)
FORCE 10 FROM NAVARONE   COL—WAR 1978
(Collins)
GOLDEN GATE, THE   ITC 1978
(Collins)
GOLDEN RENDEZVOUS   RANK 1977
(Collins)
GUNS OF NAVARONE, THE   COL 1959
(Collins)
ICE STATION ZEBRA   MGM 1968
(Collins)
LAST FRONTIER   RANK 1960
(Collins)   (*Secret Ways, The*)
PUPPET ON A CHAIN   SCOTIA-BARBER 1971
(Collins)

MACLEAN, Alistair (*Continued*)
RIVER OF DEATH   CANNON 1986
(Doubleday, N.Y.)
SOUTH BY JAVA HEAD   FOX 1959
(Collins)
WHEN EIGHT BELLS TOLL   RANK 1971
(Collins)
WHERE EAGLES DARE   MGM 1969
(Collins)

McLELLAN, C.M.S.
BELLE OF NEW YORK, THE (P)   MGM 1952
(French)

MacLEOD, Robert
APPALOOSA, THE   UI 1966
(Muller)   (*Southwest to Sonora*)
CALIFORNIO, THE   FOX 1969
(Coronet) *also published under film title*: (*100 Rifles*)
Gold Lion Books

McMURTRY, Larry
HORSEMAN, PASS BY   PAR 1963
(Hamilton)   (*Hud*)
LAST PICTURE SHOW, THE   COL 1972
(Sphere)
LEAVING CHEYENNE   GALA 1975
(Popular Library, N.Y.)   (*Lovin' Molly*)

McNALLY, Terrence
RITZ, THE (P)   COL—WAR 1976
(Dodd, N.Y.)

McNEILE, Herman Cyril *see* **'SAPPER'** *pseud.*

McNEILL, Elizabeth
9½ WEEKS   PALACE 1986
(Sphere)

McNEILL, Janet
CHILD IN THE HOUSE   EROS 1956
(Hodder & Stoughton)

McNULTY, John Lawrence
3RD AVENUE, NEW YORK   PAR 1947
(Little, Brown, Boston)   (*Easy Come, Easy Go*)

McPARTLAND, John
KINGDOM OF JOHNNY COOL, THE   UA 1964
(Muller)   (*Johnny Cool*)
NO DOWN PAYMENT   FOX 1957
(Macdonald)

MACREA, Arthur
TRAVELLER'S JOY (P)   GFD 1951
(French)

McCRUM, Robert
IN THE SECRET STATE   BBC 2 1985 (TV)
(Hamilton)

McSHANE, Mark
PASSING OF EVIL, THE   NATIONAL GENERAL
(Cassell)   LECTURES 1969
       (*Grasshopper, The*)
SEANCE ON A WET AFTERNOON   RANK 1964
(Cassell)

McSWIGAN, Marie
ALL ABOARD FOR FREEDOM   TIGON 1968
(Dent)   (*Snow Treasure*)

McVEIGH, Sue
GRAND CENTRAL MURDER   MGM 1942
(Houghton, Mifflin, Boston)

McVICAR, John
McVICAR HIMSELF   BRENT WALKER 1980
(Hutchinson)

MACAULAY, David
CATHEDRAL   UNICORN 1984
(Collins)

MADDUX, Rachel
WALK IN THE SPRING RAIN, A   COL 1969
(Doubleday, N.Y.)

MAETERLINCK, Maurice
BLUE BIRD, THE (P)   FOX 1940
(Various)   FOX 1976

MAHER, Marty *and* **CAMPION, Nardi Reeder**
BRINGING UP THE BRASS   COL 1954
(McKay, N.Y.)   (*Long Gray Line*)

MAIER, William
PLEASURE ISLAND   PAR 1953
(Wingate)   (*Girls of Pleasure Island*)

MAILER, Norman
AMERICAN DREAM, AN   WAR 1966
(Deutsch)   (*See You in Hell, Darling*)
EXECUTIONER'S SONG, THE   GOLDFARB 1982
(Arrow, N.Y.)
MARILYN: THE UNTOLD STORY   RANK 1980
(Warner, N.Y.)
NAKED AND THE DEAD, THE   WAR 1958
(Wingate)
TOUGH GUYS DON'T DANCE   CANNON 1986
(Random, N.Y.)

MAINE, Charles Eric
MIND OF MR. SOAMES, THE   COL 1969
(Panther)

MAINWARING, Daniel *see* **HOMES, Geoffrey** *pseud.*

MAJOR, Charles
WHEN KNIGHTHOOD WAS IN
FLOWER   RKO 1953
(Grayson)   (*Sword and the Rose, The*)

MALAMUD, Bernard
ANGEL LEVINE   UA 1970
(*In* Magic Barrel, The: Eyre &
Spottiswoode)
FIXER, THE   MGM 1969
(Eyre & Spottiswoode)
NATURAL, THE   COL—EMI—WAR 1984
(Chatto & Windus)

MALLESON, Lucy Beatrice *see* **GILBERT, A.** *pseud.*

AUTHOR AND ORIGINAL TITLE	FILM TITLE

MALLORY, Jay
SWEET ALOES
(Cassell)

WAR 1936
(*Give Me Your Heart*)

MALORY, *Sir* Thomas
LE MORTE D'ARTHUR
(Various)

MGM 1954
(*Knights of the Round Table, The*)
COL—EMI—WAR 1981
(*Excalibur*)

NAMET, David
SEXUAL PERVERSITY IN CHICAGO
(Grove, N.Y.)

TRI-STAR 1986
(*About Last Night*)

MANDIARGUES, Andre Pieye de
GIRL ON THE MOTOR CYCLE, THE
(Calder)

BL 1965

MANHOFF, Bill
OWL AND THE PUSSYCAT, THE (P)
(French)

COL 1970

MANKIEWICZ, Donald
TRIAL
(Deutsch)

MGM 1955

MANKOWITZ, Wolf
KID FOR TWO FARTHINGS, A
(Deutsch)
MAKE ME AN OFFER
(Deutsch)

INDEPENDENT 1954

BL 1954

MANN, Edward Beverly
STAMPEDE
(Triangle Bks., N.Y.)

ABP 1950

MANN, Heinrich
BLUE ANGEL
(Jarrolds)

PAR 1930
FOX 1959

MANN, Thomas
DEATH IN VENICE
(Penguin)
DOKTOR FAUSTUS
(Secker & Warburg)

WAR 1971

SAFIR 1983

MANN, Thomas (*Continued*)
  FELIX KRULL: CONFIDENCE MAN   SAFIR 1983
  (Secker & Warburg)   (*Confessions of Felix Krull*)
  MAGIC MOUNTAIN, THE   SAFIR 1983
  (Secker & Warburg)

MANNIX, Daniel
  FOX AND THE HOUND   DISNEY 1981
  (Various)

MANTLEY, John
  SNOW BIRCH, THE   FOX 1959
  (Joseph)   (*Woman Obsessed, The*)
  27TH DAY   COL 1957
  (Joseph)

MARASCO, Robert
  BURNT OFFERINGS   UA 1976
  (Coronet)
  CHILD'S PLAY (P)   PAR 1972
  (Random House, N.Y.)

MARCH, William
  BAD SEED, THE   WAR 1956
  (Hamilton)

MARCUS, Frank
  KILLING OF SISTER GEORGE, THE
  (P)   CINERAMA 1968
  (French)

MARKS, Leo
  GIRL WHO COULDN'T QUITE, THE
  (P)   MONARCH 1949
  (French)

MARKSON, David
  BALLAD OF DINGUS MAGEE, THE   MGM 1970
  (Blond)   (*Dirty Dingus Magee*)

MARLOWE, Christopher
  DR. FAUSTUS (P)   BL 1966
  (Various)   COL 1968
    (*Tragical History of . . .*)

MARLOWE, Derek
DANDY IN ASPIC, A   COL 1968
(Gollancz)
ECHOES OF CELANDINE   CINEGATE 1977
(Penguin)   (*Disappearance, The*)

MARLOWE, Hugh
CANDLE FOR THE DEAD, A   MONARCH 1969
(Abelard-Schuman)   (*Violent Enemy, The*)

MARQUAND, John Phillips
H.M. PULHAM, ESQ.   MGM 1941
(Hale)
LATE GEORGE APLEY, THE   FOX 1947
(Hale)
MELVILLE GOODWIN, USA   WAR 1956
(Hale)   (*Their Secret Affair*)
POLLY FULTON   MGM 1949
(Hale) *Title in U.S.A.* B.F.'s Daughter
STOPOVER TOKYO   FOX 1957
(Collins)
THANK YOU, MR. MOTO   FOX 1937
(Jenkins)

MARRIC, J.J. *pseud.*
GIDEON'S DAY   COL 1958
(Hodder & Stoughton)

MARRIOTT, Anthony
NO SEX PLEASE—WE'RE BRITISH   COL—WAR 1974
(P)
(French)

MARRYAT, Frederick
MR. MIDSHIPMAN EASY   ATP 1935
(Various)   (*Midshipman Easy*)

MARSH, Ronald
IRENE   ARGYLE 1950
(Chatto & Windus)

MARSHALL, Bruce
RED DANUBE   MGM 1949
(Constable)

MARSHALL, Catherine
STORY OF PETER MARSHALL THE   FOX 1954
(Davies)   (*Man Called Peter, A*)

MARSHALL, Edison
JEWEL OF MAHABAR   FOX 1953
(Hodder & Stoughton)   (*Treasure of the Golden Condor*)
VIKING, THE   UA 1958
(Muller)   (*Vikings, The*)
YANKEE PASHA   GFD 1954
(Redman)

MARSHALL, James Leslie
SANTA FE   COL 1951
(Random House, N.Y.)

MARSHALL, James Vance
RIVER RAN OUT OF EDEN, A   NEW REALM 1984
(Heinemann)   (*Golden Seal, The*)
WALKABOUT   FOX 1971
(Joseph) *Originally titled*: The Children

MARSHALL, Peter
RAGING MOON, THE   MGM 1971
(Tandem)

MARSHALL, *Mrs.* Rosamund
BRIXBY GIRLS, THE   MGM 1960
(Redman)   (*All the Fine Young Cannibals*)
KITTY   ABP 1953
(Collins)

MARSHALL, Samuel Lyman A.
PORK CHOP HILL   UA 1959
(Panther)

MARTIN, Archibald Edward
CURIOUS CRIME   EXCLUSIVE 1955
(Muller)   (*Glass Cage, The*)

MARTIN, George Victor
FOR OUR VINES HAVE TENDER
GRAPES   MGM 1945
(Joseph)   (*Our Vines Have Tender Grapes*)

MARTON, George *and* **MERAY, Tibor**
  CATCH ME A SPY   RANK 1971
  (W.H. Allen)

MASEFIELD, John
  BOX OF DELIGHT, THE   BBC 1984 (TV)
  (Heinemann)

MASON, Alfred Edward Woodley
  AT THE VILLA ROSE   AB 1940
  (Hodder & Stoughton)
  DRUM, THE   UA 1938
  (Hodder & Stoughton)   (*Drums*)
  FIRE OVER ENGLAND   UA 1937
  (Hodder & Stoughton)
  FOUR FEATHERS, THE   PAR 1930
  (Hodder & Stoughton)   UA 1939
                               IFD 1955
                               (*Storm Over the Nile*)
                               TRIDENT BARBER 1978
  HOUSE OF THE ARROW   AB 1940
  (Hodder & Stoughton)   ABP 1953

MASON, Howard *pseud.*
  PHOTOFINISH   WAR 1959
  (Joseph)   (*Follow That Horse*)

MASON, Richard
  SHADOW AND THE PEAK, THE   RANK 1958
  (Collins)   (*Passionate Summer*)
  WIND CANNOT READ, THE   RANK 1958
  (Hodder & Stoughton)
  WORLD OF SUZIE WONG, THE   PAR 1959
  (Collins)

MASSIE, Christopher
  CORRIDOR OF MIRRORS   GFD 1948
  (Faber)
  PITY MY SIMPLICITY   PAR 1945
  (Faber)   (*Love Letters*)

MASSIE, Robert K.
  NICHOLAS AND ALEXANDRA   COL 1971
  (Gollancz)

MASTERS, John
BHOWANI JUNCTION   MGM 1955
(Joseph)

MASTERSON, Whit
ALL THROUGH THE NIGHT   WAR 1956
(W.H. Allen)   (*Cry in the Night, A*)
BADGE OF EVIL   UN 1958
(Corgi)   (*Touch of Evil*)
EVIL COME, EVIL GO   FOX 1963
(W.H. Allen)   (*Yellow Canary, The*)

MASTERTON, Graham
MANITOU, THE   ENTERPRISE 1978
(Pinnacle, N.Y.)

MATHER, Anne
LEOPARD IN THE SNOW   ANGLO—CANADIAN 1977
(Mills & Boon)

MATHESON, Richard
BEARDLESS WARRIORS   RANK 1966
(Corgi)   (*Young Warriors*)
BID TIME RETURN   CIC 1980
(Sphere)   (*Somewhere in Time*)
HELL HOUSE   FOX—RANK 1973
(Corgi)   (*Legend of . . .*)
I AM LEGEND   GOLDEN ERA 1964
(Bantam, N.Y.)   (*Last Man on Earth, The*)
    COL—WAR 1971
    (*Omega Man, The*)

INCREDIBLE SHRINKING MAN,
THE   RANK 1957
(*In* Born of Man and Woman:
Chamberlain Press, Philadelphia)

MAUGHAM, Robin
LINE ON GINGER   BL 1953
(Chapman & Hall)   (*Intruder, The*)
ROUGH AND THE SMOOTH, THE   MGM 1959
(Chapman & Hall)
SERVANT, THE   WAR 1963
(Heinemann)

MAUGHAM, William Somerset

ASHENDEN (Heinemann)	GB 1936 (*Secret Agent*)
BEACHCOMBER (Heinemann)	PAR 1938 (*Vessel of Wrath, The*)
CHRISTMAS HOLIDAY (Heinemann)	UN 1944
ENCORE (Heinemann)	GFD 1951
HOME AND BEAUTY (P) (Heinemann)	COL 1948 (*Too Many Husbands*) COL 1954 (*Three for the Show*)
HOUR BEFORE THE DAWN (Doubleday, N.Y.)	PAR 1944
LETTER, THE (P) (Heinemann)	PAR 1929 WAR 1940
MOON AND SIXPENCE, THE (Heinemann)	UA 1942
NARROW CORNER (Heinemann)	WAR 1933
OF HUMAN BONDAGE (Heinemann)	RKO 1934 WAR 1946 MGM 1963
OUR BETTERS (P) (Heinemann)	RKO 1933
PAINTED VEIL, THE (Heinemann)	MGM 1934 MGM 1957 (*Seventh Sin, The*)
PAINTED VEIL, THE (P) (Heinemann)	MGM 1934 MGM 1957 (*Seventh Sin, The*)
QUARTETTE (Heinemann)	GFD 1949
RAIN (P) (French)	UA 1932 COL 1954 (*Miss Sadie Thompson*)
RAZOR'S EDGE, THE (Heinemann)	FOX 1946 COLGEMS 1983
SACRED FLAME, THE (P) (Heinemann)	WAR 1929 WAR 1935 (*Right to Live, The*)
TRIO (Heinemann)	GFD 1950

MAUGHAM, William Somerset (*Continued*)
VESSEL OF WRATH   GFD 1954
(Heinemann)   (*Beachcomber*)

MAUDLIN, William Henry
UP FRONT   UI 1951
(Various)

MAUPASSANT, Guy de
BEL AMI   UA 1947
(Various)   (*Private Affairs of Bel Ami*)

MAURIAC, François
THÉRÈSE   GALA 1965
(Eyre & Spottiswoode)

MAVOR, Osborne Henry *see* **BRIDIE, James** *pseud.*

MAXFIELD, Henry S.
LEGACY FOR A SPY   WAR 1966
(Heinemann)   (*Double Man, The*)

MAXIM, Hiram Percy
SO GOES MY LOVE   UN 1946
(World, N.Y.) *Originally called*: Genius
in the Family

MAXWELL, Gavin
RING OF BRIGHT WATER   RANK 1968
(Longmans)

MAXWELL, William Babington
RAGGED MESSENGER, THE   COL 1930
(Butterworth)   (*Madonna of the Streets*)

MAYER, Edwin Justus
FIREBRAND, THE (P)   UA 1934
(French)   (*Affairs of Cellini*)

MAYNARD, Nan
THIS IS MY STREET   WAR 1963
(Corgi)

MAYO, James
HAMMERHEAD   COL 1968
(Heinemann)

MAYSE, Arthur
DESPERATE SEARCH   MGM 1952
(Harrap)

MEAD, Shepherd
HOW TO SUCCEED IN BUSINESS
WITHOUT REALLY TRYING   UA 1966
(Macdonald)

MEERSCH, Maxence van der
BODIES AND SOULS   MGM 1949
(Pilot Press)   (*Doctor and the Girl, The*)

MELDAL-JOHNSEN, Trevor
ALWAYS   CANNON 1984
(Avon, N.Y.)

MELVILLE, Alan
CASTLE IN THE AIR (P)   ABP 1952
(French)
SIMON AND LAURA (P)   RANK 1955
(French)

MELVILLE, Herman
BILLY BUDD   ANGLO—ALLIED 1962
(Various)
MOBY DICK   WAR 1930
(Various)   (*Sea Beasts, The*)
    WAR 1954
TYPEE   RANK 1964
(Various)   (*Enchanted Island*)

MERAY, Tiber *see* **MARTON, George** *jt. author*

MERCER, Charles
RACHEL CADE   WAR 1960
(Collins)   (*Sins of Rachel Cade, The*)

MERCER, David
MORGAN—A SUITABLE CASE FOR
TREATMENT (P)   BL 1966
(Calder)

MERGENDAHL, Charles
BRAMBLE BUSH, THE   WAR 1959
(Muller)

MÉRIMÉE, Prosper
COLOMBA   RKO 1951
(Hamilton)   (*Vendetta*)
TAMANGO   COL 1959
(Blackie)

MERIVALE, Bernard
UNGUARDED HOUR, THE (P)   MGM 1936
(French)

MERLE, Robert
DAY OF THE DOLPHIN, THE   UA 1973
(Weidenfeld & Nicolson)
MALEVIL   POLYGRAM 1981
(Warner, N.Y.)
WEEKEND AT ZUYDCOOTE   FOX 1965
(Lehmann)   (*Weekend at Dunkirk*)

MERRIAM, Robert E.
BATTLE OF THE BULGE   CINERAMA 1965
(Panther)

MERRITT, Abraham
BURN, WITCH BURN   MGM 1936
(Methuen)   (*Devil-doll, The*)

METALIOUS, Grace
PEYTON PLACE   FOX 1957
(Muller)
RETURN TO PEYTON PLACE   FOX 1960
(Muller)

MEYER, Nicholas
SEVEN-PER-CENT SOLUTION, THE   UN 1977
(Dutton, N.Y.)

MEYNELL, Laurence W.
BREAKING POINT, THE   BUTCHER 1960
(Collins)
CREAKING CHAIR, THE   AA 1953
(Collins)   (*Street of Shadows*)
HOUSE IN MARSH ROAD, THE   GN 1960
(Collins)
ONE STEP FROM MURDER   GN 1959
(Collins)   (*Price of Silence, The*)

MICHAEL, George
AFRICAN FURY   ABP 1955
(Joseph)
MICHAELS IN AFRICA, THE   NEW REALM 1962
(Muller)   (*Drums of Destiny*)

MICHAEL, Judith
DECEPTIONS   BBC 1986 (TV)
(Sphere)

MICHENER, James Albert
BRIDGES AT TOKO-RI, THE   PAR 1954
(Secker & Warburg)
CARAVANS   BORDEAUX FILMS 1979
(Random House, N.Y.)
HAWAII   UA 1965
(Secker & Warburg)   UA 1970
       (*Master of the Islands*)
RETURN TO PARADISE   UA 1953
(Random House, N.Y.)
SAYONARA   WAR 1957
(Secker & Warburg)
SPACE   PAR 1985
(Secker & Warburg)
TALES FROM THE SOUTH PACIFIC   TODD AO 1958
(Collins)   (*South Pacific*)
UNTIL THEY SAIL   MGM 1957
(*In* Return To Paradise: Secker &
Warburg)

MIDDLETON, Edgar
POTIPHAR'S WIFE   POWERS 1932
(Laurie)   (*Her Strange Desire*)

MILES, Bernard
LOCK UP YOUR DAUGHTERS (P)   COL 1968
(French)

MILES, Richard
THAT COLD DAY IN THE PARK   COMMONWEALTH 1969
(Souvenir Press)

MILLAR, Ronald
FRIEDA (P)   EALING 1947
(English Theatre Guild)

MILLER, Alice Duer
AND ONE WAS BEAUTIFUL   MGM 1940
(Methuen)
GOWNS BY ROBERTA   RKO 1935
(Various)   (*Roberta*)
      MGM 1952
      (*Lovely to Look At*)
MANSLAUGHTER   PAR 1930
(*In* Summer Holiday: Dodd, N.Y.)

MILLER, Alice Duer *and* **THOMAS, A.E.**
COME OUT OF THE KITCHEN (P)   PAR 1930
(French)   (*Honey*)

MILLER, Arthur
CRUCIBLE, THE (P)   FILMS DE FRANCE 1957
(Secker & Warburg)   (*Witches of Salem, The*)
DEATH OF A SALESMAN (P)   COL 1951
(Cresset Press)
VIEW FROM THE BRIDGE, A   TRANSCONTINENTAL 1961
(Penguin)

MILLER, Henry
QUIET DAYS IN CLICHY   MIRACLE FILMS 1974
(Calder)
TROPIC OF CANCER   PAR 1969
(Calder)

MILLER, Warren
COOL WORLD, THE   WISEMAN 1963
(Secker & Warburg)

MILLIGAN, Spike
"ADOLF HITLER—MY PART IN HIS
DOWNFALL"   UA 1972
(Joseph)

MILLIGAN, Spike *and* **ANTROBUS, John**
BED SITTING ROOM, THE   UA 1969
(M. & J. Hobbs)

MILLIN, Sarah Gertrude
RHODES   GB 1936
(Chatto & Windus)

MILLS, Hugh
PRUDENCE AND THE PILL   FOX 1968
(Triton)

MILLS, James
PANIC IN NEEDLE PARK, THE   FOX 1971
(Sphere)
REPORT TO THE COMMISSIONER   UN 1975
(Farrar, N.Y.)

MILLS, Mervyn
LONG HAUL, THE   COL 1957
(Pan)

MILNE, Alan Alexander
DOVER ROAD (P)   RKO 1934
(*In* Chief Contemporary Dramatists: (*Where Sinners Meet*)
Houghton, Mifflin, Boston)
FOUR DAYS' WONDER   UN 1937
(Methuen)
MICHAEL AND MARY (P)   UN 1932
(Chatto & Windus)
PERFECT ALIBI, THE (P)   RKO 1931
(*In* Four Plays: Putnam, N.Y.)
WINNIE THE POOH AND THE
HONEY TREE   DISNEY 1965
(Methuen)

MINNEY, Raleigh James
CARVE HER NAME WITH PRIDE   RANK 1957
(Newnes)
NOTHING TO LOSE   ABP 1952
(Macdonald)   (*Time Gentlemen, Please!*)

MINNEY, R.J. *see* **LIPSCOMB, W.P.** *jt. author*

MISENHEIMER, M. *see* **POWERS, A.** *jt. author*

MISHIMA, Yukio
RUNAWAY HORSES: TEMPLE OF
THE GOLDEN PAVILION   COL—EMI—WAR 1985
(Knopf, N.Y.: Putnam, N.Y.)   (*Mishima*)
SAILOR WHO FELL FROM GRACE
WITH THE SEA, THE   FOX—RANK 1976
(Putnam, N.Y.)

MITCHELL, Don
  THUMB TRIPPING   AVCO EMBASSY 1972
  (Cape)

MITCHELL, James
  RED\FILE FOR CALLAN, A   EMI 1974
  (Simon & Schuster, N.Y.)   (*Callan*)

MITCHELL, Julian
  ANOTHER COUNTRY (P)   GOLDCREST 1983
  (French)

MITCHELL, Margaret
  GONE WITH THE WIND   MGM 1939
  (Macmillan)

MITCHELL, Mary
  WARNING TO WANTONS, A   AQUILA 1949
  (Heinemann)

MITFORD, Nancy
  BLESSING, THE   MGM 1959
  (Hamilton)   (*Count Your Blessings*)

MOGGACH, Deborah
  TO HAVE AND TO HOLD   LWT 1986 (TV)
  (Penguin)

MOISEIWITSCH, Maurice
  SLEEPING TIGER, THE   INSIGNIA FILMS 1954
  (Heinemann)

MOLL, Elick *see* **TARADASH, D.** *jt. author*

MOLNAR, Ferenc
  GOOD FAIRY (P)   UN 1934
  (Crown, N.Y.)
  GUARDSMAN, THE (P)   MGM 1941
  (Macy-Masius, N.Y.)   (*Chocolate Soldier, The*)
  LILIOM (P)   FOX 1930
  (*In* Treasury of the Theatre, Vol. 2:
  Simon & Schuster, N.Y.)
  OLYMPIA (P)   PAR 1960
  (Brentano, N.Y.)   (*Breath of Scandal, A*)

SWAN, THE (P)   UA 1930
(Longmans, N.Y.)   (*One Romantic Night*)
                                      MGM 1956

MONAGHAN, James [Jay]
  LAST OF THE BADMEN   ABP 1949
  (Bobbs-Merrill, Indianapolis)   (*Bad Men of Tombstone*)

MONKS, John *and* FINKLEHOFFE, Fred R.
  BROTHER RAT (P)   WAR 1938
  (Random House, N.Y.)   WAR 1952
                                      (*About Face*)

MONRO, Robert
  FRENCH MISTRESS, A (P)   BL 1960
  (French)

MONSARRAT, Nicholas
  CRUEL SEA, THE   GFD 1952
  (Cassell)
  SOMETHING TO HIDE   AVCO EMBASSY 1973
  (Pan)
  STORY OF ESTHER COSTELLO,
  THE   COL 1957
  (Cassell)

MONTAGUE, Ewen Edward Samuel
  MAN WHO NEVER WAS, THE   FOX 1955
  (Evans)

MONTEILHET, Hubert
  RETURN FROM THE ASHES   UA 1965
  (Panther)

MONTGOMERY, Lucy Maud
  ANNE OF GREEN GABLES   RKO 1934
  (Harrap)   SULLIVAN 1985 (TV)
  ANNE OF WINDY POPLARS   RKO 1940
  (Harrap) *Also published as* Anne of
  Windy Willows

MONTI, Carlotta *and* RICE, C.
  W.C. FIELDS AND ME   UN 1976
  (Joseph)

MOODY, Laurence
 RUTHLESS ONES, THE   FOX 1971
 (Hale)   (*What Became of Jack and Jill?*)

MOODY, Ralph
 LITTLE BRITCHES   DISNEY 1971
 (Harcourt, Brace, N.Y.)   (*Wild Country, The*)

MOODY, William Vaughan
 GREAT DIVIDE, THE   IN 1930
 (Macmillan)

MOON, Laura
 DARK STAR   MGM 1930
 (Gollancz)   (*Min and Bill*)

MOONEY, Michael M.
 HINDENBURG, THE   CIC 1975
 (Hart-Davis)

MOORCOCK, Michael
 FINAL PROGRAMME, THE MGM—EMI 1973
 (Alison & Busby)

MOORE, Brian
 LUCK OF GINGER COFFEY, THE BL 1965
 (Deutsch)

MOORE, George
 ESTHER WATERS   WESSEX 1948
 (Various)
 ESTHER WATERS (P)   WESSEX 1948
 (Heinemann)

MOORE, Grace
 YOU'RE ONLY HUMAN ONCE WAR 1953
 (Invincible Press)   (*So This is Love*)

MOORE, Harry T.
 PRIEST OF LOVE, THE   ENTERPRISE 1981
 (Heinemann)

MOORE, Robin
 DUBAI   AMERICAN COMMUNICATION
 (Doubleday, N.Y.)   1980

550

FRENCH CONNECTION, THE   FOX 1971
(Hodder & Stoughton)
GREEN BERETS, THE   WAR 1968
(Crown, N.Y.)

MOORE, Ruth
SPOONHANDLE   FOX 1948
(Grosset, N.Y.)   (*Deep Waters*)

MOOREHEAD, Alan
RAGE OF THE VULTURE, THE   PAR 1951
(Hamilton)   (*Thunder in the East*)

MORANTE, Elsa
ARTURO'S ISLAND   GALA 1963
(Collins)

MORAVIA, Alberto
APPOINTMENT AT THE BEACH   COMPTON 1965
(*In* Fetish, The: Secker & Warburg)   (*Naked Hours, The*)
CONFORMIST, THE   CURZON 1971
(Penguin)
LIE, THE   SELVAGGIA 1986
(Woodhill, N.Y.)
TIME OF INDIFFERENCE   CONT 1967
(Secker & Warburg)
WOMAN OF ROME, A   EXCLUSIVE 1956
(Secker & Warburg)

MORAY, Helga
UNTAMED   FOX 1955
(Museum Press)

MORELL, Parker
DIAMOND JIM   UN 1935
(Hurst & Blackett)

MORGAN, Albert
GREAT MAN, THE   UI 1956
(Dutton, N.Y.)

MORGAN, Charles
FOUNTAIN, THE   RKO 1934
(Macmillan)

MORGAN, Joan
   THIS WAS A WOMAN (P)   FOX 1948
   (French)

MORIER, James Justian
   ADVENTURES OF HAJJI BABA OF
   ISPAHAN   FOX 1954
   (Modern Library, N.Y.)   (*Adventures of Hajji Baba, The*)

MORLEY, Christopher Darlington
   KITTY FOYLE   RKO 1940
   (Lippincott, Philadelphia)

MORLEY, Edward *and* **LANGLEY, Noel**
   EDWARD, MY SON (P)   MGM 1948
   (French)

MORLEY, Walter
   GENTLE BEN   PAR 1968
   (Dutton, N.Y.)   (*Gentle Giant*)

MORPURGO, Michael
   FRIEND OF FOE   CFF 1982
   (Macmillan)

MORRELL, David
   FIRST BLOOD   ORION 1982
   (Pan)

MORRIS, Colin
   RELUCTANT HEROES (P)   ABP 1951
   (English Theatre Guild)

MORROS, Boris
   MY TEN YEARS AS A COUNTERSPY   RANK 1960
   (Laurie)   (*Confessions of a Counterspy*)

MORROW, Honore
   ON TO OREGON   HEMDALE 1974
   (Morrow, N.Y.)   (*Seven Alone*)

MORTIMER, John
   DOCK BRIEF, THE (P)   MGM 1962
   (Elek)

AUTHOR AND ORIGINAL TITLE	FILM TITLE
PARADISE POSTPONED (Penguin)	EUSTON 1986 (TV)
MORTIMER, Penelope PUMPKIN EATER, THE (Penguin)	BL 1963
MOSEL, Ted DEAR HEART (P) (Obolensky, N.Y.)	WAR 1964
MOSLEY, Leonard CAT AND THE MICE, THE (Barker)	BL 1960 (*Foxhole in Cairo*)
MOSLEY, Nicholas ACCIDENT (Hodder & Stoughton)	MONARCH 1967
MOSS, Arthur *and* **MARVEL, Evelyn** LEGEND OF THE LATIN QUARTER (W.H. Allen)	COL 1950 (*Her Wonderful Lie*)
MOSS, W. Stanley ILL MET BY MOONLIGHT (Corgi)	RANK 1956
MOTLEY, Willard KNOCK ON ANY DOOR (Collins) LET NO MAN WRITE MY EPITAPH (Collins)	COL 1949 COL 1960 (*Reach for Tomorrow*)
MOTTRAM, Ralph Hale SPANISH FARM, THE (Chatto & Windus)	EXCELLENT 1930 (*Roses of Picardy*)
MOWAT, Farley NEVER CRY WOLF (Bantam, N.Y.)	DISNEY 1983
MOYZISCH, L.C. OPERATION CICERO (Wingate)	FOX 1952 (*Five Fingers*)

MUHAMMAD, Ali
  GREATEST, THE   COL—WAR 1977
  (Hart-Davis)

MULFORD, Clarence Edward
  BAR 20   UA 1943
  (Hodder & Stoughton)
  BAR 20 RIDES AGAIN   PAR 1935
  (Hodder & Stoughton)
  COTTONWOOD GULCH   PAR 1937
  (Hodder & Stoughton)   (*North of Rio Grande*)
  HOP-ALONG CASSIDY   PAR 1935
  (Hodder & Stoughton)
  HOP-ALONG CASSIDY RETURNS   PAR 1936
  (Hodder & Stoughton)
  ROUND-UP, THE   PAR 1937
  (Hodder & Stoughton)   (*Hills of Old Wyoming*)
  TRAIL DUST   PAR 1936
  (Hodder & Stoughton)

MULLEN, Pat
  MAN OF ARAN   GB 1934
  (Faber)

MULVIHILL, William
  SANDS OF THE KALIHARI   PAR 1965
  (Longmans)

MUNDY, Talbot
  KING OF THE KHYBER RIFLES   FOX 1954
  (Hutchinson)

MUNRO, James
  INNOCENT BYSTANDERS   SCOTIA BARBER 1972
  (Barrie & Jenkins)

MURDOCH, Iris
  BELL, THE   BBC 1982 (TV)
  (Chatto & Windus)
  SEVERED HEAD, A   COL 1969
  (Chatto & Windus)

MURDOCH, Iris *and* PRIESTLEY, J.B.
  SEVERED HEAD, A (P)   COL 1969
  (Chatto & Windus)

MURPHY, Audie
TO HELL AND BACK   UI 1955
(Hammond)

MURPHY, Dennis
SERGEANT, THE   WAR 1968
(Sphere)

MURPHY, Robert
MOUNTAIN LION, THE   DISNEY 1972
(Dutton, N.Y.)   (*Run, Cougar, Run*)

MURPHY, Warren *and* **SAPIN, Richard**
REMO   RANK 1985
(Fiesta, N.Y.)

MURRAY, John *and* **BORET, Allen**
ROOM SERVICE (P)   RKO 1944
(Random House, N.Y.)   (*Step Lively*)

MURRAY, William
SWEET RIDE, THE   FOX 1968
(W.H. Allen)

MUSMANNO, Michael A.
TEN DAYS TO DIE   INTERCONTINENTAL 1955
(Davies)

MYERS, Elizabeth
MRS. CHRISTOPHER   GFD 1951
(Chapman & Hall)   (*Blackmailer*)

MYRER, Anton
BIG WAR, THE   FOX 1958
(Hamilton)   (*In Love and War*)

N

NABOKOV, Vladimir
DESPAIR   GALA 1978
(Putnam, N.Y.)
LAUGHTER IN THE DARK   UA 1969
(Weidenfeld & Nicolson)

NABOKOV, Vladimir (*Continued*)
  LOLITA   MGM 1962
  (Corgi)

NARCEJAC, T. *see* **BOILEAU, P.** *jt. author*

NASH, N. Richard
  RAINMAKER, THE (P)   PAR 1956
  (Random House, N.Y.)

NASH, N. Robert
  GIRLS OF SUMMER (P)   PAR 1959
  (French, N.Y.)

NASH, O. *see* **PERELMAN, S.J.** *jt. author*

NATHAN, Robert
  BISHOP'S WIFE, THE   RKO 1947
  (*In* Barley Fields: Constable)
  ONE MORE SPRING   FOX 1950
  (Cassell)
  PORTRAIT OF JENNIE   SELZNICK 1948
  (Heinemann)

NATHANSON, E.M.
  DIRTY DOZEN, THE   MGM 1966
  (Barker)

NAUGHTON, Bill
  ALFIE (P)   PAR 1965
  (French)
  ALFIE   PAR 1965
  (MacGibbon & Kee)
  ALL IN GOOD TIME (P)   BL 1966
  (French)   (*Family Way, The*)
  SPRING AND PORT WINE (P)   AA 1969
  (French)

NAUGHTON, Edmund
  McCABE   WAR 1972
  (Panther)   (*McCabe and Mrs. Miller*)

NEBEL, Frederick
  SLEEPERS EAST   FOX 1934
  (Collins)

NEELY, Richard
INNOCENTS WITH DIRTY HANDS   FOX—RANK 1975
(Star)

NEIDER, Charles
AUTHENTIC DEATH OF HENDRY
JONES, THE   PAR 1960
(Harper, N.Y.)   (*One Eyed Jacks*)

NEMEROV, Howard
HOMECOMING GAME, THE   WAR 1960
(Gollancz)   (*Tall Story*)

NEMIROWSKY, I.
DAVID GOLDEN   BL 1950
(Constable)   (*My Daughter Joy*)

NESBIT, Edith
RAILWAY CHILDREN, THE   MGM 1970
(Various)

NESS, Eliot *and* **FRALEY, Oscar**
UNTOUCHABLES, THE   WAR 1959
(Messner, N.Y.)   (*Scarface Mob, The*)

NEUMANN, Robert
QUEEN'S DOCTOR, THE   BL 1959
(Gollancz)   (*King in Shadow*)

NEVINS, Frank J.
YANKEE DARED, A   REP 1950
(Chicago, Published by the author)   (*Transcontinental express*)

NEWMAN, Andrea
THREE INTO TWO WON'T GO   UI 1968
(Triton)

NEWMAN, Bernard
THEY SAVED LONDON   EROS 1957
(Hamilton)

NEWMAN, G.F.
SIR, YOU BASTARD   COL—WAR 1974
(W.H. Allen)

NIALL, Ian *pseud.*
NO RESTING PLACE   ABP 1951
(Heinemann)
TIGER WALKS, A   DISNEY 1964
(Heinemann)

NIALL, Michael
BAD DAY AT BLACK ROCK   MGM 1955
(Muller)

NICHOLS, John
STERILE CUCKOO, THE   PAR 1969
(Pan)   (*Pookie*)

NICHOLS, Peter
DAY IN THE DEATH OF JOE EGG
(P)   COL 1971
(Faber)   (*Joe Egg*)
NATIONAL HEALTH, THE (P)   COL—WAR 1973
(Faber)

NICHOLSON, Meredith
HOUSE OF THE THOUSAND
CANDLES, THE   REP 1936
(Black)

NICHOLSON, Robert
MRS. ROSS   UA 1966
(Constable)   (*Whisperers, The*)

NICOLAYSEN, Bruce
PERILOUS PASSAGE, THE   HEMDALE 1978
(Playboy, N.Y.)   (*Passage, The*)

NIELAND, D'Arcy
SHIRALEE, THE   MGM 1957
(Angus & Robertson)

NIELSON, Helen
MURDER BY PROXY   EXCLUSIVE 1954
(Gollancz)

NIGGLI, Josephine
MEXICAN VILLAGE, A   MGM 1953
(Sampson Low)   (*Sombrero*)

NIJINSKY, Romolo
NIJINSKY
(AMS Press, N.Y.)

PAR 1980

NIKLAUS, Thelma
TAMAHINE
(Lane)

WAR 1963

NILES, Blair
CONDEMNED TO DEVIL'S ISLAND
(Cape)

UA 1939
(*Condemned*)

NOBLE, Hollister
WOMAN WITH A SWORD
(Doubleday, N.Y.)

RKO 1952
(*Drums in the Deep South*)

NOBLE, W. *see* **HERLIHY, J.L.** *jt. author*

NOEL, Sterling
HOUSE OF SECRETS, THE
(Deutsch)

RANK 1956

NOLAN, Jeanette
GATHER YE ROSEBUDS
(Appleton, N.Y.)

PAR 1948
(*Isn't it Romantic?*)

NOLAN, William F. *and* **JOHNSON, G.**
LOGAN'S RUN
(Gollancz)

MGM 1976

NORDEN, Peter
MADAME KITTY
(Abelard-Schuman)

FOX 1977
(*Salon Kitty*)

NORDHOFF, Charles Bernard *and* **HALL, James Norman**
BOTANY BAY
(Chapman & Hall)

PAR 1952

HIGH BARBAREE, THE
(Faber)

MGM 1947

HURRICANE
(Chapman & Hall)

UA 1937
ITC 1980

MUTINY ON THE BOUNTY
(Chapman & Hall)

MGM 1935
MGM 1962

NO MORE GAS
(Chapman & Hall)

RKO 1942
(*Tuttles of Tahiti, The*)

NORRIS, Charles Gilman
SEED   UN 1931
(Heinemann)

NORRIS, Kathleen
BEAUTY'S DAUGHTER   FOX 1935
(Murray)   (*Navy Wife*)
PASSION FLOWER   MGM 1930
(Murray)
SECOND HAND WIFE   FOX 1933
(Murray)
WALLS OF GOLD   FOX 1933
(Murray)

NORTH, Sperling
LITTLE RASCAL   DISNEY 1969
(Brockhampton)   (*Rascal*)
SO DEAR TO MY HEART   RKO 1948
(Odhams)

NORTON, Mary
BEDKNOB AND BROOMSTICK DISNEY 1971
(Dent)

NORWAY, Nevil Shute *see* **SHUTE, Nevil** *pseud.*

NOVELLO, Ivor
I LIVED WITH YOU (P)   GB 1935
(Methuen)
SYMPHONY IN TWO FLATS (P) GFD 1931
(*In* Three Plays: Methuen)
TRUTH GAME, THE (P)   MGM 1932
(French, N.Y.)   (*But the Flesh is Weak*)

NUGENT, E. *see* **THURBER, J.** *jt. author*

O

O'BRIEN, Edna
COUNTRY GIRLS, THE   CHANNEL 4 1983 (TV)
(Penguin)
LONELY GIRL, THE   UA 1964
(Cape)   (*Girl with Green Eyes*)

O'BRIEN, Kate
  THAT LADY   FOX 1954
  (Heinemann)

O'BRIEN, Robert C.
  MRS. FRISBY AND THE RATS OF
  NIMH   UIP 1982
  (Gollancz)   (*Secret of Nimh, The*)

O'BRINE, Mannering
  PASSPORT TO TREASON   EROS 1956
  (Hammond)

O'CASEY, Sean
  JUNO AND THE PAYCOCK (P)   BI 1930
  (Macmillan)
  JUNO AND THE PAYCOCK   BI 1930
  (Macmillan)
  MIRROR IN MY HOUSE   MGM 1964
  (Macmillan)   (*Young Cassidy*)
  PLOUGH AND THE STARS (P)   RKO 1936
  (Macmillan)

O'CONNOR, Edwin
  LAST HURRAH, THE   COL 1958
  (Pan)

O'CONNOR, Elizabeth
  IRISHMAN, THE   SOUTH AUSTRALIA FILMS 1978
  (Angus & Robertson)

O'CONNOR, Flannery
  WISE BLOOD   ARTIFICIAL EYE 1979
  (Farrar, N.Y.)

O'DELL, Scott
  ISLAND OF THE BLUE DOLPHINS   RANK 1964
  (Constable)

ODETS, Clifford
  BIG KNIFE, THE (P)   UA 1955
  (Random House, N.Y.)
  CLASH BY NIGHT (P)   RKO 1952
  (Random House, N.Y.)

ODETS, Clifford (*Continued*)
  GOLDEN BOY (P)   COL 1938
  (Gollancz)
  WINTER JOURNEY (P)   PAR 1954
  (Viking, N.Y.)   (*Country Girl, The*)

ODLUM, Jerome
  EACH DAWN I DIE   WAR 1939
  (Various)

O'DONNELL, Peter
  MODESTY BLAISE   FOX 1965
  (Souvenir Press)

O'FLAHERTY, Liam
  INFORMER, THE   RKO 1935
  (Cape)

OGBURN, Charlton
  MERRILL'S MARAUDERS   WAR 1962
  (Hodder & Stoughton)   (*Marauders, The*)

O'GRADY, Rohan
  LETS KILL UNCLE   UI 1967
  (Longmans)

O'HARA, John
  BUTTERFIELD 8   MGM 1960
  (Cresset Press)
  FROM THE TERRACE   FOX 1960
  (Cresset Press)
  PAL JOEY (P)   COL 1957
  (Cresset Press)
  RAGE TO LIVE, A   UA 1964
  (Cresset Press)
  TEN NORTH FREDERICK   FOX 1958
  (Cresset Press)

O'HARA, Mary *pseud.*
  GREEN GRASS OF WYOMING FOX 1949
  (Eyre & Spottiswoode)
  MY FRIEND FLICKA   FOX 1943
  (Eyre & Spottiswoode)
  THUNDERHEAD—SON OF FLICKA FOX 1945
  (Eyre & Spottiswoode)

'OLIVIA' *pseud.*
OLIVIA   FILMS DE FRANCE 1950
(Hogarth Press)

OLLIVANT, Alfred
OWD BOB   GB 1937
(Various)

OLSEN, Theodore V.
SOLDIER BLUE   AVCO EMBASSY 1971
(White Lion Pubs.)
STALKING MOON, THE   WAR 1968
(Sphere)

O'NEILL, Eugene Gladstone
AH WILDERNESS (P)   MGM 1935
(Cape)   MGM 1948
       (*Summer Holiday*)
ANNA CHRISTIE (P)   MGM 1930
(Random House, N.Y.)
DESIRE UNDER THE ELMS (P)   PAR 1958
(Cape)
EMPEROR JONES (P)   UA 1933
(Cape)
HAIRY APE, THE (P)   UA 1944
(Cape)
ICEMAN COMETH, THE (P)   AMERICAN FILM THEATRE 1975
(Cape)
LONG DAY'S JOURNEY INTO
NIGHT (P)   FOX 1962
(Cape)
LONG VOYAGE HOME, THE (P)   UA 1940
(Various)
MOURNING BECOMES ELECTRA   RKO 1948
(P)
(Cape)
STRANGE INTERLUDE (P)   MGM 1932
(Cape)

ONSTOTT, Kyle
DRUM   PAR 1976
(Pan)
MANDINGO   PAR 1975
(Pan)

OPPENHEIM, Edward Phillips
AMAZING QUEST OF MR. ERNEST
BLISS, THE   KLEMENT 1936
(Hodder & Stoughton)   (*Amazing Quest, The*)
GREAT IMPERSONATION, THE   UN 1935
(Hodder & Stoughton)   UN 1942
LION AND THE LAMB, THE   COL 1931
(Hodder & Stoughton)
STRANGE BOARDERS OF PALACE
CRESCENT   GB 1938
(Hodder & Stoughton)   (*Strange Boarders*)

ORCZY, *Baroness* **Emmuska**
ELUSIVE PIMPERNEL, THE   BL 1950
(Hutchinson)
EMPEROR'S CANDLESTICKS, THE   MGM 1937
(Hodder & Stoughton)
SCARLET PIMPERNEL, THE   UA 1935
(Hodder & Stoughton)   LONDON F.P. 1982

O'ROURKE, Frank
BRAVADOS, THE   FOX 1958
(Heinemann)
GREAT BANK ROBBERY, THE   WAR 1969
(Sphere)
MULE FOR THE MARQUESA, A   COL 1966
(Fontana)   (*Professionals, The*)

ORTON, Joe
ENTERTAINING MR. SLOANE (P)   WAR 1969
(Hamilton)
LOOT (P)   BL 1972
(Methuen)

ORWELL, George *pseud.*
ANIMAL FARM   ABP 1954
(Secker & Warburg)
1984   ABP 1956
(Gollancz)

OSBORN, John Jay
PAPER CHASE   FOX 1974
(Houghton, Mifflin, Boston)

OSBORN, Paul
ON BORROWED TIME (P)   MGM 1939
(Dramatists, N.Y.)
WORLD OF SUZIE WONG, THE (P)   PAR 1959
(Random House, N.Y.)

OSBORNE, Hubert
SHORE LEAVE (P)   MGM 1954
(French, N.Y.)   (*Hit the Deck*)

OSBORNE, John
ENTERTAINER, THE (P)   BL 1960
(Evans)   SEVEN KEYS 1975
INADMISSIBLE EVIDENCE (P)   PAR 1968
(Faber)
LOOK BACK IN ANGER (P)   ABP 1959
(Faber)
LUTHER (P)   SEVEN KEYS 1973
(Faber)

OSBOURNE, L. *see* **STEVENSON, R.L.** *jt. author*

OSTENSO, M. *see* **KENNY, E.** *jt. author*

OUIDA
DOG OF FLANDERS, A   RKO 1935
(Chatto & Windus)   FOX 1959
UNDER TWO FLAGS   FOX 1936
(Chatto & Windus)

OURSLER, Fulton
GREATEST STORY EVER TOLD,
THE   UA 1965
(Worlds Work)

OVERHOLSTER, Wayne D.
CAST A LONG SHADOW   UA 1959
(Ward Lock)

OWEN, Frank
EDDIE CHAPMAN STORY, THE   AA 1967
(Hamilton)   (*Triple Cross, The*)

OWEN, Guy
BALLAD OF THE FLIM-FLAM MAN
(Macmillan)   FOX 1966
      (*Flim-Flam Man, The*)

OWENS, Rachelle
FUTZ AND WHAT CAME AFTER (P)   COMMONWEALTH 1969
(Random House, N.Y.)   (*Futz*)

P

PACKER, Joy
NOR THE MOON BY NIGHT   RANK 1958
(Eyre & Spottiswoode)

PAGANO, Jo
CONDEMNED, THE   UA 1951
(Invincible Press)   (*Sound of the Fury, The*)

PAGE, Elizabeth
TREE OF LIBERTY   COL 1940
(Collins)   (*Howards of Virginia, The*)

PAGE, Gertrude
PADDY THE NEXT BEST THING   FOX 1933
(Hurst & Blackett)

PAGE, Marco
FAST COMPANY   MGM 1939
(Heinemann)   (*Fast and Loose*)

PAGE, Thomas
HEPHAESTUS PLAGUE, THE   PAR 1975
(Putnam)   (*Bug*)

PALEY, Frank
RUMBLE ON THE DOCKS   COL 1957
(Crown, N.Y.)

PALMER, John Leslie *see* **BEEDING, Francis** *pseud.*

PALMER, Stuart
PUZZLE OF THE BRIAR PIPE   RKO 1936
(Collins)   (*Murder on a Bridle Path*)

PUZZLE OF THE PEPPER TREE   RKO 1935
(Jarrolds)   (*Murder on a Honeymoon*)

PAPASHVILY, George *and* **PAPASHVILY, Helen**
ANYTHING CAN HAPPEN   PAR 1952
(Heinemann)

PARGETER, Edith
SPANIARD'S CURSE, THE   BL 1957
(Heinemann)   (*Assize of the Dying, The*)

PARKER, Gilbert
TRANSLATIONS OF A SAVAGE   PAR 1935
(Methuen)   (*Behold My Wife*)

PARKER, Louis N.
JOSEPH AND HIS BRETHREN (P) COL 1954
(Bodley Head)

PARKS, Gordon
LEARNING TREE, THE   WAR 1969
(Hodder & Stoughton)

PARKS, L.A.
IT WAS FUN WORKING AT THE
WHITE HOUSE   BBC 2 1984 (TV)
(Fleet, N.Y.)   (*Backstairs at the White House*)

PARRISH, Ann
ALL KNEELING   RKO 1950
(Benn)   (*Born to be Bad*)

PARROTT, Ursula
STRANGERS MAY KISS   MGM 1931
(Cape)

PASCAL, Ernest
MARRIAGE BED, THE   PAR 1931
(Allen & Unwin)   (*Husband's Holiday*)

PASTERNAK, Boris
DOCTOR ZHIVAGO   MGM 1965
(Collins)

PATON, Alan
CRY, THE BELOVED COUNTRY   BL 1951
(Cape)

PATRICK, John
TEAHOUSE OF THE AUGUST
MOON, THE (P)   MGM 1957
(Heinemann)

PATRICK, Vincent
POPE OF GREENWICH VILLAGE,   MGM/UA 1984
THE
(Hodder & Stoughton)

PATTEN, Lewis B.
LAW OF THE GUN   UI 1969
(Four Square Books)   (*Death of a Gunfighter*)

PATTERSON, Harry
TO CATCH A KING   GAYLORD 1983
(Hutchinson)

PATTON, Frances Gray
GOOD MORNING, MISS DOVE   FOX 1955
(Gollancz)

PAYNE, Laurence
NOSE ON MY FACE, THE   BL 1963
(Hodder & Stoughton)   (*Girl in the Headlines*)

PAYNE, Stephen
BLACK ACES   UN 1937
(Wright & Brown)

PEAKE, Mervyn
MISTER PYE   CHANNEL 4 1986 (TV)
(Penguin)   (*Mr. Pye*)

PEARCE, Donn
COOL HAND LUKE   WAR 1968
(Penguin)

PEARL, H. *see* **ABERSON, Helen** *jt. author*

PEARSON, William
FEVER IN THE BLOOD   WAR 1960
(Macmillan)

PECK, Richard H.
ARE YOU IN THE HOUSE ALONE   ITV 1984 (TV)
(Dell, N.Y.)

PENROSE, Valentine
BLOODY COUNTESS, THE   RANK 1970
(Caldar & Boyars)   (*Countess Dracula*)

PERCY, Edward
SHOP AT SLY CORNER, THE (P)   BL 1946
(French)

PERCY, Edward *see* **DENHAM, R.** *jt. author*

PERCY, Edward *and* **DENHAM, Reginald**
LADIES IN RETIREMENT (P)   COL 1941
(Random House, N.Y.)

PERDUE, Virginia
HE FELL DOWN DEAD   WAR 1946
(Doubleday, N.Y.)   (*Shadow of a Woman*)

PERELMAN, Sidney Joseph *and* **NASH, Ogden**
ONE TOUCH OF VENUS (P)   UN 1948
(Little, Brown, Boston)

PERKINS, Grace
NO MORE ORCHIDS   COL 1932
(Wright & Brown)

PERKINS, Kenneth
DESERT VOICES   ABP 1952
(Wright & Brown)   (*Desert Pursuit*)

PERRY, George
BLUEBELL   BBC 1986 (TV)
(Pavilion)

PERRY, George Sessions
  HOLD AUTUMN IN YOUR HANDS   UA 1945
  (Sun Dial, N.Y.)   (*Southener, The*)

PERRY, J. *see* **FARRELL, M.J.** *jt. author*

PERTWEE, Michael
  DON'T JUST LIE THERE, SAY
  SOMETHING (P)   RANK 1975
  (French)
  NIGHT WAS OUR FRIEND (P)   MONARCH 1951
  (English Theatre Guild)

PERTWEE, Roland
  HEAT WAVE (P)   WAR 1931
  (*In* Five Three-act Plays: French, N.Y.)   (*Road to Singapore*)
  PARAGON, THE (P)   ABP 1948
  (*In* Plays of the Year 1948–49: Elek)   (*Silent Dust*)
  PINK STRING AND SEALING WAX
  (P)   EALING 1946
  (English Theatre Guild)

PERTWEE, Roland *and* **DEARDEN, Harold**
  INTERFERENCE (P)   PAR 1935
  (French, N.Y.)   (*With Regret*)

PETERS, Stephen
  PARK IS MINE, THE   RAMBLE 1985
  (Blondi & Briggs)

PETERSON, Louis S.
  TAKE A GIANT STEP (P)   UA 1959
  (French, N.Y.)

PETERSON, Ralph
  SQUARE RING, THE   GFD 1953
  (Barker)

PETIEVICH, Gerald
  TO LIVE AND DIE IN LA   MGM/UA 1985
  (Arbor, N.Y.)

PETRAKIS, Harry Mark
  DREAM OF KINGS, A   WAR 1969
  (Barker)

PETRONIUS
  SATYRICON   UA 1970
  (Various)   (*Fellini Satyricon*)

PHILLIPS, Mickey
  PICK UP STICKS   RANK 1972
  (Joseph)   (*Cherry Picker, The*)

PHILLPOTTS, Eden
  FARMER'S WIFE, THE (P)   ABP 1940
  (French)
  YELLOW SANDS, THE (P)   AB 1938
  (Duckworth)

PICK, J.B.
  LAST VALLEY, THE   CINERAMA 1971
  (Sphere)

PIERSON, *Mrs.* Louise
  ROUGHLY SPEAKING   WAR 1945
  (Simon & Schuster, N.Y.)

PIKE, Robert, L.
  MUTE WITNESS (P)   WAR 1968
  (Deutsch)   (*Bullitt*)

PILKINGTON, Roger
  NEPOMUK OF THE RIVER   CINERAMA 1965
  (Macmillan)   (*Golden Head, The*)

PINCHON, Edgcomb
  ZAPATA, THE UNCONQUERABLE   FOX 1952
  (Doubleday, N.Y.)   (*Viva Zapata*)

PINERO, *Sir* Arthur Wing
  ENCHANTED COTTAGE, THE (P)   RKO 1945
  (Heinemann)
  MAGISTRATE, THE (P)   PAR 1940
  (Heinemann)   (*Those were the Days*)
  SECOND MRS. TANQUERAY, THE
  (P)   VANDYKE 1952
  (Heinemann)

PINTER, Harold
  BETRAYAL (P)   VIRGIN 1983
  (Eyre-Methuen)

PINTER, Harold (*Continued*)
  BIRTHDAY PARTY, THE (P)   CINERAMA 1968
  (Methuen)
  CARETAKER, THE (P)   BL 1963
  (Grove Press, N.Y.)
  HOME COMING, THE (P)   SEVEN KEYS 1973
  (Grove, N.Y.)
  KIND OF ALASKA, A (P)   CENTRAL TV 1985 (TV)
  (Grove, N.Y.)

PIPER, Anne
  SWEET AND PLENTY   AVCO EMBASSY 1969
  (Heinemann)   (*Nice Girl Like Me, A*)

PIPER, Evelyn
  BUNNY LAKE IS MISSING   COL 1965
  (Secker & Warburg)
  NANNY, THE   WAR 1965
  (Secker & Warburg)

PLATH, Sylvia
  BELL JAR, THE   AVCO EMBASSY 1978
  (Harper, N.Y.)

PLATT, Kin
  BOY WHO COULD MAKE HIMSELF
  DISAPPEAR, THE   MGM—EMI 1972
  (Chilton, Philadelphia)   (*Baxter*)

PODHAJSKY, Alois
  WHITE STALLIONS OF VIENNA,
  THE   DISNEY 1963
  (Harrap)   (*Flight of the White Stallions, The*)

POE, Edgar Allan
  BLACK CAT, THE   UN 1934
  (*In* Tales of Mystery and Imagination: WAR 1963
  Various)   (*Tales of Terror*)
  CALYPSO   BL 1956
  (*In* Best Tales: Various)   (*Gold Bug, The*)
  CASE OF DR. VALDEMAR   WAR 1963
  (*In* Tales of Mystery and Imagination: (*Tales of Terror*)
  Various)
  FALL OF THE HOUSE OF USHER,   AA 1960
  THE
  (Various)

MASQUE OF THE RED DEATH, THE   AA 1964
(Various)
MORELLA   WAR 1963
(*In* Tales of Mystery and Imagination: (*Tales of Terror*)
Various)
MURDERS IN THE RUE MORGUE   UN 1932
(Various)   WAR 1954
                                    (*Phantom of the Rue Morgue*)
                                    AMERICAN INT 1971
                                    (*Murder . . .*)
MYSTERY OF MARIE ROGET   UN 1942
(Various)
OBLONG BOX, THE   AA 1969
(Collins)
PIT AND THE PENDULUM, THE   AA 1961
(*In* Tales of Mystery and Imagination:
Various)
PREMATURE BURIAL, THE   AA 1962
(*In* Tales of Mystery and Imagination:
Various)
RAVEN, THE   UN 1955
(Various)
TELL-TALE HEART, THE   ABP 1960
(*In* Tales of Mystery and Imagination:
Various)

POLLINI, Francis
PRETTY MAIDS ALL IN A ROW   MGM—EMI 1971
(Spearman)

POLOK, Chaim
CHOSEN, THE   CONTEMPORARY 1982
(Fawcett, N.Y.)

PONICSAN, Darryl
CINDERELLA LIBERTY   FOX 1974
(Harper, N.Y.)
LAST DETAIL   COL 1973
(Dial Press, N.Y.)

PORTER, Eleanor H.
POLLYANNA   DISNEY 1960
(Harrap)

PORTER, Gene Stratton *see* **STRATTON-PORTER, Gene**

PORTER, Katherine Anne
SHIP OF FOOLS   COL 1964
(Secker & Warburg)

PORTER, William Sidney *see* **HENRY, O.** *pseud.*

PORTIS, Charles
NORWOOD   PAR 1971
(Cape)
TRUE GRIT   PAR 1969
(Cape)   UN 1975
                                 (*Rooster Cogburn*)

POSNER, Richard
SEVEN-UPS, THE   FOX—RANK 1974
(Futura)

POST, *Sir* **Laurens van der**
SEED AND THE SOWER, THE   CINAVENTURE 1983
(Hogarth)   (*Merry Christmas, Mr. Lawrence*)

POTTER, Stephen
GAMESMANSHIP   WAR 1960
(Hart-Davis)   (*School for Scoundrels*)
LIFEMANSHIP   WAR 1960
(Hart-Davis)   (*School for Scoundrels*)
ONEUPMANSHIP   WAR 1960
(Hart-Davis)   (*School for Scoundrels*)

POWELL, Jonathan *see* **CHAMPION, Bob** *jt. author*

POWELL, Michael
GRAF SPEE   RANK 1956
(Hodder & Stoughton)   (*Battle of the River Plate, The*)

POWELL, Richard
PHILADELPHIAN, THE   WAR 1959
(Hodder & Stoughton)   (*City Jungle, The*)
PIONEER GO HOME   UA 1962
(Hodder & Stoughton)   (*Follow that Dream*)

POWERS, Art *and* **MISENHEIMER, M.**
FRAMED   CIC 1974
(Pinnacle, N.Y.)

PRAAG, Van Van
DAY WITHOUT END   UA 1957
(Sloane, N.Y.)   (*Men in War*)

PRATT, Theodore
BAREFOOT MAILMAN, THE   COL 1951
(Cassell)
MR. WINKLE GOES TO WAR   COL 1944
(Duell, N.Y.)

PREEDY, George *pseud.*
GENERAL CRACK   WAR 1930
(Lane)

PRESNELL, Frank G.
SEND ANOTHER COFFIN   UA 1939
(Heinemann)   (*Slightly Honourable*)

PRESSBURGER, Emeric
KILLING A MOUSE ON SUNDAY   COL 1964
(Harcourt, N.Y.)   (*Behold a Pale Horse*)

PRICE, Richard
BLOODBROTHERS   COL—WAR 1978
(Bantam, N.Y.)
WANDERERS, THE   WAR 1980
(Avon, N.Y.)

PRIESTLEY, John Boynton
BENIGHTED   BL 1963
(Heinemann)   (*Old Dark House, The*)
DANGEROUS CORNER (P)   RKO 1943
(French)
GOOD COMPANIONS, THE   FOX 1933
(Heinemann)   ABP 1957
INSPECTOR CALLS, AN (P)   BL 1954
(French)
LABURNUM GROVE (P)   ATP 1935
(Heinemann)
LET THE PEOPLE SING   BN 1942
(Heinemann)
LOST EMPIRES   GRANADA 1985 (TV)
(Heinemann)
OLD DARK HOUSE, THE   UN 1932
(Harper, N.Y.)   BL 1963

PRIESTLEY, John Boynton (*Continued*)
  THEY CAME TO A CITY (P)   EALING 1945
  (Heinemann)
  WHEN WE ARE MARRIED (P)   BN 1943
  (Heinemann)

PRIESTLEY, J.B. *see also* **MURDOCH, Iris** *jt. author*

PRIESTLEY, John Boynton *and* **KNOBLOCK, Edward**
  GOOD COMPANIONS, THE (P)   FOX 1933
  (French, N.Y.)   ABP 1957

PRINCE, Peter
  GOOD FATHER, THE   FILM FOUR 1986
  (Carroll & Graf, N.Y.)

PRITCHETT, V.S.
  WEDDING, THE   TYNE-TEES 1983 (TV)
  (*In* Selected Stories: Chatto & Windus)

PROCHAU, William
  TRINITY'S CHILD   TRI-STAR 1984
  (Putnam, N.Y.)   (*Grand Tour, The*)

PROCTER, Maurice
  HELL IS A CITY   WAR 1959
  (Hutchinson)

PROKOSCH, Frederic
  CONSPIRATORS, THE   WAR 1944
  (Chatto & Windus)

PROUTY, Olive
  NOW, VOYAGER   WAR 1942
  (Hodder & Stoughton)
  STELLA DALLAS   UA 1937
  (Hodder & Stoughton)

PRYCE, Myfanwy
  LADY IN THE DARK, THE   PAR 1944
  (Lane)

PUDNEY, John
  NET, THE   GFD 1952
  (Joseph)

AUTHOR AND ORIGINAL TITLE	FILM TITLE

THURSDAY ADVENTURE
(Evans)

BL 1955
(*Stolen air-liner*)

PUGH, Marshall
COMMANDER CRABB
(Macmillan)

ROMULUS 1958
(*Silent Enemy, The*)

PUIG, Manuel
KISS OF THE SPIDER WOMAN
(Knopf, N.Y.)

PALACE 1985

PUSHKIN, Aleksandr Sergieevich
CAPTAIN'S DAUGHTER, THE
(Various)
QUEEN OF SPADES, THE
(Various)

PAR 1959
(*Tempest*)
AB 1949

PUZO, Mario
GODFATHER, THE
(Heinemann)

SICILIAN, THE
(Linden, N.Y.)

PAR 1971
CIC 1974
(*Godfather Part II, The*)
EMI 1986

PYLE, Ernest Taylor
HERE IS YOUR WAR
(Various)
STORY OF G.I. JOE, THE
(Various)

INT 1951
(*War Correspondent*)
UA 1945

PYLE, Howard
MEN OF IRON
(Various)

UI 1954
(*Black Shield of Falworth, The*)

Q

QUEEN, Ellery *pseud.*
ELLERY QUEEN, MASTER
DETECTIVE
(Grosset, N.Y.)
PENTHOUSE MYSTERY
(Grosset, N.Y.)

COL 1940

COL 1941
(*Ellery Queen and the Penthouse
Mystery*)

QUEEN, Ellery *psued.* (*Continued*)
 PERFECT CRIME   COL 1941
 (Grosset, N.Y.)   (*Ellery Queen and the Perfect Crime*)
 SPANISH CAPE MYSTERY, THE REP 1935
 (Gollancz)
 TEN DAYS WONDER   HEMDALE 1971
 (Gollancz)

QUEFFELEC, Henri
 ISLE OF SINNERS   REGENT 1952
 (Verschoyle)

QUENEAU, Raymond
 ZAZIE   CONNOISSEUR 1962
 (Lane)

QUENTIN, Patrick *pseud.*
 BLACK WIDOW   FOX 1954
 (Simon & Schuster, N.Y.)
 MAN IN THE NET, THE   UA 1958
 (Gollancz)
 PUZZLE FOR FIENDS   AA 1958
 (Gollancz)   (*Strange Awakening, The*)

R

RAE, John
 CUSTARD BOYS, THE   GALA 1962
 (Hart-Davis)   (*Reach for Glory*)
           FOREST HILL 1980

RAINE, William McLeon
 RAWHIDE JUSTICE   GFD 1955
 (Hodder & Stoughton)   (*Man from Bitter Ridge*)

RAMAGE, Jennifer *see* **MASON, Howard** *pseud.*

RAMATI, Alexander
 BEYOND THE MOUNTAINS AMERICAN INT 1968
 (Penguin)   (*Desperate Ones, The*)
 WHILE THE POPE KEPT SILENT CANNON 1985
 (Allen & Unwin)   (*Assisi Underground, The*)

RAND, Ayn
FOUNTAINHEAD, THE   WAR 1949
(Cassell)
NIGHT OF JANUARY 16TH (P)   PAR 1941
(Longmans, N.Y.)

RANDALL, Bob
FAN, THE   CIC 1981
(Random House, N.Y.)

RANDALL, Florence E.
WATCHER IN THE WOODS   DISNEY 1982
(Atheneum, N.Y.)

RANSLEY, Peter
PRICE, THE   CHANNEL 4 1985 (TV)
(Corgi)

RANSOME, Arthur
SWALLOWS AND AMAZONS   EMI 1973
(Cape)

RANSOME, Stephen *pseud.*
HEARSES DON'T HURRY   FOX 1942
(Doubleday, N.Y.)   *(Who is Hope Schuyler?)*

RAPHAEL, Frederic
OXBRIDGE BLUES   BBC 1984 (TV)
(Penguin)
RICHARD'S THINGS   SOUTHERN 1980
(Cape)
TWO FOR THE ROAD   FOX 1967
(Cape)

RAPHAELSON, Samuel
ACCENT ON YOUTH (P)   PAR 1935
(French)   PAR 1959
                (But Not For Me)
HILDA CRANE (P)   FOX 1956
(Random House, N.Y.)
JAZZ SINGER   EMI 1980
(University of Wisconsin)
PERFECT MARRIAGE, THE (P)   PAR 1946
(Dramatists, N.Y.)
SKYLARK (P)   PAR 1941
(Various)

RASCOVICH, Mark
  BEDFORD INCIDENT, THE   BL 1964
  (Secker & Warburg)

RATTIGAN, Terence
  BEQUEST TO THE NATION (P)   UN 1972
  (Hamilton)
  BROWNING VERSION, THE (P)   GFD 1951
  (French)
  DEEP BLUE SEA, THE (P)   FOX 1955
  (Hamilton)
  FRENCH WITHOUT TEARS (P)   PAR 1940
  (French)
  SEPARATE TABLES (P)   UA 1958
  (French)
  WHILE THE SUN SHINES (P)   ABP 1947
  (Hamilton)
  WHO IS SYLVIA (P)   BL 1954
  (Hamilton)   (*Man Who Loved Redheads, The*)
  WINSLOW BOY, THE (P)   INTERNATIONAL 1949
  (Hamilton)

RAUCHER, Herman
  SUMMER OF '42   WAR 1971
  (W.H. Allen)

RAVEN, Simon
  DOCTORS WEAR SCARLET   GN 1970
  (Panther)   (*Incense for the Damned*)

RAWLINGS, *Mrs.* Marjorie
  MOCKING BIRD   EMI 1984
  (St. Simon's Island: Ga)   (*Cross Creek*)
  YEARLING, THE   MGM 1946
  (Heinemann)

RAWLS, Wilson
  WHERE THE RED FERN GROWS   EMI 1974
  (Doubleday, N.Y.)

RAWSON, Clayton
  DEATH FROM A TOP HAT   MGM 1939
  (Collins)   (*Miracles for Sale*)
  NO COFFIN FOR THE CORPSE   FOX 1942
  (Little, Brown, Boston)   (*Man Who Wouldn't Die, The*)

RAWSON, Tabor
I WANT TO LIVE   UA 1958
(Muller)

RAY, Rene
STRANGE WORLD OF PLANET X,
THE   EROS 1958
(Jenkins)

RAYMAN, Sylvia
WOMEN OF TWILIGHT (P)   ROMULUS 1952
(Evans)

RAYMOND, Ernest
BERG, THE (P)   BI 1930
(Benn)   (*Atlantic*)
FOR THEM THAT TRESPASS   ABP 1949
(Cassell)
TELL ENGLAND   CAPITOL 1931
(Cassell)

RAYMOND, Moore
SMILEY   FOX 1955
(Sylvan Press)

RAYNER, Denys Arthur
ESCORT   FOX 1957
(Kimber)   (*Enemy Below, The*)

READ, Piers P.
MARRIED MAN, A   LWT 1985 (TV)
(Avon, N.Y.)

REAGE, Pauline
STORY OF O, THE   NEW REALM 1976
(Olympia)

REBETA, Joyce
CRACKER FACTORY, THE   BBC 1984 (TV)
(Bantam, N.Y.)

REED, Barry
VERDICT, THE   FOX 1983
(Bantam, N.Y.)

REED, J.D.
  FREEFALL   BARBER 1981
  (Delacorte, N.Y.)   (*Pursuit*)

REED, Mark White
  YES, MY DARLING DAUGHTER (P)   WAR 1939
  (French, N.Y.)

REED, Myrtle
  SPINNER IN THE SUN   FOX 1929
  (Putnam)   (*Veiled Woman*)

REESE, John
  LOOTERS, THE   UN 1973
  (Hale)   (*Charley Varrick*)

REID, P.R.
  COLDITZ STORY, THE   BL 1954
  (Hodder & Stoughton)

REID, Robert
  MADAME CURIE   BBC 1984 (TV)
  (Collins)

REMARQUE, Erich Maria
  ALL QUIET ON THE WESTERN
  FRONT   UN 1930
  (Putnam)   ITC 1980
  ARCH OF TRIUMPH   UA 1948
  (Hutchinson)   HTV 1984 (TV)
  FLOTSAM   UA 1941
  (Hutchinson)   (*So Ends Our Night*)
  HEAVEN HAS NO FAVOURITES   COL—WAR 1977
  (Harcourt, N.Y.)   (*Bobby Deerfield*)
  ROAD BACK   UN 1937
  (Putnam)
  THREE COMRADES   MGM 1938
  (Hutchinson)
  TIME TO LOVE AND A TIME TO DIE
  (Hutchinson)   RANK 1957

RESKO, John
  REPRIEVE   WAR 1962
  (MacGibbon)

RESNIK, Muriel
SON OF ANY WEDNESDAY (P)   WAR 1966
(Stein & Day, N.Y.)   *(Any Wednesday)*
TURQUOISE BIKINI, THE   WAR 1968
(Transworld)   *(How Sweet It Is)*

REUBEN, David
EVERYTHING YOU WANTED TO
KNOW ABOUT SEX BUT WERE
AFRAID TO ASK   UA 1972
(W.H. Allen)

RHODES, Denys
SYNDICATE, THE   WAR 1968
(Four Square Books)

RHODES, Eugene Manlove
PASO POR AQUI   UA 1948
(Houghton, Mifflin, Boston)   *(Four Faces West)*

RHYS, Jean
QUARTET   FOX 1981
(Harper, N.Y.)

RICE, Alice Caldwell
MRS. WIGGS OF THE CABBAGE
PATCH   PAR 1934
(Grosset, N.Y.)

RICE, Craig
HAVING WONDERFUL CRIME   RKO 1945
(Nicholson & Watson)
HOME SWEET HOMICIDE   FOX 1946
(World, N.Y.)
LUCKY STIFF, THE   UA 1948
(World, N.Y.)

RICE, Elmer L.
ADDING MACHINE (P)   RANK 1970
(*In* Seven Plays: Viking, N.Y.)
COUNSELLOR AT LAW (P)   UN 1933
(Gollancz)
DREAM GIRL (P)   PAR 1947
(Coward-McCann, N.Y.)

RICE, Elmer L. (*Continued*)
SEE NAPLES AND DIE (P)   WAR 1931
(French, N.Y.)   (*Oh! Sailor, Behave!*)
STREET SCENE (P)   UA 1931
(French, N.Y.)

RICHARDSON, Henry Handel
GETTING OF WISDOM, THE   TEDDERWICK 1979
(Heinemann)
MAURICE GUEST   MGM 1954
(Heinemann)   (*Rhapsody*)

RICHARDSON, Samuel
PAMELA   MGM—EMI 1973
(Various)   (*Mistress Pamela*)

RICHLER, Mordecai
APPRENTICESHIP OF DUDDY   RANK 1975
KRAVITZ, THE
(Deutsch)

RICHMAN, Arthur
NOT SO LONG AGO (P)   COL 1953
(French, N.Y.)   (*Let's Do It Again*)

RICHTER, Conrad Michael
LIGHT IN THE FOREST, THE   DISNEY 1958
(Gollancz)
SEA OF GRASS   MGM 1947
(Constable)
TRACEY CROMWELL   UI 1955
(Knopf, N.Y.)   (*One Desire*)

RIDLEY, Arnold
BEGGAR MY NEIGHBOUR (P)   GFD 1953
(Evans)   (*Meet Mr. Lucifer*)
GHOST TRAIN, THE (P)   GFD 1931
(French, N.Y.)   GFD 1941
KEEPERS OF YOUTH   POWERS 1932
(Benn)

RIDLEY, Arnold *and* **BORER, Mary**
TABITHA (P)   GN 1966
(French)   (*Who Killed the Cat?*)

RIGBY, Kay *and* **ALLEN, R.S.**
  HILL, THE   MGM 1965
  (Mayflower)

RIMMER, Robert H.
  HARRAD EXPERIMENT, THE   FOX 1974
  (New English Library)

RINEHART, Mary Roberts
  BAT, THE   UA 1931
  (Cassell)   (*Bat Whispers, The*)
  BAT, THE (P)   WAR 1959
  (French)
  CASE OF ELINOR NORTON, THE   FOX 1935
  (Cassell)
  LOST ECSTASY   PAR 1931
  (Doran, N.Y.)   (*I Take This Woman*)
  MISS PINKERTON   WAR 1941
  (Various)   (*Nurse's Secret, The*)
  TISH CARRIES ON   MGM 1942
  (Cassell)   (*Tish*)

ROARK, Garland
  FAIR WIND TO JAVA   REP 1953
  (Falcon Press)
  WAKE OF THE RED WITCH   REP 1948
  (Aldor)

ROBB, John *pseud.*
  PUNITIVE ACTION   UA 1955
  (Hamilton)   (*Desert Sand*)

ROBBINS, Harold
  ADVENTURERS, THE   PAR 1968
  (Blond)
  BETSY, THE   UA 1978
  (New English Library)
  CARPETBAGGERS, THE   PAR 1963
  (Blond)   PAR 1963
                         (*Nevada Smith*)
  LONELY LADY, THE   COL—EMI—WAR 1983
  (PB., N.Y.)
  NEVER LOVE A STRANGER   ABP 1957
  (Corgi)

ROBBINS, Harold (*Continued*)
79 PARK AVENUE   UN 1977
(New English Library)
STILETTO   AVCO EMBASSY 1970
(Mayflower)
STONE FOR DANNY FISHER, A   PAR 1958
(Hale)   (*King Creole*)
WHERE LOVE HAS GONE   PAR 1964
(Blond)

ROBERTS, Carl Eric Bechofer
DON CHICAGO   BN 1945
(Jarrolds)

ROBERTS, Denys
SMUGGLERS CIRCUIT   BL 1958
(Methuen)   (*Law and Disorder*)

ROBERTS, Elizabeth Maddox
GREAT MEADOW, THE   MGM 1931
(Cape)

ROBERTS, Kenneth
CAPTAIN CAUTION   UA 1940
(Collins)
LYDIA BAILEY   FOX 1952
(Collins)
NORTH-WEST PASSAGE   MGM 1940
(Collins)   MGM 1959
     (*Frontier Rangers*)
     MGM 1959
     (*Mission of Danger*)

ROBERTS, Richard Emery
GILDED ROOSTER, THE   COL 1955
(Laurie)   (*Last Frontier, The*)
SECOND TIME ROUND   FOX 1961
(Pocket Bks.)
Previously Published as
Star in the West

ROBERTSON, Willard
MOONTIDE   FOX 1942
(Hamilton)

ROBESON, Kenneth
DOC SAVAGE—THE MAN OF
BRONZE   COL—WAR 1975
(Corgi)

ROBINSON, Budd *see* **AMATEAU, R.** *jt. author*

ROBINSON, Frank
POWER, THE   MGM 1968
(Sphere)

ROBINSON, Henry Morton
CARDINAL, THE   COL 1963
(Macdonald)

ROBINSON, Lennox
BIG HOUSE, THE   MGM 1930
(Macmillan)

ROBINSON, Marilynne
HOUSEKEEPING   CANNON 1986
(Farrar, N.Y.)

ROBSON, Norman *see* **ROBB, John** *pseud.*

ROCHE, Arthur Somers
CASE AGAINST MRS. AMES, THE   PAR 1936
(Melrose)

ROCHE, Mazo de la
JALNA   RKO 1935
(Macmillan)

ROCK, Philip
EXTRAORDINARY SEAMAN   MGM 1967
(Souvenir Press)

RODGERS, Mary
FREAKY FRIDAY   DISNEY 1976
(Hamilton)

ROE, Vingle
GOLDEN TIDE, THE   REP 1953
(Cassell)

ROFFEY, Jack
  HOSTILE WITNESS (P)   UA 1968
  (Evans)

ROGERS, Thomas
  PURSUIT OF HAPPINESS, THE   COL 1971
  (Bodley Head)

ROHMER, Sax
  DAUGHTER OF THE DRAGON   PAR 1931
  (Cassell)
  DRUMS OF FU MANCHU   REP 1943
  (Cassell)
  MASK OF FU MANCHU   MGM 1932
  (Cassell)
  MYSTERY OF DR. FU MANCHU   PAR 1929
  (Methuen)   (*Mysterious Dr. Fu Manchu*)
  RETURN OF DR. FU MANCHU   PAR 1930
  (*In* Book of Dr. Fu Manchu, The:
  Hurst & Blackett)

ROIPHE, Anne Richardson
  UP THE SANDBOX   CINERAMA 1973
  (Secker & Warburg)

ROMERO, George A.
  MARTIN   MIRACLE FILMS 1979
  (Futura)

RONALD, James
  MEDAL FOR A GENERAL, A   BN 1944
  (Hodder & Stoughton)
  THEY CAN'T HANG ME   UN 1939
  (Rich & Cowan)   (*Witness Vanishes, The*)
  THIS WAY OUT   UN 1944
  (Rich & Cowan)   (*Suspect, The*)

ROOK, David
  BALLAD OF THE BELSTONE FOX,
  THE   FOX—RANK 1972
  (Hodder & Stoughton)   (*Belstone Fox, The*)
  WHITE COLT, THE   COL 1969
  (Hodder & Stoughton)

ROONEY, Philip
  CAPTAIN BOYCOTT   INDIVIDUAL 1947
  (Talbot Press)

ROOTES, Nina
  FROG PRINCE, THE   WAR 1985
  (Arrow)

RORICK, Isabel Scott
  MR. AND MRS. CUGAT   PAR 1942
  (Jarrolds)   (*Are Husbands Necessary?*)

ROSE, Alexander
  FOUR PUNTERS ARE MISSING PAR 1963
  (Hamilton)   (*Who's Got The Action?*)

ROSE, Anna Perrott
  ROOM FOR ONE MORE   WAR 1952
  (Houghton, Mifflin, Boston)

ROSE, Edward Everett
  REAR CAR (P)   MGM 1934
  (French, N.Y.)   (*Murder in the Private Car*)

ROSNY, J.H.
  QUEST FOR FIRE   FOX 1982
  (Ballantine, N.Y.)

ROSS, J. *see* **ADLER, R.** *jt. author*

ROSS, Martin *see* **SOMERVILLE, E.** *jt. author*

ROSS, Sam
  HE RAN ALL THE WAY   UA 1951
  (Farrar, N.Y.)

ROSSNER, Judith
  LOOKING FOR MR. GOODBAR CIC 1978
  (Cape)

ROSTAND, Esmond
  CYRANO DE BERGERAC (P)   UA 1950
  (*In* A Treasury of the Theatre: Simon & RKO 1985
  Schuster, N.Y.)

ROSTAND, Robert
KILLER ELITE, THE   UA 1976
(Dell, N.Y.)

ROSTEN, Leo
CAPTAIN NEWMAN, M.D.   UI 1963
(Gollancz)

ROTH, Arthur
TERRIBLE BEAUTY, A   UA 1960
(Hutchinson)

ROTH, Lillian
I'LL CRY TOMORROW   MGM 1955
(Gollancz)

ROTH, Philip
GOODBYE, COLUMBUS   PAR 1969
(Deutsch)
PORTNOY'S COMPLAINT   COL—WAR 1972
(Cape)

ROUSSIN, Andre
LITTLE HUT, THE (P)   MGM 1957
(Random House, N.Y.)

RUARK, Robert
SOMETHING OF VALUE   MGM 1957
(Hamilton)

RUBIN, Theodore I.
LISA AND DAVID   BL 1963
(Macmillan)   (*David and Lisa*)

RUESCH, Hans
RACER, THE   FOX 1954
(Hurst & Blackett)   (*Racers, The*)
       FOX 1958
       (*Men Against Speed*)
TOP OF THE WORLD   RANK 1960
(Gollancz)   (*Savage Innocents, The*)

RUGGLES, Eleanor
PRINCE OF PLAYERS   FOX 1954
(Davies)

RULE, Jane
 DESERT OF THE HEART   MGM 1985
 (Tallhassee: Fl)   (*Desert Hearts*)

RUNYON, Damon
 BLOODHOUNDS OF BROADWAY   FOX 1952
 (Various)
 JOHNNY ONE-EYE   UA 1950
 (*In* Runyon à la carte: Constable)
 LEMON DROP KID, THE   PAR 1951
 (*In* Guys and Dolls: Lippincott,
 Philadelphia)
 MONEY FROM HOME   PAR 1953
 (Various)

RUNYON, Damon *and* LINDSAY, Howard
 LAST BATTLE, THE   WAR 1938
 (Collins)   MGM 1968
 SLIGHT CASE OF MURDER, A (P)   WAR 1952
 (Dramatists, N.Y.)   (*Stop, You're Killing Me*)

RUSSELL, John
 WHERE THE PAVEMENT ENDS   PAR 1930
 (Butterworth)   (*Sea God, The*)

RUSSELL, Mary Annette Beauchamp Russell, *Countess see* **'ELIZABETH'** *pseud.*

RUSSELL, Ray
 INCUBUS   NEW REALM 1982
 (Sphere)

RUSSELL, Sheila MacKay
 LAMP IS HEAVY, A   RANK 1956
 (Angus & Robertson)   (*Feminine Touch, The*)

RUSSELL, Willy
 EDUCATING RITA (P)   RANK 1983
 (French)

RYAN, Cornelius
 BRIDGE TOO FAR, A   UA 1977
 (Hamilton)
 LAST BATTLE, THE   MGM 1968
 (Collins)

RUSSELL, Willy (*Continued*)
LONGEST DAY, THE   FOX 1962
(Gollancz)

RYAN, J.M.
BROOK WILSON LTD   COL 1969
(Hodder Fawcett)

RYAN, Patrick
HOW I WON THE WAR   UA 1967
(Muller)

                              S

ST. LAURENT, Cecil
CAROLINE CHERI   WAR 1968
(Heinemann)

SABATINI, Rafael
BLACK SWAN, THE   FOX 1942
(Hutchinson)
CAPTAIN BLOOD   IN 1935
(Hutchinson)
CAPTAIN BLOOD RETURNS   COL 1952
(Hutchinson)   (*Captain Blood Fugitive*)
COLUMBUS   GFD 1949
(Hutchinson)   (*Christopher Columbus*)
FORTUNES OF CAPTAIN BLOOD,
THE   COL 1950
(Hutchinson)
SCARAMOUCHE   MGM 1952
(Hutchinson)
SEA HAWK, THE   WAR 1940
(Various)   CANNON 1985

SACHER-MASOCH, Leopold
VENUS IN FURS   COMMONWEALTH 1970
(Various)

SACKLER, Howard
GREAT WHITE HOPE, THE (P)   FOX 1971
(Faber)

SACKEVILLE-WEST, V.
ALL PASSION SPENT   BBC 1986 (TV)
(Virago)

SADLEIR, Michael
FANNY BY GASLIGHT   GFD 1944
(Constable)   BBC 1982 (TV)

SAGAN, Carl
COSMIC CONNECTION   POLYGRAM 1982
(Macmillan)   (*Contact*)

SAGAN, Françoise
AIMEZ-VOUZ BRAHMS?   UA 1961
(Murray)   (*Goodbye Again*)
BONJOUR TRISTESSE   COL 1957
(Murray)
CERTAIN SMILE, A   FOX 1958
(Murray)
HEART KEEPER, THE   FOX 1969
(Murray)

SAINT-EXUPERY, Antoine
LITTLE PRINCE, THE   CIC 1974
(Various)

SALAMANCA, J.R.
LILITH   BL 1963
(Heinemann)
LOST COUNTRY, THE   FOX 1961
(Four Square Books)   (*Wild in the Country*)

SALE, Richard
NOT TOO NARROW, NOT TOO
DEEP   MGM 1940
(Cassell)   (*Strange Cargo*)
OSCAR, THE   PAR 1965
(Cassell)
WHITE BUFFALO, THE   EMI 1978
(Simon & Schuster, N.Y.)

SALTEN, Felix
BAMBI   RKO 1942
(Various)

SALTEN, Felix (*Continued*)
  FLORIAN   MGM 1940
  (Cape)
  PERRI   DISNEY 1957
  (Cape)

SALTER, James
  HUNTERS, THE   FOX 1958
  (Heinemann)

SANDERS, George
  STRANGER AT HOME   EXCLUSIVE 1954
  (Pilot Press)   (*Stranger Came Home*)

SANDERS, Lawrence
  ANDERSON TAPES, THE   COL 1971
  (Coronet)
  FIRST DEADLY SIN, THE   CIC 1981
  (Star)

SANDOZ, Mari
  CHEYENNE AUTUMN   WAR 1964
  (McGraw-Hill, N.Y.)

SANDS, Leslie
  INTENT TO MURDER (P)   EROS 1952
  (English Theatre)   (*Another Man's Poison*)

SANDSTROM, Flora
  MADNESS OF THE HEART   TC 1949
  (Cassell)
  MIDWIFE OF PONT CLERY UA 1961
  (Cassell)   (*Jessica*)
  MILK WHITE UNICORN, THE BN 1947
  (Cassell)   (*White Unicorn, The*)

SANFORD, Harry *and* **LAMB, H.**
  EMPORIA   PAR 1967
  (Hale)   (*Waco*)

SANSOM, William
  LAST HOURS OF SANDRA LEE,
  THE   BL 1965
  (Hogarth Press)   (*Wild Affair, The*)

SAPERSTEIN, David
  COCOON   FOX 1984
  (Granada)

SAPIN, Richard *see* **MURPHY, Warren** *jt. author*

'SAPPER' *pseud.*
  BULLDOG DRUMMOND AT BAY   REP 1937
  (Hodder & Stoughton)
  CHALLENGE, THE   PAR 1938
  (Hodder & Stoughton)   (*Bulldog Drummond in Africa*)
  FEMALE OF THE SPECIES   PAR 1937
  (Hodder & Stoughton)   (*Bulldog Drummond Comes Back*)
  TEMPLE TOWER   PAR 1939
  (Hodder & Stoughton)   (*Bulldog Drummond's Secret Police*)
  THIRD ROUND, THE   PAR 1938
  (Hodder & Stoughton)   (*Bulldog Drummond's Peril*)

SAROYAN, William
  HUMAN COMEDY, THE   MGM 1943
  (Faber)
  TIME OF YOUR LIFE (P)   UA 1948
  (Faber)

SARTRE, Jean-Paul
  CHIPS ARE DOWN, THE   LOPERT 1949
  (Rider)
  LOSER WINS (P)   FOX 1964
  (Hamilton)
  RESPECTABLE PROSTITUTE, THE
  (P)   GALA 1955
  (*In* No Exit and 3 Other Plays: Vintage
  Bks., N.Y.)

SAUNDERS, Hilary St. George
  RED BERET, THE   COL 1953
  (Joseph)

SAUNDERS, Hilary St. George *see also* **BEEDING, Francis** *pseud.*

SAUNDERS, John Monk
  DAWN PATROL, THE   IN 1930
  (Queensway Press)   WAR 1938

SAVAGE, Mildred
PARRISH   WAR 1960
(Longmans)

SAVORY, Gerald
GEORGE AND MARGARET (P)   WAR 1940
(French)

SAXON, Lyle
LAFITTE THE PIRATE   PAR 1938
(Appleton, N.Y.)   (*Buccaneer, The*)

SAXON, Peter
DISORIENTATED MAN, THE   AMERICAN INT 1969
(Baker)   (*Scream and Scream Again*)

SAYERS, Dorothy Leigh
BUSMAN'S HONEYMOON   MGM 1940
(Gollancz)   (*Busman's Holiday*)

SAYERS, Dorothy Leigh *and* **BYRNE, M. St. Clare**
BUSMAN'S HONEYMOON (P)   MGM 1940
(Harcourt, N.Y.)   (*Busman's Holiday*)

SCHAEFER, Jack Warner
BIG RANGE   FOX 1953
(Deutsch)   (*Silver Whip, The*)
COMPANY OF COWARDS   MGM 1965
(Mayflower)
MONTE WALSH   CINEMA CENTER 1969
(Deutsch)
SHANE   PAR 1953
(Deutsch)

SCHANBERG, Sydney
DEATH AND LIFE OF DITH PRAN,   WAR 1984
THE   (*Killing Fields, The*)
(Pan)

SCHARY, Dore
SUNRISE AT CAMPOBELLO (P)   WAR 1960
(Random House, N.Y.)

SCHAUFFLER, Elsie
PARNELL (P)   MGM 1937
(Gollancz)

SCHIROKAUER, Alfred
  PAIVA: QUEEN OF LOVE   GFD 1948
  (Jarrolds)   *(Idol of Paris, The)*

SCHISGAL, Murray
  LUV (P)   BL 1966
  (Coward-McCann, N.Y.)
  TYPISTS AND THE TIGER, THE (P)   COL 1968
  (Cape)   *(Tiger Makes Out)*

SCHISGALL, Oscar *see* **HARDY, Stuart** *pseud.*

SCHNITZLER, Arthur
  LA RONDE   BL 1964
  (HCC Bks.)
  MERRY GO ROUND   COMMERCIAL 1951
  (Weidenfeld & Nicolson)   *(La Ronde)*

SCHOLEFIELD, Alan
  VENOM   HEMDALE 1982
  (Heinemann)

SCHOTT, Max
  MURPHY'S ROMANCE   COL—EMI—WAR 1985
  (Capra: Santa Barbara)

SCREIBER, Flora R.
  SYBIL   BARBER—DANN 1979
  (Warner, N.Y.)

SCHULBERG, Bud Wilson
  HARDER THEY FALL, THE   COL 1956
  (Lane)
  SOME FACES IN THE CROWD   WAR 1957
  (Lane)   *(Face in the Crowd, A)*

SCHULMAN, Arnold
  HOLE IN THE HEAD, A (P)   UA 1959
  (Random House, N.Y.)

SCHULMAN, Irving
  CHILDREN OF THE DARK   WAR 1955
  (World, N.Y.)   *(Rebel Without a Cause)*

SCHWEIZER, Richard
  LAST CHANCE, THE   MGM 1945
  (Drummond *and* Secker & Warburg)

SCORTIA, T. *and* **ROBINSON, F.**
  GLASS INFERNO, THE   COL—WAR 1975
  (Hodder & Stoughton)   (*Towering Inferno, The*)

SCOTT, Allan *and* **HAIGHT, George**
  GOODBYE AGAIN (P)   WAR 1941
  (French, N.Y.)   (*Honeymoon for Three*)

SCOTT, J.D.
  SEA WYF AND BISCUIT   FOX 1957
  (Heinemann)   (*Sea-wife*)

SCOTT, Paul
  RAJ QUARTET, THE   GRANADA 1983 (TV)
  (Heinemann)   (*Jewel in the Crown, The*)
  STAYING ON   GRANADA 1985 (TV)
  (Heinemann)

SCOTT, Robert Lee
  GOD IS MY CO-PILOT   WAR 1945
  (Hodder & Stoughton)

SCOTT, *Sir* **Walter**
  IVANHOE   MGM 1951
  (Various)
  QUENTIN DURWARD   MGM 1955
  (Various)   (*Adventures of Quentin Durward*)
  TALISMAN, THE   WAR 1954
  (Various)   (*King Richard and the Crusaders*)

SCUDDER, Kenyon Judson
  PRISONERS ARE PEOPLE   WAR 1954
  (Doubleday, N.Y.)   (*Unchained*)

'SEAMARK' *pseud.*
  MAN THEY COULDN'T ARREST,
  THE   GB 1933
  (Hodder & Stoughton)

SEARLS, Henry
   CROWDED SKY, THE   WAR 1960
   (Harper, N.Y.)

SECONDARI, John
   COINS IN THE FOUNTAIN   FOX 1954
   (Eyre & Spottiswoode)   (*Three Coins in the Fountain*)
                    FOX 1965
                    (*Pleasure Seekers, The*)

SEELEY, Clinton
   STORM FEAR   UA 1955
   (Holt, N.Y.)

SEGAL, Erich Wolf
   LOVE STORY   PAR 1970
   (Hodder & Stoughton)
   MAN, WOMAN AND CHILD   COL—EMI—WAR 1983
   (Granada)
   OLIVER'S STORY   CIC 1979
   (Harper, N.Y.)

SEGALL, Harry
   HALFWAY TO HEAVEN (P)   COL 1941
   (French)   (*Here Comes Mr. Jordan*)

SEGHERS, Anna
   SEVENTH CROSS, THE   MGM 1944
   (Hamilton)

SELINKO, Annemarie
   DÉSIRÉE   FOX 1954
   (Heinemann)

SELTZER, David
   OMEN, THE   FOX 1976
   (Futura)

SEMPLE, Lorenzo
   GOLDEN FLEECING, THE (P)   MGM 1961
   (French, N.Y.)   (*Honeymoon Machine, The*)

SETON, Anya
   DRAGONWYCK   FOX 1946
   (Hodder & Stoughton)

599

SETON, Anya (*Continued*)
  FOXFIRE   UI 1954
  (Hodder & Stoughton)

SETON, Ernest Thompson
  BIOGRAPHY OF A GRIZZLY, THE   DISNEY 1969
  (Hodder & Stoughton)   (*King of the Grizzlies*)
  BIOGRAPHY OF A SILVER FOX,
  THE   DISNEY 1962
  (Appleton)   (*Silver Fox and Sam Davenport*)
  LOBO AND OTHER STORIES   DISNEY 1962
  (Hodder & Stoughton)   (*Legend of Lobo, The*)

SETON, Graham *pseud.*
  W PLAN   RKO 1931
  (Butterworth)

SEWARD, Florence A.
  GOLD FOR THE CAESARS   MGM 1963
  (Redman)

SEWELL, Anna
  BLACK BEAUTY   FOX 1946
  (Various)   TIGON 1971

SEYMOUR, Gerald
  GLORY BOYS, THE   YORKSHIRE TV 1984 (TV)
  (Random House, N.Y.)
  HARRY'S GAME   YORKSHIRE 1982 (TV)
  (Collins)

SEYMOUR, Henry
  INFERNAL IDOL   EMI 1974
  (Avon, N.Y.)   (*Craze*)

SHAFFER, Anthony
  SLEUTH (P)   FOX 1972
  (Calder)

SHAFFER, Peter
  AMADEUS (P)   ORION 1983
  (Penguin)
  EQUUS   UA 1977
  (Deutsch)
  FIVE FINGER EXERCISE (P)   COL 1962
  (French)

AUTHOR AND ORIGINAL TITLE	FILM TITLE
PRIVATE EAR, THE (P)	UI 1967
(French)	(*Pad, The (and how to use it)*)
PUBLIC EYE, THE (P)	UN 1972
(French)	(*Follow Me*)
ROYAL HUNT OF THE SUN, THE (P)	
(Pan)	RANK 1968

SHAGAN, Steve

FORMULA, THE	MGM 1980
(Bantam, N.Y.)	
SAVE THE TIGER	PAR 1973
(Joseph)	

SHAKESPEARE, William

ANTONY AND CLEOPATRA (P)	RANK 1972
(Various)	
AS YOU LIKE IT (P)	FOX 1936
(Various)	
HAMLET (P)	TC 1948
(Various)	CLASSIC CINEMAS 1964
	COL 1969
HENRY V (P)	TC 1945
(Various)	
JULIUS CAESAR (P)	MGM 1953
(Various)	MGM 1969
KING LEAR (P)	COL 1970
(Various)	GRANADA 1982 (TV)
	CANNON 1986
MACBETH (P)	REP 1951
(Various)	BL 1960
	COL—WAR 1971
MERCHANT OF VENICE, THE (P)	PRECISION 1974
(Various)	
MIDSUMMER NIGHT'S DREAM, A	
(P)	WAR 1935
(Various)	EAGLE 1969
	MAINLINE 1985
OTHELLO (P)	UA 1956
(Various)	EAGLE FILMS 1966
	EUROCINE 1982 (TV)
	(*Othello the Black Commando*)
RICHARD III (P)	BL 1955
(Various)	

SHAKESPEARE, William (*Continued*)
  ROMEO AND JULIET (P)   MGM 1936
  (Various)   GFD 1954
                                 GALA 1956
                                 RANK 1966
                                 PAR 1968
  TAMING OF THE SHREW, THE (P)   INVICTA 1933
  (Various)   MGM 1953
                                 (*Kiss me Kate*)
                                 COL 1966
  TEMPEST, THE (P)   RAFTERS 1969
  (Various)   MAINLINE 1979
  WINTER'S TALE, A (P)   WAR 1968
  (Various)

SHAPIRO, Lionel
  SEALED VERDICT   PAR 1948
  (Doubleday, N.Y.)
  SIXTH OF JUNE, THE   FOX 1956
  (Collins)   (*D Day Sixth of June*)

SHARP, Don
  CONFLICT OF WINGS   BL 1954
  (Putnam, N.Y.)

SHARP, Margery
  CLUNY BROWN   FOX 1946
  (Collins)
  NUTMEG TREE   MGM 1948
  (Various)   (*Julia Misbehaves*)
  RESCUERS AND MISS BIANCA, THE DISNEY 1977
  (Dell, N.Y.)   (*Rescuers*)

SHARPE, Tom
  BLOTT ON THE LANDSCAPE   BBC 1985 (TV)
  (Secker & Warburg)

SHAW, Charles
  HEAVEN KNOWS, MR. ALLISON   FOX 1957
  (Muller)

SHAW, George Bernard
  ANDROCLES AND THE LION (P)   RKO 1952
  (Constable)
  ARMS AND THE MAN (P)   GB 1932
  (Various)   ARGENT 1982 (TV)

CAESAR AND CLEOPATRA (P)   PASCAL 1945
(Various)
DEVIL'S DISCIPLE, THE (P)   UA 1959
(Constable)
DOCTOR'S DILEMMA, THE (P)   MGM 1958
(Constable)
GREAT CATHERINE (P)   WAR 1968
(Constable)
HOW HE LIED TO HER HUSBAND
(P)   BI 1931
(Constable)
MAJOR BARBARA (P)   PASCAL 1941
(Various)
MILLIONAIRESS, THE (P)   FOX 1960
(Constable)
PYGMALION (P)   MGM 1938
(Constable)   WAR 1964
       (*My Fair Lady*)
SAINT JOAN (P)   UA 1957
(Constable)

SHAW, Irwin

GENTLE PEOPLE, THE (P)   WAR 1941
(Dramatists, N.Y.)   (*Out of the Fog*)
IN THE FRENCH STYLE   COL 1963
(*In* Tip of a Dead Jockey: Cape)
RICH MAN, POOR MAN   ABC 1975 (TV)
(Cape)
THEN WE WERE THREE   UA 1969
(*In* Tip of a Dead Jockey: Cape)   (*Three*)
TWO WEEKS IN ANOTHER TOWN   MGM 1962
(Cape)
YOUNG LIONS, THE   FOX 1957
(Cape)

SHAW, Robert

HIDING PLACE, THE   PAR 1964
(Chatto & Windus)   (*Situation Hopeless but not Serious*)

SHEARING, Joseph *pseud.*

AIRING IN A CLOSED CARRIAGE   TC 1948
(Hutchinson)   (*Mark of Cain*)
BLANCHE FURY   CINEGUILD 1948
(Heinemann)

SHEARING, Joseph *pseud.* (*Continued*)
FOR HER TO SEE   PAR 1948
(Hutchinson)   (*So Evil My Love*)
MOSS ROSE   FOX 1947
(Heinemann)

SHECKLEY, Robert
GAME OF X, THE   DISNEY 1981
(*In* Wonderful World of Robert Sheckley: (*Condorman*)
Sphere)
PRIZE OF PERIL, THE   SAADA 1983
(*In* Wonderful World of Robert Sheckley:
Sphere)

SHEEAN, Vincent
FOREIGN CORRESPONDENT   UA 1940
(Hamilton)
Originally published as: In Search of History

SHELDON, Charles Monroe
IN HIS STEPS   GN 1936
(Warne)

SHELDON, Sidney
BLOODLINE   CIC 1979
(Morrow, N.Y.)   (*Sidney Sheldon's Bloodline*)
MASTER OF THE GAME   ROSEMOUNT 1984
(Collins)
NAKED FACE, THE   CANNON 1983
(Morrow, N.Y.)
OTHER SIDE OF MIDNIGHT, THE   FOX 1977
(Hodder & Stoughton)
RAGE OF ANGELS   NBC 1983 (TV)
(Morrow, N.Y.)

SHELLABARGER, Samuel
CAPTAIN FROM CASTILE   FOX 1948
(Macmillan)
PRINCE OF FOXES   FOX 1949
(Macmillan)

SHELLEY, Mary Wollstonecraft
FRANKENSTEIN   WAR 1931
(Dent)   WAR 1957
                                  (*Curse of Frankenstein, The*)
                                  YORKSHIRE TV 1984 (TV)

SHELLEY, P.B.
ZASTROZZI   CHANNEL 4 1986 (TV)
(Various)

SHELLEY, Sidney
McKENZIE BREAK, THE   UA 1971
(Sphere)

SHEPARD, S.
FOOL FOR LOVE (P)   CANNON 1986
(San Francisco: Cal)

SHERLOCK, John
ORDEAL OF MAJOR GRIGSBY, THE   CINERAMA 1969
(Hutchinson)   (*Last Grenade, The*)

SHERMAN, Richard
TO MARY—WITH LOVE   FOX 1936
(Faber)

SHERRIFF, Robert Cedric
BADGERS GREEN (P)   HIGHBURY 1949
(Gollancz)
HOME AT SEVEN (P)   BL 1951
(Gollancz)
JOURNEY'S END (P)   TIFFANY 1930
(Gollancz)   EMI 1976
                    (*Aces High*)

SHERRIFF, Robert Cedric *and* **BARTLETT, Vernon**
JOURNEY'S END   TIFFANY 1930
(Gollancz)

SHERRY, Edna
SUDDEN FEAR   RKO 1952
(Hodder & Stoughton)

SHERRY, Gordon
BLACK LIMELIGHT (P)   ALL 1939
(French)

SHERWIN, David
IF   GB 1967
(Sphere)

SHERWOOD, Robert Emmet
  ABE LINCOLN OF ILLINOIS (P)   RKO 1940
  (Scribner, N.Y.)   (*Abe Lincoln in Illinois*)
  IDIOT'S DELIGHT (P)   MGM 1939
  (Heinemann)
  PETRIFIED FOREST, THE (P)   WAR 1936
  (Scribner, N.Y.)   WAR 1945
        (*Escape in the Desert*)
  QUEEN'S HUSBAND, THE (P)   RKO 1931
  (Scribner, N.Y.)   (*Royal Bed*)
  REUNION IN VIENNA (P)   MGM 1933
  (Scribner, N.Y.)
  ROAD TO ROME, THE (P)   MGM 1954
  (French, N.Y.)   (*Jupiter's Darling*)
  THIS IS NEW YORK (P)   PAR 1932
  (Scribner, N.Y.)   (*Two Kinds of Women*)
  WATERLOO BRIDGE (P)   UN 1930
  (Scribner, N.Y.)   MGM 1940
        MGM 1955
        (*Gaby*)

SHIBER, *Mrs.* **Ella**
  PARIS-UNDERGROUND   UA 1945
  (Harrap)

SHIEL, M.P.
  PURPLE CLOUD, THE   MGM 1959
  (Gollancz)   (*World, the Flesh and the Devil, The*)

SHIELS, George
  PROFESSOR TIM (P)   RKO 1957
  (Macmillan)

SHIRREFS, Gordon Donald
  TRAILS END   ABP 1957
  (Avalon, N.Y.)   (*Oregon Passage*)

SHORT, Luke *pseud.*
  AMBUSH   MGM 1950
  (Collins)
  CORONER CREEK   COL 1948
  (Collins)
  HIGH VERMILION   PAR 1951
  (Collins)

SILVER ROCK   REP 1954
(Collins)   (*Hell's Outpost*)
STATION WEST   RKO 1948
(Collins)
VENGEANCE VALLEY, THE   MGM 1950
(Collins)

SHULMAN, Irving
AMBOY DUKES, THE   UI 1949
(Doubleday, N.Y.)   (*City Across the River*)
CHILDREN OF THE DARK   UA 1959
(Holt, N.Y.)   (*Cry Tough*)
HARLOW   PAR 1964
(Mayflower Bks.)
NOTORIOUS LANDLADY, THE   COL 1962
(Gold Medal Bks.)

SHULMAN, Max
'RALLY ROUND THE FLAG, BOYS!'   FOX 1958
(Heinemann)

SHULMAN, Max *and* **SMITH, Robert Paul**
TENDER TRAP (P)   MGM 1955
(Random House, N.Y.)

SHUTE, Nevil *pseud.*
LANDFALL   AB 1948
(Heinemann)
NO HIGHWAY   FOX 1951
(Heinemann)
ON THE BEACH   UA 1959
(Heinemann)
PIED PIPER   FOX 1942
(Heinemann)
TOWN LIKE ALICE, A   RANK 1956
(Heinemann)   BBC 1984 (TV)

SIDNEY, Margaret *pseud.*
FIVE LITTLE PEPPERS AND HOW
THEY GREW   COL 1939
(Various)

SIENKIEWICZ, Henryk
QUO VADIS   IN 1929
(Various)   MGM 1949
                                   CHANNEL 4 1986 (TV)

SILLIPHANT, Stirling
  MARACAIBO   PAR 1958
  (Farrar, N.Y.)

SILLITOE, Alan
  GENERAL, THE   UI 1968
  (W.H. Allen)   (*Counterpoint*)
  LONELINESS OF THE LONG-
  DISTANCE RUNNER, THE   BL 1962
  (W.H. Allen)
  RAGMAN'S DAUGHTER, THE   FOX 1972
  (W.H. Allen)
  SATURDAY NIGHT AND SUNDAY
  MORNING   BL 1960
  (W.H. Allen)

SILVER, Joan *and* **GOTTLIEB, Linda**
  LIMBO   UN 1972
  (Heinemann)

SIMENON, Georges
  ACT OF PASSION   CP 1952
  (Routledge)   (*Forbidden Fruit*)
  BATTLE OF NERVES, A   BL 1950
  (Routledge)   (*Man on the Eiffel Tower, The*)
  BOTTOM OF THE BOTTLE   FOX 1955
  (*In* Tidal Wave: Doubleday, N.Y.) (*Beyond the River*)
  BROTHER RICO   COL 1957
  (*In* Tidal Wave: Doubleday, N.Y.)
  MAN WHO WATCHED THE TRAINS
  GO BY   EROS 1952
  (Routledge)
  MONSIEUR LA SOURIS   COL 1951
  (Gallimard, Paris)   (*Midnight Episode*)
  NEWHAVEN–DIEPPE   AB 1947
  (Routledge)   (*Temptation Harbour*)
  STRANGERS IN THE HOUSE   RANK 1966
  (Routledge)   (*Stranger in the House*)

SIMMONS, Anthony
  OPTIMISTS OF NINE ELMS, THE SCOTIA BARBER 1974
  (Methuen)

SIMON, Neil
  BAREFOOT IN THE PARK (P)　　　PAR 1966
  (French, N.Y.)
  CALIFORNIA SUITE (P)　　　　　COL 1979
  (Random House, N.Y.)
  CHAPTER TWO (P)　　　　　　COL—EMI—WAR 1980
  (Random House, N.Y.)
  COME BLOW YOUR HORN (P)　　PAR 1963
  (Doubleday, N.Y.)
  GINGERBREAD LADY (P)　　　　COL 1981
  (French)　　　　　　　　　　　(*Only When I Laugh*)
  I OUGHT TO BE IN PICTURES (P)　TCF 1982
  (Random, N.Y.)
  LAST OF THE RED HOT LOVERS (P)　PAR 1972
  (Random House, N.Y.)
  PLAZA SUITE (P)　　　　　　　PAR 1972
  (French)
  PRISONER OF SECOND AVENUE (P)　COL—WAR 1975
  (Random House, N.Y.)
  SUNSHINE BOYS, THE　　　　　CIC—MGM 1975
  (Random House, N.Y.)

SIMON, Roger L.
  BIG FIX, THE　　　　　　　　CIC 1979
  (Pocket Books, N.Y.)
  HEIR (P)　　　　　　　　　　UA 1971
  (Macdonald)　　　　　　　　(*Jennifer on my Mind*)

SIMON, S.J. *see* **BRAHMS, C.** *jt. author*

SIMPSON, *Mrs.* **C. Fraser**
  FOOTSTEPS IN THE NIGHT　　　AUTEN 1932
  (Methuen)

SIMPSON, Helen
  SARABAND FOR DEAD LOVERS　EL 1949
  (Heinemann)
  UNDER CAPRICORN　　　　　WAR 1949
  (Heinemann)　　　　　　　　SOUTH AUSTRALIA FILMS 1983

SIMPSON, H. de G. *see* **DANE, C.** *jt. author*

SIMPSON, Norman Frederick
  ONE WAY PENDULUM　　　　UA 1964
  (Grove Press, N.Y.)

SIMPSON, Reginald *and* **DRAWBELL, J.W.**
WHO GOES NEXT? (P)   FOX 1938
(French)

SINCLAIR, Harold
HORSE SOLDIERS, THE   UA 1959
(Muller)

SINCLAIR, Upton
GNOMOBILE   DISNEY 1966
(Laurie)
WET PARADE   MGM 1932
(Laurie)

SINGER, Howard
WAKE ME WHEN IT'S OVER   FOX 1960
(Putnam, N.Y.)

SINGER, Isaac B.
MAGICIAN OF LUBLIN, THE   CENTURY CINEMAN 1979
(Cape)

SINGER, Loren
PARALLAX VIEW, THE   CIC 1974
(Doubleday, N.Y.)

SIODMAK, Carl
DONOVAN'S BRAIN   BL 1963
(Corgi)   (*Vengeance*)

SITWELL, *Sir* **Osbert**
PLACE OF ONE'S OWN, A   GFD 1945
(Macmillan)

SJOWALL, Maj *and* **WAHLOO, Peter**
LAUGHING POLICEMAN, THE   FOX 1974
(Gollancz)   (*Investigation of Murder*)

SKIDELSKY, Simon Jasha *see* **SIMON, S.J.** *pseud.*

SKINNER, C.O. *see also* **TAYLOR, S.A.** *jt. author*

SKINNER, Cornelius Otis *and* **KIMBROUGH, Emily**
OUR HEARTS WERE YOUNG AND   PAR 1944
GAY
(Constable)

SKINNER, M.L. *see* **LAWRENCE, David Herbert** *jt. author*

SKLAR, G. *see* **CASPARY, V.** *jt. author*

SLADE, Bernard
SAME TIME NEXT YEAR (P)   CIC 1979
(Dell, N.Y.)

SLADE, C. Jope *see* **JOPE-SLADE, C.**

SLATER, Humphrey
CONSPIRATOR   MGM 1949
(Lehmann)

SLATER, Montague
ONCE A JOLLY SWAGMAN   WESSEX 1949
(Lane)

SLATER, Nigel
MAD DEATH OF NIGEL   BBC (Scotland) 1985 (TV)
(Granada)

SLAUGHTER, Frank Gill
DOCTOR'S WIVES   COL 1971
(Arrow)
SANGAREE   PAR 1953
(Jarrolds)
WARRIOR, THE   RKO 1956
(Doubleday, N.Y.)   (*Naked in the Sun*)

SLOANE, William
EDGE OF RUNNING WATER, THE   COL 1941
(Methuen)   (*Devil Commands, The*)

SLOMAN, R. *see* **DOBIE, L.** *jt. author*

SMALL, Austin J. *see* **'SEAMARK'** *pseud.*

SMITH, Alson Jesse
BROTHER VAN   BL 1957
(Various)   (*Lawless Eighties, The*)

SMITH, Anthony
BODY, THE   KESTREL—ANGLO EMI 1971
(Allen & Unwin)

SMITH, Betty
JOY IN THE MORNING   MGM 1965
(Heinemann)
TREE GROWS IN BROOKLYN, A FOX 1945
(Heinemann)
Originally Published as:
A Tree Grows in the Yard

SMITH, Dodie [Dorothy Gladys]
CALL IT A DAY (P)   WAR 1937
(Gollancz)
DEAR OCTOPUS (P)   GFD 1943
(Heinemann)
ONE HUNDRED AND ONE
DALMATIANS   DISNEY 1960
(Heinemann)

SMITH, Dorothy Gladys *see* **ANTHONY, C.L.** *pseud.*

SMITH, *Lady* **Eleanor**
BALLERINA   COL 1941
(Gollancz)   (*Men in her Life*)
CARAVAN   FOX 1934
(Hutchinson)   EL 1947
MAN IN GREY, THE   GFD 1943
(Hutchinson)
RED WAGON   ALL 1938
(Gollancz)

SMITH, Frederick E.
633 SQUADRON   UA 1964
(Hutchinson)

SMITH, Harry Allen
RHUBARB   PAR 1951
(Barker)

SMITH, Martin C.
  GORKY PARK   ORION 1983
  (Collins)
  NIGHTWING   COL—EMI—WAR 1980
  (Norton, N.Y.)

SMITH, Robert K.
  JANE'S HOUSE   COL 1983
  (Pan)

SMITH, Shelley *pseud.*
  BALLAD OF THE RUNNING MAN   COL 1963
  (Hamilton)   (*Running Man, The*)

SMITH, Stephen P.
  OFFICER AND A GENTLEMAN, AN   COL 1984
  (Avon, N.Y.)

SMITH, Terence L.
  THIEF WHO CAME TO DINNER   COL—WAR 1973
  (Doubleday, N.Y.)

SMITH, Thorne
  NIGHT LIFE OF THE GODS   UN 1935
  (Methuen)
  TOPPER   MGM 1937
  (Methuen)
  TOPPER TAKES A TRIP   UA 1939
  (Methuen)
  TURNABOUT   UA 1940
  (Methuen)

SMITH, Wilbur
  GOLD MINE   HEMDALE 1974
  (Heinemann)   (*Gold*)
  SHOUT AT THE DEVIL   HEMDALE 1976
  (Heinemann)

SMITTER, Wessel
  DETROIT, F.O.B.   PAR 1941
  (Dent)   (*Reaching For the Sun*)

SNEIDER, Vern J.
  TEAHOUSE OF THE AUGUST
  MOON, THE   MGM 1957
  (Macmillan)

SNEIDER, Vera J. (*Continued*)
  BEGINNERS LUCK   AA 1959
  (Collins)   (*Desperate Man, The*)

SOLZENITSYN, Alexander
  ONE DAY IN THE LIFE OF IVAN
  DENIZOVICH   CINERAMA 1971
  (Bodley Head)

SOMERVILLE, Edith *and* **ROSS, Martin**
  EXPERIENCES OF AN IRISH RM   CHANNEL 4 1982 (TV)
  (Dent)

SOPHOCLES
  OEDIPUS REX (P)   OEDIPUS REX 1956
  (Various)   UI 1968
                              (*Oedipus the King*)

SOUSA, John Philip
  MARCHING ALONG   FOX 1952
  (Hale)

SOUTAR, Andrew
  DEVIL'S TRIANGLE   FOX 1932
  (Hutchinson)   (*Almost Married*)

SOUTHARD, Ruth
  NO SAD SONGS FOR ME   COL 1950
  (Doubleday, N.Y.)

SOUTHERN, Terry
  MAGIC CHRISTIAN, THE   COMMONWEALTH 1969
  (Deutsch)

SOUTHERN, Terry *and* **HOFFENBERG, M.**
  CANDY   CINERAMA 1968
  (Geis)

SPARK, Muriel
  ABBESS OF CREWE, THE   SCOTIA BARBER 1976
  (Viking, N.Y.)   (*Abbess, The*: also filmed *Nasty*
                            Habits)

  PRIME OF MISS JEAN BRODIE, THE FOX 1969
  (Macmillan)

SPEARMAN, Frank Hamilton
  WHISPERING SMITH   FOX 1935
  (Grosset, N.Y.)   (*Whispering Smith Speaks*)
                       PAR 1948

SPENCE, Hartzell
  ONE FOOT IN HEAVEN   WAR 1941
  (Harrap)

SPENCE, R.
  GORILLA (P)   WAR 1931
  (French)   WAR 1939

SPENCER, Elizabeth
  LIGHT IN THE PIAZZA   MGM 1962
  (Heinemann)

SPENCER, Scott
  ENDLESS LOVE   BARBER 1981
  (Knopf, N.Y.)

SPIGELGASS, Leonard
  MAJORITY OF ONE, A (P)   WAR 1961
  (French, N.Y.)

SPILLANE, Mickey
  GIRL HUNTERS, THE   FOX 1964
  (Barker)
  I, THE JURY   UA 1953
  (Barker)   COL—EMI—WAR 1982
  KISS ME DEADLY   UA 1954
  (Barker)
  LONG WAIT, THE   UA 1954
  (Barker)
  MY GUN IS QUICK   UA 1957
  (Barker)

SPRIGG, C. St. John
  PERFECT ALIBI   RKO 1931
  (Eldon)

SPRING, Howard
  FAME IS THE SPUR   TC 1947
  (Collins)   BBC 1982 (TV)

SPRING, Howard (*Continued*)
MY SON, MY SON   UA 1940
(Collins)
Originally Published as:
O, Absolom!

SPYRI, Johanna
HEIDI   FOX 1937
(Various)   UA 1954
     HANNA-BARBER 1982
     (*Heidi's Song*)

STACPOOLE, Henry de Vere
BLUE LAGOON   INDIVIDUAL 1949
(Various)   COL 1980

STAHL, Ben
BLACKBEARD'S GHOST   DISNEY 1968
(Houghton, Mifflin, Boston)

STALLINGS, L. *see* **ANDERSON, M.** *jt. author*

STANDISH, Robert
ELEPHANT WALK   PAR 1954
(Davies)

STANTON, Will
GOLDEN EVENINGS OF SUMMER,
THE   DISNEY 1974
(Lancer, N.Y.)   (*Charley and the Angel*)

STARK, Richard
OUTFIT, THE   MGM 1973
(Coronet)
POINTBLANK   MGM 1967
(Coronet)
SPLIT, THE   MGM 1968
(Hodder Fawcett)

STEAD, Christine
FOR LOVE ALONE   WARRANTY (AUSTRALIA) 1985
(Angus & Robertson)

STEELE, Wilbur Daniel
WAY TO THE GOLD, THE   FOX 1957
(Doubleday, N.Y.)

STEIGER, B. *and* **MANE, C.**
  VALENTINO   UA 1977
  (Corgi)

STEIN, J. *see* **GLICKMAN, W.** *jt. author*

STEIN, Sol
  MAGICIAN, THE   FOX 1972
  (New English Library)

STEINBECK, John
  CANNERY ROW   MGM 1981
  (Heinemann)
  EAST OF EDEN   WAR 1954
  (Heinemann)
  FORGOTTEN VILLAGE, THE   MGM 1941
  (Viking, N.Y.)
  GRAPES OF WRATH, THE   FOX 1940
  (Heinemann)
  MOON IS DOWN, THE   FOX 1943
  (Viking, N.Y.)
  OF MICE AND MEN   UA 1939
  (Heinemann)
  OF MICE AND MEN (P)   UA 1939
  (Covici, N.Y.)
  PEARL, THE   RKO 1948
  (Heinemann)   RKO 1954
  RED PONY, THE   BL 1949
  (Viking, N.Y.)   BL 1976
  TORTILLA FLAT   MGM 1942
  (Grosset, N.Y.)
  WAYWARD BUS, THE   FOX 1957
  (Heinemann)

STEPHENSON, Carl
  LEININGEN VERSUS THE ANTS PAR 1953
  (*In* Bedside Esquire: Barker)   (*Naked Jungle, The*)

STERLING, T.
  EVIL OF THE DAY, THE   UA 1966
  (Penguin)   (*Honey Pot, The*)

STERN, David
  FRANCIS   UI 1949
  (Farrar, N.Y.)

STERN, Gladys Bronwyn
UGLY DACHSHUND, THE   DISNEY 1966
(Cassell)
WOMAN IN THE HALL, THE   GFD 1947
(Cassell)

STERN, Richard M.
TOWER, THE   COL—WAR 1975
(Pan)   (*Towering Inferno, The*)

STEVENS, Leslie
LOVERS, THE (P)   RANK 1965
(French)   (*War Lord, The*)

STEVENSON, Robert Louis
BLACK ARROW   COL 1948
(Various)   DISNEY 1985 (TV)
BODY SNATCHER   RKO 1945
(Various)
CATRIONA   RANK 1972
(Harrap)
DR. JEKYLL AND MR. HYDE   PAR 1932
(Various)   PAR 1937
          MGM 1941
          COL 1959
          (*Two Faces of Dr. Jekyll, The*)
EBB TIDE   PAR 1947
(Various)   (*Adventure Island*)
KIDNAPPED   FOX 1938
(Various)   MON 1949
          DISNEY 1959
          RANK 1972
MASTER OF BALLENTRAE, THE   WAR 1953
(Various)   CBS 1983 (TV)
ST. IVES   COL 1949
(Various)   (*Secret of St. Ives, The*)
SIRE OF MALETROIT'S DOOR, THE   UI 1951
(*In* New Arabian Nights: Various)   (*Strange Door, The*)
SUICIDE CLUB, THE   MGM 1936
(Various)   (*Trouble for Two*)
TREASURE ISLAND   MGM 1934
(Various)   RKO 1949
          MGM—EMI 1971
          CANNON 1986
TREASURE OF FRANCHARD   UI 1952
(Various)   (*Treasure of Lost Canyon*)

STEVENSON, Robert Louis *and* **OSBOURNE, Lloyd**
WRONG BOX, THE   COL 1965
(Longmans)

STEWART, Donald Ogden
MR. AND MRS. HADDOCK
ABROAD   PAR 1931
(Doran, N.Y.)   (*Finn and Hattie*)

STEWART, Fred
MUSTARD   FOX 1971
(Joseph)   (*Mephisto Waltz, The*)
SIX WEEKS   POLYGRAM 1983
(Corgi)

STEWART, Mary
MOON-SPINNERS, THE   DISNEY 1964
(Hodder & Stoughton)

STEWART, Michael
HELLO DOLLY! (P)   FOX 1968
(D.B.S. Pubs., N.Y.)

STEWART, Ramona
DESERT FURY   PAR 1947
(World, N.Y.)
POSSESSION OF JOEL DELANEY,
THE   SCOTIA BARBER 1971
(Deutsch)

STINETORF, Louise A.
WHITE WITCH DOCTOR   FOX 1953
(Westminster Press, Philadelphia)

STODDART, Dayton
PRELUDE TO NIGHT   EL 1948
(Coward-McCann, N.Y.)   (*Ruthless*)

STOKER, Bram
DRACULA   UI 1931
(Rider)   UI 1957
       EMI 1973
       CIC 1979
       KODIAK 1979
       (*Dracula Sucks*)

STOKER, Bram (*Continued*)
  DRACULA'S GUEST   UN 1936
  (Jarrolds)   (*Dracula's Daughter*)
  JEWEL OF THE SEVEN STARS   MGM—EMI 1971
  (Jarrolds)   (*Blood from the Mummy's Tomb*)
      COL—EMI—WAR 1980
      (*Awakening, The*)

STOKES, Sewell
  ISADORA DUNCAN   UI 1969
  (Pan)   (*Isadora*)

STOKES, S. *see* **JOPE-SLADE, C.** *jt. author*

STONE, Gene *and* **COONEY, R.**
  WHY NOT STAY FOR BREAKFAST
  (P)   ENTERPRISE 1979
  (French)

STONE, *Mrs.* **Grace**
  BITTER TEA OF GENERAL YEN,
  THE   COL 1933
  (Bobbs-Merrill, Indianapolis)

STONE, Irving
  AGONY AND THE ECSTACY, THE   FOX 1964
  (Collins)
  FALSE WITNESS   REP 1941
  (Doubleday, N.Y.)   (*Arkansas Judge*)
  IMMORTAL WIFE   FOX 1953
  (Invincible Press)   (*President's Lady, The*)
  LUST FOR LIFE   MGM 1956
  (Lane)

STONE, Robert
  DOG SOLDIERS   UA 1978
  (Secker & Warburg)   (U.S. title: *Who'll Stop The Rain?*)
  HALL OF MIRRORS, A   PAR 1972
  (Bodley Head)   (*Wusa*)

STONELEY, Jack
  JENNY'S WAR   HTV 1985 (TV)
  (Hamlyn)

STONG, Philip
CAREER   RKO 1939
(Grosset, N.Y.)
STATE FAIR   FOX 1945
(Grosset, N.Y.)   FOX 1962
STRANGER'S RETURN   MGM 1933
(Harcourt, N.Y.)

STOREY, David
IN CELEBRATION (P)   SEVEN KEYS 1976
(Cape)
THIS SPORTING LIFE   RANK 1962
(Longmans)

STOREY, Robert
TOUCH IT LIGHT (P)   BRYANSTON 1960
(French)   (*Light Up the Sky*)

STORY, Jack Trevor
LIVE NOW, PAY LATER   REGAL FILMS 1962
(Secker & Warburg)
MIX ME A PERSON   BL 1962
(Corgi)
TROUBLE WITH HARRY, THE   PAR 1955
(Boardman)

STOUT, Rex
FER DE LANCE   COL 1936
(Cassell)   (*Meet Nero Wolfe*)
LEAGUE OF FRIGHTENED MEN,
THE   COL 1937
(Cassell)

STRABEL, Thelma
REAP THE WILD WIND   PAR 1942
(Collins)

STRAIT, R. *see* **CLOONEY, R.** *jt. author*

STRAKER, J.F.
HELL IS EMPTY   RANK 1967
(Harrap)

STRATTON-PORTER, Gene
FRECKLES   FOX 1960
(Hodder & Stoughton)

STRATTON-PORTER, Gene (*Continued*)
GIRL OF THE LIMBERLOST, A   MON 1934
(Hodder & Stoughton)
HARVESTER, THE   REP 1936
(Hodder & Stoughton)
HER FATHER'S DAUGHTER   MON 1940
(Murray)   (*Her First Romance*)
KEEPER OF THE BEES   MON 1935
(Hutchinson)
LADDIE   RKO 1935
(Murray)
MICHAEL O'HALLORAN   REP 1937
(Murray)   MON 1949

STRAUB, Peter
FULL CIRCLE   CIC 1978
(Cape)   (*Julia*)
GHOST STORY   UN 1981
(Coward-McCann, N.Y.)
SHADOWLANDS   BBC 1985 (TV)
(Collins)

STREATFEILD, Noel
AUNT CLARA   BL 1954
(Collins)

STREET, Arthur George
STRAWBERRY ROAN   BN 1944
(Faber)

STREET, James Howell
GOODBYE MY LADY   WAR 1956
(Invincible Press)
TAP ROOTS   UI 1948
(Sun Dial Press, N.Y.)

STREETER, Edward
FATHER OF THE BRIDE   MGM 1950
(Hamilton)
MR. HOBBS' HOLIDAY   FOX 1962
(Hamilton)   (*Mr. Hobbs Takes a Vacation*)

STRIEBER, Whitley
HUNGER   UIP 1983
(Morrow, N.Y.)

WOLFEN, THE   COL—EMI—WAR 1980
(Morrow, N.Y.)

STRINDBERG, Johann August
DANCE OF DEATH, THE (P)   PAR 1969
(*In* Eight Famous Plays: Duckworth)
FATHER, THE (P)   BBC 2 1985 (TV)
(*In* Eight Famous Plays: Duckworth)
FATHER, THE (P)   GALA 1981
(*In* Eight Famous Plays: Duckworth) (*Lonely Hearts*)
MISS JULIE (P)   LF 1951
(Dent)   TIGON 1972

STRODE, William Chetham *see* **CHETHAM-STRODE, William**

STRONG, Austin
SEVENTH HEAVEN, THE (P)   FOX 1937
(French, N.Y.)

STRONG, Leonard Alfred George
BROTHERS, THE   FOX 1947
(Gollancz)

STRUTHER, Jan
MRS. MINIVER   MGM 1942
(Chatto & Windus)

STUART, Aimee
JEANNIE (P)   TANSA 1942
(Hamilton)   ABP 1957
                     (*Let's be Happy*)

STUART, Aimee *and* **STUART, Philip**
NINE TILL SIX (P)   ATP 1932
(French, N.Y.)

STUART, Donald
SHADOW, THE   GLOBE 1936
(Wright & Brown)

STUART, Ian
SATAN BUG, THE   UA 1964
(Collins)

STUART, William
NIGHT CRY   FOX 1950
(Dial Press, N.Y.)   (*Where the Sidewalk Ends*)

STURE-VASA, Mary *see* **O'HARA, Mary** *pseud.*

STURGES, Preston
STRICTLY DISHONOURABLE (P)   UN 1931
(Liveright, N.Y.)   MGM 1951

STYRON, William
CONFESSIONS OF NAT TURNER,
THE   FOX 1969
(Cape)
SOPHIE'S CHOICE   ITC 1982
(Bantam, N.Y.)

SUKENICK, Ronald
OUT   CINEGATE 1982
(Swallow)

SULLIVAN, Tom *and* **GILL, Derek**
IF YOU COULD SEE WHAT I HEAR
(New American Library, N.Y.)   SUNN—CLASSIC 1982

SULZBERGER, Cyrus L.
MY BROTHER DEATH   BORDER 1965
(Hamilton)   (*Take Me While I'm Warm*)

SUMMERS, Richard Aldrich
VIGILANTE   WAR 1952
(Duell, N.Y.)   (*San Francisco Story, The*)

SUMNER, *Mrs.* Cid Ricketts
QUALITY   FOX 1949
(Dymock)   (*Pinky*)
TAMMY TELL ME TRUE   RANK 1961
(Bobbs-Merrill, Indianapolis)

SUSANN, Jacqueline
LOVE MACHINE, THE   COL 1971
(W.H. Allen)
ONCE IS NOT ENOUGH   PAR 1975
(W.H. Allen)

624

VALLEY OF THE DOLLS   FOX 1968
(Cassell)

SWANN, Francis
OUT OF THE FRYING PAN (P)   UA 1943
(French, N.Y.)

SWANSON, Neil Harmon
FIRST REBEL, THE   RKO 1939
(Grosset, N.Y.)   (*Allegheny Uprising*)
UNCONQUERED   PAR 1947
(Doubleday, N.Y.)

SWARTHOUT, Gladys
BLESS THE BEASTS AND
CHILDREN   COL 1971
(Secker & Warburg)

SWARTHOUT, Glendon
SHOOTIST, THE   PAR 1976
(Doubleday, N.Y.)
THEY CAME TO CORDURA   COL 1959
(Heinemann)
WHERE THE BOYS ARE   MGM 1960
(Heinemann)

SWIFT, Jonathan
GULLIVER'S TRAVELS   PAR 1939
(Various)   COL 1959
                                   (*Three Worlds of Gulliver, The*)
                                   EMI 1976

SWIFT, Kay
WHO COULD ASK FOR ANYTHING
MORE   RKO 1950
(Simon & Schuster, N.Y.)   (*Never a Dull Moment*)

SWIGGETT, Howard
POWER AND THE PRIZE, THE   MGM 1956
(Hodder & Stoughton)

SYLVAINE, Vernon
AREN'T MEN BEASTS   AB 1937
(Jenkins)

SYLVAINE, Vernon (*Continued*)
   AREN'T MEN BEASTS (P)   AB 1937
   (French)
   AS LONG AS THEY'RE HAPPY (P)   GFD 1954
   (French)
   ONE WILD OAT (P)   EROS 1951
   (French)
   SPOT OF BOTHER, A (P)   AB 1938
   (French)
   WARN THAT MAN (P)   AB 1942
   (French)
   WILL ANY GENTLEMAN . . .? (P)   ABP 1953
   (French)
   WOMEN AREN'T ANGELS (P)   AB 1943
   (French)

SYLVESTER, Robert
   BIG BOODLE, THE   UA 1957
   (Random House, N.Y.)   (*Night in Havana*)
   ROUGH SKETCH   COL 1949
   (Dial Press, N.Y.)   (*We Were Strangers*)

SYMONS, Julian
   NARROWING CIRCLE, THE   EROS 1955
   (Gollancz)

SYNGE, J.M.
   PLAYBOY OF THE WESTERN   CHANNEL 4 1986 (TV)
   WORLD, THE (P)
   (Methuen)

SYRETT, Netta
   PORTRAIT OF A REBEL   RKO 1936
   (Bles)

T

TALESE, Guy
   HONOR THY FATHER   FOX 1973
   (Souvenir Press)

TANIZAKI, Junichiro
   BUDDHIST CROSS, THE   CANNON 1986
   (Putnam, N.Y.)   (*Berlin Affair, The*)

KEY, THE   ENTERPRISE 1985
(Putnam, N.Y.)

TANNER, Edward Everett *see* **DENNIS, Patrick** *pseud.*

TARADASH, Daniel *and* **MOLL, Elick**
STORM CENTRE   COL 1956
(Panther)

TARKINGTON, Booth
ALICE ADAMS   RKO 1935
(Odyssey Press, N.Y.)
CLARENCE (P)   PAR 1937
(French, N.Y.)
GENTLE JULIA   FOX 1936
(Grosset, N.Y.)
LITTLE ORVIE   RKO 1940
(Heinemann)
MAGNIFICENT AMBERSONS, THE RKO 1942
(Grosset, N.Y.)
MONSIEUR BEAUCAIRE   PAR 1946
(Grosset, N.Y.)
PENROD   WAR 1937
(Hodder & Stoughton)   (*Penrod and Sam*)
                 WAR 1953
                 (*By the Light of the Silvery Moon*)
PENROD AND SAM   IN 1931
(Hodder & Stoughton)
SEVENTEEN   PAR 1940
(Grosset, N.Y.)
SEVENTEEN (P)   PAR 1940
(French, N.Y.)

TARLOFF, Frank
GUIDE FOR THE MARRIED MAN, FOX 1968
THE
(Price, Sterm, Sloan, Los Angeles)

TATE, Sylvia
FUZZY PINK NIGHTGOWN, THE UA 1957
(Harper, N.Y.)

TAYLOR, A.J.P.
HOW WARS END   CHANNEL 4 1985 (TV)
(Hamilton)

TAYLOR, Bernard
GODSEND, THE   CANNON 1980
(Avon, N.Y.)

TAYLOR, Kressman
ADDRESS UNKNOWN   COL 1944
(Hamilton)

TAYLOR, Robert
JOURNEY TO MATECUMBRE DISNEY 1976
(New American Library, N.Y.) (*Treasure of Matecumbre*)

TAYLOR, Robert Louis
TRAVELS OF JAIMIE McPHEETERS,
THE   MGM 1964
(Macdonald)   (*Guns of Diablo*)

TAYLOR, Rosemary
CHICKEN EVERY SUNDAY FOX 1948
(Methuen)   FOX 1956
          (*Hefferan Family, The*)

TAYLOR, Samuel A.
FIRST LOVE (P)   AVCO EMBASSY 1971
(Dramatists, N.Y.)   (*Promise at Dawn*)
HAPPY TIME, THE (P)   COL 1952
(Dramatists, N.Y.)
SABRINA FAIR (P)   PAR 1954
(Random House, N.Y.)

TAYLOR, Samuel A. *and* **SKINNER, C.O.**
PLEASURE OF HIS COMPANY, THE
(P)   PAR 1959
(Heinemann)

TAYLOR, Samuel Woolley
MAN WITH MY FACE, THE UA 1951
(Hodder & Stoughton)

TEICHMAN, Howard *and* **KAUFMAN, George S.**
SOLID GOLD CADILLAC, THE (P) COL 1956
(Random House, N.Y.)

TEILHET, Darwin L.
MY TRUE LOVE   UI 1952
(Gollancz)   (*No Room for the Groom*)

628

TELFER, Daniel
  CARETAKERS, THE   UA 1962
  (Macdonald)   (*Borderlines*)

TEMPLE, Joan
  NO ROOM AT THE INN (P)   BN 1948
  (*In* Embassy Successes, Vol. 2: Sampson
  Low)

TEMPLE, William F.
  FOUR-SIDED TRIANGLE   EXCLUSIVE 1952
  (Long)

TEMPLETON, Charles
  KIDNAPPING OF THE PRESIDENT,
  THE   BORDEAUX FILMS 1981
  (Avon, N.Y.)

TERASAKI, Gwen
  BRIDGE TO THE SUN   MGM 1961
  (Joseph)

TERHUNE, Albert Payson
  TREVE   UN 1937
  (Grosset, N.Y.)   (*Mighty Treve, The*)

TERROT, Charles
  ALLIGATOR NAMED DAISY, AN RANK 1955
  (Collins)
  ANGEL WHO PAWNED HER HARP,
  THE   BL 1954
  (Collins)

TEVIS, James H.
  ARIZONA IN THE '50s   DISNEY 1964
  (University of New Mexico Press,   (*Tenderfoot*)
  Albuquerque)

TEVIS, Walter
  HUSTLER, THE   FOX 1961
  (Joseph)
  MAN WHO FELL TO EARTH, THE BL 1976
  (Pan)

TEY, Josephine
  BRAT FARRAR   HAMMER 1958
  (Davies)   BBC 1986 (TV)
  FRANCHISE AFFAIR, THE   ABP 1951
  (Davies)

THACKERAY, William Makepeace
  BARRY LYNDON   WAR 1974
  (Various)   (*Luck of . . .*)
  VANITY FAIR   HOL 1932
  (Various)   RKO 1935
                      (*Becky Sharp*)

THAYER, Tiffany
  CALL HER SAVAGE   FOX 1932
  (Long)

THEROUX, Paul
  SAINT JACK   NEW WORLD 1979
  (Ballantine, N.Y.)

THIELE, Colin
  BLUE FIN   SOUTH AUSTRALIA FILMS 1978
  (Collins)

THIGPEN, Corbett H. *and* **CLECKLEY, Harvey M.**
  THREE FACES OF LOVE, THE   FOX 1957
  (Secker & Warburg)

THOMAS, Basil
  BOOK OF THE MONTH (P)   AA 1959
  (French)
  SHOOTING STAR (P)   ADELPHI 1953
  (Deane)   (*Great Game, The*)

THOMAS, Brandon
  CHARLEY'S AUNT (P)   COL 1930
  (French, N.Y.)   FOX 1941

THOMAS, Craig
  FIREFOX   COL—EMI—WAR 1982
  (Joseph)

THOMAS, Dylan
  MOUSE AND THE WOMAN, THE   FACELIFT FILMS 1981
  (*In* The Short Stories of . . .: Dent)

UNDER MILK WOOD (P)   RANK 1971
(Dent)

THOMAS, Gordon *and* **WITTS, M.**
DAY THE WORLD ENDED, THE   COL—EMI—WAR 1980
(Stein & Day, N.Y.)   (*When Time Ran Out*)
VOYAGE OF THE DAMNED   ITC 1976
(Hodder & Stoughton)

THOMAS, Leslie
DANGEROUS DAVIES—THE LAST
DETECTIVE   INNER CIRCLE 1980
(Eyre & Methuen)
STAND UP VIRGIN SOLDIERS   COL—WAR 1977
(Eyre & Methuen)
VIRGIN SOLDIERS, THE   COL 1969
(Constable)

THOMAS, Ross
SPY IN THE VODKA   PAR 1969
(Hodder & Stoughton)   (*Cold War Swap, The*)

THOMPSON, Ernest
ON GOLDEN POND   CIC 1981
(Dodd, N.Y.)

THOMPSON, Jim
GETAWAY, THE   CINERAMA 1972
(W.H. Allen)

THOMPSON, J. Lee
MURDER WITHOUT CRIME (P)   ABP 1950
(French)

THOMPSON, Morton
NOT AS A STRANGER   UA 1955
(Joseph)

THOMPSON, Thomas
CELEBRITY   NBC 1984 (TV)
(Doubleday, N.Y.)

THORN, Ronald Scott
FULL TREATMENT, THE   COL 1960
(Heinemann)

THORN, Ronald Scott (*Continued*)
UPSTAIRS AND DOWNSTAIRS   RANK 1959
(Spearman)

THORNBURG, Newton
CUTTER AND BONE   UA 1981
(Heinemann)   (*Cutter's Way*)

THORNDIKE, Russell
DR. SYN   GB 1937
(Various)   DISNEY 1963

THORNE, Anthony
BABY AND THE BATTLESHIP, THE   BL 1956
(Heinemann)
SO LONG AT THE FAIR   GFD 1950
(Heinemann)

THORP, M. *see* **LAVIN, N.** *jt. author*

THORP, Roderick
DETECTIVE, THE   FOX 1968
(Corgi)

THURBER, James
MY LIFE AND HARD TIMES   FOX 1941
(Hamilton)   (*Rise and Shine*)
SECRET LIFE OF WALTER MITTY   RKO 1949
(*In* Modern American Short Stories:
World, N.Y.)

THURBER, James *and* **NUGENT, Elliot**
MALE ANIMAL, THE (P)   WAR 1942
(Random House, N.Y.)   WAR 1952
      (*She's Working Her Way Through
      College*)

THURMAN, Judith
ISAK DINESEN: THE LIFE OF A
STORYTELLER   UN 1985
(Weidenfeld & Nicolson)   (*Out of Africa*)

THURSTON, Ernest Temple
WANDERING JEW, THE (P)   OLY 1935
(Putnam)

THYNNE, Alexander
　BLUE BLOOD   NATION WIDE 1974
　(Sphere)

TICKELL, Jerrard
　APPOINTMENT WITH VENUS   GFD 1951
　(Hodder & Stoughton)
　HAND AND THE FLOWER, THE   GFD 1953
　(Hodder & Stoughton)   (*Day to Remember, A*)
　ODETTE, G.C.   BL 1950
　(Chapman & Hall)

TIDMARSH, E.V.
　IS YOUR HONEYMOON REALLY
　NECESSARY? (P)   ADELPHI 1953
　(Deane)

TIDYMAN, Ernest
　SHAFT   MGM 1971
　(Joseph)

TILSLEY, Frank
　MUTINY   COL 1962
　(Eyre & Spottiswoode)   (*H.M.S. Defiant*)   .

TINNISWOOD, Peter
　MOG   LWT 1985 (TV)
　(Hodder & Stoughton)

TIPPETTE, Giles
　HARRY SPIKES   UA 1974
　(Futura)   (*Spikes Gang, The*)

TITUS, Eve
　BASIL OF BAKER STREET   DISNEY 1986
　(Archway, N.Y.)   (*Great Mouse Detective, The*)

TOBY, Mark
　COURTSHIP OF EDDIE'S FATHER,
　THE   MGM 1963
　(Gibbs & Phillips)

TOLKIEN, J.R.R.
　FELLOWSHIP OF THE RINGS, THE:
　TWO TOWERS, THE   UA 1980
　(Allen & Unwin)   (*Lord of the Rings*)

TOLLER, Ernst
PASTOR HALL (P)   UA 1940
(Lane)

TOLSTOY, Leo Nikolaevich
ANNA KARENINA   MGM 1935
(Various)   BL 1948
RESURRECTION   UN 1931
(Various)   UA 1934
                            (*We Live Again*)
WAR AND PEACE   PAR 1956
(Macmillan)

TOMS, Bernard
STRANGE AFFAIR, THE   PAR 1968
(Constable)

TOOMBS, Alfred
RAISING A RIOT   BL 1954
(Hammond)

TOPKINS, Katherine
KOTCH   CINERAMA 1972
(Panther)

TOTHEROH, D.
DEEP VALLEY   WAR 1947
(Hutchinson)

TOWNSEND, Sue
SECRET DIARY OF ADRIAN MOLE,
AGED 13¾   THAMES TV 1985 (TV)
(Methuen)

TRACY, Don
CRISS CROSS   UI 1949
(Constable)

TRAHEY, Jane
LIFE WITH MOTHER SUPERIOR   COL 1965
(Joseph)   (*Trouble with Angels, The*)

TRAIL, Armitage
SCARFACE   UA 1932
(Long)

TRANTER, Nigel
  BRIDAL PATH, THE   BL 1959
  (Hodder & Stoughton)

TRAPP, Maria Augusta
  STORY OF THE TRAPP FAMILY
  SINGERS   FOX 1965
  (Bles)   (*Sound of Music, The*)

TRAVEN, Bruno
  BRIDGE IN THE JUNGLE, THE   UA 1971
  (Cape)
  TREASURE OF SIERRA MADRE   WAR 1948
  (Cape)

TRAVER, Robert *pseud.*
  ANATOMY OF MURDER   COL 1959
  (Faber)

TRAVERS, Ben
  BANANA RIDGE (P)   ABP 1941
  (French)
  CUCKOO IN THE NEST   GB 1938
  (Lane)
  CUCKOO IN THE NEST (P)   GB 1938
  (Bickers)
  PLUNDER (P)   WILCOX 1937
  (Bickers)
  ROOKERY NOOK   MGM 1930
  (Lane)
  ROOKERY NOOK (P)   MGM 1930
  (Bickers)
  THARK (P)   GB 1932
  (Bickers)

TRAVERS, P.L.
  MARY POPPINS   DISNEY 1964
  (Penguin)

TREGASKIS, Richard William
  GUADALCANAL DIARY   FOX 1943
  (Wells & Gardner)

TREVANION
  EIGER SANCTION, THE   CIC 1975
  (Heinemann)

TREVOR, Elleston *pseud.*
BIG PICK-UP   MGM 1958
(Heinemann)   (*Dunkirk*)
FLIGHT OF THE PHOENIX, THE   FOX 1965
(Heinemann)
PILLARS OF MIDNIGHT   RANK 1963
(Heinemann)
QUEEN IN DANGER   EXCLUSIVE 1953
(Boardman)   (*Mantrap*)

TRINIAN, John
BIG GRAB, THE   GALA 1963
(Pyramid Bks.)   (*Big Snatch, The*)

TROLLOPE, Anthony
BARCHESTER TOWERS   BBC 1982 (TV)
(Various)   (*Barchester Chronicles*)
MALACHI'S COVE   PENRITH 1978
(Various)   (*Seaweed Children, The*)
WARDEN, THE   BBC 1982 (TV)
(Various)   (*Barchester Chronicles*)

TROY, Una
WE ARE SEVEN   ABP 1958
(Heinemann)   (*She Didn't Say No*)

TROYAT, Henri
MOUNTAIN, THE   PAR 1956
(Allen & Unwin)

TRUESDELL, Jane
BE STILL MY LOVE   PAR 1949
(Boardman)   (*Accused, The*)

TRUMBO, Dalton
JOHNNY GOT HIS GUN   RANK 1971
(Corgi)

TRUSS, Seldon
LONG NIGHT, THE   AA 1958
(Hodder & Stoughton)   (*Long Knife, The*)

TRYON, Thomas
CROWNED HEADS   MAINLINE 1979
(Fawcett, N.Y.)   (*Fedora*)

636

OTHER, THE   FOX 1972
(Knopf, N.Y.)

TRZCINSKI, E. *see* **BEVAN, D.** *jt. author*

TRZEBINSKI, Errol
SILENCE WILL SPEAK   UN 1985
(Heinemann)   (*Out of Africa*)

TUCHMAN, Barbara W.
AUGUST 1914   RANK 1964
(Constable)   (*Guns of August, The*)

TUCKER, Augusta
MISS SUSIE SLAGLE'S   PAR 1945
(Grosset, N.Y.)

TULLY, Jim
BEGGARS OF LIFE   PAR 1928
(Chatto & Windus)

TURGANEV, Ivan
FIRST LOVE   CHANNEL 4 1986 (TV)
(Hogarth)   (*Summer Lightning*)

TURKUS, Burton *and* **FEDER, Sid**
MURDER, INCORPORATED   FOX 1960
(Gollancz)

TURNER, Ethel
ONE WAY TICKET   COL 1935
(Constable)

TURNEY, Catherine
OTHER ONE, THE   FOX 1957
(Holt, N.Y.)   (*Back from the Dead*)

TWAIN, Mark *pseud.*
CELEBRATED JUMPING FROG OF
CALAVERAS   COL 1948
(Various)   (*Best Man Wins, The*)
HUCKLEBERRY FINN   MGM 1939
(Various)   (*Adventures of Huckleberry Finn*)
          MGM 1960
          UA 1974

TWAIN, Mark *pseud.* (*Continued*)
MILLION POUND NOTE   GFD 1953
(*In* Man That Corrupted Hadleyburg:
Harper, N.Y.)
PRINCE AND THE PAUPER   WAR 1937
(Chatto & Windus)   DISNEY 1961
                          FOX 1977
                          (U.S. Title: *Crossed Swords*)

TOM SAWYER   UA 1938
(Various)   (*Adventures of Tom Sawyer*)
                          UA 1973

YANKEE AT THE COURT OF KING
ARTHUR, A   FOX 1931
(Chatto & Windus)   (*Connecticut Yankee*)
YANKEE AT KING ARTHUR'S
COURT   DISNEY 1980
(Various)   (*Spaceman and King Arthur, The*)

TWISS, Clinton
LONG, LONG TRAILER, THE   MGM 1954
(Crowell, N.Y.)

TYLER, Poyntz
GARDEN OF CUCUMBERS, A   UA 1968
(Gollancz)   (*Fitzwolly Strikes Back*)

U

ULLMAN, James Ramsey
BANNER IN THE SKY   DISNEY 1959
(Collins)   (*Third Man on the Mountain*)
WHITE TOWER, THE   RKO 1950
(Collins)
WINDOM'S WAY   RANK 1957
(Collins)

UNEKIS, Richard
CHASE, THE   FOX 1974
(Walker, N.Y.)   (*Dirty Mary, Crazy Larry*)

UPDIKE, John
RABBIT, RUN   WAR 1969
(Deutsch)

URIS, Leon
  ANGRY HILLS, THE   MGM 1959
  (Wingate)
  BATTLE CRY   WAR 1954
  (Wingate)
  EXODUS   UA 1960
  (Wingate)
  TOPAZ   UI 1968
  (Kimber)

USTINOV, Peter
  ROMANOFF AND JULIET (P)   RANK 1961
  (Random House, N.Y.)

V

VACHELL, Horace Annesley
  CASE OF LADY CAMBER, THE (P)   BI 1932
  (French)   (*Lord Camber's Ladies*)

VALE, Martin *pseud.*
  TWO MRS. CARROLLS, THE (P)   WAR 1947
  (Allen & Unwin)

VALENS, E.G.
  LONG WAY UP, A   UN 1975
  (Harper, N.Y.)   (*Window in the Sky, A*)

VAN ATTA, Winfred
  SHOCK TREATMENT   FOX 1964
  (Doubleday, N.Y.)
  WINTER MEETING   WAR 1948
  (Collins)

VANBRUGH, *Sir* **John**
  RELAPSE, THE (P)   COL 1968
  (Various)   (*Lock Up Your Daughters*)

VANCE, Ethel *pseud.*
  ESCAPE   MGM 1940
  (Collins)

VANCE, Louis Joseph
LONE WOLF RETURNS, THE   COL 1936
(Grosset, N.Y.)

VANE, Sutton
OUTWARD BOUND (P)   WAR 1930
(Boni, N.Y.)   WAR 1944
          (*Between Two Worlds*)

VAN GREENAWAY, Peter
MEDUSA TOUCH, THE   ITC 1978
(Stein & Day, N.Y.)

VAN LOON, Hendrik Willem
STORY OF MANKIND, THE   WAR 1957
(Harrap)

VASQUEZ-FIGUEROA, Alberto
EBANO   COL—EMI—WAR 1978
(Hale)   (*Ashanti*)

VASSILIKOS, Vassili
Z   WAR 1969
(Macdonald)

VAUGHAN THOMAS, Wynford
ANZIO   COL 1968
(Longmans)   (*Battle for . . .*)

VAUS, Jim *jun.*
WHY I QUIT SYNDICATED CRIME   EXCLUSIVE 1955
(Van Kempen, Wheaton, Ill.)   (*Wiretapper, The*)

VECSEY, G. *see* **LYNN, L.** *jt. author*

VEILLER, Bayard
TRIAL OF MARY DUGAN (P)   MGM 1929
(French, N.Y.)

VEILLER, *Mrs.* **Marguerite** *see* **VALE, Martin** *pseud.*

VERNE, Jules
AROUND THE WORLD IN 80 DAYS   UA 1957
(Various)   (*Round the World in 80 Days*)

CAPTAIN GRANT'S CHILDREN   DISNEY 1962
(Various)   (*In Search of the Castaways*)
FIVE WEEKS IN A BALLOON   FOX 1962
(Various)
FROM THE EARTH TO THE MOON
(Various)   RANK 1958
JOURNEY TO THE CENTRE OF THE
EARTH   FOX 1959
(Various)   CANNON 1986
LIGHTHOUSE AT THE END OF THE
WORLD   MGM 1972
(Sampson Low)   (*Light at the Edge of the World, The*)
MASTER OF THE WORLD   AA 1961
(Sampson Low)
MICHAEL STROGOFF   RKO 1937
(Sampson Low)   (*Soldier and the Lady, The*)
MYSTERIOUS ISLAND   COL 1962
(Dent)
SOUTHERN STAR MYSTERY, THE   COL 1969
(Arco)   (*Southern Star, The*)
20,000 LEAGUES UNDER THE SEA   DISNEY 1954
(Various)   DISNEY 1979

VERNER, Gerald
MEET MR. CALLAGHAN (P)   EROS 1954
(French)
SHOW MUST GO ON, THE   APEX 1952
(Wright & Brown)   (*Tread Softly*)
WHISPERING WOMAN, THE   AA 1953
(Wright & Brown)   (*Noose for a Lady*)

VERNEUIL, Louis
JEALOUSY (P)   PAR 1929
(French, N.Y.)   WAR 1946
                                  (*Deception*)

VICKERS, Roy
GIRL IN THE NEWS   FOX 1941
(Jenkins)

VIDAL, Gore
BEST MAN, THE (P)   UA 1968
(Little, Brown, Boston)
MYRA BRECKENRIDGE   FOX 1969
(Blond)

VIDAL, Gore (*Continued*)
VISIT TO A SMALL PLANET (P)   PAR 1959
(Little, Toronto)

VINTON, Iris
FLYING EBONY   DISNEY 1971
(Macdonald)   (*Mooncussers, The*)

VIZINCZEY, Steven
IN PRAISE OF OLDER WOMEN   COL—EMI—WAR 1978
(Macmillan)

VOELKER, John D. *see* **TRAVER, Robert** *pseud.*

VOGEL, Klaus
VIRGIN WITCH   TIGON 1970
(Corgi)

VONNERGUT, Kurt
SLAPSTICK   INTERNATIONAL PICTURE
(Delacorte, N.Y.)   SHOW 1981
SLAPSTICK   LORIMAR 1984
(Cape)   (*Slapstick of Another Kind*)
SLAUGHTERHOUSE-FIVE *or*   UN 1972
CHILDREN'S CRUSADE, THE
(Cape)

VOSPER, Frank
LOVE FROM A STRANGER (P)   UA 1937
(French)   REN 1949
     (*Stranger Walked In, A*)

MURDER ON THE SECOND FLOOR
(P)   WAR 1941
(French)

VULLIAMY, C.E.
DON AMONG THE DEAD MEN   BL 1964
(Joseph)

W

WADDELL, Martin
OTLEY   COL 1969
(Hodder & Stoughton)

WADE, Arthur Sarsfield *see* **ROHMER, Sax** *pseud.*

WADE, Kevin
KEY EXCHANGE (P)   FOX 1985
(Avon, N.Y.)

WADELTON, Thomas Dorrington
LITTLE MR. JIM   MGM 1946
(Coward-McCann, N.Y.)   (*Army Brat*)

WAGER, Walter
TELEFON   CIC 1978
(Barker)
VIPER THREE   HEMDALE 1977
(Macmillan)   (*Twilight's Last Gleaming*)

WAGONER, David
ESCAPE ARTIST, THE   POLYGRAM 1982
(Ballentine, N.Y.)

WAINWRIGHT, John
BRAINWASH   GALA 1982
(Macmillan)   (*Inquisitor, The*)

WAKEFIELD, Dan
STARTING OVER   PAR 1980
(Dell, N.Y.)

WAKEMAN, Frederic
HUCKSTERS, THE   MGM 1947
(Falcon Press)
SAXON CHARM, THE   UI 1948
(Rinehart, N.Y.)
SHORE LEAVE   FOX 1957
(Farrar, N.Y.)   (*Kiss them for me*)

WALKER, Alice
COLOR PURPLE, THE   WAR 1986
(Harbrace, N.Y.)

WALKER, David E.
ADVENTURE IN DIAMONDS   RANK 1958
(Evans)   (*Operation Amsterdam*)
      RANK 1966
      (*Man could get Killed, A*)
GEORDIE   BL 1955
(Collins)

WALKER, David, E. (*Continued*)
  HARRY BLACK   FOX 1958
  (Collins)

WALKER, Gerald
  CRUISING   LORIMAR 1980
  (W.H. Allen)

WALLACE, Edgar
  CALENDAR, THE (P)   GFD 1932
  (French)   GFD 1948
  CALENDAR, THE   WW 1932
  (Collins)   (*Bachelor's Folly*)
  CASE OF THE FRIGHTENED LADY,
  THE (P)   BL 1940
  (French, N.Y.)   (*Frightened Lady, The*)
  CLUE OF THE TWISTED CANDLE,
  THE   AA 1960
  (Newnes)
  CRIMSON CIRCLE, THE   NEW ERA 1930
  (Hodder & Stoughton)
  DAFFODIL MYSTERY   BL 1961
  (Ward Lock)   (*Devil's Daffodil, The*)
  DEBT DISCHARGED, A   AA 1961
  (Ward Lock)   (*Man Detained*)
  FACE IN THE NIGHT   AA 1960
  (Long)   (*Malpas Mystery, The*)
  FEATHERED SERPENT, THE   COL 1932
  (Hodder & Stoughton)   (*Menace, The*)
  FLAT TWO   AA 1962
  (Long)
  FOUR JUST MEN, THE   EALING 1939
  (Various)   (*Secret Four, The*)
  GREEN PACK, THE   BL 1936
  (Hodder & Stoughton)
  GREEN PACK, THE (P)   BL 1936
  (French)
  GREEN RIBBON, THE   AA 1962
  (Hutchinson)   (*Never Back Losers*)
  GUNNER, THE   AA 1962
  (Long)   (*Solo for Sparrow*)
  JACK O'JUDGEMENT   AA 1962
  (Ward Lock)   (*Share Out, The*)
  KATE PLUS TEN   WAINWRIGHT 1938
  (Ward Lock)

AUTHOR AND ORIGINAL TITLE	FILM TITLE
LONE HOUSE MYSTERY, THE (Collins)	AA 1961 (*Attempt to Kill*)
MAN AT THE CARLTON (Hodder & Stoughton)	AA 1961 (*Man at the Carlton Tower*)
MAN WHO BOUGHT LONDON (Ward Lock)	AA 1962 (*Time to Remember*)
MAN WHO KNEW, THE (Newnes)	AA 1960 (*Partners in Crime*)
MAN WHO WAS NOBODY, THE (Newnes)	AA 1960
MIND OF MR. REEDER, THE (Hodder & Stoughton)	RAYMOND 1939 (*Mind of Mr. J.G. Reeder, The*)
NORTHING TRAMP, THE (Hodder & Stoughton)	GB 1937 (*Strangers on a Honeymoon*)
RINGER, THE (P) (Hodder & Stoughton)	ID 1932 MON 1939 (*Phantom Strikes, The*) LF 1952
RINGER, THE (Hodder & Stoughton)	ID 1932 MON 1939 (*Phantom Strikes, The*) LF 1952
ROOM 13 (Allied Press)	ALL 1941 (*Mystery of Room 13*)
SANDERS OF THE RIVER (Ward Lock)	UA 1935 PLANET 1963 (*Death Drums Along the River*) BL 1964 (*Coast of Skeletons*)
SINISTER MAN, THE (Hodder & Stoughton)	AA 1961
SQUEAKER, THE (Hodder & Stoughton)	GB 1937 UA 1937 (*Murder on Diamond Row*)
SQUEAKER, THE (P) (Hodder & Stoughton)	GB 1937
TERROR, THE (Collins)	ALL 1941
THREE OAK MYSTERY, THE (Ward Lock)	AA 1960 (*Marriage of Convenience*)
TRAITOR'S GATE (Hodder & Stoughton)	COL 1965

WALLACE, Francis
  KID GALAHAD   WAR 1937
  (Hale)   UA 1962

WALLACE, Irving
  CHAPMAN REPORT, THE   WAR 1962
  (Cassell)
  MAN, THE   PAR 1972
  (New English Library)
  PRIZE, THE   MGM 1963
  (Cassell)
  SEVEN MINUTES, THE   FOX 1971
  (New English Library)

WALLACE, Lew
  BEN HUR   MGM 1931
  (Various)   MGM 1959

WALLACH, Ira
  MUSCLE BEACH   MGM 1966
  (Gollancz)   (*Don't Make Waves*)

WALLANT, Edward Lewis
  PAWNBROKER, THE   PAR 1964
  (Gollancz)

WALLER, Leslie
  HIDE IN PLAIN SIGHT   CIC 1980
  (Dell, N.Y.)

WALLIS, Arthur James *and* **BLAIR, Charles F.**
  THUNDER ABOVE   RANK 1960
  (Jarrolds)   (*Beyond the Curtain*)

WALLIS, James Harold
  ONCE OFF GUARD   RKO 1944
  (Jarrolds)   (*Woman in the Window, The*)

WALPOLE, *Sir* **Hugh**
  MR. PERRIN AND MR. TRAILL   TC 1948
  (Various)
  VANESSA   MGM 1935
  (Macmillan)

WALSH, Maurice
QUIET MAN, THE   REP 1952
(Angus & Robertson)
TROUBLE IN THE GLEN   REP 1954
(Chambers)

WALSH, Thomas
NIGHTMARE IN MANHATTAN   PAR 1950
(Little, Brown, Boston)   (*Union Station*)

WALTARI, Mika
SINUHE, THE EGYPTIAN   FOX 1954
(Putnam)   (*Egyptian, The*)

WALTER, Eugene
EASIEST WAY, THE (P)   MGM 1931
(*In* Best Plays of 1909–10: Dodd, N.Y.)

WALTON, George *see* **ADLEMAN, R.H.** *jt. author*

WALTON, Todd
INSIDE MOVES   BARBER 1981
(New American Library, N.Y.)

WAMBAUGH, Joseph
BLACK MARBLE, THE   AVCO 1980
(Dell, N.Y.)
BLUE NIGHT   BUTCHER 1973
(Joseph)
CHOIR BOYS, THE   GTO 1977
(Weidenfeld & Nicolson)
GLITTER DOME, THE   EMI 1984
(Morrow, N.Y.)
NEW CENTURIANS, THE   COL 1972
(Little, Brown, Boston)   (*Precinct 45—Los Angeles Police*)
ONION FIELD, THE   AVCO 1979
(Delacorte, N.Y.)

WARD, Brad
MARSHAL OF MEDICINE HAT, THE
(Hodder & Stoughton)   COL 1955
                                (*Lawless Street, A*)

WARD, Mary Jane
SNAKE PIT, THE   FOX 1948
(Cassell)

WARD, Robert
CATTLE ANNIE AND LITTLE
BRITCHES   HEMDALE 1980
(Ace, N.Y.)

WARNER, Douglas
DEATH OF A SNOUT   RANK 1963
(Cassell)   *(Informer, The)*

WARNER, Rex
AERODROME, THE   BBC 1983 (TV)
(Oxford U.P.)

WARNER, Sylvia Ashton *see* **ASHTON-WARNER, S.**

WARREN, Charles Esme Thornton *and* **BENSON, James**
ABOVE US THE WAVES   GFD 1954
(Harrap)

WARREN, Charles Marquis
ONLY THE VALIANT   WAR 1950
(Macmillan, N.Y.)

WARREN, Robert Penn
ALL THE KING'S MEN   COL 1949
(Eyre & Spottiswoode)
BAND OF ANGELS   WAR 1956
(Eyre & Spottiswoode)

WASSERMAN, Dale
MAN OF LA MANCHA (P)   UA 1972
(Random House, N.Y.)

WATERHOUSE, Keith *and* **HALL, Willis**
BILLY LIAR (P)   WAR 1962
(Joseph)

WATERS, F. *see* **BRANCH, H.** *jt. author*

WATKIN, Lawrence Edward
ON BORROWED TIME   MGM 1939
(Davies)

WATKYN, Arthur
  FOR BETTER, FOR WORSE (P)   ABP 1954
  (*In* Plays of the Year 1952–53: Elek)

WAUGH, Alec
  GUY RENTON   FOX 1960
  (Consul Bks.)   (*Circle of Deception*)
  ISLAND IN THE SUN   FOX 1957
  (Cassell)

WAUGH, Evelyn
  BRIDESHEAD REVISITED   ITV 1982 (TV)
  (Penguin)
  DECLINE AND FALL   FOX 1968
  (Chapman & Hall)   (*. . . of a Birdwatcher*)
  LOVED ONE, THE   MGM 1965
  (Chatto & Windus)

WAUGH, Hillary
  SLEEP LONG, MY LOVELY   BL 1962
  (Gollancz)   (*Jigsaw*)

WEATHER, P. *see* **CARY, F.L.** *jt. author*

WEBB, Charles
  GRADUATE, THE   UA 1968
  (Penguin)
  MARRIAGE OF A YOUNG
  STOCKBROKER, THE   FOX 1971
  (Deutsch)

WEBB, Mary
  GONE TO EARTH   BL 1950
  (Cape)

WEBB, Richard *see* **QUENTIN, Patrick** *pseud.*

WEBSTER, Jean
  DADDY LONG LEGS   FOX 1955
  (Hodder & Stoughton)

WEIDMAN, Jerome
  I CAN GET IT FOR YOU
  WHOLESALE   FOX 1951
  (Heinemann)   (*This is my Affair*)

WELDON, Fay
LIFE AND LOVES OF A SHE-DEVIL   BBC 1986 (TV)
(Hodder & Stoughton)

WELLES, Orson
MR. ARKADIN   WAR 1955
(W.H. Allen)   (*Confidential Report*)

WELLES, Patricia
BOB AND CAROL AND TED AND
ALICE   COL 1970
(Corgi)

WELLMAN, Paul Iselin
BRONCO APACHE   UA 1954
(News of the World)   (*Apache*)
CHAIN, THE   COL 1952
(Laurie)
COMANCHEROS, THE   FOX 1961
(Doubleday, N.Y.)
IRON MISTRESS   WAR 1952
(Laurie)
JUBAL TROOP   COL 1956
(Grosset, N.Y.)   (*Jubal*)
WALLS OF JERICHO, THE   FOX 1949
(Laurie)

WELLS, Herbert George
DOOR IN THE WALL, THE   ABP 1956
(*In* Short Stories: Benn)
FIRST MEN IN THE MOON, THE   COL 1963
(Various)
HISTORY OF MR. POLLY   TC 1949
(Various)
INVISIBLE MAN, THE   UA 1933
(Various)   BBC 1984 (TV)
ISLAND OF DR. MOREAU, THE   EROS 1959
(Heinemann)   (*Island of Lost Souls*)
          AMERICAN INTERNATIONAL
          1977
KIPPS   FOX 1941
(Various)
MAN WHO COULD WORK
MIRACLES, THE   AU 1937
(Cresset Press)

650

PASSIONATE FRIENDS, THE   CINEGUILD 1949
(Benn)
SHAPE OF THINGS TO COME, THE   UA 1936
(Hutchinson)   (*Things to Come*)
THINGS TO COME (P)   UA 1936
(Cresset Press)   BARBER DANN 1979
TIME MACHINE, THE   MGM 1960
(Heinemann)
VALLEY OF THE ANTS, THE   BRENT WALKER, 1978
(Fontana)   (*Empire of the Ants*)
WAR OF THE WORLDS   PAR 1953
(Heinemann)

WELLS, Lee Edwin
DAY OF THE OUTLAW   UA 1959
(Hale)

WERBELL, F. *and* CLARKE, T.
LOST HERO, THE   BERYL—STONEHENGE 1985
(McGraw, N.Y.)   (*Wallenberg: The Lost Hero*)

WERFEL, Franz V.
SONG OF BERNADETTE, THE   FOX 1943
(Hamilton)

WESKER, Arnold
KITCHEN, THE (P)   BL 1961
(Faber)

WEST, Jessamyn
FRIENDLY PERSUASION   MGM 1956
(Hodder & Stoughton)

WEST, Morris L.
BIG STORY, THE   GALA 1964
(Heinemann)
NAKED COUNTRY   NEW SOUTH WALES 1984
(Coronet)
SHOES OF THE FISHERMAN, THE   MGM 1972
(Heinemann)

WEST, Nathaniel
DAY OF THE LOCUST   PAR 1974
(Penguin)

WEST, Nathaniel (*Continued*)
MISS LONELYHEARTS   UA 1959
(Grey Walls Press)   (*Lonely Hearts*)

WEST, Rebecca
RETURN OF THE SOLDIER   BRENT WALKER 1981
(Virago)

WEST, Stanley
AMOS   PRECISION 1985 (TV)
(Rawson, N.Y.)

WESTBROOK, Robert
MAGIC GARDEN OF STANLEY
SWEETHEART, THE   MGM 1970
(W.H. Allen)

WESTERBY, Robert
WIDE BOYS NEVER WORK   COL 1956
(Methuen)   (*Soho Incident*)

WESTHEIMER, David
VON RYAN'S EXPRESS   FOX 1964
(Joseph)

WESTLAKE, Donald E.
BANK SHOT, THE   UA 1974
(Simon & Schuster, N.Y.)
BUSY BODY, THE   PAR 1968
(Boardman)
BUTCHER'S MOON   EMI 1983
(Coronet)   (*Slayground*)
COPS AND ROBBERS   UA 1974
(Hodder & Stoughton)
HOT ROCK   FOX 1972
(Hodder & Stoughton)   (*How to Steal a Diamond in Four
          Uneasy Lessons*)

WESTON, John
HAIL, HERO   CINEMA CENTER 1969
(Mackay, N.Y.)

WEYMAN, Stanley John
UNDER THE RED ROBE   FOX 1937
(Various)

WHARTON, *Mrs.* **Edith Newbold**
AGE OF INNOCENCE   RKO 1934
(Appleton, N.Y.)
CHILDREN, THE   PAR 1929
(Appleton, N.Y.)   (*Marriage Playground*)
OLD MAID, THE   WAR 1939
(Grosset, N.Y.)

WHARTON, William
BIRDY   TRI STAR 1984 (TV)
(Knopf, N.Y.)

WHEATLEY, Dennis
DEVIL RIDES OUT, THE   ABF 1971
(Hutchinson)
EUNUCH OF STAMBOUL, THE   HOB 1939
(Hutchinson)   (*Secret of Stamboul, The*)
FORBIDDEN TERRITORY   HOFFBERG 1938
(Hutchinson)
TO THE DEVIL A DAUGHTER   EMI 1976
(Hutchinson)
UNCHARTERED SEAS   WAR 1968
(Hutchinson)   (*Lost Continent, The*)

WHEELER, H. *see* **BURDICK, E.** *jt. author*

WHIPPLE, Dorothy
THEY KNEW MR. KNIGHT   GFD 1946
(Murray)
THEY WERE SISTERS   GFD 1945
(Murray)

WHITE, Alan
LONG DAY'S DYING, THE   PAR 1968
(Hodder & Stoughton)

WHITE, E.B.
CHARLOTTE'S WEB   SCOTIA BARBER 1972
(Penguin)

WHITE, Ethel Lina
HER HEART IN HER THROAT   PAR 1945
(Grosset, N.Y.)   (*Unseen, The*)
SOME MUST WATCH   RKO 1946
(Ward Lock)   (*Spiral Staircase, The*)

WHITE, Ethel Lina (*Continued*)
SPIRAL STAIRCASE, THE   COL—WAR 1975
(Ward Lock)
WHEEL SPINS, THE   MGM 1938
(Collins)   (*Lady Vanishes, The*)
      RANK 1979
      (*Lady Vanishes, The*)

WHITE, Grace Miller
TESS OF THE STORM COUNTRY   FOX 1960
(Various)

WHITE, James Dillon
MAGGIE, THE   EALING 1954
(Heinemann)

WHITE, Jon Manchip Ewbank
MARK OF DUST   EXCLUSIVE 1954
(Hodder & Stoughton)   (*Mask of Doubt*)

WHITE, Lionel
CLEAN BREAK   UA 1956
(Boardman)   (*Killing, The*)
MONEY TRAP   MGM 1965
(Boardman)

WHITE, Robb
OUR VIRGIN ISLAND   BL 1958
(Gollancz)   (*Virgin Island*)
UP PERISCOPE   WAR 1958
(Collins)

WHITE, Theodore Harold
MOUNTAIN ROAD, THE   COL 1959
(Cassell)
ONCE AND FUTURE KING, THE   WAR 1966
(Collins)   (*Camelot*)
SWORD IN THE STONE, THE   DISNEY 1963
(Collins)

WHITE, William Lindsay
JOURNEY FOR MARGARET   MGM 1942
(Hurst & Blackett)
THEY WERE EXPENDABLE   MGM 1945
(Hamilton)

WHITEHEAD, Donald
  FBI STORY, THE   WAR 1958
  (Panther)

WHITEMORE, L.H.
  SUPER COPS, THE   MGM 1974
  (Futura)

WHITING, John
  DEVILS, THE (P)   WAR 1971
  (French)

WIBBERLEY, Leonard
  MOUSE THAT ROARED, THE   UA 1962
  (Bantam)   (*Mouse on the Moon*)
  WRATH OF GRAPES   COL 1959
  (Hale)   (*Mouse that Roared, The*)

WICKER, Tom
  TIME TO DIE   ITV 1985 (TV)
  (Bodley Head)   (*Attica*)

WIGGIN, *Mrs.* Kate Douglas
  MOTHER CAREY'S CHICKENS   DISNEY 1963
  (Hodder & Stoughton)   (*Summer Magic*)
  REBECCA OF SUNNYBROOK FARM
  (Various)   FOX 1932
      FOX 1938
  TIMOTHY'S QUEST   PAR 1936
  (Partridge)

WILDE, Hagar *and* EUNSON, Dale
  DEAR EVELYN (P)   UA 1944
  (French)   (*Guest in the House*)

WILDE, Oscar
  CANTERVILLE GHOST, THE   MGM 1944
  (Collins)
  IDEAL HUSBAND, AN (P)   BL 1948
  (Methuen)
  IMPORTANCE OF BEING EARNEST,
  THE (P)   GFD 1952
  (Heinemann)
  LADY WINDERMERE'S FAN (P)   FOX 1949
  (Methuen)

WILDE, Oscar (*Continued*)
LORD ARTHUR SAVILE'S CRIME   UN 1943
(Various)   (*Flesh and Fantasy*)
PICTURE OF DORIAN GRAY, THE   MGM 1945
(Unicorn Press)   HEMDALE 1973
                                    (*Dorian Gray*)
SALOME (P)   CANNON 1986
(Various)

WILDER, Joan
ROMANCING THE STONE   FOX 1984
(Corgi)

WILDER, Margaret Applegate
SINCE YOU WENT AWAY   UA 1944
(McGraw-Hill, N.Y.)

WILDER, Robert
AND RIDE A TIGER   UI 1958
(W.H. Allen)   (*Stranger in my Arms, A*)
FLAMINGO ROAD   WAR 1949
(Grosset, N.Y.)
FRUIT OF THE POPPY   MGM 1968
(W.H. Allen)   (*Heroin Gang, The*)
WRITTEN ON THE WIND   UN 1956
(Corgi)

WILDER, Thornton Niven
BRIDGE OF SAN LUIS REY, THE   MGM 1929
(Longmans)   UA 1944
MATCHMAKER, THE (P)   PAR 1958
(French)
OUR TOWN (P)   UA 1940
(Coward-McCann, N.Y.)

WILDER, William *and* **DIAMOND, I.A.L.**
SOME LIKE IT HOT   UA 1959
(Panther)

WILK, Max
DON'T RAISE THE BRIDGE LOWER
THE RIVER   BL 1967
(Heinemann)

WILKERSON, David
CROSS AND THE SWITCHBLADE,
THE   FOX 1970
(Oliphants)

WILKINS, Vaughan
KING RELUCTANT, A   RANK 1957
(Cape)   (*Dangerous Exile*)

WILKINSON, G.R.
MONKEYS, THE   DISNEY 1967
(Macdonald)   (*Monkeys, Go Home*)

WILLARD, John
CAT AND THE CANARY, THE (P) UN 1930
(Hudson)   (*Cat Creeps, The*)
          PAR 1939
          GALA 1981

WILLEFORD, Charles
COCKFIGHTER   EMI 1974
(Crown, N.Y.)

WILLIAMS, Alan
SNAKE WATER   UI 1968
(Panther)   (*Pink Jungle, The*)

WILLIAMS, Ben Ames
LEAVE HER TO HEAVEN FOX 1945
(Hale)
STRANGE WOMAN, THE UA 1946
(Houghton, Mifflin, Boston)

WILLIAMS, Brock
EARL OF CHICAGO   MGM 1940
(Harrap)
UNCLE WILLIE AND THE BICYCLE
SHOP   ABP 1953
(Harrap)   (*Ain't Life Wonderful*)

WILLIAMS, Charles
DON'T JUST STAND THERE RANK 1969
(Cassell)

WILLIAMS, Emlyn
CORN IS GREEN, THE (P)   WAR 1945
(Heinemann)
LIGHT OF HEART, THE (P)   FOX 1942
(Heinemann)
NIGHT MUST FALL (P)   MGM 1937
(Gollancz)   MGM 1964
SOMEBODY WAITING (P)   HARLEQUIN 1957
(Dramatists, N.Y.)   (*Time Without Pity*)

WILLIAMS, Eric
WOODEN HORSE, THE   BL 1950
(Collins)

WILLIAMS, Gordon M.
MAN WHO HAD POWER OVER
WOMEN, THE   AVCO EMBASSY 1970
(Secker & Warburg)
SIEGE AT TRENCHER'S FARM, THE   CINERAMA 1971
(Mayflower)   (*Straw Dogs*)

WILLIAMS, Hugh *and* **WILLIAMS, Margaret**
GRASS IS GREENER, THE (P)   UI 1960
(Gollancz)

WILLIAMS, H.V. *see* **BENTHAM, J.** *jt. author*

WILLIAMS, Jay
SOLOMON AND SHEBA   UA 1959
(Macdonald)

WILLIAMS, John
NIGHT SONG   FILM 2 1969
(Collins)   (*Sweet Love, Bitter*)

WILLIAMS, *Mrs.* Rebecca
FATHER WAS A HANDFUL   MGM 1941
(Joseph)   (*Vanishing Virginian, The*)

WILLIAMS, Tennessee
BABY DOLL (P)   WAR 1956
(Secker & Warburg)
CAT ON A HOT TIN ROOF (P)   MGM 1958
(Secker & Warburg)

GLASS MENAGERIE, THE (P)   WAR 1950
(Lehmann)
MILK TRAIN DOESN'T STOP HERE
ANYMORE (P)   UI 1968
(Secker & Warburg)   (*Boom*)
NIGHT OF THE IGUANA, THE (P)   MGM 1963
(Secker & Warburg)
ORPHEUS DESCENDING (P)   UA 1960
(Secker & Warburg)   (*Fugitive Kind, The*)
PERIOD OF ADJUSTMENT (P)   MGM 1962
(Secker & Warburg)
ROMAN SPRING OF MRS. STONE,
THE   WAR 1961
(Ace)
ROSE TATTOO, THE (P)   PAR 1954
(Secker & Warburg)
STREETCAR NAMED DESIRE, A (P)   WAR 1951
(Lehmann)   PSO 1984
SUDDENLY LAST SUMMER (P)   COL 1959
(Secker & Warburg)
SUMMER AND SMOKE (P)   PAR 1962
(*In* Four Plays: Secker & Warburg)
SWEET BIRD OF YOUTH (P)   MGM 1962
(Secker & Warburg)
THIS PROPERTY IS CONDEMNED   PAR 1966
(P)
(New Directions, Norfolk, Conn.)

WILLIAMS, Valentine
CROUCHING BEAST, THE   OLY 1936
(Hodder & Stoughton)

WILLIAMS, Wirt
ADA DALLAS   MGM 1960
(Muller)

WILLIAMSON, Henry
TARKA THE OTTER   RANK 1978
(Cape)

WILLINGHAM, Calder
END AS A MAN   COL 1957
(Barker)
STRANGE ONE, THE (P)   COL 1957
(Grosset, N.Y.)   (*End as a Man*)

WILLIS, Ted
  HOT SUMMERNIGHT (P)   RANK 1961
  (French)   (*Flame in the Streets*)
  MAN-EATER   BBC 1984 (TV)
  (Pan)   (*Maneaters are Loose!*)

WILSON, Angus
  OLD MAN AT THE ZOO, THE   BBC 1983 (TV)
  (Penguin)

WILSON, Cherry
  EMPTY SADDLES   UN 1936
  (Ward Lock)

WILSON, Colin
  SPACE VAMPIRES   CANNON 1985
  (Random House, N.Y.)   (*Lifeforce*)

WILSON, Donald Powell
  MY SIX CONVICTS   COL 1952
  (Hamilton)

WILSON, Harry Leon
  BUNKER BEAN   RKO 1936
  (Lane)
  MERTON OF THE MOVIES   PAR 1932
  (Cape)   (*Make Me a Star*)
  RUGGLES OF RED GAP   PAR 1935
  (Various)

WILSON, John
  HAMP (P)   WAR 1965
  (Evans)   (*King and Country*)

WILSON, John Raven
  MASK, THE   BL 1958
  (Heinemann)   (*Behind the Mask*)

WILSON, Sandy
  BOY FRIEND, THE (P)   MGM—EMI 1971
  (Penguin)

WILSON, Sloan
  MAN IN THE GREY FLANNEL SUIT,   FOX 1956
  THE
  (Cassell)

WILSON, S.J.
TO FIND A MAN   COL—WAR 1971
(W.H. Allen)

WILSTACH, Frank
WILD BILL HICKOK   PAR 1936
(Sun Dial, N.Y.)   (*Plainsman, The*)

WINSOR, Kathleen
FOREVER AMBER   FOX 1947
(Macdonald)

WINTER, Keith
SHINING HOUR, THE (P)   MGM 1938
(Heinemann)

WINTERTON, Paul *see* **BAX, Roger** *pseud.*

WINTON, John
WE JOINED THE NAVY   WAR 1962
(Joseph)

WISEMAN, Nicholas Patrick Stephen *Cardinal*
FABIOLA   BL 1951
(Various)

WISEMAN, Thomas
ROMANTIC CONGRESSWOMAN,
THE   FOX—RANK 1975
(Cape)

WISTER, Owen
VIRGINIAN, THE   PAR 1929
(Various)

WITTS, M. *see* **THOMAS, G.** *jt. author*

WODEHOUSE, Percival Grenville
DAMSEL IN DISTRESS, A   RKO 1937
(Jenkins)
GIRL ON THE BOAT, THE   UA 1962
(Jenkins)
PICCADILLY JIM   MGM 1936
(Jenkins)

WODEHOUSE, Percival Grenville (*Continued*)
SUMMER LIGHTNING   BD 1932
(Jenkins)
THANK YOU, JEEVES   FOX 1936
(Jenkins)

WOHL, Burton
COLD WIND IN AUGUST   UA 1961
(Mayflower)

WOLF, Alice *see* **CARTER, Angela** *jt. author*

WOLFE, Tom
RIGHT STUFF   COL—EMI—WAR 1982
(Cape)

WOLFE, Winifred
ASK ANY GIRL   MGM 1959
(Hammond)
IF A MAN ANSWERS   RANK 1962
(Hammond)

WOLFERT, Ira
AMERICAN GUERILLA IN THE
PHILIPPINES   FOX 1950
(Gollancz)   (*I Shall Return*)
TUCKER'S PEOPLE   MGM 1949
(Gollancz)   (*Force of Evil*)

WOLFF, Maritta Martin
WHISTLE-STOP   UA 1946
(Constable)

WOLFF, Ruth
ABDICATION, THE   COL—WAR 1974
(Paperback Library)

WOLFORD, Nelson *and* **WOLFORD, Shirley**
SOUTHERN BLADE, THE   COL 1967
(Morrow, N.Y.)   (*Long Ride Home, The*)

WOLLASTON, Nicholas
ECLIPSE   GALA 1976
(Macmillan)

WOLPERT, Stanley
NINE HOURS TO RAMA   FOX 1962
(Hamilton)

WOOD, Christopher
SPY WHO LOVED ME, THE   UA 1977
(Cape)

WOOD, Clement Biddle
WELCOME TO THE CLUB   COL 1970
(Panther)

WOOD, Derek *and* **DEMPSTER, Derek**
NARROW MARGIN, THE   UA 1969
(Arrow)   (*Battle of Britain, The*)

WOOD, *Mrs.* **Henry**
EAST LYNNE   FOX 1931
(Various)   TIFFANY 1931
     (*Ex-flame*)

WOOD, Michael
IN SEARCH OF THE TROJAN WAR   BBC 2 1985 (TV)
(BBC)

WOOD, William
MANUELA   BL 1957
(Hart-Davis)

WOODS, William Howard
EDGE OF DARKNESS   WAR 1943
(Grosset, N.Y.)

WOODWARD, R. *see* **BERNSTEIN, C.** *jt. author*

WOOLF, Virginia
TO THE LIGHTHOUSE   BBC 1982 (TV)
(Dent)

WOOLL, Edward
LIBEL (P)   MGM 1959
(French)

WOOLLARD, Kenneth
  MORNING DEPARTURE (P)   GFD 1950
  (French)

WOOLRICH, Cornell
  BLACK ALIBI   RKO 1943
  (Simon & Schuster, N.Y.)   (*Leopard Man, The*)
  BLACK ANGEL   UN 1946
  (Doubleday, N.Y.)
  BLACK CURTAIN, THE   PAR 1942
  (Grosset, N.Y.)   (*Street of Chance*)

WOOLRICH, Cornell *see also* **IRISH, William** *pseud.,* **HOPLEY, George** *pseud.*

WOUK, Herman
  CAINE MUTINY, THE   COL 1954
  (Cape)
  MARJORIE MORNINGSTAR   WAR 1957
  (Cape)
  WINDS OF WAR, THE   PAR 1983 (TV)
  (Collins)
  YOUNGBLOOD HAWKE   WAR 1963
  (Cape)

WREN, Percival Christopher
  BEAU GESTE   PAR 1939
  (Murray)   UI 1966
     BBC 1984 (TV)
  BEAU IDEAL   RKO 1931
  (Murray)
  BEAU SABREUR   PAR 1928
  (Murray)

WRIGHT, Harold Bell
  CALLING OF DAN MATTHEWS,
  THE   COL 1936
  (Hodder & Stoughton)
  MINE WITH THE IRON DOOR, THE
  (Appleton, N.Y.)   COL 1936
  SHEPHERD OF THE HILLS, THE   PAR 1941
  (Grosset, N.Y.)

WRIGHT, Richard
  NATIVE SON   CLASSIC 1951
  (Gollancz)

WRIGHT, S. Fowler
DELUGE, THE   RKO 1933
(Allied Press)

WYLIE, Ida Alexa Ross
KEEPER OF THE FLAME   MGM 1942
(Cassell)
PILGRIMAGE   FOX 1933
(Cassell)
YOUNG IN HEART, THE   UA 1938
(Cassell)

WYLIE, Philip
NIGHT UNTO NIGHT   WAR 1949
(Farrar, N.Y.)

WYLIE, Philip *see also* **BALMER, E.** *jt. author*

WYNDHAM, John
DAY OF THE TRIFFIDS, THE   RANK 1962
(Joseph)   BBC 1982 (TV)
MIDWICH CUCKOOS, THE   MGM 1960
(Joseph)   (*Village of the Damned, The*)

WYNETTE, Tammy
STAND BY YOUR MAN   JNP 1981
(PB, N.Y.)

WYNNE, Barry
COUNT 5 AND DIE   FOX 1957
(Souvenir Press)

WYNNE, Greville
MAN FROM MOSCOW, A   BBC 1985 (TV)
(Arrow)   (*Wynne and Penkovsky*)

WYSS, Johann David
SWISS FAMILY ROBINSON   RKO 1940
(Various)   DISNEY 1960
                               DISNEY 1977

Y

YAFA, Stephen
THREE IN THE ATTIC   WAR 1968
(Sphere)

YALLOP, David
BEYOND REASONABLE DOUBT   J & M FILMS 1980
(Hodder & Stoughton)

YARDLEY, Herbert O.
AMERICAN BLACK CHAMBER,
THE   MGM 1935
(Faber)   (*Rendezvous*)

YEATS-BROWN, Francis
BENGAL LANCER   PAR 1935
(Gollancz)   (*Lives of a Bengal Lancer, The*)

YERBY, Frank
FOXES OF HARROW, THE   FOX 1947
(Heinemann)
GOLDEN HAWK, THE   COL 1952
(Heinemann)
SARACEN BLADE, THE   COL 1954
(Heinemann)

YORDAN, Philip
ANNA LUCASTA (P)   COL 1949
(Random House, N.Y.)
MAN OF THE WEST   MGM 1957
(Deutsch)   (*Gun Glory*)

YORGASON, Blaine
WINDWALKER   PACIFIC INTERNATIONAL 1981
(Bookcraft, Salt Lake City)

YORK, Andrew
ELIMINATOR, THE   UA 1968
(Hutchinson)   (*Danger Route*)

YOUNG, Desmond
ROMMEL   FOX 1951
(Collins)   (*Rommel—Desert Fox*)

YOUNG, Francis Brett
   MAN ABOUT THE HOUSE, A   LF 1947
   (Heinemann)
   MAN ABOUT THE HOUSE, A (P)   LF 1947
   (Sampson Low)
   MY BROTHER JONATHAN   AB 1948
   (Heinemann)   BBC 1985 (TV)
   PORTRAIT OF CLARE   ABP 1949
   (Heinemann)

YOUNG, Kendall
   RAVINE, THE   RANK 1971
   (Pan)   (*Assault*)

YOUNG, Stark
   SO RED THE ROSE   PAR 1935
   (Cassell)

Z

ZELAZNY, Roger
   DAMNATION ALLEY   FOX 1978
   (Putnam, N.Y.)

ZETTERLING, Mai
   NIGHT GAMES   GALA 1966
   (Constable)

ZIEGLER, Isabelle Gibson
   NINE DAYS OF FATHER SERRA   FOX 1955
   (Longmans)   (*Seven Cities of Gold*)

ZIEMER, Geogor
   EDUCATION FOR DEATH   RKO 1943
   (Constable)   (*Hitler's Children*)

ZINDEL, Paul
   EFFECT OF GAMMA RAYS ON
   MAN-IN-THE-MOON MARRIGOLD,
   THE (P)   FOX—Rank 1972
   (French)

ZOLA, Emile
   KILL, THE   COL 1967
   (Arrow)   (*Game is Over, The*)

ZOLA, Emile (*Continued*)
  LA BÊTE HUMAINE   COL 1954
  (Various)   (*Human Desire*)
  NANA   MGM 1933
  (Elek)   GALA 1955
                                          CANNON 1983

ZWEIG, Arnold
  CASE OF SERGEANT GRISCHA,
  THE   RKO 1930
  (Secker)

ZWEIG, Stefan
  BEWARE OF PITY   TC 1946
  (Cassell)
  LETTER FROM AN UNKNOWN
  WOMAN, A   UI 1948
  (Cassell)   UB 1979
  MARIE ANTOINETTE   MGM 1938
  (Cassell)

CHANGE OF ORIGINAL TITLE INDEX

*Film companies frequently change the
original title of the book or play on
screening. This alphabetical index gives
the author's original and published title
of his work, followed by the screen
title where the two differ.*

A

ABBESS OF CREWE, THE
Spark, M.

ABC MURDERS, THE
Christie, A.

ABE LINCOLN OF ILLINOIS (P)
Sherwood, R.E.

ABZ OF LOVE, THE
Hegeler, I. *and* S.

ACACIA AVENUE (P)
Constanduros, M. *and* D.

ACCENT ON YOUTH (P)
Raphaelson, S.

ACT OF MERCY
Clifford, F.

ACT OF PASSION
Simenon, G.

"ADDIE PRAY"
Brown, J.D.

ADIOS
Bartlett, L. *and* V.S.

ADOBE WALLS
Burnett, W.R.

ADVENTURE IN DIAMONDS
Walker, D.E.

ADVENTURE IN DIAMONDS
Walker, D.E.

**ADVENTURES OF HAJJI BABA OF
ISPAHAN**
Morier, J.

ABBESS, THE
SCOTIA-BARBER 1976
(*U.K. Title:* NASTY HABITS)

ALPHABET MURDERS, THE
MGM 1966

ABE LINCOLN IN ILLINOIS
RKO 1940

LANGUAGE OF LOVE
GN 1971

29 ACACIA AVENUE
COL 1945

BUT NOT FOR ME
PAR 1959

GUNS OF DARKNESS
WAR 1964

FORBIDDEN FRUIT
CP 1952

PAPER MOON
PAR 1973

LASH, THE
IN 1931

ARROWHEAD
PAR 1953

OPERATION AMSTERDAM
RANK 1958

MAN COULD GET KILLED, A
RANK 1966

**ADVENTURES OF HAJJI BABA,
THE**
FOX 1954

ADVENTURES OF ROBINSON CRUSOE, THE Defoe, D.	**MISS ROBINSON CRUSOE** FOX 1954
ADVENTURES OF THE FIVE ORANGE PIPS, THE Doyle, *Sir* A.C.	**HOUSE OF FEAR** UN 1945
AFRICAN BUSH ADVENTURES Hunter, J.A.	**KILLERS OF KILIMANJARO** COL 1959
AFTER ALL (P) Druten, J. van	**NEW MORALS FOR OLD** MGM 1932
AFTER THE FUNERAL Christie, A.	**MURDER AT THE GALLOP** MGM 1963
AGONY COLUMN Biggers, E.D.	**PASSAGE FROM HONG KONG** WAR 1941
AH WILDERNESS (P) O'Neill, E.G.	**SUMMER HOLIDAY** MGM 1948
AIMEZ-VOUS BRAHMS? Sagan, F.	**GOODBYE AGAIN** UA 1961
AIRING IN A CLOSED CARRIAGE Shearing, J.	**MARK OF CAIN** TC 1948
ALLAN QUATERMAIN Haggard, *Sir* H.R.	**KING SOLOMON'S TREASURE** BARBER ROSE 1979 **QUATERMAIN** CANNON 1985
ALASKA Beach, R.E.	**SPOILERS, THE** UN 1942
ALEXANDRIA QUARTET Durrell, L.	**JUSTINE** FOX 1969
ALGONQUIN PROJECT, THE Nolan, F.	**BRASS TARGET** MGM 1978
ALICE IN WONDERLAND Carroll, L.	**ALICE** HEMDALE 1980

ORIGINAL TITLE	FILM TITLE
ALICE SIT BY THE FIRE (P) Barrie, *Sir* J.M.	**RENDEZVOUS** PAR 1950
ALIEN, THE Davies, L.P.	**GROUNDSTAR CONSPIRACY,** **THE** RANK 1972
ALL ABOARD FOR FREEDOM McSwigan, M.	**SNOW TREASURE** TIGON 1968
ALL BRIDES ARE BEAUTIFUL Bell, T.	**FROM THIS DAY FORWARD** RKO 1946
ALL IN GOOD TIME (P) Naughton, B.	**FAMILY WAY, THE** BL 1966
ALL KNEELING Parrish, A.	**BORN TO BE BAD** RKO 1950
ALL ON A SUMMER'S DAY Garden, J.	**DOUBLE CONFESSION** ABP 1950
ALL THINGS BRIGHT AND BEAUTIFUL Herriot J.	**IT SHOULDN'T HAPPEN TO A VET** EMI 1976
ALL THROUGH THE NIGHT Masterton, W.	**CRY IN THE NIGHT, A** WAR 1956
AL SCHMID, MARINE Butterfield, R.P.	**PRIDE OF THE MARINES** WAR 1945
AMAZING QUEST OF MR. ERNEST **BLISS, THE** Oppenheim, E.P.	**AMAZING QUEST, THE** KLEMENT 1936
AMBOY DUKES, THE Shulman, I.	**CITY ACROSS THE RIVER** UI 1949
AMERICA, AMERICA Kazan, E.	**ANATOLIAN SMILE, THE** WAR 1964
AMERICAN BLACK CHAMBER, THE Yardley, H.O.	**RENDEZVOUS** MGM 1935

AMERICAN DREAM, AN Mailer, N.	**SEE YOU IN HELL, DARLING** WAR 1966
AMERICAN GUERILLA IN THE PHILIPPINES Wolfert, I.	**I SHALL RETURN** FOX 1950
AMERICAN TRAGEDY, AN Dreiser, T.	**PLACE IN THE SUN, A** PAR 1951
AMERIKA Zafka, F.	**CLASS RELATIONS** ARTIFICIAL EYE 1985
ANATOMY OF A CRIME Dinneen, J.F.	**SIX BRIDGES TO CROSS** GFD 1954
ANATOMY OF ME Hurst, F.	**IMITATION OF LIFE** RANK 1959
AND RIDE A TIGER Wilder, R.	**STRANGER IN MY ARMS, A** UI 1958
AND THEN THERE WERE NONE Christie, A. (*Originally published as: Ten Little Niggers*)	**AGATHA** COL—EMI—WAR 1979
AND THEY SHALL WALK Kenny, *Sister and* Ostenso, M.	**SISTER KENNY** RKO 1946
ANIMAL KINGDOM (P) Barry, P.	**ONE MORE TOMORROW** WAR 1948
ANNA AND THE KING OF SIAM Landon, M.	**KING AND I, THE** FOX 1956
ANNIVERSARY WALTZ (P) Fields, J. *and* Chodorov, J.	**HAPPY ANNIVERSARY** UA 1959
ANOINTED, THE Davis, C.B.	**ADVENTURE** MGM 1945
ANY WEDNESDAY (P) Resnik, M.	**BACHELOR GIRL APARTMENT** WAR 1966

ANZIO
Vaughan Thomas, W.

BATTLE FOR ANZIO, THE
COL 1968

APACHE RISING
Albert, M.

DUEL AT DIABLO
UA 1966

APPALOOSA
MacLeod, R.

SOUTHWEST TO SONORA
UI 1966

APPLESAUCE
Conners, B.

BRIDES ARE LIKE THAT
IN 1936

APPOINTMENT AT THE BEACH
Moravia, A.

NAKED HOURS, THE
COMPTON 1965

APPOINTMENT IN ZAHREIN
Barrett, M.

ESCAPE FROM ZAHREIN
PAR 1962

APRON STRINGS (P)
Davis, D.

VIRTUOUS HUSBAND
UN 1931

ARIZONA IN THE '50s
Tevis, J.H.

TENDERFOOT
DISNEY 1964

AROUSE AND BEWARE
Kantor, M.

MAN FROM DAKOTA
MGM 1940

ASHENDEN
Maugham, W.S.

SECRET AGENT
GB 1936

ASK AGEMEMNON
Hall, J.

GOODBYE GEMINI
CINERAMA 1970

ASPERN PAPERS, THE
James, H.

LOST MOMENT, THE
UN 1947
ASPERN
CONNOISSEUR 1981

ASPHALT JUNGLE, THE
Burnett, W.R.

CAIRO
MGM 1963
COOL BREEZE
MGM—EMI 1972

ASSIZE OF THE DYING, THE
Pargeter, E.

SPANIARD'S CURSE
BL 1957

675

ORIGINAL TITLE	FILM TITLE
AUGUST 1914 Tuchman, B.W.	**GUNS OF AUGUST, THE** RANK 1964
AUNTIE MAME Dennis, P.	**LUCY MAME** WAR 1974
AUTHENTIC DEATH OF HENDRY JONES, THE Neider, C.	**ONE EYED JACKS** PAR 1960
AUTUMN (P) Kennedy, M.	**THAT DANGEROUS AGE** LF 1949
AWAKENING, THE Chopin, K.	**END OF AUGUST, THE** ENTERPRISE 1981

B

BABY JANE Farrell, H.	**WHATEVER HAPPENED TO BABY JANE?** WAR 1962
BABYLON REVISITED Fitzgerald, F.S.	**LAST TIME I SAW PARIS, THE** MGM 1954
BACK OF SUNSET Cleary, J.	**SUNDOWNERS, THE** WAR 1960
BADGE OF EVIL Masterson, W.	**TOUCH OF EVIL** UN 1958
BADMAN Huffaker, C.	**WAR WAGON** UI 1966
BALLAD OF CAT BALLOU Chanslor, R.	**CAT BALLOU** COL 1965
BALLAD OF DINGUS MAGEE, THE Markson, D.	**DIRTY DINGUS MAGEE** MGM 1970
BALLAD OF THE BELSTONE FOX, THE Rook, D.	**BELSTONE FOX, THE** FOX—RANK 1972

ORIGINAL TITLE	FILM TITLE
BALLAD OF THE RUNNING MAN, THE Smith, S.	**RUNNING MAN, THE** COL 1963
BALLERINA Smith, *Lady* E.	**MEN IN HER LIFE** COL 1941
BANNER IN THE SKY Ullman, J.R.	**THIRD MAN ON THE MOUNTAIN** DISNEY 1959
BARCHESTER TOWERS Trollope, A.	**BARCHESTER CHRONICLES, THE** BBC 1982 (TV)
BARRY LYNDON Thackeray, W.M.	**LUCK OF BARRY LYNDON, THE** WAR 1974
BAR SINISTER, THE Davies, R.H.	**IT'S A DOG'S LIFE** MGM 1955
BASEMENT ROOM, THE Greene, G.	**FALLEN IDOL, THE** FOX 1948
BASIL OF BAKER STREET Titus, E.	**GREAT MOUSE DETECTIVE, THE** DISNEY 1986
BAT, THE Rinehart, M.R.	**BAT WHISPERS, THE** UA 1931
BATTLE OF NERVES, A Simenon, G.	**MAN ON THE EIFFEL TOWER,** **THE** BL 1950
BATTLE OF THE VILLA FIORITA, THE Godden, R.	**AFFAIR AT THE VILLA FIORITA,** **THE** WAR 1964
BEACHCOMBER Maugham, W.S.	**VESSEL OF WRATH, THE** PAR 1938
BEARDLESS WARRIORS Matheson, R.	**YOUNG WARRIORS** RANK 1966
BEAST MUST DIE, THE Blake, N.	**KILLER** CINECENTA 1969

BEAUTY Baldwin, F.	**BEAUTY FOR SALE** MGM 1933
BECAUSE OF THE CATS Freeling, N.	**RAPE, THE** MIRACLE FILMS 1976
BEFORE THE FACT Iles, F.	**SUSPICION** RKO 1941
BEGGAR MY NEIGHBOUR Ridley, A.	**MEET MR. LUCIFER** GFD 1953
BEGINNERS LUCK Somers, P.	**DESPERATE MAN, THE** AA 1959
BEHOLD WE LIVE (P) Druten, J. van	**IF I WERE FREE** RKO 1933
BEL AMI Maupassant, G. de	**PRIVATE AFFAIRS OF BEL AMI,** **THE** UA 1947
BELLA DONNA Hitchens, R.	**TEMPTATION** COL 1930
BELVEDERE Davenport, *Mrs.* G.	**SITTING PRETTY** FOX 1948
BENGAL LANCER Yeats-Brown, F.	**LIVES OF A BENGAL LANCER,** **THE** PAR 1935
BENIGHTED Priestley, J.B.	**OLD DARK HOUSE, THE** BL 1963
BE PREPARED Cochran, R.E.	**MISTER SCOUTMASTER** FOX 1953
BE READY WITH BELLS AND DRUMS Kata, E.	**PATCH OF BLUE** MGM 1966
BERG, THE (P) Raymond, E.	**ATLANTIC** BI 1930

BERLIN HOTEL
Baum, V.

HOTEL BERLIN
WAR 1945

BERLIN MEMORANDUM, THE
Hall, A.

QUILLER MEMORANDUM, THE
JARFID 1966

BE STILL MY LOVE
Truesdell, J.

ACCUSED, THE
PAR 1949

BETHNAL GREEN
Fisher, M.

PLACE TO GO, A
BL 1964

BETTER ANGELS, THE
McCarry, C.

MAN WITH THE DEADLY LENS, THE
COL—EMI—WAR 1982

BETTER THAN LIFE
Bromfield, L.

IT ALL CAME TRUE
WAR 1940

BEWARE OF CHILDREN
Anderson, V.

NO KIDDING
AA 1960

BEYOND THE MOUNTAINS
Ramati, A.

DESPERATE ONES, THE
AMERICAN INT 1968

BID TIME RETURN
Matheson, R.

SOMEWHERE IN TIME
CIC 1980

BIG BOODLE, THE
Sylvester, R.

NIGHT IN HAVANA
UA 1957

BIG GRAB, THE
Trinian, J.

BIG SNATCH, THE
GALA 1963

BIG PICK-UP
Trevor, E.

DUNKIRK
MGM 1958

BIG RANGE
Schaefer, J.W.

SILVER WHIP, THE
FOX 1953

BIG STICK-UP AT BRINK'S
Behn, N.

BRINK'S JOB, THE
COL—EMI—WAR 1979

BIG STORY, THE
West, M.L.

CROOKED ROAD, THE
GALA 1964

BIG TOWN, THE Lardner, R.W.	**SO, THIS IS NEW YORK** UA 1948
BIG WAR, THE Myrer, A.	**IN LOVE AND WAR** FOX 1958
BIOGRAPHY (P) Behrman, S.N.	**BIOGRAPHY OF A BACHELOR GIRL** MGM 1934
BIOGRAPHY OF A GRIZZLY, THE Seton, E.T.	**KING OF THE GRIZZLIES** DISNEY 1969
BIOGRAPHY OF A SILVER FOX, THE Seton, E.T.	**SILVER FOX AND SAM DAVENPORT** DISNEY 1962
BIRD'S NEST, THE Jackson, S.	**LIZZIE** MGM 1957
BIRTHDAY (P) Ackland, R.	**HEAVEN CAN WAIT** FOX 1943
BITTER SAGE Gruber, F.	**TENSION AT TABLE ROCK** RKO 1956
BLACK ALIBI Woolrich, C.	**LEOPARD MAN, THE** RKO 1943
BLACKBURN'S HEADHUNTERS Harkins, P.	**SURRENDER—HELL** ABP 1959
BLACK CAT, THE Poe, E.A.	**TALES OF TERROR** WAR 1963
BLACK CURTAIN, THE Woolrich, C.	**STREET OF CHANCE** PAR 1942
BLACKJACK HIJACK Einstein, J.	**NOWHERE TO RUN** MGM 1978 (TV)
BLANK WALL Holding, *Mrs*. E.	**RECKLESS MOMENT, THE** COL 1949

BLESSING, THE Mitford, N.	**COUNT YOUR BLESSINGS** MGM 1959
BLESS THIS HOUSE (P) Evans, E.E.	**ROOM IN THE HOUSE** MON 1955
BLIND LOVE Cauvin, P.	**LITTLE ROMANCE, A** COL—EMI—WAR 1979
BLOOD BROTHER Arnold, E.	**BROKEN ARROW** FOX 1950 FOX 1958
BLOOD OF ISRAEL, THE Groussard, S.	**21 HOURS AT MUNICH** ALPHA 1976
BLOOD ON HER SHOE Field, M.	**GIRL WHO DARED, THE** REP 1944
BLOODY COUNTESS, THE Penrose, V.	**COUNTESS DRACULA** RANK 1970
BLUE DENIM (P) Herlihy, J.L. *and* Noble, W.	**BLUE JEANS** FOX 1959
BOARDING PARTY Leasor, J.	**SEA WOLVES, THE** RANK 1980
BODIES AND SOULS Meersch, M. van der	**DOCTOR AND THE GIRL, THE** MGM 1949
BODY SNATCHERS, THE Finney, J.	**INVASION OF THE BODY SNATCHERS, THE** COL 1956
BOOK OF DANIEL, THE Doctorow, E.L.	**DANIEL** PAR 1983
BOOK OF THE MONTH (P) Thomas, B.	**PLEASE TURN OVER** AA 1959
BORDER JUMPERS, THE Brown, W.C.	**MAN OF THE WEST** UA 1958

ORIGINAL TITLE	FILM TITLE
BORDER LEGION Grey, Z.	**LAST ROUND-UP, THE** PAR 1934
BOTTLETOP AFFAIR, THE Cotler, G.	**HORIZONTAL LIEUTENANT, THE** MGM 1962
BOWERY TO BELLEVUE Barringer, E.D.	**GIRL IN WHITE** MGM 1952 **SO BRIGHT THE FLAME** MGM 1952
BOY WHO COULD MAKE HIMSELF DISAPPEAR, THE Platt, K.	**BAXTER!** MGM—EMI 1972
BRAINWASH Wainwright, J.	**INQUISITOR, THE** GALA 1982
BRAVE COWBOY, THE Abbey, E.	**LONELY ARE THE BRAVE** UI 1962
BREATH OF SPRING (P) Coke, P.	**WE'RE IN THE MINK** RANK 1959
BREWSTER'S MILLIONS McCutcheon, G.B.	**THREE ON A SPREE** UA 1961
BRICK FOXHOLE, THE Brooks, R.	**CROSSFIRE** RKO 1947
BRIDE COMES TO YELLOW SKY, THE Crane, S.	**FACE TO FACE** RKO 1952
BRINGING UP THE BRASS Maher, M. *and* Campion, N.R.	**LONG GRAY LINE** COL 1954
BRIXBY GIRLS, THE Marshall, P.P.	**ALL THE FINE YOUNG CANNIBALS** MGM 1960
BROKEN DISHES (P) Flavin, M.	**TOO YOUNG TO MARRY** WAR 1931 **LOVE BEGINS AT 20** IN 1936

BROKEN GUN L'Amour, L.	**CANCEL MY RESERVATION** MGM—EMI 1972
BRONCO APACHE Wellman, P.I.	**APACHE** UA 1954
BROOK WILSON LTD Ryan, J.M.	**LOVING** COL 1969
BROTHER RAT (P) Monks, J. *and* Finklehoffe, F.F.	**ABOUT FACE** WAR 1952
BROTHER VAN Smith, A.J.	**LAWLESS EIGHTIES, THE** BL 1957
BROWN ON 'RESOLUTION' Forester, C.S.	**SINGLE HANDED** FOX 1952
BRUTE, THE Cars, G. des	**GREEN SCARF, THE** BL 1954
BUDDHIST CROSS, THE Tanizaki, J.	**BERLIN AFFAIR, THE** CANNON 1986
BUDDWING Hunter, E.	**MISTER BUDDWING** MGM 1967 **WOMAN WITHOUT A FACE** MGM 1968
BUGLE'S WAKE Brandon, C.	**SEMINOLE UPRISING** EROS 1955
BUILD-UP BOYS, THE Kirk, J.	**MADISON AVENUE** FOX 1960
BURDEN OF PROOF Barlow, J.	**VILLAIN** MGM—EMI 1971
BURNING HILLS L'Amour, L.	**APACHE TERRITORY** COL 1958
BURN, WITCH, BURN Merritt, A.	**DEVIL-DOLL, THE** MGM 1936

BUSMAN'S HONEYMOON
Sayers, D.L.

BUSMAN'S HOLIDAY
MGM 1940

BUTCHER'S MOON
Westlake, D.

SLAYGROUND
EMI 1983

BUT FOR THESE MEN
Drummond, J.D.

HEROES OF THE TELEMARK
RANK 1965

BUT GENTLEMEN MARRY BRUNETTES
Loos, A.

**GENTLEMEN MARRY
BRUNETTES**
UA 1955

C

CADDIE WOODLAWN
Brink, C.R.

CADDIE
HEMDALE 1976

CALENDAR, THE
Wallace, E.

BACHELOR'S FOLLY
WW 1932

CALIFORNIO, THE
MacLeod, R.

100 RIFLES
FOX 1969

CALL FOR THE DEAD
Le Carré, J.

DEADLY AFFAIR, THE
BL 1966

CALL GIRL, THE
Greenwald, H.

GIRL OF THE NIGHT
WAR 1960

CALL IT TREASON
Howe, G.L.

DECISION BEFORE DAWN
FOX 1951

CAME THE DAWN
Bax, R.

NEVER LET ME GO
MGM 1953

CANDLE FOR THE DEAD, A
Marlowe, H.

VIOLENT ENEMY, THE
MONARCH 1969

CAPPY RICKS
Kyne, P.B.

AFFAIRS OF CAPPY RICKS, THE
REP 1937

CAPPY RICKS COMES BACK
Kyne, P.B.

CAPPY RICKS RETURNS
REP 1935

ORIGINAL TITLE	FILM TITLE
CAPTAIN BLIGH AND MR. CHRISTIAN Hough, R.	**BOUNTY, THE** COL—EMI—WAR 1984
CAPTAIN BLOOD RETURNS Sabatini, R.	**CAPTAIN BLOOD, FUGITIVE** COL 1952
CAPTAIN GRANT'S CHILDREN Verne, J.	**IN SEARCH OF THE CASTAWAYS** DISNEY 1962
CAPTAIN HORNBLOWER, R.N. Forester, C.S.	**CAPTAIN HORATIO** **HORNBLOWER, R.N.** WAR 1951
CAPTAIN'S DAUGHTER, THE Pushkin, A.S.	**TEMPEST** PAR 1959
CARAVAN TO CARNAL, A Clou, J.	**CONQUEROR, THE** RKO 1955
CAREFUL MAN, THE Denning, R.	**ARRIVEDERCI, BABY!** PAR 1967
CARL AND ANNA Frank, L.	**AS YOU DESIRE ME** MGM 1932
CARNIVAL Mackenzie, *Sir* C.	**DANCE PRETTY LADY** BI 1931
CARPETBAGGERS, THE Robbins, H.	**NEVADA SMITH** PAR 1963
CARRIAGE ENTRANCE Banks, P.	**MY FORBIDDEN PAST** RKO 1951
CASE FILE: FBI Gordon, *Mrs.* M. *and* Gordon, G.	**DOWN 3 DARK STREETS** UA 1954
CASE OF CHARLES DEXTER, THE Lovecraft, H.P.	**HAUNTED PALACE, THE** AMERICAN INT 1963
CASE OF DR. VALDEMAR, THE Poe, E.A.	**TALES OF TERROR** WAR 1963
CASE OF LADY CAMBER, THE (P) Vachell, H.A.	**LORD CAMBER'S LADIES** BI 1932

ORIGINAL TITLE	FILM TITLE
CASE OF NEED, THE Hudson, J.	**CAREY TREATMENT, THE** MGM—EMI 1972
CASE OF THE CARETAKER'S CAT, THE Gardner, E.S.	**CASE OF THE BLACK CAT** IN 1936
CASE OF THE CONSTANT GOD King, R.	**LOVE LETTERS OF A STAR** UN 1936
CASE OF THE FRIGHTENED LADY, THE Wallace, E.	**FRIGHTENED LADY, THE** BI 1941
CASTING THE RUNES James, M.R.	**NIGHT OF THE DEMON** COL 1957
CASTLE MINERVA Canning, V.	**MASQUERADE** UA 1965
CAT AND THE CANARY, THE Willard, J.	**CAT CREEPS, THE** UN 1930
CAT AND THE MICE, THE Mosley, L.	**FOXHOLE IN CAIRO** BL 1960
CATRIONA Stevenson, R.L.	**KIDNAPPED** RANK 1972
CELEBRATED JUMPING FROG OF CALAVERAS Twain, M.	**BEST MAN WINS, THE** COL 1948
CENTURIANS, THE Larteguy, J.	**LOST COMMAND** COL 1966
CHAIR FOR MARTIN ROME, THE Helseth, H.E.	**CRY OF THE CITY** FOX 1948
CHALLENGE, THE 'Sapper'	**BULLDOG DRUMMOND IN AFRICA** PAR 1938
CHAMPION'S STORY Champion, B. *and* Powell, J.	**CHAMPIONS** EMBASSY 1983

ORIGINAL TITLE	FILM TITLE
CHARIOTS OF THE GODS Daniken, E.	**MYSTERIES OF THE GODS** EMI 1976
CHARLIE AND THE CHOCOLATE FACTORY Dahl, R.	**WILLIE WONKA AND THE CHOCOLATE FACTORY** PAR 1971
CHARLIE M Freemantle, B.	**CHARLIE MUGGIN** EUSTON FILMS 1979
CHASE, THE Unekis, R.	**DIRTY MARY, CRAZY LARRY** FOX 1974
CHAUTUAQUA Keene, D. *and* Babcock, D.	**TROUBLE WITH GIRLS, THE** MGM 1969
CHICKEN EVERY SUNDAY Taylor, R.	**HEFFERAN FAMILY, THE** FOX 1956
CHILDREN, THE Wharton, E.	**MARRIAGE PLAYGROUND, THE** PAR 1929
CHILDREN ARE GONE, THE Cavanaugh, A.	**DEADLY TRAP** NATIONAL GENERAL 1972
CHILDREN OF LIGHT Lawrence, H.L.	**DAMNED, THE** BL 1963
CHILDREN OF THE DARK Schulman, I.	**REBEL WITHOUT A CAUSE** WAR 1955 **CRY TOUGH** UA 1959
CHILDREN OF THE NIGHT (P) Lortz, R.	**VOICES** HEMDALE 1973
CHILDREN'S HOUR, THE (P) Hellman, L.F.	**THESE THREE** UA 1936 **LOUDEST WHISPER, THE** UA 1962
CHILLY SCENES OF WINTER Beattie, A.	**HEAD OVER HEELS** UA 1979

ORIGINAL TITLE	FILM TITLE
CHINESE ROOM, THE Connell, V.	**IN THE CHINESE ROOM** FOX 1959
CHRIST IN CONCRETE Di Donato, P.	**GIVE US THIS DAY** GFD 1949
CHRISTMAS AT CANDLESHOE Innes, M.	**CANDLESHOE** DISNEY 1977
CHRISTMAS CAROL, A Dickens, C.	**SCROOGE** REN 1951 FOX 1970 **CHRISTMAS PRESENT, A** CHANNEL 4 1985 (TV)
CHRISTOPHER BLAKE (P) Hart, M.	**DECISION OF CHRISTOPHER BLAKE, THE** WAR 1948
CHRONICLES I The Bible	**KING DAVID** UIP 1985
CIRCLES ROUND THE WAGON Gipson, F.B.	**HOUND DOG MAN** FOX 1959
CLAUDELLE Caldwell, E.	**YOUNG AND EAGER** WAR 1961
CLEAN BREAK White, L.	**KILLING, THE** UA 1956
CLEMENTINE Goodin, P.	**MICKEY** ABP 1950
CODE OF THE WEST Grey, Z.	**HOME ON THE RANGE** PAR 1935
COINS IN THE FOUNTAIN Secondari, J.	**THREE COINS IN THE FOUNTAIN** FOX 1954
COLOMBIA Merimée, P.	**VENDETTA** RKO 1951
COLOR OUT OF SPACE Lovecraft, H.P.	**MONSTER OF TERROR** AMERICAN INT 1965

COLOSSUS Jones, D.F.	**FORBIN PROJECT, THE** UN 1972
COLOURS OF THE DAY, THE Gary, R.	**MAN WHO UNDERSTOOD WOMEN** FOX 1959
COLUMBUS Sabatini, R.	**CHRISTOPHER COLUMBUS** GFD 1949
COMANCHE Appel, D.	**TONKA** DISNEY 1958
COME BE MY LOVE Davis, *Mrs.* L.	**ONCE MORE MY DARLING** UI 1949
COME OUT OF THE KITCHEN (P) Miller, A.D. *and* Thomas, A.E.	**HONEY** PAR 1930
COMMANDER CRABB Pugh, M.	**SILENT ENEMY, THE** ROMULUS 1958
COMMANDOS, THE Arnold, E.	**FIRST COMES COURAGE** COL 1943
COMMISSIONER, THE Dougherty, R.	**MADIGAN** UI 1968
COMPANIONS OF JEHU, THE Dumas, A.	**FIGHTING GUARDSMAN** COL 1945
COMPLETE STATE OF DEATH, A Gardner, J.	**STONE KILLER, THE** COL 1973
COMRADE JACOB Caute, D.	**WINSTANLEY** THE OTHER CINEMA 1975
CONDEMNED, THE Pagano, J.	**SOUND OF FURY, THE** UA 1951
CONDEMNED TO DEVIL'S ISLAND Niles, B.	**CONDEMNED** UA 1939
CONFESSIONS FROM THE POP SCENE Lea, T.	**CONFESSIONS OF A POP PERFORMER** COL—WAR 1975

ORIGINAL TITLE	FILM TITLE
CONFESSIONS OF A NIGHT NURSE Dixon, R.	**ROSIE DIXON—NIGHT NURSE** COL—WAR 1977
CONGO LANDING Burtis, M.	**CONGO MAISIE** MGM 1940
CONNECTICUT YANKEE IN KING ARTHUR'S COURT Twain, M.	**SPACEMAN AND KING ARTHUR, THE** DISNEY 1980
CONTINUOUS KATHERINE MORTENHOE, THE Complan, D.	**DEATH WATCH** CONTEMPORARY 1979
CONVICT HAS ESCAPED, A Budd, J.	**THEY MADE ME A FUGITIVE** WAR 1947
COSMIC CONNECTION Sagan, C.	**CONTACT** POLYGRAM 1982
COTTONWOOD GULCH Mulford, C.E.	**NORTH OF RIO GRANDE** PAR 1937
COURT CIRCULAR Stokes, S.	**I BELIEVE IN YOU** EALING 1953
CRAIG'S WIFE (P) Kelly, G.	**HARRIET CRAIG** COL 1950
CREAKING CHAIR, THE Meynell, L.W.	**STREET OF SHADOWS** AA 1953
CRIME OF SYLVESTRE BONNARD, THE France, A.	**CHASING YESTERDAY** RKO 1935
CROWNED HEADS Tryon, T.	**FEDORA** MAINLINE 1979
CROWTHERS OF BANKDAM, THE Armstrong, T.	**MASTER OF BANKDAM, THE** ALL 1947
CRUCIBLE, THE (P) Miller, A.	**WITCHES OF SALEM, THE** FILMS DE FRANCE 1957

ORIGINAL TITLE	FILM TITLE
CRY TOUGH Shulman, I.	**RING, THE** UA 1953
CUP AND THE SWORD, THE Hobart, A.T.	**THIS EARTH IS MINE** UI 1959
CURE OF THE FLESH Cozzens, J.G.	**DOCTOR BULL** FOX 1933
CURIOUS CRIME Martin, A.E.	**GLASS CAGE, THE** EXCLUSIVE 1955
CUSTARD BOYS, THE Rae, J.	**REACH FOR GLORY** GALA 1962
CUTTER AND BONE Thornburg, N.	**CUTTER'S WAY** UA 1981

D

DADDY AND I Jordan, E.G.	**MAKE WAY FOR A LADY** RKO 1936
DAFFODIL MYSTERY Wallace, E.	**DEVIL'S DAFFODIL, THE** BL 1961
DAMN YANKEES (P) Adler, R. *and* Ross, J.	**WHAT LOLA WANTS** WAR 1958
DARK ANGEL Kaus, G.	**HER SISTER'S SECRET** PRC 1946
DARKEST HOUR McGivern, W.P.	**HELL ON FRISCO BAY** WAR 1955
DARK FANTASTIC Echard, M.	**LIGHTNING STRIKES TWICE** WAR 1951
DARKNESS I LEAVE YOU Hooke, N.W.	**GYPSY AND THE GENTLEMAN,** **THE** RANK 1957
DARK STAR Moon, L.	**MIN AND BILL** MGM 1930

DARLING BUDS OF MAY, THE
Bates, H.E.

MATING GAME, THE
MGM 1959

DAS FEUERSCHIFF
Lenz, S.

LIGHTSHIP, THE
RANK 1985

DAVID GOLDEN
Nemirowsky, I.

MY DAUGHTER JOY
BL 1950

DAWN OF RECKONING
Hilton, J.

RAGE IN HEAVEN
MGM 1941

DAY IN THE DEATH OF JOE EGG (P)
Nichols, P.

JOE EGG
COL 1971

DAY IS OURS, THE
Lewis, H.

MANDY
GFD 1952

DAY OF THE ARROW
Loraine, P.

EYE OF THE DEVIL
MGM 1968

DAY THE CENTURY ENDED, THE
Gwaltney, F.I.

BETWEEN HEAVEN AND HELL
FOX 1956

DAY THE WORLD ENDED, THE
Thomas, G. *and* Witts, M.

WHEN TIME RAN OUT
COL—EMI—WAR 1980

DAY WITHOUT END
Praag, V.V.

MEN IN WAR
UA 1957

DEAD DON'T CARE, THE
Latimer, J.

LAST WARNING, THE
UN 1939

DEADFALL
Laumer, K.

PEEPER
FOX—RANK 1975

DEADLIER THAN THE MALE
Gunn, J.E.

BORN TO KILL
RKO 1947

DEAR EVELYN (P)
Wild, E. *and* Eunson, D.

GUEST IN THE HOUSE
UA 1944

DEATH AND LIFE OF DITH PRAN, THE
Schanberg, S.

KILLING FIELDS, THE
WAR 1984

ORIGINAL TITLE	FILM TITLE
DEATH AND THE SKY ABOVE US Garve, A.	**TWO-LETTER ALIBI** BL 1962
DEATH AT SHINGLE-STRAND Capon, P.	**HIDDEN HOMICIDE** RANK 1958
DEATH FROM A TOP HAT Rawson, C.	**MIRACLES FOR SALE** MGM 1939
DEATH HAS DEEP ROOTS Gilbert, M.	**GUILTY?** GN 1956
DEATH IN CALIFORNIA Barthel, J.	**DEATH IN CANAAN, A** BBC 1985 (TV)
DEATH IN CAPTIVITY Gilbert, M.	**DANGER WITHIN** BL 1958
DEATH IN DEEP SOUTH Greene, M.	**THEY WON'T FORGET** WAR 1937
DEATH IN ROME Katz, R.	**MASSACRE IN ROME** GN 1975
DEATH IN THE FAMILY, A Agee, J.	**ALL THE WAY HOME** PAR 1963
DEATH IN TIGER VALLEY Campbell, R.	**GIRL FROM MANDALAY** REP 1936
DEATH OF A COMMON MAN Holdridge, D.	**END OF THE RIVER, THE** ARCHERS 1947
DEATH OF A SNOUT Warner, D.	**INFORMERS, THE** RANK 1963
DEATH OF GRASS Christopher, J.	**NO BLADE OF GRASS** MGM—EMI 1972
DEBT DISCHARGED, A Wallace, E.	**MAN DETAINED** AA 1961
DECAMERON, THE Boccaccio, G.	**DECAMERON NIGHTS** EROS 1953

ORIGINAL TITLE	FILM TITLE
DECAMERON, THE (*Continued*) Boccaccio, G.	**LOVE BOCCACCIO STYLE** PRODUCTION ASSOCIATES 1977
DECLINE AND FALL Waugh, E.	**DECLINE AND FALL . . . OF A** **BIRDWATCHER** FOX 1968
DEEP ARE THE ROOTS (P) D'Usseau, A. *and* Gow, J.	**TOMORROW THE WORLD** UA 1944
DEL PALMA Kellino, P.	**LADY POSSESSED, A** REP 1951
DESERT GUNS Frazee, S.	**GOLD OF THE SEVEN SAINTS** WAR 1961
DESERT OF THE HEART Rule, J.	**DESERT HEARTS** MGM 1985
DESERT VOICES Perkins, K.	**DESERT PURSUIT** ABP 1952
DESTRY RIDES AGAIN Brand, M.	**DESTRY** UI 1954
DEUX FRÈRES Dumas, A. *père*	**CORSICAN BROTHERS, THE** WAR 1968 CBS 1985 (TV)
DEVIL AND DANIEL WEBSTER, THE Benet, S.V.	**ALL THAT MONEY CAN BUY** RKO 1941
DEVILDAY MADHOUSE Hall, A.	**MADHOUSE** EMI 1974
DEVILS OF LOUDUN, THE Huxley, A.	**DEVILS, THE** WAR 1971
DEVIL'S OWN, THE Curtis, P.	**WITCHES, THE** HAMMER 1966
DEVIL'S TRIANGLE Soutar, A.	**ALMOST MARRIED** FOX 1932

ORIGINAL TITLE	FILM TITLE
DICE OF GOD, THE Birney, H.	**GLORY GUYS** UA 1965
DILDO CAY Hayes, N.	**BAHAMA PASSAGE** PAR 1941
DISORIENTATED MAN, THE Saxon, P.	**SCREAM AND SCREAM AGAIN** AMERICAN INT 1969
DIVING FOR ADVENTURE Hass, H.	**UNDER THE CARIBBEAN** BL 1954
DO ANDROIDS DREAM OF ELECTRIC SHEEP? Dick, P.K.	**BLADE RUNNER** COL—EMI—WAR 1982
DOCTOR ON TOAST Gordon, R.	**DOCTOR IN TROUBLE** RANK 1970
DOCTORS ON HORSEBACK Flexner, J.T.	**BIG JACK** MGM 1949
DOCTORS WEAR SCARLET Raven, S.	**INCENSE FOR THE DAMNED** GN 1970
DOCTOR WEARS THREE FACES, THE Bard, M.	**MOTHER DIDN'T TELL ME** FOX 1950
DOLLAR BOTTOM AND TAYLOR'S FINEST HOUR Kennaway, J.	**CHARIOTS OF FIRE** ALLIED STARS 1981
DOMBEY AND SON Dickens, C.	**RICH MAN'S FOLLY** PAR 1931
DOMINO PRINCIPLE, THE Kennedy, A.	**DOMINO KILLINGS, THE** ITC 1978
DON AMONG THE DEAD MEN Vulliamy, C.E.	**JOLLY BAD FELLOW, A** BL 1964
DON CAMILLO AND THE PRODIGAL SON Guareschi, G.	**RETURN OF DON CAMILLO, THE** MIRACLE FILMS 1954

DON CARELESS
Beach, R.E.

AVENGERS, THE
REP 1950

DON DESPERADO
Foreman, L.L.

SAVAGE, THE
PAR 1952

DONOVAN'S BRAIN
Siodmak, C.

VENGEANCE
BL 1963

DOUBLE DEALERS
Klein, A.

COUNTERFEIT TRAITOR, THE
PAR 1962

DOUBLE TAKE
Huggins, R.

I LOVE TROUBLE
COL 1948

DOVER ROAD (P)
Milne, A.A.

WHERE SINNERS MEET
RKO 1934

DRACULA
Stoker, B.

DRACULA SUCKS
KODIAK 1979

DRACULA'S GUEST
Stoker, B.

DRACULA'S DAUGHTER
UN 1936

DREADFUL SUMMIT
Ellin, S.

BIG NIGHT, THE
UA 1951

DREAMLAND
Kelland, C.B.

STRIKE ME PINK
UA 1936

DR. JEKYLL AND MR. HYDE
Stevenson, R.L.

TWO FACES OF DR. JEKYLL, THE
COL 1959

DR. KILDARE'S TRIAL
Brand, M.

**PEOPLE VERSUS DR. KILDARE,
THE**
LOE 1941

DRUM, THE
Mason, A.E.W.

DRUMS
UA 1938

DUBLIN NIGHTMARE
Loraine, P.

NIGHTMARE IN DUBLIN
RANK 1957

DUNBAR'S COVE
Deal, B.

WILD RIVER
FOX 1960

DURIAN TREE, THE
Keon, M.

7th DAWN, THE
UA 1964

E

EASTER DINNER, THE
Downes, D.

PIGEON THAT TOOK ROME, THE
PAR 1962

EAST LYNNE
Wood, *Mrs.* H.

EX-FLAME
TIFFANY 1931

EASY AND HARD WAYS OUT
Grossbach, R.

BEST DEFENCE
UIP 1984

EBANO
Vasquez-Figueroa, A.

ASHANTI
COL—EMI 1979

EBB TIDE
Stevenson, R.L.

ADVENTURE ISLAND
PAR 1947

ECHOES OF CELANDINE
Marlowe, D.

DISAPPEARANCE, THE
CINEGATE 1977

EDDIE CHAPMAN STORY, THE
Owen, F.

TRIPLE CROSS, THE
AA 1967

EDGE OF DOOM
Brady, L.

STRONGER THAN FEAR
RKO 1952

EDGE OF RUNNING WATER, THE
Sloane, W.

DEVIL COMMANDS, THE
COL 1941

EDUCATION FOR DEATH
Zeimer, G.

HITLER'S CHILDREN
RKO 1943

EFF OFF
Hutson, S.

**CLASS OF MISS MacMICHAEL,
THE**
GALA 1980

8 MILLION WAYS TO DIE
Block, L.

STAB IN THE DARK
PSO 1985

ELEMENTAL, THE
Chetwynd-Hayes, R.

FROM BEYOND THE GRAVE
EMI 1974

ORIGINAL TITLE	FILM TITLE
ELEPHANT IN WHITE, THE Brahms, C. *and* Simon, S.J.	**GIVE US THE MOON** GFD 1944
ELIMINATOR, THE York, A.	**DANGER ROUTE** UA 1968
ELIZABETH THE QUEEN (P) Anderson, M.	**PRIVATE LIVES OF ELIZABETH AND ESSEX, THE** WAR 1939
EMPEROR'S SNUFF BOX, THE Carr, J.D.	**THAT WOMAN OPPOSITE** MON 1957
EMPORIA Sanford, H. *and* Lamb, M.	**WACO** PAR 1967
ENIGMA SACRIFICE Barak, M.	**ENIGMA** COL—EMI—WAR 1982
ENTER SIR JOHN Dane, C. *and* Simpson, H. de G.	**MURDER** BI 1930
ENVY MY SIMPLICITY Barton, R.	**KILLER WALKS, A** GN 1952
EPISODE OF SPARROWS, THE Godden, R.	**INNOCENT SINNERS** RANK 1957
EPITAPH FOR AN ENEMY Barr, G.	**UP FROM THE BEACH** FOX 1964
EPITAPH FOR A SPY Ambler, E.	**HOTEL RESERVE** RKO 1944
ERASMUS WITH FRECKLES Hasse, J.	**DEAR BRIGITTE** FOX 1965
ESCAPE ALONE Howarth, D.	**WE DIE ALONE** REN 1959
ESCAPE OF THE AMETHYST, THE Earl, L.	**YANGTSE INCIDENT** BL 1957
ESTHER, RUTH AND JENNIFER Davies, J.	**NORTH SEA HIJACK** CIC 1980

EUNUCH OF STAMBOUL, THE Wheatley, D.	**SECRET OF STAMBOUL, THE** HOB 1939
EVENT 1000 Lavallee, D.	**GRAY LADY DOWN** CIC 1977
EVENTS WHILST GUARDING THE BOFORS GUN (P) McGrath, J.	**BOFORS GUN** UI 1968
EVIL COME, EVIL GO Masterson, W.	**YELLOW CANARY, THE** FOX 1963
EVIL OF THE DAY, THE Sterling, T.	**HONEY POT, THE** UA 1966
EXECUTIONER, THE Macdonald, J.D.	**CAPE FEAR** UI 1962
EXECUTION OF CHARLES HORMAN, THE Hauser, T.	**MISSING** POLYGRAM 1982
EXILE, AN Jones, M.	**I WALK THE LINE** COL 1971
EXPENDABLE MAN, THE Hughes, D.B.	**HANGED MAN, THE** RANK 1964
EXPERIMENT IN SINCERITY Erskine, J.	**LADY SURRENDERS, A** UN 1930
EXPLOITS OF BRIGADIER GERARD, THE Doyle, *Sir* A.C.	**ADVENTURES OF GERARD, THE** UA 1970

F

FABRICATOR, THE Hodges, H.	**"WHY SHOULD I LIE?"** MGM 1980
FACE IN THE NIGHT Wallace, E.	**MALPAS MYSTERY, THE** AA 1960

FALSE WITNESS
Stone, I.

ARKANSAS JUDGE
REP 1941

FAMILY SKELETON
Disney, D.M.

STELLA
FOX 1950

FAMOUS
Benet, S.V.

JUST FOR YOU
PAR 1952

FAREWELL, MY LOVELY
Chandler, R.

FALCON TAKES OVER, THE
RKO 1942
MURDER, MY SWEET
RKO 1944

FAREWELL TO WOMEN
Collinson, W.

MOGAMBO
MGM 1953

FAST COMPANY
Page, M.

FAST AND LOOSE
MGM 1939

FAST TIMES AT RIDGEMONT HIGH
Crowe, C.

FAST TIMES
UIP 1982

FATHER, THE (P)
Strindberg, A.

LONELY HEARTS
GALA 1981

FATHER BROWN STORIES
Chesterton, G.K.

FATHER BROWN
COL 1954

FATHER SKY
Freeman, D.

TAPS
FOX 1982

FATHER WAS A HANDFUL
Williams, *Mrs*. R.

VANISHING VIRGINIAN, THE
MGM 1941

FEATHERED SERPENT, THE
Wallace, E.

MENACE, THE
COL 1932

FELIX KRULL, CONFIDENCE MAN
Mann, T.

CONFESSIONS OF FELIX KRULL
SAFIR 1983

FELLOWSHIP OF THE RING, THE
Tolkien, J.R.R.

LORD OF THE RINGS
UA 1980

FEMALE OF THE SPECIES, THE
'Sapper'

**BULLDOG DRUMMOND COMES
BACK**
PAR 1937

FER DE LANCE
Stout, R.

MEET NERO WOLFE
COL 1936

FIDDLER'S GREEN
Gann, E.K.

RAGING TIDE, THE
UI 1951

FIESTA
Hemingway, E.

SUN ALSO RISES, THE
FOX 1957
NBC 1984 (TV)

FIFTYMINUTE HOUR, THE
Lindner, R.

PRESSURE POINT
UA 1963

52 PICK-UP
Leonard, E.

AMBASSADOR, THE
CANNON 1984

FIGHTING CARAVANS
Grey, Z.

WAGON WHEELS
PAR 1934

FINAL DIAGNOSIS, THE
Hailey, A.

YOUNG DOCTORS, THE
UA 1961

FINAL NIGHT
Gaines, R.

FRONT PAGE STORY
BL 1953

FINNEGAN'S WAKE
Joyce, J.

PASSAGES FROM JAMES JOYCE'S
. . .
CONT 1969

FIREBRAND, THE (P)
Mayer, E.J.

AFFAIRS OF CELLINI
UA 1934

FIRES OF YOUTH
Collier, J.L.

DANNY JONES
CINERAMA 1972

FIRST AND LAST, THE
Galsworthy, J.

TWENTY-ONE DAYS
LF 1940

FIRST LOVE (P)
Taylor, S.

PROMISE AT DAWN
AVCO EMBASSY 1971

FIRST LOVE
Turganev, I.

SUMMER LIGHTNING
CHANNEL 4 1986 (TV)

FIRST REBEL, THE
Swanson, N.H.

ALLEGHENY UPRISING
RKO 1939

FIRST TRAIN TO BABYLON
Ehrlich, M.

NAKED EDGE, THE
UA 1961

FLAMING LANCE
Huffaker, C.

FLAMING STAR
FOX 1960

FLOTSAM
Remarque, E.M.

SO ENDS OUR NIGHT
UA 1941

FLOWERS FOR ALGERNON
Keyes, D.

CHARLY
CINERAMA 1968

FLYING EBONY
Vinton, I.

MOONCUSSERS, THE
DISNEY 1971

FLYING SAUCERS FROM OUTER SPACE
Keyhoe, D.E.

**EARTH VERSUS THE FLYING
SAUCERS**
COL 1956

F.O.B. DETROIT
Smitter, W.

REACHING FOR THE SUN
PAR 1941

FOG FOR A KILLER
Graeme, B.

OUT OF THE FOG
GN 1962

FOGHORN, THE
Bradbury, R.

**BEAST FROM 20,000 FATHOMS,
THE**
WAR 1953

FOOLS PARADISE
Grubb, D.

FOOLS PARADE
COL 1971

FORBIDDEN GARDEN, THE
Curtiss, U.

**WHATEVER HAPPENED TO AUNT
ALICE?**
PALOMAR 1969

FOR HER TO SEE
Shearing, J.

SO EVIL MY LOVE
PAR 1948

FOR LOVE OR MONEY (P)
Herbert, F.H.

THIS HAPPY FEELING
RANK 1958

**FOR OUR VINES HAVE TENDER
GRAPES**
Martin, G.V.

**OUR VINES HAVE TENDER
GRAPES**
MGM 1945

FORSYTE SAGA
Galsworthy, J.

THAT FORSYTE WOMAN
MGM 1949

FORTRESS IN THE RICE
Appel, B.

CRY OF BATTLE
WAR 1964

FORTY WHACKS
Homes, G.

CRIME BY NIGHT
WAR 1946

FOUR FEATHERS, THE
Mason, A.E.W.

STORM OVER THE NILE
GFD 1955

4.50 FROM PADDINGTON
Christie, A.

MURDER SHE SAID
MGM 1961

FOUR JUST MEN, THE
Wallace, E.

SECRET FOUR, THE
MON 1940

FOUR PUNTERS ARE MISSING
Rose, A.

WHO'S GOT THE ACTION?
PAR 1963

FRANKENSTEIN
Shelley, M.W.

CURSE OF FRANKENSTEIN, THE
WAR 1957

FREEDOM TRAP
Bagley, D.

MACKINTOSH MAN, THE
COL—WAR 1973

FREEFALL
Reed, J.D.

PURSUIT
BARBER 1981

FRIEND IN NEED, A
Coxhead, E.

CRY FROM THE STREETS, A
EROS 1958

FRIESE-GREENE
Allister, R.

MAGIC BOX, THE
BL 1951

**FROM THE MIXED-UP TALES OF MR.
BASIL FRANKWESTER**
Konigsburg, E.L.

HIDEAWAYS
UA 1973

FROM THIS DARK STAIRWAY
Eberhart, M.G.

MURDER OF DR. HARRIGAN
IN 1936

FRONT PAGE, THE (P)
Hecht, B. *and* MacArthur, G.

HIS GIRL FRIDAY
COL 1940

FRUIT OF THE POPPY
Wilder, R.

HEROIN GANG, THE
MGM 1968

FUGUE IN TIME
Godden, R.

ENCHANTMENT
RKO 1949

FURNISHED ROOM, THE
Del Rivo, L.

WEST II
WAR 1963

FUTZ AND WHAT CAME AFTER
Owens, R.

FUTZ
COMMONWEALTH 1969

G

GABRIEL HORN
Holt, F.

KENTUCKIAN, THE
UA 1955

GAMBLER AND OTHER STORIES, THE
Dostoevski, F.M.

GREAT SINNER, THE
MGM 1949

GAME OF X, THE
Sheckley, R.

CONDORMAN
DISNEY 1981

GAMESMANSHIP
Potter, S.

SCHOOL FOR SCOUNDRELS
WAR 1960

GARDEN OF CUCUMBERS, A
Tyler, P.

FITZWOLLY STRIKES BACK
UA 1968

GASLIGHT (P)
Hamilton, P.

MURDER IN THORNTON SQUARl
MGM 1944

GATHER YE ROSEBUDS
Nolan, J.

ISN'T IT ROMANTIC?
PAR 1948

ORIGINAL TITLE	FILM TITLE
GAUCHO Childs, H.	**WAY OF A GAUCHO** FOX 1952
GAY BANDIT OF THE BORDER Gill, T.	**GAY CABALLERO** FOX 1932
GENERAL, THE Sillitoe, A.	**COUNTERPOINT** UI 1968
GENTLE BEN Morley, W.	**GENTLE GIANT** PAR 1968
GENTLE PEOPLE, THE (P) Shaw, L.	**OUT OF THE FOG** WAR 1941
GETAWAY Charteris, L.	**SAINT'S VACATION, THE** RKO 1941
GHOSTS Barber, A.	**AMAZING MR. BLUNDEN, THE** HEMDALE 1972
GINGERBREAD LADY (P) Simon, N.	**ONLY WHEN I LAUGH** COL 1981
GIOCONDA SMILE, THE Huxley, A.L.	**WOMAN'S VENGEANCE, A** UN 1947
GILBERT AND SULLIVAN BOOK, THE Baily, L.	**STORY OF GILBERT AND SULLIVAN, THE** BL 1953
GILDED ROOSTER, THE Roberts, R.E.	**LAST FRONTIER, THE** COL 1955
GILLIGAN'S LAST ELEPHANT Hanley, G.	**LAST SAFARI, THE** PAR 1968
GIRL CRAZY (P) Bolton, G. *and* McGowan, J.	**WHEN THE BOYS MEET THE GIRLS** MGM 1965
GIRL NAMED FATHOM, A Forester, L.	**FATHOM** FOX 1968

ORIGINAL TITLE	FILM TITLE
GIRL ON A WING Glemser, B.	**COME FLY WITH ME** MGM 1963
GIRL ON THE VIA FLAMINIA, THE Hayes, A.	**ACT OF LOVE** UA 1954
GLASS INFERNO, THE Scortia, T. *and* Robinson, F.	**TOWERING INFERNO, THE** COL—WAR 1975
GLENDOWER LEGACY, THE Gifford, T.	**DIRTY TRICKS** FILM PLAN 1980
GLORY FOR ME Kantor, M.	**BEST YEARS OF OUR LIVES, THE** RKO 1946
GOD AND MY COUNTRY Kantor, M.	**FOLLOW ME, BOYS** DISNEY 1967
GODFATHER, THE Puzo, M.	**GODFATHER PART II, THE** CIC 1974
GOLD BUG, THE Poe, E.A.	**CALYPSO** BL 1956
GOLDEN EVENINGS OF SUMMER, THE Stanton, W.	**CHARLEY AND THE ANGEL** DISNEY 1974
GOLDEN FLEECING, THE (P) Semple, L.	**HONEYMOON MACHINE, THE** MGM 1961
GOLDEN HERD Carroll, C.	**SAN ANTONE** REP 1952
GOLDEN PORTAGE, THE Case, R.O.	**GIRL FROM ALASKA, THE** REP 1942
GOLDEN TIDE, THE Roe, V.	**PERILOUS JOURNEY, A** REP 1953
GOLD FISH BOWL, THE McCall, M.	**IT'S TOUGH TO BE FAMOUS** IN 1932
GOLD HUNTERS, THE Curwood, J.O.	**TRAIL OF THE YUKON** MONOGRAM 1949

ORIGINAL TITLE	FILM TITLE
GOLD MINE Smith, W.	**GOLD** HEMDALE 1974
GONE TO TEXAS Carter, F.	**OUTLAW JOSEY WALES, THE** COL—WAR 1976
GOODBYE AGAIN (P) Scott, A. *and* Haight, G.	**HONEYMOON FOR THREE** WAR 1941
GOODBYE PICCADILLY, FAREWELL **LEICESTER SQUARE** La Bern, A.	**FRENZY** RANK 1971
GOODBYE TO THE HILL Dunne, L.	**PADDY** FOX 1969
GO TO THY DEATHBED Forbes, S.	**REFLECTION OF FEAR, A** COL—WAR 1972
GOWNS BY ROBERTA Miller, A.D.	**ROBERTA** RKO 1935 **LOVELY TO LOOK AT** MGM 1952
GRAF SPEE Powell, M.	**BATTLE OF THE RIVER PLATE,** **THE** RANK 1956
GRAND DUKE AND MR. PIMM, THE Hardy, L.	**ALL THIS AND MONEY TOO** UA 1963
GREAT ADVENTURE Bennett, A.	**HIS DOUBLE LIFE** PAR 1933 **HOLY MATRIMONY** PAR 1943
GREAT CROONER, THE Kelland, C.B.	**MR. DODD TAKES THE AIR** WAR 1937
GREAT DINOSAUR ROBBERY, THE Forrest, D.	**ONE OF OUR DINOSAURS IS** **MISSING** DISNEY 1975
GREAT TRAIN ROBBERY, THE Crichton, M.	**FIRST GREAT TRAIN ROBBERY** UA 1979

GREEN GODDESS, THE
Archer, W.

ADVENTURES IN IRAQ
WAR 1943

GREEN HAT, THE
Arien, M.

WOMAN OF AFFAIRS, A
MGM 1929
OUTCAST LADY
MGM 1935
WOMAN OF THE WORLD
MGM 1935

GREEN RIBBON, THE
Wallace, E.

NEVER BACK LOSERS
AA 1962

GREYFRIAR'S BOBBY
Atkinson, E.

CHALLENGE TO LASSIE
MGM 1949

GRIMMS' FAIRY TALES
Grimm, J. *and* Grimm, W.

**WONDERFUL WORLD OF THE
BROTHERS GRIMM, THE**
MGM 1962

GUARDSMAN, THE (P)
Molnar, F.

CHOCOLATE SOLDIER, THE
LOE 1941

GULLIVER'S TRAVELS
Swift, J.

**THREE WORLDS OF GULLIVER,
THE**
COL 1959

GUN, THE
Forester, C.S.

PRIDE AND THE PASSION, THE
UA 1957

GUN CRAZY
Kantor, M.

DEADLY IS THE FEMALE
UA 1949

GUN DOWN
Garfield, B.

LAST HARD MAN, THE
FOX—RANK 1976

GUN FOR SALE, A
Greene, G.

THIS GUN FOR HIRE
PAR 1942
SHORT CUT TO HELL
PAR 1957

GUNNER, THE
Wallace, E.

SOLO FOR SPARROW
AA 1962

GUNS OF THE RIO CONCHOS
Huffaker, C.

RIO CONCHOS
FOX 1964

GUY RENTON
Waugh, A.

CIRCLE OF DECEPTION
FOX 1960

H

HALFWAY TO HEAVEN (P)
Segall, H.

HERE COMES MR. JORDAN
COL 1941

HALL OF MIRRORS, A
Stone, R.

WUSA
PAR 1972

HAMLET, THE
Faulkner, W.

LONG, HOT SUMMER, THE
FOX 1957

HAMP (P)
Wilson, J.

KING AND COUNTRY
WAR 1965

HAND AND THE FLOWER, THE
Tickell, J.

DAY TO REMEMBER, A
GFD 1953

HAPPY HOOKER, THE
Hollander, X.

MY PLEASURE IS MY BUSINESS
MIRACLE FILMS 1975

HAPPY NOW I GO
Charles, T.

WOMAN WITH NO NAME, THE
ABP 1950

HARM'S WAY
Bassett, J.

IN HARM'S WAY
COL 1965

HARP THAT ONCE, THE
Hall, P.

RECKONING, THE
COL 1969

HARRISON HIGH
Farris, J.

BECAUSE THEY'RE YOUNG
COL 1960

HARRY SPIKES
Tippette, G.

SPIKES GANG, THE
UA 1974

HAUNTING OF HILL HOUSE, THE
Jackson, S.

HAUNTING, THE
MGM 1963

HAWAII Michener, J.A.	**MASTER OF THE ISLANDS** UA 1970
HEADED FOR A HEARSE Latimer, J.	**WESTLAND CASE, THE** UN 1937
HEARSES DON'T HURRY Ransome, S.	**WHO IS HOPE SCHUYLER?** FOX 1942
HEAT WAVE (P) Pertwee, R.	**ROAD TO SINGAPORE** WAR 1931
HEAVEN HAS NO FAVOURITES Remarque, E.M.	**BOBBY DEERFIELD** COL—WAR 1977
HEDDA GABLER (P) Ibsen, R.	**HEDDA** SCOTIA BARBER 1977
HE FELL DOWN DEAD Perdue, V.	**SHADOW OF A WOMAN** WAR 1946
HEIDI Spyri, J.	**HEIDI'S SONG** HANNA-BARBERA 1982
HEIR Simon, R.L.	**JENNIFER ON MY MIND** UA 1971
HELLCATS OF THE SEA Lockwood, C.A. *and* Adamson, H.C.	**HELLCATS OF THE NAVY** COL 1957
HELLER WITH A GUN L'Amour, L.	**HELLER IN PINK TIGHTS** PAR 1960
HELL HOUSE Matherson, R.	**LEGEND OF HELL HOUSE** FOX—RANK 1973
HEPHAESTUS PLAGUE, THE Page, T.	**BUG** PAR 1975
HERBERT WEST—THE **RE-ANIMATOR** Lovecraft, H.P.	**RE-ANIMATOR** EMPIRE 1985
HERE IS YOUR WAR Pyle, E.T.	**WAR CORRESPONDENT** INT 1951

HER FATHER'S DAUGHTER Stratton-Porter, G.	**HER FIRST ROMANCE** MON 1940
HER HEART IN HER THROAT White, E.L.	**UNSEEN, THE** PAR 1945
HERO, THE Lampell, M.	**SATURDAY'S HERO** COL 1951
HEROES OF THE YUCCA, THE Barrett, M.	**INVINCIBLE SIX, THE** PAR 1968
HE WAS FOUND IN THE ROAD Armstrong, A.	**MAN IN THE ROAD, THE** GN 1956
HIDING PLACE, THE Shaw, R.	**SITUATION HOPELESS BUT NOT SERIOUS** PAR 1964
HIGH CAGE Frazee, S.	**HIGH HELL** PAR 1958
HIGH COMMISSIONER, THE Cleary, J.	**NOBODY RUNS FOREVER** RANK 1968
HIGH PAVEMENT Bonett, E.	**MY SISTER AND I** GFD 1948
HIGH ROAD, THE (P) Lonsdale, F.	**LADY OF SCANDAL, THE** MGM 1930
HIGH SIERRA Burnett, W.R.	**I DIED A THOUSAND TIMES** WAR 1955
HIGH WINDOW, THE Chandler, R.	**BRASHER DOUBLOON, THE** FOX 1947
HIGH WRAY Hughes, K.	**HOUSE ACROSS THE LAKE, THE** ABP 1954
HIJACKED Harper, D.	**SKYJACKED** MGM 1972
HIS LAST BOW Doyle, *Sir* A.C.	**SHERLOCK HOLMES AND THE VOICE OF TERROR** UN 1942

HOW SAY YOU? (P)
Brooke, H. *and* Bannerman, K.

PAIR OF BRIEFS
RANK 1961

HUMAN KIND, THE
Baron, A.

VICTORS, THE
BL 1963

HUNDRED MILLION FRAMES, A
Berna, P.

HORSE WITHOUT A HEAD, THE
DISNEY 1963

I

I AM A CAMERA (P)
Druten, J. van

CABARET
CINERAMA 1972

I AM A FUGITIVE FROM THE CHAIN GANG
Burns, R.T.

I AM A FUGITIVE
WAR 1932

I AM LEGEND
Matheson, R.

LAST MAN ON EARTH, THE
GOLDEN ERA 1964
OMEGA MAN, THE
COL—WAR 1971

I CAN GET IT FOR YOU WHOLESALE
Weidman, J.

THIS IS MY AFFAIR
FOX 1951

IF ONLY THEY COULD TALK
Herriot, J.

ALL CREATURES GREAT AND SMALL
EMI 1974

I, JAMES LEWIS
Gabriel, G.W.

THIS WOMAN IS MINE
UN 1941

ILIAD
Homer

ULYSSES
ARCHWAY 1954

I MARRIED A DEAD MAN
Irish, W.

NO MAN OF HER OWN
PAR 1950

IMMORTAL WIFE
Stone, I.

PRESIDENT'S LADY, THE
FOX 1953

IMPATIENT VIRGIN
Clarke, D.H.

IMPATIENT MAIDEN
UN 1932

IMPRESARIO
Hurock, S. *and* Goode, R.

TONIGHT WE SING
FOX 1953

IN MY SOLITUDE
Leslie, D.S.

TWO LEFT FEET
BL 1965

INTENT TO MURDER (P)
Sands, L.

ANOTHER MAN'S POISON
EROS 1952

INTERFERENCE (P)
Pertwee, R. *and* Dearden, H.

WITH REGRET
PAR 1935

INTERNS, THE
Frede, R.

NEW INTERNS, THE
COL 1964

INTERRUPTION, THE
Jacobs, W.W.

FOOTSTEPS IN THE FOG
COL 1955

IN THE HEART OF THE COUNTRY
Coetzee, J.M.

DUST
DASKA FILMS 1985

IN THE HEAT OF THE SUMMER
Katzenbach, J.

MEAN SEASON
ORION 1985

INTRUDER, THE
Beaumont, C.

STRANGER, THE
GN 1963

ISADORA DUNCAN
Stokes, S.

ISADORA
UI 1969

ISAK DINESEN
Thurman, J.

OUT OF AFRICA
UN 1985

ISLAND OF DR. MOREAU, THE
Wells, H.G.

ISLAND OF LOST SOULS
EROS 1959

IT DEPENDS WHAT YOU MEAN (P)
Bridie, J.

FOLLY TO BE WISE
BL 1952

**IT'S A 2ft. 6in. ABOVE THE GROUND
WORLD (P)**
Laffan, K.

LOVE BAN, THE
BL 1972

IT'S A VET'S LIFE
Duncan, A.

IN THE DOGHOUSE
RANK 1961

IT SHOULDN'T HAPPEN TO A VET
Herriot, J.

ALL CREATURES GREAT AND SMALL
EMI 1974

IT WAS FUN WORKING AT THE WHITE HOUSE
Parks, L.A.

BACKSTAIRS AT THE WHITE HOUSE
BBC 2 1984 (TV)

I'VE GOT MINE
Hubler, R.G.

BEACHHEAD
UA 1953

IVY GARLAND, THE
Hoyland, J.

OUT OF THE DARKNESS
CFF 1985

I WAKE UP SCREAMING
Fisher, S.

VICKI
FOX 1953

J

JACKDAWS STRUT
Henry, H.

BOUGHT
WAR 1931

JACK O'JUDGEMENT
Wallace, E.

SHARE OUT, THE
AA 1962

JACK'S RETURN HOME
Lewis, T.

GET CARTER
MGM 1971

JEALOUSY (P)
Verneuil, L.

DECEPTION
WAR 1946

JEANNIE (P)
Stuart, A.

LET'S BE HAPPY
ABP 1957

JENNY ANGEL
Barber, E.O.

ANGEL BABY
CONT 1961

JEST OF GOD, A
Laurence, M.

RACHEL, RACHEL
WAR 1968

JET STREAM
Ferguson, A.

MAYDAY—40,000 FT.
COL—WAR 1976

ORIGINAL TITLE	FILM TITLE
JEWEL OF MAHABAR Marshall, E.	**TREASURE OF THE GOLDEN CONDOR** FOX 1953
JEWEL OF THE SEVEN STARS Stoker, B.	**BLOOD FROM THE MUMMY'S TOMB** MGM—EMI 1971 **AWAKENING, THE** COL—EMI—WAR 1980
JOANNA GODDEN Kaye-Smith, S.	**LOVES OF JOANNA GODDEN, THE** GFD 1947
JOAN OF LORRAINE (P) Anderson, M.	**JOAN OF ARC** RKO 1948
JOURNEY TO MATECUMBRE Taylor, R.L.	**TREASURE OF MATECUMBRE** DISNEY 1976
JOY HOUSE Keene, D.	**LOVE CAGE, THE** MGM 1965
JUBAL TROOP Wellman, P.I.	**JUBAL** COL 1956
JULIA Straub, P.	**FULL CIRCLE** CIC 1978
JUPITER LAUGHS (P) Cronin, A.J.	**SHINING VICTORY** WAR 1941
JURY, THE Bullet, G.	**LAST MAN TO HANG** COL 1956
JUSTIN BAYARD Cleary, J.	**DUST IN THE SUN** WAR 1958
JUSTINE De Sade, *Marquis*	**CRUEL PASSION** FOX—RANK 1975

K

KENNEL MURDER CASE, THE Dine, S.S. van	**CALLING PHILO VANCE** WAR 1940

716

KESTREL FOR A KNAVE, A Hines, B.	**KES** UA 1969
KILL, THE Zola, E.	**GAME IS OVER, THE** COL 1967
KILLING A MOUSE ON SUNDAY Pressburger, E.	**BEHOLD A PALE HORSE** COL 1964
KILLING FROST, THE Catto, M.	**TRAPEZE** UA 1956
'KIND SIR' (P) Krasna, N.	**INDISCREET** WAR 1958
KINGDOM OF JOHNNY COOL, THE McPartland, J.	**JOHNNY COOL** UA 1964
KING OF HEARTS (P) Kerr, J. *and* Brooke, H.	**THAT CERTAIN FEELING** PAR 1956
KING RELUCTANT, A Wilkins, V.	**DANGEROUS EXILE** RANK 1957
KING SOLOMON'S MINES Haggard, *Sir* H.R.	**WATUSI** MGM 1958
KISS OF DEATH Bachmann, L.	**DEVIL MAKES THREE, THE** MGM 1952
KISS THE BLOOD OFF MY HANDS Butler, G.	**BLOOD ON MY HANDS** UI 1949
KON-TIKI EXPEDITION Heyerdahl, T.	**KON-TIKI** RKO 1951
KOSYGIN IS COMING Ardies, T.	**RUSSIAN ROULETTE** FOX—RANK 1975

L

LA BÊTE HUMAINE Zola, E.	**HUMAN DESIRE** COL 1954

LADIES IN RETIREMENT (P)
Denham, R. *and* Percy, E.

MAD ROOM, THE
COL 1968

**LADY IN THE CAR WITH GLASSES AND
A GUN, THE**
Japrisot, S.

LADY IN THE CAR
COL 1969

LADY OF THE CAMELLIAS, THE
Dumas, A.

CAMILLE
MGM 1936
ROSEMOUNT 1984 (TV)

LAFITTE, THE PIRATE
Saxon, L.

BUCCANEER, THE
PAR 1938

LAMENT FOR MOLLY MAGUIRES
Lewis, A.H.

MOLLY MAGUIRES, THE
PAR 1969

LAMP IS HEAVY, A
Russell, S.M.

FEMININE TOUCH, THE
RANK 1956

LAST ADAM
Cozzens, J.G.

DR. BULL
FOX 1933

LAST FRONTIERS
MacLean, A.

SECRET WAYS, THE
RANK 1960

LAST HOURS OF SANDRA LEE, THE
Sansom, W.

WILD AFFAIR, THE
BL 1965

LAST JEWS IN BERLIN, THE
Gross, L.

FORBIDDEN
ENTERPRISE 1984 (TV)

LAST OF MRS. CHEYNEY, THE (P)
Lonsdale, F.

LAW AND THE LADY, THE
MGM 1951

LAST OF THE BAD MEN
Monoghan, J.

BAD MEN OF TOMBSTONE
ABP 1949

LAST OF THE MOHICANS
Cooper, J.F.

LAST OF THE REDSKINS
COL 1949

LATE BOY WONDER, THE
Hall, A.

THREE IN A CELLAR
NEW REALM 1970

ORIGINAL TITLE	FILM TITLE
LAUGHING POLICEMAN, THE Sjowall, M. *and* Wahoo, P.	**INVESTIGATION OF MURDER** FOX 1974
LAW MAN Leighton, L.	**STAR IN THE DUST** UN 1956
LAW OF THE GUN Patten, L.B.	**DEATH OF A GUNFIGHTER** UI 1969
LAWRENCEVILLE SCHOOL TALES Johnson, O.	**HAPPY YEARS, THE** MGM 1950
LEADING LADY (P) Gordon, R.	**ACTRESS, THE** MGM 1953
LEATHER STOCKING TALES Cooper, J.F.	**TOMAHAWK TRAIL, THE** UA 1950
LEAVING CHEYENNE McMurtry, L.	**LOVIN' MOLLY** GALA 1975
LEGACY OF A SPY Maxfield, H.S.	**DOUBLE MAN, THE** WAR 1966
LEGEND OF THE LATIN QUARTER Moss, A. *and* Marvel, E.	**HER WONDERFUL LIE** COL 1950
LEININGEN VERSUS THE ANTS Stephenson, C.	**NAKED JUNGLE, THE** PAR 1953
LE MORTE D'ARTHUR Malory, *Sir* T.	**KNIGHTS OF THE ROUND TABLE** MGM 1954 **EXCALIBUR** COL—EMI—WAR 1981
LESSON IN LOVE, A Baird, M.T.	**CIRCLE OF TWO** BORDEAUX FILMS 1981
LET ME COUNT THE WAYS De Vries, P.	**HOW DO I LOVE THEE?** CIRO 1970
LETTER, THE (P) Maugham, W.S.	**UNFAITHFUL, THE** WAR 1947

ORIGINAL TITLE	FILM TITLE
LETTER TO FIVE WIVES, A Klempner, J.	**LETTER TO THREE WIVES, A** FOX 1948
LIFE AND DEATH OF THE WICKED **LADY SKELTON, THE** King-Hall, M.	**WICKED LADY, THE** GFD 1946 CANNON 1982
LIFE AND TIMES OF CLEOPATRA, THE Franzero, C.M.	**CLEOPATRA** FOX 1963
LIFEMANSHIP Potter, S.	**SCHOOL FOR SCOUNDRELS** WAR 1960
LIFE OF DAVID HAGGART, THE Haggart, D.	**SINFUL DAVEY** UA 1969
LIFE WITH MOTHER SUPERIOR Trahey, J.	**TROUBLE WITH ANGELS, THE** COL 1965
LIGHTHOUSE AT THE END OF THE **WORLD** Verne, J.	**LIGHT AT THE EDGE OF THE** **WORLD, THE** MGM 1972
LIGHT OF DAY, THE Ambler, E.	**TOPKAPI** UA 1964
LIGHTS OUT Kendrick, B.H.	**BRIGHT VICTORY** UI 1951
LIKES OF 'ER, THE (P) McEvoy, C.	**SALLY IN OUR ALLEY** RKO 1932
LINE ON GINGER Maugham, R.	**INTRUDER, THE** BL 1953
LIONS AT THE KILL Catto, M.	**SEVEN THIEVES** FOX 1960
LISA AND DAVID Rubin, T.I.	**DAVID AND LISA** BL 1963
LITTLE BRITCHES Moody, R.	**WILD COUNTRY, THE** DISNEY 1971

ORIGINAL TITLE	FILM TITLE
LITTLE LAMBS EAT IVY (P) Langley, N.	**FATHER'S DOING FINE** ABP 1952
LITTLE MR. JIM Wadelton, T.D.	**ARMY BRAT** MGM 1946
LITTLE RASCAL North, S.	**RASCAL** DISNEY 1969
LITTLE SISTER, THE Chandler, R.	**MARLOWE** MGM 1969
LIVING AND THE DEAD, THE Boileau, P. *and* Narcejac, T.	**VERTICO** GALA 1958
LIZARD'S TAIL, THE Brandel, M.	**HAND, THE** SERENDIPITY 1981
LOBO AND OTHER STORIES Seton, E.T.	**LEGEND OF LOBO, THE** DISNEY 1962
LOCK AND THE KEY, THE Gruber, F.	**MAN IN THE VAULT** RKO 1957
LODGER, THE Lowdnes, *Mrs.* M.B.	**PHANTOM FIEND, THE** OLY 1935 **MAN IN THE ATTIC, THE** FOX 1953
LONDON WALL (P) Druten, J. van	**AFTER OFFICE HOURS** MGM 1935
LONE HOUSE MYSTERY, THE Wallace, E.	**ATTEMPT TO KILL** AA 1961
LONELY GIRL, THE O'Brien, E.	**GIRL WITH GREEN EYES** UA 1964
LONELY SKIER, THE Innes, H.	**SNOWBOUND** RKO 1948
LONG HAUL Bezzerides, A.I.	**THEY DRIVE BY NIGHT** WAR 1940

ORIGINAL TITLE	FILM TITLE
LONG NIGHT, THE Truss, S.	**LONG KNIFE, THE** AA 1958
LONG WAY UP, A Valens, E.G.	**WINDOW TO THE SKY, A** UN 1975
LOOK OF EAGLES Foote, J.T.	**KENTUCKY** FOX 1938
LOOTERS, THE Reese, J.	**CHARLEY VARRICK** UN 1973
LORD ARTHUR SAVILE'S CRIME Wilde, O.	**FLESH AND FANTASY** UN 1943
LORD EDGWARE DIES Christie, A.	**THIRTEEN AT DINNER** WAR 1985
LORD GOD MADE THEM ALL, THE Herriot, J.	**ALL CREATURES GREAT AND SMALL** BBC 1985 (TV)
LOSER WINS (P) Sartre, J-P.	**CONDEMNED OF ALTONA, THE** FOX 1964
LOSS OF ROSES, A (P) Inge, W.	**WOMAN OF SUMMER** FOX 1963
LOST COUNTRY, THE Salamanca, J.R.	**WILD IN THE COUNTRY** FOX 1961
LOST ECSTASY Rinehart, M.R.	**I TAKE THIS WOMAN** PAR 1931
LOST HERO Werbell, F. *and* Clarke, T.	**WALLENBERG: THE LOST HERO** BERYL-STONEHENGE 1985 (TV)
LOST IN THE STARS (P) Anderson, M.	**CRY, THE BELOVED COUNTRY** BL 1951
LOTTIE AND LISA Kastner, E.	**PARENT TRAP, THE** DISNEY 1961

LOUIS BERETTI Clarke, D.H.	**BORN RECKLESS** FOX 1930
LOVE AND FORGET Drawbell, J.W.	**LOVE STORY** BI 1941
LOVE FROM A STRANGER (P) Vosper, F.	**STRANGER WALKED IN, A** REN 1949
LOVE FROM EVERYBODY Hanley, C.	**DON'T BOTHER TO KNOCK** WAR 1961
LOVERS, THE (P) Stevens, L.	**WAR LORD, THE** RANK 1965
LULLABY, THE (P) Knoblock, E.	**SIN OF MADELON CLAUDET** MGM 1931

M

McCABE Naughton, E.	**McCABE AND MRS. MILLER** WAR 1972
McLEOD'S FOLLY Bromfield, L.	**JOHNNY VAGABOND** UA 1943
McVICAR BY HIMSELF McVicar, J.	**McVICAR** BRENT WALKER 1980
MADAME BOVARY Flaubert, G.	**UNHOLY LOVE** HP 1932
MADAM KITTY Norden, P.	**SALON KITTY** FOX 1977
MADAM TIC-TAC (P) Cary, F.L. *and* Weathers, P.	**NO ROAD BACK** RKO 1956
MAGISTRATE, THE (P) Pinero, *Sir* A.W.	**THOSE WERE THE DAYS** PAR 1940
MAGNIFICENT DEVILS Crockett, L.H.	**PROUD AND PROFANE** PAR 1956

MAIN STREET Lewis, S.	**I MARRIED A DOCTOR** IN 1936
MAJOR THOMPSON LIVES IN FRANCE Daninos, P.	**FRENCH ARE A FUNNY RACE,** **THE** (*USA Title*) CONTINENTAL 1957
MAJOR THOMPSON LIVES IN FRANCE Daninos, P.	**DIARY OF MAJOR THOMPSON,** **THE** GALA 1957
MAKE ROOM, MAKE ROOM! Harrison, H.	**SOYLENT GREEN** MGM—EMI 1973
MAKE YOU A GOOD WIFE Foldes, Y.	**MY OWN TRUE LOVE** PAR 1948
MALACHI'S COVE Trollope, A.	**SEAWEED CHILDREN, THE** PENRITH 1978
MALE ANIMAL, THE (P) Thurber, J. *and* Nugent, E.	**SHE'S WORKING HER WAY** **THROUGH COLLEGE** WAR 1952
MALTESE FALCON, THE Hammett, D.	**SATAN MET A LADY** FIRST NATIONAL 1937 **BLACK BIRD, THE** COL—WAR 1975
MAN, THE (P) Dinelli, M.	**BEWARE MY LOVELY** RKO 1952
MAN ABOUT A DOG, A Coppel, A.	**OBSESSION** GFD 1949
MAN AT THE CARLTON Wallace, E.	**MAN AT THE CARLTON TOWER** AA 1961
MAN-EATER Willis, T.	**MANEATERS ARE LOOSE!** BBC 1984 (TV)
MAN FROM MOSCOW, A Wynne, G.	**WYNNE AND PENKOVSKY** BBC 1985 (TV)

724

ORIGINAL TITLE	FILM TITLE
MAN IN CHARGE Jessup, R.	**YOUNG DON'T CRY, THE** COL 1957
MAN IN HALF MOON STREET, THE (P) Lyndon, B.	**MAN WHO COULD CHEAT DEATH, THE** PAR 1959
MAN IN POSSESSION, THE (P) Harwood, H.M.	**PERSONAL PROPERTY** MGM 1937
MAN IN THE IRON MASK, THE Dumas, A.	**FIFTH MUSKETEER, THE** SASCHA WIEN 1978
MAN OF PROPERTY, THE Galsworthy, J.	**FORSYTE SAGA, THE** MGM 1949
MAN OF THE WEST Yordan, P.	**GUN GLORY** MGM 1957
MAN RUNNING Jepson, S.	**STAGE FRIGHT** WAR 1949
MANSON MURDERS, THE Bugliosi, V. *and* Gentry, C.	**HELTER SKELTER** HEMDALE 1976
MANTRAP Lewis, S.	**UNTAMED** PAR 1940
MAN WHO BOUGHT LONDON, THE Wallace, E.	**TIME TO REMEMBER** AA 1962
MAN WHO KNEW, THE Wallace, E.	**PARTNERS IN CRIME** AA 1960
MAN WHO ROCKED THE BOAT, THE Keating, W.J. *and* Carter, R.	**SLAUGHTER ON 10th AVENUE** UI 1957
MANY SPLENDOURED THING, A Han Suyin	**LOVE IS A MANY SPLENDOURED THING** FOX 1955
MARBLE FOREST Durrant, T.	**MACABRE** ABP 1957

ORIGINAL TITLE	FILM TITLE
MARIA CHAPDELAINE Hemon, L.	**NAKED HEART, THE** BL 1950
MARION'S WALL Finney, J.	**MAXIE** RANK 1985
MARK OF DUST White, J.M.E.	**MASK OF DOUBT** EXCLUSIVE 1954
MARK OF ZORRO McCulley, J.	**MARK OF THE RENEGADE** UI 1951
MARRIAGE BED, THE Pascal, E.	**HUSBAND'S HOLIDAY** PAR 1931
MARSHAL OF MEDICINE BEND, THE Ward, B.	**LAWLESS STREET, A** COL 1955
MARTIN ARROWSMITH Lewis, S.	**ARROWSMITH** UA 1931
MARTIN EDEN London, J.	**ADVENTURES OF MARTIN EDEN, THE** COL 1942
MARY ANN Karmel, A.	**SOMETHING WILD** UA 1962
MARY DEARE, THE Innes, H.	**WRECK OF THE MARY DEARE, THE** MGM 1959
MASH Hooker, R.	**M.A.S.H.** FOX 1969
MASK, THE Wilson, J.R.	**BEHIND THE MASK** BL 1958
MATTER OF CONVICTION, A Hunter, E.	**YOUNG SAVAGES, THE** UA 1960
MAURICE GUEST Richardson, H.H.	**RHAPSODY** MGM 1954

ME AND THE ARCH KOOK PETULIA Haase, J.	**PETULIA** WAR 1968
MEET A BODY (P) Launder, F. *and* Gilliat, S.	**GREEN MAN, THE** BL 1956
MEET THE TIGER Charteris, L.	**SAINT MEETS THE TIGER, THE** REP 1943
MEGSTONE PLOT, THE Garve, A.	**TOUCH OF LARCENY, A** PAR 1959
MELVILLE GOODWIN, USA Marquand, J.P.	**THEIR SECRET AFFAIR** WAR 1956
MEMOIRS OF A BRITISH AGENT Lockhart, *Sir* R.H.B.	**BRITISH AGENT** IN 1934
MEMOIRS OF A PHYSICIAN Dumas, A.	**BLACK MAGIC** UA 1949
MEMORY OF LOVE Breuer, B.	**IN NAME ONLY** RKO 1939
MEN OF IRON Pyle, H.	**BLACK SHIELD OF FALWORTH, THE** UI 1954
MERRILL'S MARAUDERS Ogburn, C.	**MARAUDER, THE** WAR 1962
MERRY GO ROUND Schnitzler, A.	**LA RONDE** COMMERCIAL 1951
MERTON OF THE MOVIES Wilson, H.L.	**MAKE ME A STAR** PAR 1932
METHINKS THE LADY Endore, G.	**WHIRLPOOL, THE** FOX 1951
MEXICAN, THE London, J.	**FIGHTER, THE** UA 1952
MEXICAN VILLAGE, A Niggli, J.	**SOMBRERO** MGM 1953

MICHAELS IN AFRICA, THE
Michael, G.

DRUMS OF DESTINY
NEW REALM 1962

MICHAEL STROGOFF
Verne, J.

SOLDIER AND THE LADY, THE
RKO 1937

**MIDNIGHT LADY AND THE MOURNING
MAN, THE**
Anthony, D.

MIDNIGHT MAN, THE
UN 1974

MIDWIFE OF PONT CLERY
Sandstrom, F.

JESSICA
UA 1961

MIDWICH CUCKOOS, THE
Wyndham, J.

VILLAGE OF THE DAMNED, THE
MGM 1960

**MILK TRAIN DOESN'T STOP HERE ANY
MORE (P)**
Williams, T.

BOOM
UI 1968

MILK WHITE UNICORN, THE
Sandstrom, F.

WHITE UNICORN, THE
CORFIELD 1947

MILLS OF GOD, THE
Lothar, E.

ACT OF MURDER, AN
UN 1948

MILLSTONE, THE
Drabble, M.

TOUCH OF LOVE, A
BL 1969

MIND OF MR. REEDER, THE
Wallace, E.

MIND OF MR. J.G. REEDER, THE
RAYMOND 1939

MIRROR CRACK'D FROM SIDE TO SIDE
Christie, A.

MIRROR CRACK'D, THE
EMI 1981

MIRROR IN MY HOUSE
O'Casey, S.

YOUNG CASSIDY
MGM 1962

MISCHIEF
Armstrong, C.

DON'T BOTHER TO KNOCK
FOX 1952

MISS BISHOP
Aldrich, *Mrs.* B.

CHEERS FOR MISS BISHOP
UA 1941

ORIGINAL TITLE	FILM TITLE
MISS LONELYHEARTS West, N.	**LONELYHEARTS** UA 1959
MISS MARPLE Christie, A.	**MURDER AHOY** MGM 1964
MISS PINKERTON Rinehart, M.R.	**NURSE'S SECRET, THE** WAR 1941
MISTER MOSES Catto, M.	**MR. MOSES** UA 1965
MISTER PYE Peake, M.	**MR. PYE** CHANNEL 4 1986 (TV)
MISTY OF CHINCOTEAGUE Henry, M.	**MISTY** FOX 1961
MOCKINGBIRD Rawlings, M.K.	**CROSS CREEK** EMI 1984
MOLL FLANDERS Defoe, D.	**AMOROUS ADVENTURES OF** **MOLL FLANDERS, THE** PAR 1964
MONEY DOESN'T MATTER (P) D'Alton, L.L.	**TALK OF A MILLION** ABP 1951
MONKEY PLANET Boulle, P.	**PLANET OF THE APES** FOX 1968
MONKEYS, THE Wilkinson, G.R.	**MONKEYS, GO HOME!** DISNEY 1967
MONSIEUR LA SOURIS Simenon, G.	**MIDNIGHT EPISODE** COL 1951
MONSIGNORE Leger, J.A.	**MONSIGNOR** FOX 1983
MOON OVER MULBERRY STREET (P) Cosentino, N.	**WOMAN IN THE DARK** REP 1952
MORALS OF MARCUS ORDAYNE Locke, W.J.	**MORALS OF MARCUS, THE** GB 1935

MORELLA Poe, E.A.	**TALES OF TERROR** WAR 1963
MORTGAGE ON LIFE Baum, V.	**WOMAN'S SECRET, A** RKO 1949
MOTHER CAREY'S CHICKENS Wiggin, K.D.	**SUMMER MAGIC** DISNEY 1963
MOUNTAIN LION, THE Murphy, R.	**RUN, COUGAR, RUN** DISNEY 1972
MOUNTAINS ARE MY KINGDOM Hardy, S.	**FORBIDDEN VALLEY** UN 1938
MOUNTEBANK Locke, W.J.	**SIDESHOW OF LIFE** WAR 1931
MOUSE THAT ROARED, THE Wibberly, L.	**MOUSE ON THE MOON** UA 1962
MOVING TARGET, THE Macdonald, R.	**HARPER** WAR 1967
MR. AND MRS. CUGAT Rorick, I.S.	**ARE HUSBANDS NECESSARY?** PAR 1942
MR. AND MRS. HADDOCK ABROAD Stewart, D.O.	**FINN AND HATTIE** PAR 1931
MR. ANGEL COMES ABOARD Booth, C.G.	**JOHNNY ANGEL** RKO 1945
MR. ARKADIN Welles, O.	**CONFIDENTIAL REPORT** WAR 1955
MR. BUNTING AT WAR Greenwood, R.	**SALUTE JOHN CITIZEN** BN 1942
MR. HOBBS' HOLIDAY Streeter, E.	**MR. HOBBS TAKES A VACATION** FOX 1962
M. RIPOIS AND HIS NEMESIS Hemon, L.	**KNAVE OF HEARTS** ABP 1954

ORIGINAL TITLE	FILM TITLE
MR. ISAACS Crawford, F.M.	**SON OF INDIA** MGM 1931
MR. JUSTICE HOLMES Biddle, F.	**MAGNIFICENT YANKEE, THE** MGM 1950
MR. MIDSHIPMAN EASY Marryat, F.	**MIDSHIPMAN EASY** ATP 1935
MR. PROHACK Bennett, A.	**DEAR MR. PROHACK** GFD 1949
MRS. FRISBY AND THE RATS OF NIMH O'Brien, R.C.	**SECRET OF NIMH, THE** UIP 1982
MRS. CHRISTOPHER Myers, E.	**BLACKMAILER** GFD 1951
MRS. McGINTY'S DEAD Christie, A.	**MURDER MOST FOUL** MGM 1963
MRS. ROSS Nicholson, R.	**WHISPERERS, THE** UA 1966
MULE FOR THE MARQUESA, A O'Rourke, F.	**PROFESSIONALS, THE** COL 1966
MURDER FOR A WANTON Chambers, W.	**SINNER TAKE ALL** MGM 1936
MURDER FOR THE MILLIONS Chapman, R.	**MURDER REPORTED** COL 1957
MURDER IN AMITYVILLE Holzer, H.	**AMITYVILLE II: THE POSSESSION** COL—EMI—WAR 1982
MURDER IN THE BUD Bottome, P.	**DANGER SIGNAL** WAR 1945
MURDER MISTAKEN (P) Green, J.	**CAST A DARK SHADOW** EROS 1935
MURDER OF STEPHEN KESTER Ashbrook, H.	**GREEN EYES** CHESTERFIELD 1934

ORIGINAL TITLE	FILM TITLE
MURDER OF THE CIRCUS QUEEN, THE Abbot, A.	**CIRCUS QUEEN MURDER** COL 1933
MURDER ON THE WILD SIDE Jacks, J.	**BLACK EYE** COL—WAR 1973
MURDERS IN THE RUE MORGUE Poe, E.A.	**PHANTOM OF THE RUE MORGUE** WAR 1954
MUSCLE BEACH Wallach, I.	**DON'T MAKE WAVES** MGM 1966
MUSTARD Stewart, F.	**MEPHISTO WALTZ** FOX 1971
MUTE WITNESS (P) Pike, R.L.	**BULLITT** WAR 1968
MUTINY Tisley, F.	**H.M.S. DEFIANT** COL 1962
MY BROTHER DEATH Sulzberger, C.L.	**TAKE ME WHILE I'M WARM** BORDER 1965
MY EARLY LIFE Churchill, *Sir* W.S.	**YOUNG WINSTON** COL—WAR 1972
MY LIFE Duncan, I.	**ISADORA** UI 1969
MY LIFE AND HARD TIMES Thurber, J.	**RISE AND SHINE** FOX 1941
MY OLD MAN Hemingway, E.	**UNDER MY SKIN** FOX 1950
MYSTERY IN FLORENCE Fenton, E.	**ESCAPADE IN FLORENCE** DISNEY 1963
MYSTERY OF DR. FU MANCHU Rohmer, S.	**MYSTERIOUS DR. FU MANCHU** PAR 1929
MYSTERY OF HUNTING'S END Eberhart, M.G.	**MYSTERY HOUSE** WAR 1938

MY TEN YEARS AS A COUNTERSPY
Morros, B.

CONFESSIONS OF A COUNTERSPY
RANK 1960

MY THREE ANGELS (P)
Husson, A.

WE'RE NO ANGELS
PAR 1955

MY TRUE LOVE
Teilhet, D.L.

NO ROOM FOR THE GROOM
UI 1952

N

NARROW MARGIN, THE
Wood, D. *and* Dempster, D.

BATTLE OF BRITAIN, THE
UA 1969

NEPOMUK OF THE RIVER
Pilkington, R.

GOLDEN HEAD, THE
CINERAMA 1965

NEST IN A FALLING TREE
Cowley, J.

NIGHT DIGGER, THE
MGM 1971

NEW CENTURIANS
Wambaugh, J.

PRECINCT 45—LOS ANGELES POLICE
COL 1972

NEWHAVEN–DIEPPE
Simenon, G.

TEMPTATION HARBOUR
AB 1947

NEWTON LETTER, THE
Banville, J.

REFLECTIONS
ARTIFICIAL EYE 1984

NEXT-TO-LAST TRAIN RIDE, THE
Dennis, C.

FINDERS KEEPERS
RANK 1984

NICE ITALIAN GIRL, A
Christman, E.

DANGEROUS LOVE
BRUT 1978
DON'T STEAL MY BABY
BBC 1985 (TV)

NICHOLAS NICKLEBY
Dickens, C.

LIFE AND ADVENTURES OF NICHOLAS NICKLEBY
PRIMETIME 1984 (TV)

NIGHT BUS Adams, S.H.	**IT HAPPENED ONE NIGHT** COL 1934
NIGHT CRY Stuart, W.L.	**WHERE THE SIDEWALK ENDS** FOX 1950
NIGHT DARKENS THE STREETS La Bern, A.J.	**GOOD-TIME GIRL** GFD 1948
NIGHTMARE Blaisdell, A.	**FANATIC** COL 1965
NIGHTMARE IN MANHATTAN Walsh, T.	**UNION STATION** PAR 1950
NIGHT OF THE TIGER, THE Dawlen, A.	**RIDE BEYOND VENGEANCE** COL 1966
NIGHT OF WENCELAS Davidson, L.	**HOT ENOUGH FOR JUNE** RANK 1963
NIGHT SONG Williams, J.	**SWEET LOVE, BITTER** FILM 2 1969
NINE DAYS OF FATHER SERRA Ziegler, I.G.	**SEVEN CITIES OF GOLD** FOX 1955
NO BEAST SO FIERCE Bunker, E.	**STRAIGHT TIME** COL—WAR 1978
NOBODY LOVES A DRUNKEN INDIAN Huffaker, C.	**LAST WARRIOR, THE** WAR 1970
NOBODY ORDERED WOLVES Dell, J.	**DARK MAN, THE** GFD 1951
NO COFFIN FOR THE CORPSE Rawson, C.	**MAN WHO WOULDN'T DIE, THE** FOX 1942
NO DIFFERENCE TO ME Hambledon, P.	**NO PLACE FOR JENNIFER** ABP 1949
NOMADS OF THE NORTH Curwood, J.O.	**NORTHERN PATROL** ABP 1954

734

ORIGINAL TITLE	FILM TITLE
NOMADS OF THE NORTH (*Continued*) Curwood, J.O.	**NIKKI, WILD DOG OF THE NORTH** DISNEY 1961
NO MEDALS (P) McCracken, E.	**WEAKER SEX, THE** TC 1948
NO MORE GAS Nordhoff, C.B. *and* Hall, J.N.	**TUTTLES OF TAHITI, THE** RKO 1942
NO NIGHTINGALES Brahms, C. *and* Simon, S.J.	**GHOSTS OF BERKELEY SQUARE, THE** BN 1947
NO ORCHIDS FOR MISS BLANDISH Chase, J.H.	**GRISSOM GANG, THE** CINERAMA 1971
NO PLACE FOR WOMEN Gill, T.	**TROPIC ZONE** PAR 1953
NOR PERFUME NOR WINE Bonner, C.	**ADAM HAD FOUR SONS** COL 1941
NORTH AVENUE IRREGULARS Hill, A.F.	**HILL'S ANGELS** DISNEY 1980
NORTHING TRAMP, THE Wallace, E.	**STRANGERS ON A HONEYMOON** GB 1937
NORTH OF BUSHMAN'S ROCK Harding, G.	**RIDE THE HIGH WIND** BUTCHER 1965
NORTH OF 36 Hough, E.	**CONQUERING HORDE** PAR 1931
NORTH WEST PASSAGE Roberts, K.	**FRONTIER RANGERS** MGM 1959 **MISSION OF DANGER** MGM 1959
NORWICH VICTIMS, THE Beeding, F.	**DEAD MEN TELL NO TALES** ALL 1939
NOSE ON MY FACE, THE Payne, L.	**GIRL IN THE HEADLINES** BL 1963

NOTHING TO LOSE Minney, R.J.	**TIME GENTLEMEN, PLEASE!** ABP 1952
NOT SO LONG AGO (P) Richman, A.	**LET'S DO IT AGAIN** COL 1953
NOT TOO NARROW, NOT TOO DEEP Sale, R.	**STRANGE CARGO** MGM 1940
NOW BARABBAS (P) Home, W.D.	**NOW BARABBAS WAS A ROBBER** WAR 1949
NURSE IS A NEIGHBOUR Jones, J.	**NURSE ON WHEELS** WAR 1963
NUTMEG TREE Sharp, M.	**JULIA MISBEHAVES** MGM 1948

O

ODOUR OF VIOLETS Kendrick, B.H.	**EYES IN THE NIGHT** MGM 1942
OEDIPUS REX (P) Sophocles	**OEDIPUS THE KING** UI 1968
OFF-ISLANDERS, THE Benchley, N.	**RUSSIANS ARE COMING—THE RUSSIANS ARE COMING, THE** UA 1966
OFF THE RECORD (P) Hay, I. *and* King-Hall, S.	**CARRY ON ADMIRAL** REN 1957
OIL FOR THE LAMPS OF CHINA Hobart, A.T.	**LAW OF THE TROPICS** WAR 1941
OLD ACQUAINTANCE (P) Druten, J. van	**RICH AND FAMOUS** MGM 1981
OLD CURIOSITY SHOP Dickens, C.	**MISTER QUILP** EMI 1975
OLDEST CONFESSION, THE Condon, R.	**HAPPY THIEVES, THE** UA 1961

ORIGINAL TITLE	FILM TITLE
OLD JUDGE PRIEST Cobb, I.S.	**SUN SHINES BRIGHT, THE** REP 1953
OLD LADY SHOWS HER MEDALS, THE (P) Barrie, *Sir* J.M.	**SEVEN DAYS LEAVE** PAR 1930
'OLD LADY 31' (P) Crothers, R.	**CAPTAIN IS A LADY, THE** MGM 1940
OLD MAN MINICK Ferber, E.	**EXPERT, THE** WAR 1932
OLIMPIA Cole, B.	**BOBO, THE** WAR 1967
OLIVER TWIST Dickens, C.	**OLIVER** COL 1968
OLYMPIA (P) Molnar, F.	**BREATH OF SCANDAL, A** PAR 1960
ONCE AND FUTURE KING, THE White, T.H.	**CAMELOT** WAR 1966
ONCE OFF GUARD Wallis, J.H.	**WOMAN IN THE WINDOW, THE** RKO 1944
ONE MAN'S SECRET Davis, S.	**MAN IN THE SHADOW** AA 1957
ONE PAIR OF FEET Dickens, M.	**LAMP STILL BURNS, THE** TC 1943
ONE STEP FROM MURDER Meynell, L.	**PRICE OF SILENCE, THE** GN 1959
ONEUPMANSHIP Potter, S.	**SCHOOL FOR SCOUNDRELS** WAR 1960
ON MONDAY NEXT (P) King, P.	**CURTAIN UP** GFD 1952
ON THE TRAIL Harris, F.	**COWBOY** COL 1957

ON TO OREGON Morrow, H.	**SEVEN ALONE** HEMDALE 1974
ON TRIAL London, A.	**L'AVEU** WAR 1970
OPERATION CICERO Moyzisch, L.C.	**FIVE FINGERS** FOX 1952
OPERATION TERROR Gordons, The	**GRIP OF FEAR, THE** COL 1962
OPERATOR, THE Amateau, R. *and* Robinson, B.	**WHERE DOES IT HURT?** HEMDALE 1971
ORCHARD WALLS, THE (P) Delderfield, R.F.	**NOW AND FOREVER** ABP 1955
ORDEAL, THE Collins, D.	**SHIP FROM SHANGHAI** MGM 1930
ORDEAL OF MAJOR GRIGSBY, THE Sherlock, J.	**LAST GRENADE, THE** CINERAMA 1969
ORPHEUS DESCENDING (P) Williams, T.	**FUGITIVE KIND, THE** UA 1960
OTHER MAN, THE Turney, C.	**BACK FROM THE DEAD** FOX 1957
OTTER'S STORY Liers, E.	**FLASH THE OTTER** DISNEY 1969
OUR VIRGIN ISLAND White, R.	**VIRGIN ISLAND** BL 1958
OUT OF THE FRYING PAN (P) Swann, F.	**YOUNG AND WILLING** UA 1943
OVER THE RIVER Galsworthy, J.	**ONE MORE RIVER** UN 1934
OX-BOX INCIDENT, THE Clark, W. van T.	**STRANGE INCIDENT** FOX 1943

P

ORIGINAL TITLE	FILM TITLE
PAID IN FULL Cronin, M.	**JOHNNY ON THE SPOT** FANCEY 1954
PAINTED VEIL, THE Maugham, W.S.	**SEVENTH SIN, THE** MGM 1957
PAIVA: QUEEN OF LOVE Schirokauer, A.	**IDOL OF PARIS, THE** GFD 1948
PARAGON, THE (P) Pertwee, R. *and* Pertwee, M.	**SILENT DUST** ABP 1952
PART-TIME WIVES Baldwin, F.	**WEEK-END MARRIAGE** IN 1932
PASO POR AQUI Rhodes, E.M.	**FOUR FACES WEST** UA 1948
PASSING OF EVIL, THE McShane, M.	**GRASSHOPPER, THE** NATIONAL GENERAL LECTURES 1969
PASSING OF THE BLACK EAGLE Henry, O.	**BLACK EAGLE** COL 1948
PASSPORT TO OBLIVION Leasor, J.	**WHERE THE SPIES ARE** MGM 1965
PATROL Macdonald, P.	**LOST PATROL** RKO 1934
PATTERN OF ISLANDS Grimble, *Sir* A.	**PACIFIC DESTINY** BL 1956
PATTON: ORDEAL AND TRIUMPH Farago, L.	**PATTON: LUST FOR GLORY** FOX 1970
PEABODY'S MERMAIDS Jones, G.P. *and* Jones, C.B.	**MR. PEABODY AND THE** **MERMAID** UN 1948
PENROD Tarkington, B.	**BY THE LIGHT OF THE SILVERY** **MOON** WAR 1953

739

ORIGINAL TITLE	FILM TITLE
PENROD (*Continued*)	**PENROD AND SAM** WAR 1937
PENTHOUSE MYSTERY Queen, E.	**ELLERY QUEEN AND THE** **PENTHOUSE MYSTERY** COL 1941
PENTIMENTO Hellman, L.	**JULIA** FOX 1977
PERFECT CRIME Queen, E.	**ELLERY QUEEN AND THE** **PERFECT CRIME** COL 1941
PERILOUS PASSAGE, THE Nicolayson, B.	**PASSAGE, THE** HEMDALE 1978
PERSISTENT WARRIORS, THE (P) Arundel, E.	**GREEN FINGERS** BN 1947
PERSONS IN HIDING Hoover, J.E.	**QUEEN OF THE MOB** PAR 1940 **PAROLE FIXER** PAR 1940
PETRIFIED FOREST, THE (P) Sherwood, R.E.	**ESCAPE IN THE DESERT** WAR 1945
PHANTOM CROWN Harding, B.	**JUAREZ** WAR 1939
PHILADELPHIAN, THE Powell, R.	**CITY JUNGLE, THE** WAR 1959
PHILADELPHIA STORY, THE (P) Barry, P.	**HIGH SOCIETY** MGM 1956
PHOTO FINISH Mason, H.	**FOLLOW THAT HORSE!** WAR 1959
PICK UP STICKS Phillips, M.	**CHERRY PICKER, THE** RANK 1972
PICTURE OF DORIAN GRAY Wilde, O.	**DORIAN GRAY** HEMDALE 1973

ORIGINAL TITLE	FILM TITLE
PIGEON FLY HOME Liggett, T.	**PIGEON THAT WORKED A MIRACLE, THE** DISNEY 1958
PILGRIM'S PROGRESS Bunyan, J.	**DANGEROUS JOURNEY** CHANNEL 4 1985 (TV)
PILLARS OF MIDNIGHT, THE Trevor, E.	**80,000 SUSPECTS** RANK 1963
PIONEER GO HOME Powell, R.	**FOLLOW THAT DREAM** UA 1962
PITY MY SIMPLICITY Massie, C.	**LOVE LETTERS** PAR 1945
PLACE TO HIDE, A Gillham, B.	**BREAKOUT** CFTF 1984
PLEASURE ISLAND Maier, W.	**GIRLS OF PLEASURE ISLAND, THE** PAR 1953
POLONAISE Leslie, D.	**SONG TO REMEMBER, A** COL 1945
POLTERGEIST, THE (P) Harvey, F.	**THINGS HAPPEN AT NIGHT** REN 1947
PORTRAIT OF A REBEL Syrett, N.	**WOMAN REBELS, A** RKO 1936
POTIPHAR'S WIFE Middleton, E.	**HER STRANGE DESIRE** POWERS 1932
POWER AND THE GLORY, THE Greene, G.	**FUGITIVE, THE** RKO 1947
PRELUDE Abrahall, C.H.	**WHEREVER SHE GOES** ABP 1950
PRELUDE TO NIGHT Stoddart, D.	**RUTHLESS** EL 1948
PRETTY POLLY BARLOW Coward, N.	**PRETTY POLLY** RANK 1967

PRISONERS ARE PEOPLE
Scudder, K.J.

UNCHAINED
WAR 1954

PRISONERS OF QUAI DONG, THE
Kolpacoff, V.

PHYSICAL ASSAULT
TITAN 1973

PRIVATE EAR, THE (P)
Shaffer, P.

PAD, THE
UI 1967

PRIVATE LIFE
Hackney, A.

I'M ALRIGHT JACK
BL 1959

PROCANE CHRONICLE, THE
Bleeck, O.

ST. IVES
COL—WAR 1976

PSYCHE '63
Ligneris, F.

PSYCHE '59
BL 1964

PUBLIC EYE, THE (P)
Shaffer, P.

FOLLOW ME
UN 1972

PUNITIVE ACTION
Robb, J.

DESERT SAND
UA 1955

PURPLE CLOUD, THE
Shiel, M.P.

**WORLD, THE FLESH AND THE
DEVIL, THE**
MGM 1959

PUZZLE FOR FIENDS
Quentin, P.

STRANGE AWAKENING, THE
AA 1958

PUZZLE OF THE BRIAR PIPE
Palmer, S.

MURDER ON A BRIDLE PATH
RKO 1938

PUZZLE OF THE PAPER TREE
Palmer, S.

MURDER ON A HONEYMOON
RKO 1935

PYGMALION (P)
Shaw, G.B.

MY FAIR LADY
WAR 1964

PYLON
Faulkner, W.

TARNISHED ANGELS
UI 1957

Q

'Q' SHIPS AND THEIR STORY
Chatterton, E.K.

BLOCKADE
RKO 1928

QUALITY
Sumner, *Mrs.* C.R.

PINKY
FOX 1949

QUEEN IN DANGER
Trevor, E.

MANTRAP
EXCLUSIVE 1953

QUEEN'S DOCTOR, THE
Neumann, R.

KING IN SHADOW
BL 1959

QUEEN'S HUSBAND, THE (P)
Sherwood, R.E.

ROYAL BED
RKO 1931

QUEEN WAS IN THE PARLOUR, THE (P)
Coward, N.

TONIGHT IS OURS
PAR 1933

QUENTIN DURWARD
Scott, *Sir* W.

ADVENTURES OF QUENTIN DURWARD, THE
MGM 1955

R

RACER, THE
Ruesch, H.

RACERS, THE
FOX 1954
MEN AGAINST SPEED
FOX 1958

RAGE OF THE VULTURE, THE
Moorehead, A.

THUNDER IN THE EAST
PAR 1951

RAGGED MESSENGER, THE
Maxwell, W.B.

MADONNA OF THE STREETS
COL 1930

RAIN (P)
Maugham, W.S.

MISS SADIE THOMPSON
COL 1954

RAINBIRD PATTERN, THE
Canning, V.

FAMILY PLOT
UN 1976

RAINS CAME, THE
Bromfield, L.

RAINS OF RANCHIPUR, THE
FOX 1955

RAJ QUARTET
Scott, P.

JEWEL IN THE CROWN, THE
GRANADA 1984

RAPE UPON RAPE (P)
Fielding, H.

LOCK UP YOUR DAUGHTERS
COL 1968

RAPTURE IN MY RAGS
Hastings, P.

RAPTURE
FOX 1964

RASHOMON (P)
Kanin, F. *and* Kanin, M.

OUTRAGE
MGM 1964

RATMAN'S NOTE BOOK
Gilbert, S.

WILLARD
CINERAMA 1971

RAVINE, THE
Young, K.

ASSAULT
RANK 1971

RAWHIDE JUSTICE
Raine, W.M.

MAN FROM BITTER RIDGE, THE
GFD 1955

REAR CAR (P)
Rose, E.E.

MURDER IN THE PRIVATE CAR
MGM 1934

RECOLLECTIONS OF VESTA TILLEY
De Frece, *Lady*

AFTER THE BALL
BL 1957

RED FILE FOR CALLAN, A
Mitchell, J.

CALLAN
EMI 1974

RELAPSE, THE (P)
Vanbrugh, *Sir* J.

LOCK UP YOUR DAUGHTERS
COL 1968

RELATIONS ARE BEST APART (P)
Lewis, E.

WHAT EVERY WOMAN WANTS
ADELPHI 1954

RENFREW'S LONG TRAIL
Erskine, L.Y.

DANGER AHEAD
MON 1940

RENFREW RIDES AGAIN
Erskine, L.Y.

FIGHTING MAD
MON 1939

RENFREW RIDES NORTH
Erskine, L.Y.

YUKON FLIGHT
MON 1940

RENFREW RIDES THE RANGE
Erskine, L.Y.

CRASHING THRU'
MON 1939

REPORT TO THE COMMISSIONER
Mills, J.

OPERATION UNDER COVER
UN 1975

REPUTATION FOR A SONG
Grierson, E.

MY LOVER, MY SON
MGM 1969

REQUIEM FOR A NUN
Faulkner, W.

SANCTUARY
FOX 1960

RESCUERS AND MISS BIANCA, THE
Sharp, M.

RESCUERS
DISNEY 1977

RESTLESS
Macdonald, J.P.

MAN TRAP
PAR 1961

RETRIBUTION
Curwood, J.O.

TIMBER FURY
EAGLE—LION 1950

RETURN TO WOODS
Hodson, J.L.

KING AND COUNTRY
WAR 1965

RINGER, THE (P)
Wallace, E.

PHANTOM STRIKES, THE
MON 1939

RING FOR CATTY (P)
Cargill, P. *and* Beale, J.

TWICE ROUND THE DAFFODILS
AA 1962

RIPLEY'S GAME
Highsmith, P.

AMERICAN FRIEND, THE
CINEGATE 1978

RIPPER FROM RAWHIDE
Cushman, D.

TIMBERJACK
REP 1954

RIVER RAN OUT OF EDEN, A
Marshall, J.V.

GOLDEN SEAL, THE
NEW REALM 1984

ROAD TO ROME, THE (P)
Sherwood, R.E.

JUPITER'S DARLING
MGM 1954

ORIGINAL TITLE	FILM TITLE
ROAD TO SAN JACINTO Foreman, L.L.	**ARROW IN THE DUST** ABP 1954
ROAD TO SOCORRO, THE Locke, C.O.	**MANHUNT** FOX 1958
ROGUE MALE Household, G.	**MANHUNT** FOX 1941
ROME HAUL Edmonds, W.D.	**FARMER TAKES A WIFE, THE** FOX 1953
ROMMEL Young, D.	**ROMMEL—DESERT FOX** FOX 1951
ROOM SERVICE (P) Murray, J. *and* Boret, A.	**STEP LIVELY** RKO 1944
ROOM 13 Wallace, E.	**MYSTERY OF ROOM 13** ALL 1941
ROSALIND (P) Barrie, *Sir* J.M.	**FOREVER FEMALE** PAR 1953
ROSE AND THE FLAME, THE Lauritzen, J.	**KISS OF FIRE** GFD 1955
ROUGHSHOD Fox, N.A.	**GUNSMOKE** GFD 1952
ROUGH SKETCH Sylvester, R.	**WE WERE STRANGERS** COL 1949
ROUND THE WORLD IN 80 DAYS Verne, J.	**AROUND . . .** UA 1957
ROUND-UP, THE Mulford, C.E.	**HILLS OF OLD WYOMING** PAR 1937
ROYAL CANADIAN MOUNTED POLICE Fetherstonhaugh, R.C.	**NORTH WEST MOUNTED POLICE** PAR 1940
ROYAL FAMILY, THE (P) Kaufman, G.S. *and* Ferber, E.	**ROYAL FAMILY OF BROADWAY** PAR 1930

RUNAWAY HORSES
Mishima, Y.

MISHIMA
COL—EMI—WAR 1985

RUNNING SCARED
Burmeister, J.

TIGERS DON'T CRY
RANK 1978

RUTHLESS ONES, THE
Moody, L.

WHAT BECAME OF JACK AND JILL?
FOX 1971

S

SACAJAWEA OF THE SHOSHONES
Emmons, D.G.

FAR HORIZONS, THE
PAR 1955

SACRED FLAME (P)
Maugham, W.S.

RIGHT TO LIVE, THE
WAR 1935

SAGA OF BILLY THE KID
Burns, W.N.

BILLY THE KID
MGM 1941

SAINT JOHNSON
Burnett, W.R.

LAW AND ORDER
UN 1932

SALUTE TO THE GODS
Campbell, *Sir* M.

BURN 'EM UP O'CONNOR
MGM 1939

SAMUEL I & II
The Bible

KING DAVID
UIP 1985

SANCTUARY
Faulkner, W.

STORY OF TEMPLE DRAKE, THE
PAR 1933

SANDERS OF THE RIVER
Wallace, E.

COAST OF SKELETONS
BL 1964
DEATH DRUMS ALONG THE RIVER
PLANET 1963

SAN QUENTIN
Duffy, C. *and* Jennings, D.

MEN BEHIND BARS
ABP 1954
STEEL CAGE, THE
GN 1956

ORIGINAL TITLE	FILM TITLE
SATURDAY'S CHILDREN (P) Anderson, M.	**MAYBE IT'S LOVE** WAR 1930
SATYRICON Petronius	**FELLINI SATYRICON** UA 1970
SCARLET PIMPERNEL OF THE VATICAN Gallagher, H.J.	**SCARLET AND THE BLACK** ITC 1983 (TV)
SCOTT AND AMUNDSEN Huntford, R.	**LAST PLACE ON EARTH, THE** RENEGADE FILM 1984 (TV)
SEA OF TROUBLES Duras, M.	**SEA WALL** RANK 1957
SEA WOLF, THE London, J.	**WOLF LARSEN** ABP 1959
SEA WYF AND BISCUIT Scott, J.D.	**SEA-WIFE** FOX 1957
SECOND MAN (P) Behrman, S.N.	**HE KNEW WOMEN** RKO 1930
SECRET AGENT, THE Conrad, J.	**SABOTAGE** REP 1939
SEED AND THE SOWER, THE Post, *Sir* L. van der	**"MERRY CHRISTMAS, MR. LAWRENCE"** CINEVENTURE 1983
SEE NAPLES AND DIE (P) Rice, E.	**OH! SAILOR, BEHAVE!** WAR 1931
SEND ANOTHER COFFIN Presnell, F.G.	**SLIGHTLY HONOURABLE** UA 1939
SENTIMENTALISTS Collins, D.	**SAL OF SINGAPORE** PATHE 1929 **HIS WOMAN** PAR 1931
SERGEANT YORK AND HIS PEOPLE Cowan, S.K.	**SERGEANT YORK** WAR 1941

ORIGINAL TITLE	FILM TITLE
SERVICE (P) Anthony, C.L.	**LOOKING FORWARD** MGM 1933
7½ CENTS Bissell, R.P.	**PAJAMA GAME** WAR 1957
SEVEN DAYS TO A KILLING Egleton, C.	**BLACK WINDMILL, THE** PAR 1974
SEVEN KEYS TO BALDPATE Biggers, E.D.	**HOUSE OF THE LONG SHADOWS** CANNON 1982
SEVEN MEN AT DAYBREAK Burgess, A.	**OPERATION DAYBREAK** COL—WAR 1975
SEVEN PILLARS OF WISDOM Lawrence, T.E.	**LAWRENCE OF ARABIA** BL 1962
SEXUAL PERVERSITY IN CHICAGO Mamet, D.	**ABOUT LAST NIGHT** TRI-STAR 1986
SHADES WILL NOT VANISH Fowler, H.M.	**STRANGE INTRUDER** ABP 1957
SHADOW AND THE PEAK, THE Mason, R.	**PASSIONATE SUMMER, THE** RANK 1958
SHADOW RANGE Bishop, C.	**COW COUNTRY** ABP 1953
SHALL I EAT YOU NOW? (P) Gebler, E.	**HOFFMAN** WAR 1969
SHAPE OF THINGS TO COME Wells, H.G.	**THINGS TO COME** UA 1936
SHATTERED Dwyer, E.R.	**PASSENGERS** COL—WAR 1976
SHE DIED YOUNG Kennington, A.	**YOU CAN'T ESCAPE** ABP 1955
SHE LET HIM CONTINUE Geller, S.	**PRETTY POISON** FOX 1968

ORIGINAL TITLE	FILM TITLE
SHETLAND BUS, THE Howarth, D.	**SUICIDE MISSION** EROS 1957
SHOOTING STAR (P) Thomas, B.	**GREAT GAME, THE** ADELPHI 1953
SHORE LEAVE (P) Osborne, H.	**HIT THE DECK** MGM 1954
SHORE LEAVE Wakeman, F.	**KISS THEM FOR ME** FOX 1957
SHORN LAMB, THE Locke, W.J.	**STRANGERS IN LOVE** PAR 1932
SHOW MUST GO ON, THE Verner, G.	**TREAD SOFTLY** APEX 1952
SHOW-OFF, THE (P) Kelly, G.	**MEN ARE LIKE THAT** PAR 1929
SHUTTERED ROOM, THE Lovecraft, H.P.	**DUNWICH HORROR** AMERICAN INT 1969
SIEGE AT DANCING BIRD, THE LeMay, A.	**UNFORGIVEN, THE** UA 1960
SIEGE AT TRENCHER'S FARM, THE Williams, G.M.	**STRAW DOGS** CINERAMA 1971
SIEGE OF BATTERSEA, THE Holles, R.	**GUNS AT BATASI** FOX 1964
SIGNS OF LIFE Elliott, S.	**"CAREFUL HE MIGHT HEAR YOU"** SYME 1983
SILENCE WILL SPEAK Trzebinski, E.	**OUT OF AFRICA** UN 1985
SILENT REEFS Cottrell, D.	**SECRET OF THE PURPLE REEF, THE** FOX 1960
SILVER ROCK Short, L.	**HELL'S OUTPOST** REP 1954

ORIGINAL TITLE	FILM TITLE
SING A SONG OF MURDER Langham, J.R.	**NIGHT IN NEW ORLEANS, A** PAR 1942
SINISTER ERRAND Cheyney, P.	**DIPLOMATIC COURIER** FOX 1952
SIN OF SUSAN SLADE, THE Hume, D.	**SUSAN SLADE** WAR 1962
SINUHE, THE EGYPTIAN Waltari, M.	**EGYPTIAN, THE** FOX 1954
SIRE OF MALETROIT'S DOOR, THE Stevenson, R.L.	**STRANGE DOOR, THE** COL 1949
SIR, YOU BASTARD Newman, G.F.	**TAKE, THE** COL—WAR 1974
SISTER CARRIE Dreiser, T.	**CARRIE** PAR 1950
SIX DAYS OF THE CONDOR Grady, J.	**3 DAYS OF THE CONDOR** PAR 1975
SIXTEEN HANDS Croy, H.	**I'M FROM MISSOURI** PAR 1939
SIXTH OF JUNE Shapiro, L.	**D-DAY THE SIXTH OF JUNE** FOX 1956
SKIN DEEP Kelland, C.B.	**FOR BEAUTY'S SAKE** FOX 1941
SKINNER'S DRESS SUIT (P) Dodge, H.I.	**SKINNER STEPS OUT** UN 1929
SKYSCRAPER Baldwin, F.	**SKYSCRAPER SOULS** MGM 1932
SLAPSTICK Vonnegut, K.	**SLAPSTICK OF ANOTHER KIND** LORIMAR 1984
SLEEP LONG, MY LOVELY Waugh, H.	**JIGSAW** BL 1962

ORIGINAL TITLE	FILM TITLE
SLIGHT CASE OF MURDER, A (P) Runyon, D. *and* Lindsay, H.	**STOP, YOU'RE KILLING ME** WAR 1952
SMALL MIRACLE, THE Gallico, P.	**NEVER TAKE NO FOR AN ANSWER** INDEPENDENT 1951
SMALL MIRACLE (P) Krasna, N.	**FOUR HOURS TO KILL** PAR 1935
SMALL WOMAN, THE Burgess, A.	**INN OF THE SIXTH HAPPINESS, THE** FOX 1958
SMUGGLERS CIRCUIT Roberts, D.	**LAW AND DISORDER** BL 1957
SNAKE WATER Williams, A.	**PINK JUNGLE, THE** UI 1968
SNOW BIRCH, THE Mantley, J.	**WOMAN OBSESSED, THE** FOX 1959
SOBBIN' WOMEN, THE Benet, S.V.	**SEVEN BRIDES FOR SEVEN BROTHERS** MGM 1954
SOLDIER'S PLAY, A (P) Fuller, C.	**SOLDIER'S STORY, A** COL—EMI—WAR 1985
SOLID! SAID THE EARL Carstairs, J.P.	**YANK IN ERMINE, A** MON 1955
SOMEBODY WAITING (P) Williams, E.	**TIME WITHOUT PITY** HARLEQUIN 1957
SOME FACES IN THE CROWD Schulberg, B.W.	**FACE IN THE CROWD, A** WAR 1957
SOME MUST WATCH White, E.L.	**SPIRAL STAIRCASE, THE** RKO 1946
SOMEONE IS KILLING THE GREAT CHEFS OF EUROPE Lyons, N. *and* Lyons, I.	**TOO MANY CHEFS** LORIMAR 1978

752

SOMETIMES A GREAT NOTION Kesey, K.	**NEVER GIVE AN INCH** RANK 1972
SON OF ANY WEDNESDAY (P) Resnik, M.	**ANY WEDNESDAY** WAR 1966
SOPHIA LIVING AND LOVING Hotchner, A.E.	**SOPHIA LOREN—HER OWN STORY** BBC 1985 (TV)
SORT OF TRAITORS, A Balchin, N.	**SUSPECT** BL 1960
SOUND OF HUNTING, A (P) Brown, H.	**EIGHT IRON MEN** COL 1952
SOUND OF MURDER, THE (P) Fairchild, W.	**LAST SHOT YOU HEAR, THE** FOX 1969
SOUTHERN BLADE, THE Wolford, N. *and* Wolford, S.	**LONG RIDE HOME, THE** COL 1967
SOUTHERN STAR MYSTERY, THE Verne, J.	**SOUTHERN STAR, THE** COL 1969
SPACE VAMPIRES, THE Wilson, C.	**LIFEFORCE** CANNON 1985
SPANISH FARM, THE Mottram, R.H.	**ROSES OF PICARDY** EXCELLENT 1930
SPARRERS CAN'T SING (P) Lewis, S.	**SPARROWS CAN'T SING** WAR 1962
SPHINX HAS SPOKEN, THE Dekobra, M.	**FRIENDS AND LOVERS** RKO 1931
SPINNER IN THE SUN Reed, M.	**VEILED WOMAN** FOX 1929
SPINSTER Ashton-Warner, S.	**TWO LOVES** MGM 1960
SPLENDID CRIME, THE Goodchild, G.	**PUBLIC DEFENDER** RKO 1931

753

SPOONHANDLE
Moore, R.

DEEP WATERS
FOX 1948

SPORTING PROPOSITION, A
Aldridge, J.

RIDE A WILD PONY
DISNEY 1975

SPRING CLEANING (P)
Lonsdale, F.

WOMEN WHO PLAY
GB 1932

SPY IN THE VODKA
Thomas, R.

COLD WAR SWAP, THE
PAR 1969

SQUARE CIRCLE, THE
Carney, D.

WILD GEESE II
COL—EMI—WAR 1985

SQUEAKER, THE
Wallace, E.

MURDER ON DIAMOND ROW
UA 1937

STAB IN THE DARK
Block, L.

8 MILLION WAYS TO DIE
PSO 1985

STAGE TO LORDSBURGH
Haycox, E.

STAGECOACH
UA 1939

STAMBOUL TRAIN
Greene, G.

ORIENT EXPRESS
FOX 1934

STARS IN THEIR COURSES, THE
Brown, H.

EL DORADO
PAR 1967

STATE OF THE UNION (P)
Lindsay, H. *and* Crouse, R.

WORLD AND HIS WIFE
MGM 1948

STELLA
Hartog, J. de

KEY, THE
COL 1958

STERILE CUCKOO, THE
Nichols, J.

POOKIE
PAR 1969

STILL LIFE (P)
Coward, N.

BRIEF ENCOUNTER
CINEGUILD 1946

STILL MISSING
Gutcheon, B.

WITHOUT A TRACE
FOX 1983

ORIGINAL TITLE	FILM TITLE
ST. IVES Stevenson, R.L.	**SECRET OF ST. IVES, THE** COL 1949
STONE FOR DANNY FISHER, A Robbins, H.	**KING CREOLE** PAR 1958
STOP AT A WINNER Delderfield, R.F.	**ON THE FIDDLE** AA 1961
STORY OF IVY, THE Lowndes, *Mrs.* M.B.	**IVY** UI 1947
STORY OF PETER MARSHALL, THE Marshall, C.	**MAN CALLED PETER** FOX 1954
STORY OF THE TRAPP FAMILY SINGERS Trapp, M.A.	**SOUND OF MUSIC, THE** FOX 1965
STORY OF ZARAK KHAN, THE Bevan, A.J.	**ZARAK** COL 1956
STRANGE BOARDERS OF PALACE CRESCENT Oppenheim, E.P.	**STRANGE BOARDERS** GB 1938
STRANGE ONE, THE (P) Willingham, C.	**END AS A MAN** COL 1957
STRANGER AT HOME Sanders, G.	**STRANGER CAME HOME** EXCLUSIVE 1954
SUBMISSION OF A LAZY WRESTLER Drexler, R.	**BELOW THE BELT** PRODUCTION ASSOCIATES 1982
SUICIDE CLUB, THE Stevenson, R.L.	**TROUBLE FOR TWO** MGM 1936
SURVIVOR, THE Eisner, J.	**CHILDREN'S WAR, THE** STAFFORD 1984
SUSPENSE Graeme, B.	**FACE IN THE NIGHT** GN 1956

ORIGINAL TITLE	FILM TITLE
SWAMP WATER Bell, V.	**LURE OF THE WILDERNESS** FOX 1952
SWAN, THE (P) Molnar, F.	**ONE ROMANTIC NIGHT** UA 1930
SWEET ALOES Mallory, J.	**GIVE ME YOUR HEART** WAR 1936
SWEET AND PLENTY Piper, A.	**NICE GIRL LIKE ME, A** AVCO EMBASSY 1969
SWIFT WATER Annixter, P.	**THOSE GALLOWAYS** DISNEY 1965
SYLVESTER Hyams, E.	**YOU KNOW WHAT SAILORS ARE** GFD 1953
SYMBOL, THE Bessie, A.	**SEX SYMBOL, THE** WAR 1974

T

TABITHA (P) Ridley, A. *and* Borer, M.	**WHO KILLED THE CAT?** GN 1966
TALENTED MR. RIPLEY, THE Highsmith, P.	**PURPLE NOON** HILLCREST 1961
TALES FROM THE SOUTH PACIFIC Michener, J.A.	**SOUTH PACIFIC** TODD AO 1958
TALISMAN, THE Scott, *Sir* W.	**KING RICHARD AND THE CRUSADERS** WAR 1954
TAMPICO Hergesheimer, J.	**WOMAN I STOLE, THE** COL 1933
TARZAN OF THE APES Burroughs, E.R.	**GREYSTOKE** WAR 1984
TEACHER I PASSED THIS WAY Ashton-Warner, S.	**SYLVIA** ENTERPRISE 1985

TELL-TALE HEART, THE
Poe, E.A.

CALYPSO
BL 1956

TEMPLE OF THE GOLDEN PAVILION
Mishima, Y.

MISHIMA
COL—EMI—WAR 1985

TEMPLE TOWER
'Sapper'

**BULLDOG DRUMMOND'S
SECRET POLICE**
PAR 1939

TEN AGAINST CAESAR
Granger, K.R.G.

GUN FURY
COL 1954

TEN LITTLE NIGGERS
Christie, A.

AND THEN THERE WERE NONE
ABP 1965

TEN PLUS ONE
McBain, E.

WITHOUT APPARENT MOTIVE
FOX 1972

TEN SECOND JAILBREAK
Asinof, E.

BREAKOUT
COL—WAR 1975

TENTACLES
Lyon, D.

**HOUSE ON TELEGRAPH HILL,
THE**
FOX 1951

TENTACLES OF THE NORTH
Curwood, J.O.

SNOW DOG
ABP 1951

TESHA
Barcynska, *Baroness*

WOMAN IN THE NIGHT, THE
WW 1929

TESS OF THE D'URBERVILLES
Hardy, T.

TESS
COL 1979

**THANKS GOD, I'LL TAKE IT FROM
HERE**
Allen, J. *and* Livingstone, M.

WITHOUT RESERVATION
RKO 1946

THAT UNCERTAIN FEELING
Amis, K.

ONLY TWO CAN PLAY
BL 1961
HTV 1986 (TV)

THEN WE WERE THREE
Shaw, I.

THREE
UA 1969

THERE'S ALWAYS JULIET (P) Druten, J. van	**ONE NIGHT IN LISBON** PAR 1941
THERE WAS A FAIR MAID DWELLING Delderfield, R.F.	**DIANA** BBC 1984 (TV)
THERE WAS A LITTLE MAN Jones, G.P. *and* Jones, C.B.	**LUCK OF THE IRISH** FOX 1948
THESE OUR LOVERS Fineman, I.	**LOVERS MUST LEARN** WAR 1962
THEY CAN'T HANG ME Ronald, J.	**WITNESS VANISHES, THE** UN 1939
THEY CRACKED HER GLASS SLIPPER Butler, G.	**THIRD TIME LUCKY** ANGOFILM 1948
THEY DREAM OF HOME Busch, N.	**TILL THE END OF TIME** RKO 1946
THEY KNEW WHAT THEY WANTED (P) Howard, S.C.	**LADY TO LOVE, A** MGM 1930
THEY WALK ALONE (P) Catto, M.	**DAUGHTER OF DARKNESS** PAR 1948
THEY WHO SERVE Jennings, D.K.	**MASTER SPY** GN 1962
THIEVES' MARKET Bezzerides, A.I.	**THIEVES' HIGHWAY** FOX 1949
3rd AVENUE, NEW YORK McNulty, J.L.	**EASY COME, EASY GO** PAR 1947
THIRD ROUND, THE 'Sapper'	**BULLDOG DRUMMOND'S PERIL** PAR 1938
13TH MAN, THE Bloom, M.T.	**LAST EMBRACE, THE** UA 1984
THIS FOR REMEMBRANCE Clooney, R. *and* Strait, R.	**ROSIE** FRIES 1982 (TV)

ORIGINAL TITLE	FILM TITLE
THIS IS NEW YORK (P) Sherwood, R.E.	**TWO KINDS OF WOMEN** PAR 1932
THIS STORY OF YOURS (P) Hopkins, J.	**OFFENCE, THE** UA 1972
THIS WAS MY CHOICE Gouzenko, I.	**IRON CURTAIN** FOX 1948
THIS WAY OUT Ronald, J.	**SUSPECT, THE** UN 1944
THOMASINA Gallico, P.	**THREE LIVES OF THOMASINA, THE** DISNEY 1963
THOUSAND PLAN, THE Barker, R.	**1,000 PLANE RAID, THE** UA 1968
THOUSAND SHALL FALL, A Habe, H.	**HANGMEN ALSO DIE** UA 1943
THREE CUPS OF COFFEE Feiner, R.	**WOMAN'S ANGLE, A** ABP 1951
THREE GODFATHERS, THE Kyne, P.B.	**HELL'S HEROES** UN 1930
THREE MEN IN THE SNOW Kastner, E.	**PARADISE FOR THREE** MGM 1938
THREE MUSKETEERS, THE Dumas, A.	**FOUR MUSKETEERS, THE** FOX—RANK 1974
THREE OAK MYSTERY, THE Wallace, E.	**MARRIAGE OF CONVENIENCE** AA 1960
THREE WEIRD SISTERS, THE Armstrong, C.	**CASE OF THE WEIRD SISTERS, THE** BN 1948
THUNDER ABOVE Wallis, A.J. *and* Blair, C.F.	**BEYOND THE CURTAIN** RANK 1960

ORIGINAL TITLE	FILM TITLE
THURSDAY ADVENTURE Pudney, J.	**STOLEN AIR-LINER, THE** BL 1955
TIGER AMONGST US, THE Brackett, L.	**13 WEST STREET** BL 1962
TIME OF THE CUCKOO, THE (P) Laurents, A.	**SUMMER MADNESS** UA 1955
TIME OUT FOR GINGER Alexander, R.	**BILLIE** UA 1965
TIME TO DIE Wicker, T.	**ATTICA** ITV 1985 (TV)
TINKER, THE (P) Dobie, L. *and* Sloman, R.	**WILD AND THE WILLING, THE** RANK 1962
TISH MARCHES ON Rinehart, M.R.	**TISH** MGM 1942
TO DUSTY DEATH McCutcheon, H.	**PIT OF DARKNESS** BUTCHER 1961
TO ELVIS WITH LOVE Canada, L.	**TOUCHED BY LOVE** COL 1980
TO HAVE AND HAVE NOT Hemingway, E.	**BREAKING POINT, THE** WAR 1950 **GUN RUNNERS, THE** SEVEN ARTS 1958
TOM JONES Fielding, H.	**BAWDY ADVENTURES OF . . .** CIC 1976
TOOMAI OF THE ELEPHANTS Kipling, R.	**ELEPHANT BOY** UA 1937
TOP OF THE WORLD Ruesch, H.	**SAVAGE INNOCENTS, THE** RANK 1960
TORCH-BEARERS (P) Kelly, G.	**DOUBTING THOMAS** FOX 1935

ORIGINAL TITLE	FILM TITLE
TOUCH IT LIGHT (P) Storey, R.	**LIGHT UP THE SKY** BRYANSTON 1960
TOUCH OF THE LION'S PAW, A Lambert, D.	**ROUGH CUT** PAR 1980
TOWER, THE Stern, R.M.	**TOWERING INFERNO, THE** COL—WAR 1975
TRACY CROMWELL Richter, C.	**ONE DESIRE** UI 1955
TRAGICAL HISTORY OF DOCTOR **FAUSTUS, THE (P)** Marlowe, C.	**DOCTOR FAUSTUS** COL 1968
TRAILS END Shirrefs, G.D.	**OREGON PASSAGE** ABP 1957
TRANSLATIONS OF A SAVAGE Parker, G.	**BEHOLD MY WIFE** PAR 1935
TRAVELLING LADY, THE (P) Foote, H.	**BABY, THE RAIN MUST FALL** COL 1965
TRAVELS OF JAIMIE McPHEETERS, **THE** Taylor, R.L.	**GUNS OF DIABLO** MGM 1964
TREASURE OF FRANCHARD Stevenson, R.L.	**TREASURE OF THE LOST** **CANYON, THE** UI 1952
TREE OF LIBERTY Page, E.	**HOWARDS OF VIRGINIA, THE** COL 1940
TREVE Terhune, A.P.	**MIGHTY TREVE, THE** UN 1937
TRIAL, THE Kafka, F.	**INSURANCE MAN, THE** BBC 2 1986 (TV)
TRIAL BY TERROR Gallico, P.	**ASSIGNMENT—PARIS** COL 1952

ORIGINAL TITLE	FILM TITLE
TRILBY Du Maurier, G.	**SVENGALI** WAR 1931 REN 1954
TRINITY'S CHILD Prochau, W.	**GRAND TOUR, THE** TRI-STAR 1984
TRUE GRIT Portis, C.	**'ROOSTER COGBURN** UN 1975
TRUMPETS OF COMPANY K Chamberlain, W.	**IMITATION GENERAL** MGM 1958
TRUTH GAME, THE (P) Novello, I.	**BUT THE FLESH IS WEAK** MGM 1932
TUCKER'S PEOPLE Wolfert, I.	**FORCE OF EVIL** MGM 1949
TURN OF THE SCREW, THE James, H.	**INNOCENTS, THE** FOX 1961
TURQUOISE BIKINI, THE Resnik, M.	**HOW SWEET IT IS** WAR 1968
TWENTY PLUS TWO Gruber, F.	**IT STARTED IN TOKYO** WAR 1961
TWENTY THOUSAND STREETS UNDER THE SKY Hamilton, P.	**BITTER HARVEST** RANK 1962
TWILIGHT OF HONOUR Dewlen, A.	**CHARGE IS MURDER, THE** MGM 1963
TWIN SOMBREROS Grey, Z.	**GUN FIGHTERS** COL 1947
TWO HOURS TO DOOM George, P.	**DR. STRANGELOVE; OR HOW I LEARNED TO STOP WORRYING AND LOVE THE BOMB** COL 1963
TWO O'CLOCK COURAGE Burgess, G.	**TWO IN THE DARK** RKO 1936

TYPEE
Melville, H.

ENCHANTED ISLAND
WAR 1958

TYPISTS AND THE TIGER, THE (P)
Schisgal, M.

TIGER MAKES OUT, THE
COL 1968

U

UNCHARTERED SEAS
Wheatley, D.

LOST CONTINENT, THE
WAR 1968

UNCLE HARRY (P)
Job, T.

STRANGE AFFAIR OF UNCLE HARRY, THE
UN 1945

UNCLE WILLIE AND THE BICYCLE SHOP
Williams, B.

AIN'T LIFE WONDERFUL
ABP 1953

UNCOMMON DANGER
Ambler, E.

BACKGROUND TO DANGER
WAR 1943

UNDERCOVER CAT
Gordons, The

THAT DARN CAT
DISNEY 1964

UNEASY FREEHOLD
Macardle, D.

UNINVITED, THE
PAR 1944

UNEXPECTED MRS. POLLIFAX, THE
Colman, D.

MRS. POLLIFAX—SPY
UA 1971

UNINVITED, THE
Chitterden, F.

STRANGER IN TOWN
EROS 1957

UNJUST SKIES, THE
Delderfield, R.F.

DIANA
BBC 1984 (TV)

UNTAMED, THE
Brand, M.

FAIR WARNING
FOX 1931

UNTOUCHABLES, THE
Ness, E. *and* Fraley, O.

SCARFACE MOB, THE
WAR 1959

ORIGINAL TITLE	FILM TITLE
URGENT HANGMAN, THE Cheyney, P.	**MEET MR. CALLAGHAN** EROS 1954
USELESS COWBOY, THE LeMay, A.	**ALONG CAME JONES** RKO 1945

V

VALLEY OF THE ANTS Wells, H.G.	**EMPIRE OF THE ANTS** BRENT WALKER 1978
VANITY FAIR Thackeray, W.M.	**BECKY SHARP** RKO 1935
VANITY ROW Burnett, W.R.	**ACCUSED OF MURDER** REP 1956
VENGEANCE OF PRIVATE POOLEY, THE Jolly, C.	**STORY OF PRIVATE POOLEY, THE** CONTEMPORARY 1962
VESSEL OF WRATH Maugham, W.S.	**BEACHCOMBER** GFD 1954
VICTORY Conrad, J.	**DANGEROUS PARADISE** PAR 1930
VIEW FROM POMPEY'S HEAD Basso, H.	**SECRET INTERLUDE** FOX 1955
VIGILANTE Summers, R.A.	**SAN FRANCISCO STORY, THE** WAR 1952
VIKING, THE Marshall, E.	**VIKINGS, THE** UA 1958
VIPER THREE Wager, W.	**TWILIGHT'S LAST GLEAMING** HEMDALE 1977
VISION QUEST Davis, T.	**CRAZY FOR YOU** GUBER PETERS 1985
VISITORS, THE Benchley, N.	**SPIRIT IS WILLING, THE** PAR 1968

VOLPONE (P)
Jonson, B.

HONEY POT, THE
UA 1966

W

WAGES OF FEAR
Arnaud, G.

SORCERER, THE
CIC 1978

WAILING ASTEROID, THE
Leinster, M.

TERRONAUTS, THE
AVCO EMBASSY 1967

WAITING FOR A TIGER
Healey, B.

TASTE OF EXCITEMENT
MONARCH 1969

WAKING, THE
Figes, E.

NELLY'S VERSION
MITHRAS 1983

WARDEN, THE
Trollope, A.

BARCHESTER CHRONICLES, THE
BBC 1982 (TV)

WARRIOR, THE
Slaughter, F.G.

NAKED IN THE SUN
RKO 1956

**WARTIME ADVENTURES OF
PRESIDENT JOHN F. KENNEDY, THE**
Donovan, R.J.

PT 109
WAR 1963

WASHINGTON SQUARE
James, H.

HEIRESS, THE
PAR 1949

WATCHER IN THE SHADOWS
Household, G.

DEADLY HARVEST
BBC 1984 (TV)

WATER IS WIDE, THE
Conroy, P.

CONRACK
FOX 1974

WATERLOO BRIDGE (P)
Sherwood, R.

GABY
MGM 1955

WAY OUT, THE
Graeme, B.

DIAL 999
AA 1955

WE
Lindbergh, C.A.

SPIRIT OF ST. LOUIS, THE
WAR 1956

ORIGINAL TITLE	FILM TITLE
WE ARE SEVEN Troy, U.	**SHE DIDN'T SAY NO!** ABP 1958
WEDNESDAY'S CHILD (P) Atlas, L.	**CHILD OF DIVORCE** RKO 1946
WEEKEND AT ZUYDCOOTE Merle, R.	**WEEKEND AT DUNKIRK** FOX 1965
WEEK-END GIRL Fabian, W.	**WEEK-ENDS ONLY** FOX 1932
WEEP NO MORE Coffee, L.	**ANOTHER TIME, ANOTHER PLACE** PAR 1958
WELCOME TO HARD TIMES Doctorow, E.L.	**KILLER ON A HORSE** MGM 1966
WEREWOLF OF PARIS, THE Endore, G.	**CURSE OF THE WEREWOLF, THE** RANK 1960
WHAT CAN YOU DO? Leigh, J.	**MAKING IT** FOX 1971
WHAT SAY THEY (P) Bridie, J.	**YOU'RE ONLY YOUNG TWICE** ABP 1952
WHEELER-DEALERS, THE Goodman, G.J.W.	**SEPARATE BEDS** MGM 1964
WHEEL SPINS, THE White, E.L.	**LADY VANISHES, THE** MGM 1938 RANK 1979
WHEN KNIGHTHOOD WAS IN FLOWER Major, C.	**SWORD AND THE ROSE, THE** RKO 1953
WHEN KNIGHTHOOD WAS IN FLOWER (P) Kester, P.	**SWORD AND THE ROSE, THE** RKO 1953
WHERE THE PAVEMENT ENDS Russell, J.	**SEA GOD, THE** PAR 1930

766

ORIGINAL TITLE	FILM TITLE
WHILE THE POPE KEPT SILENT Ramati, A.	**ASSISI UNDERGROUND, THE** CANNON 1985
WHISPERING SMITH Spearman, F.H.	**WHISPERING SMITH SPEAKS** FOX 1935
WHISPERING WOMAN Merner, G.	**NOOSE FOR A LADY** AA 1953
WHITE COLLARS (P) Ellis, E.	**IDLE RICH** MGM 1929 **RICH MAN, POOR GIRL** MGM 1938
WHITE SOUTH, THE Innes, H.	**HELL BELOW ZERO** COL 1953
WHITE STALLIONS OF VIENNA, THE Podhajsky, A.	**FLIGHT OF THE WHITE STALLIONS, THE** DISNEY 1963
WHO COULD ASK FOR ANYTHING MORE Swift, K.	**NEVER A DULL MOMENT** RKO 1950
WHO GOES THERE? Campbell, J.W.	**THING FROM ANOTHER WORLD, THE** RKO 1951
WHO IS SYLVIA? (P) Rattigan, T.	**MAN WHO LOVED REDHEADS, THE** BL 1954
WHO LIE IN GAOL Henry, J.	**WEAK AND THE WICKED, THE** ABP 1953
WHO RIDES WITH WYATT? Henry, W.	**YOUNG BILLY YOUNG** UA 1969
WHO WAS THAT LADY I SAW YOU WITH? (P) Krasna, N.	**WHO WAS THAT LADY?** COL 1960
WHY I QUIT SYNDICATED CRIME Vaus, J. *Jun.*	**WIRETAPPER, THE** EXCLUSIVE 1955

WIDE BOYS NEVER WORK Westerby, R.	**SOHO INCIDENT** COL 1956
WILD BILL HICKOK Wilstach, F.	**PLAINSMAN, THE** PAR 1936
WILD CALENDAR Block, L.	**CAUGHT** MGM 1948
WILDFIRE Grey, Z.	**RED CANYON** UN 1949
WILLIE BOY Lawton, H.	**TELL THEM WILLIE BOY IS HERE** RANK 1969
WILLING FLESH Heinrich, W.	**CROSS OF IRON** EMI 1976
WILL SUCCESS SPOIL ROCK HUNTER? **(P)** Axelrod, G.	**OH! FOR A MAN!** FOX 1957
WINE AND THE MUSIC, THE Barrett, W.C.	**PIECES OF DREAMS** UA 1975
WINSTON AFFAIR, THE Fast, H.	**MAN IN THE MIDDLE** FOX 1963
WINTER JOURNEY (P) Odets, C.	**COUNTRY GIRL, THE** PAR 1954
WINTER WEARS A SHROUD Chapman, R.	**DELAVINE AFFAIR, THE** MON 1954
WISDOM OF FATHER BROWN, THE Chesterton, G.K.	**FATHER BROWN, DETECTIVE** PAR 1935
WISTERIA COTTAGE Coates, R.M.	**EDGE OF FURY** UA 1958
WITCHES MILK De Vries, P.	**PETE 'N' TILLIE** UN 1972
WITHIN THE TIDES Conrad, J.	**LAUGHING ANNE** REP 1953

ORIGINAL TITLE	FILM TITLE
WOMAN IN RED, THE Gilbert, A.	**MY NAME IS JULIA ROSS** COL 1945
WOMAN WITH A SWORD Noble, H.	**DRUMS IN THE DEEP SOUTH** RKO 1952
WOMEN, THE (P) Boothe, C.	**OPPOSITE SEX, THE** MGM 1956
WONDERFUL WIZARD OF OZ, THE Baum, L.F.	**WIZ, THE** DISNEY 1979
WORLD IN MY POCKET, THE Chase, J.H.	**ON FRIDAY AT 11** BL 1961
WRATH OF GRAPES Wibberley, L.	**MOUSE THAT ROARED, THE** COL 1959

Y

YANKEE AT THE COURT OF KING ARTHUR, A Twain, M.	**CONNECTICUT YANKEE** FOX 1931 **SPACEMAN AT KING ARTHUR'S COURT** DISNEY 1980
YANKEE DARED, A Nevins, F.J.	**TRANSCONTINENTAL EXPRESS** REP 1950
YANKEE FROM OLYMPUS Bowen, C.D.	**MAN WITH THIRTY SONS, THE** MGM 1952
YEAR OF THE ANGRY RABBIT, THE Braddon, R.	**NIGHT OF THE LEPUS** MGM—EMI 1972
YEAR OF THE BIG CAT, THE Dietz, L.	**BIG CAT** DISNEY 1974
YEAR OF THE HORSE, THE Hatch, E.	**HORSE IN THE GREY FLANNEL SUIT, THE** DISNEY 1968
YEARS ARE SO LONG, THE Lawrence, J.	**MAKE WAY FOR TOMORROW** PAR 1937

ORIGINAL TITLE	FILM TITLE
YEA, YEA, YEA McGill, A.	**PRESS FOR TIME** JARFID 1966
YEKL Cahan, A.	**HESTER STREET** CONNOISSEUR 1975
YELLOW FEVER Larteguy, J.	**NOT FOR HONOUR AND GLORY** COL 1965
YELLOWLEG Fleischman, A.S.	**DEADLY COMPANIONS, THE** WAR 1961
YEOMAN'S HOSPITAL Ashton, H.	**WHITE CORRIDORS** GFD 1951
YOUNG APOLLO, THE Gibbs, A.H.	**MEN OF TOMORROW** MUNDUS 1935
YOUNG ARCHIMEDES Huxley, A.L.	**PRELUDE TO FAME** GFD 1950
YOUNG LOVE Allen, J.	**YOUNG HAVE NO TIME, THE** CROSS CHANNEL 1959
YOUNG MAN WITH A HORN Baker, D.	**YOUNG MAN OF MUSIC** WAR 1950
YOU'RE BEST ALONE Curtis, P.	**GUILT IS MY SHADOW** ABP 1950
YOU'RE ONLY HUMAN ONCE Moore, G.	**SO THIS IS LOVE** WAR 1953

Z

ZAPATA, THE UNCONQUERABLE Pinchon, E.	**VIVA ZAPATA!** FOX 1952